YOUNG WRITERS

CALYPSO

KENT

First published in Great Britain in 1997 by
POETRY NOW YOUNG WRITERS
1-2 Wainman Road, Woodston,
Peterborough, PE2 7BU
Telephone (01733) 230748

HB ISBN 1 86188 315 3
SB ISBN 1 86188 310 2

FOREWORD

Every day, each year the Young Writers' entry sack seems to multiply. Not only do we find the quantity accumulating but progressively we find the standard of young people's poetry growing increasingly eminent.

This is a commendable reflection on authors and English teachers alike. There is no question that a good English teacher produces a good young creative writer, and young people with a passion for poetry are flourishing and at last are being encouraged.

Editing Calypso *Kent* was an editorial nightmare - we found ourselves somewhat spoilt for choice, but thoroughly enjoyed it nonetheless. Featuring poems by young people aged 11-18 years old,some with special needs, the Calypso books contain one of the most diverse ranges of poetry on the market today. Some are complex, emotional and close to the heart, others are simple, light-hearted, and invariably humorous, all demonstrate a good use of language and literary skills. Many illustrate concerns, both socially and environmentally that are fresh in all of our minds. All, I believe, allow the reader access to the minds of today's youth - ultimately proving the power of the pen.

CONTENTS

Highsted Grammar School

Highworth Grammar School For Girls

THE POEMS

LIFE

You only live once,
or so they say.
To come back as a animal
or some kind of prey.

An eagle gliding through the wind,
zooming down towards the land.
Sitting on the branch of the old oak tree,
No-one to bother you, just sweet harmony.

Well back to now,
This is how it is -

You're born, you have light,
You have food, you have drink.

You grow up, you're happy.
You start working, get somewhere in life.

Then . . . you die

Sadness is a virtue, as life keeps rolling on.
Pittance is a Sunday, as the days they've come and gone.

Addiction is a promise, the needle is the key.
Satisfy your hunger, and soon you will be free.

The end is near, and lies are bound.
So look south, to the promise you have found.

Your soul will rot, beneath the grave.
The memory of the good times, you will save.

So venture north, sail the crimson sea.
That's when you'll know, your soul is free.

And when you're dead, you'll venture on,
Towards that hooded crimson sun.

Claire Louise Reynolds (15)

BROWN

An owl perched upon a hollow tree branch thinks
mysterious thoughts,
Armies of wood-lice stagger and reel as a foot stamps
the debris below,
Plump raisins shrivel in their leathery cases,
Humans tan in the blazing sunset,
Moths surround the dim light as they flap their soft
powdered wings,
Honey gloops in the reflection of the silver spoon,
Lonely sounds drift from the grandfather clock,
Coca Cola fizzes up and flows into another world of
colours,
Logs burn away as the last prayers are chanted,
Autumn leaves float into a crunch of golden stalks,
Canes smack onto plastic desks,
Chocolate breaks into cubes of melting flow,
A third place trophy is hoisted into the air as the
crowd roars,
Cockroaches scuttle up along a wooden staircase,
Mud landscapes tumble into a thick lake of flowing
slime,
Lonely piano music plays as the last farewell shiver
is sent down your spine,
Left over ale stagnates in a musty cellar,

These are the colours of brown.

Anna Jones (10)

Bookworm

Bookworm Bookworm
Hiding in a book
You'll never find him
Wherever you look.

Look in the cupboards
Look in the drawers
Have you found him yet
He might be behind the door.

Look over here
Look over there
Is he behind the chair?
I promise you'll never find him
Looking here there and everywhere.

Now you've looked everywhere
Do you give up?
You'll never find him
He's in a book
Called Bookworm's Hiding.

Carly Hughes (11)

In The Middle Of It All

Caught in the middle of a storm at sea,
Caught in the middle of a great rock lee.
Caught in the middle of a storm that's set,
Caught in the middle of a trawler's net.

Caught in the middle of a school of whales,
Caught in the middle of great big sails.
Caught in the middle of a broken boat,
Caught in the middle of a wet and heavy coat.
I wish I wasn't here, but somewhere else instead!

Amelia Mankelow

THE BEACH

Sitting on the sandy beach listening to the waves,
watching the sun go down as the wild wind begins to howl.
The waves splashing up against the shingle.
Sitting eating an ice-cream as the moon begins to set,
as the sea starts getting closer and the sun disappears.
The birds are hovering over the golden sand.
The sound of the sea and the birds make lovely sounds
as though there were a stereo playing classical music in a
long distance.
Night time's here, it's getting cold, the tide is in,
it's time to go.

Carl Fox (14)
Abbey School

IF I WAS A BIRD

If I was a bird in the sky, what would I see.
Would I see the cars when I look from above.
Would I see the plants, blossom in the light.
Would I see the rivers flowing.
Would I see the tide of the oceans rise and fall
Would I see the animals crawl and hunt for food.
If I was a bird in the sky, what would I see.
Would I see the building tall or small.
Houses, bungalows, even sky scrapers.
Could I fly as high as them.
Would I see any of these if I was a bird.

Lee Suter (13)
Abbey School

FEAR

It's quiet,
I wish you could hear me,
Shout for you,
As loud as I can.

I asked for your help,
But you just ran away,
Help they're after me,
And they're getting closer.

Bang goes a gun,
But you kept on running,
It misses,
But next time I might not be so lucky.

The gun goes off again,
But this time it does not miss,
Straight into my leg,
But on you kept running.

They come beside me,
And point a gun at my head,
But where are you,
Safe I suppose.

The gun goes off one last time,
The pain is really bad,
But do you care,
The answer must be no.

What happened that night doesn't matter now,
As my life has been taken,
You may think that you're safe,
But be careful as they will find you one day.

Maria Carlton (16)
Abbey School

THE BADGER

I saw a badger the other day,
It said I'm sorry I can not stay,
I've got to walk along my way
But I'm being chased away
Why can't you let me be,
I don't want to have to flee!

Stuart Hills (11)
Angley School

THE ELEPHANT

The elephant will be extinct.
If we don't use our heads and think.
Of ways to stop the poachers' guns from
Stopping all their harmless fun.

They're beautiful and large in size
The creamy tusks are the killers' prize.
So stop the killing and the waste.
Before it's all too late.

Joshua Marriott (11)
Angley School

THE HORSE

The horse is very beautiful,
Full of elegance as he gallops across the fields,
Stunning as he jumps,
His coat shining in the sun,
His long mane and tail flowing out behind him,
His strong and graceful body,
Gliding effortlessly through the air,
A horse is my best friend.

Kerrie Tyler (11)
Angley School

WHALE

Minke Whale is my name,
And eating little fish is my game,
I know that sounds kind of mean
But I really am squeaky clean
The thing I don't understand is this,
If humans are so nice to hug and kiss,
Why do they bother to shoot at me,
When all I want to do is live in harmony,
I never never try to harm them,
But still they persist and come again,
If the poachers come every day,
The whales will be killed and die away,
And then there will be no-one left to see,
Swimming in the deep blue sea.

Emily Martinez (11)
Angley School

DOLPHINS

Dolphins are friendly and playful.
Gorgeous swimming in the sea.
Soft and elegant dancing and diving happily.
Dazzling day-dreaming dolphins.

Samantha Burton (11)
Angley School

ON TO THE KINGDOM

She lay upon a sheet of snow,
Her clothes were soaked right through,
Two swollen eyes gazed up at stars,
As chattering lips turned blue,

The lightest one shone twice as bright,
Like hope from a pitch black hole,
She knew deep down what that star was,
Her passed-on mother's soul.

And all the sky seemed to lighten up,
Like children having fun,
A calming voice then rose above,
'Come, my daughter, come.'

At dawn the next morning she lay dead,
Sprawled out, no airs or grace,
But passers-by were comforted,
By the smile upon her face.

Chelsea Reay (11)
Angley School

TIGERS

Tigers, tigers running free.
Why can't people let them be.
Man always kills things.
Just to satisfy his greed.
He will see that he was wrong.
No more tigers wild and free.
What a shame this would be.

Timothy P Beeken (11)
Angley School

THE SEA TURTLE

I live in the Caribbean, far far away,
      in golden sand my eggs I lay.

They hatch together ping pang pong,
      and scuttle to the sea singing a song.

There they will travel far away from me,
      diving and splashing in the big blue sea.

I cry to my children please watch out,
      turtles be careful humans are about.

Swim fast swim deep and take no risk,
      or your flesh will be eaten and shells a dish.

Alex Humphrey (11)
Angley School

GENTLE GIANTS

The gentle giants gliding through the still
sparkling water of the ocean
Crashing through the waves
Calling each other with their high pitch voices
Splashing and dancing elegantly in the
glittering sea
Softly gliding happily they swim
But . . .
In the distance mankind
Armed at the ready
To take these wonderful creatures' lives away
Crashing through the waves but this time in fear
To get away from these killers, murderers,
destroyers and life threateners.
The gun goes off.
Whales splash!
Full of fear
Trying to escape their death
Mankind succeeded this time they caught one.
A mother, her child is a stray an orphan
her mother is dead.
Swimming through a blood red sea crying for her mum.
These mammals are endangered we have to save them.
Stop mankind killing them
They are wonderful creatures maybe one day
we will see and hear them having fun.

Jessica Stone (12)
Angley School

OASIS

Round our way
Some might say
Oasis are supersonic
Down at Digsy's Diner
They drink champagne supernovas
They will never slide away
Cos they're my wonder walls
They're definitely, maybe
Getting better man
They won't look back in anger
Whatever you say
They will live forever
Even when they're married with children.

Becky Joy (11)
Angley School

THE RHINO

The giant grey rhino,
Standing up straight,
Sharp horn gleaming,
In the red hot sun,
Suddenly up ahead,
He sees a hunter,
Charges full speed,
To save his kind,
Hunter turns and runs in fright,
The rhino is safe,
But not for long.

Tom Robinson (11)
Angley School

ARCHERY

I do archery,
It is a good sport,
I do it every Saturday,
We all stand in a line,
Getting ready to shoot,
We all pull our bows back,
As far as we can,
Off the arrows go,
As fast as a jet,
Slamming into the boss,
Hooray! Hooray! It's gone in the middle,
I've got a gold!

Claire Kenward (11)
Angley School

DOLPHINS

Fishing boats with their fishing nets
Catching tuna to eat
Dolphins splashing in the sea
Just wishing they could be
Happy like me
Are just caught instead
Killed and died instead.

Kelly Wilson (11)
Angley School

SQUARE MEAL

A man bought a pet hyena
And then he bought a flock.
He fed them all on Oxo Cubes
And made a laughing stock.

Timothy Found (11)
Angley School

A CHRISTMAS POEM

Christmas day is here again,
The rain has turned to snow,
Snowflakes fall like leaves from trees;
The white roofs of houses glow.

Stockings hanging over the fireplace,
Waiting for Santa to bring;
Presents, oranges, nuts and games,
While carol singers sing.

Mince pies, cakes and Christmas puds;
Turkey for Christmas dinner,
Christmas cake for after tea,
No-one getting thinner!

Excited children unwrapping gifts
Smiling faces all around,
Night-time falls, kids in bed,
Not a peep in sound!

Carly Robinson (13)
Astor School

DAYDREAMING

Sitting in a classroom bored out of your mind,
You are writing out a story on A4 lined.
Your hands are getting tired, your eyes are getting weak,
All your dreams and thoughts are now beginning to leak
A knight in shining armour bursts through the door,
He trips over his shield and falls to the floor.
You are filled with laughter, your eyes are filled with tears,
The boring old English room now disappears.
The knight walks towards you, his arms open wide,
He takes you in his arms, and swings you to one side.
He tries to kiss you but you sneeze,
He lays you down with perfect ease.
You suddenly hear your teacher shout,
'What are you doing lying about?
You say you are sorry, you will pay more attention,
'OK! You are forgiven but you're in detention.'

Claire Green & Hannah Buckett (15)
Astor School

THE EVENING ROSE

The evening rose scarlet and stained,
That gently flows in the trickling rain,
Sometimes pink sometimes white
It holds a delicate pose
And dances in the evening light
Beauty is the rose.

An attractive plant with leaves as shields
No wishes to grant in the glistening fields,
Wonderful not withering whilst other plants doze,
Not this silent living beauty is the rose.

Kate Ogilvie (13)
Astor School

I HOPE

I hope that one day I shall say
That was me in a famous way
I wish that I could go out and play
Like the big boys and girls do today
All I do is sleep and eat
Clean my face and wash my feet
What I really want to do
Is be myself - wouldn't you?
I really hate my awful pram
Which is smelly inside and is a cram
My shoes are small, I cannot reply
All I have to do is cry.
But then she says 'Hungry Frank?'
But I think 'The *shoe* you plank?'
Why don't I have a CD player. Can't you see?
A fridge or a colour TV.
That Sega Mega Drive I saw in the store.
A motor racing drive on my very own floor.
But my mum has this stupid plan
To get this rubbish action man.
Or Jack in the box which I really hate
A pathetic doll that won't inflate.
I hope I get to the age when I can get this stuff
Being a one year old really is tough!
So next time you see a baby cry
What they're saying is buy, buy, buy.
Don't just think for yourself, wait and see
Or else you'll end up just like me!

Simon Brett (13)
Astor School

BONFIRE NIGHT

Hear that bang, hear that crash,
The oohs, the aahs, look at that!
The noise, the laughter, all the fun,
Bonfire night has just begun.

I have just arrived here with my cousin,
Cor, the bonfire is as hot as an oven.
Hot-dogs, burgers, cups of soup,
See that rocket loop-the-loop.

Flashing, flaring, fireworks fizzing
Listen to those sausages sizzling.
The catherine-wheel is a sparkling star,
Oh, why didn't I get my gloves from the car?

The flames of the fire are tickling the guy,
His face is contorted, we all know why,
Just like an inferno, explosions all round,
I think I'll get a sausage, I've got a pound.

I love the smell of burning wood,
Which makes me feel really good.
Wow, look at the one, really bright,
I could watch these fireworks all the night.
Just watch him light that massive rocket
Amazing colours that stream out of it.
It looks like a million lights or stars dropping
out of the sky.
Gee, just look how the fireworks fly.

It really has been a beautiful night,
But the bonfire now is barely alight.
The rain is making me feel really damp
and soggy,
Exactly like a smelly moggy.

Although tonight has been really great,
Roll on next year, I can't wait.

Jodie Stables (12)
Astor School

MY LITTLE CHERUB

Gentle baby lying there
Sleeping on without care,
My love for you is as deep as the sea
You mean so very much to me.
Your little eyes that shine so bright
Every time I come in sight.
Your tiny hands reach out each day
For something new with which to play.
Your ears resemble little shells,
Your laughter that of pealing bells.
Your hair is as soft, as soft can be
The tiny dimples in your knee.
The way you learn the simple things
The happiness to me it brings
I know that you will grow up fine
Little darling, because you're mine.

Natalie Danko (13)
Astor School

WHATEVER HAPPENED TO SOME OF MY TOYS?

Whatever happened to my favourite ted
Who always sat at the bottom of my bed
He was golden brown and very soft
But when I got older he moved to the loft

Whatever happened to my Thunder Cat toys
Who were loved and envied by all little boys
Then they went where no other toy would dare
This was it, they were off to the boot fair

Whatever happened to my Turtle Sewer
When the Turtles fought, the enemy got fewer and fewer
I'm saving these toys for years to come
And maybe my children will play with them and have fun

Whatever happened to my Matchbox cars
I used to play with them for hours and hours
I used to have several dozen
But now I've given them all to my cousin

What ever happened to my hundreds of Lego bricks
I think there was that many, honest, no tricks
They are in a big box in the corner of my room
Gathering dust in the depths of the gloom.

Lee Vickery (13)
Astor School

I CAN'T

I can't forgive you for what you have done,
I can't bring back the stars, moon or sun.
I can't feel anything for anyone else,
I can't forgive you for being yourself.

I can't get over this anger and pain
I can't see it's my loss and her gain
I can't get over what you mean to me
I can't realise that I'm not who your heart can see.

Hannah Bird (15)
Aylesford School

FAREWELL

If your dreams fade
If your dreams turn to nothing,
Or if they just disappear.
Then something will tell you it is time to leave
To a land far away from here
Where there is nothing to fear.
We shall all end up there
But each when we are called upon
It is soon my time to depart
No more dream,
No more nothing
So I shall say farewell,
To the ones I love.

Claudia Edmondson (14)
Benenden School

A TRANCE-LIKE SPELL

Let your mind break free
Let your spirit dance with forbidden joy
The abstractness of life is an
Everlasting jungle of destruction.

My mind is a maze
Which even I get lost in
My mind is a forest
Which even I get lost in.

The powers of above
Are cornering me from the
Rest of the world
Trapped in an anxiety of destruction.

My mind is a maze
Which even I get lost in
My mind is a forest
Which even I get lost in.

A solution of wisdom and power
A solution of eternal desire
Let the world forever burn in rage and fire.

My mind is a maze
Which even I get lost in
My mind is a forest
Which even I get lost in.

Faezeh Faiz (14)
Benenden School

NIGHT SKIES

One step taken from gym
I am short of breath.
Hot air of gym radiates through my body.
Winds that touch my sweating skin
Brings freshness to me.
Is this a peace?

Suddenly from somewhere one can not tell,
Little temptation visits me.
The real form which attracts my sight, like magnet,
Is the night skies.
As I look up, I'm dragged into the world.

Stopping walk, I glare at the skies.
The stars surround me.
Soon they are likely to swoop upon me.
They flock from all quarters.
In spite of deep darkness,
They flash on me, twinkling.

I feel like the protagonist under the spotlight.
They await my world.
In the delicate mood, I sing. I dance.

But sudden silence!
With consciousness, I look around my real world.
No audience waits for me.
I'm the only protagonist of ego in loneliness.

Seo-Young Cho (15)
Benenden School

WHY ME?

Why me? I keep asking, why me?
Please just give me a rest,
I really just want to enjoy life,
Must I constantly be put to the test?

Nobody knows what it's like,
Nobody understands how I feel,
Nobody can ever imagine
That it is so very real.

I wake up every morning,
Just hoping it's gone away,
I get dressed - it's the same old story,
It's there for another day.

It's constantly sitting on me,
It's always by my side,
It's walking in my shadow,
There's nowhere I can hide.

Let me go that's all I ask,
Let me go far away from it,
Let me go and come back someone different,
But please, don't let me fall into the pit.

Will I ever be how I want to be,
Will someone ever want to know me,
I want people to look deep inside,
Not just take me for what they first see.

Who cares what I look like outside?
Who cares if I'm fat or thin?
I care, you care, doesn't everyone?
Nobody bothers to have a deeper look in!

Nikki Bush (16)
Bedgebury School

THE POEM

This is a poem,
Which is not very long,
The rhythm's not right
And the words are all wrong.
The rhyme scheme may be, simple to see,
So why is it all such a muddle to me.
The lines have got longer
But this one is short.
This poem is pointless,
Is that what you thought,
I'm sorry you think that
But it's not really my fault
The blame lies with you Miss
It's the way I've been taught.

John Lockley (16)
Borden Grammar School

WHO IS THIS CREATURE

It preys on children and their fears,
Leaving each and everyone in tears;
It's wicked, ugly, evil and scary,
If you see it then you'd better be wary;
It gives out homework, ten hours per day,
Leaving no spare time to play;
It punishes kids for being slack,
Won't think twice about giving a 'whack';
It finds its pleasure in being cruel,
It acts in a way as its fuel;
The question is what is this creature?
The answer's simple - the English Teacher!

Clive Bennett (10)
Borden Grammar School

THE TEMPEST

I sensed the storm . . .
Then . . . I heard it approaching!
Then all of a sudden, and thundery, like a pulsating and throbbing beat,
The storm emerged, and covered me in a deep black cloak of dark and
morose terror.
The smoky sky as replete and dark as night,
Was swirling in mystifying and mesmerising patterns,
As if it was delaying itself for something - it was.
All of a sudden the storm flashed with a sudden savage light,
Lighting up the dark and gloomy night.
The wind then began to howl around,
Ripping up objects from the ground.

But then the leaves from the trees fell to the ground,
Ever so inaudibly, there was no sound.
I could not believe I was still alive,
Having survived the terrible wind, I kissed the ground.
Then the ground rumbled, as if a herd of wildebeest were approaching I
wish it was so, but it was not.
Then thunder clapped again and again,
Torrents of rain engulfed me, so hard, that I grimaced in pain,
Never would I go out in a storm again.
But suddenly the rain did ease,
The peace settled on the leaves,

All the birds returned to the trees,
Once again could I go in peace.
The once violent clouds - now broken, did drift by,
In the ironic quietness of this murderous midday sky.

Christopher Read (17)
Borden Grammar School

THE NOT SO GREAT WAR!

Standing in the trench, with mud all around,
Nothing to hear but the deafening sound.
Of German big guns pounding your head,
Surrounded by people, but all your mates dead.

In the front line, it is now getting dark,
Pray to God, the sniper misses his mark.
The hairs on your neck are standing tall.
Hoping that you aren't the first fool to fall.

Cowering in one long row, man after man,
I can't kill want to live all I can.
Rifles ready to go over the top,
Once we have started we know we can't stop.

We're over the top and charging along,
Through the no-man's land, no time for a song.
Machine gun bullets ripping through our flesh,
Young men are dying in the sharp, spiked mesh.

Across German lines, to do or to die,
Those who are captured, now wish they could cry
The prisoners of war, start burning their dead
We look on without a single tear shed.

Our unit is moving, further on down the line
Preparing for death, it will soon be our time.
We'll meet with dead comrades buried aloft
We stand together with helmets a'doff.

Saull Rowland White (17)
Borden Grammar School

ETERNAL BEAUTY FOR HER SOUL

Moving silently, swiftly through the night
A dark shadow eclipsed the moon
Driven by a violent hunger
It was coming for her soon.

She dreamt of youth and deals with death
Her son lay decaying in the grave
Grey hairs still visible on his rotted skin
There was nothing left to save.

Death had kept to its word
Eternal beauty for her soul
The angels watched intently
It was time to pay the toll.

A life of misery and anguish
Death would appear to her as one
Its many faces screaming
They knew she wouldn't run.

Calmly stepping into the light
So pure, so sweet to smell
A mocking laughter from darkness
As she plunged straight down to hell.

Nick Jones (17)
Borden Grammar School

THE CLOCK

Tick, tock, tick tock,
The heavy pendulum swings.
Plodding through eternity.
The tall clock, once grand,
Now carries a cloak of dust.
The weight of time bears down on it
As it stands unchanging, rigid.
Generations have passed it by, watching
As it slices time into tidy amounts.
The colonies of wood-worm march on,
The mice do nibble out their holes.
The facade remains, greyer, slower,
No key to wind it up.
No polisher to bring out the shine.
The darkened wood dries and cracks.
The hands sag, the chime seems quiet.
The springs unwind, the rhythm falters.
A tick, an age to wait, a tock.
And then, one final grinding clack,
The pendulum sways itself to rest,
No power left to swing.

Michael Crane (17)
Borden Grammar School

THE SOLDIER

The weary soldier lays silently on his bed
Watching through the canvas of his tent for the early sun
Thoughts and memories flash through his head
As he wonders if by tomorrow his life will be done

He recalls the tragedies of the day before,
The close friends in his group now under forever sleep
Never again to see the people they adore
For now they are but a fallen soldier on the battlefield on a heap

Soldiers are gold they will see many lands,
Have glory, pride and riches untold,
But be the battle on a deep forest glade or some far off sands
Soldiers meet their death in poverty be they coward or bold.

The weary soldier lays silently on his bed
Listening carefully for even the slightest of breath
Home flashes into his mind and a tear from his eye was shed
No more will he see it, because of his imminent death.

Luke Galang (16)
Borden Grammar School

THE SWALLOW

Through the air the swallow flies;
Right there before my own eyes;
Ducking and diving the swallow tries,
In the sky with so many allies;

Such a thought the swallow thrives;
Up there just as high as the skies;
So unlike those evil magpies
Just the thought, one day a swallow dies.

Mark Ives (16)
Borden Grammar School

THE ROAD

I remember when this road was long,
With, oh, so many miles to go,
Great crowds of people,
Everyone turned out for the show.
But that, was years ago.

I wondered if this road could end,
What would come after - I know not now,
The miles drifted away and the curtain fell,
The crowd grew smaller,
But where they went I could not tell.

I remember - not so long ago,
When the end was in sight,
A dismal glow.
The crowd kept on walking,
But I turned off - I don't know why,
And on this rocky path I said goodbye.

The road, the show, my life,
All gone.
But somehow a part of me has gone on.
Where I am I cannot say,
I have no words to describe today.

Peter Grzeszczak (16)
Borden Grammar School

NEED FOR SPEED

The engine running, raring to go,
The adrenaline pumping,
The gasket going to blow,
I feel the need for speed.

The wheels spinning, trying to get traction,
Foot hard on the accelerator,
Dying for action,
I feel the need for speed.

The car shoots forward, I feel the thrust,
Strong smell of burning rubber,
The atmosphere made is a definite must,
I feel the need for speed.

Cars coming close soon cower,
Now into top gear,
Sheer velocity, this car has power,
I feel the need for speed.

Winding country roads up ahead,
Messages from the brain giving a warning,
Starting to panic, I'm too young to be dead,
I feel the need for speed.

Car now screaming to a halt,
Foot slams on the brake,
My body thrown forward in one huge jolt,
I feel the need for speed.

Nathan Ellinor (16)
Borden Grammar School

THE MATCH

the floodlights light the stadium so bright,
shining from the stand so high,
lighting up the deep, dark night,
blocking out the evening sky.

the grass, so green, so lush below,
untouched, yet so well worn,
the lines so white, so bright they glow,
the greenness of that huge, vast lawn.

the stand so full,
the heart of the ground,
on match day it is never dull,
however, now there's not a sound.

the goals stand proud at either end,
the wooden whiteness of the post.
the bar so strong it'll never bend,
the net, the ball's grateful host.

the crowd begins to build,
as the time approaches half-past seven.
a cheer goes up as the teams take the field.
they must feel like they're in heaven.

the whistle blows,
the match has started.
the players rush friends and foes,
everyone running whole hearted.

Shaun Wraight (17)
Borden Grammar School

LIFE

A tornado starts spiralling down,
Until one day it will hit the ground,
Life starting at the top;
Ending at the bottom.

At various points life disappears
And at others it begins to appear,
We all start at a set point down, perhaps a date
But one day we will leave the storm
And others will mourn,

This is the way of life,
Believe it if you will,
Where God comes in? It's no big deal,
Crash! Here it ends, life as we know it comes to an end.

Ravi Ahluwalia (16)
Borden Grammar School

WINTER FEAR

Summer has long gone and winter is here,
The ice forms on the pond and great danger is
Here.
As the children skate around without any fear.
Soon the sirens are sounding as the children fear
One might be drowning.
Help is at hand and the rescue was well planned.
Then everything was in hand,
And the children thought twice about skating on the
Ice.

Paul Gregory (11)
Borden Grammar School

MY BIGGEST LOVE

The love I hold for you is,
In full bloom tonight
The passion is shared by others
But is no less despite.
The emotions erupt whenever
I know you're around,
My heart skips a beat
At every sound.
The smells I know so well
Remind me of you,
The pleasure that you give me;
Oh if you only knew.
Adrenaline rush,
Runs through my veins,
With all the fun
There are some pains.
So disappointed,
As I leave,
Hope that next week
We achieve.
Waiting for the day
When I can choose,
Whether Crystal Palace
Win or lose.

James Pickard (16)
Borden Grammar School

THE SEASON OF GOODWILL

The tree stood in the corner,
The drink stood on the bar,
The nuts lay in the glass dish,
The chocolates in a jar.
The decorations sheathed
The sombre walls quite well,
The iridescent pot-pourri
Emanated redolent smells.

The revellers were trekking
From Chicago and New York,
The talented chefs were bringing
The cardamom and pork.
The family did gather
In the glowing, inviting room,
The party poppers and diaphanous hats
Were allocated - but too soon.

A crystal glass was shattered
By a clumsy, imprudent elbow,
But no-one cared, as this was the time where all fellows
Should forgive the altercations,
Should forget the petty feuds,
Should dismiss the remonstrations,
Should cease all minor disputes . . .
An onlooker ruminated from his lofty position,
'How bizarre my insignificant birth started this tradition.'

Neil Williamson (16)
Borden Grammar School

DREAMGIRL?

He stood watching her, his eyes transfixed.
He watched her long, golden hair wave in the midsummer's breeze.
He wanted to pluck up the courage to speak to her,
But his soul would not allow it.

Suddenly she turned,
Their eyes met,
It seemed like hours, in a delightful trance,
He had never seen anything as beautiful as she.
His heart started to pound as she slowly moved closer.
What should he say?
How should he act?
His feet urged him forwards, attracted to her divine grace.
With bodies intertwined, they clasped each other.

He opened his eyes and saw his mum:
'It's time to get up, you'll be late for school.'

Daniel James Hawkins (16)
Borden Grammar School

DAD

My dad's tall,
He's called Paul,
He's as thin as a two-brick wall
He plays snooker he plays pool,
But he'll never go near a swimming pool,
Football, cricket and basketball Dad's good at them all,
He's the best, better than the rest,
But he's never worn a dirty vest.

Luke Avron-Cotton (11)
Borden Grammar School

SATURDAY AND SUNDAY

The weekend's here
So where's the cheer?
It's lost with all the years of pain,
Another week lost down the drain.

He's tired now, he's feeling weak,
He knows the future's highly bleak.
He coughs, he chokes, he takes a drink
Dissolution, he's on the brink.

But no, for it's the weekend
And so some time he will spend
With loved ones, those who really care
And all his troubles they will share.

But they don't come this weekend,
Or the next, and so on goes the trend.
For this old man is on his own,
So no-one will hear him moan and groan.

So for this old man, what is a day?
Weeks all pass him by the way.
So as the end of Friday gets near,
Will he know the weekend's here?

Chris Hawkins (16)
Borden Grammar School

SNOWMAN

The excitement begins as it starts to snow,
And all the kids' faces begin to glow.
They all dress up, scarves, gloves and hats,
And run outside to the snow lying flat.

The snowman begins as a tiny ball,
But as more people help he begins to form.
The body is finished and now for the head,
But all is in vain for soon he'll be dead.

The children go in, to have a bath,
And take of the hats, gloves and scarves.
Outside the sun has begun to shine,
Nothing of the snowman is left behind.

Matthew Barraclough (15)
Borden Grammar School

RÓISÍN GREENE

Your blue eyes glowed like efflorescent lights,
Gleaming brightly in those summer nights,
We spent them together, you and me,
Those special times were filled with glee,
Your Celtic beauty embraced my heart,
How much pain I feel now we're apart,
You father, so strict how you cope I not know,
But your face never loses its golden glow,
Your beauty, it's like I've never seen,
Not even such beauty appears in my dreams,
I miss you Róisín, now you're back home,
My heart well it feels oh so alone,
I'm a troubadour, it's plain to see,
But the love I feel is retained in me.

Peter Hadley (16)
Borden Grammar School

. . . ?

The leathery red coat,
Glistens in the sharp light.
Cool, crisp and moist it holds
The fortress inside.
A solitary turret
Stands alone at
The watery ramparts
Impenetrable, at first.
The fair inhabitants
Lay motionless within.
Each one dark and hard
Ready for instant action.
Slowly it was lifted,
Into the beckoning cavern.
Then *crunch!*
As the apple was quickly devoured.

Alan Doucy (15)
Borden Grammar School

THE CITY AT NIGHT

The roar of a car,
The lights from afar,
The shouts from a bar;
As it drags through the night.

The thunder of a train,
A worksite crane,
You run for cover as it rains;
Two men in a fight.

Charles Parkinson (14)
Borden Grammar School

STAGGERED

Oh God! My aching head!
Wait. This is not my bed.
I think I'm on a train,
Stag nights, never again.
I've got to get back home,
But how? I'm all alone.
I've just found where I've gone,
A place called Bridge of Don.

Bridge of Don, where is that?
My friend is such a rat.
I bet he has great mirth,
To send me near to Perth.
I'm off the train at last,
Time to get home real fast.
A taxi's over there,
Can he take me to Ware?

'And where is Ware?' said he.
Just head towards Swanley,
And there lives my friend Pat,
She'll take me to my flat.

I arrived at the flat,
And then thanked my friend Pat.
Jumped in my wedding gear,
Thank God the church is near!
I called a cabby quick,
And promised a large tip.
We just arrived on time,
And the bride stopped to whine.
What a hullabaloo,
That ended in 'I do'.

Mark Stubberfield (15)
Borden Grammar School

OUTSIDE

The wind outside makes the bushes sway,
While the children with each other play,
And birds fly past without a care in the world,
While Frisbees and footballs are thrown and hurled.

Couples in love walk hand in hand,
Happy faces all over the land,
But as daytime turns from light to dark,
People begin to leave the park.

So darkness falls across the land,
And midnight's hour is close at hand,
Creatures and people fall asleep,
While owls search for things to eat.

Dean Zweck (14)
Borden Grammar School

THE JOURNEY TO SCHOOL

I travel to school by bus each day,
It takes 50 minutes when not delayed,
I get on at 7.41 at Minster Back Lane,
We go through Sheerness at about 5 to 8,
Some days we're early some days we're late,
We get to the bridge at 5 past 8,
On now to Sittingbourne,
We're now running late,
We all go to Borden and think it is great!

Craig Hewitt (14)
Borden Grammar School

THE BATTLE

The time was set;
Battle was to begin at three.
The two armies converged on one area:
The battlefield.

The whistle blew,
Twenty two men started to fight;
As their arsenal of supporters cheered.
It had begun.

The balance of power was ever changing,
The aim was to score one
Over the opposition and win.
The prize was victory.

Then the whistle blew again;
Ninety minutes was up.
The reds were the winners of the match,
Beating the blues three-one.

Matthew Frayne (15)
Borden Grammar School

THE PARK

As I walked through the park,
I heard a sweet bird lark,
When I looked above,
I saw a white glistening dove,
Now I am walking through a ditch,
That leads onto a football pitch,
As I come to the end of the park,
It's now getting dark,
It is time for me to go home.

Lee Fowler (14)
Borden Grammar School

ENGLISH IS SO STRANGE

English is so *strange*
A word meaning odd or *alien*
A life form from another planet like *Mars*
A chocolate *firm*
Hard, compact, *dense*
Not too *bright*
A light or the *sun*
A newspaper full of words and *letters*
Means of communication with other *people*
The dominant life form on *earth*
Soil perfect for a *plant*
Factory mill where goods are *made*
Female domestic *servant*
Someone who carries out an *order*
Tidy, *straight*
Level and in *line*
A rank, row, *cue*
Used in *snooker*
A game played all over the *earth*
The planet where I *live*
To exist and *remain*
Carry on, *continue*
To do something without a *break*
Snap, bend, *demolish*
To kill or *destroy*
Terminate.

Stephen Brown (15)
Borden Grammar School

TRAIN SET

Many years ago exactly three
        I wanted a train driven by electricity.
So imagine my surprise when each birthday came,
        And the train didn't.

Then it just so happened that despite the fuss,
        I managed to pass the eleven plus.
So imagine my surprise when the results came
        And the train didn't.

All hope departed that ever would be seen
        That locomotive in LNER green.
So imagine my surprise when my birthday came
        And so did the train.

I had a train set and could hardly wait
        To clear a space and operate.
So imagine my surprise when Dad came out
        And said it doesn't turn a wheel till we've built a layout.

We bought the MDF at six by four
        Some screws and battening galore.
So imagine my surprise when we made the base
        And ran out of track.

Back to the shop we went next week
        For a book on track layouts to seek.
So imagine my surprise when we found one
        And the layouts wouldn't fit.

We'll design our own when we get back,
        Said Dad, as we purchased a Network South East of track.
So imagine my surprise
        When it all worked.

Michael Wetjen (13)
Borden Grammar School

MINIATURISATION

Zooming up the tunnel,
Red discs all around.
Surfing on the pulses,
A distant beating sound.

Acid bubbling by me,
What a putrid smell.
Got to get out of here,
I've had enough of hell.

Zooming up the tunnel,
Red discs all around.
Surfing on the pulses,
A louder beating sound.

Soft cushions to sleep on,
Fresh air, consuming me.
I've died and gone to heaven
Living in, ecstasy.

Sucked up through a tunnel,
Red discs all around,
Surfing on the pulses
Into the beating sound.

Smacked against the side,
Smashed into a strife.
I'm pumped into a tunnel
Fighting for my life.

Sucked up through a tunnel,
Red discs all around.
Surfing on the pulses.
Away from the beating sound.

I'm in the nose, it's going to blow.
A little sneeze and out I go.

Andrew Gee (15)
Borden Grammar School

THE DENTIST

I'm getting really edgy in the waiting room,
I hope that this is over really quite soon,
Wandering to the surgery is as creepy as can be,
I'm trembling with fear with my mother close to me.

Opening the door with the dentist standing there,
She seems extremely happy and doesn't seem to care,
I sit down in the seat with my mother by my side,
I got so greatly fearful, that I very nearly cried.

She starts to search my mouth with a grin on her face,
A hole in the tooth is certainly the case,
Out came the injection and it went into my gum,
Now my mouth is feeling exceedingly numb.

She finished off my filling now it's time to go,
I looked in the mirror and it started to show,
Mother took me by the hand and said it's time to leave,
Now I've learnt my lesson no more sweets for me.

Shane Dowle (13)
Borden Grammar School

A Scramble!

A scramble has been sounded,
And the radar says we're surrounded,
Don't know what it may be,
But the captain says they'll flee.

One by one they all take off,
They glide better than a moth,
Then up and up they all go,
What to face they don't know.

All in formation what a sight,
They're all ready for a fight.
One by one they all break off,
And go in ready to shoot them off.

Then down and down they all go
Ready to give them a show,
Once they have given it all they have got,
They won't hang around to get shot.

Phillip Ratcliffe (13)
Borden Grammar School

IRAQ V KURDISTAN

Saddam thought he was a good
man,
That was till he fought the
Kurds.
He bombed their houses,
Burnt their cattle.
Shot the wives and children,
Took the men and killed them.

Once he takes Kurdistan,
he can move into Iran.

Bill Clinton has an election to
fight,
Helping the Kurds shows his
might.

For God's sake,
Let's hope he's right.

Alex Clark (14)
Borden Grammar School

BEHIND THE TEACHER'S BACK

The teacher turns to the blackboard,
And says 'I've got a knack,
To see what happens behind me,
Behind the teacher's back.'

In that case, why didn't he see me
Throwing those planes around?
Uh-oh! I think he heard us:
'You lot - don't make a sound!'

All the swots of the class
Sit copying off the board,
While the rest of us lot,
The scribblings, we've all ignored.

Flying bits of rubber
Bouncing off the walls,
Sitting having lots of fun,
Until the teacher calls:

'You lot, why don't you listen,
Why don't you pay attention?
That's it. That is the last straw
Now you're all in detention!'

Nathan Chase (15)
Borden Grammar School

THE COD

I went fishing one day, with my dog,
I cast out my strong aluminium rod,
My dog had gone off with a frog,
I felt something pull my line, oh my God.
My dog returned with a decapitated frog.
As I pulled out a king-sized cod.

I took it to the market instead of eating it for my dinner
I won a hundred pounds,
With my first prize winner,
My dog, who died, was buried in the Yorkshire Downs,
I do agree that dogs are,
Man's best friend.

Stuart Sears (13)
Borden Grammar School

DESSERT ISLAND

Came from up top, in the crows' nest,
land ahoy look out to the west.
Everyone looked and everyone saw,
this magnificent island that lay before.

We drew a little nearer,
and what did we see.
Then things became clearer,
that there were no trees.

The island was laden with goodies galore,
gateau and cakes never seen before.
Crisps, chocolates and of course beer,
there was no reason why not to live here.

Kevin Hodges (14)
Borden Grammar School

ANTS

Once a year in summertime
when it is very warm,
the tiny ants who now have wings
come out from nests in swarms.

The queen stays in the colony,
the workers can be seen
foraging for flies and mites
and honeydew to feed the queen.

Up and down, up and down
the steady army goes,
each tiny ant a signal sent,
running to and fro.

Busy, busy all day long,
each has its part to play.
A winding trail of moving parts,
busy all the day.

Stuart Roberts (13)
Borden Grammar School

FORMULA ONE RACE

The cars are all lined up ready to go.
And it is into the 37th lap and oh no!
Hill is out of the race it is down to the tyres.
Fortunately there were no fires.
He is out of the race what a blow.

And Anthony is taking the high road.
On the dashboard he recognises the code.
He puts his foot down and the brakes he hits,
And swerves into the pits.
The teeth close and . . . that spaghetti was a nice load.

David Halliday (13)
Borden Grammar School

AUTUMN SKIES

I watch the sun,
Draw across the sky,
As summer turns to autumn.

I watch the leaves,
Changing,
Changing,
Changing into golden birds,
Flying through the air.

The air feels so much colder,
Now autumn has arrived,
Leaves falling,
And birds flying.

I wonder what it would be like,
To be the leaves,
To be the birds,
To be the autumn skies.

Ben Smith (13)
Borden Grammar School

LISTEN

Listen to the beggar-man, begging in the street, 'Can you
spare some money, I need some food to eat.'
Listen to the innocent crying out in pain, and listen to the
refugees, many have been slain.
Listen to the problems of our Mother Earth, can we solve
these troubles, or will they get worse?

We have to listen and we have to give, a bit of time and
energy to help the ill live.
Our planet is ours, the earth is unique, but many lives upon
it seem very bleak:
There is pain and distress, and many people's lives are in a
horrid mess.

Stop and listen; have a look around, check things out;
put your ear to the ground.
No matter who you are or what you do; you can change
things and help, and make a difference too.

Christopher Crowley (13)
Borden Grammar School

SPACE

Space, a vast expanse of nothingness,
Nobody to talk, nothing to see,
It is a boundless wilderness,
An emptiness, unlimited.

Space, where does it begin,
Where does it end,
It seems overgrown,
But it is all around.

Space gives you the freedom to wander,
It is everywhere, we cannot see it,
Yet it is everywhere,
Does it have a start or even an end.

Space, mysterious and strange,
Just an open space,
We know quite a lot,
Yet we know very little.

Ben Brown (14)
Borden Grammar School

THE OUTSIDE WORLD

As I peer out of the window what do I see?
The industry of mankind standing in front of me.
The great main street with the canal split in two,
And on the highlands of Minster there's houses just a few.

Going throughout from left to right,
Minster is in the top right.
Repeatedly the houses continue to decrease,
Continuing to the right once more then they increase.

Approaching the lands of my home
The grasslands are separated by a holiday home,
The lands are great with pleasurable scenery,
Not to mention the variety of animals and greenery.

As I peer out of the window what do I see?
Some fields destroyed by a car yard standing in front of me.
And what site will this be in ten years?
The wonder and thought brings my eyes to tears.

Jason Newing (14)
Borden Grammar School

PAIN

I'm drifting on an ocean of fire,
The heat never seems to tire,
I'm lying on a bed of nails,
The sharpness never hails.

My heart is being pierced by a stone,
My body starts to moan and groan,
My bones crumble at a touch,
The aches and pains are too much.

My arm feels as if it is being stung by bees,
The stinging never seems to ease,
I'm swirling in a salty sea,
My body never can be free.

The aches and pains have been too much,
I cower at your every touch,
Suddenly my body feels like lead,
I crumble to the floor,

I'm dead.

Mark Thornton (13)
Borden Grammar School

CHILLI

Chilli isn't cold but it's hot,
From high above it's just a little dot,
Spicy is what it is,
Add kidney beans that does the biz.

But please beware,
If you dare,
To have a glass of water by your side,
Or the next day you'll find that you've died.

If that does the trick,
Then you will be able to pick
If you want to feed your chilli to the cat,
It will be in the air like a bat.

James Wickham (11)
Borden Grammar School

THE DUNK

I was jumping,
Never really reaching,
Adrenaline was pumping,
Just about to catch it.

I just reached it,
Throwing it, placing it,
I was dunking it,
Just like Jordan did it.

Reverse dunk, power dunk,
Anyway will do it,
Somehow it's like junk,
I don't know what to do with it.

Philip Salt (13)
Borden Grammar School

THE LIFE AND DEATH OF BRUNO

I've got a pet fish called Bruno,
to me he is numero uno.
He swims up and down without making a sound,
just like all other fishes do, you know.

He's a fraction the size of a whale,
with 2 bulging eyes, fins and a tail.
Though I call him a he, it could be a she,
I'm not sure if it's female or male.

I've tried other pets like a frog,
and my dad wouldn't buy me a dog.
Unlike all the rest my fish is the best,
when he dies he'll be flushed down the bog.

Terence Still (11)
Borden Grammar School

I Did It!

I look at the fear on its face
It has not much of it left
It just lies on its side
It breathes no longer
It is dead it's dead very dead

I did it I did it
It breathes no more because of me
I feel scared
I feel good
But I do not feel pity

I do not feel sorry
I feel glad
I feel happy it's dead
But now, now I feel something
Something strange something weird.

I know what it is,
I feel pity
I feel sad
I feel the fear it suffered
I killed it, no I killed him

I have killed someone who knew
I am scared because I killed my father.

Piers Pereira (13)
Borden Grammar School

THE BOY FROM THANET

The wickedest boy on the planet
An ugly boy who lived in Thanet
The name he went by was Lee
He was a little rebel as you will see
But this disgusting little thing
Decided to give the fire brigade a ring
He went outside and waited for
His mum to go back indoors
He started climbing up a tree
As slow and calm as could be
And as soon as he reached the top
Obviously he had to stop
Then this disgusting little louse
Crawled into a little house
And once inside his little home
He casually picked up a phone
Then he dialled 999
And started shouting down the line
I need your help, come quickly do
If I look down, I'm going to spew
I am stuck up a tree
If I don't get down I'll miss my tea
I live at number 55
This is in Thanet down Fernesway Drive
Suddenly the line went dead.

David Lyth (13)
Borden Grammar School

THE CREEPY WOOD

The creepy wood,
is a scary place
it's as if the wood
has got a face

In winter when brown leaves are on the ground,
crisp and crackling beneath my feet,
there is not a lot of animal food around
and the animals haven't got a lot to eat.

In spring the animals you can see,
but don't stay out too late in the creepy wood,
as the bravest have tried but they just flee,
without a trace or explanation.

In summer prepare for a shock,
the bats are out again.
So don't stay out more than 10 o'clock,
or this could be a pain.

In autumn things are there,
that will give you a terrible scare.
If you do go into the woods,
don't get lost or you'll meet a grizzly bear!

So remember this warning,
I hope you do,
tell all your friends,
your father and mother too.

Nick Brend (11)
Borden Grammar School

LIFE AND DEATH IN A DAY

It's in the van, nice and clean,
It looks really good, very mean,
I pull it out and start it up,
I put on my suit and rev it up.

I pull out of the pits, the back wheels spin,
The front wheels rocking, out and in.
I get on the straight, put my foot down,
The throttle gets stuck, I'm tyre wall bound.

Bang!

The go-kart stops, my heart does not,
I was OK but the engine was shot.
My dad comes over with a sack
To pick up the pieces and take them back.

The kart is bent 'twisted metal',
We chuck it in some stinging nettles
We get in the van make our way home
The kart is left there, all alone.

Leigh Howard (13)
Borden Grammar School

THE FOOTY POEM

In football why do people always shout
'Come on ref look at your watch!'?
Why not just say
'Referee it's time the match finished now.'?

In football why do people shout
'Send him off!'?
Why not just say
'That man should be given a red card.'?

In football why do people shout
'The ref needs glasses!'?
Why not just say
'Referee do you need some glasses?'?

In football why do people shout at all?
Why not just speak *quietly?*

Tom Passey (11)
Borden Grammar School

AIRLINE PILOT

Sitting at the strange steering column
In the complex complicated cockpit
Of the lovely luxurious liner.

Sitting above the tarmac waiting to
Taxi out. As clearance is given we
Begin our journey. To the start of the
Runway we crawl.

As the liner starts to gain speed
Biff, boff, bump, batter go the engines as
The liner forwards faster and faster
Flying down the runway.

Suddenly our silver bird soars
Skyward, and the appetising smell
Of supper stirs.

Time to take in the movie
Take that and relax before
Touchdown.

Jump, jerk, judder another journey over.

Ashley Eagles (13)
Borden Grammar School

THE WEATHER

The weather is a funny old thing,
one moment it's warm then it goes cold,
then when it's dry it goes wet and rainy,
I don't know what it's going to do day after day.

The weather is a funny old thing,
first it's nice and sunny, then it's horrible and cloudy.
When it's cold and snowy the sun comes out to melt
the snow,
I don't know what it's going to do day after day.

The weather is a funny old thing,
one day it's hot and sunny the next thing it's windy
and cold,
then when you're indoors because of the cold the
next minute it's hot and sunny,
I don't know what it's going to do day after day.

The weather is a funny old thing,
when forecasters predict the weather, sometimes the weather
changes and causes a lot of chaos for other people,
then when you're on the beach sunbathing a huge wave
comes over by a big gust of wind,
I don't know what it's going to do day after day.

Richard Penny (11)
Borden Grammar School

WORRIED LITTLE ELEPHANT

I'm a little elephant writing to complain,
About all those nasty poachers, they're driving us insane.
I mean, some of my herd about a week or two ago,
Were shot at by some poachers, they won't leave us alone.

They want our tusks to carve and sell,
But we want them too, and it's not hard to tell,
That we're on the brink of being wiped out,
There's not many elephants still left about.

Not like there used to be, anyway,
When there were huge herds of us walking around each day.
But in those days we were left alone,
People had no need for our precious bone.

A few months ago my brother disappeared
I hope the poachers didn't get him, it was what he most feared.
So if we all act together right now,
We might be able to show other people how.

To help us elephants wherever we may lie,
And stop these evil poachers from making us die.
So somebody please read this little bit of writing,
And maybe we could stop this unnecessary fighting.

Philip Baptie (13)
Borden Grammar School

IN LOVING MEMORY

The feet patter down the stairs,
and a familiar laugh echoes down the hall,
In marches little soldier, brave-faced
and ready for school.

Lunch is packed, and the shoes are clean,
out of the door hops the little soldier.
Skipping down the path, or running ahead,
longing to be amidst friends once more.

Into the school yard, to skip, hop or run,
with friends to play until the bell.
Lessons start with a clatter of feet,
laughs and cries mingle, like raindrops on the path outside.

A moment of madness, gunfire and bullets,
and the classroom becomes silent forever more.
Tears and sadness, panic and worry,
little solider lies asleep on the floor.

Throughout the nation, mothers mourn.
No more laughs, no patter of feet.
The classroom's quiet, and all is lost.

Broken dreams haunt the night,
and outside, an owl screams.
He pierces the night with his sorrowful screech,
for little soldier will march no more.

Julie Marsh (16)
Charles Darwin School

An Autumn Day

The smell of autumn and winter rolled
into one with the sharp, cold weather
piercing the nose and a gentle but noticeable
breeze against my face. Chirping and the
rustle of leaves, only to be sliced in two
pieces by a tornado in the form of a
metallic bird gliding across the sky. A last
leaf holds onto a tree like a child clutching
to its mother.

An artist paints the soft clouds in the sky
and someone sprays an aerosol from a plane.
An enormous clock made of clouds strikes
ten. The call of a seagull coming to its
mate and the whistle of its young for its
incoming food. The roar of a motorbike
as if a lion had just run by and the shake
of windows as a gust of wind sweeps the
seagull from its perch on an aerial, floating
like a leaf. Thousands of birds do a relay
but quickly return to their warm cosy nests.

The giggle of school children that stops
abruptly when the mistress strides up and
decides to question their work. The towering
tree, like a huge artist's palette with its
children falling from it. Trees that look
like thin lines drawn in every order imaginable.
The cup that is swaying to and fro as if by
an invisible hand. Birds chirping and pecking
at my feet.

It is peaceful here and I like it a lot.

Callum McFadyen (13)
Charles Darwin School

THE BURGLAR

Over the hedge he did *roll*
He was going to rob some poor soul,
Over his shoulder, he gives a glance
It's his first time, he takes a *chance*
He undoes the lock with a small *pin*
By now he has committed a sin
Sitting by the fire he sees her, old and frail
She's looking ill and rather *pale*
Back through the door he gets *going*
What could've happened there's no knowing.
It crossed his mind he could end up in clink
Well at least that made the burglar *think*
The poor old lady she was so sad
No harm done he felt *glad*
He did not want to be a *rat*
His conscience made sure of that.

Richard Lewin (13)
Charles Darwin School

THE MORAY EEL

Down at the bottom of the sea,
Lays a dark creature,
Ready to pounce out on anything in reach,
Lurking about the misty waters,
Hungry and eager to strike,
Mud and dust swirling around,
Then out he comes,
Out of his humble home,
Ready to catch his prey,
All fish will scatter but one,
Then everything is silent.

Natalie Parker (12)
Chatham Grammar School For Girls

WHALES AND DOLPHINS

Whales and dolphins swim in the sea,
in the ocean they dive wild and free.
Singing to the rhythm of the waves,
ducking and diving through the caves.
Playing so happily in the waves,
until a net comes crashing down,
Catching the dolphins,
hurting the whales.
Surrounding the dolphins until they can't move.
They cry in pain, they cry in vain
'Help me, help me,' they cry again.
They get dragged back to the shore
where they cry as they die.

Rachel Peat (11)
Chatham Grammar School for Girls

PANTHER NIGHT

The sky, jet *black,*
As the panther's velvet brush.
The stars, a scattered blanket of jewels,
As glowing as the panther's melting eyes,
The colour of butter.

The streets and avenues a-glow with stars,
No citizen of the city below,
Knows the Panther of the night,
Is observing them all,
Young and old.

Emma Gibson (13)
Chatham Grammar School for Girls

THE GIANT PANDA

The giant panda,
Running through the trees,
Running and chasing,
The bumble bees.
Swimming, swimming,
Swimming in the sea,
Happy as ever,
Can ever be.
Out of the water,
Back into the trees,
Then suddenly *bang!*
The giant panda ran and ran,
Scared and frightened,
Out of his wits,
Scared that he might be,
Blown to bits.
Through the water,
He swam and swam,
Will I make it?
I don't think I can!
Later that night,
He slept in his cave,
Thinking to himself,
What right have they,
To come and take us,
Take us away?
Extinction is forever!
What would you rather have?

Shelley King (12)
Chatham Grammar School for Girls

HOSPITALS

Most people hate hospitals,
But certainly not me,
I've been going there all my life,
My mother coming with me.

People say they think of death,
Whenever going near
A hospital, that helps save lives,
A thing thought of not as mere.

The click and whirr of large machines
And all the visitors' chatter
The screams of children having jabs,
And medicines to make them better.

The surgeons in their overalls
And porters dressed in white
Anaesthetists with their glasses on
And nurses being nice.

If it wasn't for the hospital,
I go to six times a year,
I probably would have died long ago,
A thought that fills me with fear.

I can't believe people who are scared of them
It is just in their mind,
One day they will be hospitalised.
It is just a case of time.

Victoria Pallot (15)
Chatham Grammar School for Girls

SILENT SUFFERING

Pain is like the invisible man,
It's there but rarely seen.
Tears fall unknowingly,
Guess what? It happened to me.

The suffering doesn't go away
It lurks in your mind,
Like an unforgiving sin,
Creeping forward, keeping time.

Drained by all the physical torment,
That comes and goes each day,
Impaired by the mental scarring
That drives others away.

Finally the torture endured departs,
Leaving behind its seal.
A scar that will not be missed,
A mark that is very real.

Sandra Marsh (14)
Chatham Grammar School for Girls

MATHS

My best subject is maths,
Maths is a wonderful thing.
It makes me proud to do it,
It makes me want to sing.

Maths, maths, give me more maths,
It makes me go all dizzy.
I love maths whatever the sum,
It makes my hair go frizzy.

Nicola Letchford (11)
Chatham Grammar School for Girls

NIGHT

The moon rises in the starry sky,
The calm beams of the moon,
Stroke the houses in their slumber.
An owl hoots in the nocturnal silence,
The trees shine silver,
They glisten in the moonlight,
The sinister shadows,
Dodge the silver beams,
Then the moon fades,
The stars melt,
The sun dawns upon us,
The dew adorns the grass,
In beads like pearls,
The calmness of the night has faded,
Into the hustle and bustle of the day.

Amy Adams (11)
Chatham Grammar School for Girls

MEMORIES

M any of them are in your mind
E verlasting
M ore and more each day
O f some special days
R emembering them
I could never forget them
E ach of them different
S omething special will always be there.

Amie Hatcher (12)
Chatham Grammar School for Girls

MY FISH

I have a fish
His name is Jaws
He has no feet
He has no paws

He can't walk
He can't speak
He can't talk
Just swims all week

I had a fish
He was called Fred
I don't have him now
Because he's dead.

Samantha James (11)
Chatham Grammar School for Girls

MY GREAT NAN

Early this century a young girl was born,
With a long life ahead of her,
Willing and strong.

A few years later she was ready for school,
To be taught Maths and English all day long.

She was fit and young then,
But now very old.
Weary and tired,
Legs not too strong.
Now it's the end,
And time to remember,
The good times from her childhood years.

Gemma Jordan (12)
Chatham Grammar School for Girls

PIP

I remember in the summer holidays of 1994,
I had a rabbit that I did adore.
He was grey and white,
clean and bright.
His name was Pip,
he was so quick.

One morning I noticed something,
which was only a little thing.
An ulcer had grown on the side of his cheek,
which made him oh so weak.
My lovely cute and cuddly pet,
we now had to take to the vet.

In the operation room,
there was a lot of gloom.
In the end it turned out right,
but he still hadn't won the fight.
I saw him there, his little head,
but then I realised he was quite dead.

Rebecca Brooker (12)
Chatham Grammar School for Girls

PENGUINS

Penguins are black and white,
Flapping wings but still no flight,
They dive into the deep blue sea,
Eating fishes one, two, three.

Penguins slide across the ice,
Thinking this is jolly nice,
They dive into the cold blue sea,
Where their hearts are filled with glee.

Stacey Bell (11)
Chatham Grammar School for Girls

A NEW BEGINNING

Another night falls,
Engulfing the sleepy village,
That lays across the horizon,
Dew settles on the grass,
And leaves rustle in the wind.

The moon climbs up,
To take his place on watch patrol,
Whilst the stars light the sky,
Shedding their natural light to passers by,
The stream flows by like silk,
Shimmering in the moonlight.

Then a glimpse of light,
Peeping over the hill,
Spreading out its long rays,
Waking up the dawn,
Whilst the moon drops like a pearl,
And the sky clears to a beautiful blue,
To start another day.

Lisa Bedelle (12)
Chatham Grammar School for Girls

MOVING

Mum is in a muddle,
Only one minute to go,
Various bits of junk,
Inside our old house,
No time to lose!
Good thing we don't move
every day!

Louisa Penman (12)
Chatham Grammar School for Girls

IN THE CLASSROOM

Miss Smith drew on the board -
A circle and a square,
And while she drew, sweet Peter Spriggs
Tugged on poor Sophie's hair.

'Argh!' She screamed,
The class all turned and saw poor Sophie crying,
'I'll get you back you horrid boy!'
Dear Peter was sent flying.

Across the room Peter flew;
He landed in a heap.
As he looked up, he saw
That Margaret Sawyers was asleep.

By now, the class (the awful lot)
Decided to join in
The argument that was going on
Between Caroline and Tim.

The noise they made was terrible;
It was a frightful scene.
The hamster poked his head out,
He was woken from his dream.

Miss Smith turned round, chalk in her hand,
'Oh dear, what's happened here?
Next time I take this class for maths,
I'll keep an open ear!'

Angela Hammond (12)
Chatham Grammar School for Girls

As I . . .

As I get up early each
morning,
I look out of my bedroom
window,
I see children playing in the
snow outside,
making snowmen and throwing
snowballs around.

As I stare and smile, I hear the
bells strike every hour,
from the church, high up in
the mountains surrounded by
clouds.

As the clouds start to move away,
you can just about see
the numbers six and eight,
but that's just only on occasions
like birthdays and Christmas.
I knew today was a special day
but I didn't know what day it
was and then I remembered it was
my birthday!

Ashley Bowden (12)
Chatham Grammar School for Girls

THE MAGICAL MIST

The fog feels like very, very soft rain
Tickling my face as I walk down the lane.
As I walk across the field there are ghostly figures
Walking towards me.
First they're there then they've gone
Into a cloud of dust.
It feels like you lose yourself into a spooky world of
The dead.
Zombie-like people walk towards you from
All directions,
The tops of the trees look like they hover in mid air.
Different shaped and sized cars and lorries
Rush by with headlights on.
As the car or lorry,
Disappears, only its tail lights can be seen.

Beckie Ferguson (11)
Chatham Grammar School for Girls

MY GRANDAD

My Grandad used to be a boxer,
lightweight you see.
He used to beat them every match
until it was time for tea.

My Grandad used to be in the war,
he used to get a truck,
and carry all the bombs,
and abide by the law.

My Grandad used to be a father,
until he died. My dad grieved,
then up popped *me!*

Sara C A Walsh (11)
Chatham Grammar School for Girls

MY FIRST BIRTHDAY PARTY!

I had my first birthday party when I was seven,
All my friends arrived early while I was still in the bath,
Yeah, it was OK, well I think it was,
I enjoyed it, I had a good laugh!

One by one I opened the presents,
A teddy bear, a book, even a Barbie doll,
I opened all eleven of them,
My favourite present was the rabbit stuck in a hole!

Next it was games time,
We played Pass the Parcel, Musical Chairs,
Musical Bumps and Musical Statues,
The prizes were all little cuddly bears!

Then it was time to eat,
We all sat around the table and tucked in,
Cakes, sandwiches, crisps and chocolate,
All different biscuits all in a tin.

Then it was time for the birthday cake,
We turned off the lights and the candles shone,
My friends sang 'Happy Birthday' to me,
I took a deep breath and the lights were gone.

Then the doorbell rang, the party had finished,
I handed the party bags one by one,
Inside were sweets, toys and some birthday cake,
They waved goodbye, and my friends were gone!

Sundeep Kaur (13)
Chatham Grammar School for Girls

My Mum, Your Mum

My mum's taller than your mum,
Yes, my mum's taller than yours.
If she grows anymore she'll reach the sky,
She'll have to stay outdoors.

My mum's older than your mum,
My mum's older than yours, OK.
All of her teeth will fall out,
She'll have to stay indoors.

My mum's prettier than your mum,
Yes, my mum's prettier than yours.
If she gets any prettier she'll win Miss World,
And go dressed in nothing but furs.

Heather Brook (11)
Chatham Grammar School for Girls

The Bull

There I was, sitting in the amphitheatre,
Looking with amazement at the bull,
At five years old I did not understand why . . .
Why a man was murdering an innocent bull
In front of an eager crowd.

The bull was reacting wildly to the red flag
And was charging towards it angrily.
I turned my head away,
I heard a cheer in the crowd as the bull was brutally
murdered.

And still to this day,
I don't understand
How people can be so cruel . . .

Joanne Braithwaite (12)
Chatham Grammar School for Girls

LIFE

Life is short,
Short as can be,
I loved my grandad and,
He loved me,
The time came he had to go,
Oh my grandad,
I loved him so,
In his grave, there he lie,
Seeing him buried, made me cry.

Michelle Monk (13)
Chatham Grammar School for Girls

MY BROTHERS, YOUR BROTHERS

My brothers are nicer than yours,
they take me out all the time,
to the park and to the fair,
I'm loved 'cos I never whine.

Yesterday my brothers and I,
went to see a football match,
my brothers are so lovely,
believe me, there's no catch.

But if I tell you the truth,
they hit me and call me names,
they're really horrible to me,
and they're not playing games.

So are mine, they don't like me,
they never take me out,
they really are so horrible,
they always scream and shout.

Kate Turner (11)
Chatham Grammar School for Girls

BEDTIME

'It's time for bed,' your mum will say
When you're a hundred miles away
Hearing the TV blare
All she'll do is stop and stare
You turn and say 'Please can I . . .'
She'll stop you there
And you'll be marching up the stair
You make a loud banging sound
Where your foot's thumping on the ground
Soon you make it to your room
All you can see is darkness and gloom
You turn on your light and see there
Is nothing but your favourite teddy bear
You climb into your soft, warm bed
Then lie down and rest your sleepy head
But then you hear a noise
Something hiding behind the toys
You scream and shout
Until someone comes out
And up the stairs to you
And then your little sister jumps up
And screams out 'Boo!'

Leyna Mendham (12)
Chatham Grammar School for Girls

SNOWFLAKE

I bought my hamster on a winter's day,
the snow was falling down.
We thought we would call him Snowflake,
because he was white and brown.

Each morning we would let him run,
round and round in his ball.
Because he was a Russian Dwarf,
he was always very small.

We would hear him scratching all night long,
playing in his cage.
In the mornings I'd wake up tired,
and sometimes in a rage.

Then one day I woke to find,
my hamster very ill.
We took him to the vet's that night,
the vet gave him a pill.

I sat up all night long and
I began to pray.
But it didn't do much good,
my hamster passed away.

I went to bed that night,
and sat and cried and cried.
Feeling sorry for myself,
that it was my hamster that had died.

Jackie Hurst (13)
Chatham Grammar School for Girls

THE FIRE

I woke from sleeping that dreadful night,
to the smell of burning wood,
I had to wake everyone else,
if only now I could.

As I climbed out of my bed,
the thick smoke made me choke,
to stay down low eyes closed tight,
was now my only hope.

I found my brother and my sister,
and then I called for my mum,
we called for what seemed ages,
but still she didn't come.

The fire engines came,
sirens wailing and lights flashing blue,
we were told we shouldn't worry,
our mum would soon be out too.

The firemen were really fast,
as they smashed down the door,
we saw two figures on the ladder,
and mum was with us once more.

Soon the fire was under control,
the flames were under cover,
we had no house and now no home,
but thankfully we still had a mother.

Gemma Hussein (12)
Chatham Grammar School for Girls

WHEN LEWIS FELL IN THE POND

There came a day,
That was bright and sunny.
There was a pond,
That was inside a school.

Some boys walked along,
Called Martyn, Tom and Lewis.
They were part of a group,
Which I also belonged to.

They asked to look at the pond,
Where the pond-monitor let them in.
Lewis looked at the fish,
While the others mucked about.

In a flash Lewis was gone,
He had fallen into the pond,
Everybody started to laugh,
Lewis turned round and blushed.

He had to borrow clothes,
From a girl!
They were too big,
And he looked like a girl!

Karen Rodgers (12)
Chatham Grammar School for Girls

MEMORIES

He was just lying there,
motionless,
in a gleaming white hospital bed,
nothing I could do would save him.
I felt helplessly hopeless.
His skin looked grey like stone and his lips were brown.
As I hurried into the ward,
he stared a hard glassy stare,
his eyes bloodshot.
I stopped,
it suddenly occurred to me he didn't know who I was!
I walked over putting out my hand to hug him,
I noticed the drip in the back of his hand.
He reached out to kiss me.
I kissed him but his lips felt cold as ice even though I felt hot.
Then I passed him his Christmas present.
I don't think he understood quite what it was.
He glanced at it and gingerly put it on the bedside table
Then two nurses came to wish him a merry Christmas,
and they handed him his Christmas dinner.
He cut a piece and put it in his mouth,
then he began to chew.
Suddenly without warning he began to choke.
My mum took me and my brother downstairs to the canteen.
A little while later we went to collect my Grandma and then
we went home.
But Christmas Day wasn't the same without him.
A few weeks later the bad news came.
I knew it would.
Although somewhere in my heart even though he is dead,
there are still the happy memories.

Claire Elliott (12)
Chatham Grammar School for Girls

THE SNOWMAN

My memories of the snowman,
I was only three years old,
My mum, dad and my brother
Helped me build it.
He wore a little red hat,
And a little yellow scarf,
I remember how my brother laughed,
I went in that night,
And the next morning I got a fright,
The snowman,
My lovely first snowman,
Had disappeared and all I found
Was the hat and scarf.
I was going to make another one
When I slipped on the ice
And broke my collar bone.
I howled and howled in pain.
I have still got that hat and scarf,
And I have got a scar on my shoulder.
Two memories of two winter days.

Annette Brinsden (13)
Chatham Grammar School for Girls

THE SEASONS

New life begins in the season of spring,
The land is rich with nature,
New buds open, their flowers blossom,
The fresh scents fill the air.

We sit and bask in the heat of the sun,
Which brightens the vast blue sky,
Dank evenings come late this day,
And autumn's on its way.

Feast your eyes on the colours of autumn,
It is a solemn season,
With saffron rays and russet leaves,
It is a joy to those who breathe.

Winter is but bleak and cold,
White snow levels the land,
The rich bright colours disappear,
But spring is close at hand.

Sarah Pettit (15) & Kate Jordan (16)
Chatham Grammar School for Girls

MAN DID IT ALL

Oil floats on once lush rivers,
Trees fall to the ground,
Animals choke on poisonous fumes,
Devastation is all around,
Coats of fur stolen by man,
Heads of animals hang on the wall,
The flea-bitten carpet, bearskin of course,
Yes, man did it all.

Killing fellow humans,
Blood lies everywhere,
Victims cower and hide,
They run away if they dare,
Rainforests are demolished,
They once stood straight and tall,
No-one seems to care anymore,
Yes, *man* did it all.

Jennifer Dyjak (13)
Chatham Grammar School for Girls

REALITY

Yesterday was a dream,
A dream of what was meant to have been,
Tomorrow is a vision,
A vision of peace,
And all that's going to be,
Today is reality,
Reality spoils your dreams and visions,
As you realise everything's the same,
And there's no-one left to blame anymore,
Reality a picture full of guns, bombs and
Conflicts.

Anisha Paddam (12)
Chatham Grammar School for Girls

TIME

Time . . . everlasting,
You can't hear it,
Smell it, feel it, see it,
But it controls the life of
            every living being.

Our lives are made up of,
Days, months, years,
We cannot escape from it,
When faced with danger,
It seems to be lost . . .

Time . . . everlasting
Or is it? How long,
Will our lives be?
Nobody knows,
Only time can tell . . .

Alexandra Steward (15)
Chatham Grammar School for Girls

GRANDMA'S MIDNIGHT CALLER

It all began when the dustbins were raided
The padding of feet across damp grass
And cold concrete slabs
The ripping of bags broke the silence

Its glowing eyes as red as hot embers
Surrounded by a sea of red fur
As bright as marigolds
A treasured sight remembered through the years

The visitor was cautious but soon grew bolder
Grandma wasn't too partial about its love
Of investigating her bin
She tried to encourage more domesticated habits

After plenty of patience and loving care
It became tame enough to feed from the hand
It dined like a king
On both sweets and savouries

But this closer relationship revealed that
The fox was riddled with mange
Like a favourite teddy
With fur worn thin through the years

But one sad night the fox failed to appear
And has not been sighted since
Grandma could only assume
It had finally lost its battle for life

And although there was no happy ending
I will always remember the night when
That beautiful wild fox came out of the darkness
And fed from my hand.

Rosemary Ellis (12)
Chatham Grammar School for Girls

IT'S A GIRL!

We were just sitting there waiting . . .
And waiting. Then there was a loud noise,
Like somebody riding a horse down
The corridor.
We stood up!
Looked round the corner,
Mum was running towards us with tears
Streaming down her face!
She was screaming
'It's a girl! It's a girl!'
'What's a girl?'
'Her name's Rebecca!'
She was screaming.
Melissa and I were jumping for joy,
But I was upset, I don't know why.
I started to cry, hoping she was OK.
I wanted to see her,
I couldn't.

Polly Rowe (12)
Chatham Grammar School for Girls

LONGING

My life, I feel has been taken away,
And now my mind can only stray,
Along Memory Lane it will surely go,
And then I know that my true emotions will show.

I'll try to hide them, but all in vain,
Because I must cry - if only to keep myself sane.
My friends I know I'm sure to miss,
Their generous smiles or a friendly kiss.

All these things have made me strong,
But in their absence my heart will long,
For all these things I loved so much,
And now their lives I just wish I could touch.

I know in my heart this is not the end,
But this thought alone could never mend,
The deep down fear that all is gone,
For this is the thought that makes me long . . .

Amanda Fairfield (14)
Chatham Grammar School for Girls

MEMORIES OF THE TEDDY BEAR!

Memories of the teddy bear
he looked sad,
Spinning in the washing machine
I was mad!

Memories of the teddy bear
he was all wet,
Dripping on the floor
I wept!

Memories of the teddy bear
sitting on my bed,
Watching him sitting there
he looked dead!

Memories of the teddy bear
I love him so much,
Sitting there on my bed
his name is Ted!

Kelly Liddle (12)
Chatham Grammar School for Girls

EMOTIONS

All around me, I see red,
whilst voices thunder that he is dead,
although emotions should be said,
I prefer for them to be read.

The clock starts to tick
and time begins to pass.
Light turns into dark
and lives shatter like glass.

Tears sting my eyes
and drop like tiny pearls,
I do not know why
but they taunt me as I cry.

He walks away so far
and rejects my love he knows,
yet there is nothing I can do
but watch him as he goes.

The pain tears right through me,
my silent anguish they cannot see,
for only those who know, can understand
what it is like to lose a man.

Shabnam Karim (15)
Chatham Grammar School for Girls

LOVE

Love is filled with everlasting dreams
Although we know our fantasies are unseen.
Secure in the hope this love will never die
Our life just seems to pass us by.

Friends, they share our happiness
They always see us at our best.
Others though, may not do so,
Their jealous thoughts, they come and go.

We're not adoring for all twelve months of the year,
Hatred and scorn, it makes us fear.
Maybe our love, it cannot last,
Have we the strength in our hearts?

Yvonne Hamill (15)
Chatham Grammar School for Girls

PERSONIFICATION

The stream is dancing on its way,
to make its peace to end the day.
It makes a wish and hopes it comes true,
a wish I don't think will ever do.

He wished for something yet was already there,
a wish for happiness, a wish for care.
And years went past and nobody knew,
about his wish for freedom, his wish to break through.

So he broke his wish, made up his mind to give up,
as he discovered the future, full of good luck.
So the stream now has a smile of a very happy face,
next time he makes a better wish, he'll take a slower
pace.

Tina-Amanda Wragg (11)
Chatham Grammar School for Girls

MY RIGHT LEG

I went riding on my bike
Along the garden path,
When suddenly I fell
And landed on a spike.

I looked down and saw
A long spike of wood,
Embedded in my leg
A dirty piece of wood.

The blood was trickling down
Down towards my foot,
My cries for help were so loud
They woke up all the town.

My mum carried me indoors
To clean my injured leg,
Then to the doctor's surgery
To heal my wounded leg.

Felicity Edmead (12)
Chatham Grammar School for Girls

ESCAPE

A land of beauty bathed by a desolate sunset,
The sensual colours of the weeping horizon,
The angry crashing of the rage-filled sea,
And the silence between you and me.

Our lives that bow to the animal kingdom,
To feel so small in the human race,
But feeling close to you my love,
And falling asleep to the stars above.

The piercing heat of the miraculous day,
The sweat that glistens upon my skin,
I feel in harmony once more,
And feel your presence for ever more.

The day you left this earth, I knew I could not stay,
In a country where memories will always reign,
A refugee in a darker distant land,
Oh sweetest Africa, you have always held my hand.

Julia Gillingham (15)
Chatham Grammar School for Girls

ARE YOU AFRAID OF THE DARK?

I remember a little girl,
We were very close,
She was petrified of darkness and monsters and
ghosts,
And at night in the darkness the shadows seemed
to loom
And her favourite doll would glare at her seeming
to plot her doom,
A shadow of a soldier,
Pointed a gun at her head,
In fear she sunk deeper into her bed,
The monster in the loft which caused her throat
to lump,
In the light of day was merely a heating pump,
The shadows of the night slowly disappeared,
And the frightening dolls no longer leered.
If you are wondering who that little girl could be
Yes, that's right, it was me!

Kim Green (12)
Chatham Grammar School for Girls

THE DOLPHINS

The sea is so vast,
But it is my home,
Home to many species,
Many are my friends,
Many are my enemies,
Many of my friends,
Have been captured or killed,
I will be soon, I know it.

I love the sea,
So big and strong,
With the waves crashing,
And the sun blazing down.
I could live forever,
If humans didn't want me,
Need me for entertainment,
They think it's fun for me,
It's not.

Their ships and yachts,
Come sailing past,
I must swim fast,
If I get caught that's it for me.
Trapped forever, please set me free.

Laura Hinchliffe (15)
Chatham Grammar School for Girls

MURDER OF A DEAD MAN

Warm, lifeless flesh,
lies upon a cold cement slab.
The biting odour of death,
snatches at the air.
A mangled expression,
creeps across the face,
of a small crippled body;
which appears misplaced.
Blood, the rich red of rubies,
flows along a rubbish-ridden gutter.
Dashing footsteps begin to slow;
the body's identity remains unknown.
A loving husband or desolate loner?
The mystery is never to be solved.
The oddity of night goes on,
unaware of the solitary alley;
where the murderer's battle,
was fought and won.
Regardless or not, of its discovery,
hopes of affection are tossed aside,
to make way,
for death and mortality.

Claire Burgess (16)
Chatham Grammar School for Girls

ME AND MY SISTER

My sister always gets me into trouble
she gets away with anything
I just get a smack
Mum's nicer to her.
My Dad's nicer to me than her
I get away with anything
I want with Dad.
My sister gets a smack.
I am really mean to her
She tries to be clever and pull faces
But I pull them back
My sister pulls the cat's tail and tells Mum I did it
I try and tell her but her answer is 'Go to
your room young lady.'
My sister does the same thing to Dad
But he just tells her off for telling tales
My sister and I are so lucky to
have understanding parents
Not!
I love my sister really.

Emily Bentley (11)
Chatham Grammar School for Girls

MOONSHINE

Magnificent, majestic moonlight
Dances with swaying finger-like branches
Earth's gleaming face glistens
Gently with joy as
Brilliantly bright stars shimmer softly.
Claw-like shadows scratch
Shatteringly at a gentle carpet of
Frothy, fluffy snow.
Frigid, frost-bitten, frozen branches
Cling firmly to night sky.
Spear-like icicles bleed
Cascading droplets, which pound a
Blemished winter's vale.

Dale Westbrook (15)
Christ Church High School

IN MY BOX

I will put in my box
A fluffy fragile rodent clouded with fur.
I will toss in my box
A gleaming sparkling coin
Bullied with chiselled engravings.
I will place in my box
A vulnerable petal graffitied with colour.
I will shape into my box
An emerald transparent blob:
A frigid versatile jelly.
I will throw in my box
A hairy sphere, covered with green velvet:
A tennis ball.

James Bryant (16)
Christ Church High School

GOD MADE PEOPLE

God created the eye, a jellied
Ball of vision, with its
Azure tinted glass-like surface, surrounding a
Mysterious tunnel of black.

He produced a cave of sparkling,
Pearl-like teeth, and
Placed within, a serpent-like
Monarch of taste.

He created the brain, a wondrous
Universe of ceaseless thoughts,
And contained it all within the
Precisely moulded head, the most
Distinctive aspect of the
Human Being.

Rebecca Wadey (15)
Christ Church High School

MOONSHINE

Moonlight skims frost-eaten branches as
Shadows multiply under the fingers of night.
Frost fondles refrigerated hills.
Stars glow like candles, illuminating the
Devilish darkness.
Frost-tinted trees tug the sky,
Dribbling dew onto silver-tinged grass.
Darkness cascades, cautiously covering the
Glittering earth.

Mark Osborne (15)
Christ Church High School

THE WONDER OF CHAOS

Wasted ground quakes in the
Doomed end of a dying world.
Stone showers contort already
Tortured terrain into excessively
Grotesque, twisted images whilst
Chaotic chasms gash the
Barren plains of destruction like
Ripped paper.
Lightning blasts from peak to peak,
Illuminating the carnage all around.
Acrid clouds of poison flow in
Vast, incandescent cracks of the
Ocean's desert.
Panicking soil disperses, releasing
Dark, dusty flatulent ether, like
Spores emitted from fungus.
Raised plateaux of splintering
Stone witness the
Planetoid's futile demise . . .

Robin Jobber & Barry Andrews (15)
Christ Church High School

FISH AND CHIPS

Entering the waiting room,
Bells signifying my entrance,
Smells of sacrificial items,
Seep across the room.
High priests approach
There to serve my order.
Watching intently, as
Hallowed haddock, coated in a
Sacrificial layer of batter, is
Plunged into the greasy depths of
Vast vats of a bubbling, boiling sea.
Bronzed bass and heated haddock,
Lie ceremoniously awaiting to be chosen.
Wedges of thickly cut potato, are
Burned and blistered in boisterous fat.
Carrying my long-awaited meal, I approach
Religious relics, pouring the
Holy salt and vinegar, purifying my meal.
Tasting contentedly the crispy chip,
Warmth and pleasure enrich my body.
And then,
Sheets of paper are all that remain.

Christopher Beach (15)
Christ Church High School

I MADE PEOPLE

I took a strong structure of silicon
Statue and constructed a fragile frame
Consisting of many hinges and a calcium cage.
Constructing a fragile face I moulded muscles
Around delicate mounds of ivory, imprisoning
Them like feathers in a puffy pillow.
I created a domed temple encasing the mature
Mind, protecting it from undesired damage or
Disturbance.
Taking many miles of winding wire, I finely
Trimmed it, making nerves for the being to feel.
I made a hand with five flexible fingers,
Linking them together with leathery ligaments.
I stitched the smooth, sensuous, sensitive skin
Tight around the brilliant body.
My final task was bathing the perfect person in
My eternal light of life.

Kristopher Bennett (15)
Christ Church High School

MY PRECIOUS LIGHT

Her skin is soft and icy white
You are definitely my precious light.
At night I stir about my bed
Wondering whether you like me
                    or hate me instead.

James Mungeam (13)
Darrick Wood School

ME AND MY DOG

Every morning he is waiting.
Waiting for me to come down.
I come down and give him his breakfast.
I then take him for a run around the fields.
When we come back he will have a drink
And laze around for the rest of the day.
Then I come back from school
And there he will be waiting jumping up by the door.
So then we go out and play 'fetch' or 'tug of war'.
My dog is a short-haired blond Labrador.
My dog is friendly although he barks at other dogs.
But I love my dog.

Liam Hather (12)
Darrick Wood School

MY PET

I have got one soft and light pet,
He is a chinchilla,
He is fast and class,
He is like a person hunting in the jungle.

He explores around the room,
He looks like he is looking for someone or something,
His fur is like cotton wool,
He loves eating raisins,

He is sweet and sensitive,
He does not smell but he can tell what is going on,
And I am happy that he is my cute, soft, fast
Chinchilla!

Jason James Bye (12)
Darrick Wood School

MY WORLD

In my world there shall be perfection,
and I shall earn it all.
I shall have big mansions,
with large stone pillars,
and I can see all the lands,
with the browny-gold sands.
My white and black horses,
which shall graze on the hill.

In my world there shall be make-believe,
with the cold blue, crystal rivers,
that run down the mountains
and the cold winter gives you the shivers,
the snow drifts down,
in tiny snowflakes,
and covers the roof of the town.

In my world there shall be love
friendly, friends,
and children who play games.
There would be . . .
no more hunger, war or suffering
and the air shall be fresh
with love and compassion.

Kerry Harding (13)
Darrick Wood School

THE LOVE FOR ANIMALS

Animals can be any size,
From tiny to big,
Too fat and wide.

They can be loveable, furry and cute,
They also get hungry,
And eat a lot of their food.

They can be smooth or hairy,
Always are nice,
And never disgusting.

You can see if they like you,
You can see if they don't,
But maybe they will like you,
Or even tickle your throat.

You can get them in the wild,
But sometimes as pets,
You can get them as a child,
And take them to the vet's.

When they are small
Cuddle them so much
And you can make them like it,
They will love you cuddling them
                    until they are tall.

When they are old,
Or when they are dead,
They turn to mould,
And rest their little heads.

Nicholas John Edwards (12)
Darrick Wood School

TEACHERS

Teachers are weird, strange people,
They sit in front of you,
And stare!
With dark, beady eyes,
And glasses which are too big for them.

Teachers are weird, strange people,
They like wearing red skirts, with purple jumpers,
That don't go!
And black tights so you can't see,
Their hairy legs.

Teachers are weird, strange people,
They make you copy from the board,
About a million words,
And expect you to finish quickly.

Teachers are weird, strange people,
They sit in their chairs with their arms folded,
And legs crossed,
Guarding their desk,
I wonder what they keep in there?
Maybe they have a secret stash of . . .
Mars bars, hidden in the drawers!

Teachers are weird, strange people,
When the bell goes, my teacher's expression changes,
A little grin appears on her face,
Maybe she will grab one of the children,
And turn them into stew,
But I don't suppose she's that good at cooking, though.

Teachers are weird strange, people,
They think they have eyes in the back of their heads!
Teachers really are the weirdest, strangest, people.

Lucy Knight (12)
Darrick Wood School

THE CITY

Clouds and clouds of thick smog,
Choking me and my dog.
Lots of cars driving past,
Going miles too fast.
All this in the city,
Dear, oh dear, what a pity.

Trains and buses rattling through,
Not stopping to wait for you.
Cafes, restaurants, pubs,
Most of them full of mugs.
All this in the city,
Dear, oh dear, what a pity.

Tubes packed, people like sardines,
Crashing, rattling, noisy machines.
Standing room only, aching feet,
Desperately hoping for a seat.
All this in the city,
Dear, oh dear, what a pity!

Richard A Witton (12)
Darrick Wood School

THE OWL

It flies through the night sky
With freedom it flies.
After a while,
In the dark dark night
it swoops down and tortures its prey.

It's white, mischievous but,
very talented.
Its sharp claws rip its prey apart.
You see it in the oak.

Sneaky but silent when it walks,
but when it calls
everyone says
it's the dreaded call from the *barn owl!*

Simon Jones (12)
Darrick Wood School

MY COCKATIEL

Her bright yellow feathers
Her light brown beak
Her dark black eyes
and her pink clawed feet.

Her ear-piercing squeal
The flap of her wings
She flies like lightning
at the strangest of things.

She sits on my shoulder
And tweaks my hair
Then suddenly stops
to look up and stare.

Her orange neon cheeks
that light up the room
When it is full
of darkness and gloom.

Her friendly nature
Is why I feel
My best friend in the world
is my *cockatiel.*

Anna Hemmings (12)
Darrick Wood School

THE PHOTO

On a country mantelpiece there sits . . .
A photo,
An old photo,
In a rusty silver frame.
It's not noticeable at first.
Behind the porcelain lady with a bunch of flowers,
And the Christmas card from years ago.
There's a man,
A handsome man,
A young handsome man wearing a uniform.
He's with a lady
But she looks sad and unhappy!
The actual photo is in black and white
But places are faded,
And places are yellow with age.
By picking up the photo you can see the back of the frame,
It is black cardboard,
And there is chalk writing,
With numbers,
But they're unreadable.
You put it back,
Step away,
How old it is no-one knows,
But surely it tells a story!

Stefanie Hardin (13)
Darrick Wood School

THE LIFE OF PEOPLE

Multi-coloured skin?
An extra layer they can take off?
Four feet perhaps?
Two they can take off and put aside,
Hair all colours,
Black, brown, blonde and red,
They dye it all as well,
Eyes they have two,
Green, grey, brown or blue.

Machines with four round wheels,
Pumps out black smog,
Tall pipes reach up to what looks like the sky,
Black smog yet again,
Big factories take up vast amounts of land.

Violence and killings, people just dying,
Bad language and cries of fear,
Kids on the streets.
There overnight,
Poor homeless people,
Nowhere to live,
Drug addicts and alcoholics,
Why were these things made?

Why can't people just accept others for
                    who and what they are?

Kirsty Moir (12)
Darrick Wood School

WHALES

Whales are sometimes scared,
And they are usually very brave,
They glide under the sea,
Like a silent giant,
But when they're young,
The poachers come,
And kill them or put them in captivity,
If this would not happen,
Think how many whales there would be,
So *set them free!*
And make their day,
Put them back in the sea,
So they can swim with their friends
Out of captivity.
They have big tails,
Which splash the sea,
So now do you see,
Why you should set them free?

Jennifer Coulman (12)
Darrick Wood School

THE VALUE OF TREES

The horse chestnut tree is a wonderful thing,
With its conkers in autumn and its beauty in spring.
The sweet chestnut tree with it beautiful bark,
And its nuts for roasting when the nights turn dark.
Why do we kill them? Why do we hurt them?
They keep us alive by breathing carbon dioxide,
The value of trees is more than a gem,
So why do we kill them?
If they keep us alive,
Why do we kill them?

Neil Murray (11)
Dartford Grammar School

UNTITLED

As I searched in the holy temples,
I saw image upon image of a man,
But I did not know him.
I heard people talking to someone above
But, though I listened,
I heard no reply.
I flew many leagues up into the air,
Looking all around me,
But I saw no-one.
I deciphered all the books of many languages,
Trying to see behind the words.
I tried to let understanding flow over me,
But it would not come.
The beauty all around me,
In the evening sky full of colour,
In the morning dew glistening in the early sunrise,
In the woodland glades once called sacred;
All this perfection surrounding me
Seemed to point towards something,
But I did not know exactly what.
Then I opened my eyes to the world around me,
As if seeing human life for the first time.
I saw the tears of grief mingle with the blood of death.
I heard cries of terror, screams of fright,
Gunshots tearing apart the air.
I felt lust and hatred, but no love.
I found only pain and confusion,
Leaving yet more questions.

Finally I looked within myself.
It was only here that I found all the answers.

Andrew Rye (16)
Dartford Grammar School

WHEN I'M OLDER . . .

When I'm older,
I want to be a star,
Someone who is famous,
Someone who'll go far,
I could be a stuntman,
Do things others wouldn't dare,
To fall out of windows,
Or even down the stairs,
I'd jump out of a plane,
That's really very high,
Or flip off a cliff,
And even try to fly,
I could go out on a stage,
And sing out very loud,
I'd try to do it perfect,
To make my family proud,
But whatever I decide to be,
I hope to do my best,
To have lots of holidays,
So I can have a rest.

Craig Thomas (11)
Dartford Grammar School

NIAGARA FALLS

An avalanche of water streaming, gushing, cascading,
flowing down from a tremendous height.
The tiniest of droplets are crashing, pouring, tumbling,
racing, stretching to reach the bottom first as they
all come down in unison.

People watching were amazed, mesmerised, thrilled,
bewildered by the beautiful sight.
They were speechless, gasping at the unbelievable waterfall,
they could hardly take their eyes off for a millisecond.

The liquid spray reaches the climax of its enterprising journey.
Thumping, bouncing, hitting, smacking; the huge puddle of water
that has been collected beneath the falling white cloud cover of
foamy water.
Frothing, splashing, bubbling, like lava.

The Falls are *never* still.

Alex Carne-Ross (11)
Dartford Grammar School

DARKNESS

Like a black tide it swallows the world,
It engulfs every town relentlessly,
As dark as a gaping chasm,
No light can pierce the gloom.
The night awakes our primal fears,
Born in a dark fearing childhood.
It is all-consuming,
Leaving nothing untouched.
A black demon touching our souls.
Like death it stalks,
Searching for souls to take,
Fighting light day in, day out,
Cursed in some places.
Worshipped in others,
Cursed,
Worshipped,
Nothingness, repetitive,
A sea of fear,
Waiting to strike.

Ian Rothwell (15)
Dartford Grammar School

RAIN

Rain doesn't always drive cars to a screeching halt,
the car choking and stuttering a wet protest.

Rain fills our water butts,
providing water without a tap.
It slides to the bottom racing, racing to reach the bottom,
joining other droplets, helping them along.

Rain doesn't always flood rivers and towns,
a driving torrent of water destroying anything standing
in its path.

Rain waters crops such as corn and barley wheat,
making the rich soil squelch underfoot.
Leaving the farmer to have a break from watering,
the water making little streams around the crops.

Rain doesn't always stop games in parks and gardens,
trainers slipping and sliding out of control.

Rain fills long-since dry lakes,
filling dry and cracked soil with glistening and clear water.
Providing animals and humans alike with precious water,
making a desert a fruitful oasis.

Rain doesn't always soak washing on lines,
sending mum running for their wet clothes cursing the
rain under her breath.

Rain cleans streets of dirt and grime,
making them silky smooth and Daz ultra white.
Leaving a strong scent of spring,
a sniff of leaves and a gulp full of a summer breeze.

Rain doesn't always rust cars and ruin statues,
making Nelson go green and a Skoda go brown.
Rain makes up with a rainbow at the end,
shining through a gloomy feeling.
Every colour reaches out to cheer us,
ending something bad entering something new.

David Riley (12)
Dartford Grammar School

THE RAINFOREST

All was quiet as the guttural call of the monkey rang
through the trees.
Splish, splosh, rain is once again clawing its way through
the canopy,
quenching the thirst of the parched, solemn bark.
Insects, bugs of all races cover the ground,
a carpet of undiscriminating life.
Suddenly, a cry of birds shattered the peace.
'Human!' called the chimpanzees.
A noise was filling every space,
the noise of falling trees.
The destruction swept across the land,
chainsaws whirring angrily,
Eating life like a gluttonous king.
Supposingly causing no man strife,
no strife to them.
They do not realise how much they depend on every single
simple stem.
Why cut us down?
Why make us frown!
Your life is nothing when not bearing our emerald gown.
You do not own us,
we are the ones wearing the crown.

Paul O'Hagan (13)
Dartford Grammar School

LIFE WEARS

Life wears
Flared trousers
Seventies clothing
King of dowsers

Death wears
Pure darkness
The banshee's call
Now: hark this

God wears
Brown robes
No earrings hang
From his ear lobes

Satan wears
A coat of scales
From his mouth
A forked tongue flails

Light wears
A yellow cardi'
No-one else
Is blessed so hearty

Darkness wears
A black suit
Wolves howl
Owls hoot

Time wears
The cloak of change
Linear existence
Is quite strange

Life Death God Satan Light Darkness Time
Heart Skull Heaven Hell Day Night Chime!

Lawrence McCarthy (12)
Dartford Grammar School

IN THE BEGINNING

Let's start at the beginning,
At the very first stage,
With Uranus and Saturn,
And the first Golden Age.

When the prophecy was told,
Saturn would be o'ercome,
By one of his own children,
Be it daughter or his son.

So he swallowed every baby,
From one to number five,
To stop the forecast coming true,
To keep himself alive.

Saturn's wife hid baby six,
Perhaps under the bed,
And dressed a rock in baby clothes,
Which Saturn gulped instead.

The sixth baby, Jupiter,
A very lucky bloke,
Grew up and made a potion,
To make his own dad choke.

Poor old Saturn felt quite sick,
And threw up on the floor,
Out of his mouth there came his kids,
Bewildered, *grown up (?)* and sore.

Let war commence! And so they fought,
And spiteful Saturn died,
Jupiter and Co had won!
A new era had arrived.

Ciaran Dachtler (13)
Dartford Grammar School

OUR UNIVERSE

Space is a lonely desolate place,
An infinite black,
A vacuum without life,
A region of everlasting sadness.

The nine swirling planets,
Orbiting the brilliant bright sun,
The moons turning, revolving,
In the darkness of space.

Debris floating, drifting forever,
Past burning stars,
Deserted ships,
And 20th century junk.

In the grimness of space,
Great fields of asteroids,
Burning comets,
Bright as flares.

And Earth,
Our home,
Green and blue in an ocean of black,
An oasis in the desert.

Jonathan Webb (13)
Dartford Grammar School

WAR!

War,
War, what's the point?
It gets nobody, anywhere.
Before. The world was full of life, beauty and health,
Before. The world was a place full of happiness and peace,
Before. This planet was a wonderful place,
But that was before, before, before.

War,
War, what's the point?
It gets nobody, anywhere.
After. All they left the next generation was an empty,
                               lifeless barren world,
After. The world left in mourning of their fellow beings,
After. The planet is left in ruins, the people's hearts torn
                               like an old rag.
But that was after, after, after.

War,
War, what's the point?
There is no point,
No point neither before, nor after.
No point starting bloodshed.
No point finishing.

War.

James Gray (12)
Dartford Grammar School

SPRINGTIME IN THE PARK

The sounds of nature are an orchestra, conducted by the wind,
The gently buzzing bees are French horns,
The pigeon's penetrating voice is an oboe,
The trumpeter is the cuckoo, heralding the spring,

The serenade of the peacocks,
The chanting of the martins,
The gently burbling waterfall,
The quiet little stream,

Happiness is everywhere,
As a squirrel scurries across the ground,
The children play merrily,
The ducklings learn to swim,

The bright sun breaks through a fluffy white cloud,
A swallow whooshes through the trees,
The leaves play the percussion,
Nature's finest concert begins.

Geoffrey Elliott (13)
Dartford Grammar School

WHY?

Who can say they've led a blameless life,
Without sorrow or shame.
Not I, I fear,
For I did wrong -
and regret it now.

Life is a precious gift,
I ruined mine.
If only what's past could be changed,
But I know it can't.

I never meant to do what I did,
It just, sort of happened.
I'm so, so sorry now,
Not that it makes a difference.

Why me?
Why him?
Why us?
Why anyone?
Why?

Adam Jacobs (12)
Dartford Grammar School

DREAM TEAM

I'm mad about football,
I play in my dreams,
I pull off my cover,
It rips at the seams,
I fall out of bed,
I kick the wall,
My dad thinks I'm crazy,
My mum says 'You fool.'
And there it ends,
My alarm goes bleep,
It's the end of the match,
Pheep! Pheeep! Pheeeeep!

Jason Tramontano (13)
Dartford Grammar School

THE HEADMASTER

It was announced on the PA
'Go to the office now.'
As I trundle through the corridor,
I wonder what I've done.
I'm biting my nails now,
My face trickling with sweat.
I turn the corner.
Twenty metres to go.
I loosen my tie.
Ten.
My shirt is sticking to my chest.
Five.
My whole body is shaking.
I knock on the door.
No answer.
I knock again.
The door opens.
'Well done,' says the voice.

Alex Jarvis (11)
Dartford Grammar School

INSIDE GRAN'S OLD CUPBOARD

Inside Gran's old cupboard
I found a battered old bugle,
Crooked and dented,
Reduced to rubbish.

Working days over
A good time ago;
It now bears the scars
Of its work years ago.

J Millard (11)
Dover Grammar School for Boys

THE MOUNTAIN

The high-pointed
Peaks in a swirly mist,
His summit under a sheet of snow,
A stream trickling down his side,
His cavernous mouth open wide,
Hungry for the dragon that once lived within,
His broken bones beside him.
The climbers who once discovered him
Now rest, weak and feeble.
The painful silence echoes from his feet, strongly
Embedded in the landscape, to his head high above the clouds.

Matthew Ayers (12)
Dover Grammar School for Boys

BOY'S FOOTBALL

It's a game for fun
Don't shout at the poor boy
Men shouting abuse,
Remember he's just a boy,
The poor boy playing in the rain,
He's standing there freezing.
Playing in that brown mud
But when that whistle goes
The boy jumps with joy
He's won the game
But think when you shout at him
And when it's wet
Just think
He's just a boy.

Ben Clutton (11)
Dover Grammar School for Boys

THE DEMON BOOK

There is a book on my shelf,
All dusty and old,
It's got devilish powers -
It's been foretold.
Although it's old,
It shines like gold,
And it never ever needs dusting.
I often hear noises,
Like the clanking of chains,
Or strange eerie voices.
The book should be burnt
But what's the point?
It can only be heard by me!

Dominic Targett (11)
Dover Grammar School for Boys

MOUNTAINS

You mountains of the world, biggest natural thing on this planet.
With names for each one, and famous ones such as Mount Everest.
There are groups of you such as the Alps or the Rockies.
With snow-capped peaks and lakes upon you.
Streams are born on you, and come gushing down,
fast and wide, as rivers.
People who climb you just for fame
Stick their country's flag at your peak.
Human beings have climbed each and every one of you.
You appear on both land and under the sea.
But how many of you have not been discovered yet?

Roy Yau (12)
Dover Grammar School for Boys

CHRISTMAS

Snow lays white on the floor,
The trees are bare after autumn colours.
The earth lays dead, but
She is just sleeping.
Leaves lie dead upon the floor.

Frost and ice both bite,
Cold winds blow a snowstorm.
A snowman stands freezing cold
With a carrot nose, and currant eyes.
A hungry robin sits on his hat.

The snow turns to ice
And children skid to school,
Snow-capped bobble hats
And white-tipped scarves,
Skidding home all alone.

Then the earth starts moving.
She is waking from her long hibernation.
The sun awakes, and draws out the earth.
Spring blossoms.

Michael Waghorn (12)
Dover Grammar School for Boys

DEATH

A sniper watches his prey,
Like a kestrel watching his dinner
Bang! The sniper's got his man.

The victim fights for life
Like an antelope being chased by a lion
Delaying the inevitable.

Matthew Coates (12)
Dover Grammar School for Boys

THE KITCHEN KNIFE

The kitchen knife lies,
Glinting in the morning sun,
Its teeth sharp,
As sharp as the point of a sword.

Its handle is smooth,
And the sun deflects off its blade,
Straight back towards the sky,
Blinding any human eye blocking its path.

Other knives envy its powers,
Its amount of use and its speed in doing a job,
Cutting through bread,
Like a chainsaw cutting through a tree.

Steven Horsler (11)
Dover Grammar School for Boys

THE CUCKOO

I'm here again,
I'm down the lane,
I'm in the woodland trees,
I'm on the hill,
I'm never still,
I'm as restless as the breeze!

All day long,
You'll hear my song!
Cuckoo! Cuckoo! Cuckoo!
So come my way,
I want to play,
At hide and seek with you!

Kirk Girdwood (13)
Dover Grammar School for Boys

THE DRAGON AT THE BOTTOM OF MY GARDEN

A dragon lies at the bottom of my garden.
He is bright gold with sparkling silver wings.
The dragon at the bottom of my garden sleeps on leaves and twigs.
He has no claws and breathes no fire.
He is as small as a lily bud.
The dragon at the bottom of my garden is a

```
    D        Y
    R      L
    A    F
    G  N
    O
```

Nicholas English (13)
Dover Grammar School for Boys

DRAGONS

Dark and mythical like a winter's night,
Furry and hot like a burning furnace,
Evil like life in hell.

Great big teeth like razor blades,
Puffing out smoke like a steam engine,
He smells like 500 cigarette butts.

Monstrous like a flame breathing crocodile,
Long necked like a giant crane,
Fearless and fire spitting like a massive volcano.

Slitted eyes that glow in the dark like cats,
Great broad wings like an eagle soaring high,
Webbed feet like a mallard duck.

Daniel Shaw (11)
Dover Grammar School for Boys

THE TOY TRAIN

Puffing around the track all day,
Pulling wagons all the way,
Around the bends and on the straights,
Pulling all the heavy freight.

It stops at the station,
For a short duration,
To pick up the commuters,
Who work on computers.

The train shunts away,
To work all day,
Speeding up as it goes,
Some of the passengers may doze.

The train dashes,
Oh no, it crashes!
But it's only a little boy,
Playing with his toy.

Ben Bridges (11)
Dover Grammar School for Boys

THE RABBIT

Rabbit, with long, quivering ears and cotton-like tail
       In the wild you would lie safely, underground.
       Perhaps under the shelter of a tree,
       You could play whenever you wanted
       Jump about, but be careful!
       Look out for hunters!
       Poachers, foxes, birds of prey!
       I would like to be a rabbit, just for a day,
       To see what's like to be small and defenceless.

Philip Milne (11)
Dover Grammar School for Boys

STORM IN A TEACUP

All appears calm, but things are not what they seem.
Clouds appear on the horizon,
An assassin sneaking up on the back of a calm day.
A gentle breeze whistles across a peaceful ocean, soothing
but misleading.
Suddenly the clouds are overhead,
The ocean is preparing for a storm.
The rain pats tentatively on the back of the sea,
The first wave crashes onto the shore,
The anger is released.

White horses charge towards the shore, stampeding towards
the cliff.
The wind charges over the waves, an army of barbarians
unleashed on a defenceless settlement.
The waves reach up as if to pull the sky into the turbulent
depths, before crashing into spray.
Lightning forks across the sky like a sword thrust into the
heart of the storm.
Thunder charges across the sky, a herd of buffalo stampeding
across stricken plains.
A ship is tossed about by the roaring giants of waves,
Thrown by the wind and dragged towards the greedy teeth
of the rocks.

From above, higher than the calls of the seagulls,
out of reach of the drenching rain and jagged lightning,
the universe looks down,
at the storm in a teacup.

Giles Barrett (12)
Dover Grammar School for Boys

THE ABANDONED SHELL

Washed up on the shore,
Under the evening sun,
Lying lifeless in the sand,
Its beauty shows no more.

The tide comes in,
Its qualities gone to waste,
It's drowned and gone forever,
No more days to face.

Until one calm summer's day,
The perfect owner strolls the land,
And notices a scaly body,
Lying lifeless in the sand.

She unearths it from the sand,
Brushes it clean on her cotton sweater,
And inspects it with her careful hands,
Then takes it home for now,
                its perfection shows.

Matthew Carley (11)
Dover Grammar School for Boys

THE FERRY

She starts the day early,
As the moon begins to fade.
She fills up her hull from bow to stern,
Her decks are filled with children.

The heavy motors begin to turn,
With a thick smell of diesel.
The vibrations begin to tremble,
We're off, leaving the harbour behind.

The froth and the wake,
Now floating away,
As she starts her journey to France.

Arrival in France means pleasure and joy,
For all the little children.
She is docked in the harbour,
She feels so light,
But no cars, no buses, no lorries, no people.

Michael Weatherley (12)
Dover Grammar School for Boys

THE DOLPHIN

Dolphins are grey like a cloudy sky
Sometimes as white as a snowflake

Streamlined like a supersonic Concorde
Gliding through the water like a submarine

It eats fish as small as a ruler
Eating them whole with its narrow snout

Finned like a normal fish or whale
And is sometimes mistaken for a shark.

But these are friendly and playful fish
If they are really fish.

But when there's babies and a shark comes round
They will gang up and ram it, top speed.

I like dolphins very much,
But do they feel about humans the same way?

Michael Flynn (12)
Dover Grammar School for Boys

EGG

Smooth like a bullet,
Fast as Ruud Gullit,
Carrying like a cargo ship,
Pointy as a sword's sharp tip.
Bouncy as a ping-pong ball,
Hollow as the school's great hall.

This is an egg,
Soft smooth and round,
It wouldn't last a second,
If it hit the ground!

Oliver Craggs (11)
Dover Grammar School for Boys

THE SPORT OF RUGBY

On the twenty-two,
He kicks it into touch,
Line out to New Zealand,
Who lose the ball for once.

The dragons swing it wide,
Out to the left wing,
Then Wayne puts it out wide again,
Leigh Davies picks the ball up,
Who drives at the defence.

Tackled by the forwards,
In comes the scrum-half,
Flings it wide to Ieaun,
Who goes under the posts.

Matthew Thomas (12)
Dover Grammar School for Boys

THE MORNING

The city at night, a forest, dark and spooky,
The sun rising, gold dust sweeping the land.
The first car, a solitary wasp,
A shop opening, a welcoming glow,
A lift rising, a way to heaven,
Smoke drifting, a cloud in the sky,
Doors slamming, thunderclaps on the street,
The street filling, dots of colour.
A clock strikes distantly, raindrops falling,
The city in daytime, a nest of ants.

Paul Witty (12)
Dover Grammar School for Boys

MY GRANDFATHER'S WATCH

My grandfather's watch,
it sleeps on a shelf,
in his looming old study,
in his creaking old house.
Coated with dust,
and covered in grime,
its existence stands still,
as the time flows by.
Through a hole in the rafters,
a gap of blue sky,
is visible to the naked eye.
A bird once flew in,
and built a nest,
but like the old house,
it's as silent as death.

Ross McNamara (11)
Dover Grammar School for Boys

CONTENTMENT

She felt happy,
like a child eating chocolate,
with a grin cracking her face.

She felt as happy,
as the sunshine,
breaking through the stormy clouds
and drying up the rain.

She felt happy,
like a dog chewing a bone,
savouring its delicious juices.

She felt happy
like a lion,
that had just caught its prey,
now able to feed her hungry cubs.

She felt as happy,
as someone who had achieved
         their greatest ambition,
to make someone happy
         and to be happy too

James Eaton (12)
Dover Grammar School for Boys

IF MY MUM WAS SUPERWOMAN

If my mum was Superwoman,
I'd be waving bye,
Because if my mum was Superwoman,
All she'd do is fly.

She'd help the Serbs in Serbia,
She'd meet the Greeks in Greece,
Because if my mum was Superwoman,
Her chores would never cease.

During the day,
My mum would save hundreds of people like you,
Then she'd come home and say to me,
'Was your day stimulating too?'

I'd then say,
'Oh yes mother my day was packed with fun and joy!'
Because if my mum was Superwoman,
I would be Superboy!

Tom Freeman (13)
Dover Grammar School for Boys

ANGER

I shout,
Yell,
Scream,
All my body tenses,
I hate it,
Can't control it,
I want to jump out,
Thump someone,
I feel strong,
Teeth grit tightly,
Tighter,
And tighter,
Don't care,
About anything,
Anyone.

Tim Wheeler (12)
Dover Grammar School for Boys

THE SUNRISE

The sun comes from its hiding place,
like a key unlocking a gateway,
opening light to the world.
The world of darkness,
has been slaughtered,
light has broken free.
Nature is alive,
the song of bird
has survived through the night.
The people are awakening
from their doomed eternal period,
of darkness and gloom.
The sun breathes life
into the world
calling for everyday life.
It slowly rises to its peak,
scaring darkness
into the form of shadow.
But like any great person,
it rises high and falls,
and prepares to rise again.

Stephen Hughes (12)
Dover Grammar School for Boys

THE TEMPEST

I walked out onto the deck,
With water splashing in my face,
The railings were rattling like a snake,
And almost falling off.

Inside was the luxury lounge,
With teachers being sick.
The boat was going up and down
Like a yo-yo on a string.

Inside the ship, there was a panic,
With items falling on the floor,
People frantically picking things up,
And replacing them on the shelves.

At last we reached the solid land,
The thunder and lightning stopped,
We were all glad to see the land
And all sped off to customs.

Philip Barnes (12)
Dover Grammar School for Boys

THE TELEVISION

Yes, come and buy the new Sony TV
with built-in video player.
What could be better than letting
another unsuspecting group of people be
exposed to endless amounts of violence and
strong language.

Little children, glued to it like flies
in a jam jar. This is the drug of the nation.
Drug abuse, fighting, assaults and murders
are just a couple of things which echo
in people's minds. Until their whole imagination
is like a cave of terror.

Day after day more radiation is fed to gormless zombies.
It can take over your life.
Trust me I know . . .

Jonathan Howlett (12)
Dover Grammar School for Boys

WHO WOULD HAVE THOUGHT?

Who would have thought
That a lump of metal, with cogs in and
straps at the side,
Would determine how the world works?
I mean it's only two inches wide,
But to some people it's a vital mechanism
that everyone relies on.
What would we do without it?
So next time you look at your watch
to see what the time is,
Don't take it for granted!

Thomas Punton (11)
Dover Grammar School for Boys

THE SALES EXECUTIVE

Dishonest and sneaky,
Tall and thin,
His job is to cheat,
And he's determined to win
The mind of a gullible customer.
This man is an excellent liar,
And he sells things that people desire.
Although his advert's a fraud.
His product's *the best*,
It beats all the rest,
It's something that everyone needs.
He's full of deceit,
Some think he's neat,
The executive salesman.

Adam MacLean (13)
Dover Grammar School for Boys

THE WORST QUESTION IN THE WORLD

When a boy was asked,
The worst question in the world,
By a towering giant,
Dressed from head to foot
In a robe of the darkest night's sky.

So many he had seen before,
Imprisoned in the giant's castle,
For eternity;
Whilst everyone had gone,
He was forgotten,
With only the tick of the clock
To remind him.

As the giant moved over to the boy,
The room screamed with silence,
Staring eyes,
Watching every movement,
Then a voice broke the silence.

'Well boy?' came a booming drum
As the giant leaned over him,
With threatening words,
And menacing eyes.
'I'll hand it in tomorrow, sir,
Promise.'

Stuart Inglis (13)
Dover Grammar School for Boys

RAINDROPS

Freezing cold all around,
softly falling,
Like a silk, waterlogged sheet,
Falling all over your shivering body.
It's strange, eerie feeling,
As the new, dark school beckons all around you.
Music playing,
Like an ancient phantom playing an ivory bone organ.

They are like misguided darts,
Facing backwards,
Falling through the early morning sky.
Almost cheek to cheek,
Falling faster and faster.
Splat! Land ho!
Miniature explosions everywhere,
Like 500 kids all throwing water bombs simultaneously.
The noise,
Slowly driving you insane.

One hits you,
Then another,
They quickly transform you from dry to drenched.
You finally reach the building,
Safe and dry.
You are soaked,
But you are inside now,
Only to hear the pitter patter,
Steadily on the old, slate roof.
All of a sudden it stops,
There is nothing.
The music has disappeared from within the air
Why is nothing so empty?
It is still dark, no-one is around,
In this vast school, not even the phantom is to be seen.
But at least I am not hounded now by the steady rhythm of raindrops.

Richard Jones (13)
Dover Grammar School for Boys

THE POCKET WATCH

A small brown box,
I open it,
Inside a golden, dusty, pocket watch,
I pick it up,
I sneeze, because of the dust.

I open the watch,
The small black hands,
Are still moving,
I can still hear the ticking,
Then it started to chime,
The chime was a small chime,
Like the sound of a bell,
A long way off.

I close the watch,
The long golden chain,
Was shining in the sunlight,
I clipped it on my jumper,
And put the watch into my pocket,
To see what it felt like in my pocket,
I took it out,
And put it back in the box,

I looked at the watch,
One last time,
Then put the lid back on the box,
Then I left it.

Nicholas Corlett (11)
Dover Grammar School for Boys

SILENCE, DEATH

Silence, death,
nothing, nothing
everything is silent
just me, all alone
buzzards flying, round and round
Silence, death
this place is like a deserted city
the trees are not a lush green
but instead a death-like black
the sky is grey
the grass is covered by a coating of mist.
Silence, death
some illness has taken the life away
I wander along a rocky path
looking at each one,
wondering who the owners are.
Silence, death
this blackened stone is meant for me
my name being engraved with a chisel
mist surrounds me
a black figure lurks forward
nearer, nearer
this is the illness that took life away
it is death
but it is not my time yet, the mist clears
I have always hated graveyards
Silence, death.

Matthew Wash (11)
Dover Grammar School for Boys

LORD OF THE DRAGONS

The dragon's scales are like gems
        Sparkling, Shining.
His body adorned with spikes,
        Sharp, Killing.
Fire spouts from his mouth,
        Hot, Glowing.
His sleep is eternal,
        Deep, Quiet.

Outside the night is passing,
        Cool, Dark.
Outside a man is searching,
        Slowly, Carefully.
His quarry is inside,
        Killer, Deadly.
His sword is by his side,
        Bright, Bejewelled.
He enters the cave,
        Worried, Alert.
The dragon awakes,
        Hateful, Raging.

The hero is dead,
        Gone, Defeated
The dragon triumphant,
        Joyful, Victorious
Curled tightly in a majestic sleep,
        Dragon, Lord.

Ben Langley (12)
Dover Grammar School for Boys

FOOTBALL'S A GAME

Football is a game of skill,
On the pitch the skills are displayed,
Own goal! It hits the post and finally it's in
Ties in the Cup,
Bring great surprise,
All the goals and saves please the crowd
Lots of fans pack the ground,
Losing, winning
Sometimes drawing.

A game of skill is football.

Goalkeeping errors lead to goals,
A football game is full of skill.
Match of the Day is on TV,
Everyone watches it at quarter to eleven.

Only the winning team gets 3 points
Fouling, a yellow card is shown, and another one,

Sent off!
Kick off starts the game,
In the changing rooms they have a team talk,
Loads of people invade the pitch,
Losing can be a terrible thing.

Richard McHugh (12)
Dover Grammar School for Boys

THE CITY AT RUSH HOUR

The city at rush hour,
As if someone had dropped an apple in a starving city,
All racing to win the prize.

A seagull flying below the clouds,
Circling around the apple,
Watching the race develop.

The people draw near,
Closing in on the prize,
And fighting each other to get there.

Then, the seagull swoops down,
Like an angel from heaven,
Snatching the prize from the people.

Joseph Messiter (12)
Dover Grammar School for Boys

THE LIBRARY

I entered in through the big brown door,
I was suddenly hit by the stillness,
There was a silence as if someone had died,
There was not a murmur anywhere.

All the books were still,
Stacked on top of each other,
All waiting for one to be picked up.

When suddenly the silence was broken,
A book had fallen and hit the ground,
It was as if a stone had hit some still water.

Nicholas Townend (12)
Dover Grammar School for Boys

THE SOLITARY LIBRARY

The large, lonely structure sits in its quake,
Boarded windows accumulate graffiti,
An endless boundary of strange books,
Which rest behind huge, wooden doors,
Dust collects on furniture,
Like bees to sticky substances
A silence which deafens,
In a block of wilderness.

Matthew Neill (13)
Dover Grammar School for Boys

THE FOX

As it entered the garden
Like a hunter hunting its prey.
It crept slowly up to the birds' food
When midnight finally came
The wind began to whistle a tune
The fox sniffed around the bins
Hunting for its midnight meal.
After the wind stopped its opera piece
The fox lay on the floor resting its tired legs
Like a bird resting its wings after a long journey.
The fox is disturbed by a mouse squeaking.
The fox lies there unseen like a grain of salt in the sea.
The fox then strikes.
Its movement is like lightning.
The mouse is then killed unaware.
He leaves the garden silently
Stroking the grass with its fur.
All that is seen is his white tipped tail
Exiting through the dark mist.

Adam Taylor (13)
Dover Grammar School for Boys

FIREWORK NIGHT IS NIGH

See those colours pop,
Whizzing in the sky,
They sparkle then they drop,
Firework night is nigh.

They go soaring up,
Soaring up so high,
Drink hot soup from a plastic cup,
Firework night is nigh.

Lighting fireworks can be hard,
Children shouldn't try,
Coloured raindrops drift to earth,
Firework night is nigh.

The fire's hot hands of flame,
Curling round the guy,
More wood on the bonfire,
Firework night is night.

Happy smiling faces,
As bonfire embers die,
It was such a jolly evening,
Firework night gone by.

Robert Oliver (12)
Dover Grammar School for Boys

PROTAGONIST

As I stand behind the curtain,
Waiting for the show to begin,
I hear people coughing.
In anticipation they wait,
For the curtain to rise,
And to catch a glimpse of me.
Who would have thought it?
Me, the protagonist.
The curtain rises,
The lights shine.
Suddenly all is a blur.
I falter, trying to remember my lines.
As my subconscious clears,
It kicks the shadow of confusion away.
I start to speak,
The play begins,
My words strike true and true.
Friends and teachers urge me on,
Filling the jug of confidence to the brim.
I continue defiantly, voice getting louder.
As the play draws to a close,
I walk to the front and bow.
An applause erupts,
Like an active volcano.
The applause continues,
Until I step back,
Then it stops abruptly.
The play is over.

James Garlick (12)
Dover Grammar School for Boys

UP ON THE SIDE

Up on the side
Where I belong
We're going fast
Wind's so strong

Waves coming up
Splash on your face
Big boats in front
Setting the pace

Getting near the first buoy
'Ready about, lee ho'
Sky's getting dark
It might rain, oh no

We're on the broad reach
'Let the jib off a bit'
Going away from the beach
To sail you need to be fit

We're nearly at the gybe mark
Sailing's easy to master
Now sky's really dark
Suddenly disaster

Capsize

Thrown into the sea
Water's so cold
Boat turns turtle
I'm trapped inside

Daniel Webb (12)
Dover Grammar School for Boys

ALTON TOWERS

'Did I really expect too much of the gruesome Nemesis?
Or was I really frightened? Ninety second of pure excitement.
God it was good! I just had to go on it again.
But I did think that my Nike shoes would tickle the blood
red water that flowed beneath us, as I flew through the air
hanging like an apple from a tree.

The path's tired me out. They lead me from canyons to woods
and different lands which were scattered in a thirty acre piece
of land.
Different people from all over the country, people with wheelchairs
and buggies walk to join the lengthy queues.

Burger bars, cola shops, too many to count were placed along
the bendy paths. The smells pushed by the calm gentle wind
followed you like a shadow, until the wind broke and the smell fell.

Gift shops and balloon shops, covered me from the cold wind
and surrounded me like a maze. I couldn't help myself, I had to go
in. The choice, loads, so much to choose from. Finally I exited the
buildings.

Our day soon comes to an end as all the rides close at five. We then
head towards a restaurant as the rain covers us like a blanket.
Chips, chips, chips. As the rain soon gets heavier we head for the hotel
I just had to explore. We took the lifts because of the unreal music.
Soon our holiday came to an end, as we kissed it goodbye.'

Luke Swan (12)
Dover Grammar School for Boys

FALLING IN

As I stepped from the boat into the
Gaping deep depths
I felt nothing but thin air.
Water lapped against my naked face,
It hit me like an icy stare.

The mop fell in, so did I.
I heard a shout and then a cry.
The ducks, they quacked indignantly.
As they were thrown into disarray
I heard myself shout 'I'm OK.'

I saw the world fly past my eyes.
A comet zooming through the sky.
Everything was clear and bright,
Like a firework in the dead of night.

Stagnant odours, diesel fumes,
Wafted to me on the air.
Mouldy mud, fresh cut lawn,
Sizzling bacon and burnt toast,
For all these smells, my nose the host.

My mouth is open,
Water floods in.
Like dam walls bursting
It tastes stale and bitter
Like an ancient lemon.

David Tilbee (12)
Dover Grammar School for Boys

THE BIG ONE

You look at the ride with an eagle eye,
You say to yourself I'm crazy to go on that.
You can see the fright on their faces,
And I say I'm not paying £3.50 to go on that.
But I still get on.

You are queuing up.
You see the fright.
Your heart's pounding ten to the dozen.
You don't believe you are going on this monstrosity of a ride.
But then you get on.

You pull away from the station, down a slope then in a can.
You get dragged up the hill as slow as a tortoise.
You look down at the town, then you look up at the slope ahead.
You are only half way up.
But then the top comes in sight.

You take your last breath and taste the sea air then the cable lets go.
You see the slope is at a 90° angle then your heart goes in your mouth
You close your eyes then open them and everything's like a blur.
But in a flash it's all over and all that for £3.50.

Graham Cutress (12)
Dover Grammar School for Boys

ADVERTISING

Advertising is to tell people what's on sale,
Chocolate, coke, ginger ale!
Big, bright billboards bearing the product's name,
Shiny, silver wrappers, exciting, eye-catching, but
expensive all the same.

Advertising on TV or in a magazine,
Companies trying to sell their sweet new treat.
Some things are so expensive people can but dream,
They want to buy everything they see advertised in the street.

Companies try to sell their product,
They really do insist.
And when customers see them they really can't resist.

Advertising is a very big business,
Can you now see.
So don't get tempted to buy,
Everything you see!

Dean Scoggins (12)
Dover Grammar School for Boys

CAMPING

Sight
Bats are flying from tree
to tree like emigrating leaves.
The ash on the burnt out
fire is glowing in the dull
black night

Hearing
Leaves are rustling in the trees.
Cats persistently wailing to
get in, like a child demanding sweets.

Touch
The cold air pierces through my
sleeping bag and has a constant
battle with warmth to make me cold.

Taste
Burnt bangers arrive red hot from
the frying pan. Little brown rolls
of meat with a dark tan.

Dean Baker (12)
Dover Grammar School for Boys

THE RADIO

Hmmm . . .
My new creation,
The perfect item
For everyone to treasure
And enjoy

My invention is the ultimate,
A truly splendid design
It may sound exaggerated
But we all need it.
It talks.
It has everything
Except wires,
Going to the mains.

For this is my invention
Of the wireless radio.

Those friendly voices
Of a local DJ
Shouting silently
Down a microphone
And playing music
You've got to buy one
For they'll be selling out
Very quickly.

Nicholas Hayward (12)
Dover Grammar School for Boys

THE UNIVERSE

I'd watch the stars
All through the night,
And wonder what they
Were for.

And then the moon
Came into mind,
Its light send down a glow.
What was it there for?

The sun came up
And bathed my face,
In warm and radiant beams.
What was it there for?

The night came and the
Moon shone and the stars
Twinkled in the sky.
What were they doing?

Then I'd wonder about the Earth,
And what made man
On this world.
The first man and woman brought
Upon the grassy plain.

Louis Myers (12)
Dover Grammar School for Boys

A STORMY SEA

I walked out onto the deck,
The wind was bitterly cold,
The boat swayed from side to side,
Making passengers inside feel sick.

The deck and railings were shaking,
The wind continually beating against them.

Inside the shop, Duty Free that is,
The till was repeating the same old ritual,
Beep, beep, beep, beep.

Walking through the noisy, congested bar,
Towards the peaceful quiet lounge,
Where people were playing cards and relaxing.

I sat down and tried not to think about my dinner,
My stomach jumping up and down as if it were on a
trampoline, in time with the ship.

Then at last we arrived at the harbour where all the thunder
and lightning,
came to an end.

The loudspeaker crackled through to the lounge,
'Would all foot passengers kindly depart,
Thank you.'

Henry Butler (12)
Dover Grammar School for Boys

Escape To The Real World

An early misty summer morning,
the cameras, crew and models ready.
A brilliant location luscious green hills
but where's that shaggy dog?

Here's the product 'Escape Jeans',
crisply ironed, pressed and looking great.
Unreal models getting fitted,
but where's that shaggy mut?

The storyline is a perfect couple,
walking the dog, smiling and laughing.
Throwing the Frisbee in the air,
but where's that shaggy pooch?

Here he comes dripping with mud.
So messy, smelly, but wait a minute,
isn't this far more natural,
come here you shaggy pup.

His paws go over the jeans,
squelching, scrabbling dripping wet.
This time the models are really laughing,
you clever shaggy hound.

The sales for 'Escape' go through the roof,
shipping, transporting around the world.
The success was due to the right approach,
and here's to the shaggy star!

Sam Jackson (12)
Dover Grammar School for Boys

The Salesman's Plague

Advertising is a gimmick or even a disease.
When the TV is turned on,
the disease is spread,
as you walk down the street,
the disease is spread.
This is a disease that cannot be cured
and people always fall into the small and
well thought out trap.
In the shops,
on the streets,
these tall dark men with salesman's smiles,
trying to sell you what seems like a
product which shall last you your life,
but in actual fact is a life lost gimmick
trying to be sold at a bargain price
because of reject.
Advertising can be hard because of
the message you have to feed through into
the little people scuttering around all day,
all night, until they finally give in and
take advantage of this gimmick,
that's when you know the strong disease is spreading.
When you see the little children
pestering their parents to see this, buy that.
Then and only then do you know you
can satisfy yourself that you have
contaminated the city with the
salesman's plague!

Andrew Ferguson (13)
Dover Grammar School for Boys

THE MESSAGE

A new sweet I advertised for a
low price of 30p.
What a bargain it was, soon the
people will see.
It's a hard old business is advertising,
but you mustn't stop working.
The message must be put across.
It costs a lot to put on show,
whether the people will like it or
not, soon I will know.
You see things advertised in different places,
You know whether they are interested
by the look on their faces.
The thick brown sweet looked inviting,
it made you want to pick it up and chew it.
I picked it up and slowly put it into
my mouth, it made my eyes and mouth water.
It was so delicious it made you want more.
I could have sat there all day eating
these lush sweets.

Gary Burdett (13)
Dover Grammar School for Boys

THE OWL

Nocturnal hunter,
Swift and silent,
Night eyes,
Sharp beak,
Cruel talons,
Stealthy wings,
Great, great hunter.

Sam Roberts (11)
Dover Grammar School for Boys

BOOKS

Books can be gory,
Books can be sad,
Books can be clever,
And some make you glad.

Books can be silly,
Books can be seen,
Some make you proud,
But some can be mean!

Well I like books
I think they are cool,
If you don't like them
I think you're a fool!

Books are great
I just don't know why
If there wasn't Roald Dahl,
I think I would die!

Casey Beer (11)
Dover Grammar School for Boy

TIME!

Time is like the biggest black hole,
It never ends it goes on and on, it's
Eternal.
If time did not exist nothing would
Happen,
Everything would stand still.
Without time Earth would not
Have been created.

Time! A very powerful thing.

Richard Leggett (12)
Dover Grammar School for Boys

ADVERTISING LIES

The new advert was unveiled today.
It cost my glorious company millions of pounds,
A total rip off some people think.
But no it's not when the money comes flooding in as our
                                    sweet goes on the market.
Adverts will appear on daytime TV on all major channels.
Billboards all over the country will be plastered with huge
                                            great posters
and
The primary papers will have adverts with their little white
                    lies dotted around beneath the front page.
All the adverts that we use all have on them 'They burst in your
                    mouth' but the sweet does no more than fizz.
We're stereotyping the little youngsters to force them to
        eat our sweets so that the money can make us forget that
                            we're rotting the children's teeth.

Gary Thomas (13)
Dover Grammar School for Boys

MY WATCH

Tick tock, tick tock
What would I do without my watch?
I would miss my bus and miss my plane
And even miss my choo choo train.
To us in England it is night
But in Australia it's full of light,
When everybody is asleep
Time goes on through the week,
Tick tock, tick tock
What would happen if time stopped?

Adam Patterson (11)
Dover Grammar School for Boys

BIO TOOTHPASTE

If you brush your teeth with this,
You won't need to go to the dentist.
Every night and every day,
Will keep bacteria away!
It will leave your mouth minty,
And make your teeth ping and twinkly!
But forget to use this paste,
Your teeth will be full of cavities,
So you better not delay,
Otherwise you will pay.
But if you brush your teeth with this,
Your mouth will be full of freshness!

Jonathan Simons (13)
Dover Grammar School for Boys

MY WATCH

'Switch it off'
Said the angry teacher,
'It's not my watch' said I
Give it here, you, you, you're in detention
Tick, tock, goes my dark black watch,
Bleep! Bleep!
Bleep! Bleep!
'Oh no,' I said
Detention time!
Waiting for my noisy watch to go bleep!
At last my expensive watch goes off
At last I can go home!

Paul Matthews (11)
Dover Grammar School for Boys

THE SELLING GAME

The new sparkling wrappers,
Eyes twinkling bright,
Kiddies pleading 'Please'
For the company's delight.

Creamy, milky chocolate,
Enough to last a day,
Used by the famous Mr X,
To satisfy his tastes.

New cars in the garage,
Rust appearing soon,
Sleigh bells in the distance,
Designer presents in the room!

People selling footballs,
People making doors,
Adverts all around us,
They're the reason for these wars.

Bosses glowing happily,
The kids are buying strong,
Empty shelves with cobwebs,
Paper on the floor,
Footballs in the garden,
Wreaths upon the door.

Oliver Lycett (12)
Dover Grammar School for Boys

WHAT IS AN ADVERT?

Adverts can be long, can be short,
They can be funny, serious or sad.
Advertising rules our lives
Convincing us to buy the merchandise.
The adverts are everywhere,
They are out to get you,
To trick you,
To fool you,
Into purchasing their product.
The advert can be catchy, boring,
Colourful, dull,
Fast or slow.
The product can be glamorous,
From a stylish dress,
To a dream home.
Or it can be dull and plain,
From a toothbrush,
To a colouring crayon.
You are attacked by giant billboards,
Or posters on the wall.
Between your favourite programmes on the box,
Or on the football field,
Players wearing the company's name.
In a magazine or paper,
They're everywhere,
You can't hide!

Sam Cairns (13)
Dover Grammar School for Boys

MY WATCH

Watches!
What a brilliant mechanism,
It tells you the time,
It tells you if you're late or early.
With the famous noise
Tick
Tock
Tick
Tock
The pattern never ends.
Different places mean
Different times.
Tick
Tock
Tick
Tock
Click!
'Oh no!'
12 o'clock,
Got to meet my boring friends.
Got to catch the regular bus.
Got to go for dinner,
Still the pattern never, ever ends.
Quickly, slowly,
Round and round the hands go.

Richard Stanley (12)
Dover Grammar School for Boys

THE BOOK THAT GETS LOST

The books are purchased from a crooked shop
Now they're left on a dusty old book shelf
No-one touches them
Two long years later . . .
Someone reads one of the dusty books
They enjoy the old thing
They read another one
One of them gets bought
The thing has lost a page in the old car
The thing has turned crooked
Not a straight page in there anymore
Left on an old bookcase
On the move to Manchester it gets
            dropped on the motorway
No-one finds it on the motorway
All the pages go missing from it
The pages are ripped in half
They have been blown all over the town
The book is put back together with all the papers inside
No-one ever wants to read it again
Then it gets taken into space by accident
Next it falls into the black hole
No-one ever reads that title again
It's the only copy
But no-one can get it back
So no-one will ever read it again.

Stuart Cullen (11)
Dover Grammar School for Boys

THE WATCH

I was bought carelessly at a boot fair,
left in a rusty tin.
Life for me is a boring one,
being broken, not very good.

I haven't got a face,
it was broken, years ago.
Just a gold-coloured frame,
and a strap left.

Oh the battery's still there,
the electrics too.
But I will never work again, I'm past my time,
and, I think the lights will go out any minute.

Kieren Ward (11)
Dover Grammar School for Boys

BICYCLES

The wheels of the bike spin like tops,
As the pedals are pushed down by feet,
Because of its aero-dynamic body,
You can always turn on the heat.

Helmets are worn to keep your head intact,
Some cycling events are really tough,
Like mountain biking and cyclo-cross,
These events can get really rough.

Skin-suit clothing and brilliant race times,
As long as you're quick you'll be fine,
You've got to have strength and stamina,
You've got to keep your bike in a straight line.

Mark Artis (12)
Dover Grammar School for Boys

BOOKS

'Books are old. I like toys Grandpa, not books.'
'Listen my boy, books are young, a fiery spirit within
them, evil dragons, graceful fairies, brave knights,
foreboding castles perched on the top of crooked
black crags. Much better than any toys!'
'OK Grandpa, I'll give them a try, but graceful
fairies?'
'Not just the fairies, every subject, brave knights,
foreboding castles, army tanks, strong action men,
Viking legends, Greek myths, twisted goblins,
cruel wars, gentle peacetimes.'
'But books are supposed to be for old people
Is that why you like them?'
'No, no I like them because they shake my
old bones with excitement, so my boy, read on.'
'Yes Grandpa.'

Stephen Newman (12)
Dover Grammar School for Boys

HERBERT'S TOME

It took me ages to read the pages
Of the thousand-paged old book.
Some great long words and names of birds
Filled up its dog-eared look.

I took a peek to try and seek
The subject of this tome
A look at the front caused me to hunt
The index for its tone.
To my dismay the book did say,
'The Life of Birds' by Herbert Floor
'A study of their lives and wives'
A boring volume, I felt sure.

I flicked the pages for simply ages,
I had to admit to myself
With one final look at this monotonous book
Its place was the back of the shelf.

Henry Bainbridge (11)
Dover Grammar School for Boys

DIGITAL WATCHES

Tick tock,
tick tock,
is no more on a digital watch.
It may look remotely small,
and exceptionally boring,
but really it's a magnificent creation.
There are lots of buttons and fiddly things,
and that bleeping noise,
oh yes! That terrible bleeping noise,
that wakes you up in the middle of the night.
I can't complain though,
my watch is the keeper of time,
it helps me everywhere I go,
I'd be lost without my watch,
I don't know what I'd do,
but I'll give you a word of advice,
you should get one too!

Alan Fletcher (11)
Dover Grammar School for Boys

THE BOOK

The book was a rusty brown book,
Its title unknown, the author unheard of.
The spine was torn, the edge all crumpled,
Like a pirate's golden treasure map.

But when you read this book,
You enter a new dimension,
A dream dimension,
A dimension, unknown, a dimension unheard of.

Fairies, knights, dragons and thieves,
Castles, lands, out of our dreams.
Kings, queens, princes, princesses,
All inside this craggy book.

Some people think it was written by wizards.
Others may think it was written by aliens.
But I know who wrote it, it was written by

> *. . . me!*

Christopher Knight (11)
Dover Grammar School for Boys

MY WATCH

Tick, tock, clock!
That's my watch, handles turning quickly,
telling me the time!

I'm watching my watch,
tiny cogs whirring round,
spinning slowly, precisely,
little knowing their impact on me
as they tick, tock, round!

Watches come in all shapes and sizes,
big, square, flat, blue, hexagonal,
green with purple polka dots!

My watch helps me all through the day,
letting me know it's not long till home time!
>   *Tick,*

>   *tock,*

>   *clock!*

Nicholas Beech (12)
Dover Grammar School for Boys

THE BOOK

Just waiting on a shelf to be read.
A dark brown book with dust covering its front,
It had cobwebs hanging off the side.
There were other books next to it,
Blue tatty and old ones,
Red paperbacks too
There were mysterious adventures, love-lives
and many more books to read to your heart's content.

But why was this book not read?
I didn't hesitate,
I reached over and grabbed it.
On the cover it said 'Very old comedy jokes,'
I turned the first page over,
The jokes were very funny indeed,
I told the librarian that I was going to take this book.
All she said was 'Alright!'

Adam Topping (11)
Dover Grammar School for Boys

ONE STEP CLOSER

Death is cruel,
But it comes to us all,
Every second of the day,
Somebody will die,
More sorrow will go into hearts of the losers,
But death will also go to the losers
Because death comes to us all.

We take the staircase to Heaven,
It's peaceful and warm,
No shouting,
No children playing,
It's complete peace.

We get to the top and see our God,
We are scared at first,
But God calms us,
And then we are accepted into Heaven,
For forever peace.

Jonathan Miles (11)
Dover Grammar School for Boys

THE TRAMP

He sits all alone on a bench in the park,
nowhere to go to when it's cold and dark.
He begs for money to buy some beer,
does no-one care? Does no-one hear?

Around the town the old tramp goes,
stamping his feet to warm his toes.
He begs for money to buy some food,
people ignore him, how very rude.

He wears lots of clothes to keep out the cold,
his body is thin and his bones are old.
He begs most politely, will no-one give?
he's hungry and thirsty, how can he live?

The tramp keeps on begging, he never gives in.
he searches through rubbish he finds in the bin.
He begs for some money to buy some beer,
doesn't anyone care? Can't anyone hear?

Daniel Stubbs (12)
Dover Grammar School for Boys

THE HOPELESS POET

I am a hopeless poet,
I can't think of a line,
I sometimes think 'Oh blow it!'
But sometimes, it's just fine.

I start with an idea,
Floating in my mind.
I try to find another word,
But then it doesn't rhyme.

I sometimes start a limerick
A funny sort of verse.
But when I reach the punch line,
It couldn't sound much worse.

I'm certainly no Shakespeare,
My imagination's vanished.
To put this gruesome story short,
I really should be banished.

Joe Burman (12)
Dover Grammar School for Boys

BOOKS GALORE

Books are cool,
Books are brill,
Think of all the time they fill,
Sunday afternoon,
Full of boredom,
Pick up a book,
And start to read.
Lots of words,
Possibly a picture.
Some are scary,
Some are fun,
Some I use to wipe my . . . oh never mind!
If it's boring,
Put it down,
And read another one.
Lots of pages,
Flick, flick, flick.
There is a whole new world,
Inside a book!

Iain Thomas (12)
Dover Grammar School for Boy

A TREE AT WINTER

Branches waving in the air,
With icicles hanging off the thicker ones,
With snow resting on the top,
On a cold winter's day.

Nothing protecting it from the deathly cold,
In a park with nobody in it,
Apart from an occasional dog-walker,
Or a keep-fit lunatic.

Snow all around on the ground,
Covering it like a soft warm blanket,
The tree has a purpose especially,
For the squirrel that's found a home.

The heavens keep beating it with snow,
But the thick trunk stands straight and firm,
But smaller trees aren't so lucky,
As ice and death creep upon them.

Sam Smith (12)
Dover Grammar School for Boys

SILENCE OF THE WORLD

The city at rush hour,
Like the stars in the sky,
Reflecting off the windows.

The corridors after assembly,
Like an ant trying to swim upstream,
Not getting anywhere.

The streets were quiet,
Like the bottom of the sea,
No sound to hear.

A bird chirped,
Like the cheer when you score a goal,
Breaking the suspense.

David Watt (12)
Dover Grammar School for Boys

AUTUMN

The wind starts to blow,
The leaves start to fall,
The stars start to glow.
The trees grow very tall.

Red and orange are the autumn colours,
It's quiet and peaceful, no-one's about,
Little animals keep warm with their mothers.
There's no-one to scream and no-one to shout.

The air smells fresh but is very polluted and dirty
It gets very cold and dark,
In the morning about five thirty.
As the dogs begin to howl and bark.

Anouska Aitkenhead (14)
Dartford West for Girls

THE FIRST DAY ON HOLIDAY

First I have to travel by train and boat.
When I get there my family and I
have to find the flat where we are going
to stay.
I stroll along the beach looking around.
I love to spend a lot of money and
time in the amusements,
play on lots of machines.
I love to spend a lot of money on a lot
of gifts.
I love to try to grab a teddy on
a teddy machine.
Time to go on to the next day.

Hayley Hockaday (11)
Eden Valley School

As Free As a Bird!

If I were a bird flying in the sky,
How high would I fly? How high
would I fly?

O to be as free as a bird,
What would I have seen what would I
have heard?

Darting around without a care,
Would I be here? Would I be there?
I'd let out a happy squawk,
But what would I talk? How would I
talk?
I'd settle down after a hard day of
flying.
But would people be spying? Would people
be spying?

Emma Clark (12)
Eden Valley School

The Elephant

Big floppy ears to keep them cool in the heat.
Spraying water like a shower head.
Trunks like spears to knock down trees.
Feet like a giant monster.
Tail swinging from side to side.
Nails like a knife to cut things down to size.
Head like a giant football.
The elephant lives everywhere in the country.
The biggest mammal in the world.

Liam Vaughan (11)
Eden Valley School

THE HERO

I'd like to be a hero,
Flying around saving people's lives,
What a wonderful life.
I'd like to be a hero,
Having special powers,
Flying over towers.
I'd like to be a hero,
Having freedom,
At the seat of your kingdom.
I'd like to be a hero,
Getting attention,
Being mentioned,
Then I awake,
Still wanting to be a hero,
Like that character *Sub-Zero!*

Saiful Ali (11)
Eden Valley School

ANOTHER SCHOOL DAY

When I was small and I just started this school
I wasn't very keen on school
so every day my heart was beating
of the greeting
of that place called school.

I'm waiting for the bell
to mark the end of hell
on this school day
the teachers will say
it's another school day on Monday.

Christian Finer (11)
Eden Valley School

A Poem Of My Name

D aniel is my name
A ngling's my game
N oisy I am
I   am good in goal at football
E lephant I am
L oving I am

G ardening I love
R obber I am
I   ce hockey I love
F lying I love.

Daniel Griffiths (11)
Eden Valley School

Working In Space

Out of the spaceship
Into our suits
Do some exercises
Get into our boots.
Look around the mountain peak
I can't hear a noise.
Just the splashing of the waterfall
You can hear the banging of the hammer
And the spraying of the foam
You can see where Pegasus
Burnt the launching zone
We made the house and made
The bridge but we still haven't
Put up our model fridge.
Out of the space ship
Into our boots and into our suits.

Matthew Simmons (13)
Eden Valley School

ALONE

My first day at school
I stood outside the gates
and wondered what my first
day would be like.
The school looked cold and
daunting and uninviting.
My stomach turned and my
heart began to beat faster and
faster.
With great effort I opened the
school gate and the path to the
school seemed long, even though
there were pupils who seemed
to know where they were going.
I opened the school front door
and looked across the hall
and saw another lonely pupil and
realised I was not all alone.

Danielle Marsh (15)
Eden Valley School

ISLAND DREAM

If I had an island far away,
Where I could escape for a couple of days,
I would lay there and listen to the
Caribbean Sea,
And hear a steel band in the distant
breeze,
Then all my troubles would disappear.

Natalie Belville (15)
Eden Valley School

THE CARP

A magnificent specimen it is,
It feeds on bollies, maggots
and bread.
A hot sunny day,
You could be in luck,
On the top with dog biscuits,
Or on the bottom with bollies,
     anything will work or do.
It moves swiftly through the water,
Looking for food on the way,
Its scaly body brushes up
against the silky weed and lilies,
Its wary eye looks out for
movement
of danger like pike. People they
say -
They are cowards of the
fresh water,
Never like to be caught or
seen,
Its big fat belly and wide
long back,
What a magnificent specimen
to see.

Simon McAvoy (15)
Eden Valley School

STRANGE PLACE

I've arrived at Isis
It's a very unusual place
I want to stay
The grass is long and blue
Strange place!

The mesa is like a table top
On the mesa it's cold and windy
We have to wear strange suits like
Spacemen
Strange place!

The houses are shell-like made from
Plastic and foam
They look like bubbles
Strange place!

The two moons of Isis
Shu and Nut
One revolves faster than the other
Tiny moons
Hidden among bright coloured stars
Isis - a beautiful but
Strange place!

Adam Wood (14)
Eden Valley School

ISIS

Here on Isis,
Space all around.
The sky is so different,
There are many strange sounds.

Ra shines brightly,
Tanning my face brown.
Grey-green grass, high up on the Mesa,
The drop of the Mesa goes down and down.

The jaggy-peaked mountains
Tower above,
The flowing cascades,
It's so lovely.

The lake is beautiful,
Surrounded by fruit trees that are so small.
The red and purple crags,
Are very deep and tall.

Different but beautiful, that's Isis.

Rebecca Richardson (13)
Eden Valley School

ISIS

Looking down from the mess,
I see range after range of mountains.
Some are jagged-peaked, some are smooth
as ice.
As I look east I see a river.
As it enters the valley it loses its impetus
and widens into a lake.
I look up into the sky.
I try to look for earth but how can I see,
it's so crowded up above.
I look down again, I notice people,
I'm not alone now.
I see a bridge, I never noticed that before.
It seems to be changing Isis.
Why do they have to build it?
Above the eastern horizon the moon rose
And one after another a little star.
It is getting dark, the noise has stopped.
Time to sleep.

Gemma Harris (14)
Eden Valley School

ISIS

Isis is a planet millions of miles away,
We came here in a rocket which took us days and days.
There are two moons Nut and Shu,
When we got out of the rocket we stood in a queue.

In the valley the oxygen is thick,
As we left Earth the rocket door went click,
The running water from the lake is pure,
The picture on the brochure was enough to lure.

We're staying here forever to start a new life,
This is more exciting than our last home in East Fife.
There are lots of jagged rocks on the floor and in the air,
There's even lots of dust floating everywhere.
The houses are made of concrete and steel,
When we were back on Earth people were getting killed.

Kevin Burgess (13)
Eden Valley School

LIFE ON ISIS

As we landed on Isis all I could see was a
mist of blue-grey coloured grass.
As I take a look around I see high
up, the Mesa, a range of mountains,
range upon range of grey coloured mountains
with a stream cascading down a trail of
jagged rocks leading into the lake.
In the distance I see a lake, blue
coloured water with the construction
of a bridge going on.
I go for a walk and see lots of settlers
just moving in and settling down.
The weather here is cold, cold as I walk.
I look up and see a girl sitting on the
Mesa watching the settlers moving in.
I walk back to my ship as I see
Ra setting and get ready to go home.

Hayley Payton (13)
Eden Valley School

CHANGE

This is free,
The place to be,
Isis is home,
I live here alone.

Slowly inexorably,
The face of the plain has changed,
This valley had lain, grass-filled,
And now it'll never be the same.

I'll never smell the fresh air,
Never smell the grass,
Just all the pollution,
The humans will bring to us.

Leave my home,
To live here alone,
Never come back.

Ruhena Khanom (13)
Eden Valley School

THE ISIS SETTLERS

Isis is an unusual place with
Its ragged cliffs and so much
Space and the sound of the
Tumbling waterfall and the
Mesa face so giant and tall
And houses of plastic so
Flimsy and small they
Might collapse and kill us
All.
There might even be germs
In the air that would get us
And that would be the end
For the Isis settlers.

Emily Jepps (13)
Eden Valley School

21ST CENTURY POEM

Through the spacecraft window I see a crystal, glinting,
transparent dome housing bright, dazzling lights.
Next to the dome a towering, black, sinister metropolis.
Fumes rise past the tiny craft, clouding it in a black
smog.
A blue shimmering light shone through the tiny window.
My legs grow weak with the gravity pulling down on me.
I glance again at the shining dome and make out tiny people
and cars shooting past.
A deep, loud, clicking sound crackles out of the speakers.

My legs give up on me as I struggle through the craft
I fall hopelessly to the floor having forgot about gravity.
All of a sudden the door oddly cranked open.
I look out of the barely open hatch. I am quickly dragged to
a white, pearly chair.
I look through the diamond, transparent dome as black clothed
poorly clad people bang angrily on the side.
I timidly cringe as guards shoo them away with a volley of
non-lethal grenades. It blocks out the hot, burning sun.
I slump down as the dome is surrounded by thick black, scowling
mobs.

I climb back into the ship with a melancholy feeling.
As I close the hatch the dome slowly crumbles to the floor.
A mixture of people and radiation sweep through it in chaos.
With a sigh I hit the retro engines.
I am not to return to this spoilt and unlawful world; *My home!*

Samuel Fagence (11)
Gravesend Grammar School For Boys

RACISM

Should people be treated equally?
Is everyone equal?
Should it matter what religion you believe in?
Should it matter what your name is?
Should it matter what colour skin you have?
We are all the same; all equal in our own right.

What would you do if you were hated for the colour of your skin?
Would you cry, or would you sit there and take it?
Do you pray to a different god?
Do you wear different clothes?
Maybe you celebrate different holidays to the kid next door.
Does it matter?

Some black kids are called names,
Some black kids are laughed at,
Some black kids are expected to mug a little old lady
          by the time they are 20 years of age,
Some black kids are beaten behind the bike sheds,
I wonder what sort of person would do that sort of thing?
I wonder, if I had black skin, would my friends still be my friends?

Dolley Jean White (15)
Highsted Grammar School

IT WASN'T ME

'It wasn't me'
Lives under the stairs.
We've never seen him,
But we know he's there.

The toast got burnt.
'It wasn't me!'
My sister cried,
'I was playing Barbies.'

The pen was leaking.
'It wasn't me!'
My brother yelled,
'I was watching TV.'

The plate got smashed.
'It wasn't me!'
My mother called,
'I was in the garden'

'Who spilt the paint
All over the carpet?'
Demanded Mum.
'Don't look at me!'

'It wasn't me'
Lives under the stairs.
We've never seen him,
But we know he's there.

Joanna Hill (13)
Highworth Grammar School for Girls

WHY ARE WE SO CRUEL?

Why are we so cruel to keep them locked up in a cage?
We all understand the animals' rage.
The lions loudly roar,
while walking on the cold brick floor.

Their forest eyes are gone,
we give people money while they con.
They can only walk a few yards up and down,
we would not like this, it would give us a frown.

Nothing to do all day,
they're just wild beasts on display.
Only lying in the heat,
with rotten smells and meat.

They remember how they chased,
their jungle prey, and raced,
leaping upon their backs,
along the grassy tracks.

But they are here instead
they would prefer to be dead
than locked in the dark den,
forgive us animals then,
we did not ever choose,
our circuses and zoos.

Ashley Hills (12)
Highworth Grammar School for Girls

To You With Love

The pain you left is washed away,
By pouring rain and endless grey,
Replaced by hate if you should hate
Or love if love so lets it be.
For daggers of the mind be such
As wounded pride, and e'er so much
Depends upon the mind of fate
And your behaviour unto me.
Together is our destiny,
Apart if you would have it so,
But by my side your path does lie,
Together, entwined, forever.

Freyja Cox Jensen (12)
Highworth Grammar School for Girls

The Candle

The candle flame flickering,
Wax melting slowly,
Dripping, gently onto the table,
The flame tenderly glows in the darkness.

The candle flickers,
The light dim,
The only light, the one of the candle,
Glowing brilliantly in the dull light.

Late at night,
The candle still burning,
Wax dripping, forming a pool,
Drip, drip, drop.

Nicola Adams (13)
Highworth Grammar School for Girls

FREEDOM

The lush, flourishing, verdant grass,
Crumples beneath the strength of my unwrinkled, bare feet,
Leaving a smooth compressed pattern of footprints behind me,
As I stroll gently into a proud life of freedom.

I run faster, faster, faster, faster
Not knowing where I am going, nor what to fear, nor caring
Never looking back or stopping once,
As I stroll gently into a proud life of freedom.

And now, fifty years on,
I am walking through my apple orchard,
Dashes of scarlet, ochre and avocado confront me,
While I pass heavily laden blackberry bushes which droop like withered
flowers.

At the end of an invisible path lies an old, ramshackle cottage,
Roof tiles missing and dusty, broken windows.
And it reminds me of the place I was running from,
As I strolled gently into a proud life of freedom.

I turn around and look behind me,
There is a smooth, compressed pattern of footprints made in the
jade grass,
And I remember . . .
That same day that I strolled gently into a proud life of freedom.

Emma Russell (12)
Highworth Grammar School for Girls

If I . . .

If I could fly, I would soar through the trees,
And talk with the beautiful birds and the bees.

If I could swim like a shark,
I would explore the underwater park.

If I could jump as high as a kangaroo,
I would jump right up to the moon.

If I could, but I can't.

If I was a stream, I would keep my water cool,
To make a perfect swimming pool.

If I was a cloud I would float around,
Raining not water but pennies and pounds.

If I was the weather, I would keep out the sun,
So all the people could have fun.

If I was, but I'm not.

Carly George (12)
Highworth Grammar School for Girls

Winter For The Homeless

I lie out in the shivering cold,
All my belongings in my arms I hold.
Gently falling from the sky is snow,
Setting softly down below.

Christmas seems to be coming near,
In homes I see a warming atmosphere.
Celluloid memory in my hand,
I wish my life had gone as planned.

Once I had a warm, caring home,
Peace - free, where no-one ever moaned.
Then my life turned to a mess
And I became homeless.

The pavement about me,
Is like a cemetery.
This cardboard basket,
Resembles a casket.

Kacy-Marie Ford (12)
Highworth Grammar School for Girls

THE ALLIGATOR

I'm going hunting down by the lake
Looking for a tasty alligator steak.
What's that I hear? A hearty bellow
It must be a female looking for a fellow.

Looking at a snout broad, flattened and round
I stand frozen not making a sound.
Mud and water plants a perfect nest
A suitable site for her eggs to rest.

For sixty days I watch alone
As the eggs are incubated in their home.
The female alligator guards the site
Caring for her young both day and night.

I change my mind my hunger gone
Hunting alligators I know is wrong.
They belong to the earth like you and me
A wonderful sight for all to see.

Zoe Cahill (12)
Highworth Grammar School for Girls

ALLEY-CAT

Slowly prowling through the night,
Giving small creatures a terrible fright,
The master gives a creepy mew,
So everyone knows he is here too.

The brown ruffled tawny fur,
Mysterious throbbing purr,
His catch of food is but a few,
As everyone knows he is here too.

Unsuspecting characters know,
That it should be time to go,
He can jump on you as quick as . . . boo!
But everyone knows he is here too.

Dreams of children, dreams of friends,
Dreams on which your life depends,
In the morning there'll be much to do,
As everyone knows he is there too.

Slowly walking as it is dawn,
The human gives a mighty yawn,
The first pigeon gives a coo,
But everyone knows he is there too.

He is finally gone, animals back,
He is back on the lonely track,
The birds . . . they all flew,
As everyone knew he was there too.

Laura Venn (12)
Highworth Grammar School for Girls

OH CRUMBS, IT'S RHUBARB

The rhubarb was growing in a village one day,
When some mean soul picked it away
He put some in a crumble and some in a pie
Little did the rhubarb know that it was to die
It got chopped into pieces as small as a bug
The poor little rhubarb just sat there and blubbed
It got put in a bowl with crumble on top
And got put in an oven and baked very hot
Then taken from the oven and dished on a plate
The poor little rhubarb now knew his fate
It then got shovelled on a fork as well as a spoon
This was the end of the rhubarb's doom
Meanwhile back in the village that day
There was some more rhubarb just picked away.

Victoria Sudlow (12)
Highworth Grammar School for Girls

MY PARENTS

My parents are like a gentle rock.
Kind, but strong.
They offer me advice and help me
When I am in trouble or I feel alone.

My parents are very generous
They provide me with the things I need
I am given gifts at Christmas and on my birthday
And provided with money for trips.

My parents are very important to me
I do not know what I would do without them
They are loving, caring and kind
My parents are important to me.

Elizabeth Griffiths (13)
Highworth Grammar School for Girls

MOVING HOUSE

Trundling along with his house on his back,
On his way to his new domain he prays,
He will not be seen by the sparrows above.
Going as fast as he possibly can,
Hoping he gets to his shelter in time,
Sixteen, Craggey Rock, Garden Avenue,
The pots and pans inside his rich brown shell crash,
His powerful body a tarnished grey.
He reaches his new humble abode safely.
Starting to unpack his dreams are shattered.
A human being finds the stone and throws it away
Far away and out of the sight of the snail,
Into the distance and far beyond his region,
He gets his things together and sets off.
Trundling along with his house on his back.

Elaine Miles (12)
Highworth Grammar School for Girls

CAT POEM

Our cat is really special to me,
and to all of my family.

He sits on my mum's lap and purrs,
as we sit down to watch Chelsea and Spurs.

He sits on the bed while I stroke his head,
and he goes to sleep in a big tired heap.

He makes a racket when he wants some food,
and if he does not he gets in a mood.

In the evening he sits in front of the fire,
all curled up for everyone to admire.

Victoria Brignall (11)
Highworth Grammar School for Girls

THE WOLF

Into the cold,
Into the ice,
Into the dark,
Into the night.

Moving slowly,
Creeping softly,
Through the shadows,
Tall and lofty.

The wolf is crouching,
He's preparing,
Leaping for his prey,
From hiding.

Satellite ears pick up,
The hare's soft heartbeat.
Eyes glint, steel blades,
Preparing for the kill.

The spring is made.
In a fleeting moment,
A single instant,
The hare's life is over.

Pearl needles sink into soft flesh,
The wolf devours the hare.
Warmth spreads through his body,
And the creature is fulfilled.

Emili Yates (13)
Highworth Grammar School for Girls

PIGS

Pigs can be pink,
Pigs can be black,
Pigs can be brown,
And hairy on their back.

Scratches, oinks and grunts,
Snuffles, squeaks and squeals,
Pigs roll in mud,
Before and after meals.

Their tails are like a snail's shell,
They can eat like a slob,
They are clean and do not smell,
And are worth more than a couple of bob.

Pigs are gluttons
Pigs don't pout,
Pigs find truffles,
With their little snouts.

Sarah Ticehurst (12)
Highworth Grammar School for Girls

A FOX'S DAY

A fox wanders lonely across the land
His mate and cubs have been ripped to pieces
By human's uncaring hand

It is the cubbing season and the hounds are eager
To get the smell of blood and the screams in their ears
Knowing if they don't their chances of survival are meagre

The fox runs on, tiring fast
The flashes of red and deafening horns
Oh no! His fate has been cast

Now lies only silence
The hunt has been called off
Oh joy! The fox runs still vibrant

But his cunning will not outrun us
For much longer now
Just because some of us like to kick up a fuss.

Natalie Hopley (12)
Highworth Grammar School for Girls

AN AUTUMN THOUGHT

Popping berries under feet,
Of mufflered men
And bundled children
Squelch and merge
With yellow leaves
And brown puddle water
A soup
Rippling a shiver of cold
Below the whirling wind
And throbbing leaves
Swiped off the trees
By drizzling rain
To form sodden banks
Of autumn.

Katy Blatt (12)
Highworth Grammar School for Girls

JULIE ROSE RACE

Today is the day of the Julie Rose Race,
The runners and spectators take their place,
Either on the Julie Rose Stadium track,
Or in the stand watching the race,
After everyone has taken their place.

The stadium is spectacular,
Not even finished yet,
But hopefully finishing is near soon - I bet,
Soon hundreds of sweaty bodies,
Steaming and weak, are on their wobbly legs.

First it is the under nines' run,
Round the track, just once,
A small boy runs,
Just one of the crowd,
Himself and his parents are very proud.

Then it is the over nines' to thirteens' race,
Including me we take our place,
Round track three times and a bit,
The pain is horrendous - I have terrible stitch,
The finish is in sight,
I get a medal at the end - so that's
Definitely alright!

Two more races to go,
First the thirteens to fifteens run,
Then the over sixteen's ten kilometre one!
One pain barrier is reached,
Then so is the next one!

The Julie Rose Race was a lot of pain,
But was also a lot of fun!

Caroline Lawlor (12)
Highworth Grammar School for Girls

CHRISTMAS IN SEPTEMBER?

Why does Christmas start in September?
I always thought it was in December.
Christmas trees, lights as well,
In popular shops, trying to sell,
Nobody, thinks it is right,
And probably think it's a horrible sight.

In Ashford, Christmas has lasted all year,
The lights just didn't disappear.
The Eurostar one, and candles too,
Were pretty at Christmas but not all year through.
Do you really think it's right,
That lights in June should be so bright?

When Christmas finishes, Easter starts,
When Easter finishes, Christmas starts.
It's a cycle to make money,
Which is *not* very funny,
As soon as Christmas ends, cream eggs
are in the shops,
Put our Christmas back to December, or
we will call the cops!

Emma Kingsnorth (12)
Highworth Grammar School for Girls

WHERE DOES MY CAT GO AT NIGHT?

I wonder if my cat raids the nearest dustbin
Searching for scraps of fish,
Then climbs to the nearest rooftop to meet her boyfriend
for a walk under the stars.

On the other hand, my cat could be fighting violently on my very own
rooftop,
Throwing cats off the roof,
Defending her territory against intruders
'til there are no cats left in town.

My cat loves to sing
So she could be in a choir,
Yowling out of tune,
Waking up the whole town.

My cat might find a cosy barn
And curl up in the straw,
Snug and warm but one eye open.
A mouse would be a tasty midnight snack.

My cat might like this exciting life
But it isn't really true.
When I go to bed she comes too
And stays with me 'til morning.
- *I think!*

Joanna Lee (11)
Highworth Grammar School for Girls

LIFE'S LITTLE MISHAPS

A child, sitting on the street.
She calls to a passer by.
'Please sir, I'm broke, I've nowt to eat!
I'm sure I'm going to die!'

> The man just hums and crosses the road.
> No sympathy or grief he showed.

'Be quiet now! Stay right by me!'
Says hunter number one.
His voice was filled with devilish glee,
As he pulls out his foot long gun.

> The ape tries all it can to hide,
> But the trigger's pulled, the poor thing died.

Along the dirty, sludgy track,
Through greenery and woods,
The heavy metal trucks are back
To collect their priceless goods.

> The sound of crashing logs is heard.
> The loss of a home to another bird.

A factory, not far away
From famous London City
Is burning things, I have to say
On Earth I take much pity.

> The fossil fuels are burnt all day,
> They poison air. The sky turns grey.

The child's still out upon the street,
The ape will be used for research.
The crashing of logs is a regular beat,
Global warming is left in the lurch.

> Life's little mishaps are a thing
> That greedy human beings bring.

Karen Jordan (12)
Highworth Grammar School for Girls

MY GRANDMOTHER

My grandmother is a beautiful woman,
Her name is Emily and that is pretty too,
She has lovely sunset coloured cheeks,
And dark jade coloured eyes.

She has wild grey curly hair,
But the strange thing is,
She has no wrinkles at all,
Even though she is eighty.

When I am in pain,
She comforts me,
And when I need aid,
She helps me,

She is very kind,
And I love her dearly,
She tells us stories,
And makes our clothes.

My grandma is a strong one,
She fights pain and troubles,
But she also cares for other people,
And helps in her community,

She is very gentle,
And cares about animals,
And how they are treated,
All in all I love her very dearly.

Anna McConnell (11)
Highworth Grammar School for Girls

PETS

Cats, dogs and hamsters,
Anything could be a pet,
Even elephants with long trunks,
That's why I intend to be a vet.

> I have got a rabbit,
> Leanne has a dog,
> Sarah's got a poodle,
> And Lucy owns a frog.

The dog barks at the boys,
The cat likes to purr.
Most make a lot of noise
But the rabbit seems not to care.

> The dog chases the cat,
> The cat will chase the bird,
> The rabbit can't run fast enough
> To keep up with the herd.

The frog eats lots of flies,
The cat eats plenty of fish,
The dog likes a juicy bone
In his special dish.

> Long haired, short haired,
> I don't really care,
> Large, small, fat or thin
> It can even fly in the air

Any pet could be your friend,
Dog, rabbit, hamster or cat,
But if ever you get fed up,
They are always welcome on my
Doormat.

Michelle Smith (11)
Highworth Grammar School for Girls

WHAT I WANT FOR CHRISTMAS SANTA

What I want for Christmas, Santa,
it's not very much,
so here is a list,
from a puppy to a hutch.

An apple would be nice,
or what about a ball,
I s'pose I could manage an orange
or a cat that's really quite small.

A bear,
a goldfish,
a basketball court,
these are a few of the things
of which I have thought.

I could have a sports car,
yes that's what I need,
a sports car would be fine,
so that's what you can buy for me,
Santa.

Catriona Blair (11)
Highworth Grammar School for Girls

THE FRIEND

As slick as an eagle
She comes round my house
Trying to open the door!
I lock it up and then try to hide on
the floor!

Every morning she walks me to school,
Hoping she would have a friend,
I try to be nice, I really do!
But somehow it comes to an end.

In all of my lessons she bugs me
and bugs me,
In the end I eventually gave in,
I play with her all of the time now,
And so she is my *friend!*

Leanne Stone (11)
Highworth Grammar School for Girls

MY CAT

My cat
Jumps and prowls,
Stalking her prey
In the long grass,
With not a sound.
Suddenly she leaps,
And strikes
Her aim.
Cleverly she pounces,
Until she wins,
Then has her reward
Of a plump mouse.

My cat
Sleeps and purrs
In a cupboard
Or an a lap,
She rubs
Our legs
And sweetly miaows,
This wild
Hunter's tamed.

Florence Nisbet (11)
Highworth Grammar School for Girls

WHAT TO DO WITH PARENTS

Now it's time for number one,
Put them in the freeze and make them go numb,
What to do with parents?

Now it's time for number two,
Stick their shoes with super glue,
What to do with parents?

Now it's time for number three,
Make them a muddy cup of tea,
What to do with parents?

Now it's time for number four,
For the very last thing pin them to the floor,
What to do with parents!

Sammy-Jo Leigh (11)
Highworth Grammar School for Girls

HIBERNATION

They poke their heads and sniff the air,
The weather is warm enough for them to bare.
They raise their heads and begin to creep,
Awakening from their long winter's sleep.

They start to creep out of their warm little nests,
And look for their friends, after their long, long rest.
They start to explore the forest so green,
The forest so lush has never been seen.

The animals are also beginning to hunt for their lunch,
They haven't had anything for at least five months.
Now they're glad they can stay with their friends,
Spring has begun and winter ends.

Samantha Speed (12)
Highworth Grammar School for Girls

HOW DO YOU WRITE A POEM?

How do you write a poem?
I really want to know.
It's going to be a winner and
It needs to be put on show.

Where do you start with a poem?
What subject shall I pick?
Hamsters, hills and heffalumps.
I shall have to make my mind up quick.

Shall I make it funny like Michael Rosen
Or as serious as Dorothy Wordsworth.
Shall I make it cheerful like Julie Holder
Or sad like Elizabeth Coatsworth.

Narrative shall my poem be
About the days of old,
Or shall it be dramatic.
I need to be told.

I could do an elegy
About someone that's dead
Or what about my thoughts and feelings
In a lyric instead,

Now I'd better write my poem,
Oh, I am a twit.
I've just read what I've written
And I've already written it.

Catherine Fagg (11)
Highworth Grammar School for Girls

COLOURS

Red is the red, red rose
or a ripe juicy apple.

White is the snow on rooftops
or ghosts in a haunted house.

Green is the newly cut grass
or leaves of trees in spring.

Gold is corn sparkling in the sunshine
or coins glittering in the sunlight.

Blue is the swimming pool
ready to dive into
or a cool glass of water

And what's orange?
Why just an orange.

Rebecca Evans (11)
Highworth Grammar School for Girls

AUTUMN

Autumn is my favourite season
For this very simple reason,
I love the colours orange and brown
And the leaves that crunch upon the ground.

The nights get dark,
The rivers overflow,
The storms brew up,
And I watch the fire glow.

The fireworks flash,
They zoom through the sky,
It begins to snow
And the moon soars high.

The lightning flashes,
The thunder rolls,
I tuck up in bed
And my dreams unfold!

Rachel Taylor (11)
Highworth Grammar School for Girls

DREAMS

Have
You ever
wondered what
happens to dreams
once you wake up? Where
do they go and how? They fly away
back to the land where they came from. The land
of dreams. Catching rides on the nearest stars and
sometimes the moon. They laugh and joke about the
things they
had made you dream, and the naughty
stars boast on how much they had scared
you. The lasiest dreams get left behind as they
have missed their rides on the stars. But they still find
something
to do. They enter your head during the day when
you're awake. But most people are able
to control them and the dreams
leave. Then when the night
arrives the dreams
return ready
for another night of mischief.

Nicola Louise Cattini (12)
Highworth Grammar School for Girls

HEDGEHOG

The hedgehog's spikes are prickly,
They are razor sharp and worse,
Curled up tight, he's quite safe,
Only one thing can harm him then,
That is humans and their inventions.

The hedgehog staggers wearily home,
After the night's great hunt,
He sleeps away the daytime,
To have energy for . . .
The next night's great hunt.

He wakes in the dusk,
He walks to search for food,
So slowly he walks,
With his usual sluggish pace,
On his regular nightly route.

He crosses the quiet road,
As he does a car comes,
He curls up tightly,
Hoping for the best,
The car's going too fast!

Samantha Holroyd (11)
Highworth Grammar School for Girls

ME AND MY BUDDY

Every Saturday I ride,
It's a hobby I love to do.
Me and my pony side by side,
My friend Louise loves it too.

I arrive at the stables at half past nine,
I can see my pony thinking, 'Oh no, it's time!'

My pony on the outside is sweet as can be,
But nobody knows him like me!

His coat is pure white,
But once he's been in a muddy field, 'Oh what a sight.'

He's the smallest of the bunch,
Even though he eats up all his lunch!

But I don't care, because he's my *buddy!*

Emilie Cross (11)
Highworth Grammar School for Girls

GONE . . .

The friendship we once had was no more;
We had a fight and you walked out that door;
We drifted apart,
Each of us ready to make a new start.
Smile and be happy you said to me -
It wasn't that easy if only you could see.
I missed you being there,
And the times we could no longer share.
I love you,
And as the days go by the more I do.
Now you've gone, I'm all alone,
But deep inside I've always known,
You've never loved me,
But maybe it was meant to be.
All I'm left with is heartache and tears,
And the future that holds my fears.
Now I've got to let go of the past,
And make these memories the very last,
I've got to look forward to what the future holds,
A whole new experience, so I'm told.

Sarah James (15)
Highworth Grammar School for Girls

IMAGINATION OF NIGHT

Wind rustles through the trees,
Dragging clouds, leaves, everything.
With a sharp glowing moon.
Able to make dark things glow.
Beating the dread darkness.

Imagination playing up,
Looking at the mid unknown.
Goblins, ghosts and scary things
Looking through the wall of darkness.
Hoping for the window of lightness.

James Eaton (15)
Holy Cross High School

SELFISH BLIND ME

My self esteem is low.
Just how deep can I go
in the ground where I lay.
If only I could find a way to
distance the fears and crowd my mind.
As I face up to the fear I realise
that I'm turning blind.
I can see I'm blind.

My eyes close once again
and my remaining senses are sharp
to sleep is to wake,
it's forever dark
to see the sun
Oh what joy it would be
Oh what I'd give to see . . .

Jonathan Huggins (16)
Holy Cross High School

BEGGAR'S CRY

Sir, sir give me a dime.
Really, I don't do crime
Please, sir, give me a dime.
the needles next to me are not mine.

Sir, sir give me a chance
the cafe closes at half past.

Sir, sir don't go away
I might not live to the next day.

Oh, no, no, no it's cold now
I've got frost growing on my eyebrow.
Oh no the subway's closed
I wish I had my home now.

Drugs are bad, but make me feel good.
I wish I never started or stop if I could

Sir, sir give me a dime
If you don't I'll become once upon a time.
Good night.

Stuart Byrne (15)
Holy Cross High School

THE SEA

The seas are changing every minute from
calm to cruel and calm once more.

Calm seas are like sheets blowing in the
wind, free from all the worries of the
world.

The sun is glinting off the surface of
the water, silently in the wind.

If only life was like the sea, the whole
world would be at peace.

Yet when I look at the sea when it is
rough, I think of unicorns running,
running from something but nobody
knows what, anxious to get away. That's
more like real life. Rough, tough and
ready for whatever lies ahead.

Caroline Renham (16)
Holy Cross High School

THE TEACHER

As I sit inside the room and stare,
I have a feeling and know she's there.
She thinks she's queen,
Above us all,
But does she know she's really quite small.
She is plump and looks quite full,
She looks harmless to one and all.
And then her shout,
Rings the air,
Now you know that she is there.

Natalie Mann (13)
Invicta Grammar School

A MILLION REASONS WHY PONIES ARE GREAT!

Everyone knows that ponies are great
They'll listen to problems and be your best mate
They'll be your best friend all for free
And what a good friend your pony can be!

Everyone knows that ponies are cool
They're friendly and big but that is not all
They'll keep you fit and looking your best
And turn you into a sporting success!

For making excuses, they are the best
And jumping large fences will really impress
They give you maturity and this can be great
When your parents won't let you party till late!

You can eat lots of junk food without getting fat
The good exercise from riding will keep you from that
But eating is the thing that makes ponies happy
Maybe that's why most ponies are fatties!

Sarah Hicks (12)
Invicta Grammar School

UP ON THE MOORS

Up on the moor where the winds
blow strong.
All of a sudden I felt something
wrong.
The air was not fresh as first I
had thought.
Oh my God it's the sandwiches
I'd brought.

Claire Elliott (13)
Invicta Grammar School

THE BLACK CHARGER

She cascades graciously through the feathery, cushiony land.
Her fleecy mane and tail combine freely with the pure sea air.
She dances elegantly like white-washed waves echoing through the sea.
Each time she exhausts her black blemished hooves, she harvests the
Crumbly curdles of sand.
She flies like a kite and continuously fights against the wind that
Tears at her face.
She carries her tail high in the rustling wind, her ears pricked up
As every sound skips past her muscular body.
The fresh sea odour tingles within her nose.
And the waves furiously lash at her magnificent limbs as she
Relentlessly polishes the salty tide like a maiden sweeping the dust.
The sooty, charcoal sky just endures over the world and the stars
Peacefully sparkle, singing their seductive song
They stand situated up in their magical world, forming a picturesque
Scene.
The black charger hurdles over the few remaining waves and departs.
Fearless, she gallops on fluently into the clean sheet of berry
Sponged horizon.

Erin Dodds (12)
Invicta Grammar School

THE HIPPO AND THE PARROT

A big, grey hippo lay in the mud;
When suddenly there was a huge thud.
The hippo turned and looked all around;
There was a bright parrot down on the ground.

'Ow' squawked the parrot. Her beak was bent;
The hippo laughed, then came a proper gent.
'How can I assist you in becoming amend?'
'The best thing you can do is be my friend!'
'So little parrot, what's your name?'

'I'm Beth, I was going to ask you the same!'
'Well I'm Big Bill, and I am ten.'
'I'll be ten soon but I don't know when.'

Big Bill and Beth played jungle seek;
Somehow this seemed to mend Beth's beak.
'Wow, Big Bill, my face is amend!
That's all thanks to you being my friend.'

Amanda Lakin (13)
Invicta Grammar School

My Garden

Stepping out into my beautiful garden,
Into a perfect scene.
Pearls of dew gather on a spider's web,
Above a blanket of green.

The weeping willow bows to the lilies,
Bobbing softly on the ripples of the pond.
The slight breeze teases the poppies,
And tugs at the daffodils of which I am fond.

The air carried the sweet smell of pollen,
Over the sunflowers, stretching to the sky.
I can taste the freshness of this morning,
But how quickly time passes by.

The hazy sun sets on my garden,
Pouring out light with an orangy glow.
And now I have to leave it lonely,
Oh, I wish I didn't have to go.

Jennifer Staunton (13)
Invicta Grammar School

TRAPPED

Around me is a circle of flames
Engulfing me in an orb of warmth
Flashes of red, yellow and orange dance around me
Jeering and sneering as
Their halos of smoke smother me
Pushing me down, down, down,
There's no way out
I'm trapped.

Jane Greenstock (13)
Invicta Grammar School

THOUGHTS

When you go to bed at night,
What's under your bed?
You might get a fright,
With all the things that fill your head,
Ghosts and ghouls and people who are dead.

Things that go bump in the night,
May give you quite a fright.
With all the things lurking around,
Try not to make a sound.

All your friends may think it's funny,
But deep down inside,
They have an upset tummy.

When you wake up in daylight
The monster will be gone
Until it's dark, at night.

Katie Coleman (12)
Invicta Grammar School

THE HERO AND THE MONSTER

Deep beneath the dark, murky sea of green,
A red trail marks where the monster has been.
The Grendel has destroyed everything in sight,
Even the men who have fought with great might.
All this has happened for countless years,
Leaving sorrowful ladies to dab their tears.
The story began when a brave hero,
Dived to challenge the demon, long ago.
He plunged through swirling, shifting waters,
Thinking only of his distressed daughters.
He saw a shipwreck; it's the monster's lair!
And slowly made towards it, with great care.
Suddenly the brute shot into the room,
And pinned the great hero, beneath the shining moon.
The Grendel was fierce and bared his teeth,
As the hero removed his sword from its sheath.
The darkness shattered as his sword came down,
But the sound was buried beneath a frown.
The monster cried loud but again was free,
The warrior was tired, and hot was he.
He lifted his sword, for a proud last time,
And brought it down, which made the monster whine.
The hairy beast's head was thrown to the ground,
And the sea grew red for miles around.
A loud cry erupted from the supporters,
As they saw him rise up from the waters
Carrying the huge head, that had been torn
From the dead brute on that jubilant morn.
That is where this epic comes to an end,
I'm sure our hero has more strength to lend!

Rachel Sear (13)
Invicta Grammar School

To Those Who Are Suffering

I dedicate this poem,
                    to people everywhere,
Victims of oppression,
                    showing that I care.
People just like us,
                    who suffer all the time,
While they are not guilty,
                    of any given crime.

Men and women young and old,
                    living in despair,
They have to cope with laws,
                    that simply are not fair.
What about the children,
                    suffering each day,
As their precious childhood,
                    slowly slips away.

We must think of them,
                    each passing day and night,
And do the best we can,
                    to rid them of their plight.
'Please help us O Allah,
                    to be mindful and to care,
To reach out far and wide,
                    to help and do our share.'

Iffat Ahmed (11)
Invicta Grammar School

MANCHESTER UNITED

They play in the colours of red and white.
To see them play is a wonderful sight.
There's Giggsy, Cantona, Beckham and May.
To see them play would make my day.

With legends such as Edwards, Law and Best.
How can you put them to the test?
Give them Newcastle, Chelsea or Liverpool
With their heads held high we'll beat them all.

For all those who died in Munich in '58
The rewards since then have been so great.
The league, the Cup and Europe too,
We've conquered them all, what else is there to do.

Stephanie Gadd (13)
Invicta Grammar School

THE AUTUMN GIRL

The autumn leaves fall gently down
modestly covering the body on the ground,
dressing her in a gown of fire
while she and the earth quietly conspire.
The autumn wind dances wild and light
stealing a lost soul far from sight,
and capturing any deathly trace
that still might remain on her face.
The autumn light still heats her lips
as flowers entwine her fingertips,
and the flowing stream that runs nearby
will steal her tears from her eyes.

Elizabeth Butler (16)
Invicta Grammar School

THINGS THAT GO BUMP!

What are the things that go bump in the night
When you're lying there alone in your bed?

Are they things crawling on the floor,
Or things made up in your head?

Are they monsters, insects, ghosts or ghouls,
Or little angels swimming in pools?

Or maybe they're just having fun
By going for a gentle run.

So what are the things that go bump in the night?
They'll all be gone when you turn on the light.

Sarah Dearling (11)
Invicta Grammar School

MONEY

To have money can be really great,
But money can't buy you an excellent mate.
Money can buy you that new black skirt,
Although it won't stop you from getting hurt.

With money you can pay the electric bill,
But money can't prevent you getting ill.
Money is something most people have got,
It could be very little or an awful lot.

Maybe money means everything to you,
It's your life, your happiness and in all you do.
Money can buy a lot of good things,
But it cannot buy the joy that life brings.

Sarah Head (13)
Invicta Grammar School

THE CONCERT

As I recall the crowds that swayed,
I write on my pencil case 'I love RK'.
The neon scenery, the flashing lights,
The hot London concerts on those summer nights.
I remember the concert as I lie on my bed,
I stare at my posters surrounding my head,
Ronan, Mikey, Stephen and Shane,
And don't forget Keith, I love him the same.
These are my idols, my life, my love,
I think as I stare at the poster above.
The group is called Boyzone, my one true passion.
They're not just a fad, a whim, or a fashion,
Their angelic voices sweep me off my feet,
When I hear them singing, my heart skips a beat.
my life would be worthless if they weren't around,
No other group can compete with their sound.
But back to the concert, I could not believe,
When the last song was sung and I had to leave,
I was upset to leave them then,
But little did I know I'd be going again!
That's right, this December, I'll go through
that once more.
Just watch them, try and stop me get through
that arena door!

Hannah Villars (13)
Invicta Grammar School

THE NATIONAL LOTTERY

Every Saturday,
It's always the same.
Most people play,
The same 'money-winning' game.

My mum and dad sit there,
Arguing over who's going to win.
When usually the tickets,
End up in the bin.

Then all is silent,
As the numbers are drawn.
And my dad's ticket,
Is ripped up and torn.

But mum just sits there,
So I ask her what's wrong.
Then she exclaims,
'I've won, I've won!'

Everyone screams,
This cannot be happening.
As my dad prances round
And my sister starts singing.

But then mum's face,
Fills with despair.
It was last week's ticket,
She was waving in the air!

Jessica Hartridge (13)
Invicta Grammar School

THE ENCHANTED LAKE

It seems like a dream
From which I never wake,
The whispering of the water
In the enchanted lake.

It has a mystic spirit
Which strikes a familiar chord,
The smell of religious incense
The sharpness of a sword.

As I stare into the water
Conclusions do I make,
The realisation of the image
In the enchanted lake.

Melanie Simpson (13)
Invicta Grammar School

NOSES

Don't you find it's really funny,
When people's noses get so runny.
Their nose gets red,
They're straight in bed.
Some get spots,
And some get lots.
But don't you find it's really cool,
When people with a nose so small,
Often want a bigger nose.
And big nosed people envy those.
So if you find your nose isn't great,
Get plastic surgery, it's not too late.

Jenni Hardes (11)
Invicta Grammar School

My Grandad

Grandad had a welcoming face,
although not at all handsome.
He had a dull forest of long ginger hair,
like straw.
His forehead, wrinkled,
looked as though it'd been there for hundreds
of years.
His cheeks sagged and flopped.
His eyebrows like golden caterpillars,
eyelashes hardly there.
His beautifully protruding eyes resembled the sea,
were easy to get lost in, almost see-through.
His ears were deep dark tunnels,
miles long,
full of folds and creases.
He had a smooth round shiny nose,
like a cherry in the winter.
His lips were always dry as a bone,
chapped, laden with cracks.
A short bristly beard grew on his square chin,
like a small hedgehog.
He had freckles on his little nose and sagging cheeks,
like gold coins had gently fallen out of the sky.
Before he died that is,
before he went to Heaven.

Joséphine Nelson (12)
Invicta Grammar School

THE DOLPHINS

As I walk into the shallows,
Of the ocean calm and still.
I look into the distance,
To scan across the greeny blue.
When suddenly I see,
My dearest wish come true.
A dolphin leaps over waves,
Of deep, silk blue.

It swiftly swims towards me,
Dancing as it rides along the sea.
How can it be so graceful?
Unlike me.
I paddle in towards it,
My heart is racing wildly.
It squeaks at me, I understand it,
Could it be beckoning me?

I get on its back,
It seems to be happy.
Then we dive through waves,
Of emerald green.
We race along waves,
Which are tipped with white.
It starts to grow dark,
The dolphin disappears, it's out of sight.

But I am snug,
And I am warm.
As I open my eyes,
I see the dawn.

Amy Duval (11)
Invicta Grammar School

THE HILL

I'm lonely . . .

It's still, quiet and peaceful,
But then there are noises,
They sit on me watching the view.

I don't mind them breathing *heavily*,
As I know they are there,
And they are keeping me company.

It turns, chilly and cold,
And the clouds are drawing in,
The sparkling emeralds fade away.

The voices stand up,
And start running like a gun being fired,
As the cool raindrops cut into their backs like swords.

It is quiet,
Please come back,
I'm lonely!

Hayley Cooper (13)
Invicta Grammar School

EXILED

I feel all empty inside,
I feel scared and I want to hide,
I'll miss everything at home,
And how I feel so alone,
There's nothing left for me.

I won't have a single friend,
Why does it feel like the end?
It feels like the walls are caving in,
I don't think I'm ever going to win,
I really don't want to move.

They don't know how I feel,
Honestly this can't be real,
I've only got my teddy left,
I've had to leave all of the rest,
Why do we have to be exiled?

Charlotte Kirkham (11)
Invicta Grammar School

FLYING

I would like to fly
Up
Into the deep blue sky
Where the clouds are puffy and white

Up into the warmth
Of the air surrounding me
Birds and insects breeze past
Pulling me after them

Then dark and coldness
As the sun becomes blocked by cloud
An uncomfortable feeling tingles down my body
As I swoop across the sky

The cloud drifts past
The sun and warmth reappears
I see the lush green grass below
Suddenly it seems much closer

I had flown
Down
On to the firm safe ground
Where the bright coloured flowers blow in the wind.

Charlotte Pomeroy (14)
Invicta Grammar School

SNOW

It falls, silently, without a word,
Swiftly laying on the frozen ground.
Children wrapped up like parcels, peacefully, playing.
Long, sharp, shining daggers hang freely from the window.
It smells of nothing,
Tastes like nothing, but
It is spectacular for all to see.
A cool, cold sense wraps around the earth like a blanket.

Then a warmness escapes,
A white flame is seen from the roaring winter fire.
The ash falls, silently,
Like *snow*.

Karen Wilson (13)
Invicta Grammar School

THE PARENTHOOD

The parenthood is worn always by a parent,
When put on makes the wearer an unbearable tyrant,
The parenthood is a hat with unbelievable powers,
The effects go on for more than many, many hours,
In fact the effects do last forever,
This is the fate the poor parent has to endeavour,
The hat is so uncomfortable it makes you want to scream,
And sometimes you wish that it is all a bad dream,
No-one knows how it gets on the poor parent's head,
It is put on when an adult becomes a parent instead,
So there you have it, the parenthood, with unfound doubt,
The parenthood should never have been found out,
The hat itself is an uncontrollable crime,
But it will last until the very end of time.

Hannah Whiteley (11)
Invicta Grammar School

A THOUSAND TEARS

My face is round, my body vast,
I'm treated as an outcast,
A pair of specs sit on my nose,
And when I run my asthma shows.

The features of my *vulgar* frame,
I sometimes think I am to blame,
For the taunting and the laughs,
My heart feels like it's broken in half.

The constant throbbing of my head,
A thousand tears I seem to shed,
Tears of sadness, exclusion and fear,
I always wish I wasn't here.

For several days the taunts go on,
I do not know where I went wrong,
I have no laughter, I have no joy,
I wish I could lie down and die.

Maybe if they listened hard,
I could play my lonely card,
Make them see my throbbing heart,
And realise I'm a work of art.

Nikki Phillips (14)
Invicta Grammar School

MY NEW SISTER

Until she came along it was alright,
Now nobody takes any notice of me.
All she does is cry and cry.
Everybody likes her and thinks she's really cute.
I think she's ugly.
I hate my baby sister.

When I come along she opens her mouth
And *screams* and *screams*.
It just isn't fair.
I always get told to be quiet.
I hate my baby sister.

When I come for a cuddle,
She's always there and gets in the way.
Mum hates me,
She only likes her.
I hate my baby sister.

Today I walked up to her,
While nobody was looking.
I peeped into the cot.
And . . .
She smiled at me.
I quite like my baby sister.

Cassie Dodd (11)
Invicta Grammar School

EXILED

I have a mixture of feelings,
I feel so alone
Without any friends
I want to go home!

No turning back.
Why is it too late?
I want back my life
The one without fate.

No-one to turn to
Why should we pay the price?
I've lost all faith,
Sometimes I hate life.

Confused by all changes
I don't understand,
New streets, new faces
Now I'm in a new land.

All my hard work
And education
Has been taken away.
No joyful salutations.

I've lost all faith
I'm all alone
I draw a tear
I want to go . . . home!

Charlotte Sinden (11)
Invicta Grammar School

The Mouse's Christmas Dinner

It was Christmas Eve and all through the house,
Not a creature was stirring, except for a mouse.
The mouse ran through his little hole,
Into the kitchen that was his goal,
He climbed up the cupboard and along to the fridge,
He edged along the narrow ridge.
With the help of a friend he pulled open the door,
He was amazed at the things he saw.
Christmas pudding and chocolate cake,
But it was the cheese he aimed to take,
He crawled up to the cheese dish and pulled off
the lid,
Behind the cheddar the Swiss cheese hid.
The little mouse pulled off a lump then off to the
cheddar to pull off a chunk,
The small brown mouse repeated this plot,
And pulled a little off the whole lot,
Taking the cheese along the ridge,
He clambered down the five foot fridge.
Along the floor the two mice scampered,
With their own cheesy Christmas hamper!

Lucy Atkinson (11)
Invicta Grammar School

How Hard It Is To Explain When You're Dead

I am so glad I am in heaven
as happy as can be
So many things fly past you
there is so much to see.

Flying all around you
the birds and flying ducks
They always say hello to you
my friends would think it sucks.

So how could I tell them
that heaven is so cracking
They would all write back to me
and say I must be joking.

So when it's time for them to die
then they will see how
They'd all be yelling back to me
we think this place is *wow*.

Rachel Jackson (11)
Invicta Grammar School

LEAVING

I'm going away, I'll miss them so,
Oh why, oh why do I have to go?
I'm excited, I'll make new friends,
So with my *friend*, I'll never make amends,
I'm annoyed with people who make me go,
Because I'll miss everything so,
I'm ever so sad, I'll miss them all,
Even the bully who took *my* ball.

But when I got there, it wasn't so bad,
In fact I was really quite glad,
I've made new friends, it now seems strange,
To think of my life before this change.

Tanya Knight-Olds (11)
Invicta Grammar School

HOMEWORK

Homework's a worry, homework's a bore,
I don't listen in lesson so it takes years more.
I'm always getting E's and on the best day D's,
Oh no I can't take much more.

I need a break,
It's all too much to take.
My brain is going round and round,
Making a funny clanging sound.
Soon my brain will stop,
But I've still got a lot,
I feel I'm going to rot.

Catriona Hithersay (11)
Invicta Grammar School

DANCE OF THE DOLPHIN

Gliding through the ocean blue,
Dancing, jumping - talking too!
Their slim wet bodies gleaming as the
brightest star,
Under the moonlight,
'There they are!'
I think of how riding them would be,
Or even one belonging to me,

But who are we to pick and choose,
Which of these creatures should be whose?

Sacha Burek (11)
Invicta Grammar School

MICE!

Down with children do them in,
Boil their bones and fry their skin,
Bish them squish them,
Mash them bash them,
Break them shake them,
Slash them mash them,
Offer them chocs with magic powder,
Say eat up then say it louder,
Cram them full of sticky eats send them home
    still guzzling sweets,
In the morning little fools go marching off
    to separate schools,
A girl feels sick and goes all pale,
'Help I think I've grown a tail!'
A boy is standing next to her,
Says 'Help I think I am growing fur!'
Oh we look like freaks there's whiskers growing
    on our cheeks,
A boy who is extremely tall says 'Help I think
    I am growing small,'
Four tiny legs begin to sprout,
From everybody round about,
But all at once all in a trice,
    there are no children only
        Mice!

Claire Barber (11)
Invicta Grammar School

SPIDERS

I really hate spiders,
Don't you?
They are big
And small,
Fat
And thin.
They crawl around the
                    kitchen bin.

They sit all day,
Waiting for prey,
For their victim
To slip on the slippery
                    silk.

When it does slip
The victim sticks.
The spider slides down
                    by its side.
Then it weaves a silky
                    sack.
And that's the end of that!

Hayley Light (11)
Invicta Grammar School

EXILED

I'm feeling sad,
I'm feeling lonely.
I've got to leave my friends behind me.

Tomorrow I'm going away,
But then again . . .
It might be exciting,
It might be thrilling,
Alas I only own 2 shillings.

What to take,
What to choose,
What to leave behind and lose.
I can't take this,
I can't take that,
I can't leave behind poor Bobo Bat!

What about my favourite book,
My old rag doll and Captain Hook,
This could be their end, their fate,
I'd really hate them to be Hitler bait!

Gemma Ludgate (11)
Invicta Grammar School

THE CHEETAH

The cheetah runs almost at the speed of light.
Like a rocket,
The dust from the desert ground collects and blows
at the cheetah's feet.
Scavenging its prey, the smaller animals of the desert,
Defenceless,
To the power and speed of the cheetah.
He spots a falcon spying on a desert rat,
Slyly he creeps up,
Closer,
Quietly until he pounces,
The falcon stands no chance,
But the rat gets away,
He'll get what he wants,
If it's there for the taking.

Jennie Hart (13)
Invicta Grammar School

WHY ME?

Why me? Why not that person down the road,
He deserves it he looks like a toad.
Now where's my teddy,
Boy, this bag's getting heavy!
All these things rushing round in my head,
It must have overheated, it's probably gone red,
Mum's rushing round trying to get organised,
Tomorrow it's all going to be goodbyes.

Well here we are,
How I'm glad we have got a car.
Just imagine walking here,
I would probably disappear,
This is a nightmare, it must be,
I'm going to wake up in a minute, you'll see,
This morning I was crying badly,
Now I think I'm dying sadly.

So this is my bedroom,
I think I'm falling to my doom,
Mum looks happy doesn't she,
But I ask myself why me?

Rosamund Selby (11)
Invicta Grammar School

FEELING LONELY

Frightened, I feel all alone
Excited, I was, but not anymore
Eating practically nothing
Lonely, with only a family to love me
In the sea of my mind
Nervous, I need someone to talk to
Getting out as quickly as possible.

*L*eaving my friends behind
*O*bviously it's not going to be easy
*N*ever returning again
*E*verybody is going to be strange
*L*iving in a different country
*Y*ears and years all on my own.

Katherine Thomas (11)
Invicta Grammar School

A SHARK

It slowly glides across the seabed,
Searching for its unsuspecting victims.
Advancing silently across the water
Slowly contemplating what prey to devour next.

It has distinguished a seal shooting by
It turns silently to keep the seal in sight
His black deadly eyes watching closely
He prepares his jaws to gorge on the seal.

It closes up on its unprepared prey
He opens his jaws; a shredding machine
The seal is ripped to shreds with razor teeth
He eats the rest in a pool of red sea.

He carries on looking, searching for the next
His victims live in anxiety, in hiding
Of this rebellious predator
This dangerous creature, the shark.

Nyssa Howarth (14)
Invicta Grammar School

THE PREZWALSKIS HORSE

Galloping wild across the moor,
My beautiful cry will be heard no more,
First it's a chase, and then it's a shot,
Then man will leave my poor body to rot.

I used to be tall, and proud, and wild,
My herd used to be, good and mild,
My challenging neigh would ring loud and clear,
To make other stallions, away from me steer.

One day I heard yet another cry,
Not of a proud horse but an unknown cry,
I listened out for another cry rare,
I then heard a crack, split the air.

I ordered my herd to retreat a small way,
But I myself foolishly wanted to stay,
I wanted to see what this new thing was,
Inside myself I felt one great big buzz.

What was this noise that shattered the peace?
Why is the silence starting to cease?
Then it came, hard, loud and clear,
Then right by my hooves, a hole did appear.

The hole which was made by this shattering shot,
The shot made me fear, but flee I would not,
I wanted to stay and see what it did,
When I had seen, I would then have it rid.

All around me, over the years,
My herd have been falling, dead it appears,
Then one day my own fate came,
I never will gallop freely again,

Galloping wild across the moor,
My beautiful cry will be heard no more,
First it's a chase, then it's a shot,
Then man will leave my poor body to rot.

Cristina Graham (14)
Invicta Grammar School

TIME

What are your thoughts on time?
My exam paper says to me.
Give me some time and I'll see!

Time is what we run our lives by,
When we're having a good time
It flies right on by.

When things aren't so great,
It's as if it were blocked by a gate
Like when it's Latin with fussy Miss Bates.

My time is ticking away,
Second by second,
Minutes just wasting away.

I've got my answer!
This time-wasting answer.
Quickly, there's just time to scribble down your answer.

Time is that thing
That just carries on going
Time after time after time.

Rozanah Brown (11)
Invicta Grammar School

THE GREAT SPIDER HUNT

I'm lying in the bath one day,
And look up at the ceiling,
I see a huge tarantula,
And really can't stop screaming.

I jump out of the bath so quick,
And grab at the towel rail,
I run along the landing,
Downstairs for Dad I wail.

Wearily he climbs the stairs
To where it was last seen
He looks up at the ceiling
To where it should have been!

He looks in all the corners
Behind the hair shampoo
Inside the shower curtain
And all the flannels too.

It's gone away it won't be back,
But then above his head,
I see the spider shiny black,
And eyes all glowing red.

I scream and shout
'Hey Dad, look out!'
He splats it with one whack
There's nothing left, it's just a mess
And that's the end of that.

Lucy Jeanes (12)
Invicta Grammar School

HAMSTER

This daytime fluffy cuddly piece of chestnut
coloured cotton wool,
becomes at night a hurrying, scurrying, clambering,
scampering bundle of fun.
He stores his food in cheeks like pouches,
and then transfers it to his burrow of dust.
The nosy pet with black, marble-like eyes
and alert ears watches our every move.
He twitches his whiskers and shuffles to his wheel,
and runs, faster, faster, faster.
The playful pet, dainty pet, cuddly pet,
is suitably named his colour - Chestnut.

Amy Jones (13)
Invicta Grammar School

THE SWAN

With a gloved hand I hold a piece of bread
Towards the white beauty gliding effortlessly along the lake
Her long, slim neck supporting her feathered head
Which dives and disappears underwater
To search and quench her hunger
I call her name and she turns
Gracefully she swims towards me
Her large black eyes alert but still wary
Deciding on whether to collect the bread
She waddles in a zigzag fashion
Careful not to get too close
Then peck! She snatches the bread from my hand
All I see is a flash of amber before she turns
Then she departs from me on orange webbed feet
And proceeds into the lake to join her young.

Gemma Scott (13)
Invicta Grammar School

BLUE

The bright blue sea laps upon the shore,
It's soothing sound penetrates sleep.
This blissful bed of sand I adore,
The day no longer looks so bleak.

The calm blue night sky shines down on me,
The clear, crisp stars give off their light.
I think to myself this has to be,
Oh thank you God for such a sight.

Vikki Arnold (13)
Invicta Grammar School

FRIENDSHIP

Friendship is everything.
Not money,
Not love,
But friendship.
It holds the key to life.
Without friendship the world would
Be a sullen place cold and
Neglected.
Friendship is the key to mankind,
No doubt about it.
It holds the key to happiness and
Joy,
It opens a doorway to love and
Compassionate people,
It holds the key.

Amie Woodward (11)
Invicta Grammar School

YELLOW

Sun,
slowly rising,
pastelly, peachy, eggshell,
welcoming, mellow, yellow,
shimmering, shining, warming,
awakening, lighting, igniting, flaring,
satsuma, melon, tropical star fruit,
kindling, fieriness, inflaming, fury,
merciless beams of fever,
scalding, burning,
furnace.

Jenni Cook (13)
Invicta Grammar School

GREY

Sitting in her flower bed,
Comfy, cosy, safe.
She sees the clouds looming ahead,
Dull, dreary, storm.
It comes drumming on the soil,
Pounding, penetrating, rain.
Then from the distance, expected, it comes,
Growling, grumbling, thunder.
Yellow forks light up the grey sky.
Sizzling, striking, lightning.
Dark clouds clear, blue skies return,
Refreshed, radiant, flower!

Becky Burbridge (13)
Invicta Grammar School

THE CUNNING FOX

The cunning fox slowly walks through the dark and dreary wood,
Not a sound can be heard except for the small cub rustling through
twigs and leaves,
Suddenly it spots its prey and a small dormouse pauses in fear,
The proud fox then brutally traps the innocent creature in torment
under its large brown paw,
The fox hears footsteps through the dark wood and raises its paw
in anxiety,
The mouse has run from its enemy fast and far away,
Closer and closer the footsteps get then *bang*,
The poor fox is no longer cunning or hungry.

Laura Thompson (14)
Invicta Grammar School

NOTHING MORE TO LIVE FOR

Nothing more to live for so we fled,
Leaving everything we had, we sped,
Cocooned in a strange place,
The whole world we had to face,
Life was cruel, brutal and savage.

Lost in a maze in my mind,
I had lost my sight I was blind.
My ears would not hear,
So the words were not clear,
I was deaf, I was dumb I was blind.

Gone, gone, gone forever,
To be seen again never,
Never to return,
Bright light ahead burn,
Life was cruel, brutal and savage.

Sarah Barton (11)
Invicta Grammar School

PURPLE MOODS

Night swamped him.
He smiled and looked up to the sky,
Blinded by boldness strength and power,
He felt weakened.
His face was expressionless,
His body frozen,
Blood coursing round his body,
The evilness within him flowed free.
Now his riches meant nothing to him,
It was obvious that he loved,
Sunsets.

Laura Birchley (13)
Invicta Grammar School

FASHION AND MYSELF

The days of gentry now are gone,
Long coats, top hats and shoes that shone.
Fashion now calls for horrid things,
Like track-suit trousers held with strings.
But I care not for fashion, I really do not care,
For scraggy clothes and trainers, as well as uncombed hair.
I carry an umbrella, and wear a blazer too,
I take great pride in daily buffing up my shoes.
My hair I like a-combing, and I take great pride,
In sweeping it all over to a parting at the side.
All boys have centre partings, except a very few,
And spit upon the floor as though there's nothing else to do.
Some walk along the High Street with such an attitude,
That I'd really like to strike them for being jolly rude.
But I shall be myself, not a conforming sheep,
Who walks round wearing clothing that looks so very cheap.

Russell Butcher (16)
Invicta Grammar School

EXILED

I came home from school one day
Suspecting nothing at all.
My Mum said out of the way!
As she came bustling down the hall.

My parents will not tell me
What is going on.
The house is topsy turvy.
How long will we be gone?

My Dad sits down to talk to me
Explaining what's gone wrong
He talks about the Nazis
And Hitler, the mean one.

'We have got five minutes.
The train it will not wait.
Hurry child, put on your coat
Or we will be late.'

Now we're at the station
Tears fill in my eyes.
As the train is leaving
I say my last goodbyes.

Emily Rayner (11)
Invicta Grammar School

WHY DO I HAVE TO GO?

Why do I have to leave my town?
Why do I have to leave my friends?
Why do I have to leave my pets?
Oh why do I have to go?

Why can't I come back and see my friends?
Why can't Hitler lose the election?
Why can't there be peace in the world?
Oh why do I have to go?

Why do I feel so miserable?
Why do I feel so cold?
Why do I feel so scared?
Oh why do I have to go?

Why does our religion have to be Jewish?
Why does our family have to suffer?
Why does my life feel so empty?
Oh why do I have to go?

Nicola Talbot (11)
Invicta Grammar School

RED

Fury, anger, hell, and fire,
These are words that red inspire.
Heat, rage, and passion,
Also fit the fashion.
Agony and distress,
A glaring, sparkling party dress.
The red sky at night,
A fierce warning light,
Red is a danger that is burning bright.

Sara Thompson (13)
Invicta Grammar School

BLUE

The sea violently crashes against the wet sand,
Furious, frenzied and fierce.
Salt fills the air and the wind hits my ears.
Churning and frothing, a dark ugly blue.
Wind whipping, whistling, surrounding and
encircling.
Shocking cold rain drenches me,
Stinging at my cheeks and soaking my feet.
I stand feeling damp, miserable and cold.
Flash! The sky illuminated brilliant white.
Streaks of lightning everywhere,
Then *boom!* The deafening noise of thunder,
The ear blasting sound makes me want to
scream.
Up above, the gloomy, depressive, dark, dark
sky,
Frowns down like an evil witch.
I slowly walk home, my shoes are squelching,
Weather still throwing at me what it can find.

Sara Mitchell (14)
Invicta Grammar School

THE RABBIT

Sitting, watching, waiting,
Nibbling on the grass,
Bouncing like a ball,
Joyfully playing.

His fur weather-worn,
And dirty from his home,
His coat is dull and roughened,
Unlike when it used to shine when he was young.

Alert, listening for enemies,
Ears pricked up as sharp as knives
Dashing, diving like a dart,
To the safety of his burrow.

His heart is beating fast and hard
Like thunder coming and going,
Quicker, slower, quicker again,
As he changes his speed to escape.

Pamela Crooks (13)
Invicta Grammar School

. . . SHEPHERD'S DELIGHT

Sadness, scold, startle, solitaire;
An arrow through my heart.
Sensational, secure, serene;
Once was, never again.

Cadaverous, cold, capsize;
My emotions drowning.
Comfort, charm, chatter, cheerfulness;
A sea of denied love.

Death, danger was there but now gone.
Don't dishearten, don't dislike.
Taste the soft and rosy passion,
Slay the fret and anger.

For remember the shepherd's rage,
Doesn't last forever.
Soon there will be red skies at night . . .
. . . Shepherd's delight.

Sheila Mangaleswaran (14)
Invicta Grammar School

EXILE

I am going somewhere new,
Away to another place
I'm finding it hard not to show
The tears upon my face.

Where will I go?
What will I see?
What is waiting
There for me?

Leaving all our friends behind,
It'll never be the same,
I can't go back and visit,
Or see them once again.

Where will I go?
What will I see?
What is waiting
There for me?

I have done nothing wrong,
You have to agree,
So God please tell me why
You have to choose me!

Leonie Savory (11)
Invicta Grammar School

WHY DO I HAVE TO GO?

I'm nervous, scared, worried,
I don't want to be hurried.
I like it here it's me,
It's where I want to be.
Although I'm really scared,
I ought to be prepared.
For surprises and bad shocks
My stomach's filled with rocks
It's hard and complicated,
I wish it could have waited,
Or never even happen.

I'm starting fresh again,
I cannot stand the pain
Somewhere new but cold,
I'm trying to be bold.
I've got to be taught
Even more than I thought.
I've got to get to know
Who I've got to follow,
I don't know what to feel,
'Cause it doesn't feel real.
What's happ'ning to my life,
It feels like a knife,
Digging into my back
I'm going to have to pack.

Kirsty Wesbroom (11)
Invicta Grammar School

SUMMER LOVE

On the mid June days,
When we sat together,
Feeling the sun's warm rays,
I remember these only
As a haze.

The nights we spent just in
each other's arms,
Wine at our lips,
And love in our heart.

The sunsets we watched,
The blood red sky,
We whispered sweet nothings,
Until the morning was nigh.

Our love will never be shy,
and I'll never make you cry,
I'll love you forever,
We'll always be together.

Julie Bacon (15)
Invicta Grammar School

WHITE

I look up and see the clouds, soft, pure and
tranquil.
The doves fly overhead temporarily breaking the
stillness.
After a second or two it returns, trapping me and
all of my thoughts for a second time.

I can feel the breeze, icy cold, making me *shiver*.
The loneliness hits me making me anxious and
isolated.
I feel dizzy then bright white lights make all of
my problems go away.

I wake up not remembering anything.
I look around me, just plain, clean walls and
ceilings.
I realise that I am in hospital.
With birth and death around me, I wonder, why
am I here?

Rachel Piper (13)
Invicta Grammar School

THE OCELOT

The sun rises, it stretches out from its corner of the tree
Its shimmering fur sparkles
Eyes, like crystals searching
Clawing its way down the tree, pouncing on land
The flexible body, like a flash is gone

Mischievous it springs onto target
And they tumble around fighting
Scratching, kicking up the dust
Then cleaning themselves with their moist rough tongues
And slinking of on their separate ways

By the wild, glistening river, he waits in ambush
Eyes roving the clear waters below
With a bolt the claw is in and out again
His victim jerks in his deadly grip
As he sniffs it then gulps it down.

As the sun's evening embers slowly go out
The cat prowls back to base
Launches back onto the tree
Curling himself into a ball buffing up his coat
Eyelids sliding over tired eyes, relaxed he drifts away.

Eleanore Varnham (13)
Invicta Grammar School

BAWD

This is not how I wish to go on
My usefulness is useless to she
Who hungers excitement
My sensibility is senseless to she
The wild cat
To be extraordinarily boring
Is not half as fun as being plainly
Bawd

From this day forth
My own causes shall be honoured
I shall cherish a frantic, frivolous lifestyle
I shall obey my promise to be
Sincerely slovenly
Until I part from this life to death

I shall prey upon my men
As wildly as the elegant she cat
Her silent crawl then her ruthless pounce
I shall devour my prey
Impulsively, unfeelingly
If the flavour does not suit my taste
I shall discard it immediately
Until the unhappy fate shall fall upon another

I shall have my men as I have my steak
Oozing hot blooded passion
Well known among the ladies
As a rarity
He shan't be a man like many
But of many

Other women shall think of me as
Uncontrolled, uncultured and unconventional
But not uncommon.

Alison Blackwell (17)
Invicta Grammar School

FEARSOME SHARK

Gliding through the dense sea
Flipping his lightweight tail from side to side
Pushing himself through the water,
Fighting a battle.
The sea creatures prudently detect him.
His streamline body
Writhes up to his next victim,
Steadily, steadily
The shark's teeth sharp long needles
Saw through the innocent fish,
Before snapping his mouth shut
Like a mouse trap
With the palatable fragment inside,
Drifting away at his ease.

Shehla Shaikh (13)
Invicta Grammar School

WHITE

A bitter winter's day.
An icy wind hitting my face,
Like a series of small, sharp, stones.
Icicles hanging from the frost-covered
roof tops,
Beautiful, shiny but sharp.
And still the wind,
Nipping at my ankles like a dog,
Unseen but still it's there like a ghostly
presence.
Following me.

Emma Pritchard (13)
Invicta Grammar School

LOOKING AT ME . . .

The bright, luminous sand,
      Looking
              D
                 O
                    W
                        N at me,

The yellow as light as sun,
      Looking
              D
                 O
                    W
                        N at me.

The feeling of reviving,
The taste of warmth around,
The smell of flowers near me,
The sound of the new born breathing their first breath,

The yellow object moving as,
I lower down my arms,
The yellow replaced with darkness,
As I close my weary eyes,
The yellow is beside me,
It's my teddy bear.

Kirsty Sutton (13)
Invicta Grammar School

THE COLOUR PURPLE

As I look into the sunset, I see colours, so many
glorious colours, reds
> *yellows*
> *oranges* and *pinks* but the one that stands
out is *purple,* that fiery *purple* that covers the sky
like the devil's

shadow.
> All of the colours start to spin, spin around
and around like T-shirts in a washing machine.
Then the volcano of colours *erupts* into my head, a
pang of frustration and pressure hits me like a
thundering headache that keeps on persisting until it
gets me down and kills me.

I wake up in a room full of *smoke*, that awful
smell so crippling that it stops me from moving but
I just manage to lift my head and see purple, so
much purple, engulfing me with its smell, that
sweet scent of sugar, nothing else but sugar and
then everything became clear, that prickling sound
of foil, it was *Cadbury's chocolate.*

>   That
lovely taste swallowed up my taste buds and
smothered my stomach in its adorable taste and as
I rock myself to sleep, fields of gold are spinning
around in my head, nothing is clear.

Amy Richardson (13)
Invicta Grammar School

BLUE

The river moved endlessly along its winding path.
Quiet in the stillness of the night, it lapped endlessly against
the grassy banks
Affecting not the structure of the bank, nor clashing with the
other twilight sounds.

Beautiful.

But as it ran into the lake it struck discord:-
For beneath the calm exterior a danger lay within
Perilous to those in blissful ignorance of the dark and murky
depths.

Lethargic.

Suddenly, without warning the lake became a seething mass
And the river, once so calm was now a surge of turmoil
Finally uprooting many tender water plants, struggling for
weeks to survive the cobalt waters.

Unmerciful.

And soon, as suddenly again the lake was still once more
The unknown creature returned to whence it came
Leaving the lake a shining, shimmering peaceful land, full of
mystery and magic.

Enigmatic.

Full of depth and deception, the colour changes to suit the mood.
Cool and calming to those in need of calming things, dismal and melancholy to those whose greatest wish is to see the sun.
Yet a lighter blue can bring great hope; a cheerful contrast to its cheerless counterpart.

Blue.

Janet Galbraith (14)
Invicta Grammar School

MY BABY SISTER

It must have started late one night,
Nine months later we had a big fright.
Out popped a head with flecks of brown hair,
Whilst I was watching Fresh Prince of Bel Air.
My dad came in red from head to toe,
Was it girl or boy I had to know.
I walked in to find my mum lost for breath,
It was another girl, we called her Beth,
Bethany Victoria Duhigg was her name,
She looked like my dad, oh what a shame!
She grew up quickly she is now two,
Her favourite word is shouting 'Boo!'
She is a pain of that I am sure,
I dread to think what she'll be like when she's four.
But after all I dearly love her,
Well she is my little baby sister.

Amanda Duhigg (13)
Invicta Grammar School

MUSIC

There are a lot of pop stars,
Who let fame go to their head
There's Noel and Liam Gallagher,
'We are best' they said.

'Take That' will always be the best band,
In Europe, Asia and Space,
East 17, Boyzone and 3T
Will never take their place.

There's a lot of solo artists,
Like Peter Andre and Sean Maguire
Who like to go alone
And up the charts go higher.

And not forgetting the girls
Louise, Alanis and Gabrielle
Who produce such excellent music
That their companies just have to sell.

As you can probably tell already
My favourite music is in the chart
And this poem tells you
How music is big in my heart.

Alex Southgate (13)
Invicta Grammar School

GREEN-FACED GREEN-EATERS!

'Everyone should eat their greens,'
That's what all mums say.
'Even if they're really mouldy,
Eat them anyway!'

When your cabbage makes you ill,
They claim you've caught the flu.
It doesn't matter, you'll be better,
In a day or two.

Three weeks now have gone past,
And still I've got the flu!
If you find me another food,
I'll thank you through and through.

Helen Leichauer (13)
Invicta Grammar School

MY TRIP TO FRANCE

As it splatters to the floor
I wondered what I did it for
Crossing the English Channel I mean
That's why I suddenly feel so green!

My throat feels like it's filled with mould
I'm shivery and very cold.

The thing that really puzzles me
Is when I'm on a ship at sea
People say that I look green
When really I'm a sort of cream!

Sarah Taylor (14)
Invicta Grammar School

THE SEASONS OF BLUE

Blue is spring:

A haze of bluebells ringing all around.
Crocuses sprouting out of the earth.
Blue tits chirpily nesting in the bird box.
Clear spring-blue skies which make me happy.

Blue is summer:

Blue and white boats bobbing on the salt blue sea.
The bright kingfisher swooping for its fish.
Sapphire delphiniums standing true and tall.
The fragrance of sweet peas all around me.

Blue is autumn:

Damson and ripening plums weighing down the trees.
The blue dullness of foggy mornings.
My blue jeans and sweatshirt keeping out the autumn
chill,
And school-blue shirts and ink now that I'm back at
school.

Blue is winter:

My cold blue nose after a wintry walk.
Shiny blue wrapped presents under the Christmas tree.
Ice-blue icicles hanging from the gutter.
The crisp-blue skies of a frosty winter day.

Blue is all around me.

Anna Lindley (14)
Invicta Grammar School

OH, WHAT A SHOCKER, MR COCKER!

Every day, I sit and gaze,
At the posters on my wall.
Jarvis stands there waving his hand,
Is he really that tall?

Is it Walkers, Discos or Skips,
That take Jarvis's fancy?
Spaghetti or tagliatelli?
Home-baked pie from Aunty Nancy's?

I wonder if when he's on stage,
Does he get really shy?
When they mention Michael,
Will he get annoyed,
And punch the keen joker in the eye?

His old clothes and leather boots,
Are well-known throughout the world.
He thinks the girls would all love him,
But has he ever pulled?

Cocker rhymes with many things,
I suppose it is pretty cool,
But is he the hard man he thinks he is
Or just a northern fool?

With 'Common People' is he taking the mick?
In the 'Year 2000' will it all be the same?
He tries to stand out from the crowd,
But, sister, what does he thinks he will gain?

Helen Wright (13)
Invicta Grammar School

THE PLACE

There's a place I go sometimes,
Whenever I feel low.
It's a place where fairies live,
And cool, sweet rivers flow.

The air I breathe is warm and clean,
The sky is bright with blue.
Sweet breezes flee through leaves on trees,
The grass is fresh with dew.

The place I sit is on a rock,
Just by the water's edge.
The river swells and swirls around,
This greyish stony ledge.

But if you listen carefully,
And lay your ear to the ground.
You'll hear a quite unusual,
But merry little sound.

For beneath the swelling river,
And the bright and brilliant stars,
There is a secret village,
Where the little people are.

Their singing cheers me endlessly,
So I'm no longer blue.
Sometimes I'll stay for days on end,
Just to hear their merry tune.

So that's why I go to this place,
Whenever I feel low,
For it's the place where fairies live,
Under the cool, sweet river's flow.

Natalie Friend (16)
Invicta Grammar School

I WISH . . .

I wish I was a dolphin
Swimming in the sea
Graceful as a dancer
Beautiful and free

I wish I was a kitten
Soft as cotton wool
Playing in the garden
With my favourite ball

I wish I was an old tree
Standing proud and tall
Waiting for the autumn
When my golden leaves will fall

I wish I was the sunshine
Spreading warmth around
Hearing children's laughter
Enjoying every sound

I wish I was a twinkling star
Glistening in the sky
Looking down upon the world
Shining up on high.

Kate Buchan (11)
Invicta Grammar School

FORBIDDEN FRIENDS

Friends is a word that shouldn't be meddled with
No-one knows its true meaning, which should be filled with promise
You can't trust a friend if they don't return it
And a no trusting friend is a friend who isn't there
You should never dabble in forbidden things
Friends should be forbidden if they don't mean a thing
They say they are there to help, when you are down
They say they'll always love you, and be around
Friends should be forbidden if they don't care
Friends who aren't there.

Ilona Taft (14)
Invicta Grammar School

WAR

The endless killing machines with their hearts
frozen over,
Stalking defenceless prey, ready to pounce,
Like a raised dagger about to strike,
Leaving a city of bloodied bodies in their trail

Bombs shattering the silent serenity,
Spreading a pattern of destruction across the
earth.
Their whisper of death still humming,
For the devil has walked today,
And the human race is gone.

Now they realise their mistake;
Now it's far beyond changing.

Jennie Sheldon (12)
Maidstone Grammar School for Girls

THE DOMESTIC CAT

Lazy cat curled up on the chair,
Fast asleep is the domestic cat,
While in the wild the wild cats are
                 always awake,
At tea-time the domestic cat wakes up and
                    eats its tea.
Wild cats hunting night and day,
Then the lazy cat wanders into its garden territory,
Chases away any bird that dares to enter,
Then curls up in the evening sun,
But the wild cat's work is not yet done.

Kathryn Holland (12)
Maidstone Grammar School for Girls

HIPPOS

They sit there all day wallowing in the mud.
The expression on their faces remind me
of when my dad thinks!

You know:
Hippos are big
Hippos are fat
They could break a strong man's back like
that!
They often have a very big nose and ears
that twitch back and forth . . .

I'd love to be a hippo!

Stefanie Pitt (11)
Maidstone Grammar School for Girls

TORTOISE

He glides through the water,
As slow as a snail on land.
His heavy shell rests on his back,
As he becomes tired from swimming.
He swims into shallow water,
Resting on the sand,
Basking in the sun,
He feels the warmth upon his back.
As the sun sets,
The night draws in.

Julie Yeomans (11)
Maidstone Grammar School for Girls

THE ANTS

It must have been at least size 9,
The shoe that killed my cousins,
They were trod upon the other day,
But we are only ants, who cares?

The babies were sitting on the grass,
And what did they see, but my mother and father
One squeeze and *poof!* They were gone,
But we are only ants, who cares?

One hungry dog, looking for a snack,
Its eyes fall upon a small black creature
Uncle was doing no harm when the jaws clamped down,
But we are only ants, who cares?

Lisa Cranney (11)
Maidstone Grammar School for Girls

THE LAST DAY AT SCHOOL

The head teacher is talking of emotions and feelings,
The parents sitting interested at the back of the hall.
The head teacher's tie filling the room with bright colours,
Making the feeling of sadness fade away.
The distinct smell of school dinners only seeming
                                                    five minutes ago,
As you look through the school,
A feeling of sadness for those leaving,
But a tingle of excitement for the year ahead.
The children are dismissed,
Leading out in classes,
The rustle of clothes,
The sound of musical instruments being packed away.
The clanging of music stands as they are being packed
                                    away for the last time this year.
As I freeze I can touch the emotions of sadness
                                            that fill the hall.
At last we are all released,
I watch the start of the line leading off,
For this is the last time I walk on this floor in an assembly.

Clare Jones (11)
Maidstone Grammar School for Girls

THE FROG

Bounding from lily pad to lily pad like a jack-in-a-box.
Its skin as smooth as silk,
But as wet as a sponge.
His hind legs as strong as an iron bar.
His skin is the most beautiful green,
Sparkling where the water has settled on his back,
And the sun's rays are hitting him.

Samantha Fallaize (12)
Maidstone Grammar School for Girls

THE LAMB

The beautiful spring lamb, bouncing, bumping
everywhere,
Fluffy and white like freshly laid snow,
The lamb's paws look like they've been dipped
in soot.

The beautiful spring lamb bouncing, bumping
everywhere,
You hear them baaing a long way away, over
the hills and far away,
They look like little clouds floating away with
legs,
They look like *spring lambs* bouncing, bumping
everywhere.

Jemma Farbrace (11)
Maidstone Grammar School for Girls

THE MOLE

As the mole scurried through the soil,
His little paws moving fast like the wind,
His small cold nose sniffing around,
Down in his home underground.

He comes to the surface, like a fish coming up for air,
And is blinded by the light,
He hurries back down into the earth,
This has been his life since birth.

He scrambles back into his bed,
And curls up in a ball,
He falls asleep so soft and sound,
Lying on the floor underground.

Sophie Tully (11)
Maidstone Grammar School for Girls

MY EXOTIC DREAM

I went to an exotic land,
In my dreams,
Everything you could wish for,
Rushing waterfalls and flowing streams.

It was very peaceful,
For I was on my own,
But for a very strange reason,
I didn't feel alone.

The fresh smell of spring,
You could tell it was here,
Badgers and rabbits,
Horses and deer.

The sun was so bright,
The air so clear,
A beautiful evening,
Was sure to be near.

The morning was wondrous,
And then I awoke,
The day lay before me,
Full of wonder and hope.

Sam Lacey (11)
Maidstone Grammar School for Girls

THE ENORMOUS CATERPILLAR

We found it on our garden path,
The funny looking thing,
But then we noticed on its back,
A tiny little sting.

Was it a worm,
Was it a snake?
Someone tell me,
For goodness sake.

I said 'Here Mum,
Look at this,
Listen carefully,
Does it hiss?'

No, it laid there,
On the ground,
Not a hiss,
Not a sound.

It moved its head,
From left to right,
It gave my sister,
Quite a fright.

My Dad came out to take a look,
My Mum just stood there and she shook,
Dad suggested 'Is it a snake?'
But then Mum just poked it with the garden rake.

We took it to the RSPCA,
And we let it go, hip, hip, hooray!

Diana Brady (11)
Maidstone Grammar School for Girls

A MAN GREY AND OLD

A man grey and old,
Sitting in the dark,
Air is all musty, mouldy, and cold,
Around the man grey and old,
Sitting in a dusty room on a cobweb-covered chair,
He is hungry, lonely and cold.
A man grey and old.

A man grey and old,
His beard is made from a silvery thread,
His blue eyes, now grey like burnt coals,
That man grey and old.
His ragged clothes are sooty and torn,
His hands are gnarled from years of hard work,
A man grey and old.

A man grey and old,
Was his life full of misery and grief?
But no-one knows, because no-one talked to
That man grey and old.
Thinking of his childhood days,
He was happy then but not now,
Poor man grey and old.

A man grey and old
Now lies peacefully down on a silky satin bed,
For eternity now, at least he is happy,
Poor man, grey and old.
Nobody knew him, and that has not changed.
Why did no-one know him, why did no-one care?
A man grey and gone.

Jenny Gray (11)
Maidstone Grammar School for Girls

A Moonlit Walk

Mysterious shadows cast downwards
onto the calm, still river
As I crossed a rustic old bridge,
the only sound that reached my ears
was the quiet rustling of leaves
or the occasional hooting of a distant owl
in search of its prey.
Only a faint flicker of light
could be seen
through the dense woodland
on the other side of the bridge.
Dare I go on?
I ventured forth.
Something moved in the dark, damp bushes.
When I spun around
a fox jumped out at me.
Relief swept over me.
I trudged on further and further
into this new, strange wood.
I was beginning to wonder,
if I'd be lost forever,
when a light came into view.
It was a warm, cosy light
and a smoking chimney to accompany it
coming from a familiar cottage.
At last I'd reached the warmth of my own home.

Charlotte Hook (11)
Maidstone Grammar School for Girls

THE GLISTENING MOON

The moon rises above the silvery
lake.
The snow-white swans swim
gracefully to shelter.
The water ripples reach out as to
touch the lake.
The sky turns midnight blue as the
stars appear in the night sky.
The moon glistens as it reflects on the
lake.
As the glistening moon sets, the fiery
sun rises once again.

Rebecca Chimnery (12)
Maidstone Grammar School for Girls

THE TWISTER

The wind moved quickly destroying all

It didn't turn to view its damage.

A lightning bolt flashes down like the
reckless dive of a kamikaze pilot.

Moving clouds, raging torrents of madness,
like two people disagreeing.

The sky is a world of rage, a world without
any silence!

Jennifer Benton (11)
Maidstone Grammar School for Girls

THE TORTOISE

The tortoise moves slowly along,
Like a queue of traffic waiting so long,

He carries his shell on his back,
Like a bent old man carrying a sack,

Powerful jaws for munching food,
Really his manners are ever so rude,

He waddles along determined to escape,
With his home on his back like a greeny brown cape,

His skin is crinkly and flaky in the sun,
Two miles per hour is the fastest he can run,

He is very bold,
And he looks so old,

He has such muddy feet,
And his pen is not neat,

When the autumn winds blow,
And it starts to snow,

He must hibernate,
Before it's too late,

But he will return next spring,
The *tortoise,* that's him!

Laura Gregson (12)
Maidstone Grammar School for Girls

WHAT ARE THEY?

They have no mind to think or speak,
They have no spine to move freely,
Their eyes are staring, they never blink,
They keep you safe in bed at night,
They are warm and comforting when close
                                    to your body,
They mean so much when so little,
They are dropped, thrown, placed under the bed,
But do you see them complaining?
What are they? I hear you ask,
I tell you, ask yourself,
I'll give you a clue,
They're cuddly and cute,
They're soft and snug,
They like a hug?
What are they?

Annabel Bashford (12)
Maidstone Grammar School for Girls

ETERNAL FLAME

Burning endlessly,
Eternal flame,
Wax trickling down,
It's a race.
Who can reach the finish line first?
The flame flickers as someone opens
and shuts a door,
Once again,
And then dead, like a thin wisp of paper,
Gone!

Rhiannon Johnson (11)
Maidstone Grammar School for Girls

WHY THE WORLD?

The world's a wonder to love and respect,
It must be looked after for the generation next!
Why do we build factories of metal and stone?
To conquer the earth and make it our own.
Why is technology moving so fast?
All this development surely can't last.
Why do so many have no job to do?
How can we know what they're going through?
Why do we fight over pieces of land?
We want the world, for want we demand.
Why do we war over matters of state?
Millions die, soon it will be too late.
Why do we cut down the life-giving trees?
Can we just do whatever we please?
Why do we pollute with poisonous gasses?
The atmosphere decays in very large masses.
Why are animals killed for their skin?
All this destruction must be a sin.
Why do some murder, plunder and steal?
They ruin our lives, well that's how I feel.
Why is there drought, hunger and pain?
All of this suffering is making no gain.
Why are there homeless out on the street
Will their lives ever be complete?
Why do the poor slave for their living?
Shouldn't the rich be loving and giving.
Look at the destruction our greed has done,
Some say there's a great future, I say there's *none!*

Gemma Tully (14)
Maidstone Grammar School for Girls

THE BLACK PANTHER

Gracefully and silently,
He creeps through the night,
Gliding in and out of shadows,
Like a weaver,
Pouncing and fighting playfully,
Like an over-sized black bouncing ball,
His green eyes penetrating through the night,
Giving off such a blinding light,
His powerful hind legs push off swiftly but
forcefully,
Pounding the floor,
Then he slows down, the earthquake is over,
In the vegetation of the woods he is safe from
the hunter,
Suddenly he plunges into the deep dark night
never to be seen *again!*
The Black Panther who roams the darkened
silent lands.

Rachelle Wan (11)
Maidstone Grammar School for Girls

FIREWORKS

Fireworks can be fierce or delicate.
I love to watch the fireworks cascade from
the night sky
Roasting jacket potatoes cook on the embers
Everyone has enjoyed the thrill of the
nearby funfair.
While fountains exquisitely burst into a hundred
thousand sparks.
Opulent sparklers light up the children's
joyful features.
Rich, red, radiant, roaring rockets explode
in the night sky.
Knowing it's all over happy faces reflect
the dying bonfire's glow.
Slowly the crowd fades away into the night.

Amy Breakwell (11)
Maidstone Grammar School for Girls

FRIENDSHIP

Being a friend with somebody can be a wonderful
thing
Quarrelling with somebody can be a sad thing
My best friend helps me when I am sad and
unhappy
Without friends you would feel lonely
Friendship can be a very special thing
I am always there to talk or just listen to my friend
Make it last forever - friendship never ends.

Gemma Scott (14)
Marjorie McClure School

SPORT

I like sports quiz programmes.
I watch Grandstand every Saturday afternoon.
I want to help out with Liverpool football team
In the future I want to be player-manager and
in the future I want to live in Liverpool when
I am a little bit older.
If I win the lottery I will take the whole school on
holiday around different places in Europe.

Marc Cadwallader (14)
Marjorie McClure School

THE GREAT FOOTBALLER

I had a dream the other night
that I was a footballer with Arsenal.
But I was different.
I was a goalie and a defender,
mid-fielder, striker and manager.
I was faster than the rest
And I cost £2,000,000,000
                    (two billion pounds!)

Jamie Watson (13)
Marjorie McClure School

THE SPACE BATTLE

It's coming! It's coming!
The big Starship is coming
With its big boosters flaming
As it goes along in Space.
Giving the commands is Commander Biggs.
The Starship is being attacked by the enemy.
The enemy suddenly communicates with
The Starship. As the enemy talked to the
Starship it fired three laser torpedoes at them.
Suddenly there was a big explosion
and the enemy was destroyed.
Everyone cheered. The enemy is destroyed.
The enemy is destroyed!
Then there were some more of them.
They were firing laser torpedoes and laser bullets at
the Starship, so the Starship fired laser torpedoes at the enemy.
Then the Starship fired a big laser beam and destroyed them.
It was the biggest explosion in the galaxy
and the enemy was destroyed.
Everyone cheered. The enemy is destroyed.
The enemy is destroyed!
Hooray! They cheered for their commander
Hip hip hooray! Hip hip hooray! -
and then they all went home.

Justin Gibson (13)
Marjorie McClure School

FROM THE HEART

Me and my friend Rebecca
do everything together
We go to parties and eat Smarties
and then we eat some cakes
We never fight
It would be a fright!
I go round her house, she comes round my house
We have lots of fun
Making things and taking things
We even try to help
It's good to have a friend you know
It's very very good.
But what I'm going to say now
is spoken from the heart.
When you have a friend like her
you must never grow apart!

Natalie Barwell (11)
Pent Valley School

NATURE'S FOREST

Hear the stream come trickling softly,
Take a quick glimpse of the rabbits
hopping by,
Listen to nature's trees already
blossomed swaying in the summer breeze,
Watch the birds flying in the sky
Singing such sweet songs as they fly by,
Smell the sweet scent of the blooming flowers,
This is where I love to be heaven
on earth among trees.

Stacey Abel (12)
Pent Valley School

SID MY FRIEND

Sid is my imaginary friend I always play with him but when
he loses a game he feels dim.
Sid and I always play with my Action Man and we always watch
videos together and we always listen to Invicta FM and listen
to my favourite songs and Sid's favourite songs as well.
We always play board games we love: playing snakes and ladders
but Sid loves playing chess, but I don't know how to play it.
I love Sid he is my best friend.
I miss him because my school took him away with a talking machine
and sucked him out of my brain.

> Sid if you read
> this please come
> back to me.

Ben Lock (12)
Pent Valley School

YOU ARE?

You are like the moon
coming out at noon

The sky is bright
like at night

The stars sparkle
like sparkling white charcoal

Your hair is so long and beautiful
so is your blue and green eyes

Your lovely hair glitters
in the sunlight
so does your sparkling earrings.

Sue Bushell (12)
Pent Valley School

HARVEST FESTIVAL

This is always a busy time
As I put pen to paper to write this rhyme.
Harvest time is here once more
Fields are ploughed, the grain in store.

We should give thanks for the sun and rain,
Which helped the crops to grow again.
Everyone gives thanks to God above,
For all his care and all his love.

If we give any food that's spare
Then the old folk can have a share
Of fruit that's ripe and vegetables too
And all the crops the farmers grew.

Now all the harvest is safely in
Congregations gather to sing
Hymns of thanks to our Lord
For the harvest that's now been stored.

Adam Mercer (11)
Pent Valley School

SIMBA

Simba's my name
Pouncing's my game
Playing with my daddy
Makes me very happy
Then I see my mummy
And she tickles my tummy
When I see Narla we
Catch a koala.

Sarah Hayden Selfridge (12)
Pent Valley School

MOVING ON

Write a poem she said,
A poem about moving on,
Do we have to go?
To a bigger school I mean,
I'll feel sad and afraid,
To leave this place,
I won't know anyone,
It will be terrible
Well I suppose it won't be that,
bad,
I'll meet new friends,
I'll have a ball,
It will be great apart from,
Hours of homework,
every night,
Getting lost every day,
But I don't mind,
That's life.

Jane Senior (11)
Pent Valley School

MY IDEA OF FAMILY LIFE

F eelings shared
A nger and sometimes happiness
M emories of the past
I n all kinds of trouble
L ove and hate
Y oung and old.

Rosanna Cox (13)
Pent Valley School

LOVE

Love is a burning ball in a heart
Keeping a friendship from falling apart.

We stick together like paper and glue
For one reason only that you love me
and I love you.
There's never a day I don't think about you,
You don't know the pain I'm going through.

Some people think that love is just a fling,
But others think it's a wonderful thing.

Kimberley Smith (14)
Pent Valley School

CHAMPION

Are you a champion,
Do you win lots of medals,
lots of trophies.
Do you always come top of
the class
Do you have lots of money and
drive a big car.
Do you win lots of races
always come first.
Do you have a good job
and live in a big house.
Do you always go to school
get good marks.
But if you're special then you're
a champion.

James Kirkham (14)
Pent Valley School

A MISSED GOODBYE

To say goodbye was all I wanted,
But now my thoughts are all haunted,
Just because of a stupid mood,
I was put off my food,
How could I have been so stupid?
I need a few lessons from God or cupid;
I stand at the top of the hill,
Or lean on the windowsill,
I am longing to see you;
Honest it's true,
Even if it's only once,
To say sorry and goodbye is what I want,
I have never really shown you my love,
And now you're too far above.
I wish you could just hold me tight
And then I would know everything was alright.
All my memories of you are good,
If I had half the chance I'd take it -
Honestly I would.

Zoe Law (15)
Pent Valley School

DO YOU CARE?

When you walk into a zoo
All the animals stare at you
I wonder what it's like in there
People don't really seem to care

They wouldn't like it if it was them
They could never see their family again
No-one thinks of them in there
Everyone just likes to stare

Where are their families and their friends
Probably altogether in their dens
There is no sadder sight to see
Than an animal, caged, never free!

Nicola Condon (14)
Pent Valley School

THE DANCING BEAR

The excruciating pain as the chain is
nailed into my sensitive nose.
As my cry is: 'Don't do this to me,
I am your friend.'
As they put me on red hot plates
burning off my seven layers of skin
showing my bones.
My cry is: 'Don't do this to my
innocent body you will kill me.'
As you whip my back to make
me move for you to laugh at my pain
My cry is: 'Don't do this to me you are
dragging the desperate life out of me.'
And as you force me to drink beer
making me angry.
My cry is: 'Don't do this to me
I am dying.'
But what you don't realise is that
if you kill me and my friends you
won't have anyone to laugh at and
cause pain to
Then what animal will you do this to?

Daniel Chapman (12)
Pent Valley School

A HOMELESS HIKER

Roaming down a big wide street,
Looking for a place to rest and sleep,
But in the distance of the dark cold night,
There was a glimmer of gleaming light.

I dropped my bags and being aware,
It could have been a thief or a smuggler's lair,
But as I edged a little closer,
It began to look like a giant toaster.

The thing was big with two little eyes,
It began to come closer it looked very shy,
It spoke in a language like never before,
Lifted me up and opened its door.

There stood inside it, were little green men,
Whom ran round in circles again and again,
One could speak English and in English he said,
'Come on in Earthling and sit on that bed.'

I wondered if I should obey the voice,
It seemed in my mind I had no choice,
I got on the bed and quietly I lie,
The next thing I know I was up in the sky.

So there I was looking up at the stars,
Wondering if the men come from Venus or Mars,
The space craft entered a thick cloud of mist,
The ship blew apart now I no longer exist.

Lee Jones (12)
Pent Valley School

FASHION

Without the pain there is no gain.
That's how to play the fashion game.
Facial make-up and creams are relaxing.
But it doesn't make up for my legs
They're waxing.

Plucking eyebrows and dyeing lashes.
And buying the latest pop group smashes.
Lovely waistcoats and long dark tails.
And multicoloured fingernails!

Without the pain there is no gain.
That's how to play the fashion game.

Katy Tingley (13)
Pent Valley School

IN LOVE WITH YOU

When I look at you I get vivid butterflies,
When you're not with me I want you,
I crave for you to touch me,
To stroke my hair, and tell me you love me,

From the first time I saw you,
I knew I had to have you,
There was this electric attraction between us,
I knew you could feel it too

All I really want to say is,
I love you,
And I know you love me too.

Lucy Charlton (14)
Pent Valley School

THE HERO

The knight in shining armour,
rides night and day, over the hills
and far away.
In the North
In the West
He rides around with his horse
with no rest, he helps people every day
to end battles, and make peace
to rest the day.
With his shining sword, and
gleaming armour
He's a hero!
For here, and forever after.

Sarah-Jayne Edwards (11)
Pent Valley School

AT THE BEACH

The sun's rays reflecting onto the sea water,
Sparkling pieces of shingle,
Scattered about on the sand,
What a wonderful day, so grand.
Yachts on the water,
Sailing gracefully at full speed.
Swimmers floating on the surface,
Shells getting caught in seaweed.
Children making sandcastles,
Right up to the blue sky,
Then a ball comes and knocks it down,
Why oh why.

Emily Brown (12)
Pent Valley School

THE LAST MAN

OK
That's it, it's all come to an end,
the last man's standing and he's definitely
not a friend.
He lays down his gun,
takes a long look around,
but all he can see, are dead
bodies on the ground,
The man seems not to notice, the fact
he's alone, he's just standing there in
a world of his own.
That man has caused frustration,
anger and pain, that man doesn't
deserve to be the last man again.

Alexandra Todd (14)
Pent Valley School

DOLPHINS

Greyish coloured creatures swimming in the sea,
They do no harm to anybody,
Killed or slaughtered they may be,
Coming from fishermen out at sea.

Cruel people just don't care,
Their bodies are washed up in the pair,
Why don't people help to care,
They are treated as if they are everywhere.

Dolphins will be extinct one day,
Then we will regret them floating away.

Jodie Duncombe (15)
Pent Valley School

IF I MOVED HOUSE . . .

If I moved house I'd take . . .
The times we ran in the corn
The times we used to canoe
In the field when it flooded.

If I moved house I'd take . . .
The helicopter seeds
And the arch of honeysuckle
That smelt so sweet.

If I moved house I'd take . . .
The mossy greenhouse
And the weeping willow that
Hung over the pond.

But I wouldn't take . . .
The smoke from next door
When she has a fire.
Or the black cat that knocked over
Our gnomes.

If I moved house I'd take . . .
My grandpa's flower beds
And my family that I love.

If I moved house I'd take . . .
The sound of the stream.

Joanna Lock (14)
Pent Valley School

Nervous!

Shall I say Hi!
I better not No!
Hi! Hello! Bye!
Is that all we say?
Don't let our friendship go that way,

Nerves!
Is that what it is?
Why?
I'm not going to lie,
My love's the problem,
I can't deny!

My love for you feels so strong,
I didn't know love could be so wrong,
I'd do anything to be with you,
I'd give anything too,

Our friendship,
What does it mean to you?
Do I mean anything to you?

A lot of 'things' you mean to me,
'Things' I'll only ever see!

Diddy Rouge (14)
Pent Valley School

WHAT IS THAT LIGHT IN THE SKY?

What is that light in the sky?
It rises every morning,
Just as the day is dawning,
It's yellow and bright,
And can affect your sight,
Oh but what can it be?
I really can't see.

When it's glowing,
The heat is flowing,
I asked my parents to give me a clue,
but they just said 'It was to cover
a piece of faded blue.'

So I asked an old lady 'Please me' I whined,
'I don't know' she replied 'but I wish I
knew why it shines.'
I went to the library and asked 'What
is that light in the sky?'
On this subject the information was
none,
But the woman said 'I've heard it called
the sun.'

Samantha Cullen (14)
Pent Valley School

A SPANISH NIGHTMARE

I am a donkey from a desert plain
I work in bad conditions even when I'm lame.

Struggle along I will until I die
With the beating of the stick and the sun in my eye.

We are the ponies from the heart of Spain
Giving children pleasure despite our pain

A living carousel all day long
Kicked and beaten if we put a step wrong.

I have no flesh I'm just skin and bone
I search tips for food as I have no home

No-one to love me no-one to care
To those who neglect me I'm just a useless old mare.

We dream that we're happy and that we are well
But in reality we're living in hell

But with charities' money and donations from you
Maybe our dream could really come true.

Helen Cruickshank (14)
Pent Valley School

SAUSAGES

Sausages, sausages,
Bang bang bang,
Popping in the frying pan.

They make no noise until,
Bang bang,
Popping in the frying pan.

Sausages sausages,
Bang bang 'What
Need more sausages?
I'll pop to the shops.'

Gemma Thornton (12)
Pent Valley School

WINTER

With the bad weather winter finally comes,
Freezing cold feet, fingers and thumbs.

Icicles hanging from the tall bare trees,
Swinging and swaying in the freezing cold breeze.

Children playing in the bright white snow,
At night they watch it as it starts to glow.

Christmas trees twinkle on cold dark nights,
In the windows of houses they shine so bright.

Cold winds whistle through the empty white streets,
Whipping up the snow and mixing it with sleet.

How lucky we are to be at home in the warm,
While the evening shivers in the winter storm.

Helen Taylor (13)
Queen Elizabeth's Grammar School

RABBIT

At first all I saw was sadness;
Lonely faces with
Innocent eyes,
The point of life was to stare,
Blankly
At the four grey walls
That surrounded them,
Day after day,
Just sitting.

One rabbit was different, though -
His fluffy nose was
As soft as an Eider duck's down,
His eyes like little sequins,
Sparkling and dancing
At me.

His lopped ears
Were perfectly formed,
Like a carefully
Hand-made mitten.

And so I crouched down
On the dusty floor
And smelled his
Sweet rabbit breath,
And put my gloved finger
To the smeary glass.
The rabbit hopped up,
Eagerly sniffing,
Knowing that I
Would choose
Him.

Kate Fisher (13)
Queen Elizabeth's Grammar School

NEPTUNE'S DOMAIN

Sand strongholds crumble and melt
Into the boiling rip tide,
Fortresses conquered by Neptune's armies.

Rain cascades from the open, murky grey sky,
With the ferocity of an aerial assault,
Bombarding the submerged beach with liquid missiles.

The lashing wind whips the bubbling ocean
Into devastating blue-green towers of destruction,
As if conducting an orchestra into a mighty climax.

Neptune's domain coils and twists itself into a raging tidal,
As if angered by the atrocious conditions,
Barraging the rocky cliffs with torrents of foamy blows.

David Balchin (13)
Queen Elizabeth's Grammar School

THE MEANING OF LIFE

Why are we born and why are we here?
Is there a God whom people should fear?
Are we governed by some unknown being
Controlling our minds without us seeing?

Who knows what direction our lives will take,
The important decisions we'll have to make?
Do we exist as part of a plan,
Or is it just chaos, revolving round man?

Until after death we all have to wait
To discover our purpose and ultimate fate.
Does it all end when it's our turn to die -
Is the answer revealed to the big question 'Why?'

John Voller (14)
Queen Elizabeth's Grammar School

AN EMPTY HOUSE

It stood there, just across the road,
Missing tiles and peeling paint,
Its blind windows gazing across an overgrown garden.
There were three of us: Emma, Nichola and I,
We crept into the shadowed garden,
Past rampant ivy scaling the cheap walls,
Hedgerows full of bright bramble berries,
Each one a purple reflection,
Of the house's past, better days.
An old man, caring for each withered plant,
In his single flower bed.

Ducking under a cracked pipe, dripping rusty red,
We gained the house.
Our eyes screwed up we peered through a tarnished window,
Its frame spotted with mildew,
Inside.
The dark hid shady objects,
Broken chairs, a useless cooker,
Half a porcelain head, its one eye staring,
The rest smashed into sharp shards.

Where was the man now, moved away, living with family?
A worse thought, what if he was dead!
His cold body on the house's cold floor,
His white ghost still tending with withered plants,
In his dead flower bed.

We looked down, suddenly scared,
Under each soiled shoe lay a small mound,
Of once dug earth, where plants used to grow.
Six shoes churned up the messy path,
As we ran from the broken window, home.

Elizabeth Rivers (15)
Queen Elizabeth's Grammar School

SEA AT SUNSET

Walking along the sandy beach,
The sea lashing at my bare feet,
Running my hands along the pure sand,
The colours in the sky, red, orange and purple,
The enormous yellow and red sun,
Half still shining, half hidden by the sea,
With its reflections displaying on its surface,
In front of it, a black shadow like a silhouette,
On a tanker ship, far out in the distance,
With the black, shadowed seagulls,
Flying, floating above it,
The colours of the deep sea,
Its blue and greens mixing together,
The sound, soft, calming,
Accompanied by a gentle breeze,
Blowing my hair across my face,
The freedom of being by myself, just me,
Then, finally, one more moment of light,
The darkness arrives.

Claire George (13)
Queen Elizabeth's Grammar School

THE WOLVES OF ELLESMERE ISLAND

Silver claws and plain, shameless eyes
A dry lust for blood fills the air around
Skin-piercing teeth, set, ready to murder
Their prey's life ends in one savage bound.

Creatures panic, fleeing, young and old
With a blind clueless fear, growing heavy like lead
Something adds voice to pain and peril
Somewhere unknown, a victim lies dead.

The assassin escapes, well fed but unseen
Leaving one trace of death; in its call.
Eerie, empty, lifeless and clear
Filled with fear, animals stumble and fall

Covered by night, without mercy or guilt
Wind destroys scent, fresh snow covers tracks.
Never seen are those silver claws
Or the shameless eyes that deny a look back
At their murders on the Island of Ellesmere.

Delia Norman (14)
Queen Elizabeth's Grammar School

A WINTER'S SUNSET

There's a chill in the air
The sun low in the winter sky,
Shining brighter as it falls.
Trees become silhouettes
Against the orange glow.

Footsteps echo
As red cheeked children
Run home.
Their breath steaming
Into the cold air.

Long shadows fade
At the end of a short
Winter's day.

Katharine Bryant (13)
Queen Elizabeth's Grammar School

THE STALLION

The tall, black stallion stood at the head of his herd,
Like a General, at the head of his army.
I observed the magnificent creatures intently,
As they grazed upon the dewy moor, like a gang of lawnmowers.
Never did they all feed, there was always one,
Keeping a look out for danger.
I slowly approached the stallion.
As I did so, he rose his head and challenged me by stamping his hoof.
He pricked his ears and snorted.
His breath lingered in the air, white as the morning frost.
He pawed the ground and tossed his head.
I moved closer.
By now the whole herd were aware of my presence.
The stallion, reared, arched his neck and galloped off.
The whole herd followed him.
The sound of their thundering hooves were deafening,
But yet, extremely peaceful.
Their motion was like the rolling waves of the ocean.
Their flowing manes and tails, flapping in the wind.
They were so strong, but yet so painfully elegant.
I watched them gallop over the hill,
Until all I could hear was the distant thundering,
Of their careering and exultant hooves.
Their lungs filled with the joy of freedom.

Paul Barkaway (13)
Queen Elizabeth's Grammar School

Bullying: My Torment

I am in a crowded room, alone.
Deaf whispers all around.
Blurred images dance before me
I wipe a tear from my cheek
Silence falls as I approach.
'What's so funny?' I enquire.

My questioning causes further, amusement.
These chuckles are at my expense.
A so-called friend stabs me in the back
His words are the tools of my torment.
The laughter is louder now
Madness more powerful.

Each smile cuts, like a knife.
Slicing me open
Reality fades from view
Hell takes control
My mind is in pieces
Broken
They've crushed my heart
My soul
My *life!*

I am in a crowded room, alone.
I smile
A cruel, bloody smile,
I laugh
An evil, unholy laugh.
I pull the trigger.
Those who once mocked me
Now *stained* with my blood.

John Justice (17)
Rainham School for Girls

HUNGRY

They shout, 'Please give us food!'
But we give them nothing,
They shout, 'Help us please!'
But we don't,
You see their bones sticking out because they've got no food,
You feel sorry but you don't do anything,
They're dying because of you.

They shout, 'Please have mercy on us!'
We don't listen,
They shout, 'Feed us! Please feed us,'
But what do we know with our three meals a day?
Hot steaming plates of tasty food that makes our mouths water,
While all the time in the back of our minds,
We can hear their pitiful cries,
'Give me food!'
'Feed me!'
'Help me!'
'Don't let me starve!'

But what do we do?
We eat our food and let them die.

Elizabeth Mant (11)
Rainham School for Girls

ANIMALS IN CAPTIVITY

They've lost their freedom,
Man spoilt their fun,
There, the animals in captivity,
With nowhere to run,

People walk past,
They stop and stare,
The animals look back,
Dreaming for care!

The animals keep on trying,
But then give up hope,
Man's spoilt their lives,
And now they cannot cope.

Shelley Willson (13)
Rainham School for Girls

GARY

I have an older brother,
Gary is his name,
he moans and shouts,
then makes me tea,
are brothers all the same?

He's really good at football,
and any sporty game,
he thinks he is fantastic,
are brothers all the same?

He's good at trampolining,
to be champion is his aim,
he trains so hard, no pain, no gain,
are brothers all the same?

He helps me with my homework,
I like to pick his brain,
he's got it wrong, I get the blame,
are brothers all the same?

I have an older brother,
Gary is his name,
he teases me and calls me names,
but I love him all the same.

Claire Smith (13)
Rainham School for Girls

SAD AND LONELY THOUGHTS

By the shore I stray each day,
Inquisitive to know what the people say.
Roaming the beach each day,
Destined to stay, never to move away.
Man will shudder at my presence,
And I will look at their magnificence.
Not one day will pass by without a sigh.

Charlotte Corthorn (12)
Rainham School for Girls

ROSES

In my garden
there are pretty
flowers,
that rise like
sudden beauty
showers.

Roses and
Marigolds,
what a sweet
smell they hold,

but these are
two special
flowers in my
garden.

Sophie Acheson (11)
Rainham School for Girls

HARVEST POEM

H ave time to give people a thought.
A utumn days are here.
R eaping the harvest, farmers work until late.
V arious colours of leaves falling off the trees
  looking like a mass of carpet as they fall to the floor.
E lderly and poor please give them a little more.
S oon winter will come and their fingers could
  start to get numb.
T ake time to think how much we have as they have
  nothing except the future to look forward to.

Louise Myatt (13)
Rainham School for Girls

AUTUMN IS HERE

Autumn is the time of year
when little animals disappear.
They hide away in the ground
to keep themselves safe and sound.

Autumn is the time of year
when all the leaves disappear.
Their colours will change and rearrange
before they die and say goodbye.

Autumn is the time of year
when the days are short and disappear.
The nights grow long, it may seem wrong,
but this is autumn you need not fear.

Janine Griffiths (12)
Rainham School for Girls

THE NEW SCHOOL

Up at seven thirty,
Run for the bus,
Mustn't be late,
Or there'll be a fuss.

Hundreds gathered,
Together in the hall,
Class by class,
Waiting for the call.

Mine is a mobile,
A kind of hut,
A little cool in winter,
So keep the door shut.

We move around for lessons,
From block to block,
With a map to help us,
We're still a lost flock.

Time has passed so quickly
It's the end of the day,
The pips have gone,
Time to be on our way.

Hollie Allen (11)
Rainham School for Girls

My First Day

I rushed round this morning packing my bag,
making sure that everything had the right tag,
I sat down to breakfast of toast and tea,
wondering if everyone was as nervous as me.

When I get to the school, we all meet in the hall,
looking around me I feel so small.
Into the classrooms we all go,
our new timetables the teacher will show.

I find out that I am to learn French,
and when I go out I sit on the bench,
I meet my new friends and have a good talk,
then round the school we go for a walk.

For a first day it wasn't too bad,
it certainly didn't make me feel bad.

Zoe Brown (12)
Rainham School for Girls

Helpless Children

Children so hungry
So thin and bare
It looks as if there is nothing really there,
I feel so helpless what can I do?
Put some money in a box,
So you can buy some food.
We see so many poor people
Crying,
It is sad because your friends are dying.

Holly Reid (11)
Rainham School for Girls

LONELINESS

Alone and just left with my own thoughts.
Lonely, cold and confused in the darkness of this place,
The memories of my family lay with me always.
To dream of comfort and of light
that always seems to be out of reach,
The pain of loneliness will never fade
as I struggle on through life.
All that I wish for is to see a brighter day
before I go far away,
To see a flower bloom in the spring,
To see a tomorrow and feel no sorrow.
To feel the heat of the sun and coldness of the wind,
just to get out of the darkness of these four dark walls.

Donna Evans (14)
Rainham School for Girls

THE PARROT

The parrot squawks and jumps about
feeling trapped cos he's not allowed out,
sad confused and full of rage,
lonely and lost, trapped in his cage.
He often wishes that he could fly,
up above in the clouds in the deep
blue sky; sadly though, this cannot be,
for this parrot is someone's pet you
see. However, life for him is not so
bad, he's loved very much so don't
be sad.

Gemma Nicholls (12)
Rainham School for Girls

COCKTAIL OF EMOTION

What's going on in my head?
I wonder what life would be like if I were dead.
Happier people, faces alight,
It's alright. I'm not there. I cannot bite.
Sitting around the Christmas tree,
Presents for Mum and Dad . . . but none for me.
Life would be better without me.

What would life be like without me?
No need to worry about *my* GCSE.
Kinder people about the school,
After all, I'm just a drop in that great big pool.
No-one needs me.
Can't you see?
You don't need anyone,
Except your family.

So many times I have dreamt of being dead,
So many unspoken words left unsaid.
Is life worth living, if you're destined to die,
And become another star in that big black sky?
Nobody needs me.

I've said everything I need to say.

Nothing has been left unsaid.

Now I may die.

Gemma Fuller   (15)
Rainham School for Girls

LOVE, LIFE, DREAMS AND LIES

My love for you is too unreal,
It comes and goes and soon I'll
know it's hard to cope when
you are gone.
It feels like love with all my
heart and I'm ready to take
the pain.

Life can be hard and complex
too, and soon enough it will
fall through. When times are
hard nothing makes sense,
troubles revolve inside your
head.

Dreams are real or so you
think, never to be found out or
so you wish, people's thoughts
mixed with your cares, brings
out the troubles in the air.

Lies come through in times of
pain, you are saying you'll
never do that again, I know
you will but I hope you won't,
but love's too strong which
makes it hard to cope.

The look in your eyes makes
me want to believe, but
somewhere deep inside me,
I won't let go of the thoughts
inside my head, and if I do I
may just regret, the love I've
had deep inside me will mean
more to me than you'll ever
see.

Jane Woolterton (15)
Rainham Schoolfor Girls

GHOSTLY NIGHT

Ghostly night
Ghostly fright
Is it them or just my sight?
People scream
People run
Is it people having fun?

Hiding underneath the quilt
Do they ever feel the guilt?
Do they roam around the street?
All you hear is their feet.

But maybe I could be mistaken
It could have been something I have taken
Are there footprints in the snow?
Is it them, I shall never know.

Nikki Savage (11)
Rainham School for Girls

HELPLESS CHILDREN . . . !

Helpless children
suffering every day.
Poor helpless children
dying of disease
Hungry, neglected children
needing our help
Disabled, helpless children.
Poor and dying of starvation
They need a doctor?
Why not go to a doctor?
They are too tired to move
Their bones stick out and,
the swelling hurts. They
need our love or they soon
will be dead.

Amy Dobinson (11)
Rainham School for Girls

FIREWORKS

Fireworks, fireworks lighting up the sky,
With a pop and a bang above the Guy,
Flashes of golden-orange and red,
and explosions loud enough to wake the dead.
Children amazed with the colourful rockets,
keeping their hands warm in their pockets.
But sadly, it's now time to say goodbye
to the marvellous display that was up so high.

Adrianna Allman (12)
Rainham School for Girls

BE FIREWORK SAFE

The sky will light up on Tuesday night
And smoke will fill the air
For Tuesday night is firework night
And we ask you to take care

Don't be foolish be firework safe
Use a taper and gloved hand
Read the instructions before you start
And be careful where you stand

Keep them in a safe dry place
In a sturdy box or tin
Ensure the lid is kept in place
In case a stray spark should get in

Place them firm in earth or sand
and skyward point your rockets
Never hold fireworks in your hand
or put them in your pockets

A firework should not be thrown
It's a risk you should not take
The life it ruins could well be your own
Please don't make that mistake

Never return when you've set one alight
If you think that it's gone out
You may get burned or lose your sight
It may be your light that goes out.

Danielle McBride (11)
Rainham School for Girls

THE ALLEY

On a dark dreary night,
I wander through the alley.
Dirty cans amuse themselves,
as they wildly roll about.
Sweet wrappers curl up on
the side of the path
as if too cold to straighten out.

I walk along the dark alley while the
overlapping trees seem to be
whispering goodnight,
as they rustle their leaves.
The street lamps shine brightly
as I walk under them,
like a bright summer's night.

I look at the house as they switch
off their lights. I feel cold and scared.
The wired fence bends rapidly as
the wind blows it,
I feel my dark shadow leading me
through the alley, I feel the wild wind
running through my hair.

Then the rain starts to beat on the floor,
It sounds like a drum, getting louder and louder.
Then all of a sudden a crash of
thunder and a flash of light follows
me to the end of the alley.

Charlotte Patching (12)
Rainham School for Girls

THE GHOST CHILD

I am a ghost child,
And I want to be free,
I am lost and helpless,
And no-one can see me,
But I know that Minty has the key.
I am lonely,
with no ghost children around me,
Minty, Minty set me free.
If not I will be locked up for eternity.
I scream,
and my voice echoes,
Minty, Minty,
help me, help me.
Why me?
I wish I could be free.

Gemma Gray (12)
Rainham School for Girls

ROCKETS

Rockets that are flying in every direction so high,
They fly as they let out everything they have,
Sparkling colours fill the sky like an orchard
blooming in the night sky,
when the booming colours fall once more
as the last firework goes up
The guy is left to die,
All alone . . .

Nicola Watts (11)
Rainham School for Girls

THE KESTREL

Soaring in the sky above his prey.
Searching through the grass and hay.
Looking for the meal that would last him the day
The missile was off, the target locked on
With a blink of an eye the target had gone.

This bird is a savage a ravenous wild beast
No effort or skill is needed for a feast.
One poor little rabbit, mice or vole,
The beast will eat them, yes eat them whole.

The bird hunts the weak, lame and ill.
Hunting for food and not for the thrill.
The prey he gets is to feed his young,
Because they will be doing what he has once done.

This beast does not struggle, it lives like a king
And soars in the sky above everything.
His young will someday be like him,
Rabbits and voles they will be hunting.

Peter Jones (13)
Ravens Wood School for Boys

FITBA!

The young striker was as fast as a bullet,
His dreads resembled that of Ruud Gullit.
He ran down the left wing quick as a laser,
He backed into the defence sharp as a razor.

The ball shot right into the back of the net,
Will there be another goal yet?
As the ball shot in the lions roared,
They were pleased he had finally scored.

The goal must've taken a lot of skill
As the score tallied up to five-nil.
When the referee blew his whistle,
The winners were Partick Thistle.

Michael Cooper (14)
Ravens Wood School for Boys

THE SCHOOL CARETAKER

He wears a greasy uniform
and looks like an undertaker.
He's more scary than a horror film,
he is the school caretaker.

In the corner of the playground,
he stands and begins to stare.
He wears a big black dustman's hat
to cover his red hair.

He gives us all detentions,
especially to little boys.
He confiscates our comics
and all our favourite toys.

He's not really all that bad
for he's given Mamma a kiss.
He's invited her for tea today,
but she said she'll give it a miss.

Simon Peacock (13)
Ravens Wood School for Boys

THE PWACHE

Deep beneath the sea so blue
Crawls a deadly creature.
The Pwache.
Not any bigger than a horse
Or any smaller than a dog.

Four legs he has
And a head like a pear
All over his body
He has some skin
Just like an elephant's

As strong as ten bears
And as graceful as an eagle
He lives a very lively life,
Prowling for his prey.
With his large beady eyes
He can watch all around for movement
He can surely kill.
The Pwache has one danger
Just like any other creature.
Yes man!
They can tie him.
They can cut him.
And when he comes to the surface
His head is parted from his neck
In one powerful blow
And the Pwache is no more.

Michael Jackson (12)
Ravens Wood School for Boys

ON THE SLAYING OF A DRAGON

Whoosh! The dragon flames exhaled,
A passing train was derailed,
The wooden huts razed to the ground,
A thousand people must have frowned.

Upon this word the scene is set,
The dragon soon will regret
The day it cast its misty gaze,
Upon the village of St Mays.

The leaders called a gathering
Of people hungry for the killing,
Already armed with forks and rakes,
A motley crew this group does make.

Onward towards the dragon's cave,
Faces worn and faces grave,
Outside the mouth of the black hole,
People want the dragon's soul.

The dragon comes out from his lair,
Not knowing what's to come,
With flailing claws and fiery breath,
He kills them one by one.

The last man left, a well fought slayer,
Comes to claim a prize,
Climbs a stone and is met
With the dragon's deep, black eyes.

The dragon's neck is vulnerable,
The slayer knows this well.
The sword goes in, so does a claw,
And both descend to hell.

Tom Evans (12)
Ravens Wood School for Boys

LIFE

Life is like a corridor.
Long and straight with doors either side.
You need keys for the doors which you get
                        at school or at work,
and they lead on to other things.

          A corridor is straight but life is not,
          it can take many different paths
          depending on how you wish to live.
          If only it was so simple.

Life is like a roulette wheel,
you earn your chips at school,
you make a choice and hope for the best,
and pray that you might win.

          Roulette is just a game
          as long as you don't bet it all
          there'll always be another chance.
          If only it was so easy.

Life is like swimming the sea,
if you choose the right way
you'll have help every day,
if not you're against the current.
It won't be fair, you'll get nowhere
and be left there all alone.

          Life's not so bad,
          it's not so sad,
          as long as you make it right.
          You'll have other chances
          to make life how you want it
          and settle down in the end.

Lee Piotrowski (13)
Ravens Wood School for Boys

THE APPETISER

Lurking in the darkness,
Unseen by its prey,
As it moves into his trap,
He waits,
For the perfect moment.
And then he pounces,
He claws its face,
He snaps its neck,
He tastes victory.
Taking his meal into the darkness,
He eats,
He sleeps,
He wakes again with a hunger.

Christopher Hollister (13)
Ravens Wood School for Boys

FAT BLOKE

Trudges
A tank rolling down the street
Each thundering footstep
An earthquake
Tight fitting clothes
That stretch
Like skin over a drum
Chins hang
Like fat fruits
Wobbles
A jelly on legs
Ridiculed
A freak in the circus
That is modern society.

Michael Cutting (14)
Ravens Wood School for Boys

UNTITLED

I will sail the seven seas
And sail the ocean wide
With the wind behind there is no stopping me
I will sail round the world and back again
To go back to my beloved wife.

Daryl Gallagher (14)
Rowhill School

THE NAUGHTY TREE

The tree lets its branches sway to and fro.
It lets the wind guide it throughout its life.
It is like a big hand searching for things
Wanting freedom.
Not to be stuck to the ground for the rest of its life.
Wanting to be like all the other children and animals
Have legs and arms scream and shout.
It whispers like a naughty child
On a cold dark night
When its meant to be tucked up in bed.
The tree is like a thick stick
With a tangled ball of wool at the top.
Trying to find the right path.
It stretches and stretches so far
until it can't take anymore
Snaps!
All it wanted
was to be free.

Sophie Parsons (12)
St Anselm's Catholic School

THE SUN

       Bright yellow
like a golden coin,
sitting in the middle of nowhere,
beaming down on me,
like my mum when she's proud of me.

       Gleaming red,
as it rises, and sinks,
up and down,
like a yo-yo
every day.

       Dazzling white,
burning into my eyes,
like a hot needle
piercing through
as it penetrates the mist,
like a cat creeping through the long grass,

       Its rays reaching out,
warming me,
like my Dad's hand comforting me,
then scorching hot,
sun burning me,
like boiling water on my skin.

Charles Casey (12)
St Anselm's Catholic School

A FRIENDSHIP STRAIGHT FROM THE HEART

I've never felt as close to anyone as I have to you,
You're part of my life that I'll never forget,
I can't leave you, to be honest it makes me scared,
That one day I'll have to say goodbye,
And take that chance that we may never meet again.
Our voices will never talk, the way they used to talk;
Our ears will never hear, like they used to hear;
Our eyes will never see, the things they used to see;
Our laughter will never sound the way it did;
Our tears will never fall the way they used to fall;
And our hearts will never beat in time,
To the rhythm of life, the life we had together.
All these things will never be the same without you.
You're everything to me, even if you don't realise it now,
You will some day.
You understand me like no-one else could ever understand,
We've reached a level beyond the clouds, for you and me for eternity.
Even when you've gone you're still there,
The memories will stay forever,
Our friendship will never die.
Whenever I need you a presence will occur,
And I know that you are always there and I needn't be scared.

Jo Brown (15)
St Anselm's Catholic School

THE DUNBLANE TRAGEDY

After what happened it will never be the same,
this is no game,
Those little children are no longer alive,
you killed them when they were only five.
You whisper through the trees,
to my friends and me,
a ghostly howl which we try to ignore.
Why did you do it?
What did they do to you?
It's not only me you hurt,
It's the whole world too.

Melissa Drinkwater (12)
St Anselm's Catholic School

BLUE SKY, DARK LAND

She sat on the cold, hard stone,
and started to weep,
she was half awake,
and half asleep.
People walked past as if she wasn't there,
some people even just looked and stared.
She looked at the blue sky,
it was so pretty,
high above the ugly old city.
Can't you just have spared a little bed,
for then today she might not have been dead.

Jessie Dubieniec (13)
St Anselm's Catholic School

SHOPPING WITH MUM

Mum, can I have sweets today?
No you cannot have sweets.
Mum can I have a packet of crisps today?
No you cannot have a packet of crisps.
Mum can I have a doughnut today?
No you cannot have a doughnut.
Mum can I have a cake today?
No you cannot have a cake.
Mum can I go into McDonald's today?
No you cannot have a McDonald's today.
Mum can I have a Wimpy today?
No you cannot have a Wimpy.
Mum can I have a Burger King today?
No you cannot have a Burger King.
Mum can I have fish and chips today?
Yes you can have fish and chips.

Alan Cooper (13)
St George's School

FOOTBALL

Football is my favourite game,
To play it or watch it, I like both the same.
My team is *Everton*, they play in blue,
I know all the players, both old and new.

Neville Southall is our hero,
When he's in goal the *opposition scores zero*.
With Duncan Ferguson and Michael Branch,
The other team doesn't stand a chance.

Nicholas Chessun (12)
St Gregory's School

THE RAINFOREST

Just south of the equator a rainforest lies,
in the sweltering heat and the bright blue skies.
The Yanomamo's tribe works hard to survive,
building huts and hunting to keep themselves alive.

The great gigantic python with its horrible slimy slither
gracefully he cools himself in the Amazon river.
The red and black tree-frog with his deadly venomous sting,
lives up in the canopy, where you can see everything.

The monkeys and baboons swing from tree to tree
using all their limbs and joints to dangle crazily.
The tiger stalks the jungle at the end of the day
being a monstrous predator and waiting for his prey.

The beetle chooses to appear when the weather is fine
crawling up and snatching grapes from the dangling vine.

The sloth climbs up the tree trunk in his usual
prolonged manner,
like a lazy side-winder crossing the Savannah.

Diggers come from time to time and wipe out half
the forest,
Chopping trees down and carting them off in their big
and dirty lorries.
Killing all the animals and nearly every tribe,
Spoiling this enchanted place, too lovely to describe.

Benedict Holme (13)
St Gregory's School

HOME

I walk in, a sigh of relief
I couldn't wait to get home
Feeling bored, nothing to do
I'll go for a little roam.

In the cupboard, in the fridge
Looking for something to eat
Ah ha! Found something
Now I'll sit down and rest my feet.

Just as I start to relax
I need to get up to turn on the TV
Then I spot the remote control
Quick, simple and easy.

I think I hear something
Is someone calling me?
Oh yes, it's mum
What's for tea?

I go up to my room
From my bag I get my books
I'd better do my English homework
Or she'll give me evil looks.

Later I go to bed
Got school the next day
Tomorrow I'll get home
And do the same as today.

D McDonagh (13)
St Gregory's School

THE MOON AT NIGHT

The moon at night
gives the most tremendous light
It lights up the sky
and glistens in my eye.
The moon looks like a lump of cheese
do you think the mice are pleased?
I gaze away into the splendid night
while the moon gives off a wonderful light.
One man called Neil went up there
in 1969
I bet he had the most fascinating time.
When I woke in the morning
I had the most terrible fright
because the big white thing that gave off light
had disappeared from the night.

Oliver Grinsell (12)
St Gregory's School

THE TEACHER

S he stares as if she's
   hunting for prey.
H er eyes are more evil
   than the clothes she
   has on today.

H er hair is like she has
   had an electric shock.
S he must have looked in
   the mirror and seen
   her nylon yellow frock.

H er breath is like a
   smelly fish.
S he's like a dog just
   been let off the leash.
T hat's a teacher
   in our school.
E veryone hates her
   she's so cruel.

Tammy Powell (13)
St Gregory's School

BEING THE GREATEST

Football is my life
I will never have a wife
She will never put up with the mud
This week I lost another stud.

On Saturday we are playing a very good team
If we win it will be like a dream.
But if we lose we are out of the Cup
But it will only be a small hiccup.

This week it's my turn to wash the kit,
Last time my mum nearly had a fit
There was so much mud and grass to get out
The washing machine took a week to sort out.

My medals and trophies are my pride and joy
I really enjoy playing for Rusthall Boys
This week I must try to play my best
And then one day play as well as George Best

If I practise my skills every day of the year
Not smoke cigarettes or drink a lot of beer
I will be able to play football for a very long time
Or at least until I reach my prime.

Stuart Waters (12)
St Gregory's School

MY FRIEND

So full of life was she,
So alive and yet so free,
Her spirit soared across the sky
Almost as if the girl could fly.
So happy was she,
More happy than we could ever be,
Always a smile for you,
And nothing was too much to do,
She was a perfect friend,
Until one day, her life did end,
And now her spirit really flies,
Across the world's bluest skies,
She watches over us I know,
For her memory will never go.
So sweet and oh, so kind,
She was the bestest friend you'd ever find.

Lorraine Scutt (16)
St John Fisher School

DESTRUCTION

As our earth moves round the golden sun,
It and our time is slowly moving to the end.
This earth upon which we do too much depend,
The problems we ignore and which we shun.
Our leaders who say they are doing their best
Seem to be sitting around for years too long.
Their failing meetings we see through the press -
Their eyes blind to the planet going wrong.
Our own contributions to the halting of time
As the fruits and breath of the earth do fade.
Like sitting ducks we wait for a sign
That will put an end to the mess we've made.
We are breaking the bridge over troubled water,
To which we could fall to a premature slaughter.

Claire Stevens (16)
St John Fisher School

AUTUMN LEAVES

The yearly flurry of colours,
When leaves turn into flames,
And forests are lit up with colours,
Autumn is here again.
The crackle of leaves on the forest floor,
Means the year is dying,
The wind pushes them into
Their tree trunk coffin,
Autumn is here again.
The leaves are dying limp and poor,
And a golden carpet
Covers the forest floor.
Their leafy skeletons,
Edged with lace,
Know their destiny is coming,
Autumn is here again.

Jeff Knott (11)
Sir Roger Manwood's School

CATS

Cats move with elegance as they walk,
Sophisticated in the way they stalk.
Cats can go where people can't,
They communicate in a feline chant.
They climb up high on your roof top or shed,
The night is all theirs when we drift off in bed.

Caroline Loveridge (12)
Swadelands Comprehensive School

AUTUMN TO WINTER

Autumn time is coming
the Americans call it Fall.
The leaves are falling on the ground,
and laying on the wall.

The leaves they sound all crunchy
crispy to the ear.
But now it's getting very cold,
Winter's nearly here.

Winter's here now,
and so is Christmas.
We send our letters up the chimney,
and wait and see what he will bring us.

We wake up on Christmas Day,
and look at all our presents.
Then for lunch we have roast turkey,
or we have roast pheasant.

Caroline Washington (12)
Swadelands Comprehensive School

PENZANCE BEACH

I love the sound and smell of Penzance Beach.
The crashing waves against the rocks.

The sea slowly pulling at the rocks like a
hungry little fox.
I like the sight of people queuing for
a bite to eat.
They get a bit of a fright when
the shop has closed.
I like the smell of salt, seaweed and
sweets galore, it makes me want to stay
some more.
When the tide is going out, nobody
else is about.
When all is quiet and is still I wave
my arms like a little windmill.
I love the sound and smell of
           Penzance Beach.

Jane Burgess (12)
Swadelands Comprehensive School

THE LOLLIPOP LADY

She gets up early every day
Has some breakfast and makes her way
White coat and 'stop' sign at the ready
One mum, one girl, one boy and his teddy.

Whatever the weather she waits at the gates.
She waits for the children
Whether they are early or late
The last little boy crosses the road
Her shift now complete she returns home.

Washing, polishing and ironing to do
The lollipop lady has plenty to do
She finishes just as she falls into her chair
With her chores all now complete
She makes some tea and rests her feet.

The time goes quick she's off again
Puts on her coat with a cheerful grin.

Emma Soames (12)
Swadelands Comprehensive School

I DREAM

I dream I'm Davy Crocket, the man who shows no fear.
The roughest, toughest fighter on the Indian frontier.
I fight them Indians my own way. You ought to know me chaps.
I catch them in the forest with my brilliant booby traps.

I dream that I'm the genius Napoleon with an army at my back.
With all my strongest leaders I am ready to attack.
All my men just captured them. They're tied up inside sacks.
I load all my muskets full of tacks. No kidding, it's a fact.

When I wake up, I knock my cup over.
I find that I am travelling all the way to Dover.
When we arrive in France, I really start to dance.
Then we see a castle and someone throws a lance.
Then people playing football score, I start to dream once more.

Alistair Inkersole (12)
Swadelands Comprehensive School

THE BABY SISTER

When my baby sister was born,
I dropped her she had a nasty fall,
At first I loved her,
Then I hated her,
I wish she was never born.

I'm sure my head will soon explode,
All she does is shriek and groan,
At night I lay awake in my bed,
Wah, shut up or I'll shoot you dead.

She's driving me crazy,
She'll have to go,
I'll lock her in the shed,
No-one will ever know.

My plan didn't work,
I got grounded for a month,
Oh damn,
I'll have to think of another plan.

But as I try to sell her,
Drown her and kill her,
I notice that now she's older,
She's not so bad.

I've changed my mind,
I like her really,
Now she's older,
And not driving me silly.

Emma Neaves (12)
Swadelands Comprehensive School

SCHOOL

School, such a dull place,
always have to be on time,
all people put on a sad face,
If I get one more line
I'll be unable to take the strain.
The teachers are a pain -
they drive you insane!
All the detentions,
I'm sure I'll crack.
Been talking too much,
sent to the back.
Lunch is the best thing,
Music is a bore,
or is it because I can't sing?
Can't draw, can't do art,
Maths is OK but you have to be smart.
Science is exciting,
except for the writing
What do I think about school?
well, all in all,
I'd say it's OK,
Too bad we don't get any pay!

Sarah Compson (12)
Swadelands Comprehensive School

THE RAIN

Why do children like the rain,
When parents think it's such a pain?
Under an umbrella they all huddle,
Trying to avoid every puddle.
Down, down comes the rain,
Why doesn't it go down the drain?
I don't think the rain is slowing,
Like a river the rain is flowing.
Windows mist up on the train,
The only view is the rain.
The train seems to go in slow motion,
As it approaches the murky station.
At the station the children play,
Splish and splash on this rainy day.
Why do children like the rain,
When parents think it's such a pain?

Mark Conyers (12)
Swadelands Comprehensive School

THE NIGHT BEFORE CHRISTMAS

Christmas is coming, Christmas is near,
Here comes Grandad, with all the beer!
Placing the presents around the tree,
I hope that big one is for me!
Tonight all the reindeers will come
If we leave a carrot for everyone,
All too soon it will snow,
And the strong winds will blow,
While we wrap up warm,
Against the cold winter's storm.

Charlotte Sim (13)
Swadelands Comprehensive School

TIMBUCKTOO

I've been lots of places,
Heard lots of songs;
Seen lots of faces.
My most favourite place of all -
Is where the cows play ball,
Where the giraffes aren't tall.
And where gorillas dress like you and me
It's one place that you've got to see.

That place is called Timbucktoo
Where a snake will wear a shoe,
Where cats talk,
Teddy bears walk.
The sun won't sleep,
Children won't weep.
Where bees don't sting
Where dogs go ding-a-ling
          Timbucktoo
Is it the place for you?

Mary Ann Palmer (13)
Thamesview High School

THE MYSTERIOUS ANIMAL

It's black and white
With an orange beak
And amazing eyes to seek.
There are many kinds
With cute behinds
and the kind of body
that attracts flies.
It swims through the water
fast and swift hunting
for food, for example fish.
It has sly eyes
that slide from side to side
and fast feet
that travel far and wide.
It has wings
not pairs of hands
that help it travel in the arctic sands.
It moves slow
waddling from side to side
moving further every stride.
It's amazingly fat not thin
This animal is a *penguin!*

Robert Roberts (12)
The Archbishop's School

FRIENDS

Primroses, roses and daisies too.
All smell different, with different colours too.
Some friendships last and others don't
While flowers just sit and dote.
That is why I'm sad to say,
I will do the same some day.
For when I'm old,
I'll look nice and feel like spice,
But just like flowers all life ends,
That is why we should be nice to our friends.

For friends are good and very kind,
They help you along when you're behind.
They are there when you need to talk,
But flowers just make you smile,
So do some friends for a while.
Flowers are bright when some friends are dull.
So cheer up and life will be neat.
For you are still on your feet.
Also please remember what I've said
Friends are there but so are flowers
So no need to be down.
Be like a clown.

Sarah Fuller (14)
The Archbishop's School

SAVE THE DOLPHINS!

Swimming, gliding, through the water,
Shimmering, shining, sparkling sun!
Tumbling, jumping, all over each other,
Playful faces, even their mothers!
Blue and grey in their colour.
Soft, slippery skin, like a snake's,
Tails nearly as big as lakes!
When the never-ending fun is here,
You will know the dolphin's near!
Always loving, never fearing,
Of the creatures that may be peering.
Jumping up, jumping down,
Water splashing all around!
Even the ferocious serious shark is smiling
'Be nice, ha, he's lying!'
Dolphins jumping, dolphins flying!
For their agility, the shark is vying!
Then on the horizon a fishing boat looms,
With it, its nets which then cause doom!
Its black shape is so ghostly,
The surprise it brings isn't hostly!
Creatures rush, creatures hurry,
Fish swim, all in a flurry!
Of these dolphins one is left,
Leaving the others all bereft!
No longer the fun and happy feeling,
Everyone's senses now are reeling!

Robyn Felix (12)
The Archbishop's School

WE ARE SAILING . . .

We are sailing . . .
. . . and it is beautiful!
Our boat has sails with bright colours.
Blue sea all around.
Warm and lovely sunshine.
Very peaceful and quiet.
We feel relaxed,
and the breeze refreshes us.

Beautiful dolphins swim and jump.
We swim with the dolphins
and catch fish with colours like rainbows.

We are sailing away
into orange sun sparkling on the water.
Soon the sun will go down behind the waves.
Everything is calm and quiet
We are sleepy on our boat.
It was a long day.
We are sailing away
We are happy.

Soon the moon will come up
and silver light will sparkle on the water.
We will sail far far away
towards the moon.
We will sail under stars
- stars like shiny drawings on the black sky.

Then in the morning
we will hear the first bird sing.
And the sea will sparkle in the morning
when the new sun comes up.

Daniel Ailey, Doraine La Touche, Kamaljit Bhania, & Wayne Oliver
(14) The Royal School for Deaf Children, Margate

A Day To Remember

I'm so nervous I can't eat,
And last night I couldn't sleep,
The gymkhana is on today,
Prizes rosettes all the way.

At his stable bright and early,
I'll plait his mane although it's curly,
Lots of ribbon and elastic bands
To tack him up I'll need more hands.

Already 9 o'clock, I must hurry,
Now I'm really starting to worry,
Will I finish him in the time?
I must really make him shine.

The first class is at 9,
Tack and turnout he looks fine,
The next class is at 10,
It's best rider and then,

At clear round jumping, we jumped clear,
First at bending, what a cheer,
We came second at all the rest,
I know you tried your very best,

Darling I love you, you're my star,
Seven rosettes piled up in the car,
They will go up on my wall,
And to you I owe it all.

Claire Wakefield (13)
Tunbridge Wells Girls' Grammar School

DEAR DIARY

I write in you dear diary,
To tell of the people I've met,
To record the things that I've seen and done,
In the hope that I'll never forget.

To let my life trot by
Is a fear to last life-long.
Turn back to see the hazy shades
Of things that have been and gone.

A memory's like a flower,
The seed of a moment grows.
It shoots, it blooms, it wilts, it dies,
To the stub of a rotting rose.

So write and keep on writing,
Cling, our time flies fast,
But while you scribble down your life,
The present may have passed.

Claire Leigh (15)
Tunbridge Wells Girls' Grammar School

PORT OUT STARBOARD HOME

Three cheers my hearty shipmate,
Take your first step on board,
      We'll sail through the ocean far and wide,
      We'll take to the sea with all our pride,
      We'll travel the world from side to side,
When we start on our journeys abroad.

Exploring foreign countries
Through seas both calm and rough,
      Working by day and relaxing by night,
      Being friends to the end without a fight,
      If we all work together it will be just right,
Though we'll need to be skilful and tough.

Say farewell to your family and friend,
Set sail on the silver sea,
You'll return like a dove that has reached the end,
Of his long and tiresome journey.

So at last my hearty shipmate,
You've taken that first step on board,
      We're sailing through the sea with all our pride,
      We're travelling the ocean far and wide,
      Let us venture the world from side to side,
Now that we're on our journeys abroad.

Emma Stewart (12)
Tunbridge Wells Girls' Grammar School

DUNBLANE

A minute's silence is
A silence full of pain
Too short a remembrance
For the children of Dunblane.

And while we all go on with life
And things are just the same
There speaks a voiceless sorrow
For the children of Dunblane.

The children were all playing
Just like any normal day
But life's game was cut short
For the children of Dunblane

Their blood has disappeared
And is washed out, by the rain,
But the scars are never-ending
For the parents of Dunblane

A silent scream, a brutal death
Not just a playground game
'Lost but not forgotten'
Are the children of Dunblane.

Emma Jones (14)
Tunbridge Wells Girls' Grammar School

LULLABY

Lay me down as if I were,
A baby so asleep,
Dig a hole and put me in,
- A rag doll in a heap.
Sow some seeds around my grave,
Chalk my name in white,
Wave a silk above the stone,
As if a dove to flight.
Stand beyond and watch me there
- Cherish all our love,
Although I'm lying in that pit,
I'm watching from above.
Throw a piece of silver birch,
Painted in the frost,
Watch it land beyond my place,
The wind will wish it lost.
The sun will set beneath the clouds
With one last, warming ray,
Blow a kiss unto my soul,
And slowly walk away.

Louise Clarke (16)
Tunbridge Wells Girls' Grammar School

PARENTS' DIVORCE

I was too young to remember it all.
I was just a child, knew nothing about love.
My parents were in love, that's all I recall.
That and the passion, that's what made their love.
Then came the arguments; they were just hell.
Shouting and yelling that's what it was like,
Hearing the 'discussions' - there goes the bell,
Round one is over, all dressed in Nike.
Then came the French, so we couldn't understand.
It's for the best couldn't make head nor tail;
Sitting in the doorway, hiding tears with my hands,
Some marriages worked: my parents just failed.
Then dad moved out; it was for the best,
Shame that their love turned into a mess.

Jo Goudie (15)
Tunbridge Wells Girls' Grammar School

OPA

'I'm here,' calmly I comfort, but I shivered with fear.
Don't go, echoed my thoughts, our time is not enough.
'No response,' many said. But I saw the glist'ning tear.
Your face relaxed peace radiated as from a dove:
Pain of losing sharply engraved on my heart.
I grasped your hand, as a drowning man clings to life,
Courage, love to your form I would impart
but you sink away, agony sliced like a knife
I cry! So much love had I still to give
I weep! You've gone, leaving void emptiness in me;
Is life for me to battle through, though you no longer live?
　　　　You may be gone, but are with me even now.
　　　　Opa, ik hou altijd van jou.

Suzanne Jenkins (16)
Tunbridge Wells Girls' Grammar School

UNREQUITED LOVE

Passion inside me, burns vibrant as fire,
So strong, yet it cannot capture your love.
My heart is filled with an immense desire
To become part of you. Oh! God above,
He must hear my prayers, 'Please save me from death,'
For it's a disease that cannot be cured.
Without you I can't live - Oh! Give me breath,
For this pain I can no longer endure.
So many hot tears I have shed o'er you,
How soaked is my pillow, yet I am parched.
You cause me such grief, if only you knew,
The agony, knowing I have no chance.
      Yet I'm so sure we're meant for each other,
      Is there no way you can be my lover?

Rebecca Armstrong (15)
Tunbridge Wells Girls' Grammar School

DEPRIVATION

Deny a man of simple possessions;
Refuse pleasure in civilisation,
Dispossess his feelings and emotions.
You impose on him all the privations.
Incite the mental degeneration,
Contemplate deplorable toleration,
Perceive mankind: is of distortion;
Sufferings of your moral corruption.
Comprehend man in state - deprivation -
Withdrawal of his entire meaning,
You own nothing to apply prevention,
A man's life appears now non-existing.
      Decipher this, your debauched act,
      And consider society intact.

Joanna Dunning (15)
Tunbridge Wells Girls' Grammar School

THE STRAWBERRY

Lusciously red with yellow speckles
and the green leaf gently rested over
the trunk of the magnificent red. Then
as you lift the strawberry towards
your mouth, you take a whiff
of heaven as it passes your nose.
So delightful the smell that
you have to put it in your
mouth. Mmmm. The scrumptious
taste, You must have
another.

Stuart Caw (12)
Tunbridge Wells Grammar School for Boys

THE CHOCOLATE POEM

I have a big present, very big
I quickly open it . . .
It's a massive 1kg bar of Dairy Milk Chocolate!
I can smell the chocolate through the box and the wrapping
The nicest smell of chocolate ever.
I open it frantically, the smell is unbearably good
I take a bite . . . I'm in heaven,
Luxurious, so thick, chunky and creamy,
My mouth begins to drool, I want more and more.

Eventually I've finished,
All that luxurious chocolate gone,
Just a kilogram lump of fat now
I feel ill, very sick indeed,
It doesn't taste that good in my mouth now.

Lawrence Anderson (12)
Tunbridge Wells Grammar School for Boys

DIGGING

When you dig, in the ground,
You'd be surprised at what could be found.
When you dig, in the ground,
You could find things you never thought were around.
When the shovel hits the turf,
What surprising things you could unearth.
When you dig around, dig around.

Smell the musty smell,
See the wildlife crawl around.
There are many things you can find,
From a Roman coin to a key to a door,
But it's not always what you are looking for.
Or as the weight of turf is set upon,
You could hear the call, of a time long gone.

As the soggy earth on the piles get higher,
As the hole gets deeper, deeper, deeper.
You could find the relics of ancient times.
When you dig around, dig around,
In the ground,
Never knowing what could be found.

James Phillips (13)
Tunbridge Wells Grammar School for Boys

DIGGING

'Caterpillar' the name that everyone knows,
Huge great machines with power that shows.
They go up and down digging all day,
They're the best things for it the workmen would say.
They do the job well and are built really strong,
They can do almost anything and it never goes wrong.

Digging all day, a spade hits the ground,
As it does this, it makes a loud clonking sound.
Dig out lots of soil,
In the hope to find some oil.
And that is the stuff that you have found,
When it comes shooting, up from the ground.

James Gayler (13)
Tunbridge Wells Grammar School for Boys

THE LOOMING LION

The looming lion sits around
waiting for its prey.
Deciding on which animal
It will stalk that day.

Looming through the bushes,
Lunging through the grass,
If you are not careful
It might bite you on
the arm.

Lions don't come from Anglia,
or Londis corner shops,
Lions come from Africa
And they eat gazelle chops

Here ends my poem of lions
And if you ever meet one
Watch out, just be careful
Or you'll end up in his tum.

David McPherson (13)
Tunbridge Wells Grammar School for Boys

DIGGING

The war is in full flight,
The men can't wait to fight,
So if the women plant the seed,
We will have the food we need.

The planes are overhead,
So pull the flowers from the bed,
Let the women dig and dig,
To grow our vegetables nice and big.

They're digging on the farms,
While the men are away at arms,
The women's forks will keep us healthy,
With the beautiful crops a plenty.

Jonathan Owen (12)
Tunbridge Wells Grammar School for Boys

THE HUNTER

It swims where no animals see
It moves silently through the murky water
It hears the activity of the birds in the trees above
It swims around the bend and spots an elephant herd
Its senses are zooming, its stomach is rumbling
It sees the lone baby elephant
It aims its nose like the barrel of a gun
It opens its jaws and strikes
A nearby elephant charges towards it
The croc gives in and swims silently away
It swims around the next bend and sees a herd of hippos
There is a baby standing on its own.

Matt Plimmer (14)
Tunbridge Wells Grammar School for Boys

THE BIG EXCUSE

'Homework boy!'
'Oh dear,'
'My dog ate it sir!'
''E did sir.'
'What!'
''Onest sir'
'Right, detention!'
'Knew I wouldn't get away with it!'

Gareth West (11)
Tunbridge Wells Grammar School for Boys

THE KANGAROO

I've been to Dublin, Tokyo, Chinatown, Moscow, Timbuktu,
I've been anywhere and everywhere, I'm telling you the truth
I thought I'd seen it all before I travelled to the Bush-land
And it was there I saw a kangaroo leaping swiftly over the red sands

Her movement was so graceful, her posture so distinct,
The joey in her stomach pouch was cute beyond belief
Its mother seemed protective, her wide eyes scanning the land
And if you live in the Northern Territory, I think you'd understand

The kangaroo is a marsupial with features truly blue
I think you would agree with me if you were to see one, too
The only thing that bugged me was the way they stopped to stare
Though by this point you're staring back, too bewildered to even care

After this encounter, I know now I was wrong
I haven't seen it all before, that's why I wrote this song
And if you wish to see a roo in it's natural habitat
Australia is the way to go, I'll proudly tell you that!

Alec MacFarlane (13)
Tunbridge Wells Grammar School for Boys

DIGGING

Obscene stories
Past lives long forgotten
Old friends long gone
The journalists go deeper
Digging the dirt

They grasp at anything,
A worm of scandal,
A snail of outrage,
The journalists go deeper
Digging the dirt

Not with a shovel or spade do they dig
But a pen, paper, telephone or computer
Contacting 'old friends'
The journalists go deeper
Digging the dirt

Can it go on?
Or will they dig too deep?
So deep they cannot get out
The journalists go deeper
Digging the dirt.

Benjamin Poxon (12)
Tunbridge Wells Grammar School for Boys

ANGER

Anger strikes you,
Like thunder from the skies,
And lashes out at you like rain.
It is a candle,
Fluttering in the moonlight,
That never goes out.

Freddie Staermose-Johnson (11)
Tunbridge Wells Grammar School for Boys

DIGGING

The war is coming.
The Germans are running
With their guns and bombs.
To destroy our homes.

The planes fly over.
Dropping bombs upon Dover.
They dodge the flak.
As our men attack.

Dig for victory.
If you want to win.
Dig for victory.
To save your skin.

Plant your seed.
If you want to feed.
Dig the land.
Sow the seed by hand.

The farmers are there to harvest the crop.
Ready and waiting to feed the flock.
Greens, carrots, spuds.
Are dug up from the mud.

The harvest is done.
The war is won.
It's all over now.
God knows how.

Ben Robinson (12)
Tunbridge Wells Grammar School for Boys

PIZZA AND CHIPS

I sit at the table, I lick my lips
A plate full to bursting of pizza and chips.
I snatch for the vinegar I slosh it all on,
And within seconds half of it's gone.

I reach for a chip I give it a dip,
Oh yummy, yummy it's off to my tummy.

Half of the pizza was all that was left,
Now I'm gonna commit a pizza theft.
I run to the freezer open the door,
I take out a pizza then more and more.

I open the oven chuck 'em all in,
Put all the rubbish in the litter bin,
Don't wanna be a thug or a litter bug.

I put on my oven-gloves, so not to burn myself,
I take four plates off the shelf.

I turn around and fall over,
All because of my stupid dog Rover.
My precious pizza's all over the floor
I jump up and down with rage and kick the door.

I kick it so much it comes off its hinges
My mum comes in, then she winges.

'What have you done you stupid boy, now I'll have to
clear it all up, you're grounded for a century!'

'Sorry' I said.

Alex Pomeroy (11)
Tunbridge Wells Grammar School for Boys

COOKED PINEAPPLE

I like it at my grandad's,
Cooked pineapple for tea.
Especially with icing sugar,
And squirty whipped cream.
Just him and I like it
Just grandad and me.

He puts it on the barbecue,
For about a minute.
Then you can sniff the sweet, sweet smell,
Coming from within it.
The golden-brown pineapple,
Melts the squirty cream.
Just him and I like it
Grandad and me.

Then as the icing sugar and cream begin to melt,
Bite into the pineapple
And let the flavour out.
I love it at my grandad's
Cooked pineapple for tea.
Just him and I like it,
Grandad, and me.

Samuel Parkin (11)
Tunbridge Wells Grammar School for Boys

THE BLACKCURRANT BUSH

All year I watch it grow
It sits alone
Uncared for and unattended
Waiting for summer to come to ripen its fruit.

Summer comes
The bowls are empty
But soon to be full of luscious blackcurrants,
The currants are sticky and soft to touch
The mouth is as red as a rose.
Upon a crust of smooth brown pastry
The currants are placed and baked in an oven,
A family sit down to enjoy the feast
But the feast is yet soon gone.

Gradually the bush begins to wilt
The currants are starting to die
They can't wait till next year
When they will be in yet another pie.

Thomas Batchelor (12)
Tunbridge Wells Grammar School for Boys

PRISONER

P eanuts is all I have
R otten rat food all around
I want to cry but I might die
S lowly I can see
O pening. Am I free?
N o
E scape I must
R ight I'm going through. Yes yes I'm
                                    free.

Andrew Fielding (11)
Walmer School

A CAT'S LIFE

There's a black cat sleeping by the fire,
Peacefully sleeping on a rug,
The moon shines with a silvery glow,
It brings little light through the small window,
But the cat is happy, at peace and content,
Slowly rises the sun, gradually she climbs the sky,
Bringing light to the world,
The cat wakes hearing the bird's sweet song,
He watches a mouse scamper over the floor,
He crouches,
His tail swishes from side to side,
The mouse looks up and gives a small squeak,
But the cat is so strong and the mouse is too weak,
The poor mouse is now no more,
Except for her tail that lays on the floor,
This routine is kept daily,
But the cat's growing old,
He can't keep it up much more,
The winter is cold and the wind brings a chill,
But the cat lays by the fire, as always he will,
The fire is now out, but the cat is still there,
The moon may not shine,
And the sun may not rise,
But the cat remains there,
Sleeping by the fire.

Holly Workman (11)
Weald of Kent Grammar School

INFORMATION

We hope you have enjoyed reading this book - and that you will continue to enjoy it in the coming years.

If you like reading and writing poetry drop us a line, or give us a call, and we'll send you a free information pack.

Write to :-

Young Writers Information
1-2 Wainman Road
Woodston
Peterborough
PE2 7BU

EUROPE
WITHOUT FRONTIERS

THE IMPLICATIONS
FOR HEALTH

London School of Hygiene and Tropical Medicine
Second Annual Public Health Forum

E U R O P E
WITHOUT FRONTIERS

THE IMPLICATIONS
FOR HEALTH

Edited by
Charles E.M. Normand and Patrick Vaughan

*London School of Hygiene
and Tropical Medicine*

JOHN WILEY & SONS

Chichester · New York · Brisbane · Toronto · Singapore

Other Wiley Editorial Offices

John Wiley & Sons, Inc., 605 Third Avenue,
New York, NY 10158–0012, USA

Jacaranda Wiley Ltd, G.P.O. Box 859, Brisbane,
Queensland 4001, Australia

John Wiley & Sons (Canada) Ltd, 22 Worcester Road,
Rexdale, Ontario M9W 1L1, Canada

John Wiley & Sons (SEA) Pte Ltd, 37 Jalan Pemimpin #05–04,
Block B, Union Industrial Building, Singapore 2057

Library of Congress Cataloging-in-Publication Data
London School of Hygiene and Tropical Medicine Public Health Forum
(2nd : 1992 : London, England)
Europe without frontiers : the implications for health / London
School of Hygiene and Tropical Medicine Second Annual Public Health
Forum : edited by Charles E.M. Normand and Patrick Vaughan.
p. cm.
Includes bibliographical references and index.
ISBN 0 471 93759 2 (cloth)—ISBN 0 471 93761 4 (pbk.)
1. Medical policy—Europe—Congresses. 2. Public health—
International cooperation—Congresses. 3. Public health—Europe—
Congresses. I. Normand, Charles E.M. II. Vaughan, Patrick.
III. Title.
[DNLM: 1. Delivery of Health Care—trends—Europe—congresses.
2. Health Policy—trends—Europe. 3. International Cooperation—
congresses. 4. Public Health—trends—Europe—congresses. WA 30
L847e]
RA395.E85L65 1993
362.1'094—dc20
DNLM/DLC
for Library of Congress   92–49575
CIP

British Library Cataloguing-in-Publication Data

A catalogue record for this book is
available from the British Library

ISBN 0 471 93759 2 (cloth)
0 471 93761 4 (pbk)

Typeset in 10/12 Times by Photo·graphics, Honiton
Printed and bound in Great Britain by
Biddles Ltd, Guildford and King's Lynn

Contents

Contents

Contributors

E. Donald Acheson Visiting Professor in International Public Health, Department of Public Health and Policy, London School of Hygiene and Tropical Medicine, Keppel Street, London WC1E 7HT, UK

Jo E. Asvall Regional Director for Europe, World Health Organization, Scherfigsvej 8, DK-2100 Copenhagen Ø, Denmark

Francesco Auxilia Medical Assistant, Ospedale Maggiore di Milano, Direzione Sanitaria, via F Sforza 35, 20122 Milano, Italy

Christopher L.R. Bartlett Director, Public Health Laboratory Service, Communicable Diseases Surveillance Centre, 61 Colindale Avenue, London NW9 5EQ, UK

Eva Belicza Department of Social Medicine, University Medical School, PO Box 2, H-4012 Debrecen, Hungary

Virginia Berridge Senior Lecturer in History, Department of Public Health and Policy, London School of Hygiene and Tropical Medicine, Keppel Street, London WC1E 7HT, UK

Ferenc Bojan Head, Department of Social Medicine, University Medical School, PO Box 2, H-4012 Debrecen, Hungary

Martin Bojar Minister of Health of the Czech Republic, Ministry of Health of the Czech Republic, Palackého nám. 4, 128 01 Praha 2, CSFR

Nick Bosanquet Professor of Health Policy, Royal Holloway and Bedford New College, University of London, Department of General Practice, Lisson Grove Health Centre, Gateforth Street, London NW8 8EG, UK

Helmut Brand Head, Environmental Health Unit, Public Health Department, Kreis Minden-Lübbecke, Gesundheitsamt, Portastrasse 13, D-4950 Minden, Germany

David J. Briggs Head, Department of Geographical and Environmental Sciences, University of Huddersfield, Queensgate, Huddersfield HD1 3DH, UK

Stefano Capri Lecturer in Health Economics, Institute of Biometrics, University of Milan and National Cancer Institute, via Venezian 1, 20133 Milano, Italy

Merce Casas Manager, IASIST SA, Ronda Universidad 23 3° 2ª B, 08007 Barcelona, Spain

Silvana Castaldi Health Management Board, Ospedale Maggiore di Milano, Direzione Sanitaria, via F Sforza 35, 20122 Milano, Italy

Czesław Czabała Deputy Director for Research, Institute of Psychiatry and Neurology, al. Sobieskiego 1/9, 02-957 Warszawa, Poland

Helen Dolk Lecturer in Environmental Epidemiology, Department of Public Health and Policy, London School of Hygiene and Tropical Medicine, Keppel Street, London WC1E 7HT, UK

Richard Doll Consultant, Imperial Cancer Research Fund, Cancer Studies Unit, Harkness Laboratory, Radcliffe Infirmary, Oxford OX2 6HE, UK

Nicholas Dorn Development Director, Institute for the Study of Drug Dependence, 1 Hatton Place, London EC1N 8ND, UK

Janice L. Dreachslin Associate Professor of Health Care Administration, Penn State Great Valley, Graduate Management Programs, 30 East Swedesford Road, Malvern 19355 Pennsylvania, USA

M.N. Graham Dukes Professor of Drug Policy Studies, University of Groningen, Unit for Drug Policy Studies, Anton Deusinglaan 1, 9713 Groningen, The Netherlands

Paul Elliott Senior Lecturer in Epidemiology, Department of Public Health and Policy, London School of Hygiene and Tropical Medicine, Keppel Street, London WC1E 7HT, UK

Michael J. Gibney Associate Professor of Nutrition, Department of Clinical Medicine, Division of Nutritional Sciences, Trinity College Medical School, St James Hospital, Dublin 8, Ireland

Cees Goos Regional Advisor, Abuse of Psychoactive Drugs, World Health Organization, Regional Office for Europe, Scherfigsvej 8, DK-2100 Copenhagen Ø, Denmark

Alastair M. Gray Research Associate (Economics), Centre for Socio-Legal Studies, Wolfson College, Oxford OX2 6UD, UK

Louise J. Gunning-Schepers Professor of Social Medicine, Institute of Social Medicine, University of Amsterdam, Meibergdreef 15, 1105 AZ Amsterdam, The Netherlands

Felix Gurtner Professor, Department of Social and Preventive Medicine, University of Berne, Finkenhubelweg 11, 3012 Berne, Switzerland

Piroska Hajdu Department of Social Medicine, University Medical School, PO Box 2, H-4012 Debrecen, Hungary

Elizabeth Hayes Health Programme Coordinator, International Organization of Consumers Unions, Emmastraat 9, 2595 EG The Hague, The Netherlands

Bruno Hubert Bureau Maladies Transmissibles, Direction Générale de la Santé, 1 Place de Fontenoy, 75350 Paris 07 SP, France

Suraiya Ismail Senior Lecturer in Nutrition Policy, Department of Public Health and Policy, London School of Hygiene and Tropical Medicine, Keppel Street, London WC1E 7HT, UK

Ghada Karmi Consultant in Public Health Medicine, Public Health Directorate, North West/North East Thames Regional Health Authorities, 40 Eastbourne Terrace, London W2 3QR, UK

Martti Kekomäki Coordinator Research and Development, National Agency for Welfare and Health, Siltasaarenkatu 18 C, Box 220, 00531, Helsinki, Finland

Ilona Kickbusch, Director, Lifestyles and Health, World Health Organization Regional Office for Europe, Scherfigsvej 8, DK-2100 Copenhagen Ø, Denmark

Lenore Kohlmeier Head, Department of Epidemiology, Institute of Social Medicine and Epidemiology, Federal Health Office, Berlin, General Pape Strasse 64, D-1000 Berlin 42, Germany

Paula T. Kokkonen Deputy Director General, National Agency for Welfare and Health, Siltasaarenkatu 18 C, Box 220, 00531 Helsinki, Finland

Juris Krúminš Associate Professor, Department of Statistics and Demography, University of Latvia, Rainis Blvd. 19, Riga 226098, Latvia

Reiner Leidl Professor, Department of Health Economics, University of Limburg, PO Box 616, 6200 MD Maastricht, The Netherlands

Martin McKee Senior Lecturer in Public Health Medicine, Department of Public Health and Policy, London School of Hygiene and Tropical Medicine, Keppel Street, London WC1E 7HT, UK

Klim McPherson Professor of Public Health Epidemiology, Department of Public Health and Policy, London School of Hygiene and Tropical Medicine, Keppel Street, London WC1E 7HT, UK

Béatrice Majnoni d'Intignano Professor of Economics, Universités Paris XII, Faculté de Sciences Economiques et de Gestion, Paris/Saint-Maur, 58 Avenue Didier, 94210 La Varenne St Hilaire, France

Péter Makara Director, National Institute for Health Promotion, H-1062 Budapest, Andrássy út. 82, 1378 Pf. 8, Hungary

Klaus Mäkelä Research Director, Finnish Foundation for Alcohol Studies, Kalevankatu 12, 00100 Helsinki, Finland

John S. Marsh Professor, Department of Agricultural Economics and Management, University of Reading, 4 Earley Gate, Whiteknights Road, PO Box 237, Reading, Berkshire RG6 2AR, UK

Christoph E. Minder Department of Social and Preventive Medicine, University of Berne, Finkenhubelweg 11, 3012 Berne, Switzerland

Rafael Nájera Director General, Instituto de Salud Carlos III, Ministerio de Sanidad y Consumo, Carretera de Majadahonda a Pozuelo Km 2, Majadahonda 28220 Madrid, Spain

Demetra Nicolaou Department of Social Sciences and Administration, London School of Economics and Political Sciences, Houghton Street, London WC2A 2AE (also at London School of Hygiene and Tropical Medicine)

Charles E.M. Normand Professor of Health Policy, Department of Public Health and Policy, London School of Hygiene and Tropical Medicine, Keppel Street, London WC1E 7HT, UK

Vasso Papandreou Commissioner for Social Affairs, Commission of the European Communities, Rue de la Loi 200, Wetstraat 200, B-1049 Brussels, Belgium

Victoria L. Phillips Centre for Socio-Legal Studies, Wolfson College, Oxford OX2 6UD, UK

Karin Poulton Nursing Officer, Department of Health, Eileen House, 80–94 Newington Causeway, London SE1 6EF, UK

Peter Reuter Senior Economist/Co-Director, Drug Policy Research Center, The Rand Corporation, 2100 M Street NW, Washington DC 20037-1270, USA

Gualtiero Ricciardi Lecturer, University of Cassino, via L Chiala 125, 00139, Roma, Italy

Michel Rotily Director, Centre Alpin de Recherche Epidemiologique et de Prevention Sanitaire, BP 217X, 38043 Grenoble Cedex, France

Colette Roure Technical Adviser, Bureau maladies transmissibles, Direction générale de la Santé, 1 Place de Fontenoy, 75350 Paris 07 SP, France

Susana Sans Senior Lecturer in Epidemiology, Department of Public Health and Policy, London School of Hygiene and Tropical Medicine, Keppel Street, London WC1E 7HT, UK

Richard Shepherd Head, Food Choice Section, AFRC Institute of Food Research, Shinfield, Reading, Berkshire RG2 9AT, UK

Fahreddin Tatar School of Social Studies, Nottingham University, University Park, Nottingham NG7 2RD, UK

David G. Taylor Fellow in Health Policy Analysis, King's Fund Institute, 126 Albert Street, London NW1 7NF, UK

Andrew Trigg Lecturer in Economics, Royal Holloway and Bedford New College, University of London, Egham Hill, Egham, Surrey TW20 0EX, UK

Denny H. Vågerö Reader in Medical Sociology, Swedish Institute for Social Research, Stockholm University, S-10691 Stockholm, Sweden

Wilhelm van Eimeren Director, MEDIS Institute, GSF-Research Center for Environment and Health, Ingolstädter Landstrasse 1, D-8042 Neuherberg, Germany

Patrick Vaughan Professor of Health Care Epidemiology and Head, Department of Public Health and Policy, London School of Hygiene and Tropical Medicine, Keppel Street, London WC1E 7HT, UK

Danuta Wiewiora Health Economist, Centre for Postgraduate Studies, The Polish Medical Association, 05-420 Józefów, ul. Mickiewicza 2, POB no. 1, Poland

Marjorie Zernott Director of Classification Development, Commission on Professional and Hospital Activities, 1105 Eisenhower Place, PO Box 304, Ann Arbor, Michigan 48106 0303, USA

Foreword

I am very happy to have this opportunity to write a foreword for this book which is based on an important forum sponsored by the European Community, called 'Europe Without Frontiers: the Implications for Health'.

The countries of Europe find themselves, to an ever-increasing extent, faced with both old and new problems in public health. To mention only a few: the consequences of ageing populations; increased mobility of the workforce; increasing numbers of people travelling; consequences of environmental and social changes on health; changes in working practices; increased food production and wider distribution; and the threats posed by people's lifestyles, such as cancers, cardiovascular diseases, AIDS and drugs.

However, despite all these important challenges to the health of our people, another more welcome development can be seen. It is increasingly being realized throughout Europe that an effective public health response to these problems must involve cooperation between States and the coordination of efforts across national boundaries.

In recent years both statutory authorities and health professionals have been placing a greater emphasis on good international relationships in health. This is evident, for example, in the growing exchange and dissemination of information about health problems and policies, as well as in the creation of networks of individuals and institutions in the field of public health. I am sure that the Forum and this volume will play a useful part in this process, both by raising awareness of particular problems and, just as important, by pointing the way towards possible solutions.

Commissioner V. Papandreou

Preface

In early 1991, when the meeting was being planned, we were conscious that the changing map of Europe would have significant implications for the health of Europeans and that these had not yet been systematically explored. The development of a single market in the EC countries, the removal of the barrier between East and West, and the closer links between the EC and the EFTA countries would all be expected to increase the flow of people, goods and services between the countries of Europe. With this will come planned and unplanned effects on public health. What was not expected at that time was the disintegration of Yugoslavia and the USSR, with the emergence of many new countries and the re-emergence of ethnic rivalries and conflicts.

Europe without frontiers was designed as a working conference for leading policy-makers and researchers in the field of public health. The Forum set out to explore the practical issues of health and health care provision and the need for greater coordination and cooperation throughout Europe. *The objectives of the Forum were to*:

- Review existing knowledge, understanding and current research.
- Identify the implications for policy development in Europe.
- Develop implementation strategies for policy changes.
- Set objectives and timetables for European health in the late 1990s.
- Identify areas requiring further research.

The meeting consisted of plenary and workshop sessions. Papers were invited from leading researchers and policy-makers as a basis for discussion in the workshops, and additional papers were provided by participants. The workshop participants were asked to report back with a brief statement of their current position, the need for measures to develop policy, and the needs for further research to inform policy-making. Where possible they were asked to identify who or which organizations should be taking the next steps.

No single organization has a mandate for European health policy. The Council of Europe has a long history in the area of public health, but the EC has been involved in issues on the movement of health care professionals, control of licit and illicit substances, food standards and more recently public health. However, the EC has had only a limited involvement in health services and the control of the environmental hazards within and between countries. Some existing policies fail to meet existing challenges and do little to anticipate the new ones. For example, arrangements for access to health services within the EC aim to accommodate those who travel and need care, but not those who travel to receive care or to provide care. Policies on illicit drugs focus on the limited scope for supply reduction and control strategies. Policies on pharmaceuticals, whilst protecting consumers, encourage free trade and attempt to protect the industry, a mixture that is unlikely to survive the pressures of a free market. The voice of the consumer (and indeed the voice of the people) is likely to get lost in the processes of intergovernmental policy-making. Where possible, that policy-making should be at local or national level; it is clear that many public health issues will be sensibly tackled for part or all of Europe, and better procedures are needed.

Following the euphoria of the emergence of the new democracies of central and eastern Europe, the full extent of their health problems is becoming clear. Life expectancy is lower than in western countries, with some obvious problems of high smoking rates, poor diets, exposure to environmental hazards, shortages of drugs and poor health services. Problems of drug abuse and related problems of HIV infection are becoming very serious in some countries. Two challenges have emerged—to develop policies that address public health problems across national boundaries (e.g. air and water pollution) and to support the new democracies in tackling the public health issues that face their countries. The West needs to share experiences, make information available, and provide financial assistance. The learning should not be one-way. The social and political climate may allow innovative and imaginative policies from which the West can learn.

The papers included in this volume reflect the varying history, traditions and approaches in health policy across Europe. Every attempt has been made to allow the original voices to be heard, but even so several interesting contributions had to be left out for lack of space.

Certain major themes have emerged. Differences within Europe, along with lower frontiers, are a source of challenges for policy-makers. Free movement of professionals makes it more difficult to plan for the needs of individual countries, and surpluses and shortages may become international problems. Good health services will attract patients and must be paid for. But differences also offer great opportunities for research, when similar people do different things that produce natural experiments. However, identifying issues, developing policies, and carrying out research are all hampered by poor information and inconsistencies in data. In many areas standardization and agreement on definitions would lead to great dividends for research and policy development.

Europe without frontiers aimed to be the start of this process. Two hundred and ten people from 23 countries came together to share experiences and ideas, suggest ways to proceed and identify areas for the future research agenda. New alliances and working relationships have been formed and some new projects will result. It was a first step, but an important one. We are grateful to those who made it possible, with organizational and financial help; in particular staff at the London School of Hygiene and Tropical Medicine and the King's Fund College, London; our sponsors who were the Commission of the European Communities; the Department of Health; the North West and North East Thames Regional Health Authorities; the Health Education Authority, London; the British Council; and the Kellogg Company of Great Britain. But the success of the meeting is due mainly to the positive and open-minded participation of the main speakers and the delegates.

CHARLES E. M. NORMAND
PATRICK VAUGHAN

INTRODUCTION

Europe without frontiers

Martin Bojar

Minister of Health of the Czech Republic

Europe without frontiers is the dream for central Europe and a nightmare for west Europeans: Europe without frontiers, for drug smugglers, prostitutes, HIV victims, and IRA or ETA terrorists, but I still believe it is a dream and a promise. I must confess that our views and hopes are deeply influenced by central European cultural, historical and geopolitical experience. Previous socialist neighbours and Soviet slaves, such as Poland and Hungary, share our experience to a great extent. We all share a tension and nervousness with states of the former Soviet Union and the Balkans. Baltic nations especially share the Polish experience in many respects and we should not ignore the fact that help will be needed from different parts of Europe. From an older historical perspective, before the different political and economic developments in the last 70 years, Czechoslovakia also shares many common features with Austria and Germany—our neighbours and traditional rivals, and present and future partners.

After the Second World War the central and eastern European nations quickly fell behind the defeated and war-destroyed Germany, Austria and Italy. However, I should mention that these countries have, on the other hand, experienced some rapid developments—high rates of abortion, suicide, alcoholism, tumours and many other of civilization's illnesses. This happened in spite of (or maybe because of) the fact that Czechoslovakia and other Soviet satellites quickly developed centralized, state-run national health care systems.

It is necessary to stress that the totally state-run and state-controlled health and social services face a profound crisis. This crisis is not of the same magnitude in Hungary, Czechoslovakia or Poland; however, it has the same rules and is closely linked to the decline in health status of the populations of the countries of central Europe. The decline in health status is tightly linked to the enormous environmental problems that have been totally neglected for decades. In all the countries of central Europe we can identify the same social transformation trends, but with differences in timing and degree. The transformation programme prepared for the Czech health

Europe Without Frontiers. Edited by C.E.M. Normand and P. Vaughan
© 1993 John Wiley & Sons Ltd

care system has many common features in its proposed plans for Israel, the UK or Scandinavian countries.

We are facing the same problems and using the same tactics as our Hungarian and Polish colleagues, but the stage of our central European illness is substantially different. Please remember it is not a 'flu; it looks like polio—it is highly contagious in all aspects of our lives; it is sometimes dirty. We have high aspirations and high expectations but many of us suffer from low motivation, and one of the most dangerous factors is the eagerness to get rich quickly. There are plenty of health problems in this part of Europe. Governments, parliaments, and non-governmental bodies are developing health and social service systems in a period of great instability and the transition to a market economy. I would like to stress that our goal is a genuine market economy. The problem is how to respect social and environmental demands. We have to explain to our radical prophets of the market economy that health care and social care cannot be treated in the same way as a business.

The Czech health system can be used to typify these profound changes. The previous regime used to boast that its health care system offered high-quality accessible and completely free health care. It was a frequent slogan, and the most dangerous 'newspeak'. The previous regime believed that quantity (number of vets or number of educated doctors) was more important than the human approach. The quality of Czech health and social care today faces fierce criticism. Critics exaggerate in some respects, but overall the criticism is valid. Many disadvantages and failures of the strictly centralized and state-controlled health care system have finally become apparent. The health system shares many problems with other so-called non-productive sectors. Many people in our country believe that health care is a non-productive and begging sector that should not be given priority now. We suffer from low professional motivation, low motivation of health consumers to participate in health promotion and health protection. This problem is linked to the prejudice that health is free. We face problems of low salaries for health providers combined with the surplus of health providers in secondary health care, especially in the hospitals. There is an abundance of beds of medium or of low quality that are misused by health providers and health authorities, as well as by the health consumers, because we still believe that health care is free. We must try to resuscitate the system that has offered low-quality health care relative to western European standards only because of previous regime ostentation to quality, quantity to the real human approach. During the past 20 years the quality of health care has become more and more problematic and uncertain, but I should add that the quality of our lives in central Europe has also become more problematic.

The relatively good medical care standards in many areas are only comparable to conditions prevailing in advanced European countries 10 or

15 years ago. Data on the decline in health status of the Czechoslovak population, especially child sickness rates and cancers and their geographical distribution, were so alarming that formal authorities kept them secret for 45 years. The result of epidemiological and sociological studies that focused on living conditions of different at-risk social groups—such as children, the elderly and the disabled—were also banned or safely modified. Results from environmental studies I cite are typical for all the countries of central Europe. To stress the importance in taking a critical approach when addressing the health and social sector, it is necessary to criticize carefully successes and failures of the first stage of the transformation process, and compare these results in other countries. Soon we shall want to share our experience with our colleagues in the newly independent Baltic republics. Nowadays we have contacts with Polish and other friends, but we have lost our contacts with colleagues from Yugoslavia. Introducing the health insurance scheme and the private sector, as well as a completely free choice of health providers and hospitals, is a brand new change in our lives in Czechoslovakia, and a brand new phenomenon for a great part of our population. However I should add it is a risky strategy.

Choice of doctor was more or less a possibility also before November 1989—families who knew the new ropes could arrange it. There was an unofficial private health market, estimated to be worth between 200 and 300 million US dollars, representing one-fifth of the total health care budget in my country. The transformation programme of the Czech health care system began some time in the 1980s via a document from Charter 77. The first version of the transformation programme was published just before the free elections in 1990.

The basic aims of the Czech reform system can be summarized in a few sentences. We believe it is necessary to create a democratized health care system, combining public, private and state sectors—a completely new phenomenon in our country. It is necessary to revitalize the idea of a health and social insurance scheme that had a long tradition, and a high reputation in our country, to guarantee adequate health care for citizens. To create an independent private health sector there is a need to specify the rights and duties of medical professionals and their customers. Health promotion and disease prevention programmes are needed, and we must educate politicians about their importance. Communities will have to implement the principle of health prevention and public health policy on rare or specific conditions. Health care should be provided to well-informed and free citizens. We need community-based models in various areas of the health sector. We started this part of the resource financing, and during the past four months four new laws have been passed in the Czech national council—the health insurance company act, the health insurance scheme act, the health services act that completely destroyed the state monopoly, and the model of the socialized health system and the health law that is extremely important, and deals with health care provided by the non-state health sectors. There are new laws concerning public health protection, control of drugs and drug abuse, education of health professionals, and a new abortion law is under discussion in the Czech government and Czech parliament. We are in the last phase of these discussions. The new health insurance company started in January 1992. It is only partially functional because we are still awaiting the new taxation scheme.

The health sector will undergo one of the most challenging and fundamental transformation processes. Revitalized and active information systems are very important tools, and we have risked much in giving up parts of it at the regional and district levels. We know we can pay a high price for a strong and sometimes irrational tendency to decentralize everything too hastily. Health statistics will be restructured. The transformation of the Czech health system is undoubtedly risky in some respects, and the changes may be unpopular. Unpopular steps and decisions must be made despite the coming elections.

Steps in the transformation of society and public health are closely linked to the transformation of the economy, and the development of public and environmental health policies in other European countries. We exchange problems with Germany and Austria, with whom we share the same borders. We breathe the same air. Exchange of information is vitally needed.

Financial resources of this sector are limited, and there are now many international and government-funded agencies providing consulting and counselling activities. Sometimes we feel that some of these projects of public health, health care, health financing and environmental protection, even those properly funded, could be more effective were there better coordination between WHO, the EC, USAID and other agencies.

I would like to summarize by saying that our response should be aimed at reduction of differences in the quality and availability of health care in the whole of Europe, a Europe without real frontiers even in health and social care. We should struggle for coordination of the simultaneous transformation of activities relating to health and the health sector. We are stepping forward to the new undivided Europe without barriers, and with fewer differences in approaches to the economy. Public health and health care cannot be isolated in any European country. They cannot be isolated from health care and educational systems in any European country. Let us hope that in the next three to five years the countries of central Europe and the western European nations will cooperate more effectively in this field. I believe it is a promise for European nations, for a Europe without frontiers for free citizens, and does not constitute a free route for smugglers and terrorists.

The implications for health

J.E. Asvall

Regional Director for Europe, World Health Organization, Copenhagen, Denmark

It is a particular pleasure for me to represent the World Health Organization, and I should like to start by congratulating the London School of Hygiene and Tropical Medicine, and in particular Professor Richard Feachem, as well as the other supporters of this conference, for their initiative.

Our old Europe is developing at such a breathtaking speed these days that we hardly have time to digest a new development before it becomes 'old' and replaced by something different. We are witnessing a situation which, in large parts of the European region, is chaotic and driven by forces that hardly seem manageable—ethnic and national pride, a widespread thirst for change, a sudden economic collapse and a desperate yearning for freedom—all of which send Europe reeling. In this situation it is indeed opportune to take a step back and try to discern what are the forces at work, where do the major trends go. This we must do if we want to find a way through the crisis that is shaking Europe at this historical turning point, as we enter the last decade of the twentieth century.

A crisis, however, is not necessarily only a negative event; in old Asian culture the sign of crisis was composed of two other signs—one for 'danger' and one for 'opportunity'. The challenge in our crisis situation today is how to grab the unique opportunity of a Europe laid open by the disappearance of old impenetrable frontiers, exploiting *ad maximum* the newfound political will for *real* change and to push vigorously those solutions that are truly effective in health development. Now is the time for the more fundamental changes!

The political map of Europe

Which Europe are we talking about? Today there are many Europes; there is the European Community, the European economic space, the geographical Europe, etc. However, when you invite the Regional Director for WHO in Europe to speak, you will not be surprised that the Europe I will talk about is the European Region of WHO—the 850 million people living on a land mass stretching from Greenland to the Mediterranean and eastwards to the

Europe Without Frontiers. Edited by C.E.M. Normand and P. Vaughan
© 1993 John Wiley & Sons Ltd

Pacific shores of the Russian Federation; this is the area for which we are responsible in WHO's Regional Office in Copenhagen. If you ask me how many member states we have, I cannot tell you; we had 31 in November 1991, 30 in December 1991, 34 at the end of January 1992. Today, 13 April 1992, the number depends on how many applications for WHO membership have left capitals of the new countries emerging from the former Soviet Union, on their way to the Secretary-General of the United Nations. What I *do* know is that, in this year, 1992, the number of our member states will probably grow from 30 to 45 or even 50—depending on events in the coming months. This, as we all know, comes as a result of extraordinary political developments which started in the middle of the 1980s and rose to a crescendo during the past two years.

While, for more than 40 years, after the Second World War, Europe was divided into two sharply defined areas—the Communist bloc and the 'western bloc'—today's picture is dramatically different. We see many groupings, some very strong, some weak, but all of them rapidly changing, creating new and sometimes surprising alliances. Strongest no doubt is the European Community, where the 12 member states, through the Maastricht Agreement, are expanding the basis for their cooperation decisively, moving towards an organization that spreads its influence on national developments in many walks of life, including public health. Its membership will surely also grow, but prognoses indicate a little slower than many would like; perhaps including some 20 of WHO's likely 50 European member states by the year 2000. The European Economic Area (EEA), encompassing the European Community and EFTA countries, has recently emerged as a kind of 'economic halfway house' between the countries of these two organizations.

The Council of Europe is also increasing its membership, and will probably, before too long, comprise most of the countries that are members of WHO's European Region, with which it cooperates extensively in health matters. The OECD has for a long time had a strong health economics mandate for its member states from Europe and beyond. The Nordic Council, with its five member states, has quite extensive cooperation in health and social matters, while the Baltic area now seems to re-emerge as an entity of much collaboration, as witnessed by the recent Baltic Conference and by cooperative efforts in environmental health and in WHO's Healthy Cities movement.

In the south, the past year has seen the re-emergence of the old Balkans as a united focus for cooperation, including health matters, among six of our countries; recently Ministers of Health and also representatives of medical associations have come together to see how they can cooperate and support each other. Finally, during the past two months, the collapse of the Soviet Union has revealed a long-dormant, strong historical, cultural, emotional and religious link between Turkey and six of the former Asian republics of the Soviet Union—Azerbaijan, Uzbekistan, Kyrghyzstan, Tadjikistan, Kazakhstan and Turkmenistan.

The economic situation and its consequences

What are the factors that shape European societies today? How do they influence risk factors to health and health development possibilities?

First, the economic outlook is rather grim. The strong growth shown by western Europe for many years—particularly by economically leading countries such as Germany, Sweden and Switzerland—has recently shown signs of a downturn. Growth in western Europe in 1991 is unlikely to have averaged much more than 1%, a sharp deceleration from the average of 2.6% in 1990 and even higher figures during the 1980s; however, recent forecasts show some optimism, with perhaps a 2% growth rate in the years ahead. However, for the countries of central and eastern Europe the situation is bleak. The fall in their industrial output is now disastrous; some 10% in the former Soviet Union, 20% in the rest of eastern Europe and 50% in the former German Democratic Republic during 1991, for instance. The fall in total output in central and eastern European countries is now so large that they are close to the dreaded economic depression of the 1930s.

The effects on health risk factors are several. From a situation of no unemployment only two years ago, the total number of unemployed in central and eastern Europe today is probably more than 7 million, representing 2% of the labour force in Romania, 10% in Poland, 15% in Yugoslavia—and quickly rising in many areas. Galloping inflation in a number of these countries—66% in Poland, 400% in Yugoslavia and some 360% in the former Soviet Union in 1991—has led to a rapid decline in living standards, an increase in poverty groups and a critical worsening of living conditions, particularly for vulnerable groups, such as the elderly and single mothers. In some areas, such as Albania, the breakdown of society's infrastructure and functioning has reached chaotic proportions, with a virtual standstill of public functions, including serious disturbance in the functioning of many hospitals and health centres. Part of this is due to the sudden disappearance of agricultural cooperatives which were the financial basis for many social and health care institutions throughout the country. In many CCEE countries we have seen an acute lack of the most essential commodities, including drugs, vaccines and basic medical supplies. This in turn increases the risk for infectious diseases and malnutrition, and it sharply decreases the quality and accessibility of the most basic health and social services in many areas. This has to do with many factors—old machines, no spare parts, no basic materials, collapse of work discipline, disappearance of the COMECON soft currency trade arrangements, etc.

Another great danger in the present situation is the effect on the mood of people. For decades the hundreds of millions of people in central and eastern Europe have been anxiously waiting for political freedom, expecting democracy to bring a rapid and tangible improvement in their daily lives. The present desperate economic situation and the prospect in many of the countries—but not all—of a further deterioration before a turn-around can occur, now presents a real danger, undermining support for the new reform processes and increasing the attractions of simplistic solutions. This threatens the social health fabric, increasing the risk of alienation, of the young in particular, leading to criminality, risk of drug abuse, depression and other threats to health.

In this situation only a radically different attitude from western European countries can help the situation. This help must not only include the most urgently needed supplies and equipment but, and above all, it must encourage investment and give the trade preferences that are fundamental to help the countries of central and eastern Europe start producing goods that can be sold with profit, turning their economies around and recreating a basis for new optimism and development.

This will require a political will beyond what is currently apparent; necessitating financial resources at the level of the Marshall plan that helped western Europe break out of its severe depression after the Second World War.

The health status of Europe

What is the health status of Europe today? Since 1984 all our 31 member states have utilized the same set of basic indicators to measure progress towards the 38 European Health-for-All targets, monitoring and evaluating systematically their own health development—while the Regional Office has done the same at the European level. In 1991 we finished our second European-wide evaluation and presented the results to all European countries in an extensive document at the Regional Committee in Lisbon. What were the results? As always, there was not a uniform picture; in some areas progress has been good, in others less so, and in some it is deteriorating.

Towards which targets has good progress been made? Briefly, one could say that there has been a very encouraging improvement in health policy development, good progress in controlling accidents and specific infectious diseases, a substantial rise in life expectancy and a similar decrease in infant and maternal mortality and, in parts—but not all parts—of Europe, an improvement in cardiovascular diseases. Furthermore, the speed of improvement is rising with respect to maternal mortality, cardiovascular diseases, accidents, suicide and water supply and sanitation.

On the other hand, little or no overall progress has been made with regard to equity and health, cancer mortality, appropriate use of health care technologies, providing health services according to needs, etc.

Furthermore, the AIDS epidemic has grown from around 2000 six years ago to almost 70 000 today—and the total number of HIV-infected persons in Europe is estimated at more than half a million. While there are some encouraging signs that there may be an effect from the preventive measures initiated for high-risk populations as from the middle of the 1980s, there are indications of a growing heterosexual spread in some areas; a disturbing fact. Even more worrisome, a series of factors—rapid increase in travel, change in cultural and social patterns, increasing drug abuse and criminality, insufficient hygiene standards in health care settings—today, make many areas of central and eastern Europe potentially very high-risk situations, where only vigorous preventive measures instituted immediately can prevent what otherwise may become a very serious increase in HIV infection for the 415 million people in this part of our region. This is why WHO's Regional Office for Europe has started a special emergency programme for AIDS prevention in central and eastern Europe.

Factors that influence future health development possibilities

What can we do to improve the health situation in Europe? Is it madness to believe that we *can* influence the health and well-being of 850 million people in 50 countries? Should we just sit back, close our eyes and say 'let it take its own course, there is nothing we can do about it anyhow'?

No; that is not an option! On the contrary, I firmly believe we *can* move things, because we have been able to do so in the past; furthermore, the present opening-up to a 'Europe without frontiers' adds a whole new dimension which is extremely positive. What are some of the important factors in this change?

First, today there is not only a political change that permits people to travel abroad and see for themselves; more important, there is a *mental change* for more openness. Today we are throwing overboard our past blind beliefs in ideologies and demanding clear facts, openly searching for the best results, no matter where they may be.

This is not only a new openness in central and eastern Europe, where the police state for many decades repressed any re-thinking, it is also a new openness in western Europe. Let us admit it; for many years the different parts of western Europe had a blind belief that *their* model—the Scandinavian, the pluralistic, the British, etc.—was, by definition, the best, a view more rooted in cultural and political traditions and beliefs than in open and unbiased evaluations.

There is no doubt that the landmark decision of the European countries in 1984 to openly share a large amount of basic information—through a set of common Health For All indicators that could show progress or lack of it in each country—has been a major factor in this development. This new attitude brought periodically to the fore a large amount of new information which stimulated governments to search actively for new ideas in other models; a process taking place not only in central and eastern Europe, but also in Germany, The Netherlands, the United Kingdom, and Sweden, to mention but a few.

A *second* important factor of change is the recent tearing down of the old political divide, the 'Iron Curtain'. This has led to a new solidarity and a willingness for direct help across old frontiers. This process, in my view, has not yet gone far enough; ideally, the donor countries in the west should provide more of their assistance through an integrated, neutral programme for helping central and eastern European countries, while in reality a lot of current assistance is still through bilateral efforts that tend to 'sell' the specific system that prevails in a particular donor country.

A *third* important asset in the present situation is that Europe has tremendous resources, both intellectual and economic, that can be mobilized for better health. We have a vast potential of scientific educational institutions all over Europe, and we have extensive networks of organizations, professional ones and others.

Finally, and particularly challenging, we have a European population which is currently adrift, in search of new orientations and new goals. With the end of the 'cold war', the hedonistic attitude to life as a venture of economic exploitation and easy luxury is increasingly being felt as insufficient to meet the basic human aspirations of large groups of our society. Herein lies a vast potential for action, not least at local level—people 'out there' are desperately waiting to be challenged, stimulated and inspired for action!

The need for a common vision in health development

What do we need to exploit the situation?

First, we need *a common vision in health*. If we want to 'move' Europe, 'move' societies and 'move' individuals, we must provide a clear vision of where we want to go. This vision must outline a strategy which makes it possile for *all* concerned—countries, institutions, organizations and individuals—to see not only how they themselves can be part of the movement, but how they can play a meaningful role in it. It must be a vision broad enough to be relevant for large parts of societies but specific enough to be an inspiration for the many subgroups of it; it must be clear enough to provide guidance on where to go, but vague enough to stimulate curiosity for finding new solutions and better approaches to solve the problems.

In Europe today we are fortunate that we do indeed already *have* such a common vision, and that this is a vision which is specifically designed on the basis of European problems, European specificities and European possibilities today. When, in 1984, all the 31 countries of the European Region adopted their common policy in health, they did so on the basis of four years of extensive scientific and political work, and they drafted a policy in health for Europe as a whole and an inspirational framework for each country to reshape its own.

In the years that have passed since then, this policy has been endorsed by all European countries and served as an inspirational guide for the formulation of similar national policies in two-thirds of our member states. It has been officially endorsed by the Council of Europe and by all European medical, nursing and pharmaceutical associations, as well as by European associations of medical deans, medical education, schools of public health, medical sociology and many specialized professional groups. Updated by a decision of the 31 countries in September 1991, this policy now also creates a common framework for WHO's new 'Eurohealth' programme of assistance in health to central and eastern European countries, adopted by the European Regional Committee of WHO in September of 1991.

This European Health-For-All (HFA) policy is particularly important at present, when the economic situation both in eastern and western parts of our region tends to be such an overriding concern—to the detriment of solidarity with vulnerable and high-risk groups, and pushing health and equity to the back-burner of national policies and priorities. HFA's strong emphasis on equity, being the first of the 38 European HFA targets, is particularly important just now to keep a strong and clear voice in the defence of the weak, in the present harsh economic realities of central and eastern Europe—as indeed it is also inside the more affluent countries.

Building partnerships for health

A *second* thing we need to move Europe forward in health is a *strong mechanism for bringing our potential resources to bear in more coherent and harmonious ways*. In the past, health developments have too often been fragmented and confined primarily inside individual countries, where firmly entrenched special-interest groups or unwilling political leadership have often killed new initiatives and ideas by 'nipping them in the bud' before they have gained strength to grow. With the new open Europe, national frontiers no longer will be effective barriers, and there will be a new opportunity for developing wide collaborative networks among partners from many countries that can draw on each other's experiences, be mutually supportive and join forces in developing new and better solutions.

This philosophy of *building partnerships for health* has been a strong element in the strategy that the European Office of WHO has elaborated in the past five years—with considerable success. All European *governments* are now closely linked through the work of the Regional Committee of the Regional Office for Europe, where every year they meet for a week to share experiences of their individual efforts to develop national health systems in line with the joint HFA policies they made together in 1984 and 1991. *Cities*, increasingly important both politically and as economic and administrative entities (now comprising more than half of Europe's population) have been brought together in WHO's Healthy Cities network of cities pledged to implement the European HFA policies in their own area. Now comprising almost 500 cities and probably reaching some 50 million people directly, the Healthy Cities movement is fast becoming one of the largest public health experiments ever.

Another network now starts to link European *schools* together through our Health Promoting Schools project, and a third—at the moment comprising 27 *hospitals*—reaches out through the Health Promoting Hospitals initiative. Even more important may become our latest initiative, a new Healthy *Worksite* project, which is already starting to network labour organizations, industries and occupational health specialists, throughout the region—again to apply the HFA principles at the local worksite where people spend such a large proportion of their lives.

Our *professional networks* now comprise a new European Forum of National Medical Associations and WHO which, for five years, has brought all European Medical Associations into an organized framework of collaboration from all over Europe. A similar forum to spread the HFA movement has recently been created between WHO and all national pharmaceutical associations, while for several years all European national nursing associations and WHO have worked intimately together to develop nursing in Europe to respond to the HFA challenge. During the past two years very close cooperation between national diabetes organizations, Ministries of Health and WHO, has been established in order to give reality to the implementation of improved health for Europe's 30 million diabetics, through the so-called St Vincent Declaration of the International Diabetes Federation and the European Regional Office of WHO.

These collaborative efforts have tremendous potential for health development in Europe as they help to spread rapidly the basic strategies on how to approach health development better, in line with official policies developed by all the countries together. Thus, it creates a rapidly growing, flexible web of countries, organizations, institutions, groups and individuals, that bring together, in an organized fashion, experiences in health development— whether in lifestyles and health, environment and health, or health services development areas—from all over Europe. These networks are now ready to absorb new members from central and eastern European countries, providing a much more integrated and systematic form of cooperation than the *ad-hoc* and individual assistance currently given by particular countries, associations and donor agencies.

Bringing the economic resources for health development assistance to countries of central and eastern Europe together

Third, what Europe needs in the years ahead to exploit the 'Europe without frontiers' situation is a better mechanism to pull together the economic resources available for assistance in health development for the central and eastern European countries.

As regards economic assistance, at the moment there are a number of major organizations, and many countries, working to support the countries of central and eastern Europe. The World Bank offers large-scale loans for health assistance, for example, to Poland and Romania; the European Bank for Reconstruction and Development in London devotes 40% of its loans to infrastructure development including the environment; the one billion ECU European PHARE programme will commit perhaps 10% of its 1992 budget to health; the World Health Organization has a budget of approximately $2 million for the biennium; the Council of Europe is funding a fellowship programme; a large number of non-governmental organizations of different kinds contribute also. In addition, a considerable number of European member states—and some from outside the region—are providing millions of dollars of support. A new initiative, from the 'G-7' group has announced a large aid package for the Commonwealth of Independent States to a total sum of $24 billion, some of which will be credit to allow the republics of the CIS to buy pharmaceuticals and medical supplies.

Of these different organizations, WHO is the only one that provides assistance according to an overall policy directly linked to the one decided by all European countries for Europe as a whole. At the moment there is no agreement between all the different organizations on providing assistance through one, coordinated programme per country according to a clear set of priorities for health development. Of course, this happens to various extents in the receiving countries, but experience clearly shows that this is not always an easy situation for them to handle. The Regional Committee has therefore agreed to a principle whereby WHO establishes liaison officers in countries, to try to help bring more coordinated support to the individual countries. Such liaison officers have now been set up in six central and eastern European countries and new ones are about to be appointed. However, it is clear that a more structured agreement between WHO, the EC, the European Bank of Reconstruction and Development, etc. will facilitate this coordination, and we are currently exploring such ideas.

Exploring better research and development

Another opportunity for the new Europe lies in better coordination of the resources that are available for research and development in all European countries—not only in the central and eastern European ones. For this purpose the Regional Office for Europe and DG-XII of the European Community have established cooperation through mutual representation in our research committees, and a special liaison person named by the European Community. This has led to a good dialogue, but there is very considerable scope for much closer cooperation among the major organizations and institutions dealing with research and development in health.

A stronger advocacy and a stronger movement for health

As regards the EC countries, there is no doubt that the new public health mandates given to the European Community, through the Maastricht Agreement, will help channel more resources, in a more purposeful manner, for research and development inside the European Community itself. However, the Maastricht Agreement can also improve substantially the possibilities for health advocacy. At the moment, as I have already said, the Regional Office for Europe of the World Health Organization reaches out to ministers of health, other ministries, professional groups, subnational organizations and cities, research and development institutes, with the HFA message. The European Community, with its strong mandates for imposing supranational legislations and regulations on its member countries, can now strengthen its possibilities for health advocacy as well. The Council of Europe, with its direct link to national parliamentarians in all member states and its own Parliamentary Assembly, has also a very important network. There is no doubt that closer cooperation between the three could lead to a much more purposeful, broader range of networks for health development initiatives—for instance, supporting initiatives to regulate tobacco advertisement, pricing, principles of smoke-free areas, etc. I am pleased to inform you that we have agreed with the Council of Europe to undertake such closer cooperation, while negotiations with the European Community have been awaiting the conclusion of the Maastricht Agreement.

How can we *bring all this together*? How can we 'make it swing', how can we give it the sound professional support it needs, how can we keep the momentum going—not only at European level, not only at national level, but down to every local community throughout our continent? As I have already mentioned, it is my firm conviction that only a common policy can really do that. Only a common policy can be the inspiration and the tool that we use to give a shared direction, stimulating a thousand and one organizations to make a thousand and one moves—towards the same objective; *not* through the maze of a huge bureaucratic system but by stimulating partners to network through voluntary agreements. This means also that we must be able to explain that policy to a vast number of people and organizations, and we must give to each of them a sense of ownership— if not, they will fail to feel that this is 'theirs' and follow-up will not be effective.

That is why WHO believes so strongly that using the principle of *target setting*—with different levels but similar types of targets at European, national and local levels—is such an important developmental mechanism. It was a long and hard fight from 1980 to 1984 to have that principle accepted for the European Region as a whole. Today, however, no-one questions the correctness of the decision of the 34th session of the Regional Committee; nor is its impact on subsequent development in Europe in dispute—mention of the European HFA policy and targets is made in every new government health policy in this region, and in thousands of health development projects, articles and documents of public health in our member states. It has taken a long time for countries to truly accept the same philosophy but, during the past few years, the principle of target setting has finally been accepted as one of the major tools in health development in many countries of the region.

The public health leadership

In the end it is *people* that make the difference, people that make things move. In the development of the new 'Europe without frontiers', the public health professionals must be the true leaders, the catalysts, the skilled technicians who know the principles and can apply the methods that are appropriate for the situation at hand. That is why the Regional Committee for Europe has so strongly emphasized the need to strengthen countries' infrastructure of public health through the provision of professionals who are properly trained in the HFA development philosophy. In that context I am very pleased to be here in the United Kingdom, where the recommendations of the so-called Acheson Commission have led to an important strengthening of the public health infrastructure in this country— an initiative which has reverberated throughout Europe and has already influenced thinking in other countries as well.

However, we are not only talking about development inside countries, but of strengthening the overall European movement for better health. That is why we, in WHO, firmly believe that only a more consolidated European initiative towards the training of public health professionals that are truly capable of leading a HFA development, can bring us forward. With this in mind we have worked intensely with the Association of Schools of Public Health of the European Region (ASPHER) to try to develop together the concept of a European Master of Public Health, thus lifting the level of public health knowledge all over Europe to a new and more uniform level. This work has not been easy; as always, many institutions tend to be jealous about their philosophies and teaching programmes—and that is understandable. However, I believe our goal in this area is so important that it should receive a much stronger commitment from the many European schools of public health. I should like to use this occasion to thank the London School of Hygiene and Tropical Medicine for its input to the process so far, and to encourage the School and its Board to throw their full weight behind this development, which can be such a crucial contribution to European health development in the decades to come!

I wish you all success with this meeting and hope you will all have interesting and challenging discussions in the days ahead.

MAJOR ISSUES FOR EUROPEAN PUBLIC HEALTH

Diversity and similarity of health: organization, practice and assessment

Klim McPherson

London School of Hygiene and Tropical Medicine, UK

Introduction

European traditions, beliefs and practices of health, health provision and health behaviour have evolved in an extraordinarily independent manner. Clearly for some neighbouring countries which have exchanged populations over the centuries this is not so true, but nonetheless these traditions across the whole expanse of Europe are enormously disparate. What are we to make of these differences now that there is a systematic tendency towards some sort of unified whole? Do these differences reflect genuine preferences or just a series of historically determined accidents.

One thing is certain: controls on costs are inexorably going to raise questions of effectiveness and then of value for money, and these questions will inexorably highlight these differences. First cherished (and sometimes unquestioned) notions of the utility of hospital care will be threatened by observed differences in population admission rates.

For more than 60 years, ever since the work of Glover (1938) on British school children in Kent, the facts of variations in the provision of hospital care, unexplained by commensurate morbidity differences, have been known. While expenditure on cure remained relatively unquestioned, however, such information could be ignored in the knowledge that tonsillectomy was benign, cheap and discretionary, and hence marginal to the main thrust of curative services.

However, following in that tradition, but taking full advantage of modern information systems, epidemiologists and health policy analysts have since the early 1970s been systematically pursuing this approach (Table 1). They have documented and questioned the range of standardized rates of various reasons for hospitalization, for example, between small areas served generally by a single hospital (McPherson *et al.* 1982).

Europe Without Frontiers. Edited by C.E.M. Normand and P. Vaughan
© 1993 John Wiley & Sons Ltd

Table 1 Admission rates, per 100 000 per annum

	USA	UK	Netherlands	Norway	France	Italy	Germany
Hysterectomy	557	250	381	150	?	?	?
Appendicectomy	130	131	149	120	?	?	?
CBPG	61	6	5	13	?	?	?
Prostatectomy	308	144	116	238	?	?	?

From McPherson (1989), with permission
? = data not available in these countries

The point of this paper is to illustrate and identify the range of differences that exist in the way that health care is provided. This is obviously important because health care and health services are expensive, may not be effective and indeed may not be benign, but effectiveness is too often assumed on grounds of 'intrinsic' plausibility. Hospital expenditures are often seen as beyond discretion or culture or tradition, and to be a matter largely for science.

Increasingly, however, decisions have to rest on more than just the plausibility of some net health gain, but on the precise relationship of the expected size of that gain with the price of achieving it. Such decisions will then inevitably involve, if only implicitly, public policy issues concerning particular social, health and individual priorities.

What emerges initially from this work, unfortunately, is not answers to these policy questions but an empirical emphasis on the importance and relevance of the questions themselves. More importantly such research provides dispassionate assessment of the extent of scientific uncertainties that allow what will increasingly be seen as exogenous and perhaps irrelevant factors to influence important policy decisions.

Hysterectomy is a frequently studied hospital admission, because it could be driven by consumer preferences and because its small area variation is typical of most procedure-specific admissions. Variations between countries are interesting (Figure 1) and no evidence can be adduced suggesting any important demand component in the determination of these rates (Coulter *et al.*, 1988). Even Bunker's study in the 1970s suggested the excess among doctors' wives could be determined by availability rather than preference (Bunker and Brown, 1974).

Many have studied the enormous differences in systems of health care delivery and expenditures between countries, to emerge with only weak conclusions on efficient organization (Aaron and Schwartz, 1984). Others have analysed the policy choices for health promotion between Britain and the US to better understand the complex interaction between public policy, politics, society and health beliefs and behaviour (Leichter, 1991).

Increasing costs, increasing concern about quality and the expectations of

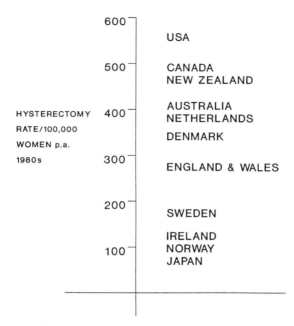

Figure 1 Hysterectomy rate by country in the middle 1980s

consumers will continue to drive the enquiry—but the research agenda requires direction. Much needs to be done in expanding the public health function in Europe and building on the major traditions of research and collaboration to set about solving the major health questions of our time.

European public health research

By far the largest single cost of health care is the cost of hospitalization. Workers such as Wennberg and colleagues, in attempting to enlighten the debate surrounding the determinants of the decisions to admit to hospital, are able to distinguish quite neatly the relative importance of consumer preferences based on their perceived needs and supplier dominance, at least as far as decisions for hospitalization are concerned (Wennberg, 1990).

This work demonstrates that variations of the kind seen in the 1930s for tonsillectomy are the rule and not the exception, and that they largely represent consequences of the different but often strongly held view of clinicians. Moreover measures of morbidity, need or demand do not correlate well with utilization.

This is extremely important in understanding the nature of contemporary European health care, and the strongest evidence for supplier dominance,

Table 2 Per capita hospital expenditure rates, 1982 (US$)

	Boston	New Haven
Expenditure	889	451
Medicare reimbursements	2647	1561

From Wennberg *et al.* (1987), by permission of *The Lancet*

based on scientific uncertainties as opposed to scientific ignorance, can be extrapolated from a study of the health care in two of America's most prestigious medical institutions, Yale and Harvard (Wennberg *et al.*, 1987). The findings that the citizens of Boston receive hospitalization expenditures per capita which are nearly twice as much (Table 2) as the demographically similar citizens of New Haven (Table 3), demonstrates the nature of this uncertainty.

In New England the citizens of Boston were being admitted much more commonly than the citizens of New Haven for medical back problems, carotid endarterectomy and D&Cs. But the New Haven citizens also underwent more tonsillectomies and coronary bypass surgery than those in Boston. These hospitalizations cost, in the early 1980s, $890 and $450 per capita per annum respectively, with no concomitant differences in health. Moreover the differences in hospital supply and utilization were neither suspected nor understood by the professionals, and least of all by the consumers.

Such differences are bound to be just as common through Europe and generally the explanations will be the same. The evidence on hospitalization for particular conditions, for which there are data, strongly supports such a view, as do the enormous differences in aggregate health sector expenditures (Figure 2). The history of our cultures strongly suggests even greater, and possibly unmeasured, differences.

If this is true of hospitalization in two of the world's most prestigious medical centres then it is not difficult to imagine the differences that must

Table 3 Population characteristics, 1982

	Boston	New Haven
Percentage aged over 65	13.5	12.9
Percentage black	18.7	21.4
Median family income (US$)	17 000	17 000
Percentage below poverty	15	14
Hospital beds per 1000	4.5	2.9

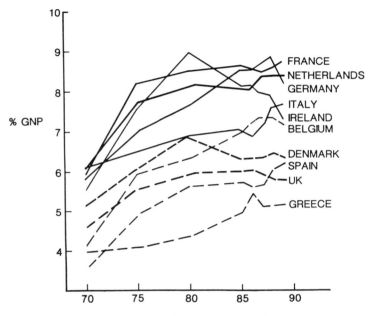

Figure 2 Percentage of GNP spent on health care

exist in health promotion practices and in health behaviour. With small area analysis in a single country it has been possible to determine that clinical uncertainty is dominant, and that there are many important uncertainties in the provision of medical care.

Studies in a single country, as in the USA, moreover might disclose many other interesting possible determinants of the health care decision. One of these is the effects and constraints of the organization of health care itself, that is policies and traditions about reimbursement, manpower, capital expenditure, primary care, research priorities, etc. Equally important are the implied, and indeed the real, preferences of consumers faced with medical uncertainties, in so far as they are aware of them. These are likely to be strongly determined by both culture and history. Both of these are possibly the most crucial and enigmatic aspects of the health care debate, in all its manifestations, facing Europeans into the next century.

We know in Europe that quite enormous variations exist in expenditures both as a proportion of GNP and per capita on purchasing power parity exchanges. Enormous variations exist on per capita surgical use rates, on length of stay, on manpower densities, on the role of primary care and so on (Poullier, 1991). But there are also variations with respect to the traditions and expectations of the consumers, on almost every dimension. What is now required is a sophisticated attempt to disentangle this web of complex information in order to learn.

The traditions of public health are poised to address the issues in the ideal situation of existing diversity and increasing international collaboration. It is inefficient to look for causal associations where there are few or minor differences in 'exposure'. The historical diversities of Europe are an under-exploited natural experiment. There are, of course, many important and unanswered questions; not least is the relationship between health and health care. Work on hospitalization, for instance, uncovers massive differences in utilization and therefore expenditure, but few measured differences in aggregate outcome.

On the other hand observational monitoring of mortality in the US (Hahn *et al.*, 1990), for example, uncovers large and systematic differences in standardized mortality rates for common diseases, the large proportion of which is preventable in principle by eliminating or reducing known risk factors for chronic disease (Table 4). Thus we already understand essentially the method of reducing mortality and hence a major burden of illness, in western society. Largely this is little or nothing to do with health services as we know them.

The implications on research policy and organizational priorities must be becoming clearer. Information from the *European Atlas of Avoidable Deaths* (Holland, 1988) begins to enlighten the policy options and the research priorities. Work recently published comparing (what used to be) the two halves of Europe and North America with respect to changes in mortality, provides enormous insight into the political and social possibilities for health gain (Boys *et al.*, 1991) (Table 5). Interestingly all of this evidence strongly supports the arguments of McKeown (1979), which have been well understood in the public health world for a long time. The opportunities for contemporaneous validation and detailed exploration have never been better.

Table 4 US studies: mortality from nine common diseases in US states

	Rate/100 000	% Average
Highest state	483.1	113
US average	427.4	100
Lowest state	304.7	71
Lowest rate for each disease	284.1	66
Elimination of greatest attributable risk factor	224.5	53

From Hahn *et al.* (1990), with permission
Age-adjusted rate per 100 000

Table 5 Changes in standardized mortality rates between 1970–74 and 1985–87 (percentages)

	Total	Amenable	Non-amenable	IHD
Hungary	17	−15	29	26
East Germany	−4	−27	3	1
West Germany	−27	−62	−19	−20
England and Wales	−22	−50	−15	−16
USA	−26	−51	−22	−10

From Boys *et al.* (1991), with permission

Conclusions

Increasingly many of the implicit assumptions about health care, at least on the margins of illness where there is nonetheless much expenditure, are being questioned. This process is inexorable, simply because resources are limited. Hence much variation in hospital admissions without concomitant evidence about need or about outcome will not be countenanced for too long. Where the health information systems are deficient they will be improved. Where the uncertainties are important and long-standing their investigation will not be resisted.

In Europe now, precisely because of our heterogeneous history and culture, the opportunities for powerful public health research and health services research to investigate important questions of cost-effectiveness are too great to be missed (Figure 3). The relevance of the questions is not in doubt, and I am sure that the whole of Europe shares a similarity of purpose to maximize health gain efficiently for its people.

To pursue this strategy does require basic epidemiological understanding, and hence methodological exploitation as well as international collaboration. Firstly it is important to acknowledge that medical certainty can and does coexist with overwhelming evidence for real scientific uncertainty (from variation studies for instance) because decisions have to be made (even under conditions of uncertainty), and possibly even because therapeutic effectiveness is thus enhanced (Inglefinger, 1980; Thomas, 1987). Such a realization should be no threat to medical hegemony, once its nature is understood.

However, the incentive to evaluate may thus be illegitimately diminished. Moreover randomized clinical trials can only ethically be conducted in circumstances of quite explicit and demonstrable medical uncertainty. There is thus likely to be (and indeed is) a large middle ground between those medical decisions which are entirely based on sound scientific evidence, with well-understood patient preferences, and those for which the uncertainty is dominant and acknowledged (McPherson, 1989), and hence well investigated.

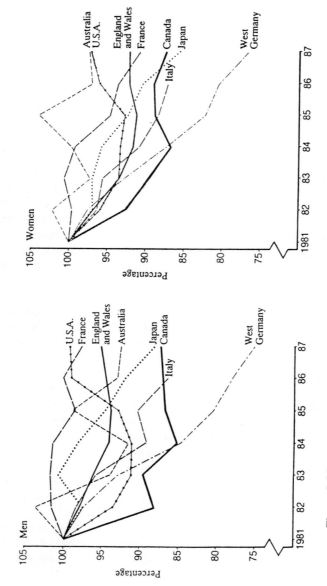

Figure 3 Mortality rates for selected countries, men and women aged 15–44, 1981–1987

This middle ground will typically exist at the 'margins' of symptomatology for common conditions. That is among patients deemed in some cultures to be ambiguously in need of hospitalization whereas in others they warrant medical or watchful attention only (Payer, 1989). The investigation of this uncertain middle ground will have to be made largely using non-experimental methods (see Appendix).

The main interest of new European collaboration is to provide a framework whereby insights into efficacy (and hence efficiency) can be routinely derived using observational methods in circumstances where experimental investigation seems unethical, but where the natural variations are large. Initially it might only be a matter of setting up well-directed databases in circumstances of large practice style differences which are unlikely to confound the comparison of outcome. This methodology is in its infancy, but experience is accumulating (General Accounting Office, 1992).

Similarly the epidemiology of common diseases can be very efficiently investigated by design considerations which maximize the range of putatively harmful or beneficial exposures. In Europe it must be true that the variety of dietary and other exposures, which are correlated strongly with culture and history, are less confounded with illness across countries than they would be within countries. Thus case–control and cohort studies across countries in Europe are likely to provide epidemiological evidence unobtainable elsewhere and at any other time.

Lastly as the nature of the real uncertainties becomes better understood as part of this process, so the role of the consumer will become much more dominant in all aspects of health care decision-making. The challenge then is in understanding the nature and determinants of individual utilities and preferences, and in informing public policy accordingly. Such studies are difficult to do, of course, and are seldom thought worthwhile in the present climate. Perhaps it will turn out that enlightened health policy would then continue to emphasize hospital care at the margin of illness and disparage social policies designed to prevent disease. If such policy were based on evidence and genuine preferences, who could possibly object?

Appendix: Methodological developments

1. The ability to make inferences from observed outcome difference among patient groups treated differently, derived from databases or longitudinal studies, requires significant development. This hinges on the ability to measure and adjust for aspects of case-mix (indices of prognosis) which might affect outcome, and which are related systematically to treatment choices. The statistical models are well developed for performing the appropriate calculations but their utility depends on the specific interrelationships between case-mix, outcomes and treatment.

2. In outcome research in clinical medicine the methodological problems are more acute than in observational epidemiology because treatment choices are made

with and for particular patients largely to influence outcome. In observational epidemiology the classical problems of confounding are less severe because the determination of choice of exposure (as opposed to exposure) being investigated rarely (it is assumed) has any relationship to subsequent disease outcome, and hence will only be confounded with outcome through some other, and often secondary, mechanism.

3. Thus disentangling the choice of a treatment for a particular patient from its therapeutic effect will always be difficult when comparing treatment effects (Byar, 1980). If the reason has nothing to do with intrinsic prognosis, as in randomized comparison, then comparison of outcomes between treatments is entirely valid. But outside such studies the therapeutic decisions will usually be made on the basis of other characteristics of the patients which will clearly influence outcome whatever the treatment.

4. In these circumstances we know that apparently exhaustive case-mix adjustments can still sometimes leave large residual outcome differences which can logically be attributed to nothing other than (unmeasured) differences in case-mix (Coronary Drug Project Research Group, 1980). In the CDP, adjustment for 40 potent prognostic indicators among men receiving *placebo* in a secondary CHD prevention trial made little difference to the substantial and highly significant mortality difference observed between adherers and non-adherers. Hence firm conclusions are bound to be elusive, in general (McPherson and Bunker, 1991). There are two possible and important exceptions to this general rule.

5. Firstly in circumstances where the proportion of variance in outcome (however measured) explained by measurable co-morbidity is high, statistical adjustment for these variables may be extremely potent and hence yield approximately unconfounded comparisons of treatment. Secondly this may be particularly relevant when a dominant determinant of treatment choice at some symptomatic threshold is some aspect of practice style related to geography, education or organization, and not to individual patient prognosis.

6. Clearly such notions can be tested in specific instances by comparison of observational contrast, adjusted for co-morbidity, with randomized trials of the same contrast, where they exist. It is not difficult to imagine circumstances where the benefits associated with intervention are thought to be finely balanced for a range of indications. In such circumstances some would intervene early in the range and others much later; the classical interventionist versus conservative approach. Then the decision might be independent of intrinsic prognosis for the marginal patient.

7. Thus the exploitation of data for comparisons between countries or areas with different rates requires to be developed (Anonymous, 1989). When there are large international differences in use rates, as well as small area variations, and where case-mix adjustment is inconclusive, pseudo-randomization strategies may be necessary. This approach requires identification, in a low-use country, of people who would be admitted to hospital for treatment in a high-use country, and identification of those who are admitted in both countries.

8. Such a strategy depends on the ability to identify unadmitted patients with relevant symptoms in low-use areas who, it must be convincingly argued, would have been admitted/treated in a high-use area. In principle, since in the UK admission rates are generally low and data systems in primary care well developed, there are enormous opportunities to simulate the control arm of 'unethical' clinical trials. They would be unethical paradoxically because well-

established ethical practice in one area would often be deemed to be quite unethical as a clinical policy in another (Anonymous, 1990).

9. It would be sensible to investigate admissions for mild cardiovascular and cerebrovascular symptoms, menorrhagia, prolapse, problems of micturition, cataract, low back pain, cataract and cholecystitis. Such methodology requires assiduous record-keeping in general practice of patient consultations, and will require clerks to ensure that all eligible patients are included. In some circumstances existing diagnostic indexes could be used, for routine computerization of all consultations is becoming increasingly common.

10. As an example of this methodology, in Canada cholecystectomy rates are nearly three times as common as in the UK, with no concomitant evidence of commensurate morbidity (McPherson et al., 1985). By identifying twice as many people with relevant symptoms in general practice in the UK than there are admissions for surgery per 100 000 population in a year, then it can be inferred that such a cohort (including both people with and without surgery) could be comparable with people receiving cholecystectomy in Canada.

Collaboration with colleagues will then provide indices of outcome, possibly many years after the index operation (Roos et al., 1989) using linked claims data. This could be compared with concurrent data on the identified linked cohort of UK patients, only one-third of whom underwent surgery.

11. Prospective randomized controlled trials can then be initiated when the explicit uncertainty uncovered by the above analyses is sufficient to enable clinicians to allocate patients randomly to decide the issue, free of confounding and therefore reliably. Clearly not only does there need to be sufficient uncertainty, but also the therapeutic question has to be of sufficient consequence to justify a randomized trial.

References

Aaron HJ and Schwartz WB (1984) *The Painful Prescription: Rationing Hospital Care*. Brookings Institute, Washington, DC.

Anonymous (1989) Databases for health care outcomes. *Lancet*, 2, 195–196

Anonymous (1990) Medical ethics: should medicine turn the other cheek? *Lancet*, 336, 846–847

Boys RJ, Forster DP and Jozan P (1991) Mortality from causes amenable and non-amenable to medical care: the experience of Eastern Europe. *British Medical Journal*, 303, 879–883

Bunker JP and Brown B (1974) The physician as an informed consumer of surgical services. *New England Journal of Medicine*, 290, 1051–1055

Byar DP (1980) Why data bases should not replace randomised clinical trials. *Biometrics*, 36, 337–342

Coronary Drug Project Research Group (1980) *Influence of adherence to treatment and response of cholesterol on mortality in the Coronary Drug Project*. New England Journal of Medicine, 303, 1038–1041

Coulter A, McPherson K and Vessey M (1988) Do British women undergo too many or too few hysterectomies? *Social Science and Medicine*, 27, 987–994

General Accounting Office (1992) *Cross Design Synthesis. A new strategy for medical effectiveness research*. US General Accounting Office (March), Washington

Glover JA (1938) The incidence of tonsillectomy among school children. *Proceedings of the Royal Society of Medicine*, 31, 1219–1236

Hahn RA, Teutsch SM, Rothenberg RB and Marks JS (1990) Excess deaths from nine chronic diseases in the United States, 1986. *Journal of the American Medical Association*, *264* (20), 2654–2659

Holland WW (ed.) (1988) *European Community Atlas of Avoidable Deaths*. Oxford University Press, Oxford

Ingelfinger FJ (1980) Arrogance. *New England Journal of Medicine*, *303*, 1507–1511

Leichter HM (1991) *Free to be Foolish. Politics and health promotion in the United States and Great Britain*. Princeton University Press, Princeton

McKeown T (1979) *The Role of Medicine*. Blackwell, Oxford

McPherson K (1989) International difference in medical care practices. *Health Care Financing Review Annual Supplement*, pp. 9–20

McPherson K and Bunker J (1991) Health information as a guide to the organization and delivery of services. In Holland W, Knox G and Detels D (eds) *Oxford Textbook of Public Health*. Vol 21, pp. 67–79, Oxford University Press, Oxford

McPherson K, Wennberg JE, Hovind OB and Clifford P (1982) Small area variations in the use of common procedures: An international comparison of New England and Norway. *New England Journal of Medicine*, *307*, 1310–1314

McPherson K, Strong PM, Jones L and Britton BJ (1985) Do cholecystectomy rates correlate with geographic variations in the prevalence of gallstones. *Journal of Epidemiology and Community Health*, *39*, 179–182

Payer L (1989) *Medicine and Culture. Notions of health and sickness in Britain, the US, France and West Germany*. Victor Gollancz

Poullier, JB (ed.) (1991) *OECD Compendium of Health Care*, Paris

Roos NP, Wennberg JE, Malenka DJ *et al*. (1989) Mortality and reoperation after open and transurethral resection of the prostate for benign prostatic hyperplasia. *New England Journal of Medicine*, *320*, 1120–1124

Thomas KB (1987) General practice consultations: Is there any point in being positive? *British Medical Journal*, *294*, 1200–1202

Wennberg JE (1990) Small area analysis and the medical care outcome problem. In *AHCPR Conference Proceedings: Research Methodology; strengthening causal interpretations of non experimental data*. US Department of Health and Human Services, Washington, D.C., pp. 177–206

Wennberg JE, Freeman JL and Culp WJ (1987) Are hospital services rationed in New Haven or overutilised in Boston. *Lancet*, *1*, 1185–1189

Discussion

Merce Casas, *Ronda Universidad, Barcelona, Spain*

There is scientific evidence of variability in health and health services; as this is a result of complex relationships among medical knowledge and decisions, political and social processes, we are facing an exciting challenge.

To face this challenge there is a gift to help us with the situation and that is a privileged field for research. As clearly pointed out by Professor McPherson, diversity in Europe makes a privileged field for research, as it offers many opportunities for quasi-experimental design, in some cases where there are no other opportunities for ethical approaches.

The opportunities that European countries can offer for research are really important due both to the country differences in factors with potential contributions to health, and to the recent movement towards increasing commonality in policies that affect health and health services in different ways.

To miss these opportunities could merit social disapproval. Efficiency in using limited resources is an obvious aim, but it is especially critical when we are talking about a public service, as is the case in most of Europe. The guarantee of efficiency can be seen, then, as the basis of legitimacy for the system. Increasing health care costs have led to the high priority being given to these topics, placing them in political agendas and public debate. All politicians, health administrators and health professionals should pay attention and feel co-responsible for that.

Previous experiences of collaboration in research at the European level have, in fact, shown the potential of the approach. The OECD must be mentioned as one of the pioneers in collecting and analysing health databases at an international level, with the result of important contributions to the knowledge of health services and to the agenda for new research. The EC has been playing an important role in proving the advantages of European collaboration in research and development.

The establishment of homogeneous economic and social policies with health implications opens new approaches. The current process of adopting homogeneous taxation in EC countries offers the opportunity to explore the degree of influence of price in the consumption of tobacco and alcohol, for example, as it will imply no changes in some countries, while in others there will be large price increases. Regulations in other related aspects, such as in the promotion of these products, can also offer situations with important potential for research.

Freedom of movement will probably favour the interests of increasing knowledge on the characteristics, performance and costs of health services.

In health services, use and cost variation has already been demonstrated, and there is a need for increasing the knowledge of its causes. Relevant decisions can be related to it. As a first approach three kinds of hypotheses can be formulated: (a) the variations indicated by the statistics do not correspond to real differences in use and practices; (b) if they correspond, the differences can be due to differences in practices that cannot be sustained by scientifically demonstrated efficacy, and must result from uncertainty; and (c) if one practice is sustainable, inefficiency can be established.

Some studies have pointed out important differences in medical practices for pathologies with well-defined treatment patterns. In these cases uncertainty does not seem to be the underlying problem, and inefficiency can be suggested. This can then be felt as a threat to medical hegemony, and it is an important point to keep in mind as something to explain clearly, and to avoid. Doctors are the only ones who can decide on the more convenient patterns for treating patients and, thus, support information has to be seen as an important tool to help them in clinical decision-making, and not as a threat.

A similar problem that can be found when facing the pooling of data from different countries is that of some reluctance to contribute on the part of professionals and institutions involved: researchers, epidemiologists and administrators.

One of the most important contributions that analysis of existing data can make is to improve the current knowledge generating hypotheses for new research.

Undoubtedly all perspectives opened by this kind of approach need to be focused carefully. New problems such as confidentiality and database security should be dealt with as they arise.

Finally, we have a role to play in applying the concept of efficiency to research, too, and should be critical of our own approaches and priorities. In that sense debate will arise around at least a couple of issues: prioritizing topics for research and establishing fair ways for financing this international cooperation.

Legal and economic issues in European public health

Paula T. Kokkonen and Martti Kekomäki

National Agency for Welfare and Health, Helsinki, Finland

Introduction: health issues and the moving legislative focus

Economic issues and commercial policies have been and will be the driving force in the EC. Aspects relating to social policy and health have thus been regarded as subordinate and complementary to these main issues. Correspondingly, it has been agreed that social and health policies should primarily be based on national solutions. These, in turn, are strongly influenced by national values, practices, traditions and economy.

Despite this basic constellation, clearly more direct attention is being paid to social and health issues in the EC currently than during the days of the Treaty of Rome in 1957. The extant sectoral policy in 1977–1978 was transformed into a more global one when the Health Ministers decided on the development of three policy areas: (a) the economic aspects of health, development of costs and consumption of medicines; (b) health information, tobacco abuse, drugs and food; and (c) mutual assistance in cases of disasters and particularly serious illnesses.

Since that time there have been several research and development programmes oriented to the 'most important health problems'. These include research on cancer and AIDS, action on age-, environment- and lifestyle-related health problems, improvement and efficient use of health resources, research and development of medical technology, research on health care organizations and care delivery and research on radiation risks.

At the beginning of 1988 the Commission laid down the broad lines of Community social policy for the years ahead. The five guiding principles are: (a) encouraging the improvement in living and working conditions, (b) ensuring conditions for free movement of persons, (c) preparing the ground for the necessary adjustments, (d) strengthening economic and social cohesion, and (e) promoting dialogue between the two sides of industry.

The Social Charter of the Community, approved in 1989, takes into account the needs and financing of the health care of the freely moving

Europe Without Frontiers. Edited by C.E.M. Normand and P. Vaughan
© 1993 John Wiley & Sons Ltd

labour force. It is interesting to note that the early draft referred to 'citizens', and the final text to 'workers'. Ethical and legal problems relating to health care have an increasingly high visibility in the ministers' biannual meetings, held since 1986. This is important, as the full consequences of the internal market in the field of health—on the health of the population and health-related services—are as yet unknown (Leidl, 1991).

From the public health point of view it is most fundamental that, in their Council meeting held on 11 November 1991, the health ministers of the Community stated that 'The Council of Ministries for Health should be able to discuss aspects of *any decision with health implications to be taken at the Community level*'. Extrapolating from this statement we could hope that health-related views in legislation will gain in importance towards the end of the decade.

When writing this text the European Economic Community (EC) plans to become a political union. The Intergovernmental Conferences on Political Union and Economic and Monetary Union reached in the Maastricht Summit (9–10 December, 1991) an agreement on the Draft treaty on European Union. This 'Draft Union Treaty', signed in February 1992, states among other things as follows:

> This treaty marks a new stage in a process leading gradually to a Union with a *federal goal*. The main objectives are: to promote economic and social progress which is balanced and sustainable, in particular through the creation of an area without internal frontiers, through the strengthening of economic and social cohesion and the establishment of economic and monetary union ultimately including a single currency in accordance with the provisions of the present Treaty.

According to Article 3 of the Treaty the activities of the Community shall among other things include: (a) the elimination . . . of customs duties and quantitative restrictions on the import and export of goods, and of all other measures having equivalent effect; (c) an internal market characterized by the abolition . . . of obstacles to the free movement of goods, persons, services and capital; (i) a policy in the social sphere comprising a European Social Fund; (j) the strengthening of economic and social cohesion; (k) a policy in the sphere of the environment; (m) the promotion of research and technological development; (n) encouragement for the establishment and development of trans-European networks; (o) a contribution to the attainment of a high level of health protection; (t) contribution to the strengthening of consumer protection.

The purpose of legislation

Political will can be changed into laws. With laws we can build structures and establish, change and nullify or abolish legal rights, we can also grant freedoms and put burdens and restraints on people and organizations, and enact penal systems. With laws we try to design the scope of the civilized society in order to guarantee that the life of the citizens would turn out favourably and be to a certain extent predictable.

Many of the member states' constitutions guarantee their citizens right to life, freedom and personal integrity. Moreover States have signed different international treaties and have bound themselves to respect certain social rights.

The goals of public health legislation in the EC

Currently, the main goals of legislative actions of the EC could include at least the following separate entities:

1. *To promote the principles of the four freedoms*; with the idea of creating free trade, coordinated legislative action has already been necessary, e.g. to provide health care services for the labour force, with special reference to the forms of financing and the quality of such services; to extend and widen the standardization of drugs, medical equipment and data processing; and to promote free movement of capital needed in health-related enterprises (e.g. the health care industry, pharmaceutical and equipment manufacturing, and the health insurance business).

   This separate goal has thus far been and still is the principal form of EC health-related legislation.

2. *To protect the population of the member states* against any unwanted effects—negative externalities—of any trade-promoting solution within the Community; as recently stated (Richards, 1991): 'the interests of industry have usually prevailed over health interests'. Trade of products with potential or proven health hazards, such as promotion (advertising) of tobacco and alcohol consumption, use of certain xenografts and products of chemical industry would serve as examples from different areas.

   This area of activity was outlined in the Council's resolution (11 November 1991) referred to above.

3. *To reduce differences in health status* within and between the member states and to rationalize health benefits obtainable through prudent organization and delivery of preventive and curative health services and health-promoting activities.

   This goal is still beyond the current scope of the Council of Ministers. However, in the long run this may be the main direction of the legislation to shift. Much depends on the commercial policies accepted in the near future. At present it is difficult to assume that equity in the health care could in the foreseeable future be an explicit goal of the Community, so much remains to be done even on the national level of the Member States (Mooney, 1983).

4. *To reduce health hazards to third parties*; any attempt to maximize economic growth may involve subcontracting with a third party; the Community is morally responsible for guaranteeing that its economic activities with non-member states do not involve any practices, which even potentially could carry a risk of negative health externalities; furthermore, the pursuit for a sustained development cannot be limited to the geographical area of the Community.

The ecological and social responsibility of developed countries such as the member states must be global (ABC, 1990)—in future this goal can be predicted to be even more important.

Ways to promote public health through legislation

The health-related policies are formulated into binding legislation by the different legislative bodies and procedures of the Community. Such harmonizing legislation must be in agreement with the constitutions of the member states as well as with the International Covenants ratified earlier by the states.

The forms of legal protection are traditionally divided into preventive and repressive measures. Both forms will be necessary to promote public health. The following examples could illuminate these measures:

Quality of health care provided is a traditional area of preventive legislation. The forms and length of formal professional education can be regulated in detail, as has already been done; in addition, certification (registration) practices can be applied to ensure that all members of the profession are qualified to practise; through recertification practices the health authorities can monitor the continuous education process of the medical professions; a wide application of the principle of consumer participation serves in part the same preventive goal.

Repressive legislation is applied as a shelter: in this example, despite all preventive legislation, situations occur where the structure, process or outcome of treatment does not fulfil the preset criteria of a high-quality treatment. The patient's right to seek remedial action is a most fundamental part of his/her legal rights. Legislation concerning withdrawal of the registration (no-fault) compensation (Kokkonen, 1989; Lahti, 1990) as well as economic and criminal sanctions form another body of repressive legislation. Analogous examples can be found in most areas of public health legislation.

When considering legal issues in public health we should remember that a great majority of the decisions affecting public health are made on domains other than health care. Examples of these domains are education, the living environment, industry, traffic, agriculture and community planning.

Economic issues in European public health

European public health services carry a century-long tradition. In addition to the organizing, financing, and controlling functions, the public sector participates in providing these services. Such a public concern and participation in traditionally market-driven economies may relate to the special nature of health services as commodities, perceived implicitly long before the birth of health economies as a separate scientific discipline (Normand, 1991). Furthermore, in the search for synergies all Western societies have taken public actions to integrate social and health care sectors, although the strength of such ties varies.

In Western societies the overall impact of health care services on the health of the population is small at the margin: aggregate health indicators are influenced more strongly by determinants relating to lifestyles and living environment. Recognizing this fact is fundamental both for the allocation of scarce societal resources and for the resultant legislation.

Two different publicly regulated health care systems have been created in Europe. While in Continental Europe the public role is limited mainly to the control of services and their reimbursement via compulsory sickness insurance (the Bismarck model; OECD, 1987), in the Nordic countries and in the UK the services are provided by the public sector, which uses income taxes in financing care (the Beveridge model).

The future of financing of European public health

The pursuit of economic stability underscores the entire EC. This limits the use of national monetary policy in handling conjectures. Because the Community will not have common budgets in the foreseeable future—in contrast to the situation in the USA—Community finance policies cannot be used to their full extent to smooth the ebb and flow of national economies. Income policies remain as the only tool of economic adaptation for the governments of member states. In the long run this fact may create pressures to move from the stiff tax-based financing gradually towards a more flexible insurance. Whichever is the form of financing, public provided health care systems seem to share currently many economic strengths and weaknesses.

The strengths of public health care

Political manageability   The political manageability of publicly provided health care is certainly important. Cost constraints have been efficiently set via global budgeting. Although the average GNP share of health care consumption is determined very strongly ($r^2 = \sim 0.80$) by the wealth—per capita GNP—of the nation, member states with central global budgeting may spend, on average, less in health care than others. Similar features are seen in the real gross domestic product elasticities of health care expenditure, which is also indicative of a more efficient cost controlling system.

Public health care is also able to allocate new resources effectively. As an example, a central fiat, fortified by legislation, may facilitate the shift of focus from specialized care to primary health care (as was done in Finland in 1972; Ministry of Social Affairs and Health, 1987).

Capital management   The public health care system has also been efficient to support natural monopolies, to exploit scale economies and to avoid duplication of services. The latter feature is exemplified by conscious concentration—regionalization—of high technology to named institutions only. Such regionalization also facilitates the attaining of measurable quality goals.

Related to the former is the sector's ability to manage its investments. Because the demand for health care services is stochastic, but predictable in the long run, the capacity can be built to meet the average demand rather than peak demand for services. Waste can thus be minimized.

Management of labour prices   The ability of the public health sector to control cost development relates in part to its monopsonistic power. Being by far the largest employer of medical manpower, the sector may influence labour prices strongly.

For similar reasons the administrative overheads of public service systems are, on average, low. This fact is in part due to the way in which public health care is financed. A tax-based financing system cuts the loading costs into a minimum.

Other functions   In tax-based financial systems the progressivity of taxation emphasizes the transfer payment character of health care financing. For example, in Finland the highest income decile alone almost covers the health care costs of the two lowest deciles. By these means of redistributional policy the public system contributes strongly to societal equity in health care.

Weaknesses of public health care

As every coin has two sides, any good intention may turn counterproductive. The economics of public health care are no exception.

Economic and managerial stiffness   A public health care system seems so far to carry structural and functional features of bureaucracy. Such structure may be strong and manageable during stable times but not flexible to meet new challenges, be they economic or functional.

Economically such an inflexibility is reflected in many ways. As was alluded to before, to make necessary cuts or to reallocate existing resources in a health care system has proved to be a formidable task during an economic recession of any depth.

The stiffness in steering is not limited to economically hard times: legally preset ways to measure productivity—the production of hospital days and clinic visits—do not call for the most efficient use of resources, such as day surgery and other forms of ambulatory treatment. In short, perverse incentives are numerous in every bureaucracy, with waste as result.

Lack of personal incentives The inability to pay extra for outstanding performance—is another feature typical of bureaucracy. When the individual achievement is not reflected in the remuneration, mediocrity and inefficiency may soon prevail. This is vividly displayed in the managerial accounting of services delivered from the public sector as compared with the same products from private health care: the negative variances in price and volume largely offset each other.

Intermingling party politics Strong political control, aiming primarily at increasing the accountability of the system towards local needs and preferences, may as well turn counterproductive. Representative administration—more clearly, party politicization—can impregnate the entire organization and create much inefficiency.

In sum, public health care has had difficulties to deal with the increasing demand for services. Long waiting lists have characterized not only operative care, but primary care as well. Queueing for services cannot be productive: patients with orthopaedic, ophthalmological and cardiac conditions amenable to surgical care but without prompt access keep binding societal resources, such as sickness compensation, home aid and relatives' work input, not to mention the patients' suffering. The probability of re-entering productive life is inversely related to the waiting time in surgery.

The future of public health care

Certain steps are about to be taken to revitalize the public health sector and its productivity. The proposed development will be similar in many countries with mainly public provision of services. Bureaucracy can be relaxed without compromising the political acccountability of the system. Both demand and supply sides can be manipulated by health-services-related legislation to improve the effectiveness and quality of care. Polarization of the health care field to service providers and purchasers, application of managerial accounting techniques, adapting capitation-based remuneration systems and other performance-based incentives, allowing for consumer choice and competition ('internal market') in service production will belong to the armamentarium of the new public health care.

Concluding statements

1. A great majority of the decisions affecting public health are made in domains other than health care.
2. In 'Western societies' the overall impact of health care services on health of the population is small—at the margin: aggregate health indicators are influenced more strongly by determinants relating to lifestyles and living environment.
3. Recognizing these facts is fundamental for the allocation of scarce resources and for drafting legislation.

References

The ABC of Community Law (1991) European Documentation. Periodical, 1991

Culyer AJ (1990) Cost containment in Europe. In Health Care Systems in Transition. The Search for Efficiency. Social Policy Studies No 7, OECD, Paris, pp. 29–40

Directory of Community Legislation in Force and other acts of the Community institutions. Official Journal of the European Communities, 17th edn, Vol I (as at 1 June 1991)

European Council, Maastricht, 11 December 1991, Presidency Conclusions, SN 271/1/91

Kokkonen P (1989) No-fault liability and patient insurance: The Finnish Patient Injury Law of 1986. International Digest of Health Legislation, 40 (1), 241–246

Lahti R (1990) Politische Implikationen und Probleme einer nationalen Patienten-rechtsgesetzgebung: Erfahrungen in Finland. In Pichler JW (Hsrd) (ed.) Ein-fuehrung in die Patientenrechtspolitik. Böhlau Vlg, Wien, pp. 73–85

Leidl R (1991) How will the single European market affect health care? British Medical Journal, 303, 1081–1082

Ministry of Social Affairs and Health (1987) Health for All by the Year 2000. The Finnish National Strategy. VAPK, Helsinki, p. 11

Mooney G (1983) Equity in health care: confronting the confusion. Efficient Health Care, 1, 179–184

Normand C (1991) Economics, health, and the economics of health. British Medical Journal, 303, 1572–1577

OECD (1987) The health systems of OECD countries. In Financing and Delivering Health Care. A Comparative Analysis of OECD Countries. OECD, Paris, pp. 24–32

Richards T (1991) Medicine in Europe: 1992 and all that. British Medical Journal, 303, 1319–1322

Smith T (1991) Medicine in Europe, European health challenges. British Medical Journal, 303, 1395–1397

Szyszczak E (1991) *Euroopan Integraatio ja suomen Oikens*, Tampereen Yliopisto Julkisoikeuden Laitos, pp. 103–120
World Health Organization, Regional Office for Europe (1991) *Health for All Policy is Finland*. WHO, ROE Copenhagen (WHO health policy reviews)

Discussion

Wilhelm van Eimeren, *Research Centre for Environment and Health, Neuherberg, Germany*

The introduction of the free flow of goods, labour force, money and services (the four freedoms) in the common market in 1993 and the decisions of Maastricht concerning EC responsibilities in the field of public health will inadvertently lead to a growing influence of the EC on health, health organization and specifically on health-related markets in the member nations. Expectations about the speed and comprehension of such changes vary considerably and are linked with hopes and anxieties.

It is therefore a natural consequence to thoroughly study the perspectives of the EC inner policies in the field of health, and in addition to review the consequencs of the EC foreign politics for the health of non-EC countries, as has been pointed out by Mme Kokkonen.

Though acknowledging the latter issue I will focus in my comments on the inner EC perspectives.

First I want to point out the fact that in the past 20 years—and certainly continuing in the coming decades—there is a strong tendency of convergence of life and lifestyle conditions in the EC. This is reflected in life expectancy, growing percentage of aged people (e.g. beyond 75), in consumption statistics, etc. There is already a rich history of EC-driven harmonization of the exposure to chemicals in food, the workplace and the environment. Though principles of health care organization and financing seemingly were not tampered with by the EC in the past, and will not be dealt with in the foreseeable future, there is a convergence of conditions or similarity of fate in the health care organization of the member nations. Regardless of the differences between tax- or insurance-financed systems, or between public, private or mixed ownership of provider institutions, doctors' incomes in the EC are converging (expressed as a relative difference to each country's average wages) and expenditures for health care seem to relate similarly to the nation's productivity. Most countries experienced only a moderate increase in acute hospital beds and simultaneously a dramatic increase in the number of doctors (mostly related to secondary care). No country is without major changes or reforms of health care financing and/or organization, and, regardless of the differences, similar techniques of cost and quality control have been discussed, experimented with or implemented.

Secondly it is true that a lot of more or less interesting differences still exist between the health care systems of EC member nations, as well as in level, trends in performance, outcome and structures. Not only can this be used—as Prof. McPherson has shown so clearly—to better understand epidemiological and socioeconomic mechanisms, but also we could view our national characteristics as parts of an inner-EC laboratory, where more and more circumstantial conditions are standardized across countries and no longer might contribute to the complexities of study designs or data interpretation. In this context we might rightly expect a strong push for the harmonization of health reporting systems by the EC's execution of the Maastricht mandate.

Third, we should not expect any substantial changes with respect to internationalization of the health care market, specifically regarding labour and services. On one hand certain areas have been harmonized long ago, and will develop further—e.g. the pharmaceutical market by the introduction of a comprehensive European drug market regulation—but on the other hand the long-existing mutual recognition of our medical education and certificates has only led to a few thousand doctors going to work outside their home country. There will be certain impacts on the private health insurance market, but this is of major interest only to those countries where private health insurers cover larger sectors of population and/or health services, as in Germany, The Netherlands and France. In addition some transnational markets will emerge in in-house chronic care, cure and rehabilitation.

Fourth, the EC will continue to exert influence through regulations that are not specifically targeted towards health care, but include it. One example of importance is the pending liability regulations which will put health consumers and providers transnationally under the same rules, meaning that professional medical behaviour will grow more alike by such pressures rather than by any specifically health-oriented European policy. What is new is the inclusion in the Maastricht mandate that any non-health-care-market-oriented activity of the community can, and hopefully will, be analysed regarding its impacts on the health of European citizens. Certainly the hundreds of millions of British pounds that are spent annually to subsidize the production and marketing of European tobacco should be discussed regarding its health impact, as well as the meagre tens of millions of pounds going into European anti-cancer programmes.

Finally, in order to put itself into the position to formulate a European health policy, and to act accordingly, the EC will have to get itself better organized. Up to now health-related EC activities are scattered over nearly all general directorates, with some larger percentage found in DG-V. But when and where the EC will be acting we know from the past: this has not to be confused with much weaker international programmes such as those launched by WHO. EC regulations have to be obeyed and EC recommendations most often find their way into our national settings. We public health scientists have to redefine our role as European. From my point of view this has to be done primarily by jointly studying the performance of our systems and agreeing on achievable goals, rather than on implementations, thus keeping up in reality, and not only in theory, that there is always more than one way to Rome.

Health promotion and disease prevention: the implications for health promotion

Ilona Kickbusch

Lifestyles and Health, Regional Office for Europe, World Health Organization, Copenhagen, Denmark

The challenge: which frontiers?

The theme of this forum is 'Europe without frontiers'. Obviously, the first association with this title is the discussion around the single European market and with European union. Such a discussion is immediately prejudiced because the name 'Europe' is usually applied only to a small group of countries. With the events of the past two years we are forced to reconsider what we mean by the term 'Europe'. The same also applies to the word 'frontiers'. When the American West was being settled there was much talk of the new and last frontiers. When we look towards eastern Europe we can see two new frontiers which are both highly relevant to health promotion.

The West's first impulse is to break down the barriers and rush in and to conquer, using the marketing strategies of major multinational companies through an assault on the lifestyles and the health of eastern Europeans— as the slogan of a cigarette company expresses it; 'Test the West'. At the same time the fear in eastern Europe is that the 'invisible wall', as Vaclav Havel called it, of a 'fortress Europe' will divide the continent along new frontiers that are drawn by poverty. Both these dimensions need all the attention that public health professionals can give—and (it should go without saying, if reality were not so different) all the cooperation and solidarity between countries and agencies that they can muster.

World Health Organization data show a difference in life expectancy between West and East of about seven years. That is the tip of an iceberg. This difference is the consequence not just of individual health behaviours, but of patterns of living and working conditions, environment, culture and political priorities that my co-speaker Peter Makara will take up in more detail. It presents a new challenge to the work of the WHO Regional Office for Europe—where I work as the Director of the Department of 'Lifestyles

Europe Without Frontiers. Edited by C.E.M. Normand and P. Vaughan

and Health'—given that the first and foremost target in our Regional Health Policy document is 'to reduce the differences in health status between countries and between groups within countries by at least 25% by the year 2000, by improving the level of health of disadvantaged nations and groups'.

The WHO strategy: common approaches for Europe

Let me first outline the role and functions of the Regional Office in order to show how health policy developments can cross frontiers.

The World Health Organization is a United Nations agency whose task is to support, develop and coordinate public health measures throughout the world—and I would like to stress that global role. This is laid down in our constitution. At present there are 170 member states. WHO is the only specialized agency of the United Nations to have a regional structure. It has six regional offices, one of which is the Regional Office for Europe in Copenhagen (WHO Europe).

1. *WHO has a role as an innovator*. In this context the greatest achievement has been to establish a consensus on a common European health policy and to have it adopted in 1985. It finds its expression in 38 targets and more than two-thirds of the member states (and there are now 34 in the European Region) have now aligned their health policies with this document. It took five years to establish consensus for this policy, and in many countries it is only now that this alignment is beginning to take effect. Updated targets were accepted by member states in September 1991.

2. *WHO's second role is one of advocacy*. This is a priority task in public health, and it is in keeping with the United Nations' stance on human rights. This enables WHO to call for a reduction in inequities and inequalities in health, not only worldwide but also within individual countries. The WHO priority is to narrow the gulf between those who are able to live long and healthy lives and those who are still not able to do so.

   WHO was the first organization to point out, on the basis of the preparatory work done for the targets, how poor the health status in eastern Europe really was. This was obvious from the available data as far back as 1984/85 and WHO said so bluntly and publicly. Of course advocacy also has a role to play in other areas, for instance the action plans on tobacco, the AIDS programme or the proposed alcohol action plan.

3. *WHO also has a consulting role*. This is particularly in the area of health policy or health infrastructures. WHO's task is to gather together models from all over the world, convert them into strategic information and, if

necessary, use that information to develop action plans. An example of this is our action plan with eastern Europe, called 'Eurohealth', which is firmly based on the bridge-building role. WHO brings together successful models and competent individuals so that they can learn from one another. And I must stress that we do *learn from one another*. Vaclav Havel repeatedly emphasizes that we must get away from the idea that it is only the East which can learn from the West; there is a great deal which the West can learn from the East.

4. *WHO's fourth role concerns activating and networking.* It has found new methods and approaches for converting new thinking into policies which are both practicable and visible: the Healthy Cities project is a key example of this. Together with the CEC and the Council of Europe we have reached European-wide agreement for health promotion in schools, which we hope will also be supported by the OECD and UNESCO. WHO is also developing European training in public health with a group of partners, including ASPHER (Association of Schools of Public Health in the European Region). This networking role offers the ideal conditions for partnerships.

There is no other organization in Europe at present that can combine innovation, advocacy, networking, activation and consulting in this proactive manner. WHO can initiate discussions which are then continued by others. The working methods leave room for a climate which is conducive to open discussion and for cooperation, which otherwise would be more difficult to establish.

A strategy for health promotion

'Lifestyles are patterns of choices made from alternatives that are available to people according to their socio-economic circumstances and to the ease with which they are able to choose certain ones over others' (Milio, 1981). Obviously, a health promotion strategy would aim to understand these patterns and make the healthier choice the easier choice. This is the key message of what has been called the New Public Health.

Most health choices are made in environments that are not conducive to health, but so far most strategies have focused on single issues or on interventions focused on individuals. The simplest examples are those strategies that see smoking or drinking as an individual behaviour, in which the person can decide to stop on his/her own will (just say no) within a social environment that explicitly (social norms, advertising) and implicitly (through accessibility, availability and affordability) encourages people to start and continue smoking.

Given the presence of these contradictions it is astounding how little effort has gone into approaching smoking and drinking as a cultural and social problem, as an accepted term of coping, as normal risk-taking behaviours—and (from a new public health point of view) as an issue that needs political commitment and intervention.

My own favourite example is the building of sewers under the major European cities 100 years ago—public health proponents urged a systematic and 'total' population approach rather than 'boil your water' campaigns. It took 50 years from Snow's investigation of the Soho outbreak of cholera and the Broad Street pump, together with a lot of political lobbying, for this population approach to be accepted. If we want to influence the health of populations today, our commitment must be just as definite and our lobbying just as consistent. However, I have yet to see all the organizations and experts lobby together for support to low-income families, better schools and education, and better housing and working conditions. The usual approach is to fight among ourselves for a greater piece of the health care cake and make do with the crumbs we get. This will not produce any large-scale effects on the population's health.

In contrast to this mode, the WHO launched the Ottawa Charter for Health Promotion in 1986, which explicitly sees health promotion as a social process of empowerment and public responsibility. The Ottawa Charter highlights the:

1. Social determinants of health.
2. Crucial role of social and economic environments that are supportive to health.
3. Process, relationships and systematic influences that create health.

Healthy public policy

Most importantly, in the present climate, the Ottawa Charter focuses on the need for public policies that support health:

> Health promotion goes beyond health care. It puts health on the agenda of policy-makers in all sectors and at all levels, directing them to be aware of the health consequences of their decisions and to accept their responsibilities for health.

Based on knowledge of the factors that constitute health, health promotion debates how we can achieve improvements in health, life expectancy and well-being within a frame of public policy and sustainability. I would like to highlight three policy areas for action that emerge as central to a health strategy:

1. Investment in those sectors and those strategies that produce the largest health gain.

2. A commitment to policies that help reshape public opinion towards major health issues.
3. A commitment to those policies that promote environments that are supportive to health.

Three lead questions must be asked: (a) Where is health created? (b) Which investments produce the largest health gain? (c) Which strategies help to reduce the health gap?

Healthy public policy questions the rationale of many aspects of the present 'health' policies and 'health' expenditures, by highlighting the declining returns to be expected from spending on health care. In most OECD countries the expenditure on non-health care areas of public policies has not kept pace with those on health care, and a fundamental imbalance has been created. Health obviously calls for investments in other sectors as well as in the 'health' sector itself. We need to revisit the birth of public health in the nineteenth century—where the obvious health improvements related to investments in physical infrastructure (housing and sewers) and social infrastructure (access to education; social insurance; social rights of women, workers and children). This link between social reform and health needs has to be re-established as a priority in health strategies, and this approach is crucial to policy options that emerge for central and eastern Europe. The question is where to invest, in view of the limited resources?

To take an example: the developed country with the highest rate of drug abuse and of HIV/AIDS invests twice as much in the medical care sector as in education—one in every five inhabitants of this country is functionally illiterate. Obviously, this relates to the fact that the medical care system has power to induce demand, contrary to the providers and receivers (teachers and students) in the education section and child care sector. In some of the richest countries in the world we are presently witnessing the paradox that the investment in health care itself becomes counterproductive for a society, since it draws resources from other sectors and other investments that would be badly needed in the context of social health strategy.

Integrated action

WHO, at a large conference in Bonn in December 1990, began to set the *Investment in Health Agenda*, and will continue this approach systematically over the next two years in a special 'investment in health' project that focuses on policies. For example, the health policy issues that emerge most consistently with regard to addictions are:

1. Family support, particularly for low-income families.

2. Education and programmes for young people.
3. Price policy that restricts access to addictive substances by young people.
4. Taxation policies that provide the resources for health promotion programmes.

Such a strategy needs to be supported by strong cultural norms that make it inappropriate to engage in certain behaviours (i.e. no smoking in public places), reduces access to alcohol and tobacco (i.e. not in every supermarket) and that there should be a strong disassociation of certain behaviours and situations (i.e. drinking and driving, and drinking and working).

It is interesting that while the multinational companies clearly use the same images around the world, the different national campaigns around the world have not been able to pool their resources. This would be an interesting challenge for the future that WHO will be exploring in Europe. We need new forms of media advocacy in order to keep up a constant public debate about what creates health and well-being, to put public pressure on political decision-makers, and to inform the community and create social pressure for health action.

In the face of this knowledge we cannot just wait for government action. Already trade unions, employers, large sickness funds and insurance companies have become active. Through an implementation strategy WHO has begun to work with a series of European-wide projects which are based in the context of social environments. 'Investment in health' becomes an issue about developing strategies that work with people in the settings of their everyday lives and as defined in the Ottawa Charter: 'enable [them] to increase control over, and to improve, their health'. This totally changes the functions and approaches of what we have called public health—it definitely takes public health outside what is presently called the 'public health infrastructure' and gets involved with those settings and actors that can influence the creation of health. These projects are called: Healthy Cities, Health Promotion Schools, Health Promotion Hospitals, and Health Promotion Companies.

'Settings for health' projects

These projects function within the overall Health for All (HFA) framework, and the 38 European HFA targets for the European Regions, which constitute a commitment to a social health strategy. More recently we have witnessed an increasing interest in HFA policy development at the subnational level, along the lines of 'healthy regions' projects. There is a network of several hundred cities developing the health agenda and we are piloting the school project in three countries. About 30 hospitals are embarking on the hospitals project—based on a two-year pilot project in Vienna. This means that we are working with a multitude of partners, for example: local politicians, representatives of trade unions, ecologists, large companies, hospital administrators, sickness funds.

The challenge is how can we transform a setting that 'constrains' health to one that 'enables' health. Most importantly, it puts health decisions in the hands of the actors in that setting, not the health promotion professionals. This can be done only through a process of organizational development within the setting, combining both a top-down and a bottom-up approach. This takes time and timing: some of our cities have taken nearly five years to establish functioning mechanisms for intersectoral work.

The programmes adhere to the following strategic guidelines for implementing a social model of health:

1. Build strategies that commence from or fully integrate the social context: aim to create supportive environments for health.
2. Build strategies that allow for social involvement and commitment, allow for social support, and help develop a sense of coherence.
3. Build strategies that allow for the development of self-esteem and sense of control and expand personal skills and explore meaning.
4. Build strategies that are explicitly linked to other social policy agendas and open the debate on investment in health and move out of the narrow 'health' field and infrastructure.
5. Build strategies that allow for pride and a sense of achievement—allow for the fact that health is not necessarily people's main aim in life.

This calls for a serious discussion on policy priorities which differentiates between social strategies *that improve health* and the expansion of health care. And this means that health promotion strategies must place themselves firmly within the first objective, and concentrate effort on shifting the public policy debate from health care to health. Only then can intersectorality truly function.

We know enough about the social determinants of health to take action— let us aim to make environments and life patterns more conducive to health and move public health back into the social policy arena, and see ourselves as advocates for a new type of health policy that focuses on health.

That truly is a key frontier that we all must cross.

References

Adelaide Recommendations: healthy public policy (1988) *Health Promotion*, 3 (2), 183–186

Badura B and Kickbusch I (eds) (1992) *The New Social Epidemiology*. WHO Regional Office for Europe, Copenhagen

Evans R and Stoddart G (1990) Producing health, consuming health care. *Social Science and Medicine*, *31*, 1347–1363

Green L and Raeburn J (1988) Health promotion—what is it? What will it become? *Health Promotion*, *3*, 151–159

Kickbusch I (1989) Good planets are hard to find. *WHO Healthy Cities Papers*, No. 5. FADL, Copenhagen.

Machnes Y (1990) Health and the allocation of public expenditure. *Health Policy*, *16*, 27–31

Milio N (1981) *Promoting Health through Public Policy*. FA Davis, Philadelphia

Ottawa Charter for Health Promotion (1986) *Health Promotion*, *1* (4), iii–v

Schieber G and Poullier JP (1991) International health spending: issues and trends. *Health Affairs*, Spring 1991

Sundsvall Statement on Supportive Environments (1992) WHO/HED/92.1, Geneva

Discussion

Péter Makara, *National Institute for Health Promotion, Budapest, Hungary*

Health promotion is, on one hand, as old as human medical thinking, if we take into account the holistic understanding of old Chinese medicine. On the other hand it is as young as a child. Ilona Kickbusch has an outstanding part in her role in developing modern health promotion ideas, implementation and practice.

I would like to start by discussing the terminology of the meeting. The London School of Hygiene and Tropical Medicine suggests the terminology of 'Europe without frontiers'. We have to think about whether this is a real description of the situation or just a dream. In social and historical sciences the centre–periphery dilemma is well known. Two thousand years ago Rome was the centre of Europe, Britannia the periphery. Since the sixteenth century western Europe has been the centre of Europe and the East the periphery, but this process took 400 years. This division of Europe is not the product of this century alone.

Yesterday we discussed the relationship between government and non-government types of organization in Europe. It is not only an East–West difference, but also a difference in historical and political traditions—a task which is carried out by a non-governmental organization (NGO) in the UK may be the responsibility of a public body in the very centralized French political system. In central and eastern Europe there are very important historical differences and sometimes we become frustrated by being lumped together. The former Soviet territories had 70 years, and other parts of central and eastern Europe 45 years of communist rule, which reduced the efficiency of health care provisions, and prevented innovation and voluntary action.

Individual lifestyles also have very deep historical roots, in particular patterns of alcohol consumption, sexual behaviour and eating habits have surprisingly long historical roots which make them difficult to change. It must also be realized that the role of the centralized state organization has very deep roots in the health field as well as others. There is a very strong scientific need for further research to improve our understanding of factors influencing behaviour and changes in behaviour.

Concerning health promotion in central and eastern European countries, we start with deteriorating trends in mortality from non-communicable diseases and in risk factors. But we have no real scientific in-depth explanation of this phenomenon. There have been investigations in cardiovascular epidemiology of the effects of cholesterol and blood pressure. The impact of the political system cannot be easily converted into the language of classical individually based epidemiology. There is a need for theoretical and empirical development of multi-level analysis, explaining the impact of macro-social factors on individual health or the modern understanding of the concept of health. There is a need for international cooperation to help to explain the effects on these countries. Waking up from communism is a real hangover feeling.

For very understandable reasons, health is on the periphery of the political decision system in central and eastern Europe. Public health and health promotion is on the periphery of the health sector. So we are on the periphery of the periphery! And that is our brilliant future. There are well-known difficulties of economic and social crisis, and great uncertainty. Our only certainty is uncertainty. There is a lot of stress and very limited skill of coping with stress. But there are some positive signs, one of which is the increasing importance of NGOs, community action and voluntary association in our society. However, I think we need to get organized, but not by importing western organization into our country. European standards are extremely important for advocating laws and policy developments. EC legislation can have a large impact on central and eastern Europe.

We have to learn to avoid the three main problems in health promotion in our countries, which are wishful thinking, patronizing attitudes and victim blaming. I would like to outline three key areas for the future of health promotion. First the equity issue. It is better not to speak about a Europe without frontiers. At least we have to avoid an increasing gap between countries and the development of a two-tier Europe. There is a controversial relationship between the effectiveness of health promotion and equity of health, because most of the tools of health promotion are effectively upper middle class. We have to face health dilemmas that are linked with poverty and deprivation, ethnic minorities like gypsies, unemployment, migration and also in sections of society where self-organizing capacity is very weak.

These are the new challenges. We have to learn from western experiences, and to adapt rather than adopt them.

We must push towards new ways of thinking in public health, towards a new public health strategy where the best setting may be a park or a street. This shows a clear need for intersectoral cooperation in our situation, within the framework of an integrated social and health policy. In Hungary in the Ministry of Welfare social policy and health policy are in the same building, but with no sign of dialogue. The second issue is linked to demography. We have to learn to work with people and not for people. It is a quite different way of thinking. There are new players in public health in Hungary. There are the old brontosaurus-like government national health service organizations, services of local government, which in Hungary are controlled by opposition parties, and the increasing role of NGOs. We have to learn to bargain, advocate and mediate for health, and take steps to empower people. We have to learn to build new alliances with green movements, which may be the best partners in this field. Accountability is important. If you are poor you have to be careful with your money. We have to persuade people that health is a good investment. We have to persuade people of the importance of planning. It is a paradox that we have lived in so-called planned economies for 40 years, but no-one had any idea about real health planning.

We have to strengthen evaluation, and in this field western help will be extremely important. We have to think more and more about cost-effectiveness of health promotion. We are sure that health promotion is at best very cost-effective, and this may be the best basis for arguing with governments. We need a European support system, and to identify the best ways of providing support and training. In the field of health promotion the cooperation in Europe is very good. WHO is playing an extremely efficient role. 'Settings' approaches are very welcome in central and eastern Europe because this is something positive, not based on 'do not do this' types of argument. It is nice to deal with children, cities and villages. We need to think of new forms of mutual learning with our western colleagues.

The year 1992 is the year of the environment, but also of Christopher Columbus. Some people say that health promotion in central and eastern Europe is a Columbus-like enterprise. Columbus never exactly defined where he was, and during his life never understood fully what he had done, but was always travelling on other people's money. This is not really applicable to us. We have to work with our problems, but our task I think is to work with faith but not illusions.

Health divergence during political division: East and West Germany— 'socioeconomic factors in health'

Lenore Kohlmeier

Institute for Social Medicine and Epidemiology, Federal Health Office, Berlin, Germany

You have entitled this meeting 'Europe without frontiers', referring in part to the loss of borders due to the completion of a common market at the end of the year, and probably in part referring to the melting of the iron curtain separating eastern and western Europe. Under the definition of a frontier as the part of a country bordering on another, we have, particularly in Germany, dropped a frontier. The frontier was the term used to indicate dead man's zone along the wall in West Germany, which has now just become a tourist curiosity.

According to a dictionary (Webster, 1983) however, a frontier is also 'any new or incompletely investigated field of learning'. From this perspective, speaking as an epidemiologist, we still face many frontiers of investigation. The loss of political borders, or their increase, as in the case of the former Soviet Union, has only confronted us with how incompletely we have investigated the health differences between East and West.

Unfortunately, few objective indicators of health status are available with which comparisons can be made. Quality of life has been generally overlooked in international comparisons (Lundberg, 1986). Length of life has been the scoreboard on which the winners and losers were measured, for what could be more important than negative trends in the development of total premature mortality? The greater life expectancy was in West Germany (WHO, 1991). A closer look at the differences in disease risk in both sides of the country, and their development over time, might shed light on possible causal factors.

At the Federal health office our concern is health of the nation; a nation whose identity has recently changed. This separation is comparable with the stories of maternal twins separated in youth and then rejoined by common will after adulthood. The health of these two adults, and their current and

Europe Without Frontiers. Edited by C.E.M. Normand and P. Vaughan
© 1993 John Wiley & Sons Ltd

future offspring, is of primary concern, the extent of social inequities an issue of political importance.

A brief history

With the political division of the country in 1948 and its physical division in 1961 a cruel experiment took place in Germany. Families were separated, but not as in the civil war, because of different beliefs. This separation was random, a throw of the dice.

Information was not openly circulated in the former East Germany. The news and press were controlled and censored, foreign newspapers were confiscated. It was illegal to watch television transmitted from the West. The open exchange of ideas, experiences and knowledge was extremely limited in a country in which the population on the whole, however, was relatively well-to-do. The attempt to indoctrinate to the belief that their system was the best and fairest lasted 40 years. Nine million East Germans were born and brought up into this system, another seven million lived with it for most of their adulthood.

It was a surprise to all when suddenly on 11 November 1989 the radio reports came that East Germans were being allowed to cross the Berlin wall at some of the checkpoints. It was a time of great joy, of a warm and open heartfelt welcome. We in the West thought the nightmare was over, the family reunited after the years held hostage; that healing would take place immediately and everything would be better for everyone. In the East they thought they would be welcomed as equals and live as West Germans in the immediate future. This has not been the case, and things are getting worse.

What one sees now is a new social structure; and with it a new language: the 'Ossies', the 'Besserwessies', and the 'Wossies'.* People from the East (Ossies) are being treated as second class citizens by the western Germans (Besserwessies). They are paid less for the same work, they are discriminated against in job competition, they have lost control of much of the industry located in their part of the country, and derogative regional stereotypes have developed. The stereotype is that Ossies are slow in learning western ways, they do not work hard enough, they have not enough initiative, do not show the ambition and drive expected of them. They do not take enough responsibility for tasks; waiting for someone else to bring them all the required tools and information to get the job done. The Besserwessies are considered arrogant and intolerant, taking their financial and employment security for granted.

---

* The term used for West Germans who are working in the East.

Eruptions of violence, pent-up anger in the East being vented against foreigners, groups of neo-nazis shocking the population, crime in general is on the rise. The acute social and economic situation can best be described as turbulent: fascinating to watch, a nightmare for a scientist to try to analyse and determine the critical factors with the hope of improving future trends.

No-one can foresee the future, we can only describe and analyse the past; and these analyses contain some surprises which are causing a rethinking of our assumptions. The patterns of disease, and the exposures influencing them, are the fields to be harvested by epidemiologists. The bias is that the West was a healthier, happier place to be.

It is now time to address the questions of who was and is healthier, what were the main factors influencing changes in the health status of the population, whether point comparisons are valid, and what developments can now be expected.

How fast did changes occur?

Life expectancies in both parts of Germany were reported to have scissored apart in the 1970s so that West Germans enjoyed almost three more years of life than their former countrymen living in the East. This large difference implied that at least some if not all important risks were lower. Didn't this prove that life was better in the West? For many years this information was used to prove that point. A closer examination of the trends, however, reveals some disturbing inconsistencies.

Mortality is a crude indicator of health. It is, however, one the most comparable measures available. Following the hypothesis that the differences in life expectancy are a result of the separation, one would have expected that age-standardized mortality was roughly equal in the 1950s or 1961, when the wall was built, at the latest. After a specific time lag one would expect improvements in the West German life expectancy which surpassed those in the East.

A look at the main causes of death among 60-year-olds, as a vulnerable group, whose deaths, however, can be considered largely premature, shows a different picture (Junge and Hoffmeister, 1992). Heart disease was actually lower in the East until 1985 among 69-year-old men, at which time a major trend change occurred in the West (Figure 1). This looks more like an effect of improved treatment, perhaps the initiation of lysis therapy, than a long-term prevention difference. East German women showed an increase in 1968 after the eighth revision of the international classification of diseases (Bundesminister, 1979) and maintained this new level with a slight decrease in trend over the following 25 years. This trend paralleled that in West German women until the figures showed a drop, as with the men in 1986.

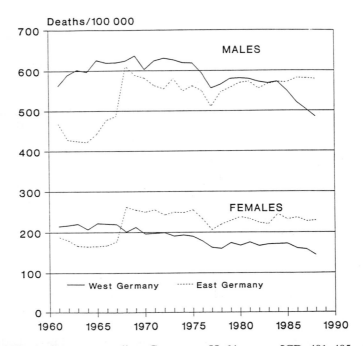

Figure 1 Heart disease mortality, Germany, 55–64 years; ICD 401–405, 410–414, 415–417, 420–429 (from department of Epidemiology, BGA, Berlin, with permission)

Liver cirrhosis deaths were greater in the West (Figure 2). The rates scissored apart after the separation, and bowed back together in the last decade. Unfavourable developments in the consumption of alcohol in the West are reflected in this disease profile.

Colon cancer shows a similar trend, with greater increases in both men and women in the West since the separation (Figure 3). Rectal cancer deaths, in contrast, are considerably lower in West Germans, and have been increasingly so since 1974, when a trend reversal occurred.

Stomach cancer death rates have been higher in the East for the past 30 years in both men and women (Figure 4), most probably reflecting the extent of refrigeration of food and the commonly used preservation methods.

Breast cancer has been consistently high in the West, with parallel increases in both sets of 60-year-old women. Part of this difference in incidence rates is due to differing age at first birth. Differences in mortality rates remain unexplained.

In all, the rates of death from a number of nutritionally related cancers were lower in the East. These include cancers of the tongue, lip and oral cavity, the oesophagus, colon and breast. The age-standardized incidence

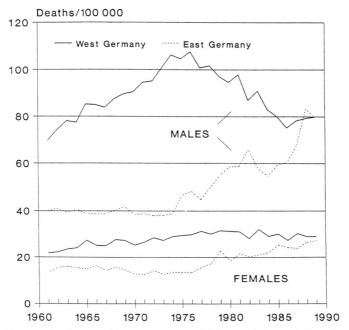

Figure 2 Liver cirrhosis mortality, Germany, 55–64 years; ICD 571 (from Department of Epidemiology, BGA, Berlin, with permission)

rates (world population distribution) were also lower in the East German cancer registers as compared with the only complete register in West Germany, that of Saarland (Schön *et al.*, 1989). Table 1 shows a 30–180% greater risk for cancer of the tongue, lip, oral cavity, pharynx (as a group), oesophagus and colon (Kohlmeier and Dortschy, 1991). The risk of breast cancer is 15% greater in the West, and the risk of cancers of all sites is 22% greater in men from the West as compared with those from the East in 1985–1987. This is in contradiction to the expectations that, because of a diet lower in fresh fruits and vegetables, and higher in saturated fats, as well as a higher level of environmental pollution, the rates should be higher.

Are the differences seen today due to diet?

There was hunger in both parts of Germany after the Second World War. Food rationing was in effect in the West until April 1950. At that time 50% of income was spent on food, as compared with 17% in 1990. In the western part of Germany the pendulum swung from hunger to excess in the early 1960s. Since 1965 the per-capita consumption trends indicate that 26%

Figure 3 Colon cancer mortality, Germany, 55–64 years, Females; ICD 152, 153 (from Department of Epidemiology, BGA, Berlin, with permission)

increases in fat intake, 20% in sugar, 29% in cholesterol consumption and 15% increases in alcohol intake have occurred (Kübler, 1988).

During the same time period, food availability and trends in consumption were quite different in East Germany, and all eastern European countries (Kohlmeier, 1991). The indicators of well-being were meat and butter availability (Ulbricht, 1991). The development of per capita intakes of meat and meat products over the past 30 years in both countries shows that the levels in the West were considerably higher until 1965, after which the average availability in the East increased so that, in 1989, 20 kilograms more were reported consumed by East Germans (Figure 5). Although there is reason to believe that figures reported to the FAO were exaggerated, the diet was clearly increasingly rich in high-fat beef and pork, and remained poor in the variety of fruits and vegetables available, the seasonal availability of foods was stronger, and the range of other food products was much more limited (Ulbricht, 1991).

If one takes a look at the risks of premature death of West and East German women it is evident that most of the major risks of death are due to nutritionally related diseases (Figure 6). Currently breast cancer is the

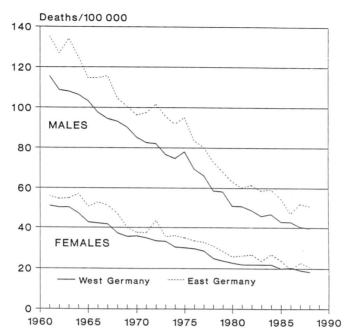

Figure 4 Stomach cancer mortality, Germany, 55–64 years; ICD 151 (from Department of Epidemiology, BGA, Berlin, with permission)

major threat for 50-year-old women from both sides of the country. Ischaemic heart disease is the second greatest problem. All of the top five causes of premature death in men and women are nutritionally related, and seven of the top eight causes are also nutritionally related. Furthermore, the rates of most of these diseases differ substantially between the two sides of the country. Still unexplained remains the degree to which these rates are due to dietary behaviour and the extent to which differences in rates are attributable to differences in food consumption patterns.

No representative information on the changes in dietary behaviour exists in the new German states. Aside from an ongoing representative survey, which will assess current disease prevalence and disease risk status as well as former dietary behaviour in 2000 adults in the new states, only sporadic results on selected individuals in specific regions have been conducted. The results of one of these is that self-reported changes in food consumption of large dimension have taken place. From a survey conducted in Potsdam in 1991 (Ulbricht *et al.*, 1991) it is seen that the largest changes are in the increased consumption of yoghurts and milk products; 88% of those interviewed report increased consumption. Tropical fruit consumption

Table 1 Age-standardized death rates* in the Union Republics according to sex (1970–1987)

Republic	1970–1971		1980–1981		1986–1987		Change 1970/1971–1986/1987	
	Males	Females	Males	Females	Males	Females	Males	Females
Russia	14.6	7.5	14.9	7.6	12.8	7.1	–	–
Ukraine	11.8	7.1	13.1	7.3	12.1	7.1	+	0
Byelorussia	9.9	6.3	12.1	6.6	11.9	6.9	+	+
Uzbekistan	8.6	5.8	11.9	7.8	11.4	7.9	+	+
Kazakhstan	11.5	6.2	13.8	8.1	12.2	6.9	+	+
Georgia	10.4	6.6	11.4	6.8	10.9	6.6	+	0
Azerbaijan	10.7	6.9	12.4	7.6	12.1	7.4	+	+
Lithuania	10.7	6.6	12.0	6.7	11.3	6.5	+	–
Moldavia	11.6	8.3	14.0	9.7	13.0	9.1	+	+
Latvia	12.3	7.3	13.7	7.5	12.7	7.5	+	+
Kirghizia	11.4	7.0	13.6	8.0	12.1	7.6	+	+
Tadjikistan	8.5	6.7	11.2	8.3	9.8	7.3	+	+
Armenia	8.6	5.8	9.0	5.8	9.1	6.0	+	+
Turkmenistan	10.4	7.2	14.2	9.4	13.3	9.6	+	+
Estonia	12.4	7.3	13.7	7.6	12.6	7.4	+	+

* Based on the 1979 USSR population age-structure, derived from *Population of the USSR*, 1987, pp. 326–341 (forthcoming).

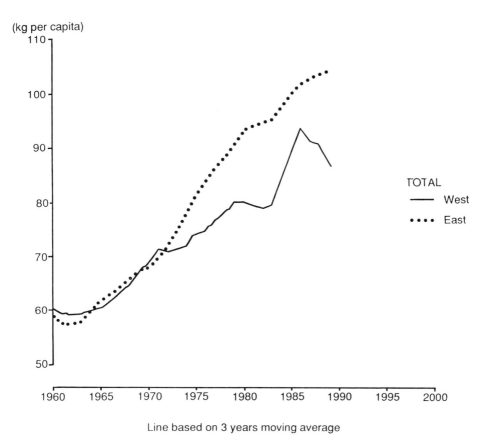

Line based on 3 years moving average

Figure 5 Red meat consumption in Germany

increased in 97% of the subjects, as did the intakes of alcoholic beverages (68%). Major switches from butter to margarine have been noted, and from white bread consumption to the use of breakfast cereals (Figure 7). Taste has been reported as the main reason for these changes, although health was given a high ranking in conjunction with the margarine and muesli increases.

The difficulty in studying the influence of diet lies in the time lag between food intake and its measurable effect on disease development. It is not only the intakes at the end of the division which are of interest, but also the time period in which changes occurred and how rapidly they occurred (Kohlmeier and Helsing, 1989). A more favourable health profile in 1989 may reflect the health environment in the 1970s, and give no indication of the trends to be expected as a result of diet and other conditions in the

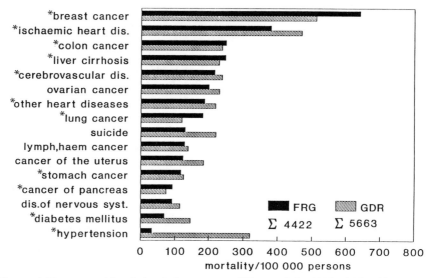

Figure 6 Ten-year risk of death for women (50 years) in 1989. * Nutrition related diseases

1980s. In other words, diets improved more rapidly in the West since the 1950s, but so did the intakes of saturated fats. Therefore the cancer rates may have increased earlier in the West than in the East. The later development of affluence may lead to continuing increases in the coming years due to past exposures. It may, however, also be that the society in the East, with all its flaws, may have been more supportive of the health of the individual.

More supportive environments in the East?

Supportive environments have become a theme of the WHO in Europe (WHO/UNEP, 1991). Environment is now being understood in the context of housing, transportation, education and food, not just in a chemical context. It can be proposed that, despite widespread news reports on secret police activities in the East, eastern Germany provided a more supportive environment than in the West. The workplace, medical services, and health insurance company (instead of 1107 as in the West) radiated an environment of protection and safety.

There was no concern about finding a job in East Germany, and no concern about becoming unemployed. The company would employ individuals and send them to school, maintaining a guaranteed workplace and paying the costs during his or her studies. The company was also involved in the

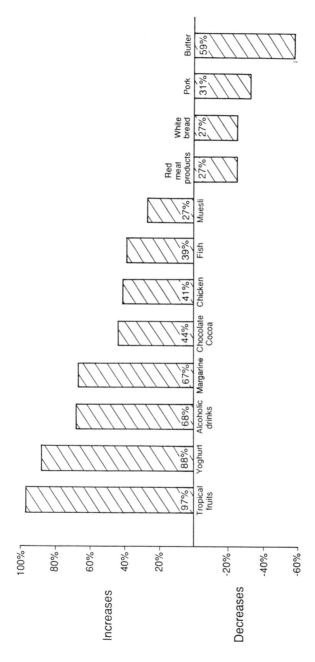

Figure 7 Reported change in consumption of specific foods in Potsdam after 1989

evaluation of apprenticeships and practical work conducted as part of the studies. The social network was much tighter than it is now.

Children were vaccinated more thoroughly in the East (Wiesner, 1991). It was not left to the initiative of the parents to know and arrange vaccinations. All children were followed medically with coordinated records, and families were reminded of vaccination appointments. Our East German neighbour never saw people sleeping on the street before the wall fell. Older persons did not fear being mugged on the street or in their own apartment houses. From many points of view the environment has become much less supportive for the individual, more supportive of productivity.

Although the field of research examining the role of social support on mortality is relatively young, a number of cohort studies have shown relationships between social support, social isolation and the risk of disease (Berkman, 1986). And risk status within a society has been closely related to social status, even in wealthy societies in which all individuals have access to the basic necessities; food, clothing and housing (Marmot *et al.*, 1987). It is argued that social gaps within societies are widening (Parmuk, 1985). Within the former West Germany, strong relationships have been reported between social status and cardiovascular risk factors (Hoffmeister *et al.*, 1992). It can therefore be expected that differences between systems contribute to differences in risk.

Another aspect which now plays an important role is that of change. Abrupt change occurred, and change itself can carry insecurity and fear. The fear of the unknown, fear of unemployment, fear of not being able to handle the new demands of a more complex society, and fear of violence and homelessness are new developments affecting the current psychological health of the population. Statistics show that former East Germans are going less often to physicians than they formerly did. They are also less frequently absent from work because of illness than they were. Is this a sign of improved health? Or is it because of fear, fear of losing their jobs? Job insecurity, after being brought up in a system which provided employment to everyone, is a source of unmeasurable anxiety.

The study of effects of fear and psychological stress on health is advancing through research on the effects of different social conditions on the immune system. Cancers and infectious diseases distinguish themselves from other prevalent diseases in that they are caused or initiated by substances foreign to the individual. The immune system's sole purpose is to identify and reject material foreign to the self. Although this system has been traditionally divided into cellular and humoral immunity and phagocytosis, the close interrelationship between these subdivisions is being increasingly recognised (Calabrese *et al.*, 1987). The level of T lymphocytes is taken as one of many measures of immune capacity. T cells mediate cellular immunity by acting on invading antigens. Both helper T lymphocytes and suppressor T cells have been shown to respond to examination stress (Kiecolt-Glaser *et al.*, 1986), bereavement (Bartrop *et al.*, 1977) and other dysphoric states. Lower helper to suppressor T cell ratios have been found in married men reporting a poorer marital quality (Kiecolt-Glaser *et al.*, 1988), and in divorced women showing continued attachments to their ex-husbands (Kiecolt-Glaser *et al.*, 1987). These and other findings provide evidence of a complex interrelationship which may well result in altered susceptibility to certain diseases under more dysphoric conditions (Kaplan, 1991).

Perhaps, from a medical point of view, prevention of disease was better in the East: through societal support, financial support, vaccination programmes, and an easily accessible health care system. In the West curative medicine, expensive and glamorous high-tech. diagnostics and treatment were better. More pharmaceuticals were available. In general treatment was more strongly supported, and maybe our economic forces drive us in this direction, to develop the expensive and neglect the basics from which little direct profit can be made. Society in East Germany may well have been more preventive in a number of ways.

Paradise lost? There is a large portion of former East German society which wishes for the old GDR with a few adaptations: they say they want the societal and ideological structure of East Germany without the Berlin wall, and with the purchasing power and options of the West and the ability to travel world-wide. Would they have been healthier without the change? Time will tell, if we install the appropriate instruments to measure change. Otherwise the knowledge of whether we are moving in a better direction, and if any advances are due to the 'system', and would not have been even more advantageous under the 'extinct' social system, will remain unanswered.

Conclusions

Undoubtedly this natural experiment provides a unique opportunity to address the questions of how strongly social environment and lifestyles in well-to-do countries affect the risk of death from specific diseases. Analysis of these developments requires the consideration of a number of constraints and potential confounding factors; these include:

1. Critical evaluation of the comparability of the historical health data produced in both countries during the past 30 years is required, as well as estimations of the extent to which biases may affect the comparisons of trends.
2. The dynamic nature of this time period, from hunger, poverty and rebuilding after the war, to wealth and excesses in the last decades, occurred with different rates and to different extents in both countries. Comparisons need to carefully consider the different timing in both countries.

3. The diseases of interest develop with long time lags between exposures and disease diagnosis or death. The influences have differing time lags. Therefore the effects of recent exposures have not yet been seen. Only under the weak assumption of steady state can conclusions about recent differences based on current health data be made.
4. The effects of radical change, independent of direction, can have a profound influence on health. These more recent changes may well interfere with health statistics in such a fashion that prior and current influences cannot be separated.

The indication that cancers of many types occurred less frequently in the East needs to be critically evaluated. If, however, time is lost until confirmation, the ability to examine causality through documentation of prior lifestyles may be lost.

References

Bartrop RW, Luckhurst E, Lazarus L et al. (1977) Depressed lymphocyte function after bereavement. *Lancet, 1*, 834–836

Berkman LF (1986) Reviews and commentary, social networks, support, and health: taking the next step forward. *American Journal of Epidemiology, 123*, 559–562

Bundesminister für Jugend, Familie und Gesundheit (eds) (1979) *Internationale Klassifikation der Krankheiten (ICD)*. Deutscher Consulting-Verlag GmbH, 9. Revision, Band 1

Calabrese JR, Kling MAF and Gold PW (1987) Alterations in immunocompetence during stress, bereavement, and depression: Focus on neuroendocrine regulation. *American Journal of Psychiatry, 144*, 9

Hoffmeister H, Hüttner H, Lopez H et al. (1992) *Sozialer Status und Gesundheit (Nationaler Gesundheits-Survey 1984–1986)*. BGA-Schriften 2

Junge B and Hoffmeister H (1992) *Mortalität an ernährungsabhängigen Krankheiten. Ernährungsbericht 1992*. Deutsche Gesellschaft für Ernährung e.V., Frankfurt a.M.

Kaplan HB (1991) Social psychology of the immune system: a conceptual framework and review of the literature. *Social Science and Medicine, 33* (8), 909–923

Kiecolt-Glaser JK, Fisher LD, Ogrocki P et al. (1987) Marital quality, marital disruption, and immune function. *Psychosomatic Medicine, 49*, 13–34

Kiecolt-Glaser JK, Glaser R, Strain E et al. (1986) Modulation of cellular immunity in medical students. *Journal of Behavioural Medicine, 9*, 5–21

Kiecolt-Glaser JK, Kennedy S, Malkoff S, Fisher L, Speicher CE and Glaser R (1988) Marital discord and immunity in males. *Psychosomatic Medicine, 50*, 213–229

Kohlmeier L (1991) Food patterns and health problems: central Europe. *Annals of Nutrition and Metabolism, 35* (suppl. 1), 22–31

Kohlmeier L and Dortschy R (1991) Diet and disease in East and West Germany. *Proceedings of the Nutrition Society, 50*, 67–75

Kohlmeier L and Helsing E (1989) Epidemiology nutrition and health. *Proceedings of the 1st Berlin Meeting on Nutritional Epidemiology*. Smith–Gordon, London, pp. 9–106

Kübler W (1988) *Entwicklung der Ernährungssituation in der Bundesrepublik Deutschland. Ernährungsbericht 1988*. Deutsche Gesellschaft für Ernährung e.V., Frankfurt a.m., pp. 15–25

Lundberg O (1986) Class and health: comparing Britain and Sweden. *Social Science and Medicine*, 23 (5), 511–517

Marmot MG, Kogevinas M and Elston MA (1987) Social/economic status and disease. *Annual Review of Public Health*, 8, 111–135

Pamuk E (1985) Social class inequality in mortality from 1921 to 1972 in England and Wales. *Population Studies*, 39, 17–31

Schön D, Bertz J and Hoffmeister H (1989) Bevölkerungsbezogene Krebsregister in der Bundesrepublik Deutschland Band 2. *MMV Medizin Verlag München*, 4/89 bga Schriften

Ulbricht G (1991) Ernährung und agrare Veredlungswirtschaft in der frühen DDR. *Agrarwirtschaft, 40* (5), 134–138

Ulbricht G, Friebe D and Bergmann M (1991) Änderungen im Verbraucherverhalten in den neuen Bundesländern/Erste Ergebnisse einer Studie in Potsdam. *AID-Verbraucherdienst, 36*, 235–240

Webster N (1983) *Webster's New Twentieth Century Dictionary of the English Language*, unabridged 2nd edn. Simon & Schuster, New York.

Wiesner GE (1991) Zur Gesundheitslage der Bevölkerung in den neuen Bundesländern. *MMV Medizin Verlag München*, 4/91 bga Schriften

World Health Organization (1991) *World Health Statistics Annual*. WHO, Geneva

World Health Organization/UNEP (1991) *Sundsvall Statement on Supportive Environments*. WHO Regional Office for Europe, Copenhagen

Discussion

Denny H. Vågerö, *Stockholm University, Sweden*

I would like to comment on Dr Kohlmeier's paper, and secondly to try to put it into the general context of East–West European comparisons.

The aim of the paper is to demonstrate how the two different political systems have led to differences in their people's health. Comparisons are made between East and West Germany with regard to the incidence and mortality of a number of diseases and, if differences are found, these are seen as support for the thesis that the separation of the two Germanies led to differences in health.

There are a number of interesting comparisons made. Each one of these merits attention in its own right. We find, for instance, that lung cancer rates are higher among East German than West German men, but for East German women they are lower than those in the West. East German women also have lower breast cancer rates, and this results in an overall cancer mortality which is lower. However, heart disease mortality is higher amongst East German women, as it is also in East German men.

My first question is how do we regard all these comparisons? Should we look for a specific set of risk factors and try to find a specific explanation for each of them? That seems to be the safest and most traditional epidemiological course of action. I have nothing against this.

Or should we look for more 'global' explanations which could help us understand the most important diseases. The rationale for doing this is the hypothesis that several explanations have more to do with the differentially developing social systems of East and West Germany from the 1950s until 1989. If the political and social systems of the two Germanies penetrated all aspects of human life, as well as the ecological system, there is justification for such 'global' comparisons and explanations.

Some environmental components or socially influenced behaviours are common to several different groups of diseases. Dr Kohlmeier in her presentation has suggested (a) nutritional factors and (b) social support. There is clear evidence that nutritional exposures, food supply and food habits changed in different ways in the two Germanies. This means that one could make a case for nutritional exposures being an underlying cause of, for instance, health differences in cardiovascular disease.

Social support, I believe, has been shown to be linked to mortality. The evidence for social support being different between the two Germanies is perhaps not very strong. It seems to be anecdotal, based on impressions rather than more rigorous documentation. However, it has been suggested by other researchers as being important in this context, for instance by Clyde Hertzman (personal communication) in studying mortality in Czechoslovakia. We would expect social support primarily to be important for cardiovascular disease where, as far as I am aware, there is the strongest evidence.

The hypothesis presented by this paper, as I see it, is this: the split of post-war Germany into East and West also led to differences in (a) food supply, and food, drinking and smoking habits; and (b) in social relations and social support, in such a way that they resulted in differences of life expectancy and specific cause mortality. If this is the case it obviously has implications for comparisons between eastern and western Europe as well.

Let us now look at the evidence and some problems inherent in Dr Kohlmeier's paper.

One of the graphs that was presented by Dr Kohlmeier showed trends in heart disease. At the beginning of the period in 1960, both men and women in East Germany had lower heart disease rates. The rate was slightly lower among women and slightly higher among men. I do not believe that this tells us much about the situation at that point in time. We cannot draw the conclusion from that single point in time that there was a more socially supportive environment in East Germany than in West Germany around 1960. We do not know what other important influences existed at that time. The 65-year-old men that were compared would have been born before the turn of the century and already would have had a long life before 1960 of which we know nothing, except for one thing: those lives had already experienced a number of events and exposures that would have, to a degree, determined the mortality that we observe for 1960.

A point comparison of this kind is certainly difficult and probably impossible. Trend comparisons are better. The trend from 1960 to 1990 demonstrates a reversal in the ranking between East and West Germany. East Germany is doing progressively worse. You could argue that this has something to do with the two political systems, and changes that take place influenced by these systems, such as, perhaps, the level of social support and social competitiveness. You have to base your arguments on trends rather than on any specific point in time.

Dr Kohlmeier also pointed out that there was a revision of the ICD classification in 1968. The leap we have on the curve may be due to diagnostic change. It would be advisable to look not only at heart disease but also at total mortality. Dr Niehoff of the Humboldt University in Berlin has demonstrated that life expectancy at birth was in fact higher in East Germany in 1970, but during the 1970s this advantage was lost, and by 1988 life expectancy at birth was better in West than East Germany (Figure 1). This is partly due to infant mortality trends, as the better East German record up to 1979 became worse after that point in time. However, comparisons of life expectancy at age 65 again demonstrate that adult mortality experience also contributes to the widening mortality gap between

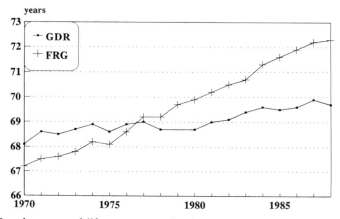

Figure 1 Development of life expectancy in the male population of the GDR and the FRG between 1970 and 1988 (from Niehoff, 1992, with permission)

East and West Germany. Thus, it seems quite likely that the reversal of the ranking in heart disease mortality demonstrated by Dr Kohlmeier is real rather than caused by changed diagnostic criteria.

We are left with the following picture: there has been a widening of the health gap between East and West Germany as measured by mortality. It embraces adult mortality and in particular heart disease mortality. It is possible that it is linked to the influences of the two political systems. The mechanisms for this influence are suggested to be firstly nutrition, secondly social support. To fit the trends of mortality we must assume that nutritional standards have become more privileged in the West and less privileged in the East. The same is true for social support, although here Dr Kohlmeier has made the suggestion that social support in the East originally was better than in the West.

I think both these factors merit attention. It is well worth finding out in what way social support, social isolation and social cohesion in the East and West did change during the enforced split of Germany, and whether these changes contributed to the observed differences in mortality. If they did, there are implications for the differential development of mortality in East and West Europe for the 1965–1980 period.

I will end on this note. Dr Asvall, from WHO, demonstrated that mortality trends in eastern and central Europe were negative with mortality increasing, while western European mortality was decreasing. I can add some new information on this topic, from the work of Drs Mezentseva and Rimachevskaya in Moscow. They demonstrate that each one of the former union republics saw an increase of adult mortality during the 1970s, and most of them during the longer 1970–1986 period (Figure 2). It is truly

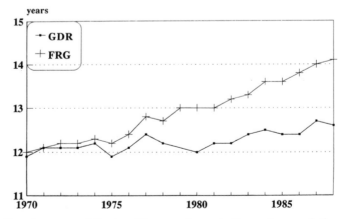

Figure 2 Development of further life expectancy in the male population aged 65 of the GDR and the FRG between 1970 and 1988 (from Niehoff, 1992, with permission)

amazing that all countries of the former communist bloc, including every republic in the former Soviet Union, should at the same time, most clearly in the 1970s, have witnessed the same negative development in mortality. It is difficult to avoid the conclusion that the fundamentally different developments in eastern and western Europe resulted in contrasting mortality trends, and that this differential development was strongly influenced by the two political systems that divided Europe after the Second World War.

References

Niehoff J (1992) In Vågerö D and Illsley R (eds), *Inequality, Health and Policy in East and West Europe* (Special issue) *International Journal of Health Science, 3,* 205–214

POLICY DEVELOPMENT FOR EUROPEAN PUBLIC HEALTH

Market for health care professionals

Health Service Workforce Planning in Europe

Karin Poulton, *Department of Health, London, UK*

Introduction

This paper raises issues concerned with the 'market' of health care professionals and its complex and dynamic relationship with health care service delivery and underlying educational needs. Much of the discussion paper draws on the author's experience as Study Director of a recently completed Council of Europe Health Workforce Planning Study (Council of Europe, Health Manpower Planning (CDSP), from draft).

The challenge

People in Europe are becoming healthier, live longer and make more demands on health services. The population's expectations are becoming more sophisticated as people become better informed and better educated. People are also more aware of environmental influences and social effects. As lifestyle changes so does the focus of health determinants. The trend emphasizing a healthy lifestyle is becoming apparent, which causes some countries to take steps to create new ways of promoting health. For example Public Health Departments are being redesigned in Sweden, Switzerland has created health promotion foundations and the United Kingdom is introducing a much stronger public health function.

Health care is moving from preoccupation with treating the sick to greater emphasis on prevention of sickness and the promotion of health. These are exciting changes, but with them comes the need for cultural and organizational changes which include the training of health care personnel, who will in future need to undertake new roles to meet the challengers of the new era of health service needs.

Success largely depends on creating a professional workforce responsive to the requirements of the future. The workforce has a constantly changing

Europe Without Frontiers. Edited by C.E.M. Normand and P. Vaughan
© 1993 John Wiley & Sons Ltd

profile but is tied to the legacy of the past. There is therefore a process of evolution to shape the profile of the future.

The World Health Organization (WHO) target 36 is of particular relevance (Alma-Ata, 1978). It states:

> Before 1990 in all member states, the planning, training and use of health manpower should be in accordance with health for all policies, with emphasis on the primary health care approach.

Workforce planning is a complex issue requiring vision and knowledge to influence and bring about desired changes. It is the umbrella activity incorporating issues of supply, demand, utilization and management of the workforce at different levels with the aim of arriving at a broad balance between the supply of and demand for qualified professional staff. In particular it tries to prevent the over-supply and shortages of graduates in professions. Because of the long lead time for training, health workforce policy decisions can have long-lasting effects on the level of availability of professional staff and market forces.

European response to health workforce challenges

Over a number of years the WHO, the Council of Europe and the European Community have held expert conferences and consultations to put professional education and training on the agenda, including the issue of EC directives concerned with nursing and medical education.

The Single European Act, designed to achieve a single market free movement by 1992 came into effect in 1987. The White Paper did not contain guidance of direct relevance to patient care for health care personnel, other than those directives already adopted prior to 1985. Doctors and nurses had such directives.

Directives for harmonization between EC member states were adopted for doctors in 1975 and for nurses in 1977, and came to serve as models for other professions. Specific training directives for general practitioners were adopted in 1986. A second general directive has been issued to deal with broad overall issues concerning harmonization between EC member states.

The EC Council set up an Advisory Committee on Medical Training (ACMT) and a Committee of Senior Officials on Public Health (SOPH) to guide developments. This suggests that broad agreement has been reached that health professional education is developing equally among states in western Europe.

In 1983 the Council of Europe Health Committee adopted a recommendation (R(83)5) on further training for nurses (CE Health, 1983). The report recommends specific training curricula for nurses having already successfully achieved their basic education and gained practical experience, and a possible international exchange to further professional experience.

In 1985 WHO published a document on health manpower requirements for the achievement of Health for All by the year 2000 through primary health (WHO, 1985). WHO produced the regulatory mechanisms for nurse training and practice, in 1986 concerning primary health and in 1988 concerning health care needs (WHO, 1986). These reports make strong recommendations concerning manpower planning and education. Amongst other things they recommended that each country must specify its own quality and quantity of health manpower requirements, that manpower planning must be integral with the health care system and have political and community commitment. Reference was also made concerning the need to strengthen continuing education and career development. The second report recommended the redirection of nurse education to prepare nurses for practice in primary health care, and to reorient regulatory mechanisms governing the function of nurses to promote their full contribution to primary health care.

In 1988 the World Federation of Medical Education held a conference which resulted in the Edinburgh Declaration. This stated that education of medical doctors should be aimed at gaining knowledge in promoting health and greater social awareness. It calls for medical education to be more responsible to the need for equality in health care, the humane delivery of health services, and the overall cost to society. It recommends 'self-help' by medical schools to bring about change, and the need for wide involvement such as intersectorial and interministerial cooperation (World Federation on Medical Education, 1988).

In 1988 in Lisbon at a WHO Ministerial consultation for medical education in Europe, Ministers of Health and Ministers of Education expressed their wish for medical education to become more relevant to health needs, and recommended a course of action in line with HFA (WHO, 1989a).

An international consultation on health manpower education for HFA was held in 1989 in Venice (WHO, 1989b) as a sequel to Lisbon 1988, and the most recent consultation on the development of a WHO Education and Training Policy for HFA document in Barcelona 1990 (WHO, 1992) is yet another part in the jigsaw of directing health education towards a model of health. At the same time WHO, the Council of Europe and the European Community (CEEC) promoted a number of other initiatives such as the European Conference for Nursing in Vienna 1988 (CEEC, 1988) which made particular reference to an innovative nursing service which should focus on health rather than disease. Patterns of work should be appropriate, efficient and conducive to primary health care. It also refers to the restructuring and reorientation and strengthening of basic nurse education programmes in order to produce professionals able to function in both hospital and community.

In 1987 the European Commission held a conference to discuss health care and nurse education in the twenty-first century, and summarized that nurses responsible for general care, even though responsive to individual countries, needed to comply with the EC directive in EC member states (77/453/EEC), which ensures the minimum guarantee of professional quality service *vis-à-vis* the care recipient. The key issues raised were health promotion and prevention, critical care and specialist nursing, new-styled teachers to respond to new needs, and the linking of theory to practice in greater 'formal' involvement of ward staff in teaching students (Commission of the European Communities, 1989).

While most of the above-mentioned conferences and constitutions concentrated on professional issues and educational reorientation of professional education, steps were also taken by Health Ministers in Europe to look at the wider issue of health manpower profiles, i.e. skill mix, volume, cost and conditions. The demographic 'time bomb' and the inter-professional imbalance of manpower raised questions of 'housekeeping', i.e. what can be done within the constraints of human and financial resources.

In 1989 a meeting was held in Paris of representatives of European Community Health Ministries (EC, 1989). The aim was to compare individual countries' health manpower situations, analyse problems and search for solutions. The main issues were the over-supply of medical doctors and the shortage of nursing staff in most EC countries. Establishment of better-trained support staff, part-time working, flexible hours, better pay, facilitating appropriate skills competencies, improving career prospects and return to nursing after a career break, were some of the possible solutions already being tried in some countries.

However, the most important and recent conference yet in the context of this study was the Council of Europe's Fourth Conference of European Health Ministers in Nicosia in October 1990. The theme was 'Health manpower: changes and challenges'. The Ministers recognized that the theme was of crucial importance for the future of health care services. The importance of a balance between health personnel to be educated and the desire by individual professions and institutions to follow attractive professional education was discussed. The main issue was the maintenance of a good-quality service and an optimal cost-effective investment in education.

Ministers considered future developments and implications for education of health care staff and addressed the following major issues: (a) demographic patterns; (b) management of human resources; (c) rising consumer expectations; (d) new developments in the area of science and technology; (e) the social environment in health; (f) the physical environment of health care; (g) the health care setting in the light of changing patterns of disease; and (h) soaring health care costs. To respond better to emerging needs, flexible training programmes based on an analysis of skills required should be developed with a continuum from basic to post-basic and in-service training. The sharing of professions' curricula should be facilitated through mutual recognition of common, or the use of identical, modules. The various curricula of health professionals should include periods of training in a number of health care services and especially those for chronically ill and dependent patients.

To ensure the necessary qualitative and quantitative recruitment of health manpower, ways of improving the image, social status and working conditions of those professional groups most affected by recruitment problems should be sought; particularly of staff working in services caring for chronically ill and dependent people.

Much of the response by the Ministers to further desirable developments revolved around the training of health staff. The focus should be on shaping the skills and competencies of health care professionals. The training and education of health staff should respond to changing technology and social developments.

As shown, these issues are gaining momentum which will increase simultaneously with greater freedom of movement for professional staff.

Health service workforce planning

As countries vary extensively in size, structure and location it is not surprising to find that the ways in which health services are financed, determined and managed are also different. Most health services are financed either wholly or in combination through central taxes, employer/employee contributions or some form of compulsory insurance. Remuneration for hospital and community health services also varies considerably. Systems are often of a highly complex nature and are likely to influence the decision of level and type of care provided, and by implication the numbers and skill mix of various health professionals required to provide this service.

The Council of Europe's study report suggests that there is a growing emphasis on health promotion and community care, in particular in primary health care. There is new emphasis on care for the elderly and mentally handicapped people in non-institutional establishments. This in itself presents a change in the numbers and skill range of professional health care personnel required.

Resourcing the growing demand for health care, along with the capacity to finance the demand of major policy, concerns all European countries.

This is likely to continue into the next century and presents a major issue. Growth in demand can be estimated from sources such as demography, advances in medical technology, changing patterns of care and the social goals and expectations surrounding health care. Technological advances and long-term care needs for the elderly will compete for scarce resources. These resources are largely represented by health care staff who will be expected to provide the service and care. Demands, in terms of workforce planning, are translated from service requirements to provider requirements. Demand for health personnel is part of the equation of balancing demand and supply, to achieve the desired size and profile of the workforce.

The Council of Europe study found that most countries interpreted demand in terms of global indicators, that is to say 'top–down', and do not undertake detailed analyses of demand indicated at operational level. The number and ratios of population to medical and nursing staff vary extensively between European countries, and there is little evidence of a uniform approach to determine demand or utilization of staff. Nevertheless it appears that there is a perceived shortage of nursing staff, and in some countries underemployment of medical staff. A demand for a health care workforce, however, has to take into consideration all groups of health care staff and support staff, including the examination of individual boundaries and range of tasks to be performed.

The professionals

Determining the supply of such a workforce has as many imponderables as assessing the demand for the workforce. Constantly evolving health care needs and skills of competencies required to meet these needs are intrinsically linked to the total socioeconomic network and values of the community which give it its unique character.

Within the European Community there is a range and variety of professionals responsible for specific aspects of health care. It would be of little value to analyse the detailed job descriptions and professional skill boundaries but the main co-professions in health number around 10 to 12. The most dominant professions are the medical, nursing, midwifery, pharmacy, dentistry, psychology, physiotherapy, occupational therapy, speech therapy and social work professions and their assistants. There are, however, new health workers evolving, such as the health care and therapy helpers to fulfil some of the demands created by gaps between professional services.

Over- and under-supply of different professional groups have been mentioned, but two key factors in terms of medical staff supply are the control of students and the reform of medical education. Most countries do not support a statutory requirement concerning the regulation of intakes to training based on the needs for the health sector. It is therefore difficult to foresee at what point the experience of unemployment will deter young people from taking up a health service career and move to other attractive careers with better employment prospects. The reform of medical education is a crucial issue in reshaping the medical profession to meet the needs of the coming century. That is 'Health For All and All For Health'.

The supply of nursing and midwifery staff is considered insufficient in almost all European countries. Nursing and midwifery professions have evolved over many years and have developed their skills and knowledge base to justify their place in the ranks of the professionals. However, throughout Europe they are at varying stages of development and academic attainment, and some are undergoing a radical reform of nurse education systems to meet the needs of future decades.

The health care professionals supplementary to medicine constitute a much smaller group, mainly educated in universities and higher education institutions. These are growing professions and, unlike nurses and doctors, the work of these professions may vary considerably between countries. Some of the work identified as a separate profession by some countries may be subsumed by other professions as part of their work in other countries.

Market opportunities for health professionals

A major factor contributing to an effective and efficient workforce is making the best use of the workforce and its skills. Retention, recruitment and the re-employment of already skilled personnel have a considerable impact on the volume of 'new recruits' requirement. Considering the increasing scarcity of skilled health care professionals, particularly in nursing, the appropriate utilization of the skilled personnel, as well as their retention, have become priority issues in many European countries. Continued and unconstrained growth in the number of doctors is a costly investment and unemployment a medical career disaster. At the same time there needs to be a growth in general practice rather than an escalation in the number of hospital doctors. A shift in balance would have a considerable effect on promoting health and primary health care.

The issue of boundaries within professions is very important, particularly between nurses, medical staff and professions supplementary to medicine. The opportunity to work as teams and with the potential of recognizing shared boundaries is important. A shortage of nursing staff may be a perceived shortage as qualified nurses are not necessarily required to meet the whole range of care needed. The growth of other professions such as physiotherapy and occupational therapy is invaluable to the overall skills distribution, best use of resources and an efficient workforce profile.

Conclusion

In a Europe without frontiers the market opportunities can be rewarding, the demand for excellence in service provision is increasing. There is much scope for interdisciplinary training and education in support of patient-centred care. Professionals need an appreciation of each other's work and goals, as increasingly the demand will be for professionals responsive to changing needs, new technologies and practices.

References

Alma-Ata (1978) *Primary Health Care.* Report of the International Conference on primary care, Alma Ata, USSR
CE Health (1983) *Further Training for Nurses in the Member States of the Council of Europe and Finland* R (*83*), 5
CEEC (1988) European Conference on Nursing, summary report. WHO ICP/HSR 329
Commission of the European Communities (CEC) (1989) Health Care and Nursing Education in the 21st century. EUR 12040EN
EC (1989) *Consultation on Health Manpower, Paris, 1989.* European Community international publication
WHO (1985) *Health Manpower Requirements for the Achievement of Health for all by the Year 2000 through Primary Health Care.* WHO Technical Report Series 717
WHO (1986) *Regulatory Mechanisms for Nursing Training and Practice Meeting Primary Health Care Needs.* WHO Technical Report Series 738
WHO (1989a) Ministerial Consultation for Medical Education in Europe Lisbon 1988. WHO EUR/1CP/HMD 115
WHO (1989b) International Consultation on Health Manpower Education for HFA Venice. WHO EUR/1CP/HMD
WHO (1992) International Consultation on Training Health Manpower Education and Policy Document, Barcelona, 1990. WHO (to be published)
World Federation on Medical Education (1988) *World Conference on Medical Education.* Report, Edinburgh

Health care labour market

Francesco Auxilia and Silvana Castaldi, *Ospedale Maggiore di Milano, Milano, Italy*

Overview

In 1978 Italy reorganized its health care and established a National Health Service (SSN). Health care was considered a public commodity granted to the whole population irrespective of income. It is largely planned centrally, with the government, parliament and the ministry of health being in charge of defining principles, general tasks and objectives of the system. Evaluation of the service also takes place on this level, using the annual reports to assess the success of the services in meeting their objectives.

Regions organize and plan the service within the framework provided by the central organizations. Regions also define district boundaries (USSL), determine the range of services to be provided and determine budgets and allocate human resources. The USSL districts provide a range of services according to regional objectives. Primary health care and emergency care at community level are provided by structures known as 'distretti'. Local authorities have basic administrative tasks to perform within the framework set by the Regional Health Authority.

Both public and private hospital services are available. The SSN hospital network includes: 972 public hospitals run by SSN directly; eight teaching hospitals; 20 public and private research hospitals; 40 religious non-profit hospitals; 643 private hospitals with SSN contracts. There is a total of 440 181 beds, of which 83.5% are public. Hospital care is free at point of service and patients can choose either a public or a private hospital. The service is funded about equally by contributions from employees and firms and by the national budget, together with some charges, 'ticket moderateur' for pharmaceuticals, laboratory, radiology and outpatient services.

People can choose their own general practitioners, who are free contractors who may enrol up to 1500 patients. If patients cannot find a GP one will be allocated to them by the USSL.

Pharmaceuticals are provided privately, but the health sector decides what may be provided and whether there will be charges and, if so, what they will be. Laboratory, radiology and other investigations are provided both by the public and private sector but public services predominate.

The medical manpower market

Health personnel are provided according to the level of health services to be assured and the establishment is centrally determined.

Figures provided by the College of Health Professionals, in a report published in 1989, estimated that there were 271 221 physicians in Italy, an increase from 262 148 in 1988. Most of these doctors are in the large conurbations of Rome, Milan and Naples. The distribution of doctors expressed per head of population over time and by region can be seen in Table 1.

Statistics produced for administrative purposes are difficult to interpret as physicians may be both SSN employees and contractors to family practice or the private sector. The most recent data show that, for 1989, 631 330 people were employed by SSN, with 13.5% being physicians, of which

Table 1 Proportion of doctors per head of the population

	1970	1986	1988	1989
Doctors per head	1:561	1:233	1:219	1:212
Northern Italy				1:230
Asti–north Italy				1:362
Southern Italy				1:216
Sicily, Sardinia				1:203
Central Italy				1:180
Bologna				1:134

59 731 out of a total of 85 396 were on full-time contracts. There were 63 807 doctors working in primary care, of whom 93% were GPs and 7% were paediatricians. The average doctor/patient ratio in primary care was 1:817—with regional variations from 1:553 in Campania (southern Italy) and 1:1785 in Autonoma di Bolzano (northern Italy). However, 30% of GPs enrolled less than 500 patients, 20% over 1500 and only 30% were within 1000–1500, the range judged to be most cost-effective.

Compared with other EC countries Italy had the lowest, and Ireland the highest, number of doctors per head of population. Italy is at the top of the range for unemployed doctors with 17%—with Germany at 8%, Spain at 4–6% and The Netherlands with 2%. Unemployment is virtually zero in the remaining countries.

Data for the decade 1976–1986 provided by the Italian Medical College shows that Italy ranked third (with 14%) in 'exporting' doctors, following Greece and Ireland. These physicians went mainly to Britain (41.5%) and Germany (42.5%); with a few to France (7%). The net inflow into Italy was only 1.2%.

A study attempting to define the needs for manpower in western Europe until 2000 estimated that Italy needed an extra 3% increase in demand and for health services to meet the increase in health care personnel, and an increase of 2% not to worsen the balance. The predicted growth rate is 2.5%. Changes in admission rates to medicine courses have contributed to maintaining this balance.

Medicine has always been a popular choice since it is perceived to have charm, prestige and economic rewards. Before the 1960s only students from the wealthier families could afford to train as doctors. In the 1960s access was opened to all students coming from secondary school. This change is readily perceivable from the growth in the numbers of graduates: 2400 in 1955; 2645 in 1965; 8590 in 1975 and reaching a peak of 14 246 in 1980 and then falling to 13 079 in 1985, and to 11 000 in 1989. Students need to pass 30 examinations in six years and then defend a thesis. Although this curriculum allowed students to register as qualified doctors a further practical and theoretical examination had to be passed to facilitate registration in the Medical College of the relevant city. To become specialists, doctors had to register for further postgraduate training.

This particular form of training did not facilitate the adjustment of numbers entering training and the number of doctors required by the SSN. Attempts were made to minimize the impact of the 'spectre' of medical unemployment by replacing it with under-employment in which many doctors do many small duties for low pay. Such under-employed doctors are particularly evident in providing 'emergency on-call services'. Data show that some 2441 emergency facilities in 1989 were covered by some 12 938 doctors. Jobs such as these are considered 'parking areas' for young doctors.

New government regulations are designed to restrict access to the medical schools and to reduce the surplus. In 1986 it was decided that each medical faculty should set a quota for the first year, and if the quota was exceeded entry would be allocated by examinations. Students attend medical school on a full-time basis for some 5500 hours of teaching. The curriculum is designed to direct students to consider all points of view. Teaching methods are changing to more problem-solving group-based teaching. The new curriculum and the under-employment of young doctors have contributed to a reduction in applicants to medical schools, and reduced the high prestige of medical studies. The total number of students enrolled in the medical faculty in Milan fell from 10 841 in 1986 to 7380 in 1990, and did not reach the quota of 650 in 1990–1991.

These changes have been predicted to reduce the number of new doctors annually from the current 9000 to 4771 by 1999. Further changes have also been introduced into the training of GPs and specialists. Specialist training will require attending and passing examinations in practical and theoretical subjects at universities or designated public structures. During this period the trainees must not work either in SSN or private practice. Trainee GPs must train for a further year in hospital and a period in practice with GPs. These two training changes are expected to eliminate the problem of under-employment among young doctors, who will be paid by the Government while they continue their training. It is unrealistic to expect that necessary funds will be available for sufficient doctors to enter into training posts.

A further uncertainty about the demand for personnel is related to the promotion of private health care and insurance schemes. A new law being discussed is aimed at restricting the possibility of SSN doctors being contracted to other clinics and with other agencies.

Dentists do not face the same problems as doctors. In the past 20 years there were very few dentists and so all new ones were easily absorbed. Most Italian people use private dentists because of poor facilities and long waiting times for SSN dentists. Recently, however, there has been an increase of 108% in the number of dentists.

Market for nurses: the reverse of the coin

In addition to the surplus of doctors the SSN has had to cope with a problem of nurse shortage. The ratio of nurses to inhabitants in Italy is only 40 per 10 000 compared to 50 in France, Germany and the UK. A further 50 000 would be required to make good this shortfall. The distribution of nurses throughout Italy is very uneven, 32/10 000 in southern Italy to 54/10 000 in northern Italy. The nurse per bed ratio varies between 58 and 69, and does not appear to be related to geographical area.

Students may enter nursing school without a high-school diploma. Students apply to nursing schools run by regional health authorities, who select the number of entrants at each school. Some schools are organized in private hospitals. After a three-year training period students may be employed as nurses and their average career tends to be short, at eight to nine years. Many studies have been undertaken to find out why this attrition occurs. The profession is not considered attractive, being too much under the control of the physicians and lacking professional autonomy. In addition they have no role in running the SSN system. It has been suggested that nurses, most of whom are female, receive poor social support for child care and so leave to get part-time jobs which fit in with family obligations. The job is also considered hard, and having little social prestige. However, more recently there has been strong competition from the private sector for nurses.

The shortage of nurses is considered by health planners as a factor limiting the development of new services. To encourage school-leavers to become nurses a grant has been introduced, and attempts have been made to improve the professional image. In addition, nursing auxiliaries have been introduced to provide help with some of the basic nursing tasks, and as an emergency measure foreign qualified workers are being encouraged to work in Italy. Finally, financial benefits have been introduced to encourage nurses to work in intensive-care units, infectious disease wards and in operating theatres. In the longer term, curriculum reform is to be embarked upon by raising the entry standards, and a university degree in nursing is being considered. These measures should go some way towards raising the status of nursing.

The conclusion is clear. The Italian health system suffers from two major personnel problems. There is an excess of doctors giving rise to a waste of resources and under-employment, and coexisting with this is the severe shortage of nurses.

Nursing in a European labour market: an economic perspective

Alastair M. Gray and Victoria L. Phillips, *Wolfson College, Oxford, UK*

Introduction

The creation of the Single European Market in 1992, and prospects of expansion in the number of member or affiliated states, will have a significant impact on many product and labour markets. Although the health care sector mainly produces an internationally non-tradable service (Lindley and Wilson, 1991), it will also be affected insofar as health care *producers* will be free to move between countries. Nurses form the largest group within this sector, and so the nursing labour market makes an interesting case study of the effect of the changing environment in Europe.

This paper discusses the factors likely to influence nurse mobility, and examines the available empirical evidence on the size and direction of labour flows. It then considers projected demographic and labour market changes in the EC and their likely implications for nursing. The relationship between employment levels of health care workers and national income and pay are examined in the next section. The paper concludes with some tentative predictions about the direction and magnitude of future nursing migration.

Determinants of migration

While the free movement of skilled workers across all of Europe has yet to be arranged, labour is mobile between countries in the EC. The Treaty of Rome declared that people should be allowed to move freely within the EC but, as recognized in Article 57, community-wide standards of training would have to be agreed on before such migration could take place.

Since 1979 general care nurses have been enabled to move freely within the EC. For example British nurses who want to work in an EC country simply request a certificate attesting to their registered status from the United Kingdom Central Council for Nursing, Health Visiting, and Midwifery (UKCC), and use it to secure a job within the Common Market. As part of this process they must register with the competent authority (normally the Ministry of Health) in the country in which they are seeking a job or have accepted employment.

Under EC regulations recognition of a nursing qualification does not depend on the nurse's ability to demonstrate linguistic competency in the language of that country, as the Treaty of Rome precludes discrimination on the basis of language. Nurses may register their qualification in any EC country, even one in which he or she does not speak the language. However, as providing proper care often depends critically on a nurse's ability to communicate with his or her patients or colleagues, it will be difficult for the nurse to secure employment without demonstrating linguistic competency. A similar system of registration could be extended to non-EC countries, but may have little effect on nurse migration.

Removing formal barriers to migration does not necessarily produce large flows of nurses moving between countries. International migration at any point in time is determined by a number of complex factors. These can be categorized as administrative/bureaucratic which encourage or discourage migration; structural/macroeconomic which create push/pull factors in both recipient and donor countries; and personal which influence the individual decision whether to migrate. The first category was discussed above, the latter two are discussed below.

At the macro level it has been suggested that the movement of nurses and physicians appears to be broadly related to levels of economic development (Mejia *et al.*, 1979). Countries with low GDP per capita sustain the largest losses relative to their domestic stock, while countries with higher GDP per capita experience net gains.

From an individual's perspective the benefits of working abroad must outweigh the costs of securing such employment if a move is to take place. Income differentials are frequently cited as a factor influencing migration. However, the relationship between income and labour mobility is not necessarily straightforward as high incomes for health workers may reduce demand and constrain employment. Other relevant factors affecting the migration decision include search costs as well as the needs of partners, spouses, and children.

Similarly, the cost–benefit calculations of employers must also produce a positive outcome if non-nationals are to be recruited and offered jobs. Employers often look to buy skills which are in short supply at home, such as Intensive Therapy Unit experience, through foreign recruitment.

Evidence on nurse migration

Evidence on nurse migration is scant and dated. The only global empirical assessment of nurse migration was published in 1979 and drew on data from 1972 (Mejia *et al.*, 1979). This study estimated that in the early 1970s an annual average of 15 000 worldwide left their country of origin or of training, and took up employment in another country; this would have been equivalent to approximately 0.5% of the world's nursing stock. Around 75% of these nurses went to three countries: the USA (5220), the UK (3267), and Canada (2866), while the three principal donor countries were the Philippines (2440), the UK (2000), and Australia (1540).

More recent information on the mobility of nurses between developed countries is available from the UKCC, which documents both the number of foreign nurses registering in the UK and the number of British nurses requesting verification of their qualifications. Table 1 combines these figures to give estimates of inflows and outflows of nurses.

The data indicate that the UK is at present a net importer of nurses from the EC, but an exporter of nurses generally. The volume in both cases is very small compared to the total nursing workforce in the UK, but locally such flows may be more important. One recent study of a cohort of nurses who took up employment at a well-known Oxford teaching hospital in the year ending June 1979, and who subsequently left their post, found that 5% emigrated to another country, while the same was true of 19% of another cohort who took up employment during the year ending in June 1985 (Phillips, 1990).

Figures on inflows to the UK may be underestimates in that they are based on trained nurses of foreign nationality registering with the UKCC, and do not include foreign nationals who enter the UK and then train as nurses. A proportion of this group many take up employment in the UK as a nurse, or they may return to their home country. Evidence from the early 1970s indicates that up to 25% of the total enrolment in UK nursing schools comprised overseas students. While it could be argued that increasing harmonization and international recognition may have reduced the number of overseas students seeking qualifications in schools in other countries, this would clearly depend on the supply of places in nurse training schools worldwide. Flows in international trainees is an area needing further research.

Table 1 Net UK gains and losses of nurses through migration

| Year | Net gains (+) and losses (−) between | |
	UK and rest of EC	UK and rest of world outside EC
1984/1985	+ 483	
1985/1986	+ 462	− 915
1986/1987	+ 297	− 969
1987/1988	+1283	− 351
1988/1989	+ 594	− 616
1989/1990	+ 591	− 71

Prospects for the EC nursing market

After expanding rapidly during the 1970s and into the early 1980s, employment in EC health systems has slowed down markedly (OECD, 1990), as Figure 1 shows. The average annual rate of growth of qualified nursing staff across the EC continues to be above the average for the health sector as a whole, but this group has also experienced a slow-down. For example, in the English NHS the number of whole-time equivalent nurses increased by 17.8% over the period 1977–1987, but a mere 1.1% of this growth occurred in the sub-period 1982–1987. The only large EC country in which this slow-down is not evident is Germany.

A slackening rate of growth of demand for nurses should have made recruitment easier, all else being equal, but some demographic changes underway in the EC are running against nursing. During the 1960s and 1970s the number of people of working age in the EC member states grew rapidly. However, as shown in Figure 2, the working-age population will grow more slowly in the period 1990–2010 or (in six of the 12 countries)

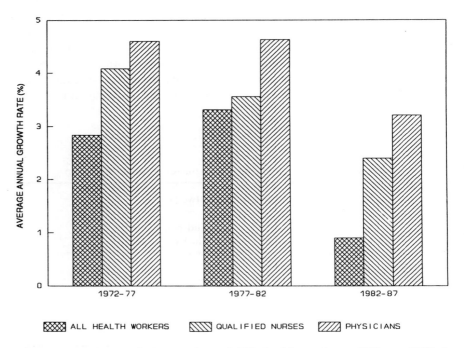

Figure 1 Annual growth in number of EC health workers, 1972 to 1987, by employment group

will become negative (OECD, 1988). Accompanying this slowdown, the average age of the workforce will rise. Meanwhile, the increasing emphasis on qualified nursing rather than the less qualified grades may concentrate nurse recruitment in the more competitive parts of the labour market. In the UK, for example, the traditional source of qualified nurse recruitment— school-leavers with some qualifications—will have fallen by 31% between 1983 and 1993. This poses stark choices for nursing: either increase its share of 18-year-old female school-leavers with the relevant qualifications from 43% to 62% (Conroy and Stidston, 1988), change its recruitment tactics, or run an annual recruitment deficit of up to 3000 recruits.

It is also worth noting that the previous historical low-point in numbers of school-leavers—during the late 1950s—marked the starting point of a significant wave of immigration to the UK, both generally and specifically of nurses (Ermisch, 1990).

Set against these problems for nursing, it should be noted that there has been a substantial increase in recent years in the participation of working-age women in the labour force (that is, the proportion of the working-age population who are in work or seeking employment). Across the EC this

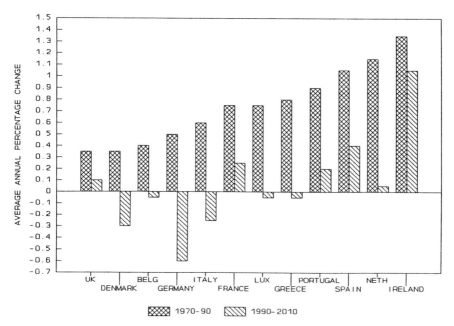

Figure 2 Growth rate in size of working-age populations, 1970–1990 and 1990–2010

rose from 37% in 1980 to 44% in 1990, equivalent to an additional 7 million workers in the Community (Commission of the European Communities, 1990). Participation rates vary substantially between EC member states, and Figure 3 shows this variation for one of the key demographic groups for nursing: females aged 25–49. Nevertheless, in the EC as a whole the participation rate of women is significantly lower than in comparable countries elsewhere, and a continued increase can be expected.

So far, the data indicate that the rate of growth of demand for nurses is slowing in the EC, the traditional sources of recruitment for trainees to nursing are declining, and female labour force participation rates are rising. Some member states may therefore find at certain points that their demand for nurses outstrips supply, creating some of the conditions to pull in labour from EC neighbours. Other member states may produce push conditions that make them suitable exporters of nursing labour. For example Ireland, an historically important source of nurse recruitment, especially to the UK, will continue over the next 20 years to have the fastest-growing population of working age in the EC, and is therefore more likely to be a nursing exporter. It is useful to identify some more systematic way of identifying countries which are most likely to exhibit these push-and-pull characteristics.

Previous research has suggested that physicians per capita and national income may be broadly related in such a way that countries above the trend

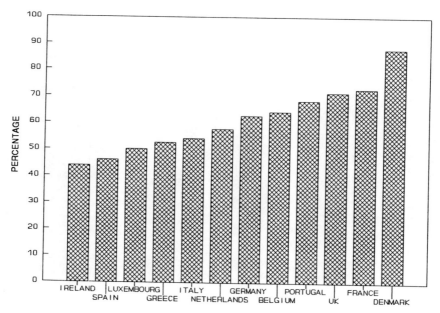

Figure 3 Activity rate of females aged 25–49 in the EC, 1988

line are more likely to experience outflows of physicians while countries below the trend line are more likely to experience inflows (Mejia *et al.*, 1979). Below, a similar analysis for qualified nurses, midwives and physicians across the countries of the European region of WHO is conducted.

Figure 4 shows the relationship between the nurse–population ratio and GNP per capita in purchasing power parity terms for 1985 or nearest year, using recent data from the OECD and WHO (OECD, 1990).

It is apparent that an approximate trend line does exist, and that the main outliers are the Scandinavian countries and Poland and Hungary, which all have significantly more nurses per capita than might be anticipated on the basis of their GDP per capita. In contrast, West Germany, Italy and Austria have somewhat fewer nurses than might be expected. If the analogy between physicians and nurses holds, and bearing in mind a number of other caveats, there may therefore be predisposing factors consistent with an expectation of, for example, some outflow of nurses from Poland and some inflow to West Germany.

Figures 5 and 6 show similar data for midwives and physicians. The most notable feature of Figure 5 is the evidence of an inverse relationship between national income and numbers of midwives. The UK and Finland are two clear exceptions to this pattern, having a much greater number of midwives than other countries at the same income level. Figure 6 suggests that the relationship between physicians and national income is positive: however, it is not statistically significant.

While at an aggregate level the relationships explored above may help to predict migration flows, at an individual level it is likely that relative pay will affect migration. There is remarkably little information about the comparative earnings of nurses in different countries, but Figure 7 pieces together some data on the earnings of newly qualified nurses in the EC in 1990, as given in a recent series of articles in the nursing press (*Nursing Times*, 1990). The figure shows the percentage difference between each country and the UK.

In terms of prevailing exchange rates, at least seven EC countries paid more than the UK to newly qualified nurses in 1990. However, when converted into purchasing power parities (Ermisch, 1990) the picture alters considerably, with only Denmark paying more than the UK to newly qualified nurses. There is thus no strong evidence that relative pay is likely to pull UK nurses towards other EC countries, and some evidence to the contrary. The unknown factor, of course, is relative productivity: in manufacturing industry the significant differences found across the EC in average wage levels are thought largely to reflect variations in labour productivity (Commission of the European Communities, 1990), but measurement of productivity in nursing or in the health sector generally is still in its infancy.

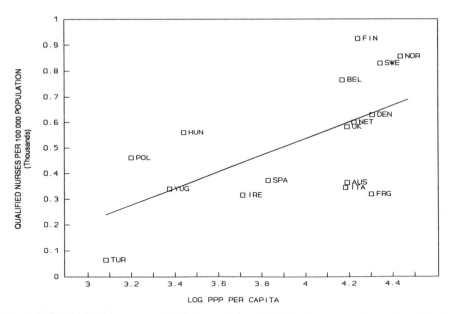

Figure 4 National income and health workers, PPP (log) per capita and qualified nurses

Regression data: Qualified Nurses
Regression variables = 1 ppp/qnpc/dependent = qnpc/method = enter
Listwise Deletion of Missing Data

Equation number 1   Dependent variable.   QNPC qualified nurses per capita
Beginning block number.   Method: Enter

Variable(s) entered on step number 1. LPPP

Multiple R	0.60655	Analysis of			
R Square	0.36790	variance		Sum of	Mean
Adjusted R	0.32275		DF	squares	square
square		Regression	1	315675.98384	315675.98384
Standard error	196.82746	Residual	14	542374.70745	38741.05053
		$F = 8.14836$		Signif. $F = 0.0127$	

Variables in the equation

Variable	B	SEB	Beta	T	Sig T
LPPP	324.388166	113.639661	0.606547	2.855	0.0127
(constant)	−761.053504	451.711010		−1.685	0.1142

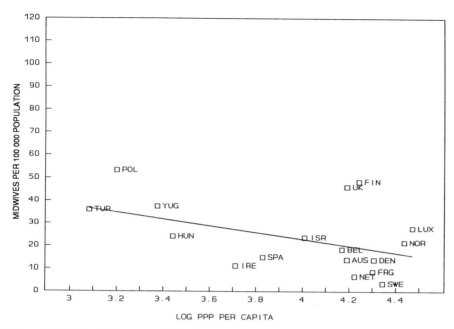

Figure 5 National income and health workers: PPP (log) per capita and midwives

Regression data: Midwives
Regression variables = mwpc/ppp/dependent = mwpc/method = enter
Listwise deletion of missing data
Equation number   Dependent variable.   MWPC midwives per capita
Beginning block number 1.   Method: Enter

Variable(s) entered on step number. LPPP

		Analysis of				
Multiple R	0.44203	variance			Sum of	Mean
R square	0.19539			DF	Squares	Square
Adjusted R square	0.14175	Regression		1	728.99070	728.99070
Standard error	14.14691	Residual		15	3002.02472	200.13498

$F = 3.64250$ Signif. $F = 0.0756$

Variables in the equation

Variable	B	SEB	Beta	T	Sig T
LPPP	−15.065358	7.893688	−0.442026	−1.909	0.0756
(constant)	83.967796	31.537518		2.662	0.0177

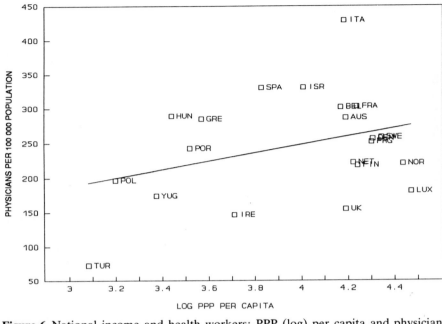

Figure 6 National income and health workers: PPP (log) per capita and physicians

Regression data: physicians
Regression variables = 1 ppp/hpc/dependent = phpc/method = enter
Listwise deletion of missing data
Equation number 1   Dependent variable.   PHPC phys per capita
Beginning block number 1.   Method: Enter
Variables(s) entered on step number 1.   LPPP

Multiple R	0.33124	Analysis of			
R Square	0.10972	variance		Sum of	Mean
Adjusted R	0.06287		DF	squares	square
square		Regression	1	13314.21302	13314.21302
Standard error	75.40451	Residual	19	108030.96605	5685.84032
		$F = 2.34164$		Signif. $F = 0.1424$	

Variables in the equation

Variable	B	SEB	Beta	T	Sig T
LPPP	60.096387	39.272445	0.331243	1.530	0.1424
(constant)	7.837480	156.142705		0.050	0.9605

Finally, Figure 8 shows the earnings of newly qualified nurses as a percentage of average earnings across the entire economy. UK nurses come fourth-top in this ranking, suggesting that the standing of nurses in the UK as measured by their position within the national pay league compares relatively favourably within the EC.

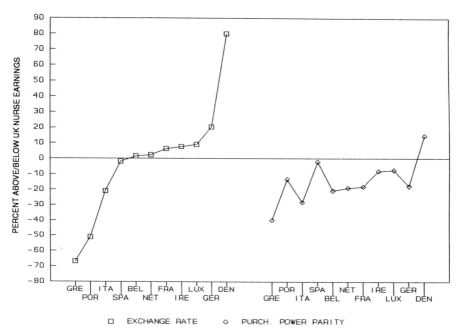

Figure 7 Relative pay of nurses in the EC: exchange rate and PPP, base UK = 0, 1990

While each of the factors examined above may exert some influence on the likelihood that a country will attract or lose health professionals, it is possible that, for any particular country, individual factors will point in different directions, thus cancelling or reinforcing each other. In order to get a clearer view of the likely *net* impact of these various factors, a composite index has been devised, in which the relative positions of a country on each of five different migration-influencing factors are calculated and averaged. The five factors are: GNP per capita in purchasing power parity (PPP) terms; the earnings of health professionals in PPP terms; the earnings of health professionals relative to the national average earnings; the ratio of those aged 65 to those of working age; and the ratio of predicted health professionals per capita to actual professionals per capita, using GNP per capita as the predictor. Each factor is given equal weighting, and if data are available for fewer than all five factors, the score is averaged over those factors for which data were available. Table 2 summarizes the results of this exercise.

On the basis of these data it would appear that, within the EC as a whole, Greece, Italy, The Netherlands and Ireland are most likely to experience a net outflow of nursing staff, while Denmark, the UK, Luxembourg and

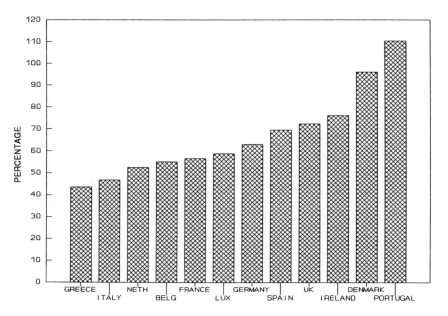

Figure 8 Earnings of newly qualified nurses as percentage of all-economy average, 1990

West Germany are most likely to experience a net inflow of nursing staff. These results, however, are tentative and clearly more information is required to develop and support these ideas in full.

Conclusions

Production of health care in the EC is almost exclusively geared to domestic markets, and so the potential impact of the Single European Market (SEM) will primarily be on movements of health workers, the single largest category of which is nursing. Many administrative and bureaucratic obstacles to nurse movement within the SEM were removed during the 1970s, while remaining cultural and other barriers are unlikely to be directly affected by the SEM.

Over the past decade the total employment of nurses has expanded, and in most cases this demand has largely been met by domestic recruitment. However, as a result of future demographic and policy changes it is possible that the demand for nurses will considerably exceed supply in some national markets. One potential adjustment mechanism would be an increase in the migration of nurses across national frontiers.

Finally, it is possible that the most important effect of the SEM on the European nursing labour market will be indirect: professional males are

Table 2 Composite index of likelihood that economic factors predispose towards emigration or immigration of professional nurses in the European Community

Country			Rank position			
	GNP per capita (PPP)	Nurse earnings (PPP)	Nurse earnings relative to national average earnings	Ratio of those aged 65 to those of working age	Ratio of predicted nurses, *cf.* GNP per capita to actual nurses, *cf.* GNP per capita	Mean rank
Belgium	6	10	9	5	8	8
Denmark	3	1	2	3	6	1
France	2	8	8	6	n.k.	6
West Germany	4	7	6	4	1	4
Greece	11	12	12	9	2	12
Ireland	10	5	3	12	3	9
Italy	7	11	11	7	n.k.	11
Luxembourg	1	4	7	2	n.k.	3
Netherlands	8	9	10	11	7	10
Portugal	12	6	1	10	n.k.	7
Spain	9	3	5	8	4	5
UK	5	2	4	1	5	2

n.k. = Not known.

most likely to move within the EC, and it is likely that nurse mobility will consequently rise in line with spouse/partner mobility.

Acknowledgements

We are grateful to the Institute of Employment Research, University of Warwick and the Equal Opportunities Commission for organizing a conference in 1991 at which some of the themes in this paper were initially developed, and to participants for valuable comments. A detailed treatment of previous research in this area, and of the legal/institutional framework, are available in the proceedings of this conference (Gray and Phillips, 1991).

References

Commission of the European Communities (CEC) (1990) *Employment in Europe 1990*. EC, Luxembourg

Conroy M and Stidston M (1988) *2001—The Black Hole: an examination of labour market trends in relation to the National Health Service*. NHS Regional Manpower Planners' Group, London

Ermisch J (1990) *Fewer Babies, Longer Lives: policy implications of current demographic trends*. Joseph Rowntree Foundation, York

Gray AM and Phillips VL (1991) Developments in specific UK labour markets: nursing. In Lindley RM and Wilson RO (eds) *Women's Employment: Britain in the Single European Market*. HMSO, London, Chap. 10

Lindley RM and Wilson RO (eds) (1991) *Women's Employment: Britain in the Single European Market*. HMSO, London

Mejia A, Pizurki H and Royston RE (1979) *Physician and Nurse Migration: analysis and policy implications*. (The WHO Multinational study of the international migration of physicians and nurses). WHO, Geneva

Nursing Times (1990) European Round-up. *Nursing Times*, 86 (48), 38–41.

OECD (1988) *Ageing Populations: the social policy implications*. OECD, Paris

OECD (1990) *Health Care Systems in Transition: the search for efficiency*. OECD, Paris

Phillips VL (1990) The labour supply decisions of nurses in Great Britain. Dissertation, University of Oxford

Workshop discussion report

Martin McKee, *London School of Hygiene and Tropical Medicine, UK*

Context

The changing nature of frontiers within Europe is providing many more opportunities for movement of health care professionals. The principal ones are within the European Community, but there are also long-standing traditions of movement between certain countries outside the European Community and others within it. Examples of the latter include movement from the British Commonwealth to the United Kingdom, Austria to Germany, and from the former French possessions to France. In the immediate future the probable enlargement of the European Community (EC) to include the European Free Trade Association (EFTA) countries will provide further opportunities, as will the opening up of borders in central and eastern Europe. In this rapidly changing situation it is difficult to predict future patterns of migration. This is especially true in the case of the countries of central and eastern Europe from which there is clearly enormous potential for movement to the wealthier countries of western Europe.

The key question that arises is the extent to which such a free movement of health care professionals will cause problems. In some countries, especially those with established systems of workforce regulations, it would appear to be of little significance. In other countries, and especially those where there is considerable potential for either emigration or immigration, it could become a substantial problem. In general, however, the impact of migration within Europe has not so far been particularly important. A major concern arises with the future opening up of borders in central and eastern Europe, and especially within the Commonwealth of Independent States, where mass emigration of health care professionals, many of whom may seek alternative employment outside the health care sector in western countries, could lead to a substantial depletion of scarce human resources.

Policy-making process

The existing policy on movement of health care professionals into and within Europe is governed by EC directives and by some bilateral arrangements, such as that between Austria and Germany. Within the EC, directives on the free movement of doctors and medical specialists have been in place since 1975. Additional directives relate to the free movement for nurses (1977) and general practitioners (1986). Many of the professions supplementary to medicine, such as physiotherapists, are covered by the General System

Directive for training courses involving three or more years of full-time education.

While international policies serve to regulate or facilitate the movement of professionals, national policies on workforce planning are of substantial importance in creating the environment within which movement takes place. Some countries have well-established and effective systems for controlling the rate of entry to the workforce, such as limits on the numbers of medical students, whereas this is lacking in others. Some countries have also sought to regulate the numbers of staff in the workforce through increasing retention, by financial and other methods. In the United Kingdom the improved pay and conditions of nurses, together with a move to a more highly qualified workforce, is an example.

EC directives provide for mutual recognition of existing qualifications in each member state so long as each qualification fulfils certain minimum criteria. Policy has been led in the past by a combination of political influences and the views of health care professionals. There has been very little input from the public or from scientific evidence on the evaluation of different training programmes and methods of delivering care. In general the development of health care policy in many countries is seen as moving from political views to those of the public, and from implicit professional views to evidence from scientific evaluation of effectiveness and appropriateness. The latter is seen in the increasing research into the appropriateness of work done by doctors and nurses in the United Kingdom.

Agenda for action

Development of policy relating to the movement of health care professionals is made especially difficult by the relative lack of accurate and timely information. The principal requirement is for the establishment of information systems and the performance of high-quality and relevant research. In the short term there are certain actions that could be taken to improve the situation.

There is very little easily available information about the position of health care professionals in different countries and their opportunities for movement. Where information has been provided, such as in the 'Who do I ask?' series produced by the permanent working group of European junior hospital doctors, it is not widely known about. The EC could commission a simple and comprehensible guide to the status of qualifications in different countries, the different roles assumed by each professional group, and a summary of the relevant directives on free movement. In this rapidly changing situation such a publication should be regularly reviewed and updated.

A brief review of the situation in different European countries reveals that professional roles differ considerably. For example, there is wide variation in the extent to which certain tasks are performed by doctors or nurses in different countries. This is an area in which evaluative research is difficult, but the existing diversity provides an opportunity to identify areas where a particular approach works well. The EC should encourage the development of a mechanism by which experience about the adoption of different professional roles could be exchanged, and generalizable models of good practice could be identified.

It is accepted that movement of health care professionals within the EC does require some degree of regulation. It is not, however, apparent that the coordination of this activity is as effective as it might be. The European Commission should examine the way in which coordination takes place, to determine the strengths and weaknesses of the existing system, and to examine ways in which it might be improved.

With regard to harmonization, while it is recognized that the quest for agreement among EC member states has necessitated the use of criteria on the length and content of curricula for mutual recognition of qualifications, there should be an attempt to move towards competencies and skills. It is recognized that this will be extremely difficult, as it may be perceived as a threat to certain existing training programmes.

The agenda for research

There are four areas in which further research is required: international comparisons of the workforce in individual countries; the movement of those seeking qualifications; the movement of those with qualifications; and the process and outcome of harmonization.

International comparisons

While a great deal of information is available on mechanisms for workforce planning in many European countries, this is not true for all of them, including some within the EC. There is a need for further descriptive work to fill the existing gaps. More information is also required on the size and nature of the workforce in different countries. It is recognized that many of the published sources of this information are inaccurate because of the exclusion of certain categories, such as physicians in private practice, or the inclusion of other categories, such as staff who are retired or who are on long-term leave. Information is also required on projected needs for the future. This has been done successfully for several European countries by the Permanent Working Group of European Junior Hospital Doctors (Saugmann, 1991), but again there are omissions for certain EC countries.

International comparisons are often dependent on the use of terms that have not been adequately defined, such as 'nurse'. There is a need for qualitative work to examine the roles undertaken by different health care professions in each country. This problem is not limited to major professional groups, but also affects the differentiation between basic-level professionals and specialists. While there is a directive on mutual recognition of medical specialist qualifications, this is recognized to have many problems as it is based on minimum standards. Many of the opportunities for free movement originally intended by those who produced the directive have not been realized.

Movement to obtain a qualification

An issue of emerging importance is whether each region or country should seek to be self-sufficient in training certain profession groups or specialists, or should it seek to have its citizens trained elsewhere? For example, medical training is not provided in Luxembourg. There is relatively little information on which to base a decision. This is already an important issue facing the countries of central and eastern Europe as they seek to rebuild their specialist training programmes in areas such as public health. There is a need for information on the comparative costs of training in different countries, and the content and quality of training.

Further information is also required on the framework within which people do travel abroad for training. There are concerns that, on the one hand, a country that trains as many of its citizens abroad may lose them to the country where they are being trained. This could lead to countries refusing to fund such training. On the other hand it may be possible to train people abroad more cheaply than it would be to establish a facility in the home country. There is little information available about the extent to which incentives or contracts are used to encourage those trained abroad to return to their country of origin after training. In all cases it is important to ensure that training provided in another country is appropriate to the needs of the country sending trainees.

A major barrier to movement for training is the extent to which different countries charge fees. For example, higher education in universities in the United Kingdom is much more expensive than in other European countries. Thus, while in theory it is relatively easy to move within the EC for postgraduate training, there are considerable financial disincentives to move to certain countries. The effects of these factors are not known, and there is a need for information on the extent to which differences in the structure and funding of higher education influence the movement of people undergoing training.

Movement with qualifications

Many of the issues involved in the movement of people with qualifications relate specifically to the process of harmonization and mutual recognition of qualifications, and will be considered under that heading. One specific area relates to the extent to which it is appropriate to provide all services on a national level, or whether it might be more appropriate for regions to form consortia which would provide particular specialized services. These might be those involving high technology and expensive capital, or those specialized in other ways, such as particular forms of rehabilitation. There are many important research questions which should influence this debate. They include the relationship between volume of work and outcome of care. There is growing evidence that better results are obtained for some procedures by those centres that undertake them frequently. Conversely there are important issues of accessibility to services and equity which must also be examined. More generally there is a need for additional research to determine which services should be regionalized and what size of population can support them.

Harmonization

Research is required into the process and outcome of harmonization. This is required to inform the debate about the extent to which free movement is actually possible, and whether mechanisms for harmonization are needed. Research into the process of harmonization should include studying why people move. Some of the factors that may be important include economic ones, including differentials in income and employment opportunities. In the former case there is a need for much more information about the actual incomes in different countries as official salaries may not accurately reflect them. Other reasons for movement may include opportunities for further training, the movement of spouses (especially in predominantly female workforces), increased job satisfaction and their access to equipment, possession of an appropriate language, traditional patterns of movement and, increasingly in the case of countries such as the former Yugoslavia and the Commonwealth of Independent States, the political environment.

In terms of the outcome of harmonization there is a need for much more information on the extent to which people are moving. What evidence there is suggests that movements are, in general, relatively small. Recognized examples include that of doctors and nurses from Ireland to the United Kingdom, from Austria to Germany, and between Belgium, France and the Netherlands. There is, however, little systematically collected evidence of the numbers of people moving. These figures must be related to the size of the existing workforce and, as was previously noted, this is not always accurately known.

Given that migration appears to be relatively small, research is required to identify the barriers to movement. Work has been done with regard to doctors (Hurwitz, 1990) but there has been relatively little work with regard to other professional groups.

Conclusions

Development of policy on the movement of health care professionals within the European Community has been complicated by the lack of relevant information and the interests of professional groups. There is a need to shift the policy-making process to one that is based on accurate information and evaluative research. Where problems arise, they often reflect difficulties with, or the absence of, national policies for workforce planning. There are many examples of good practice within Europe, but equally there are many examples that are not good. Those countries that are facing problems should seek to learn from those that have overcome them.

References

Hurtwitz L (1990) *The Free Movement of Physicians within the European Community*. Gower, Aldershot
Saugmann P (1991) *Medical Manpower in Europe*. Danish Medical Association, Copenhagen

Health services and the Single Market

EC health care systems entering the Single Market

Reiner Leidl, *University of Limburg, Maastricht, The Netherlands*

Health service issues are not yet on the European Community political agenda. This is quite surprising for a 'Single European Market' (SEM): in 1990, health care expenditure in the EC summed up to more than the gross domestic product of Belgium, Denmark, Greece, Ireland, and Luxembourg together. Yet the legal responsibilities of the Community concerning health are quite restricted. Health care is not referred to in the legal bases such as the Treaty of Rome (1957) or the Single European Act (1985).

The latter will significantly affect our societies. Also for the field of health, a number of impacts can be hypothesized. The facts that the SEM is due to start shortly, and that in December 1991 the European Council in Maastricht decided to include public health—but not health services—as a new EC responsibility, have significantly increased the need to look at health issues at the EC level. Health issues are not currently covered or controlled under the umbrella of a specific authority in the EC commission. A number of health-related activities is scattered across it, e.g. on safety and health of workers, on research on biomedical issues, or on medical informatics.

Research can take its share in identifying relevant issues in this field, analysing them and stating the need for information, evaluation and management. Health systems are a wide and complex issue; this paper will exemplify a few aspects focusing on care and its financing. It will do so looking at the health care systems in the EC, at possible impacts of SEM, and at the research and policy agenda.

Europe Without Frontiers. Edited by C.E.M. Normand and P. Vaughan
© 1993 John Wiley & Sons Ltd

EC health care systems

It is well known that significant differences exist in the organization of EC social security systems, including health care (CEC, 1988). Harmonization throughout the EC is not planned so far. Some differences with respect to organization and to performance are briefly illustrated.

One example for organizational variation within the EC is cost-sharing regulations. A recent study (MPS, 1991) investigated the existence of four types of cost-sharing (exclusion of coverage, co-payment, deductibles and fixed reimbursement) across six sectors of care (inpatient/outpatient care, dental care, drugs, medical appliances and others). None of these 24 categories had a unique solution for all member states; the most homogeneous regulation was the exclusion of insurance coverage for specific drugs. Workers migrating in the SEM face these differences as well as patients do who receive—or try to receive—services outside their home member state.

As other examples, differences in hospital financing may require cross-border patients to pay or not to pay for investment cost. In a national health service, payment may not be required at all. For a migrant worker changing the system of health risk coverage, the health insurance premium that covers inpatient care could, for example, be turned into a tax burden.

It is obvious that much detail is required in describing the definition of institutions, their interaction and regulation in different sectors of care. The standardized, comprehensive analysis of the EC health services is a huge task; first steps have recently been taken (Schneider et al., 1992).

As an example of variation in the performance of health care systems, the aggregate indicator 'health care expenditure' is taken. Its level is, as widely known, closely related to the national income of a country. Using OECD data and purchasing power parities (to account for some disturbances in exchange rates), a population weighted EC average can be calculated. It is not possible to discuss indicator and data quality issues in this paper (see e.g. Rublee and Schneider, 1991; Culyer, 1989). In the EC of 1990, health care expenditure per capita amounted to US$1067 and equalled 7.5% of the US$14 235 gross domestic product per capita (Figure 1; shares for each member state can be compared by the slopes of the lines connecting origin and observation, e.g. Greece 5.3%, France 8.9%). With the exception of Denmark and the UK, who spend relatively small amounts on health care, member states can be attributed either to a group of high-income, high-expenditure countries (upper right corner), or to a low-income, low-expenditure group (opposite corner).

During 1985–1990 most low-income countries improved their position relative to EC average, while most high-income countries did not extend their lead. Similar developments were found for health care expenditure. The greatest increase relative to the EC average for health care expenditure

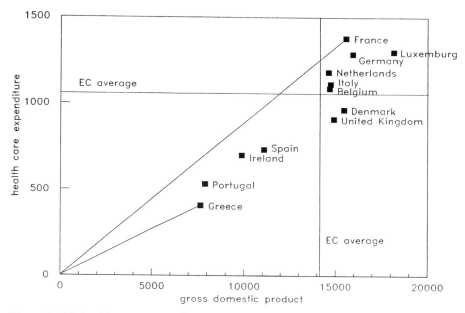

Figure 1 EC health care expenditure and gross domestic product, 1990; per capita figures in US$ (purchasing power parities) (data from OECD health data 1.01, 1991)

was achieved by Spain, the greatest decrease by Germany. In spite of this, the 1985 and 1990 versions of Figure 1 look pretty much the same; with respect to convergence, trends require more in-depth analysis. In total, the EC achieved a nominal growth of a little more than about one-third both in income and health care expenditure, the latter a little bit higher than the former (elasticity: 1.09).

Both organizational and performance differences between the health care system of member states need systematic exploration. What differences exist in premiums and benefits of health risk coverage, and what differences in the availability, access, quality, or efficiency of health services? A next issue is the effect of these differences on the behaviour of various actors in the health care system. Differences in queueing lines, cost sharing, quality of services and medical goods can make patients look for care in other member states. Differences in reimbursement, in the regulation of supply, or in quality control make providers look out for markets. Differences in expenditure levels can induce political pressure, e.g. by provider groups arguing for higher levels of quality. Differences in cost levels may be attractive for authorities shopping around for efficiency-oriented contracts for the care of their patients. Differences in health care systems can also affect the SEM, since health care expenditure is a relevant component of labour cost.

In summary, even though a harmonization is not intended, differences between EC health care systems may set incentives for interaction, and may affect the SEM. On the contrary, the relevance of the SEM for health systems is looked at next.

Developments in the SEM

The SEM can affect health and health care systems in numerous ways. One example of a direct effect on health is changes in the prices for alcohol and cigarettes due to the harmonization of tax rates (Gordon, 1988); another, even more striking one, is the subsidization of the production of tobacco, which is contrasted by a cancer programme which is less than 1% of the subsidies (Townsend, 1991). This paper looks at health care illustrating two examples: the financing of cross-border health care which seems important for free movement in a SEM, and differences in drug prices, a sector-specific issue which contrasts the economic will for a single market with the political will to keep health care financing national (for overviews on SEM impacts on health systems see Hermans *et al.*, 1992 and Leidl, 1991; for analyses of doctors' migration see Hurwitz, 1990; for impacts on the pharmaceutical industry see Burstall, 1990).

In a SEM the free movement of workers, but also other citizens, increases the chance that health care may be demanded in a member state different from the one where the patient is insured. As stated above, there may very well be incentives to do so on purpose. Twenty-year-old EC regulations (1408/71; 574/72) allow for the coverage of immediate need that occasionally occurs during a visit; in a few other specific circumstances coverage is also granted. The patient will be treated subject to the rules of the country he/she is visiting. Financing is provided first by a financial intermediary, followed by the organization covering the patient's risk in the home member state. The claims to reimburse care are nationally collected, then exchanged, negotiated on, and, not always, paid.

Commonly accepted rules on how to calculate the claims—e.g. which types of cost are accepted, which are not—are lacking. Due to bilateral agreements, some countries waive claims. Data available on exchanges suffer from a number of problems; statistics on types and quantity of services are lacking and, even in 1989, the files were not computerized. This system of exchange seems designed for few, exceptional cases, but not for a SEM with a significant potential for movements of people. Future coordination tasks can hardly be estimated on the basis of the available data, and future ways of organizing the exchange of services remain to be discussed—e.g.

by introducing a specific EC institution or, as a technical aspect, by introducing EC-wide magnetic or chip cards for patients.

In contrast to other sectors of health care, drugs have been subject to extensive EC legislative activity—because the market for pharmaceutical and medicinal products is one of those supposed to be single. EC directives and proposals for directives have dealt with safety standards, the approval of drugs, post-marketing surveillance and others. Many aspects have been standardized, or are subject to ongoing harmonization (Burstall, 1991). But when it comes to drug pricing and reimbursement, the—untouchable—national terrain of health care is reached. As a first step to screen this terrain a transparency directive came into force on 1 January 1990 which requires member states to lay open reimbursement systems and price controls for drugs.

There are significant differences in drug prices between member states. This is of obvious relevance for health care financing, and it sets incentives for government intervention. Some discussion emerged on different methods to calculate drug price indices. Figure 2 shows two calculations for a drug basket of 125 products. One calculation comes from the Bureau Européen des Unions de Consommateurs (BEUC, 1989), the other one from a German organization of pharmacists (ABDA). The ABDA study started with the BEUC figures. It then corrected the German drug basket (resulting in a decrease of the index by 2%), standardized for differences in value-added

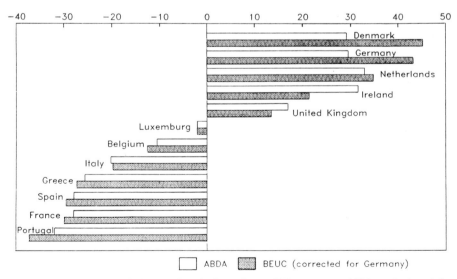

Figure 2 Difference of drug price indices from EC average, 1988; calculated by BEUC and ABDA (data from Diener, 1990)

taxes (which varied between 0% and 22%), weighted the EC average by each nation's share of the EC gross national product (between 0.1% and 25.8%), and standardized for wholesale discounts for sick funds (Diener, 1990; both calculations quoted from this study). Clearly, there is no one 'correct' way in calculating comparable drug price indices.

EC harmonization directives in the drug field are hypothesized to lower, and already to have lowered, price differentials. Different reimbursement systems, and specific product markets for each member state, may hinder the emergence of future single prices throughout the Community. The ABDA study also reported another 2% lowering of the German index figure by 1990.

The recalculation of indices by ADBA, which was induced by the high price levels published for Germany, and the time trend analysis presented, show that EC issues play a role in national health politics, and that information on EC health care systems, their organization, their performance and their reactions to SEM measures are a valuable resource. There is an obvious need to investigate the development of the drug market in the SEM from an industry perspective (looking at the number of companies, size, research and development activity, competition, etc.), but also from a health care point of view (looking at drug prices, volumes, approval, surveillance, coverage and control by health insurance, and others).

Looking at the impact of SEM, it is worth mentioning a question which exceeds the analysis of selected issues such as financing or drugs. It asks to what extent the SEM in total reduces differences between the health care systems, and refers to speculations about a convergence of EC health care systems. Convergence tendencies could emerge from an opening of the EC health care market as well as from integration of markets such as those for medical personnel, medical equipment, drugs, or complementary health insurance. Both adequate theory and empirical measurement for these questions are lacking.

Research and policy agenda

Research can provide methods and information to evaluate problems and benefits of the European integration in the health care field, and support control and decision-making concerning the impacts. A standardized description of current EC health care systems is lacking, as well as an EC health reporting system (on indicators such as sociodemography, morbidity and mortality, health care resources, utilization, and financing). The heterogeneous data available remain to be harmonized or to be documented with respect to data origin, collection, processing, quality, comparability, and representativeness. With the implementation of the SEM its effects and side-effects can be explored, identified and documented using a variety of perspectives, levels of aggregation, and methods of collecting evidence. Evaluation studies can supplement the more general monitoring. Consultancy work can support evaluation, planning, and decision-making by target groups such as administrations, industries, or professional groups. Research, it emerges from the above, can play quite an active role.

On the policy agenda a few comments are made. There is an obvious problem to which institutions' questions can be posed such as 'Which coordination activities and other health care policy measures are required?', e.g. on Community, national, regional or on a local level. For the Commission, an EC health care policy is not covered by the new public health responsibility. In spite of that, the institutions and mechanisms of coping with effects of the SEM in the field of health care have to—or implicitly will—be defined on the different levels mentioned. Public authorities responsible for health have to consider this.

The definition of an EC health care system, which may be one composed of different national systems, is still lacking. Yet the EC pluralism of interest groups conducting health care policies and politics on a European scale has already started. This can be indicated for the pharmaceutical sector, or can be found for physicians (Brearley and Gentleman, 1991). The activity of interest groups and of health authorities in member states will shape the future conduct of European elements in health care. In addition to this, a next step is the institutional set-up of the European public health responsibility. This situation sets clear tasks for health services research: to define its future role with respect to explicit EC responsibilities and, not less relevant, to support different actors in health care in coping with EC issues.

References

Brearley S and Gentleman D (1991) Doctors and the European Community. The agenda lengthens. *British Medical Journal, 302* (6787), 1221–1222

Burstall ML (1991) Europe after 1992: implications for pharmaceuticals. *Health Affairs 10* (3), 157–171

Burstall ML (1990) *1992 and the Regulation of the Pharmaceutical Industry*. IEA Health & Welfare Unit, Institute of Economic Affairs, London (IEA Health Series No. 9)

Bureau Européen des Unions de Consommateurs (BEUC) (1989) *Drug Prices and Drug Legislation in Europe*. Ref. 112/89, Brussels

Commission of the European Communities (CEC) (1988) *Comparative Tables of the Social Security Schemes*, 14th edn. Office for Official Publications of the EC, Luxembourg

Culyer AJ (1989) Cost containment in Europe. *Health Care Financing Review*, Annual Supplement, pp. 21–32

Diener F (1990) Arzneimittelpreise in der EG. *Pharmazeutische Zeitung, 135* (40), 9–16

Gordon L (1988) Abolishing fiscal frontiers in the EEC. *Tax Planning International Review*, pp. 3–8

Hermans HEGM, Casparie AF, Paelinck JHP (eds.) (1992) *Health Care in Europe after 1992*. Academic Press, Aldershot (In press)

Hurwitz L (1990) *The Free Circulation of Physicians within the European Community*. Gower, Aldershot

Leidl R (1991) How will the single European market affect health care? *British Medical Journal*, *303* (6810) 1081–1082

Medizinisch Pharmazeutische Studiengesellschaft (MPS) (1991) Jahresbericht 1990 der Medizinisch Pharmazeutischen Studiengesellschaft e.V. und der Paul Martini Stiftung, Bonn

Rublee DA and Schneider M (1991) International health spending: comparisons with the OECD. *Health Affairs*, *10* (3), 187–198

Schneider M, Dennerlein R, Koese A and Scholtes L (1992) *Health Care Systems in the EC Member States*, Elsevier, Amsterdam *Health Policy Monographs Vol 1* (Health Policy (1992) vol 20/1+2)

Townsend J (1991) Tobacco and the European common agricultural policy. *British Medical Journal*, *303* (6809), 1008–1009

Migration and Health after 1992

Ghada Karmi, *NW/NE Thames Regional Health Authorities, London, UK*

The current debate over the implications of the Single European Market (SEM) which is to be introduced on 31 December 1992 has devoted little attention to one important aspect of the proposed changes that may have considerable implications for medical services in Britain and other EC countries. This is the issue of the potential for labour migration within Europe. Although most commentators have emphasized the commercial implications of the SEM, the legislation will also provide for the free movement of people throughout the EC, without the current limitations of border controls. According to the 1987 Single European Act (SEA), the EC Internal Single Market is defined as 'an area without internal frontiers in which the free movement of goods, *persons*, services and capital is ensured'.

Thus, by the end of 1992 the SEA will complete the process of the removal of barriers on worker movement within the Community that began with the EEC Council Directive of 15 October 1968 and which has been the subject of much subsequent EEC legislation. Worker movement may well increase as a result of this, but it is far more likely to do so because of the associated economic legislation after 1992 (European Communities Commission, 1988, pp. 21–22): for example, the integration of the European economies, business merger operations across frontiers, and the opening up of major public contracts. Not only will these changes lead to differential job creation, but they will also promote a broader perception of work opportunities among the workforce in Europe and a potential for an increase in labour migration (Niessen, 1991).

The fact that the fundamental changes in the labour market which the new era will usher in must mean an increase in immigration has now been widely recognized. 'The advent of the free movement of persons in the EC post-1992 will coincide with the greatest increase in immigration pressures that has ever been seen' (Appleyard, 1991, p. 7). This reflects in part a wider anxiety about global migration trends in the 1990s. When the leaders of the most industrialized nations (G-7) met in London in July 1991, they devoted part of their discussions to 'a growing concern about world-wide migratory pressures' (*Daily Telegraph*, 21 July 1991). In Europe the anticipation of increased illegal and extra-EC migration has given rise to a sort of panic and the establishment of a special machinery to deal with it after 1992 (Widgren, 1991, p. 763). This is the Trevi group of ministers from all the EC countries who have been meeting since 1986 to agree a system of border controls against the entry of undesirable people, and is paralleled by the Schengen accords concluded between a smaller group of EC countries.

The question of which type of worker will be involved in this migration is of importance here, especially in the context of health and health service provision. Experience shows that it is the unskilled worker who is most likely to suffer disadvantage in a new country, and for whom the services need to make the greater adjustment. The assumption in Britain has been that labour movement after 1992 will be most pronounced among skilled and professional groups (DHSS, 1988). More recently an international migration seminar also concluded that the demand in Europe would be for skilled labour with a range of specialized knowledge (Appleyard, 1991, p. 65). Indeed, there may even be fierce competition world-wide to secure the most highly skilled workers, especially for a post-1992 European labour market dominated by service and information technologies. Persuasive as these arguments are, none of them is based on quantitative research and none of them negates the possibility of a concomitant increase in unskilled labour migration. This problem may arise after 1992 partly because of the effects of the SEA, but also because of the pattern in world migration.

The sources of this unskilled labour migration will be both from the EC and from outside. The legislation after 1992 will provide for EC nationals and their families to have unrestricted rights of access, domicile and work in any EC member state. Thus, a former migrant with EC nationality would have the same rights as a member of the native EC population. The point here is that former migrants are far more likely to be unskilled, even if second generation. In 1988 the European Commission denied any likelihood of an increase in such migration, arguing that migrants already in Europe were unlikely to disturb their local residence and employment patterns by further migration (European Community Commission, 1988, pp. 7–36). This assessment, however, needs to be re-examined in the light of population movements from eastern to western Europe which started in 1989. A total of 1.2 million people have already left the Warsaw Pact states and the flow from the former USSR is projected to reach 2.5 million annually (Widgren, 1990, p. 759). In 1990 more than 400 000 eastern Europeans applied for asylum status in western Europe (Salt, 1991). The impact of this new form of migration is as yet unclear, but it may well affect previous migrant groups in EC states by displacing them in the labour market: for example, a recently arrived East German worker might well be preferred to a Turkish 'guest worker', however long-standing the latter's residence in Germany had been. Displacement of this kind on a large scale may ultimately stimulate a new migration between EC states of non-European ex-migrants who are likely to be unskilled.

The other source of unskilled labour migration, deemed to be far more significant, will be that from non-EC or third countries. Although the organized hiring of foreign unskilled labour for work in Europe was said to be diminishing (Widgren, 1990, p. 753), business opportunities after 1992 will act as new magnets for low-paid workers, variously labelled 'seasonal' or 'temporary' and often illegal, who have traditionally been recruited by employers because of the reduced labour costs involved (Power, 1984, pp. 8–12). It is this illegal labour migration which exercises EC governments because it is so difficult to control. It is estimated that there are currently 1.5 million illegal immigrants in Europe, most of them in Italy, Spain and Greece—even Switzerland has 110 000 such immigrants despite stringent border controls—and this number may reach 3 million by the year 2000 (Salt, 1991). Experience shows that no border is impenetrable to this flow of illegal migrants and, while the propensity for countries to stem the tide by imposing restrictive controls over entry is understandable, it may only succeed in making such migrants 'invisible'. Such people are then pushed into irregular situations in which they are vulnerable to exploitation and, because of their illegal position, will not be able to seek help from the statutory agencies, whether in health or social services. The health implications inherent in such a situation are potentially serious. The increase in the numbers of asylum seekers in European countries can be seen as another form of migration. In 1990 there were just under half a million asylum seekers, many of whom are in reality economic migrants, and the figure is increasing (Appleyard, 1991, p. 30). Although this is not a large number, it represents a growth area for an economic migration which can by-pass the formal immigration procedures.

But it is the demographic factor which may turn out in the end to be the most significant of all. A recent Council of Europe seminar calculated that Europe's indigenous population growth, low enough already at 0.89% per year compared with a world average of 2.6% per year, will move down to zero or even minus in the next two decades. Furthermore, the population age structure will change considerably, with an increasing percentage share being taken by the over-65s who will account for more than 25% of the total by the year 2025 and a concomitant reduction in the numbers of young people. At the same time the population of the 14 non-EC countries bordering the Mediterranean is increasing by 5 million a year. The five North African countries alone will increase their populations threefold by 2025 (Escallier, 1991) and French demographers have estimated a potential emigration of 25–30 million people from North Africa in the next 30–40 years. The enormous demographic and economic imbalance between the EC states and their neighbours will constitute a powerful incentive, the so-called push factors, for migration. This trend will be augmented by the desire on the part of some European countries to arrest their demographic decline by encouraging immigration, and by the reluctance on the part of indigenous Europeans to take certain kinds of unskilled jobs. Third country migrants—the most mobile force available—are inevitably going to fill the gap, a situation which obtained even before the SEM was envisaged (Castles and Kosack, 1985).

Migration and health

In the foregoing section I have attempted to set out the arguments for a scenario of significant increase in labour migration, both legal and illegal, in a future Europe. If this speculation turns out to be correct, then the implications for health and the likely demand for health services are considerable. The link between migration and ill-health is well known, and migrants moving from one society to another face physical and psychological ill-effects (College et al., 1986) which are accentuated among unskilled migrants in disadvantaged inner cities with additional environmental health hazards. For example, 50–75% of the tuberculous infection found in immigrants to western European countries, such as North Africans in France and Asians in Britain, is acquired after arrival in the new country and is likely to be due to a combination of a poor environment and low immunity (Castles and Kosack, 1985, p. 318; Kushigemachi et al., 1984). Likewise, the incidence of sexually transmitted disease has been found to be consistently higher in immigrant single men in Britain, Holland, France, and Austria than in their indigenous counterparts (de Schryver and Meheus, 1991). This has been ascribed to the relative lack of females among these groups, who are in any case isolated and forced to live outside main society. As a result the men tend to visit prostitutes and become infected. Language difficulties and ignorance of the medical system compound the problem. The same social isolation is also likely to be the cause of the high hospitalization rate recorded among single male Algerians in France (Castles and Kosack, 1985, p. 333).

Rickets and osteomalacia constitute another hazard for migrants. In 1961 a study of North African children in France showed a 20% prevalence of rickets, by comparison with 2.8% in French children (Castles and Kosack, 1985, p. 331). In Britain, Asian immigrants are known to develop higher rates of rickets and osteomalacia because of vitamin D deficiency (Adelstein et al., 1984). The evidence seems to point to the relative lack of sunshine in Britain as the major cause for this condition. Studies on migration between Scandinavian countries showed that the health of migrants, especially those who had migrated frequently, was poorer than that of the indigenous population as measured by long-term illness, anxiety, psychosomatic illness and use of medication (Nagi and Haavio-Mannila, 1980). Other studies have found that blood pressure levels can be related to the process of migration. In a comparative study of Punjabi females carried out in London, and in the area of origin in the Punjabi State, India, it was found that blood pressure was significantly higher in the migrant group and that it was positively correlated with obesity and the length of time spent in England (Keil et al., 1980). The stress of migration and assimilation was believed to be the cause of elevated blood pressure levels in a study of immigrants in the USA, was correlated with the degree of assimilation and social support available to the immigrants (Walsh and Walsh, 1987).

The effects of the migration process on mental health have been the subject of much research. Bagley's epidemiological study of mental illness among British immigrants in London showed that those who came from Africa, India and Pakistan had the highest rates (Bagley, 1971). West Indians have an above-average admission rate to psychiatric hospitals in Britain, and their rates of schizophrenia are three to five times those for whites (Littlewood and Lipsedge, 1988). This effect seems to persist into second-generation West Indians whose admission rates for the same condition are even higher than those of their parents. In Sweden, immigrants from southern and eastern Europe were more often diagnosed as hysterical, paranoid, and hypochondriacal; they complained more commonly of somatic symptoms, and the worst affected were those who had migrated to Sweden at a younger age (Haavio-Mannila and Stenius, 1975). Immigrants to Canada suffer from various degrees of 'acculturation stress', depending on a number of factors: gender—women migrants suffer more stress than men; poor education, knowledge of English—the less, the greater the stress; and the relative importance of 'push' or 'pull' motives for migration; that is, if the migrant had been forced to escape the home country, then acculturation posed greater stress than was the case for a migrant who had migrated because of the attractions offered by the new environment (Berry et al.,

1987). Similar findings were reported from a study of depression among Mexican migrant women in the United States (Vega *et al.*, 1987).

The health service response to migration

Migrants have characteristics that can greatly affect the demand for health services. As well as being subject to the foregoing health risks, they tend to be young and to cluster in specific geographical areas. This means that they will require greater obstetrical, paediatric and dental services. Since many of the men will be working in heavy industry they are more likely to use hospital accident and emergency services. And the fact that they are geographically clustered will impose particular stress on the health services in those localities. In addition, many migrant groups have their own traditional medicine, which they tend to use on an emergency and adjuvant basis without health providers necessarily being aware of these practices. All this poses an exceptional challenge to those who have to tend to the medical needs of migrants.

To date the health service response in Britain and other European countries has not been adequate (Black, 1987). There has been no systematic policy or strategy to cater for the special needs of migrant groups, whether it be in the provision of interpreters or in the training of practitioners to understand the cultures of their patients. Mental health services are singled out as being particularly inadequate with a paucity of epidemiological research into the causes and prevalence of mental illness among migrants and a lack of collaborative work across Europe (*Lancet*, 1990). It is possible to argue that while the numbers of migrants were small relative to the 'host' population, specific service responses were not called for. In Britain this is certainly no longer the case and, if the speculation in this paper proves to be correct, no 'receiving' country in Europe can afford to neglect this area of health care any longer. What is required is a different vision of the issue to be shared across European countries which should lead to a specific strategy. Such a strategy will need to address not only the question of culture and language, but also the other features which degrade so many migrants' lives: racism and low status and the effects of poverty and social disadvantage (Johnson, 1991; Watson, 1984). Perhaps the task is too onerous for one or even a group of countries, but will require, as Appleyard says (Appleyard, 1991, p. 77), international agreements on the global reduction of economic inequality which in turn leads to migration and even greater health and social inequality.

References

Adelstein AM, Marmot MG and Bulusu L (1984) Migrant studies in Britain. *British Medical Bulletin*, *40*, 315–319

Appleyard RT (1991) *International Migration: challenge for the nineties*. International Organisation for Migration, Geneva

Bagley C (1971) Mental health in immigrant minorities. *Journal of Biosocial Science*, *3*, 449–459

Berry JW, Kim U, Minde T *et al.* (1987) Comparative studies of acculturation stress. *International Migration Review*, *21*, 512–529

Black N (1987) Migration and health. *British Medical Journal*, *295*, 566.

Castles S and Kosack G (1985) *Immigrant Workers and Class Structure in Western Europe*, 2nd edn. Oxford University Press, Oxford

College M, van Guens HA and Svensson PG (eds) (1986) *Migration and Health: towards an understanding of the health care needs of ethnic minorities*, WHO Regional Office for Europe, Copenhagen; HMSO, London

Council of Europe (1991) *Seminar on Present Demographic Trends and Lifestyles in Europe*. HMSO, London

Department of Health and Social Security (1988) *Creation of a Single European Market: implications for the Department of Health and Social Security*. Paper no. CSPRG (88)

Escallier R (1991) Demographie et migration. In L'Acoste C and L'Acoste Y (eds), *L'Etat du Maghreb*. Editions le Fennec, Paris, p. 87

European Communities Commission (1988) *Social Europe*. HMSO, London, pp. 7–36. Commission of the European Communities "Social Europe: The Social Decline of the Internal Market: Interim Report of the Interdepartmental Working Party"

Haavio-Mannila E and Stenius K (1974–1975) Mental health problems of the new ethnic minorities in Sweden. *Acta Sociologica*, *17–18*, 367–392

Johnson MR (1991) Migration and health: an overview. In Karmi G (ed.), *Health and the Movement of Labour after 1992*. King's Fund, London.

Keil JE, Britt KP, Weinrich MC *et al.* (1980) Hypertension in Punjabi females: comparison between migrants in London and natives in India. *Human Biology*, *52*, 423–433

Kushigemachi M, Schneiderman LJ and Barrett-Connor E (1984) Racial differences in susceptibility to tuberculosis: risk of disease after infection, *Journal of Chronic Diseases*, *37*, 853–862

Lancet, editorial (1990) Mental health services for migrants in Europe, *Lancet*, *336* (8720), 911–912

Littlewood R and Lipsedge M (1988) Psychiatric illness among British Afro-Caribbeans. *British Medical Journal*, *297* (6641), 135–136

Nagi SZ and Haavio-Mannila E (1980) Migration, health status and utilization of health services. *Sociology of Health and Illness*, *2*, 174–193

Niessen J (1991) The European Community after 1992 and the movement of unskilled labour. In Karmi G (ed.), *Health and the Movement of Labour after 1992*. Kings Fund Centre, London, pp. 33–43

Power J (1984) *Western Europe's migrant workers*, 2nd edn. Minority Rights Group, London, pp. 8–12

de Schryver A and Meheus A (1991) Sexually transmitted disease and migration. *International Migration*, *19*, 13–28

Salt J (1991) Current and future international migration trends affecting Europe.

Paper for the Fourth Conference of European Ministers responsible for migration affairs, Strasbourg

Vega WA, Kolody B, Valle JR (1987) Migration and mental health: an empirical test of depression risk factors among immigrant Mexican women, *International Migration Review*, *21*, 512–529

Walsh A and Walsh PA (1987) Social support, assimilation and biological effective blood pressure, *International Migration Review*, *21*, 577–591

Watson E (1984) Health of infants and use of health services by mothers of different ethnic groups in East London. *Community Medicine*, *6* (2), 127–135

Widgren J (1990) International migration and regional stability. *International Affairs*, *66*, 749–767

Regional differences in avoidable mortality in Europe

Ferenc Bojan, Piroska Hajdu and Eva Belicza, *University Medical School, Debrecen, Hungary*

Summary

The pattern of avoidable mortality in 22 European countries representing all major regions of Europe was studied for the period 1981–1989. These countries were assembled into three groups on the basis of the pattern of trends in mortality from avoidable and all other causes. The majority of the developed countries showed a continuous considerable decrease in mortality from both types of causes in men and women. Some developed countries and East Germany were found to show inconsistent trends for mortalities from avoidable or all other causes or both due to temporary increases. The trends proved to change most adversely in the former eastern bloc countries.

The levels of the age-adjusted death rates from avoidable causes also formed three distinctive groups. Fifteen developed countries had the best rates. Much higher levels of mortalities were found in most of the eastern bloc countries and Portugal. Thirdly, Hungary and Bulgaria showed strikingly high death rates from the avoidable causes.

An obvious relation was found between the levels of the latest available death rates from avoidable and all other causes in men. For women the difference between the developed and eastern bloc countries proved to be primarily avoidable mortality.

Death rates from hypertensive and cerebrovascular diseases both in men and women were the highest in the former eastern bloc countries and relatively high rates were observed in some developed countries. The death rates from cancer of cervix uteri and corpus uteri were also found to be the highest in the former eastern bloc countries and in Denmark.

Avoidable mortality without hypertensive and cerebrovascular diseases, as well as cancer of cervix uteri and corpus uteri, was also the highest in the former eastern bloc countries. Relatively high mortality from all other avoidable causes could also be found in a few other developed countries.

Our study has shown that the region of the former eastern bloc countries is far behind the (developed) rest of Europe in terms of avoidable mortality.

Introduction

Avoidable mortality is frequently analysed in many studies on the outcome of medical care (Bauer and Charlton, 1986; Bojan *et al.*, 1991; Charlton *et al.*, 1983, 1984; Gil and Rathwell, 1989; Holland, 1986, 1990; Poikolainen and Eskola, 1986; Rutstein *et al.*, 1976, 1983). These studies are all based upon the publications by Rutstein *et al.* (1976, 1980). To develop indicators of the quality of medical care they drew up lists of diseases which should not, or should only infrequently, give rise to death in the appropriate age groups. The basis for compiling such lists is that mortality from certain diseases should be wholly or substantially avoidable through appropriate and timely medical care, given the current level of knowledge and technical development.

Since the fundamental publications by Rutstein *et al.* (1976, 1980) a number of studies has been done to reveal the pattern of avoidable mortality in some individual countries (Bauer and Charlton, 1986; Charlton *et al.*, 1983, 1984, 1986; Poikolainen and Eskola, 1986), and to compare the mortality patterns in several countries, among them in the eastern and western European countries (Bojan *et al.*, 1991, Boys *et al.*, 1991; Charlton and Velez, 1986; Kunst *et al.*, 1988). Moreover, due to the 'concerted action' project in the framework of the Health Services Research Programme of the European Community an atlas of avoidable mortality in the European Community's countries (except the Mediterranean countries) in the 1970s was prepared and published (Holland, 1988). This atlas was followed by a second issue to cover the mortality data collected in the 1980s and to include the Mediterranean European community countries (Holland, 1991).

However, such a comprehensive study covering nearly all European countries and showing the mortality pattern from avoidable causes in different regions of Europe has not been done. In our present work the pattern of avoidable mortality in 22 European countries representing all major regions of Europe has been studied. The major objectives of this study were to:

1. study the trends in mortality from avoidable and all other causes and to group the countries on the basis of their mortality trends;
2. describe the age-adjusted death rates from avoidable conditions in European countries;

3. reveal the relation between the age-adjusted death rates from avoidable conditions and all other causes;
4. investigate the age-adjusted death rates from the individual major avoidable causes in the European countries.

Materials and methods

The selection of countries is shown in Figure 1. Some countries such as Albania, Belgium, Romania and Northern Ireland, and the very small countries, were excluded from this study because we could not get access to complete mortality data and their very small populations, respectively. The mortality and population data for the period 1981–1989 were collected from the *World Health Statistics Annuals* (1981–1989).

The selection of avoidable causes in this study (Table 1) was based upon the literature, generally omitting the very infrequent causes of death (e.g. diphtheria) and further omitting those causes for which avoidability lies mainly outside the health care system, such as in many forms of primary prevention (e.g. traffic accidents, lung cancer) (Holland, 1986, 1988, 1990; Rutstein *et al.*, 1976, 1980, 1983). Our previous studies (Bojan *et al.*, 1991) included abdominal hernias and Hodgkin's disease, but they were not studied here because separate data for them were not given in the *WHO Annuals*. Their very low frequency, however, would not alter the major trends for

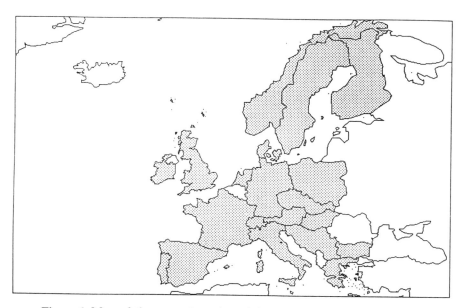

Figure 1 Map of the countries selected for the present mortality studies

Table 1 Selection of causes of death avoidable with medical treatment

Causes of death	ICD-8 code	ICD-9 code	Age group (years)
Tuberculosis	010–019	010–018	5–64
Cancer of cervix uteri	180	180	15–64
Cancer of corpus uteri	182	182	15–64
Diabetes mellitus	250	250	5–64
Chronic rheumatic heart disease	393–398	393 395–398	5–44
Hypertensive disease	400–404	401–405	5–64
Cerebrovascular disease	430–438	430–438	5–64
Acute respiratory diseases	460–466	460–466	5–49
Pneumonia	480–486	480–483 485–486	5–49
Chronic respiratory diseases	490–493	491–493	5–64
Appendicitis	540–543	540–543	5–64

avoidable mortality. In order to minimize the effect of differences in diagnostic and coding practices, mortality data on hypertensive and cerebrovascular diseases as well as cancer of cervix uteri and corpus uteri were amalgamated.

Age-adjusted mortality rates were calculated for all conditions by using the direct standardization method based on the appropriate European standard population (*World Health Statistics Annuals*, 1981–1989).

Results

To demonstrate the mortality trends from avoidable and all other causes the relative changes in the age-standardized death rates were calculated annually for the period 1981–1989 (1981 = 100%). On the basis of the trends, European countries could be separated into three groups.

The first group represented 10 countries (men) and 12 countries (women) in which a considerable continuous decrease in mortality from both avoidable and all other causes could be observed for the whole period 1981–1989 (Figure 2). The mortality from amenable causes always declined faster than the mortality from all other causes of death. However, there were notable differences among the age-adjusted rates for these countries (e.g. range for men: 30.8–85.5, for women: 24.9–60.2 per 100 000 population in 1981). None of the eastern European countries could be placed into this group.

The countries in the second group did not show a constant decrease in mortality from either avoidable or all other causes (Figure 3). In these countries temporary increases could be observed in mortalities from avoidable

Annual average of percentage charges

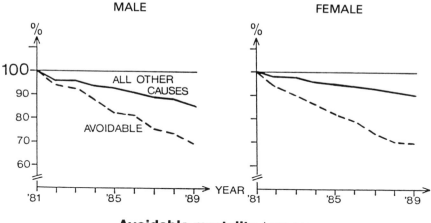

Avoidable mortality / 100 000

	1981		Latest	
	Male	Female	Male	Female
Sweden	30.8	27.8	23.8*	21.8*
Switzerland	31.5	25.6	23.6†	17.8†
France	32.9	24.9	25.7**	19.1**
England and Wales	43.0	39.3	29.5†	29.1†
West Germany	44.9	33.8	31.0†	23.4**
Ireland	47.2	42.7	32.3**	29.9**
Italy	50.0	38.4	36.0**	27.7**
Finland	52.4	31.9	41.4**	24.2**
Scotland	57.1	51.0	38.6†	38.3†
Portugal	85.5	60.2	55.8†	39.2†
Spain	–	34.6	–	25.9**
Greece	–	35.7	–	20.7**

Figure 2 Trends in age-standardized mortality in group of the countries as indicated, 1981–1989, 1981 = 100% (range of CV%: 2.8–7.5% in men; 1.7–8.8% in women). Latest recorded mortality: * 1987; ** 1988; † 1989; – no data available

or all other causes or both. Out of the former eastern bloc countries it was only East Germany that fell into this group. It should be noted that there were differences among the age-adjusted rates for these countries.

The most adverse mortality trends were in the former eastern bloc countries which formed the third group in this comparative study (Figure 4).

On the basis of the pattern of the age-adjusted death rates from avoidable causes in both men and women, European countries formed three distinctive groups (Figure 5).

Fifteen countries with the best rates in men formed a distinctive path in which two parts could be observed (Figure 5). The lower part included Switzerland, Sweden, The Netherlands, France, Greece and Norway, all with the lowest rates for avoidable mortality in Europe (the dotted area). The rates in the upper part (marked with dashed lines) were also much lower than the rates in the second group. None of the eastern European countries belonged to this group.

The eastern European countries and Portugal are gathered in the second group. In Portugal, however, the mortality rates declined fast over the whole period studied and by 1989 the Portuguese rates became lower than those of any eastern bloc countries. The third group was formed by Hungary and Bulgaria with their strikingly high death rates from avoidable causes.

The grouping of the European countries by the avoidable mortality rates in women was similar to that observed in men. There was one exception, at the beginning of the 1980s Scotland had higher avoidable death rates than those in the developed European countries, but by the end of the 1980s the rates for both Scotland and Portugal were related closely to the group of countries with low rates.

Among the former eastern bloc countries the avoidable mortality both in men and women was the lowest in the former East Germany.

Existence of an association between the levels of the latest available death rates (1987–1989) from avoidable and all other causes in the European countries has been studied. The relation between the levels of the two classes of mortalities is obvious in men (Figure 6). Men of the former eastern bloc countries are strongly separated from the men of the developed European countries by their mortalities from both avoidable and all other causes. Portugal and the former East Germany represent the transition between the two groups of countries. For women the difference proved to be primarily avoidable mortality (Figure 6).

Mortality rates from hypertensive and cerebrovascular diseases which represent more than half of the avoidable mortality have been analysed in a separate study of individual causes. At the end of the 1980s a fairly wide range for mortality rates from hypertensive and cerebrovascular diseases in both men and women could be observed (11.4 and 81.9 per 100 000 men, 7.2 and 44.9 per 100 000 women in Switzerland and Bulgaria, respectively).

Death rates from hypertensive and cerebrovascular diseases in men were the highest in the former eastern bloc countries (Figure 7). In addition, the rates proved to be relatively higher in the southern European countries,

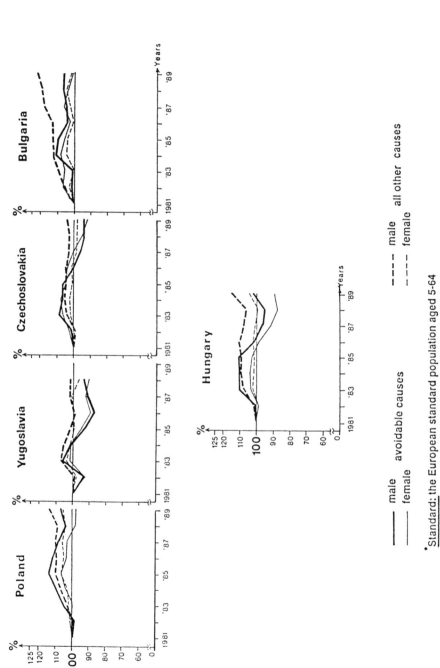

Figure 3 Trends in age-standardized mortality in some individual countries as indicated, 1981–1989; 1981 = 100%

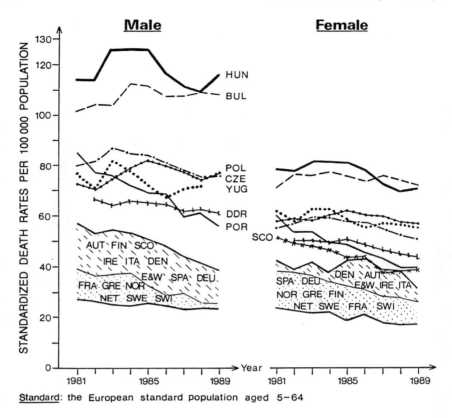

Figure 4 Trends in age-standardized mortality in some individual countries as indicated, 1981–1989; 1981 = 100%

Austria, Finland and Scotland. The mortality pattern from hypertensive and cerebrovascular diseases in women seemed to be similar to that in men, in addition to the former eastern bloc countries the death rates were relatively higher in Portugal and Scotland (Figure 8).

Regional mortality patterns from cancer of cervix uteri and corpus uteri were also analysed. At the end of the 1980s a wide range could be found in death rates from these cancers (3.5 and 14.8 per 100 000 women). The death rates from cancer of cervix uteri and corpus uteri were the highest in the former eastern bloc countries and in Denmark (Figure 9). In all these countries the death rates were higher than 10.0 per 100 000 women.

In the final analysis the death rates from avoidable causes without hypertensive and cerebrovascular diseases as well as cancer of cervix uteri and corpus uteri were studied. The mortality from all other avoidable causes

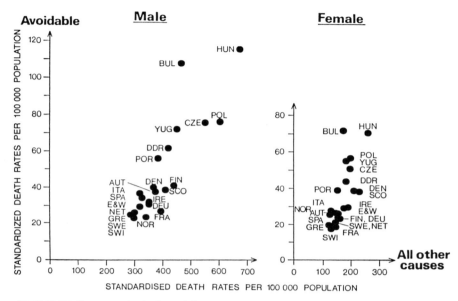

Standard: the European standard population aged 5–64

Figure 5 Trends in avoidable mortality in the studied countries, 1981–1989 (abbreviations: HUN, Hungary; BUL, Bulgaria; POL, Poland; CZE, Czechoslovakia; YUG, Yugoslavia; DDR, East Germany; AUT, Austria; DEN, Denmark; NOR, Norway; NET, The Netherlands; additional abbreviations as in legend to Figure 2)

in men and women was also the highest in the former eastern bloc countries (Figures 10 and 11). Moreover, relatively high mortality from all other avoidable causes could also be found in a few developed European countries. These death rates were relatively higher in women in Scotland, Ireland and Portugal, and in both men and women in Denmark.

In summary, in terms of the adverse trends in mortality from both avoidable and all other causes, the consistent high death rates from all avoidable mortality and selected individual causes such as hypertensive and cerebrovascular diseases, cancer of cervix uteri and corpus uteri, striking regional differences have been found between the bloc of eastern European countries and the other regions of Europe. Differences have also been found between the countries of the rest of Europe, but they proved to be inconsistent and smaller than the former ones.

Discussion

A number of previous studies have revealed considerable intra-country and inter-country differences as well as regional differences in avoidable mortality

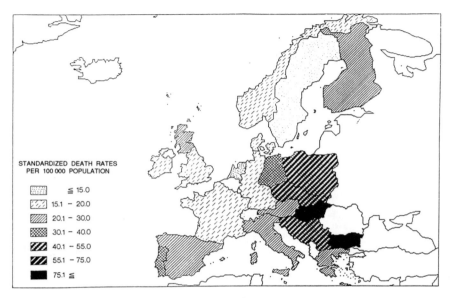

STANDARDIZED DEATH RATES
PER 100 000 POPULATION

≦ 15.0
15.1 – 20.0
20.1 – 30.0
30.1 – 40.0
40.1 – 55.0
55.1 – 75.0
75.1 ≦

Figure 6 Association between the levels of the latest available death rates (1987–1989) from avoidable and all other causes in the studied countries (abbreviations as in legends to Figures 2 and 5). Standard: the European standard population aged 5–64

(Bauer and Charlton, 1986; Bojan *et al.*, 1991; Boys *et al.*, 1991; Charlton and Velez, 1986; Charlton *et al.*, 1983, 1984, 1986; Kunst *et al.*, 1988, Poikolainen and Eskola, 1988). However, the majority of these studies on regional differences concentrated on a limited number of countries or one region in Europe such as the European community (Holland, 1988, 1991). The aim of the present study was to make as comprehensive comparison between the countries and regions of Europe as possible. Our study has shown that there is a region in Europe which is far behind the developed European countries in terms of the avoidable mortality.

A main concern in the studies on avoidable mortality is whether rates of mortality from conditions amenable to medical intervention can be interpreted as outcome indicators of the health services or whether they are under the control of a variety of socioeconomic determinants.

The concept of avoidable mortality as an outcome indicator has been frequently criticized (Carr-Hill *et al.*, 1987; Mackenbach *et al.*, 1990; Paul *et al.*, 1989). Indeed, avoidable mortality proved also to be influenced by socioeconomic factors to a large extent (Lagasse *et al.*, 1990; Mackenbach *et al.*, 1988a, b; Poikolainen and Eskola, 1988). In addition, variations in avoidable mortality could be due to variation in incidence or case fatality,

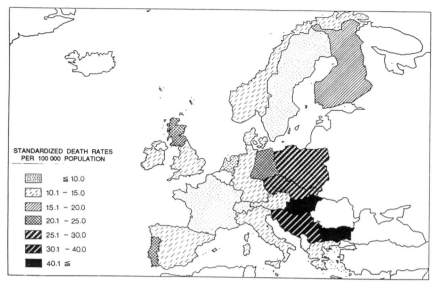

Figure 7 Mortality from hypertensive and cerebrovascular diseases in men in the studied countries, 1987–1989. Standard: the European standard population aged 5–64

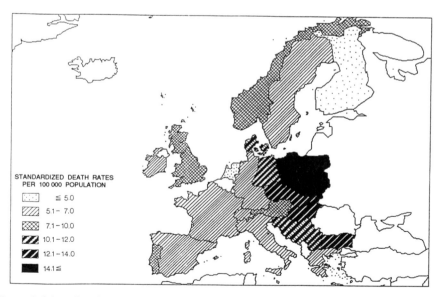

Figure 8 Mortality from hypertensive and cerebrovascular diseases in women in the studied countries, 1987–1989. Standard: the European standard population aged 5–64

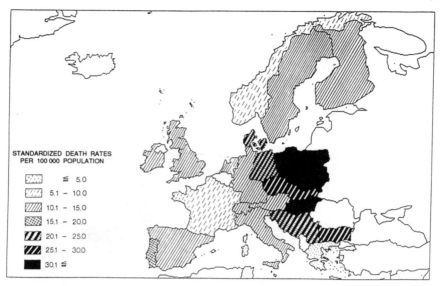

Figure 9 Mortality from cancer of cervix uteri and corpus uteri in the studied countries, 1987–1989. Standard: the European standard population aged 5–64

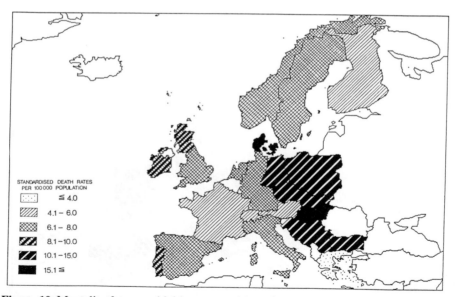

Figure 10 Mortality from avoidable causes without hypertensive and cerebrovascular diseases in men in the studied countries, 1987–1989. Standard: the European standard population aged 5–64

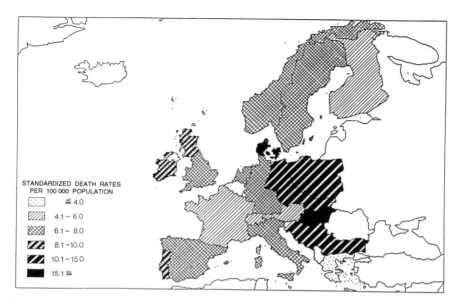

STANDARDIZED DEATH RATES
PER 100 000 POPULATION

[:::]	≤ 4.0
▨	4.1 – 6.0
▩	6.1 – 8.0
▨	8.1 –10.0
▨	10.1 –15.0
▉	15.1 ≤

Figure 11 Mortality from avoidable causes without hypertensive and cerebrovascular diseases as well as cancer of cervix uteri and corpus uteri in women in the studied countries, 1987–1989. Standard: the European standard population aged 5–64

differing certification and coding practices. Despite all these criticisms, avoidable mortality is now considered by many experts as a useful measure of outcome of medical care.

Recently Mackenbach *et al.* (1990) have reviewed the published work reporting avoidable mortality and concluded that the low levels of mortality from amenable causes which currently prevail in industrialized countries are likely to reflect, at least in part, the increased effectiveness of health services.

The former eastern bloc countries have been experiencing a very bad pattern of health status indicators (Forster and Jozan, 1990; Hajdu and Bojan, 1990) reflecting the socioeconomic problems in these countries. In these countries the health care systems have also been in crisis for a long time. Resources for health care have been very limited. Additionally, the former eastern bloc countries lacked an adequate supply of 'hard' currency to purchase advanced technology from the highly developed countries. The health care systems were centralized, fragmented, hospital-based, and badly managed. Performance and quality indicators and incentives have not been used in a systematized way (McKee, 1991).

It could be supposed that the adverse pattern of avoidable mortality in the former eastern bloc countries may reflect the deep crisis both in the health services and the socioeconomic environment. In these contexts there is much to put right in the former eastern bloc countries approaching Europe without frontiers.

Acknowledgements

This study was supported by an ETT grant from the Ministry of Welfare, Hungary (Grant No. T-10 T-460/1990). Thanks are due to Mrs Julia Moczok, Mrs Jolan Sari, Mrs Judith Szabo and Mrs Aniko Szabo for their valuable assistance.

References

Bauer RL and Charlton JRH (1986) Area variation in mortality from diseases amenable to medical intervention: the contribution of differences in morbidity. *International Journal of Epidemiology*, *15*, 408–412

Bojan F, Hajdu P and Belicza E (1991) Avoidable mortality. Is it an indicator of quality of medical care in eastern European countries? *Quality Assurance in Health Care*, *3*, 1919–2203.

Boys RJ, Forster DP and Jozan P (1991) Mortality from causes amenable and non-amenable to medical care: the experience of eastern Europe. *British Medical Journal*, *303*, 879–883

Carr-Hill RA, Hardman GF and Russel IT (1987) Variations in avoidable mortality and variations in health care resources. *Lancet*, *1*, 789–792

Charlton JRH and Velez R (1986) Some international comparisons of mortality amenable to medical intervention. *British Medical Journal*, *292*, 295–301

Charlton JRH, Hartley RM, Silver R and Holland WW (1983) Geographical variation in mortality from conditions amenable to medical intervention in England and Wales. *Lancet*, *1*, 691–696

Charlton JRH, Bauer R and Lakhani A (1984) Outcome measures for district and regional health care planners. *Community Medicine*, *6*, 306–315

Charlton JRH, Lakhani A and Aristidou M (1986) How have 'avoidable death' indices for England and Wales changed? 1974–78 compared with 1979–83. *Community Medicine*, *8*, 304–314

Forster DP and Jozan P (1990) Health in eastern Europe. *Lancet 335*, 458–460

Gil LMB and Rathwell T (1989) The effect of health services on mortality: amenable and non-amenable causes in Spain. *International Journal of Epidemiology*, *18*, 652–657

Hajdu P and Bojan F (1990) Lecture notes on social medicine. Medical demography. University Medical School of Debrecen (in Hungarian)

Holland WW (1986) The 'avoidable death' guide to Europe. *Health Policy*, *6*, 115–117

Holland WW (ed.) (1988) *European Community Atlas of Avoidable Death*. Oxford University Press, Oxford

Holland W (1990) Avoidable death as a measure of quality. *Quality Assurance in Health Care*, *2*, 227–233

Holland WW (ed.) (1991) *European Community Atlas of Avoidable Death*, 2nd edn. Oxford University Press, Oxford

Kunst AE, Looman CWN and Mackenbach JP (1988) Medical care and regional mortality differences within the countries of the European Community. *European Journal of Population*, *4*, 223–245

Lagasse R, Humblet PC, Lenaerts A, Godin I and Moens GF (1990) Health and social inequities in Belgium. *Social Science and Medicine*, *31*, 237–248

Mackenbach JP, Looman CW, Kunst AE, Habbema JDF and Van der Maas PJ (1988a) Regional differences in decline of mortality from selected conditions: The Netherlands, 1969–1984. *International Journal of Epidemiology*, *17*, 821–829

Mackenbach JP, Looman CW, Kunst AE, Habbema JD and Van der Maas PJ (1988b) Post-1950 mortality trends and medical care: gains in life expectancy due to declines in mortality from conditions amenable to medical intervention in The Netherlands. *Social Science and Medicine*, *27*, 889–894

Mackenbach JP, Bouvier-Colle MH and Jougla E (1990) 'Avoidable' mortality and health services: a review of aggregate data studies. *Journal of Epidemiology and Community Health*, *44*, 106–111

McKee M (1991) Health services in central and eastern Europe: past problems and future prospects. *Journal of Epidemiology and Community Health*, *45*, 260–265

Paul EA, Evans J, Barry J *et al.* (1989) Geographical variations in mortality from conditions amenable to medical intervention in Europe: the European Community atlas of avoidable death. *World Health Statistics Quarterly*, *42*, 42–49

Poikolainen K and Eskola J (1986) The effect of health services on mortality: decline in death rates from amenable and non-amenable causes in Finland, 1969–81. *Lancet*, *1*, 199–202

Poikolainen K and Eskola J (1988) Health services resources and their relation to mortality from causes amenable to health care intervention: a cross-national study. *International Journal of Epidemiology*, *17*, 86–89

Rutstein DD, Berenberg W, Chalmers TC, Child CG, Fishman AP and Perrin EB (1976) Measuring the quality of medical care. A clinical method. *New England Journal of Medicine*, *294*, 582–588

Rutstein DD, Berenberg W, Chalmers TC, Child CG, Fishman AP and Perrin EB (1980) Measuring the quality of medical care (second revision of Tables, May 1980). *New England Journal of Medicine*, *302*, 1146–1153

Rutstein DD, Mullan RJ, Frazier TM, Halperin WE, Melius JM and Sestito JP (1983) Sentinel health events (occupational): a basis for physician recognition and public health surveillance. *American Journal of Public Health*, *73*, 1054–1062

World Health Statistics Annual (1981–1989) World Health Organization, Geneva

Public/private mix and internal competition: aftermaths on the Single Market. The case of Italy

Stefano Capri and Gualtiero Ricciardi*, *University of Milan and National Cancer Institute, Milano, and *University of Cassino, Roma, Italy*

Introduction

The current Italian health care system is a National Health Service (INHS), created in 1978 along the lines of the British system, though with a marked decentralization of functions and responsibilities (regional governments, local health authorities).

The role of the Ministry of Health is exclusively one of providing guidelines and controls, and it has no real say in terms of the spending mechanisms of the individual regional authorities or regarding the procedures through which the health care services are offered.

The law had been designed as a remedy to the inequalities between different sectors of the population, providing all citizens with free health care of a high quality.

The goal was to guarantee all Italians an equal opportunity to maintain a good state of health, emphasizing prevention and health education, though without neglecting the areas of therapy and rehabilitation.

More than 10 years after its establishment the National Health Service has fallen decidedly short of its goals, lending itself to continuous criticism for inefficiency, inequality and corruption.

The focus of the controversy is the failure to separate between political and administrative procedures, resulting in interference by politicians who often lack expertise in the sector, but who nevertheless take part in technical and organizational decisions, using as their criteria considerations of influence-peddling and vote-getting rather than satisfaction of the needs of the population.

This situation has generated calls for reform, not only from the general public and the mass media, but also from a political force that cuts across party lines, leading to the formulation of a legislative proposal designed to guarantee that health care services be administered according to more technical, management-oriented criteria.

The public, state-sponsored system is accompanied by a richly endowed, highly developed private sector which has unique characteristics that make it a 'de-regulated but protected' sector operating in the absence of true mechanisms of competition.

The aim of this work is to provide an answer to the normative question of whether competition would be a feasible, appropriate way to improve the economic efficiency of the health care sector, given the public/private mix of its structure.

Privatization in Italy/EC comparison

Privatization of the health care system in the form of direct payment by citizens for care (private spending) has followed a completely different course in Italy than in the other EC countries; in the early 1960s the leading countries of the European Community had high levels of private spending as compared to total health care spending, except for the UK and Italy; then, while these last two countries maintained constant levels of private spending into and beyond the mid-1970s, the other countries significantly reduced their levels of private spending, though the levels were still higher than that in Italy (roughly 25% as compared to 12%) (see Figure 1). In 1978, however (with the introduction of the National Health Care Service in Italy), the stationary situation in the other European countries was contrasted by a rapid growth in private spending in Italy, which reached the average EC level in the mid-1980s (only in the UK did the low levels of the 1970s remain essentially unchanged).

In recent years, if the figure for private spending is combined with that for the resources administered directly by private suppliers (contracted services), then the trend for Italy shows the percentage of health care spending directly administered by the public sector dropping to below 50%

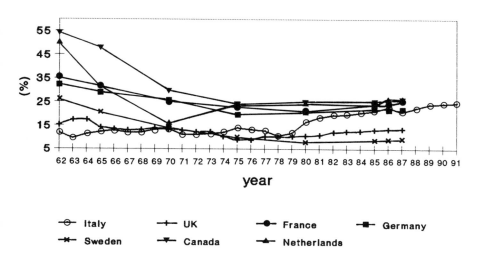

Figure 1 Private health expenditure/total, 1961–1991. * = Projected values

of total spending (see Figure 2). In other words, the Italian system would
appear to be quantitatively receptive to competition, though the market
mechanisms—both external and internal—necessary for effective compe-
tition are lacking, which results in what can be defined as the Italian
paradox.

Regional differences exist as regards the percentage of private spending:
contrary to expectations, according to which the south of the country would
be the area most prone to private spending, given the inefficiency of the
public sector, it is the more wealthy sector of Italy that spends proportionately
more on private health care, with the figure for 1990 being 30% as compared
to 15% in southern Italy and a national average of 25% (see Figure 3).

Finally, a relatively significant element is the degree to which the Italian
system is open to outside health care. Indeed, taking into consideration the
flow of spending for the care of Italian patients in EC countries, and vice-
versa, the spending figures (0.2% in 1983) show a marked imbalance in
favour of patients 'exported' as compared to those 'imported' (see Figures
4 and 5).

Perspectives for change in the EC

The overview produced by the analysis presented above shows a system
characterized by the following problems: (a) the absence of mechanisms for
competition; (b) a lack of mobility in the workforce (public sector contracts)

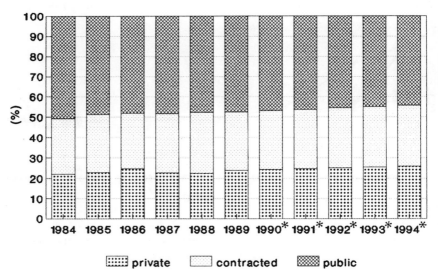

Figure 2 Health care expenditure by sector, Italy, 1984–1994. * = Projected values

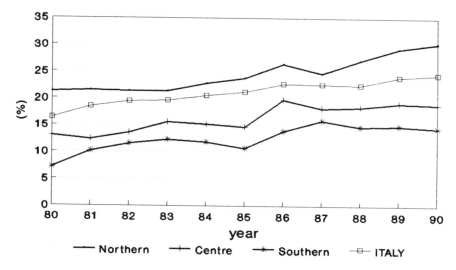

Figure 3 Private health expenditure/total, Italy, by area, 1980–1990

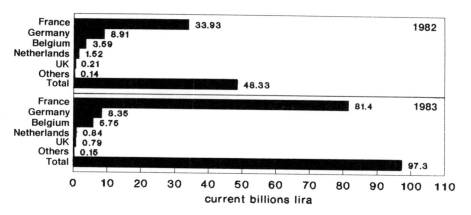

Figure 4 Government health expenditures in EC countries, 1982–1983

and a failure to hold the individual professionals responsible for their performance; (c) scarce penetration of the mechanisms of efficient administration (i.e. clinical budgeting, cost centres, etc.). A possible stimulus for change is the debate occasioned by the reform proposal.

The legislative proposal for reforming the National Health Care Service is geared towards guaranteeing that operating units receive guidance from

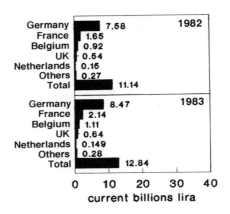

Figure 5 EC countries expenditures in Italy, 1982–1983

better-qualified sources, that are more prepared to take responsibility for their actions, and that are more likely to make independent, well-informed decisions designed to provide concrete solutions to the health care problems of the general public.

To this end the reform proposal calls for a period of transition, already under way, during which the management of the Local Health Care Units and the major hospitals is entrusted to special administrations, followed by a regularization of the situation through the appointment of a management board consisting of a general manager, a health care director and an administrative director, with the last two officials being selected by the general manager and hired on the basis of private contracts for specific periods of time, with the option of renewal—as is also the case for the general manager.

The underlying logic is similar to the thinking that produced the Griffiths Report in the UK, though it is limited to reforming the upper management of the health care system, leaving the operational and contractual structure of the system unaltered for the moment.

Though the legislative proposal is commendable for having introduced an initial series of changes into a situation that has become intolerable, it does not represent a true management approach—which, as Griffiths states, must install well-defined roles and clearly identifiable responsibilities throughout the entire health care system—but instead introduces hierarchically ordered administrative figures whose powers, though broad in theory, in practice prove significantly limited.

A specific example is personnel, which is selected, contracted and managed according to criteria typical of a highly inefficient, heavily bureaucratic public administration. In addition to this there is the extremely heterogeneous cultural, social and economic make-up of Italy, thanks to which the country is divided up into 21 different political and health care systems: one for each of the country's regions.

Indeed, as emphasized by Gwenael Pors, Europe still represents, in terms of health care, a paradox:

> There is no real common health policy in the EC. Europe is essentially an economic entity, only marginally technological, moderately social and only very slightly health-oriented.

But this situation must be subject to change, given that a growing percentage of the GNPs of the member countries are spent on health care; what is more, in the global village the errors of one country will certainly have an effect on the others.

For this reason it is to be hoped that common rules can be established on the Community level, with adequate standards being established and enforced while mechanisms for the planning, organization and management of health care services are made to function in a harmonious manner.

Privatization vs. competition: a proposal for internal competition

There has recently been debate over the need to introduce elements of competition into the field of health care, and in particular in the area of hospital care. The different positions are the result of experiences both in systems where the private sector is present to a significant degree (Enthoven, 1988, as well as in situations characterized by the presence of public health care services (or, in any event, publicly financed systems) (Saltman, von Otter, 1987, 1989, 1990; Enthoven, 1985, Department of Health, 1989; Ruttan, 1987). What is more, the reference framework is that of an equitable system, meaning one where the right to the same level of health care is guaranteed to all, regardless of their economic possibilities.

The motives underlying the introduction of competition would be: (a) achievement of greater levels of efficiency; (b) the possibility of an active role for the consumer and greater satisfaction on his or her part (exit, voice: possibility of choice); (c) expenses limited on account of greater controls resulting from the introduction of competition; (d) reduction of the role of politicians in the management of health care services.

In the opinion of Fama and Jensen (1983) the absence of a market where public-sector managers can capitalize on their performance (i.e. incentives tied to positive results) is the root cause of inefficient performance. For Alchian and Demsetz (1972) the weakening of property rights, which translates into incentives that are either lacking altogether or insufficient, explains the lower degree of efficiency of the public bureaucracy. The fact that it is almost impossible for the consumer to express dissatisfaction increases the likelihood of there being X-inefficiency, meaning behaviour on the part of health care professionals that falls below their actual production capacity:

> Considerable X-inefficiency may rise as a result of low pressure . . . low pressure on firms may exist because of considerable inability on the part of buyers of the services to understand the nature of the product. For example, this may be true of hospital services (Leibenstein, 1966, p. 604).

There would appear to be no way of identifying elements capable of increasing the participation of the consumer on the micro level, apart from the possibility of choice already present in the Italian system, though this too is limited by the various specializations in which the public sector is more technologically advanced than the private sector. Within this context it would seem advisable to publish the performance results of the various hospitals: apart from eventual effects on the financing of the hospitals this information could provide guidelines for consumer choices, as regard both individual patterns of consumption and collective choices expressed through political votes cast to change the political bureaucracy responsible for the results in terms of guaranteeing certain quantitative and qualitative levels of the services supplied.

In theory, competition does not necessarily lead to more limited rises in prices, but rather to prices that afford the consumer the highest possible level of well-being; as such, the introduction of competition does not necessarily lead to a reduction in costs (Robinson and Luft, 1987).

The concept of competition being proposed is the following: hospitals do not necessarily compete for patients (indeed, the market is characterized by limited mobility of patients), but rather they compete for the funding that can be obtained on the basis of results analysed according to identical parameters of efficiency.

Consideration should also be given to the contestability of the hospital market: in countries such as Italy the market is characterized by a low level of contestability. It is difficult to enter the market because of the high degree of regulation (permits, etc.); what is more, the limited presence of private insurance companies and the compulsory nature of the INHS health tax add to the difficulty of entering the market; it is equally difficult to pull out of the market, given the presence of sunk costs that are not easily recovered; in fact there is no competition between the public and private sectors, at least not in the most important segments of the market, meaning that competition exists only in residual segments, such as long-term hospital care and care of the elderly.

Given the above, a scenario in which public hospitals able to act independently compete with each other for market shares in a market that would already appear to offer a low degree of contestability would not seem to be a feasible solution. The proposal put forth in this work, therefore, does not involve competition for market shares, at least not directly, but rather competition for the management groups that already work in other hospitals, or that could change their sector of activity. Structured along these lines, the market would be contestable only in terms of its management, with entry into the market being open, and pull-out not entailing any costs (the losing group would leave without compromising the structure of the fixed investments or of the hospital itself). As is common knowledge, this characteristic denotes a situation of perfect competition, but what makes it a characteristic of a contestable market as well is the fact that the framework functions regardless of the number of hospitals involved or the nature of their ownership (in a certain sense there exists a public monopoly, though the individual hospital, in the person of its administrators, is characterized by its 'vulnerability to hit-and-run entry' on the part of other administrators— Baumol, 1982).

Another element of discussion in the formulation of an alternative proposal is represented by the contractual form of franchising (franchise contracts were first proposed for health care by Grant Thornton Management Consultants (1986), but were limited to health screening, or to specific services inside the hospital) between hospitals (which must obviously be granted administrative autonomy as regard all the various inputs, most importantly labour: at least in terms of establishing different salary ceilings from region to region, depending on the cost of living and the supply of labour. What is more, this would entail sacrificing the job security of public employees) and the State (which would retain ownership of the hospitals).

Under this approach the INHS would be responsible for the costs that cannot be recovered while the hospital management would work to reach a set of goals. In this way the problem of low contestability could be reduced not in terms of new hospital structure, but in terms of new management groups that would replace existing groups showing poor results. Indeed, the public authorities could hold periodic 'auctions' to find new management groups to replace those at the less efficient hospitals.

Within this proposed framework the public authorities would have to specify: (a) the qualitative characteristics of the services; (b) a definite reference framework for the investments to which commitments have been made by the public authorities for the reference period (including eventual subsidies to the private sector); (c) the transformation of personnel relations to a private-contract basis.

This proposal needs to be demonstrated rather than simply asserted. With this in mind, as stated in the Enthoven proposal commented on by Robinson and Luft (1987), the idea must be tested through pilot projects.

The approach followed in this work has presented the problem in terms of the structure to be chosen, meaning the appropriate institution (property rights, regulation), rather than in terms of the price that must be reached to reduce the scarcity and achieve the goal of greater efficiency in the hospital sector.

Setting the rules of the game in health care is a daunting task that must take into account and respect the social, cultural and economic differences between countries and, in the case of Italy, the high degree of internal diversification. But this is a task that must be confronted and brought to completion in order to avoid an enormous waste of resources, not to mention high costs in terms of social tension and inequality, given that, 'operating without rules continues to be the most difficult calling in the world'.

References

Alchian AA and Demsetz H (1972) Production, Information costs, and economic organization. *American Economic Review*, 62, 777–795

Baumol WJ (1982) Contestable markets: an uprising in the theory of industry structure. *American Economic Review*, 72, 1–15

Department of Health (1989) *Working for Patient*. HMSO, London

Enthoven AC (1985) *Reflections on the Management of the National Health Service*. Nuffield Provincial Hospitals Trust, London

Enthoven AC (1988) *Theory and Practice of Managed Competition in Health Care Finance*. North-Holland, Amsterdam

Fama EF and Jensen MC (1983) Separation of ownership and control. *Journal of Law and Economics*, 26, 301–325

Grant Thornton Management Consultants (1986) *Health Service Management. Developing Co-operation between Public and Private Hospitals*. Nuffield Provincial Hospitals Trusts, London

Himmelstein DU and Woolhander S (1986) Cost without benefit: administrative waste in U.S. health care. *New England Journal of Medicine*, 314, 441–445

Leibenstein H (1966) Allocative efficiency vs. X-efficiency, *American Economic Review*, 56, 392–415

Maynard A (1988) Privatizing the National Health Service. In Lloyds Bank annual review, *Privatization and Ownership*, Lloyd's Bank, London, pp. 47–59

OECD (1990) *Health Care Systems in Transition. The search for Efficiency*. Social Policy Studies no. 7. OECD, Paris

Parker P (1988) A free market in health care. *Lancet*, i, 1210–1214

Robinson JC and Luft HS (1987) Competition and the cost of hospital care, 1972 to 1982. *Journal of the American Medical Association*, 257, 3241–3245

Rutten FF (1987) Market strategies for publicly financed health care systems. *Health Policy*, 7, 135–148

Saltman RB and von Otter C (1987) Re-vitalizing public health care systems: a proposal for public competition in Sweden. *Public Policy*, 7, 21–40

Saltman RB and von Otter C (1989) Public competition versus mixed markets: an analytic comparison. *Health Policy*, 11, 43–55

Saltman RB and von Otter C (1990) Implementing public competition in Swedish county councils: a case study. *International Journal of Health Planning and Management*, 5, 105–116

The EC's need for a common currency in health care quality assurance

Janice L. Dreachslin and Marjorie Zernott*, *Penn State Great Valley Graduate Programs in Management, Pennsylvania, and *Commission on Professional and Hospital Activities, Michigan, USA*

Economic integration of the EC into a single community and the elimination of barriers to free trade will not result in a single health care system. However, the closer relationships among the member nations, and the members' individual desires for competitive advantage in the new market-place, will lead to an interest in comparing health care systems along cost and quality dimensions. Without a common currency for quality assurance, such comparisons will be time-consuming, costly, and of questionable validity.

Why address health data comparability in the EC?

Differences in health care expenditures at the aggregate level among the EC member nations are well documented. Total and public health care expenditures as a percentage of gross domestic product (GDP) varied from a low of 5.3% in Greece to a high of 8.6% in France in 1987, with per capita health expenditures varying between Greece's US$337 and France's US$1105. In the United Kingdom, health care expenditures as a percentage of GDP were 6.0% in 1987 or US$758 per capita (Schieber and Poullier, 1990). Culyer (1990) reports large international variations in the proportional distribution of health care expenditures among institutional, ambulatory, pharmaceutical and other components of expenditures.

The quality implications of these cost differences are significantly less well established. It is unclear whether higher health care expenditures result in significant improvements in the process and outcome of care. The data that we do have suggest that international health policy and practice variations must be more thoroughly examined in order to determine the impact of these differences on public health. As Culyer (1990, p. 39) concludes, 'Aggregate international comparisons cannot be used to indicate what health care spending ought to be, nor can they be used to prescribe its optimal growth rate. Such issues require patient and fairly detailed cost–benefit analysis of specific health care programs.'

As yet unaddressed data comparability issues stand as major constraints to meaningful cross-national, patient-level quality and resource utilization comparisons. With the formation of the EC the opportunity is here to address and, perhaps ultimately, remove this constraint to valid international comparisons of health care along a quality dimension. Data comparability is a basic and essential component of the policy agenda for public health within the EC.

Growing interest in international comparisons of quality of care is evidenced in the literature. Lomas (1990) attributes the growing international interest in quality assurance to the following three factors:

1. The consistent finding that approximately 20% of medical care is inappropriate.
2. The inability to explain variations in practice through reference to patient or facility characteristics.
3. The indications that decreased utilization due to economic or regulatory factors lead both to appropriate and inappropriate care reductions.

Adding to concerns about the relative efficiency and effectiveness of alternative models of health care delivery represented in the EC and in other democratic states, are the results of a recent consumer satisfaction survey (Blendon et al., 1990). Five EC nations—France, Italy, Netherlands, United Kingdom, and Germany—were included in the 10-nation satisfaction survey. Italy, with a national health service model, ranked most dissatisfied with their current health system among the five EC member nations studied. The Netherlands emerged as the most satisfied among the EC nations and, along with Canada, overall. Excluding the United States and Sweden from the analysis, Blendon et al. (1990) report that public satisfaction is associated with higher levels of per capita expenditures on health care.

With the exception of West Germany, over 40% of the survey respondents in each of the EC countries studied identified the need for fundamental changes in their nation's health care system. The relative dissatisfaction of survey respondents from the United States and Sweden undermines the notion that increased expenditures alone can create greater public satisfaction. What is the relationship between these public perceptions and the process and outcome of patient care?

Davis (1990, p. 114) identifies the need for international comparisons that are diagnosis-specific. 'Two types of information that would be especially valuable are research disaggregated at the diagnostic level and studies of the effectiveness of specific medical procedures and patterns of care for various diagnoses.' Evans (1988, p. 23) summarizes the current research need as follows: 'The answers at the aggregate level are already mostly in; it is time to look for God in the details.'

Evans (1988), Davis (1990), Enthoven (1990), and Schieber and Poullier (1990), all raise concerns about data comparability across countries. Differences in the definition of data elements will affect the validity of international comparisons. As Davis (1990, p. 114) states:

> Much more needs to be done to standardize definitions and reporting practices to establish comparable, timely, cross-national data bases. . . . Greater efforts should be made to conduct studies at the individual patient level, with cross-national comparison of treatment patterns, health outcomes, and costs. . . . Methodologies and data systems for making cost comparisons at the individual patient level need to be developed.

An agenda for developing QA's common currency

Establishment of the EC's common currency for quality assurance (QA) will require that consensus be achieved on all of the following:

1. The essential elements in a database for health care QA.
2. Common classification systems for key elements in the QA database.
3. Standardized conventions for coding practices to ensure data validity and reliability.

Essential data elements

Without the availability of a common set of data elements that are routinely collected in all the EC countries, international comparisons of quality and resource utilization will remain limited to broad, aggregate measures of questionable reliability and validity or to expensive, one-time studies that are difficult or costly to replicate. For quality comparisons to be specific enough to inform change in clinical practice, the common set of data elements must be collected at the patient level. Patient-level data can then be aggregated up to the level appropriate to answer the question at hand.

Dreachslin and Mendenhall (1986, p. 7) identified seven questions that a comprehensive QA data set should be able to address:

1. Who received the service?
2. What was the service?
3. How many did they receive?
4. How much did it cost?
5. When was it provided?

6. Who provided the service?
7. What were the results of diagnostic tests?

Each of these questions will require the collection of more than one data element. To address the question Who received the service? might, for example, involve the collection of data elements such as the following: ICD-9 or ICD-9-CM diagnosis codes, age, sex, town or postal code.

Agreement must be reached at the level of individual data element if valid, reliable comparisons among the EC countries are to be made on a routine basis. In Britain the Korner Report identified a national minimum data set for the NHS. The EC must, similarly, define a minimum data set that all health care facilities in all the member nations will collect and report to a central authority.

The definition of a minimum set of common data elements for the EC's health care QA comparisons is only the beginning. Without common classification systems for coding the data elements and standardized coding conventions, the validity and reliability of the resultant database will be questioned and results of analysis will not be relied upon to inform decision making.

Common classification systems

The medical record continues to serve as the source document for clinical information. Data must be abstracted from the medical record, coded, and made accessible via a computerized database. As information systems in health care facilities become more sophisticated and integrated, the order entry system will increasingly be relied upon as a source of clinical data that reduces the need for abstracting from a paper record. Regardless of how data are compiled, the selection of classification systems for common data elements to be used consistently across the EC countries is essential to the process. Such standardization will eliminate the need to design crosswalks between classification systems, e.g., ICD-9 and ICD-9-CM, and will address the associated loss of information, expense and risk of error.

The tenth revision of the International Classification of Diseases (ICD-10) is the logical choice for diagnosis coding for the EC member nations. ICD-10 will be available from 1 January 1993. But how should clinical services be coded? The WHO has not developed a numerical classification for clinical services comparable to ICD-10 for clinical diagnosis.

Meaningful international comparisons of QA and resource utilization require information about the discrete clinical services the patient received. What laboratory tests were performed? Which antibiotics were administered? In what dosage? What was the route of administration? Without these data it is not possible to compare the process of care among the EC member nations.

A focus on process, as defined by Donabedian (1968), will enable clinicians, managers, and policy-makers to explore the relationship between systematic differences in treatment paths for specific clinical conditions and patient outcome, resource utilization or cost-effectiveness. The heightened atmosphere for international cooperation generated by the EC provides health policy-makers with the opportunity to build data collection mechanisms that will allow researchers to explore the quality implications of documented cost and resource utilization differences among EC member countries.

The Commission on Professional and Hospital Activities has published a classification entitled *The International Classification of Clinical Services* (*ICCS*) (1989). This classification consists of 12 digit codes whose structure captures key aspects of clinical services that are specific to each clinical area. The coding structure for drugs, for example, captures the following: treatment category (anti-infectives, blood modifiers, hormones, etc.), drug name, route of administration (oral, topical, etc.), form (tablet, capsule, etc.), strength, and unit. The classification is in use in selected hospitals in the United States. *ICCS* and alternative classifications of clinical services that may be available need to be evaluated and pilot tested for use in building the EC's common currency for QA. A classification such as *ICCS* would standardize data commonly available through health care organizations' order entry systems. By using a system of mapping institution-specific codes to the *ICCS* codes, the need to change myriad internal collection systems could be minimized. However, the EC would still achieve a common patient-level database to be used for the type of detailed clinical comparisons being called for in the literature.

Standardized coding conventions

Even given a common set of data elements that are routinely coded using the same agreed classification schemes in each of the EC countries, the resultant EC QA database may still be invalid or unreliable without standardized coding conventions. For example, if diagnostic data are coded upon admission in one country and upon discharge in another, the resultant databases will not be comparable. A strong commitment to the integrity and importance of the data collection process is essential to building the EC's common currency for QA.

Next steps

The first step towards developing a common currency for QA in the EC is clearly that of agreeing upon a list of essential data elements that should be routinely collected for each patient encounter. A study identifying patient-level data elements that are either government-mandated or otherwise routinely collected in each member country would help inform the discussion. In addition, classification systems now in use to code common data elements in the EC member countries need to be identified, evaluated and compared. Coding conventions, educational programmes and courses of study for medical record personnel also need to be compared among the EC members.

Britain emphasized the importance of adequate information systems through funding six resource management projects (Black *et al.*, 1989; Central Consultants and Specialists Committee, 1989) in the years preceding the recent enactment of marked-based reforms within the NHS. Medical audit, i.e., QA, was an essential component of these reforms. The EC's health policy leaders might similarly fund pilot facilities in the member countries to explore the feasibility of building the EC's common currency for QA.

An EC-wide symposium on health care data would be a useful forum through which interested parties might begin the process of designing QA's common currency. The EC creates a new context for health policy-makers—a context wherein questions of relative quality and cost will be more often raised. The process of building a common currency that will allow researchers to address these questions is central to the EC's health policy agenda. The first steps towards its creation should be taken today.

References

Black A, Dearden B, Mathew D and Nichol D (1989) *The Extension of Resource Management: An audit for action.* NHS Training Authority, Bristol
Blendon RJ, Leitman R, Morrison I and Donelan K (1990) Satisfaction with health systems in ten nations. *Health Affairs, 9*, 185–192
Central Consultants and Specialists Committee (1989) *Resource Management Initiative: An evaluation of the six experimental sites by the CCSC.* British Medical Association, London
Commission on Professional and Hospital Activities (1989) *The International Classification of Clinical Services.* Commission on Professional and Hospital Activities, Ann Arbor, Michigan
Culyer AJ (1990) Cost containment in Europe. *Health Care Systems in Transition: The search for efficiency.* OECD Social Policy Studies No. 7, pp. 29–40
Davis K (1990) Respondent: What can Americans learn from Europeans? *Health Care Systems in Transition: The search for efficiency,* OECD Social Policy Studies No. 7, pp. 112–115
Donabedian A (1968) Promoting quality through evaluating the process of patient care. *Medical Care, 6*, 181–202
Dreachslin JL and Mendenhall S (1986) Seven data pieces for management. *Health Management Forum, 7* (3), 68–78
Enthoven AC (1990) What can Europeans learn from Americans? *Health Care Systems in Transition: The search for efficiency.* OECD Social Policy Studies No. 7, pp. 57–71
Evans RG (1988) Split vision: Interpreting cross-border differences in health spending. *Health Affairs (Millwood), 7* (5), 17–24

Lomas J (1990) Editorial: Quality assurance and effectiveness in health care: an overview. *Quality Assurance in Health Care*, 2 (1), 5–12

National Health Service and Community Care Act 1990. HMSO, London

Schieber, GJ and Poullier JP (1990) Overview of international comparisons of health care expenditures. *Health Care Systems in Transition: The search for efficiency.* OECD Social Policy Studies No. 7, pp. 9–16

World Health Organization (1990) The International Conference for the Tenth Revision of the International Classification of Diseases. *World Health Statistics Quarterly*, *43*, 202–285

The European community and Turkey: an assessment of Turkish health in the light of Turkish–EC relations

Fahreddin Tatar, *Nottingham University, UK*

Introduction

Turkey's adventure with the European Community could be analysed in two distinct phases. The first phase is characterized by a nationwide enthusiasm and excitement about the possibility of being a part of Europe. This would mean the realization of a long-awaited national goal, *westernization*, which was set out by the founder of the Republic, M.K. Atatürk. While Turkey is rapidly waking up from the EC dream, the second phase is emerging. This phase is characterized by disaffection with the EC since some people, including the political and administrative elite, have started to feel abandoned by the EC. Those who see the EC as a religious club more than anything else are more vociferous.

The developments in the ex-eastern bloc and especially in the former Soviet Union and the possibility of the Muslim and Turkic Republics of the former Soviet Union being able to approach Turkey has provided Turkey with an alternative. This is an alternative that will be exploited by those who feel Turkey has no place in Europe. The developments in the former Soviet Union have already started to pave the road for Turkey to establish greater economic ties with many break-away republics of the former Soviet Empire. This, in turn has placed Turkey in a much stronger position in her relations with the EC. Turkey is no longer a secular state that is squeezed between non-secular Persians and Arabs, but rather an economic bridge between Europe and the depths of Central Asia. That is why one can conclude that Turkey's chance of achieving an EC membership seems to be far greater than it has ever been.

However, is Turkey ready to exploit this evolving opportunity that has been long awaited in some specific quarters? Turkey has been waiting on the doorsteps of Europe for almost 30 years now. Has this been purely political or religious as some might like to see it? Or have there been, and are there still, some socioeconomic problems that Turkey has to solve to become a convergent State with the rest of the EC? In this paper an attempt is made to answer these and similar questions in relation to health.

Health status

Turkish people, on average, live some 11 years less than their counterparts in the EC countries. As seen from Table 1, the infant mortality rate (IMR) in Turkey is far higher than in the EC countries; while the average IMR in the EC is around 10 the figure for Turkey is reported to be 74.

The difference is not only in health status between the EC and Turkey. There are equally significant differences in demographic indicators. Population growth in Turkey, for example, is almost three times higher than that of Portugal, the country where the rate is the highest among the EC members (Table 1).

Table 1 Some comparative social and demographic indicators of EC countries and Turkey, 1988

Country	Average life expectancy (years)	Population under 16/under 5 (percentage of total)	IMR	Population growth rate, 1980–1987 (%)
Belgium	75	20.0/6.1	10	0.1
Denmark	75	19.6/5.9	8	—
France	76	22.0/6.8	8	0.4
West Germany	75	16.1/5.1	8	−0.2
Greece	76	22.0/6.0	13	0.5
Ireland	74	29.7/8.1	7	0.9
Italy	76	19.5/5.4	10	0.2
Luxembourg	74	—	9	—
Netherlands	77	19.9/6.2	8	0.4
Portugal	73	23.5/6.0	14	0.6
Spain	77	23.0/6.9	9	0.5
U.K.	75	20.2/6.5	9	0.1
EC	—	20.2/6.0	—	—
Turkey	64	37.2/12.7	74	2.3

Source: The figures have been compiled from: (a) OECD, 1990; (b) UNICEF, 1990.

Health care financing

The first obstacle that is faced by all researchers studying the Turkish health system is the lack or inaccuracy of relevant data. However, the data published by some international organizations such as the OECD, the World Bank and the World Health Organization, though slightly different one from another, could be enough to shed some light on the comparative performances of the EC countries and Turkey in health financing. According to OECD records Turkey's total health expenditure in 1987 was 3.5% of its gross domestic product (GDP). The EC countries' mean was, for the same year, 7%. In the same year the proportion of the public health expenditure to GDP in EC countries on average was 5.34%. This means that in the EC 76% of total health expenditures is from the public purse. This figure in Turkey was 41%, the same as the American figure in the same year (OECD, 1990, pp. 129–130).

Table 2 presents private health expenditure as a percentage of total health spending for EC countries and Turkey. Turkey is ahead of EC countries.

Health care organization

The most observable characteristic of the Turkish health system is its highly fragmented structure. There are multiple public and private health care providers and there is no system whereby the activities of different providers are coordinated on a macro level even within the public sphere. As far as secondary and tertiary health care is concerned, the Ministry of Health is

Table 2 Private health expenditures by country, 1987 (percentage of total)

Belgium	23
Denmark	15
France	25
Germany	22
Greece	25
Ireland	13
Italy	21
Luxembourg	8
Netherlands	26
Portugal	39
Spain	29
United Kingdom	14
EC (mean)	22
Turkey	59

Source: OECD, 1990, pp. 129–130.

the largest provider (Table 3). This is followed by the Social Insurance Organization (SIO), which provides manual workers and their dependants in both public and private sector organizations with health care. The scheme is financed mostly by the premiums paid both by employees and employers. These two largest providers are followed by medical schools, the Ministry of Defence (MoD), State Economic Enterprises (SEE), municipalities, and other ministries.

In the private hospital sector the scene is much clearer. Private sector health care organizations could be divided into four main categories: private, minorities, foreigners, and associations, which together operate less than 5% of hospital beds. Many hospitals in the private sector are non-profit-making hospitals.

Preventive medicine is provided by the Ministry of Health and some other public sector agents. With regard to primary health care services, it is the private sector which is the largest provider. Apart from a few private polyclinics there is a large number of private physicians supplying the first level of health care services. According to some estimates 44% of all physicians practise privately, including those who work also for the public sector on a part-time basis. This figure could be as high as 76% for consultants assuming that almost all private practitioners are consultants (State Planning Organisation, 1990, p. 200; State Institute of Statistics, 1990, p. 98).

Table 3 Number of health care institutions by ownership, October 1989

Institutions	Hospitals		
		Beds	
	Number	Number	Percentage
Ministry of Health	543	68 003	51.97
SIO	87	19 597	14.98
Medical schools	24	17 749	13.56
Ministry of defence	42	15 900	12.15
Private	98	3 404	2.60
SEE	15	2 146	1.64
Municipalities	5	1 160	0.89
Minorities	5	934	0.71
Other Ministries	3	780	0.60
Foreigners	8	670	0.51
Associations	9	505	0.39
Total	839	130 846	100.00

Source: Sağlık Bakanlığı, 1989.

Health coverage

In spite of many public sector health care schemes there is a large proportion of the population still with no organized health coverage. This figure is reported to be 41% of the whole population representing, some 22 million people (World Bank, 1990). It is stated that only 10 million of these people can afford to pay for themselves. The rest, however, are *de facto* provided with health care services in public facilities virtually free of charge.

Is the Turkish health system equitable?

Wagstaff *et al.* (1990, pp. 141–171) have done a comparative study on equity in the finance and delivery of health care. According to one of their analyses, as far as financing is concerned, the NHS of the United Kingdom, a predominantly general-taxation based system, was more equitable than both The Netherlands' and the United States' health care systems, which both had a greater involvement of private financing; 24% and 58% in 1975, respectively (OECD, 1990, pp. 129–130). Among the latter group, however, the researchers found that the health care system of The Netherlands was more equitable than that of the United States. For the same year, however, the share of private health expenditures in total was 52% in Turkey.

Although this and similar analyses should be treated tentatively, as these researchers themselves warn, it is believed that those systems which are financed more from private sources of finance, and especially in the form of direct household payments, are less equitable than those financed with a higher rate of public money and especially out of general taxation. It could be stated that in a country with a highly unequal income distribution, if more than half of the total health expenditures comes from out-of-pocket payments then the system should be regarded as inequitable. The system of taxation in Turkey is not particularly progressive when compared to the EC countries.

Is the Turkish health care system European?

In order to answer this question one need not undertake very detailed studies. The previous sections of this paper have outlined the major differences between Turkey and EC countries as far as both health status and health care systems are concerned. In this sense it is clear that the Turkish health system is not a European one. But, is it sensible to talk of a common European health care system while all health systems within the EC have different organizational and financial arrangements?

As has been outlined partly in the earlier sections there is a great degree of similarity among all EC countries in terms of achievements in health.

The IMR, for instance, varies between 7 in Ireland and 14 in Portugal among EC countries, whereas this figure is 74 in Turkey. While the EC countries are dealing mainly with diseases that are peculiar to industrialized societies Turkey is suffering from both this kind of diseases and others that are peculiar to the developing world.

It is very natural that each country would have a different amount and mix of health resources such as manpower, and health achievements such as a low rate of IMR reflecting different levels of development. However, the question is whether a given country has achieved as much as it should have, given its level of development. More important is whether a given country is on the right track to achieve what the front-runners in health such as the EC countries have already achieved, and learn from their mistakes so as to achieve it in a shorter span of time. It is on these issues that the claim that Turkey does not have a European health care system is based. Otherwise, the differences between Turkey and EC countries in health status have to be accepted as natural, given the different levels of development in the countries concerned.

If the level of (medical) technology employed within a country's health system can possibly be used as a criterion for being European then one cannot exclude the Turkish health system from being European, since the differences would be negligible. Similarly, the number of health professionals, especially of physicians, is increasing quite rapidly in Turkey. Since the early 1980s, increasing the number of physicians in Turkey has gained a new impetus. Under these circumstances by the year 2000 Turkey would reach a physician/population level almost comparable to EC countries. Nevertheless, such prospective developments would still not be enough to earn Turkey, as far as health is concerned, a European identity unless some fundamental differences separating the Turkish health system from its counterparts in the EC are minimized or eliminated. What are these differences?

Turkish health problems are typical developing world problems, such as high levels of IMR and child and mother death, communicable diseases, malnutrition (though not in the African sense), as well as industrialized world health problems such as cancer and circulatory diseases. All these are well reflected in the relatively low level of life expectancy in Turkey, which is around 63 years.

The Turkish health system, however, is not compatible with the needs of the country in many respects. It is a high-tech., hospital-based, and doctor-centred system. Resource allocations between geographical regions are grossly unequal, favouring urban to rural. As discussed earlier, in terms of finance it is quite inequitable with more than half of the total finance coming from private sources mostly in the form of direct payments for services. In order to reach the European health standards, and to meet the targets determined by the World Health Organization, instead of a needs-based planning approach a resource-based one has been adopted. It is because of this strategy that, while masses of rural and sometimes urban population are still suffering and dying from preventable infectious diseases, the country has been trying to deal with targets such as bed and physician per population for a long time.

Another negative element that has to be dealt with in Turkey is the issue of health coverage. Almost half of the population has no organized coverage and has to rely mainly on the Ministry of Health facilities for free services. The problem is worsened by the common lack of accessibility and availability of health facilities, particularly in rural areas.

Although the integration of public health care providers has long been a national health policy aim, and although it was reinforced by the 1982 Constitution, the Turkish health system is still as fragmented as ever. Assuming that this is a proper aim, the system is getting worse with the introduction of newly imported ideas such as self-governing hospitals. Like many other declared policies this is destined to be another item in the health policy scrap-yard of Turkey.

One of the long-standing problems of the Turkish health system is the lack of an effective information system. Although a need for a sound financial and administrative information system has always been stressed in both national and international quarters, there is still no attempt to deal with the issue. While this is being neglected all national and international efforts in the health sector to reorganize the system are still being based on usually inconsistent, inaccurate, and unreliable sources of data. And this alone seems to be the guarantee of failure in all these attempts.

A course of action for the EC and its member states, and Turkey

Turkey has close historical, socioeconomic, and political ties with both individual EC countries and the EC as a whole. These ties could be even closer with a likely decision to let Turkey enter the EC. Turkey, irrespective of its application to the EC, is under moral and social obligation to provide its citizens with a better life, and health is undoubtedly one of the most important ingredients of this. In order to fulfil this obligation Turkey has to take some radical measures, whether accepted to the EC or not. However, if joining the EC is an overriding aim for Turkey then in the health field, too, Turkey has to put its house in order to become more convergent with the rest of the Community. This would create some extra stimulus to take radical measures and execute them as fast as possible.

The EC, on the other hand, is facing two distinct possibilities. The first one is that if Turkey is ever going to be let in, then it is in the interest of the EC to help Turkey to solve its health problems as well as other socioeconomic and political ones before they become the problems of the

Community. Once in, and with the right of free labour movement across Europe, the health problems of Turks will no longer be a problem for the Turks alone, but for the whole Community.

The second possibility, however, is that even if Turkey is not thought of as a prospective member then still there are at least moral arguments for helping Turkey out of its problems. Moreover, a neighbour with severe health problems, considering the large contingents of Turkish workers in the EC countries and interflows of tourists and the like between Turkey and the EC, would be a constant threat to the health and, in turn, to the economies of the EC.

So far in this paper a brief account of problem areas in the Turkish health system has been presented. These problems are not necessarily incurable. It seems that solutions to the Turkish problems of health that are mostly a reflection of the mid-twentieth-century European health problems have been sought with the most contemporary solutions at work in Europe today. The policies being adopted, and reforms being implemented, throughout Europe today are all to deal with the problems of a developed world. That is why blind imitation of the reforms and techniques from this world would provide Turkey with a set of solutions that are not designed for the problems of the country. The question as to whether a (developing) country should follow the footsteps of the already developed ones has been a subject for ideological, political and economic discussions.[1] However, the issue here is not whether Turkey should or should not follow the footsteps of the developed world countries since the country officially has long adopted the policy of modernization through westernization in almost every aspect of life. Both 'capital' and 'cultural diffusion', the necessary ingredients of development according to Rostowian line of thinking, have been constant in Turkey for a long period of time. The issue here is rather about the way these diffusions are taking place and the effects that they have on Turkey.

The health care system and policies adopted in Turkey so far have not delivered the desired health outcomes. In fact, Turkey today has a health level that is far below its economic development level, as admitted by all parties including some international organizations like the World Bank. In terms of not only macro level indicators but also equality and equity, as has been stated earlier, the Turkish health care system has not produced any satisfactory results. This is obviously a failure in terms of policies and systems that have been adopted so far.

To say that the policies have not delivered the desired outcomes so far does not mean that there is nothing to be learned from others. Once this reality is admitted Turkey should adopt new policies that are based on her

---

1 The arguments that are centred around 'modernization' and 'dependency' theories are deliberately avoided here, due to the scope of this paper.

own human and material resources and more important, her own needs. As far as learning from outside is concerned Turkey should be extremely selective. If the developed world has to be imitated then Turkey has to look at the earlier periods that the countries of the developed world passed through a long time ago, too. Only this would give the chance to learn from the mistakes of the pioneers and avoid them. For example, Turkey should learn that unless the taxation system is improved and/or some extra measures are taken, the move to establish a universal health insurance system would increase the existing inequalities.

The EC, and other richer members of international society for that matter, on the other hand, in their relations with the Turkish health sector should, for reasons discussed earlier, also be sensitive to the real needs of the country. Turkey cannot afford to waste time and money. Instead of funding expensive projects that usually do not prioritize the needs of the country, projects that would help the country to stand on its own feet (self-reliance) in the matters concerning health policy development should be given priority. Whether this is realistic to suggest, or whether this would ever happen if it is left to the mercy of donors, are issues not dealt with here. However, if the answers to these questions are 'No, it is not', and 'No, it would not', then it means there is a lot more to be done by the recipient. In fact, in this case, *Europeanization* of the health system of Turkey would ironically be realized by distancing Turkey from both the EC and other developed countries.

References

Saglık Bakanlıgı (The Ministry of Health), Özet Saglık Istatistikleri (Summary Health Statistics). Saglık Bakanlıgı, Ankara

State Institute of Statistics (1990) *Statistical Yearbook of Turkey 1989*. SIS, Ankara

State Planning Organization (1990) *Health Sector MasterPlan Study, Report on the Current Situation*, State Planning Organization, Ankara

OECD (1990) *Health Care Systems in Transition*. OECD Social Policy Studies No. 7, Paris

UNICEF (1990) *The State of The World's Children 1990*. Oxford University Press, Oxford

Wagstaff A *et al.* (1991) Equity in the finance and delivery of health care: some tentative cross-country comparisons. In McGuire A *et al.* (eds) *Providing Health Care: The Economics of Alternative Systems of Finance and Delivery*. Oxford University Press, New York, pp. 141–171

World Bank (1990) *Issues and Options in Health Financing in Turkey*. World Bank, Washington, D.C.

From central planning to market forces: the implications for health services in Poland

Danuta Wiewiora, *The Polish Medical Association, Mickiewicza, Poland*

Introduction

Poland is undergoing a transformation from the so-called real socialism to a free market system. The public (social) sector, health service included, lags behind the relatively advanced economic and monetary changes. The old organizational and legal structures have been preserved in this sector. Such a situation has produced an acute crisis in the health care system.

How can the crisis be overcome? What type of health care system should function under the new political situation? This paper is an attempt to give an answer to this question.

Present problems in the health services

The existing Polish health care system has many deficiencies. State policies were dominant. Hospitals, outpatient clinics and special-service facilities were built and resources were centrally distributed according to predetermined budgets for health care institutions.

Health personnel policy was dominated by the requirement to educate as many doctors and nurses as possible. Lack of resources and prestige of health personnel resulted in a negative selection of candidates for medical studies and a decline in their ethical and moral standards.

Doctors did not receive sufficient information about technological and scientific progress or about new drugs. Doctrinaire education and poor research completed the bad image.

We should pay homage to those thousands of doctors who, despite the State system, were strong enough to preserve the good name of Polish medicine.

The centralized administration was expensive and ineffective and required about 20% of the total budget. The organization of services encouraged institutionalization but not the care of individuals. Patients could enter the system in different ways and could be treated by several different doctors. Naturally, in this situation the patient instead of the doctor became the coordinator of the treatment.

Health care costs bore no relationship to the achievements. The very high proportion of specialists (74% of the total number of doctors) resulted in patients being attended by specialists for illnesses that did not require such expertise. Free services at the point of consumption resulted in excessive use, and in abuse, of the health care services.

Inpatient stays in poorly managed hospitals were long and frequently were unnecessary or for social and not medical reasons. Investigations were commonly duplicated and also became a source of financial losses.

Access queues, black market, poor management and a lack of humanitarianism became common features. The patient–doctor relationship was paternalistic and far from a partnership. Medical visits frequently failed to solve the patient's actual health problems.

Other characteristics were common, such as the high frequency of breakdowns, poor performance of prevention services, and lack of health promotion programmes.

These defects resulted in an inefficient and ineffective system. It has been estimated that maybe 40% of resources were spent with no effect. No wonder that Poland, according to health indicators, is ranked as one of the unhealthiest countries in Europe.

The increasing cost of health services has only aggravated the situation. During the past two years, under the new economic policy, the government's financial capacity has decreased considerably. About US$110 per capita are spent on health care, which is less than 4% of GDP. Unfortunately, reforms of the health services have not been carried out, and the opportunity to conduct this reform, together with general economic reforms, has been lost. The implications of this are a continuing deterioration in health status, frustration among medical staff and the undermining of the authority of the State.

However, the interdisciplinary character of health services, the fact that managerial skills and technology are at a low level and that both medical and economic knowledge is required for good performance—all these things make the transformation more difficult.

Poland also lacks international models that could be adapted; but then almost every country is in search of new solutions.

Analysis of specific issues

The basic reason for the appearance of present difficulties is the fact that there are *limited resources for unlimited health needs*. The term resource should neither be understood exclusively as a certain percentage of GNP allocated for health, nor as the amount of expenditure per capita. Both values depend on the actual economic situation and actual prices and costs. They do not necessarily impact directly on the quality of health services. The lack of resources petrifies a system based on centralized budgeting, an overly developed network of health care institutions and far too many medical personnel. Some resources are wasted within this ineffective and inefficient system.

Because of the lack of money, *economic phenomena* are now dramatically evident, including the destructiveness of what we determine as 'moral hazard', or 'free service at the point of consumption' and those things that lead to a misuse of the health service. Health services are misused not only by patients who, for example, make redundant visits, but also by doctors who generate unnecessary visits when it suits them.

High and still increasing indirect costs have become a notorious phenomenon. Considerable resources are wasted because funds are raised at central level and subsequently distributed through institutional budgets, which leads to high administrative costs.

The financial crisis has caused the welfare state to collapse. The reality does not follow the constitutional provisions, nor does it conform to the promises made by State authorities and political parties. It is true that health care coverage is undergoing a deep crisis all over the world, but in a poor country with low GNP, such as Poland, it affects society in a particularly dramatic way.

In many countries the crisis in coverage has been accompanied by a decline in health insurance systems to pay the full costs. Western countries that still maintain this system preserve only its name and idea. Both the State and users make payments in addition to this form of insurance. Patients pay more and more of the costs. In Poland patients pay a central tax but they still need to meet more and more additional charges for their treatment. It is a dangerous situation. For many people these additional charges are beyond their family means, as is clearly seen for the recently passed Law of Parliament on drugs.

Analysis of some elements of the model

In health it is impossible to renounce the principle concerning the redistribution of resources. They must be transferred from better-off people to the poorer, from those who need few services to those who need them most. It is impossible to predict the health needs of a family. To meet them by means of a completely free market would mean to step back to the Middle Ages.

We know two redistribution systems: the first is based on an insurance premium paid by all citizens, and the other uses general taxation. In the face of a deep crisis in the social security system, the economic recession and the fall in average family incomes, it is not feasible for all members of Polish society to make payments for health insurance premiums. The remaining alternative is the State budget.

However, we know that State budget resources will not be sufficient.

Additional payments, regardless of taxes, will be necessary. Such payments require social justice and organizational effectiveness. It is a moral imperative that with a shortage of resources the little available should be used to meet basic needs, and the expenditure should be prioritized according to clear and strict criteria.

This cannot be done by means of a health system or by a law. Only doctors can do it, having regard to individual patient care, which suggests that funds should be given to those doctors who work as close to patients as possible, such as family doctors. The British model should be followed as an example, using the concept of family doctor budgets. A family doctor is also needed in Poland to reduce the first contact to one health worker and to take over responsibility for the organization of care and treatment from the patients.

The introduction of a so-called internal market is created when the *responsibility for resource is separated from the responsibility for services*. Therefore, some persons have resources at their disposal and someone else provides services. Between the two parties market mechanisms of supply and demand are generated with competition between suppliers. If the party disposing of resources is a family doctor he will face demand competition (free choice of doctors by patients). On the other hand, the party providing services will not have a centrally allocated budget, and will be transformed into a self-financing entity. The concept of the welfare state is preserved while allowing the market mechanisms into the game. These mechanisms should preserve the universal cover. A market mechanism, but not a free market system, will result. Such a solution shortens the resource distribution chain to the following three stages: Ministry–voivodship (local authority)–family doctor. It also reduces administrative costs and health care costs in general. It allows specialized treatment to develop at hospitals where it will be based on better technology. It also provides us with a certain organizational order because now a family doctor and not his patients will seek a hospital specialist's advice. It is also more humane and changes the doctor–patient relationship from being paternalistic and bureaucratic to a partnership.

Social welfare is undergoing crisis in Poland, together with the whole health care system. Only the return to individualization of social welfare, the involvement of the carer as a partner, or co-decider, is acceptable.

In Poland the most reasonable thing would be to separate treatment from prevention and to create a new service which I call home care. This service would integrate treatment and prevention problems, focused on patients at home, not around a health facility. I think that this service can prove effective when used in conjunction with community-run prevention and rehabilitation.

The above analysis of elements that are essential for the construction of a model health care system in Poland indicates that it is necessary to bring together holistic and individualistic ideas and to develop a flexible model, adaptable to changing financial circumstances in the State and to the financial condition of the people.

It is necessary to make use of the experience of the British health care system and to follow the principles of its last reform.

Proposed health care

The above observations suggest the following new model for the health care system in Poland:

1. Health care budget determined as a proportion of GNP.
2. Budget distributed by the Ministry through voivodships and given to family doctors using a special formula.
3. Thus, a family doctor assumes a particular position, representing both the state and the patients in his or her area. Apart from family doctors, all the remaining health care facilities (hospitals, specialists, diagnostics, dentistry, research, education) should function as self-financing entities.
4. The relationship between family doctors, who spend resources, and health care facilities, that provide all but basic services, should be based on contracts. Individual patients who are willing to cover the costs of greater comfort can supplement the resources provided by the family doctor.
5. State intervention should remain especially in the area of unique medical problems, research or education.
6. Service quality should be controlled by Medical Chambers which, above all, represent the doctor's interests and on the other hand, by a ZOZ (consolidated health care centre) which represents a patient's interest and medical needs.
7. Home care, prevention and rehabilitation should be controlled by local government (community).

The above model saves the concepts of universal cover and redistribution of resources, and simultaneously makes the health care system efficient, effective, well managed and humanitarian. It also preserves equality, accessibility and quality.

Model implementation

The principal idea for its implementation is the use of a monetary method. This allows rapid implementation in contrast to a managed reform model whose implementation tends to take longer and often becomes distorted by the pressure of particular interest groups. By the monetary method I understand that the central budget stops financing overnight health care facilities and distributes the resources among family doctors according to the number of inhabitants in their area. The appointment of family doctors also should be a result of the application of financial and market stimuli and not an effect of a centrally planned action (jobs should be well paid, there should be job satisfaction and some unemployment should be allowed among medical doctors).

I would also give the buffer role that would involve ensuring an orderly change to the new model to a ZOZ. This institution should constantly reduce its backup tasks as health care facilities become more and more self-financing, as progress in appointing family doctors takes place and as countries take over their obligations.

Adequate resources in the Ministry should allow State intervention when needs arise.

Potential obstacles for model implementation

The proposed model, if it is implemented, will challenge some interests of doctors and administration. It will certainly produce considerable unemployment among doctors. All health service employees will be affected in their response and labour patterns. Efficiency, kindness and effectiveness require completely different psychological attitudes than the ones generated by the 45 years of the communist regime. But if this transformation were possible in the business sector why should it not happen in the health care sector?

The reform itself within the model discussed above should not require additional resources. Doctors should become interested in their own further training. Computerization and data processing will depend on independent decisions of self-financing facilities. A family doctor will use the resources of existing regional outpatient clinics to provide space and equipment.

Therefore, financial resources or organizational problems will produce no obstacles for model implementation.

Acknowledgements

I owe acknowledgements to faculty members of the universities of Aberdeen, York, Birmingham, London and others which I have had the opportunity to visit several times. It is difficult not to mention Professor Enthoven, and his idea of the internal market, or Sir Roy Griffiths whose experiences were used to build the concept of home care. The model owes a lot to Professor Deker, President of the Board of Directors of Philips Company. I should mention also the British Council, who made it possible for me to complete studies of the reform and sponsored my participation at this Forum.

Workshop discussion report

Béatrice Majnoni d'Intignano, *Universités Paris, La Varenne St Hilaire, France*

What will the Europe of the Single Market be like? Prior to 1989 it was composed of a *west part*, with solid frontiers, and very heterogeneous health systems (national through taxation and compulsory health insurance funds), and an *east part*, with few or no frontiers and homogeneous health systems of national type and there was virtually no exchange between the two parts.

The 1990s will see radical change. In the west part the Single Market in the European Community (EC), the European Free Trade Association (EFTA), and the Scheengen Agreement will all relax frontiers for people, but it will not necessarily harmonize the health services. In the east part, the countries of central and eastern Europe (CCEE), new frontiers are emerging (e.g. Baltic States, Commonwealth of Independent States, CIS), national health services are changing towards a greater mix of social security and private health systems.

The general trend is towards regional provision of services. The supernational power of the EC will provide the context for the provision of services. The influence of nation states will decline. However, there will also be some moves towards diversity, with new patterns emerging in the Baltic republics, Czech and Slovak republics and the Yugoslav republics.

Due to strong demographic and economic pressure three types of *new immigrants* are emerging: skilled people inside the EC, partly skilled from CCEE to EC/EFTA, and unskilled from outside Europe.

Inside the EC the Community has been organizing the 'Coordination' of social protection for such migrations (e.g. tourists, migrant workers and retired people), so guaranteeing finance and access to care. Illegal immigrants will also partly benefit from these arrangements. In the CCEE such groups in the population could 'slip through the net' of any finance and social protection (e.g. Russian/Ukrainian immigrants).

Due to the structure of Europe three topics emerged from our workshop:

EC internal dynamics

Health is a 'non-issue' for the EC, and is perceived as only a 'component of any economic policy' (Maastricht Treaty). No harmonization can be expected in health care, but the general dynamics of the market can be expected to have powerful effects in three fields:

1. *Finance and reimbursement.* If purchasers are required to place tender

for their contracts in the EC there is a need to make costs comparable (e.g. capital included in all hospital costs); we can expect an *increase in services* available in the EC and an increase in the *demand* for new services from the poorly served countries (e.g. Italy/France for cancer treatments); we can expect a move towards the creation of standardized services (e.g. screening, bypass surgery) with monopolistic behaviour in some cases and specialties.

Is the creation of one health service crossing frontiers a goal for the twenty-first century, so as to stimulate workers' mobility? Might the EC be moving towards regulating the international provider/purchasers market? Should one health service be built? These questions need to be addressed by national governments and the EC.

2. *Evaluation of health service, quality assurance, technology assessment.* Wider assessment of forms of care, including comparative country/country studies; including the evaluation of forms of care that are not available or recognized in some countries (e.g. hypotension, spa treatment); cost-effectiveness of treatments and cost containment policies. In the national health service the purchasers' global budget will do this job. But in insurance-based systems, health ministers might be involved to protect the competitiveness of the national health enterprises in the Single Market; in the Single Market, once this was opened up, health care might be driven more by *demand* than by need, and hence there should be greater emphasis on determining 'real needs'.

3. *Population migrations.* For short stays this is presently covered by the 'coordination' privileges (between country of origin and country of destination, taking account of type of care). For long-term stays there are bilateral arrangements between governments on health insurance. It is important to ensure that people's health insurance moves with them. There is a need for greater knowledge about migration, specific health status (databases, network of experts, research and specific strategy).

Aid to CCEE

Levels of aid are low and debt is increasing. Both donor and recipient get poor value from aid. Coordination of international aid (WHO, World Bank, BERD, USA, etc.) and appropriate skills are lacking, leading to waste and duplication.

The use of people of the CCEE who have been trained abroad should be improved, aid should be linked to better-defined objectives, more partnerships should be used (EC hospitals, WHO Healthy Cities) and new roles of the states should be promoted rather than letting aid reinforce traditional forms of action. An equal democratic partnership, a clearing house for information and dissemination of experience in an understandable language, are needed. For example, research is needed to study the process and outcome of transition (for example, Hungarian health insurance) using the methods of social and contemporary history.

Information and databases

A superstructure of progress requires information. Only what is well measured is also well managed. Effectiveness and efficiency are two facets of society's concern for improved health status. Whereas some knowledge exists about resource allocation, well over two-thirds of medical procedures are not yet properly evaluated.

Two sets of data are required—on outcome of selected procedures, and on monitoring activity, expenditures and throughput. Outcome research is necessarily selective, therefore three priorities emerge: elective procedures: areas in which there are large practice variations and avoidable mortality and increased disability-free life years. Research at the European level offers a large potential for economies of scale and cross-fertilization. Diversity may enrich and accelerate the development of process and outcome research.

The best information systems will be those which focus on an integrated policy framework. Information budgets are a much smaller component of the production function in health than in most other goods and services. The enlargement of the information and research budget is desirable at all levels of government and service delivery. The European Commission's involvement in health policy is felt to be particularly uncoordinated at present.

A European health information strategy also requires better communication tools: from better definitions to the development of minimum data sets and a common stock of knowledge about health services research.

Conclusion

The main thrust of EC activities will remain in opening up market opportunities throughout any economic sector. Health as an issue still has to attract awareness. So the prolongation of protected marketing of new drugs, for example, is reflecting industrial interests much more than those of the consumer. The opening up of an international health insurance market and cross-border bids in hospital services in the future might well raise problems. These problems may be solved according to market regulations, and force national health systems to change their rules and structures. For example, French insurance companies and statutory German health insurance may begin to move into each others' markets, and this could induce financial changes as well as influence changes in the health systems. From the economic point of view there is little difference in this respect from other markets such as car manufacturers. But from the point of view of health care organization this will usher in a new phase where national policies might gradually lose control over health care provision. This is why, up to now, the EC Commission has been concentrating on marketable goods and coordination. Health care itself is still a 'non-issue' for the EC, although public health has now been included in the Maastricht Treaty.

Communicable disease control

Communicable disease control in a Europe without frontiers

Rafael Nájera, *National Institute of Health, Madrid, Spain*

The history of the control of infectious diseases is linked to the history of the movement of people and to the development of frontiers, regulations, isolation, quarantine and discrimination.

History demonstrates that advances in scientific knowledge are due to intricate patterns in which the dominant culture of society, ideology and politics play an important role. To illustrate this, cholera arrived in Bristol in 1831 and there were big disputes about the nature of the disease, between those who described it as 'cholera nostras', and those who considered it as 'cholera morbo asiaticus'. In 1883 Robert Koch discovered the organism *Vibrio cholerae* and this was accepted in academic circles by the year 1884. However, it was eight years before the International Sanitary Conference, held in Venice in 1892, adopted a resolution signed by the participant countries that cholera was a disease of the digestive tract and was transmitted by excreta and vomit. The emerging scientific culture played a role in all such discussions, and new knowledge influenced commerce through the quarantine of ships, goods and persons.

This is only one example of the reluctance to accept the germ theory of infectious diseases. As Henle pointed out in his classic 1840 essay 'On Miasmata and Contagia', previous theories from the sixteenth century, held by the so-called contagionists, stated that the disease passed directly from sick to healthy people. The identification of a germ allowed measures to be taken against it and this apparently reduced the importance of social factors. Soon epidemiologists were forced to recognize the effect of the environment, both physical and social, on the incidence of communicable and other diseases. The more recent 'web of causation' theory and the concept of 'ecological health' are some recent steps in the evolution of our understanding of the causes of disease.

Fortunately, the response to the development of the latest pandemic

Europe Without Frontiers. Edited by C.E.M. Normand and P. Vaughan
© 1993 John Wiley & Sons Ltd

disease, AIDS, is one of solidarity, even though problems due to discrimination exist and the social and economic problems associated with it also prevail. The continuing presence of infectious diseases in the world today is linked as much to the development of socioeconomic inequalities as it is to a lack of knowledge.

'Europe without frontiers' means that about 300 million people will be living together within the EC frontiers and a similar number exists in the greater Europe borders. In order to achieve unity some type of similar developments are needed, and similar standards should be used in the control of infectious diseases, in order that no uncontrolled outbreaks occur.

To this end, a good infrastructure needs to be developed consisting of standards and legislation, epidemiological surveillance networks and computerized information networks.

All this is a big challenge that requires consensus to be established by the countries in the European Community. To reach this point a Committee for Communicable Disease Control (CDCo) could be established under the auspices of the 'High Level Committee on Health' recently organized by the European Commission.

With this working structure in place an inventory of available resources for CDCo could then be done and a 'minimum requirements' type of agreement achieved. After that, the measures required to be taken for controlling specific diseases could be defined, and budgets and timetables established. Targets could be set for these activities to be achieved and an evaluation system could help in following up the efficacy and efficiency of the plan.

The discussions held at this Forum might be the beginning of such a Plan for Communicable Disease Control in Europe.

Variety of actions

The control of communicable diseases requires a large variety of different actions to be taken, according to the diversity of the agents involved and their sources. For example, the following could be considered: vaccines for measles, veterinary policy and regulations for brucellosis, abattoir control for hydatid disease, inspection of buildings for Legionnaires' disease, sanitation for typhoid fever, poultry feeding and food handling and processing for salmonellosis, health education for anisakiases, and blood screening for AIDS.

Far from being exhaustive, this list merely shows the variety of actions required for the control of communicable diseases. Many of them are not directly dependent on the health services but can be provided by other sectors such as agriculture, public works, legislation and the economy.

Epidemiological surveillance

Essential for every public health action is health information, obtained through epidemiological surveillance. Data collected from primary health services, hospitals, microbiological laboratories, networks for environmental control and for food control, can all provide the health authorities with information for judging the epidemiological situation and for decision-making about the preventive measures to be taken for disease control. This information should be returned in an analysed form to the individual centres so that they can understand their own position in relation to the total health problems.

Data for epidemiological surveillance should include not only demographic and morbidity and mortality figures, but also data on work and school absenteeism, environment, food, vector studies and data from special epidemiological investigations.

Of special interest are the data provided by laboratory studies, such as diagnostic and confirmatory tests, immunity studies, data on antibiotic resistance, results of studies with epidemiological markers and studies on molecular epidemiology and genetic and antigenic variability.

The analysis of such a range of epidemiological data provides the health authorities with general information and advice. At the same time it provides feedback information for health professionals and the community.

Models of epidemiological surveillance

Different methods for surveillance of communicable diseases exist in different countries according to the structure of their health services. In countries with a national health service, information is provided from doctors and laboratories acting as sentinels. These data are used for case–control studies, identification of trends, and for the evaluation of programmes. In countries with a greater free market health care system, surveillance is commonly based on specific sentinel groups and the data are used for identifying trends for diseases with a high incidence and for supporting mainly those intervention programmes for important diseases.

Levels of epidemiological surveillance

In the structure of health services, different levels can be identified. Communicable disease surveillance activities will be found in all of them. The first level, generally represented by the health centre, serves a population of 5000–30 000 people. It is usually the entry point to the services and provides integrated care, including health promotion and disease prevention. The identification of at-risk individuals or groups, of cases and outbreaks, is carried out mainly at this level. So too is the control of cases and contacts.

The second level is usually identified with the health area or district, commonly serving a population of 150 000–250 000 people. This is the first specialized level for epidemiological surveillance, able to identify risk-groups in the population and to provide specific support to intervention programmes. It usually has a public health laboratory and provides support for the health centres.

The third level or region represents the level of health policy, where analysis, planning and evaluation for action commonly takes place. It corresponds to the health services of autonomous governments or states in federal countries. In federal countries a fourth level of coordination corresponds to the federal government itself which, in centralized countries, undertakes general planning, decision-making and the organization of control measures.

Communicable diseases in a Europe without frontiers

When we consider the implications for health of a Europe without frontiers in relation to the control of communicable diseases, four main items need special attention.

1. *Coordination*. This is a very important prior condition for the establishment of real links between countries, and needs some previous steps for its implementation:
   (a) a definition of areas of mutual interest, such as communicable diseases, environmental problems related to them, food-related problems, health education, microbiological laboratories and an epidemiological network;
   (b) a description of all the resources in the different countries available for communicable disease surveillance, particularly epidemiological surveillance and a network of laboratories;
   (c) establishment of a standardized information format that allows for the interchange of data between the countries and, in relation to this, it is necessary to fix the minimum amount that will be provided by each country to the rest of Europe;
   (d) establishment of the basics required to develop a computerized European network for epidemiological surveillance.
2. *Equity*. It is very important to be realistic about the differences that exist between the health services, socioeconomic conditions and health infrastructure in the European countries. A priority should be greater equity if the control of communicable diseases is to be achieved. Four points are of special interest to achieve a more equitable distribution of resources:
   (a) a catalogue of available resources, material and human, should be available in the different countries;

(b) a budget needs to be assigned in each country for communicable disease control, sufficient in total amount and as a percentage of the total public health budget;

(c) the minimal objectives to be achieved in resources and budget by 1997 and the year 2000;

(d) specific and concrete commitments should be taken to overcome any deficiencies in the necessary budget.

3. *Protection of health.* For the protection of health in relation to communicable disease control some interesting aspects should be considered:

(a) the definition of the necessary indicators is necessary if the present situation is to be well described, comparisons between regions and countries are to be made, and the achievements of the established control programmes are to be demonstrated;

(b) the health measures that are to be taken for epidemiological surveillance and the control of risk factors, which are derived from environmental conditions, human behaviour or socioeconomic and cultural factors;

(c) establishment of standards for training in communicable disease control for the different cadres of health, sanitation and environmental personnel, community and social workers, health educators, food handlers, etc.;

(d) establishment of a network of public health laboratories which exchange information on methods and results.

4. *Promotion of health.* The points established in the Ottawa Charter for Health Promotion, complemented in some respects by the Conferences in Adelaide and Sundsvall, are interesting for community disease control in two respects. There is the need to build a healthy public policy, to reorientate health services, to create supportive environments, to strengthen community action and to develop healthy personal behaviours. To get to this point it will be necessary to:

(a) define the objectives, in relation to public policy devoted to improving both the physical and socioeconomic environments;

(b) link costs of medical care and preventive measures to specific diseases, as a very important element in decision-making at a high level, in order to achieve greater equity in access to healthy conditions;

(c) define the concrete activities that need to be taken, including the necessary budget provision, timetable and the evaluation criteria and mechanisms.

Proposal for minimum requirements to be achieved by consensus

Taking these ideas into consideration, I consider that it will be necessary to achieve a European consensus on the minimum requirements for a coordinated and efficient communicable disease control. These requirements should be:

1. To have a communicable disease surveillance system based on data collection and public health laboratory services.
2. To agree a list of diseases to be included in this surveillance system, together with the laboratory criteria for diagnosis.
3. To establish the control measures to be applied in relation to vaccinations, taking into account the WHO EPI programme.
4. To take specific measures to control food poisoning, selected zoonoses, 'imported' diseases, blood-borne infectious diseases, sexually transmitted diseases, nosocomial infections and transplant and immunocompromised patient-associated diseases.
5. To create a catalogue of minimum requirements for the sanitation infrastructure to be achieved by the years 1997 and 2000.
6. To select the important areas for research and the specific goals to be reached.
7. To establish the budget and time schedule for the concrete actions to be implemented to achieve the previous points.

The final and main proposal is this: under the umbrella of the 'High Level Committee on Health' of the European Community, a Committee for Communicable Disease Control should be organized which has the task of defining the minimum activities and resources that would be necessary to achieve a high level of control throughout Europe.

Communicable disease surveillance in France

Bruno Hubert and Colette Roure, *Direction Générale de la Santé, Paris, France*

Epidemiological surveillance is the systematic collection, analysis and interpretation of health statistics, their analysis and use in the evaluation of public health programmes, and rapid dissemination of the information to those who need it.

Objectives and principles of surveillance

In the field of communicable diseases, surveillance has the following objectives:

1. To know the incidence and characteristics of infectious diseases; to study their rate and geographical pattern of spread, and to predict the future pattern.
2. To put in place systems and indicators of outbreaks; to intervene early to interrupt the chain of transmission;
3. To understand risk factors in order to suggest the best measures to prevent outbreaks.
4. To evaluate preventative interventions.

Surveillance can be developed in various ways:

1. Starting with clinical and/or biological criteria (the information sources can be practising clinicians and laboratories).
2. Starting with comprehensive or sample investigation, depending on the type of disease covered:
   (a) serious and/or uncommon diseases, compulsory registration or notification;
   (b) frequent and not serious illness, starting with samples from the doctors' network or laboratories.
3. With continuous or periodic further data collection.
4. Passive (wait for information) or active (regular contact with the sources of information).
5. Possibilities at several geographical levels: national, regional, departmental or communal.
6. With the most appropriate system for transmission of information: questionnaire, telematic network, telephone.
7. If possible it is important to use at least two independent but complementary surveillance systems for the same illness. Comparisons of information obtained by these different systems of surveillance make it possible to check that the information gathered is complete and representative.

Surveillance systems in France

In recent years the surveillance of communicable diseases has experienced a significant development in France for several reasons: the observed inadequacy of surveillance almost solely based on compulsory notification of certain diseases; the growing need to evaluate health policies; the emergence of new diseases, AIDS in particular; the need to intervene in particular diseases linked to the consumption of contaminated foods. This growing need for knowledge and for action has led to a diversification of surveillance systems, the use of new methods of communication (telematic network), the preparation of protocols for intervention in the event of an outbreak and better dissemination of information.

The surveillance of communicable diseases at a national level in France relies on several information systems: notifiable diseases, national centres of reference, networks of microbiology laboratories, networks of general or specialized doctors, and investigations into particular groups of the population. The list of diseases presently under surveillance is presented in Table 1.

Compulsory notification

In order to make compulsory reporting of certain communicable diseases a more viable instrument of epidemiological surveillance, the list of diseases and the methods of notification have been reformed. The Decree (10 June 1986) stated the list of diseases that have to be notified. This list can be divided into two: the first group is diseases that justify taking steps at national or international level. These diseases must be confirmed by the appropriate national reference centre. The second group justify taking steps at a local level, or alternatively their notification is used as an evaluation instrument.

The majority of notifiable diseases are sufficiently serious to involve hospitalization, so the reporting is by the hospital doctor responsible for the treatment after the diagnosis is confirmed. In primary care only three notifiable diseases require confirmation, which are tuberculosis, brucellosis and all alimentary toxi-infections.

The reports are made on questionnaires specific to each illness and include demographic information, clinical and risk factors. These questionnaires are sent to the DDASS (medical inspectors of health and health engineers) of each department; each DDASS handles the reports and the information supplied as confidential. Every week the reports are sent to the bureau for communicable diseases at the Direction Générale de la Santé; an evaluation is carried out periodically at a national level and it is published in the *Weekly Epidemiological Bulletin* (BEH).

As with all passive systems of surveillance, the notification cannot be used to compile disease registers. Also it is important to evaluate the notification rates and in particular the representativeness of the collected information. This evaluation is possible only if other independent systems of surveillance exist for a given illness. The notification rates vary according to the illness, and they are better for very rare or very serious diseases

(100% for poliomyelitis, 85% for AIDS, 70% for meningococcal infections). The rate also varies according to department (varying between 0% and 100%). However, qualitative evaluation shows both that the data are representative, and that the notification is sufficiently consistent over time to allow analysis of trends.

Lastly, separate from the notification, practitioners are asked to report as quickly as possible to the doctor at the DDASS by telephone, telematic network or letter:

1. All severe communicable diseases in the relevant categories.
2. Cases with unusual clinical features or where the course of the disease is unknown.

The national centres of reference

The national centres of reference (CNR) are appointed for three years by order of the minister in charge of health. There are 40 centres and 17 of them are located at the Pasteur Institute in Paris. The list of centres is printed in the *BEH* No. 9/1990. The centres have the following aims:

1. Expertise: help with the identification of strains of viruses at the request of medical (or sometimes veterinary) laboratories. This work depends on the upkeep of prototype strains and/or the referencing of antisera. These activities are often the direct application of the research work in the centres.
2. Contribution to epidemiological knowledge by identifying individual strains from specimens. For this work to be effective the samples analysed at the centre must have the same strains as samples in France as a whole, and complementary information about samples such as age, sex, clinical signs of the illness, the nature of the tests, supposed origin of the contamination, etc., is necessary.
3. Awareness: each centre is bound immediately 'to inform the minister in charge of health of all verification that has been requested in their work which may have serious repercussions on the state of health of the country'. This is equally justified with groups of cases (salmonella due to the same serotype, listeria, Legionnaires' disease and in isolated cases of rare diseases (haemorrhagic viral fevers, botulism, plague, cholera, poliomyelitis).
4. To give advice on administrative matters, such as technical meetings, or for setting recommendations (malaria prophylaxis for travellers, vaccination timetable, composition of influenza vaccine, tuberculosis surveillance).

Table 1

Disease/causative organisms	International surveillance	Mandatory reporting	Sentinel networks	Laboratory networks	CNR	Other sources of information
Anaerobic (Bacteria)					*	
Arboviruses:						
Yellow Fever	*	*			*	Local networks
Dengue		*		*	*	
Botulism		*			*	
Brucellosis		*			*	Animal brucellosis
Campylobacteria				*		
Cholera	*	*			*	Vaccination records
Whooping cough					*	Vaccination records
Diptheria		*				
Acute diarrhoea			*		*	
Enteroviruses				*	*	
Haemorrhagic viral fevers	*	*			*	
Influenza	*		*		*	Prescriptions, absenteeism
Haemophilus				*	*	
Viral Hepatitis			*	*	*	Local networks, blood donations
Nosocomial infections					*	Immediate enquiries
Hydatid		*			*	Immediate enquiries
Legionella					*	
Leishmania					*	Immediate enquiries
Leptospirosis					*	
Listeriosis				*	*	Food
STD						
Chlamydia				*	*	STD clinics
Gonorrhoea		*		*	*	STD clinics
Syphilis		*		*	*	STD clinics
Male Urethritis			*			

						Notes
Meningococcal	*				*	
Mycobacterial						
Tuberculosis	*				*	Immediate enquiries
Leprosy		*			*	
Mycoses			*			Vaccination records
Mumps	*				*	
Malaria	*				*	
Pasteurella					*	
Plague	*				*	
Pneumococcus		*		*	*	Vaccination records
Poliomyelitis	*	*		*	*	Animal rabies
Rabies	*	*		*	*	
Rickettsioses		*			*	Vaccination records
Rubella		*	*	*	*	Vaccination records
Measles		*	*	*		Food
Salmonella	(*)1				*	
Shigella					*	
AIDS	*		*		*	Prevalence surveys blood donation
HIV Infections		*	*	*	*	
Staphylococcus					*	
Streptococcus		*				Vaccination records
Tetanus	*				*	Vets
Other food poisoning	*			*	*	
Toxic shock syndrome				*		Immediate enquiries
Toxoplasmosis					*	
Tuleraemia				*		
Typhus	*			*	*	

The national telematic network of communicable disease surveillance

This network was created in 1984 within the framework of a collaboration between DGS (Direction Générale de la Santé) and URBB Unité de Recherches Biomathématiques et Biostatistiques (INSERM U263). It is based on the telematic communication systems connecting different partners: the Bureau of Communicable Disease of DGS, URBB, national centres of reference, National Laboratory of Health, DDASS, 'sentinel' doctors and laboratories.

The network of 'sentinel' doctors involves 550 GPs, which represents 1% of French GPs. These unpaid doctors are recruited in such a way that the sample is representative of all French GPs (age, sex, type and place of practice). Seven communicable diseases are monitored continuously by this network. Moreover, non-routine epidemiological enquiries are carried out on request (attitude regarding vaccination, Lyme's disease). The results of the surveillance are published weekly and distributed by electronic mail, giving the spatiotemporal occurrence of the surveyed disease.

The telematic network is also used to transmit other information such as DDASS communications concerning the number of diseases notified weekly and the LNS (National Laboratory of Health) network, which is described below. In other respects such a system of communication allows the partners to communicate directly amongst themselves. This allows the 'sentinel' doctors to highlight all unusual pathological observations in their practice, and it also allows the health services to distribute their warning messages.

The National Laboratory of Health Network (LNS)

The epidemiological unit of the National Laboratory of Health alerts the network of private and public medical biology laboratories to microorganisms (bacteria or viruses) identified by their activities. This network can be divided into three categories:

1. (a) The general network links the hospital laboratories covering all of France, and provides, on a monthly basis, an exhaustive summary of organisms identified or confirmed under their administrative authority, analysing different kinds of specimens, and covering certain diseases.
   (b) The EPIVIR network (viral epidemiology) was established in 1980 and brings together specialized virology laboratories.
   (c) The EPIBAC network (bacterial epidemiology) was set up in 1983. Until 1990 it registered all the reported bacterial infections and bacterial meningitis. From 1991 it covers only systematic infections due to the following bacteria: *Haemophilus influenzae*, *Neisseria meningitides*, *Streptococcus pneumoniae*, *Streptococcus* groups A and B, *Listeria monocytogenes*.

2. Specialized networks are made up of public and private laboratories throughout France and are concerned with particular pathogenic agents diagnosed by isolation or serology: RENAGO (gonorrhoea), RENACHLA (Chlamydiae), RENASYPII (syphilis), RENAVI (HIV), RENAROUG (measles), RENARUB (rubella).
3. The warning network is linked into the national surveillance telematic and communicable disease information network. At the moment this network covers approximately 25% of hospital and bacteriological laboratories and covers infections of *H. influenza*, *L. monocytogenes* and *N. meningitides*. An automated telematic bulletin presents a continually updated synthesis of the facts.

Periodic or non-routine enquiries

Instead of continual surveillance periodic enquiries may be used:

1. If problems posed can be studied by prevalence enquiries (nosocomial infections, enquiries into HIV in hospitals, enquiries into prevalence of HIV in pregnant women).
2. To evaluate preventive actions; vaccination coverage in schools, knowledge of preventive measures (for example sexually transmitted diseases, AIDS, congenital toxoplasmosis).

Finally enquiries are sometimes carried out to discover the incidence of diseases not covered by the routine surveillance: retrospective enquiries into the toxic shock syndrome, anisakiasis, Lyme's disease.

Other sources of information

Other sources of information are used to validate indirectly the surveillance systems or the preventive actions. Data are collected by different organizations: statistical services, study and information services (SESI), National Centre for Blood Transfusion, pharmaceutical industry, Common Service No. 8 of INSERM. The information comes from:

1. Medical death certificates.
2. Sales of medicines or vaccines.
3. Screening activities:
   (a) blood donations (syphilis, hepatitis B, HIV),
   (b) sexually transmitted diseases clinics;
   (c) anti-tuberculosis services.
4. Health certificates for 24 months vaccination cover.
5. Hospital morbidity (using data on treatment from information systems).

Distribution of information

All the results of surveillance are regularly analysed and noted in the *Weekly Epidemiological Bulletin* (BEH), which is sent out to 5000 subscribers. The DDASSs have been encouraged to develop departmental epidemiological bulletins, better suited to the local epidemiological needs. Detailed regional information on AIDS is also distributed each week to those involved in surveillance (practitioners, public health professionals). Lastly, the results of surveillance in France are regularly communicated abroad by intermediaries such as WHO or by BEH who sent them to numerous national surveillance organisations.

Further Reading

Thacker SB and Berkelman RL (1988) Public Health Surveillance in the United States. *Epidemiological Reviews*, *10*, 164–190

Circulaire DGS/PGE/1CNo68 18/1/1988 relative à la déclaration obligatoire des maladies transmissibles. BEH 5/1988

Valleron A, Bouvet E, Garnerin P *et al*. (1986) Computer network for the surveillance of communicable diseases: the French experiment. *American Journal of Public Health*, *76*, 1289–1292

Chambaud L, Dab W and Hubert B (1989) Les recherches-sentinelles en France. Carateristiques actuelles et éléments de reflexion pour comprendre leurs conditions d'utilisation. *Revue du Practicien—Médécine Générale 79*, 79–86

Bouvet E, Brunet JB, Hubert B, Laporte A and Roure C (1991) Le bulletin epidemiologique hebdomadaire. *Revue du Practicien—Médécine Générale*

Workshop discussion report

Christopher L.R. Bartlett, *Communicable Disease Surveillance Centre, London, UK*

Context

Human frontiers have always been artificial barriers. Historically, the truth of this statement has been exemplified by communicable diseases, as shown during the past decade with the global spread of AIDS and the extension of cholera to the Americas.

Several factors have come into play recently which further challenge the relevance of regional or national frontiers. These are the dramatic increase in international travel, the development of even more complex and widespread food distribution networks and the opportunities presented by improved telecommunication which will help create a truly international culture.

It follows that communicable diseases will have to be controlled through more international action. The Maastricht Agreement will enable the European Commission (EC) to contribute to this control through encouraging cooperation and support. Furthermore, there is commitment to scientific collaboration in Europe among public health workers involved in communicable disease control. There is also a strong desire to develop an international training programme.

In considering our recommendations there was complete agreement that surveillance is the key to communicable disease control. The effectiveness of surveillance and investigation for the control of outbreaks for long-term prevention has been frequently demonstrated, and there is good evidence that this approach is cost-effective.

The establishment of international surveillance will increase the detection of such outbreaks at an early stage, thus enabling control measures to be implemented. Comprehensive investigation of the source may reveal hazardous practices or inadequate quality assurance which, when corrected, will contribute to long-term prevention.

Action plan

International surveillance

Our first action point identifies the means by which international surveillance may be strengthened. It is the firm view of our workshop that appropriate international policy for communicable disease control will follow upon the creation of international surveillance and not the other way round. There is considerable variation in the quality of surveillance in Europe both with the EC and between western and eastern countries. International outbreaks have been detected in some countries but remain unrecognized in others.

We recommend, therefore, that the EC, in collaboration with the European office of the World Health Organization, should facilitate the strengthening of international surveillance by:

1. (a) Encouraging a minimum standard of quality for surveillance systems in all European countries.
   (b) Harmonizing, and where appropriate standardizing, definitions and methods—this is a prerequisite for international comparison and essential to establish the correct priorities for prevention.
   (c) Developing public health laboratory networks for surveillance including reference laboratories for specific agents.
       National surveillance systems based on statutory notification by

clinicians and sentinel reporting are well established in many European countries. This is not the case for laboratory-based surveillance, although this method is often required to detect communicable disease outbreaks. Furthermore, the wider application of current microbiological reference techniques and the development and harmonization of new typing schemes will strengthen the surveillance of long term trends in infectious diseases.

2. A pilot system needs to be established and funded through EC for international surveillance of communicable diseases which is highly responsive to rapid changes in the pattern of disease and to allow effective action.

There is in existence a successful reporting system in Europe for AIDS. What is required, in addition, is a pilot system for the surveillance of infections which have shorter incubation periods. This system should be highly responsive so as to rapidly detect changes in the pattern of disease. Ideally, the data should be transmitted electronically and analysed centrally at least weekly, to identify outbreaks.

There was a lively discussion as to whether international surveillance in Europe be based on a single dedicated *centre*, or achieved by means of epidemiological networks and distributed databases; most of our group were in favour of the former.

3. (a) A technical forum for directors of surveillance/control from each country should be created at a European level to review surveillance methods and results, and to provide information and advice for international policy formulation.

(b) This forum should establish a task force of epidemiologists/microbiologists who are willing to collaborate in international field investigations of outbreaks detected through international surveillance.

Research and development

4. Research on communicable diseases and development of international surveillance and control in Europe should be recognized as priority areas for funding by the EC.

Training

5. The EC, in consultation with WHO and ASPHER, should set minimum standards for postgraduate education in communicable disease control.

6. The EC should fund a postgraduate fellowship programme to provide practical training in the necessary surveillance skills, to build expertise for the future and to foster the development of international surveillance.

Policy development

7. To assist policy development the EC should establish an advisory body to identify specific areas where communicable disease prevention could best be achieved through international action.

   It is clear that there will be economic pressures (the demand for a level playing field in the market) that will force the standardization of preventive measures. It is essential that policies on prevention are based on sound scientific evidence, from surveillance and research, which should be assembled by this body. It might also advise on priority areas for research on communicable disease control.

8. All countries in Europe, not only member states of the EC, should also benefit from these recommendations.

   A recurring theme in our deliberations was the need to strive towards equity in developing the systems for communicable disease control across the whole of Europe.

Health and the environment

Health aspects of hazardous waste disposal sites

Helmut Brand, *Kreis Minden-Luebbecke, Gesundheitsamt, Public Health Department, Minden, Germany*

Definition of hazardous waste and hazardous waste disposal sites

At the moment there is no consensus on how to define 'hazardous waste'. The definition of the European Community under the EC Directive COM (88) 399 considers waste to be hazardous if it contains anything from its scheduled list, or if it is derived from a certain process as specified in the Directive, of if it has certain defined properties which render it hazardous (European Community, 1991). Because this definition is not yet applied in all countries of the EC the term 'hazardous waste' will be used for any waste which may present a hazard to human health or the environment through either handling or disposal. This is the same working definition used by the British Medical Association in its report on hazardous waste and human health (BMA, 1991).

'Hazardous waste disposal sites' in this article are all controlled or uncontrolled and/or abandoned landfill sites that contain hazardous waste. Incineration, marine disposal or chemical or physical treatment will not be discussed.

Scope of the problem

There are no exact data on how much hazardous waste is produced. It is estimated that in 1989 there were 4.5 million tonnes in England and Wales (BMA, 1991) and 10.6 million tonnes in West Germany in the year 1985 (UBA, 1989) compared with estimated 255–275 million tonnes in the US (Office of Technology Assessment, 1983).

Surveys in several countries have been aimed at estimating the number of hazardous waste disposal sites (Table 1). The actual number is difficult to determine, because many sites operated uncontrolled, or are now inactive because they have been filled. The number of illegal operated sites is not

Europe Without Frontiers. Edited by C.E.M. Normand and P. Vaughan
© 1993 John Wiley & Sons Ltd

Table 1 Number of hazardous waste disposal sites in various countries

Country	Number of dumps	Year of survey
Austria	2 300[a]	1988
Denmark	3 115[a]	1982
France	800[a]	1982
Germany (West)	40 000[a]	1988
Netherlands	7 500[a]	1988
UK	12 000[a]	1987
USA	30 000[b]	1983

[a] Rat von Sachverstaendigen fuer Umweltfragen, 1989
[b] US Congress, Office of Technology Assessment, 1983

known. Additionally some sites operated for a very short time, and are now forgotten. They are often rediscovered when, for example, private houses are built on these sites.

Public concern on hazardous waste disposal sites

In a survey by the UK Department of the Environment disposal of hazardous waste was the public's biggest environmental concern, and was ranked higher than acid rain or pesticides (Central Statistical Office, 1990). Most people are suspicious of hazardous waste sites. The NIMBY (not in my back yard) syndrome describes people's attitudes towards the problem best (Walker, 1991). The concerns most often voiced from persons living near hazardous waste disposal sites are about cancer and adverse effects on the reproductive system (Berman and Wandersman, 1990). Another centre of concern are children, since at some waste sites, children are at increased risk of exposure due to mouthing behaviour and forms of play activities (Johnson, 1988). Often there is a discrepancy between perceived and actual risk (BMA, 1987). In a study of residents in Love Canal no association was found between the concerns expressed and actual proximity to the site; but there was a closer relation between fear of exposure and perceived distance from the site than with actual distance (Howe, 1988).

Risk assessment

To decide on the potential hazard to human populations from waste site exposures it is necessary to classify the health risks posed by the waste site. This is done by application of a health risk assessment. This term covers a broad group of laboratory, environmental, and epidemiological investigations. In contrast, a standardized risk assessment protocol refers to a set of operationally defined criteria used as the basis for site classification and decision-making with regard to potential remedial actions (Marsh and Day, 1991). An example for such a protocol is given in Table 2. Using a scoring system and a set of decision rules, sites can be classified on a priority list.

Chemicals found in hazardous waste disposal sites

In the US, 951 hazardous waste disposal sites were on the National Priority List (NPL). This comprises a list of the most dangerous sites (EPA, 1987a). The number of different compounds found at NPL sites is large and growing. For most sites it is not known exactly which chemicals are inside. Among the more commonly encountered substances (Table 3) are many that have been judged by the Environmental Protection Agency (EPA) and the Agency for Toxic Substances and Disease Registry to deserve high priority as reportable hazardous substances (Table 4) (EPA, 1987b). The chemicals

Table 2 Standardized risk assessment protocol checklist for hazardous waste disposal sites

1. Hazardous site
   Documentation of the presence of a hazardous site
   Toxicity of the five most hazardous substances on site
   Quantity of the five most hazardous substances on site
   Persistence of five most hazardous substances on site
   Concentration of five most hazardous substances on site
   Site management and substance containment
   Potential for direct access to site

2. Exposure potential of environmental pathways
   Groundwater
   Surface water
   Air
   Deposition on (in) soil off site
   Presence of food chain

3. Potential for human exposure absorption
   Presence of potentially exposed population
   Basis for evidence for human exposure/absorption
   Levels of substances found through biological sampling

4. Health effects in the exposed population
   Allegations/reports of health effects
   Results of clinical or epidemiological studies conducted
   Expectation of current acute short-term health effects
   Expectation of future chronic or long-term health effects
   Severity of public health impact of presumed health effects

From Marsh and Day (1991), by permission of National Institute of Environmental Health Sciences

Table 3 Substances commonly detected at National Priority List (NPL) sites and their concentration in groundwater

Substances	Prevalence (percentage of all sites affected)	Concentration in groundwater (ppm)	
		Average	Maximum
Halogenated hydrocarbons			
Trichloroethylene	34	3.82	790
Chloroform	21	1.46	220
Polychlorinated biphenyls	19	—	—
1,1,2,2,-Tetrachloroethane	17	9.68	21 570
1,1,1-Trichloroethane	16	1.25	618
1,2-*Trans*-dichloroethylene	12	—	—
Methylene chloride	11	11.2	7 800
1,1-Dichloroethane	9	0.31	56.1
Vinyl chloride	8	0.80	516
Carbon tetrachloride	7	0.54	20
1,2-Dichloroethane	7	6.33	440
Aromatic hydrocarbons			
Toluene	28	5.18	1 100
Benzene	24	5.0	1 200
Phenol	15	3.27	80
Ethylbenzene	13	0.65	25
Xylene	12	4.07	150
Chlorobenze[a]	7	0.10	13
Pentachlorophenol[a]	6	—	—
Metals			
Lead	31	37	31 000
Zinc and compounds	16	—	—
Cadmium	15	0.85	225
Arsenic	15	30.6	3 670
Chromium and compounds	14	—	—
Copper and compounds	11	—	—
Chromium	10	0.69	188
Mercury	9	0.34	50
Nickel and compounds	7	0.50	50
Heavy metals	7	—	—

[a] Also a halogenated compound
From Upton *et al.* (1989), by permission of the *Annual Review of Public Health*, Vol. 10, © 1989 by Annual Reviews Inc.

listed in Tables 3 and 4 are commonly also found in hazardous waste disposal sites in other countries.

Table 4 List of the 50 most hazardous substances
(Environmental Protection Agency and Agency for Toxic Substances and Disease
Registry)

Group 1	Group 2
Benzo(*a*)pyrene	Carbon tetrachloride
Dibenzo(*a,h*)anthracene	Chlordane
Benzo(*a*)anthracene	*N*-nitrosodimethylamine
Cyanide	4,4′-DDE, DDT, DDD
Dieldrin/aldrin	Chloroethane
Chloroform	Bromodichloromethane
Benzene	1,1-Dichloroethane
Vinyl chloride	Isophorone
Methylene chloride	1,2-Dichloropropane
Heptachlor/heptachlor epoxide	1,1,2-Trichlorethane
Trichloroethylene	1,1,2,2-Tetrachloroethane
N-nitrosodiphenylamine	Pentachlorophenol
1,4-Dichlorobenzene	3,3′-Dichlorobenzidine
Bis(2-ethylhexyl)phthalate	Benzidine
Tetrachloroethene	1,2-Dichloroethane
Benzo(*b*)fluoranthene	Toluene
Crysene	Phenol
p-Dioxin	Bis(2-chloroethyl)ether
Lead	2,4-Dinitrotoluene
Nickel	BHC-alpha, gamma, beta
Arsenic	Bis(chloromethyl)ether
Beryllium	*N*-nitrosodi-*n*-propylamine
Cadmium	Mercury
Chromium	Zinc
PCB-1260,54,48,42,32,21,1016	Selenium

Group 1 has higher priority than group 2
Chemicals are arrayed in each group according to increased Chemical Abstract Service number
From EPA (1987b), with permission

Human exposure

Possible means of human exposure are water, air, food and soil (Figure 1).
The most important route of exposure has been through contaminated
drinking water from groundwells. Acute toxic episodes were not reported,
but chronic exposure may cause adverse health effects. The average
concentrations of the most commonly detected chemicals in the groundwater
near hazardous waste disposal sites are given in Table 3. By leaching dumps
it is possible that large amounts of water are polluted, for example, small
amounts of halogenetic organic compounds render the source useless as
drinking water.

Contaminated soil can be a potential health hazard for small children
because of the oral intake, which is estimated to be between 200 mg/day

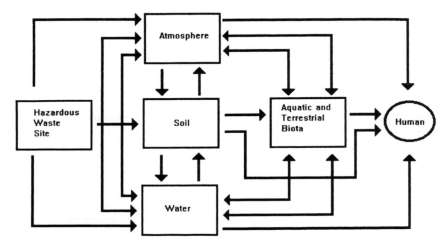

Figure 1 Routes of human exposure to toxic substances released from hazardous waste sites

and 10 g/day (Duggan and Williams, 1977; Kimbrough *et al.*, 1984). Elevated lead concentrations were found in the serum of children living near lead-polluted soil (Ewers and Brockhaus, 1987). Therefore it is important that land development does not take place on closed waste sites.

The contamination of foodstuffs by toxic chemicals is facilitated by the structure of the food chain. Therefore contaminated agricultural products can lead to an increased body burden in humans.

In waste dumps methane is produced and released in the air. For persons living next to or on such sites this can lead to adverse health effects, especially when methane or other gas can be found in the cellars of such buildings (Eickmann, 1987).

Adverse health effects

There are no studies on adverse health effects of workers accidentally exposed to hazardous waste. The numbers of workers on sites is small, the amount of time a person works is limited and the use of protective equipment is enforced (Melius, 1986). A study on workers who had been employed to inspect, evaluate and clean up hazardous waste disposal sites did not show any relationship between exposure and health effects (Favata and Gochfeld, 1989).

Contaminations with dioxin and furans seem to be ubiquitous (Czuczwa and Hites, 1986). Background concentration in humans is about 30 ng TE/kg fatty tissue in Germany (Basler *et al.*, 1991). Adverse health effects will occur from 1500 ng TE/kg fatty tissue, but physical examination of exposed persons should start with 60 ng TE/kg fatty tissue and upward. The daily intake is about 1 pg TE/kg fatty tissue. PCDD and PCDF are now usually found in hazardous waste disposal sites. The health effects of these substances—when chronic exposure takes place—are not known. A recent study on workers exposed to dioxin showed a slight but significantly higher mortality from all cancers than expected (Fingerhut *et al.*, 1991).

Relatively few investigations on health effects in populations potentially exposed to chemicals from disposal sites are published in refereed scientific journals (Upton *et al.*, 1989); most of the papers were published in the US. The majority of articles are news media reports or papers printed in the lay press. In a survey on public health investigations in the US at 21 disposal sites (UAREP, 1985; Grisham, 1986) 25 (86%) of the 29 studies were concerned with multiple chemical exposures. A measurement of body burden as an index of exposure was used in seven (33%) cases. Study design frequently took into consideration distance of residence from the disposal site.

A general medical questionnaire accompanied by a physical examination was used in nine of 29 studies. Nearly all questionnaires relied on participant recall. Another source of information was hospital or GP medical records.

Cancer incidence, reproductive outcome, neurological changes, medical care utilization and cytogenetic abnormalities are typical indicators of health effects which are used.

The main epidemiological methods were case–control studies (five studies), cross-sectional (seven studies), cohort studies (four studies) and case reports (three studies). Forty per cent of the studies reported fewer than 100 participants and only 10% included more than 1000 participants.

Nearly all these studies have been criticized because of inadequate study design, choice of health outcome and determination of exposure (Phillips and Silbergeld, 1985). To date, no sufficient evidence has been provided to support the hypothesis that a causal link exists between exposure to chemicals of a hazardous waste dump and adverse health effects, although several positive associations have been shown:

1. From 1930 to 1953 over 200 chemicals were dumped into an abandoned canal, Love Canal, in Niagara Falls, New York. The canal was later covered with earth, and a house and school were built over it. In 1978 residents of houses bordering the canal noticed odours that were traced to the chemical dump. A series of health investigations ensued. A study on cancer rates showed no consistent elevation (Janerich *et al.*, 1981). Two other studies reported adverse health effects, but there was no exact knowledge of chemical exposure in the cohorts studied. In one study a significant excess was found of low birthweight babies at the time the

dump was active (Vianna and Polan, 1984). Another study reported that some health problems, e.g. seizures, learning problems, hyperactivity, eye irritation, skin rashes, abdominal pain, and incontinence, were more prevalent in Love Canal children (Paigen *et al.*, 1985).

2. In 1979 hazardous waste was discovered near wells that supplied water to Woburn, Massachusetts. There were 32 volatile organics identified in the drinking water. Studies found elevated rates of leukaemia, perinatal deaths and congenital disorders in children (Lagakos *et al.*, 1986). However, the investigators concluded that the entire leukaemia excess was not explainable by the two contaminated wells.

3. In the Netherlands more than 250 houses were built between 1972 and 1975 on contaminated soil in the town of Lekkerklerk. It was discovered that the drinking water and underfloor voids of the houses were contaminated with hazardous substances. Residents complained of various non-specific illnesses. The area was evacuated and the site was cleaned up in 1981.

4. An incidence study revealed a significantly increased incidence of leukaemias in the district of Minden-Luebbecke, West Germany, near to a closed hazardous waste disposal site (Greiser *et al.*, 1991). Linear regression of community incidence rates with community distance to the hazardous waste disposal sites showed significant negative coefficients for leukaemias and malignant lymphomas. A case–control study and a study on birth defects in this region are in progress.

Conclusion

There are numerous hazardous waste disposal sites in Europe. They are widespread and a source of potential risk to the health of the population. The number of sites in eastern Europe cannot even be estimated at the moment. A central 'Register of Hazardous Waste Sites' on a national and European level, that includes location and compounds found at such sites, could help to provide an overview of the magnitude of the problem. This is essential for setting up priority lists for remedial actions.

There are only a few published epidemiological studies of the health effects on exposed populations. These have often been small studies in which the exposure has not been adequately characterized. There is a need for 'European Guidelines' on health impact evaluation to make efficient use of the invested resources.

With a 'Register of Hazardous Waste Sites' studies on health effects should be planned and coordinated. In this way it will be possible to improve the quality of studies and to carry out meta-analysis on the data.

The evidence to date on health effects is inconclusive. Possible health effects are decreased birthweight, increased number of malformations and certain types of cancer. Therefore there should be a surveillance system in every European state for these special health effects near hazardous waste sites.

In the planning process for new hazardous waste sites monitoring of health effects, and an initial description of the health of the people living next to the site, should be included.

References

Basler A, Greim H, Henschler D *et al.* (1991) Stellungnahme zu Dioxingehalten im Blutfett der Bevoelkerung, Berlin, 29 May 1991

Berman SH, Wandersman A (1990) Fear of cancer and knowledge of cancer: a review and proposed relevance to hazardous waste sites. *Social Science and Medicine*, *31* (1), 81–90

BMA (British Medical Association) (1987) *Living with Risk*. John Wiley, New York

BMA (British Medical Association) Professional and Scientific Division (1991) *Hazardous Waste and Human Health*. Oxford University Press, Oxford

Burke TA, Gray S, Krawiec CM, Katz RJ, Preuss PW and Paulson G (1980) An environmental investigation of clusters of leukaemia and Hodgkin's disease in Rutherford, New Jersey. *Journal of the Medical Society of New Jersey*, 77 (4), 259–64

Central Statistical Office Great Britain (1990) *Social Trends*, 20. HMSO, London

Czuczwa JM and Hites RA (1986) Airborne dioxins and dibenzofurans: sources and fates. *Environmental Science and Technology*, 20, 195–200

Duggan MJ and Williams S (1977) Lead in dusts in city streets. *Science of the Total Environment*, 7, 91–97

Eickmann, Th (1987) Bewertung des Eintrages von Luftverunreinigungen auf bzw. in den Boden im Hinblick auf die Inhalation, Ingestion und Hautkontamination des Menschen. *Schriftenreihe der VDI-Kommission Reinhaltung der Luft*, Band 5, Wirkung von Luftverunreinigungen auf den Boden, pp. 65–84

EPA (US Environmental Protection Agency) (1987a) *Background Information: National priority list, Final and Proposed Rulemaking*. US EPA, Washington, D.C. HW-8.10

EPA (US Environmental Protection Agency) (1987b) Notice of the first priority list of hazardous substances that will be the subject of toxicological profiles. *Federal Register*, 52, 12866–12874

European Community (1991) Umweltpolitik und Umweltrecht in der Europaeischen Gemeinschaft. XXIV. Gesamtbericht ueber die Taetigkeit der Europaeischen Gemeinschaft 1990, Luxemburg, Amt fuer amtliche Veroeffentlichungen der Europaeischen Gemeinschaft, 1991

Ewers U and Brockhaus A (1987) Die biologische Ueberwachung der Schadstoffbelastung des Menschen und ihre Bedeutung bei der Beurteilung umwelttoxikologischer Einfluesse. *Oeff. Gesundh.-Wes.*, 49, 639–647

Favata EA and Gochfeld M (1989) Medical surveillance of hazardous waste workers: ability of laboratory test to discriminate exposure. *American Journal of Industrial Medicine*, 15 (3), 255–265

Fingerhut MA, Halperin WE, Marlow DA *et al.* (1991) Cancer mortality in workers exposed to 2,3,7,8-tetrachlorodibenzo-*p*-dioxin. *New England Journal of Medicine*, *324* (4), 212–218

Greiser E, Lotz I, Brand H and Weber H (1991) Increased incidence of leukemia in the vicinity of a previous industrial waste dump in Northrhine Westfalia, West Germany. *American Journal of Epidemiology, 134,* 755

Grisham JW (1986) *Health Aspects of the Disposal of Waste Chemicals.* Pergamon Press, New York

Howe HL (1988) A comparison of actual and perceived residential proximity to toxic waste sites. *Archives of Environmental Health, 43* (6), 415–419

Janerich DT, Burnett WS, Feck G *et al.* (1981) Cancer incidence in the Love Canal area. *Science, 212* (4501), 1, 404–407

Johnson BL (1988) Public health effects of hazardous waste in the environment. In Abbou R (ed.) *Hazardous Waste: Detection, Control, Treatment,* World Conference Proceedings, Elsevier, Amsterdam

Kimbrough RD, Falk H, Stehr P and Fries G (1984) Health implications of 2,3,7,8-TCDD contamination of residential soil. *Journal of Toxicology and Environmental Health, 14,* 47–93

Lagakos S, Wessen B and Zelen M (1986) An analysis of contaminated well water and health effects in Woburn, Massachusetts. *Journal of the American Statistical Association, 81,* 583–614

Marsh GM and Day R (1991) A model standardized risk assessment protocol for use with hazardous waste sites. *Environmental Health Perspectives, 90,* 199–208

Melius JM (1986) Medical surveillance for hazardous waste workers. *Journal of Occupational Medicine, 28* (8), 679–683

Office of Technology Assessment (1983) *Technologies and Management Strategies for Hazardous Waste Control.* Government Printing Office, Washington, DC

Paigen B, Goldman L, Highland J, Magnani M and Steegman A (1985) Prevalence of health problems in children living near Love Canal. *Hazardous Waste and Hazardous Materials, 2,* 23–43

Phillips M and Silbergeld EK (1985) Health effects of exposure from hazardous waste site—where are we today? *American Journal of Industrial Medicine, 8,* 1–7

Rat von Sachverstaendigen fuer Umweltfragen (1989) Sondergutachten Altlasten. Rat von Sachverstaendigen fuer Umweltfragen, Wiesbaden

UAREP (Universities Associated for Research and Education in Pathology) (1985) *Health Aspects in the Disposal of Waste Chemicals.* UAREP, Bethesda, MD

UBA Umweltbundesamt (1989) *Daten zur Umwelt 1988/89.* Umweltbundesamt, Berlin

Upton AC, Kneip T and Toniolo P (1989) Public health aspects of toxic chemical disposal sites. *Annual Review of Public Health, 10,* 1–25

US Congress Office of Technology Assessment (1983) *Technologies and Management Strategies for Hazardous Waste Control.* US Government Printing Office, Washington, DC

US PHS (1983) *SPACE for Health: A System for Prevention, Assessment and Control of Exposure and Health Effects from Hazardous Sites.* US Public Health Service, Washington, DC

Vianna N and Polan A (1984) Incidence of low birthweight among Love Canal residents. *Science, 226,* 1217–1219

Walker A (1991) Health and the environment: waste disposal: fresh looks at a rotting problem. *British Medical Journal, 303* (6814), 1391–1394

Environmental pollution, human exposure and health

David J. Briggs, *University of Huddersfield, UK*

Introduction

The geography of environmental pollution

The distribution of pollution in the environment is both intricate and dynamic. Pollutants may be released into the environment in many different ways (e.g. by combustion, by spillage or leakage, as a deliberate act of disposal), from a wide array of both point and non-point sources (industrial installations, transport, agricultural activities, etc.), and in a multitude of different forms. They may be transferred through the environment by a variety of different mechanisms, along a variety of interlocking pathways, via different media, and at different rates. *En route*, they are subject to a range of different processes of dilution, deposition, decomposition and storage. Moreover, all these processes and pathways vary according to the character and level of economic activity, the climate and the terrain, and the nature of the pollutant involved. The geography of environmental pollution is thus not one geography but many, different substances having their own patterns of release and dispersal, these patterns shifting and changing over time.

The pollutants released into the environment have a wide range of known and suspected effects. Atmospheric emissions from industry and transport, for example, have been implicated in a lengthening chain of impacts: acid deposition, forest damage, acidification of soils and lakes, the loss of wildlife species and damage to buildings; stratospheric ozone depletion, global warming, vegetation change, desertification and sea-level rise. Nitrates and phosphates released by agriculture and in urban wastes have contributed to eutrophication of rivers and lakes, groundwater pollution, marine pollution and damage to ecosystems. Attempts to dispose of solid wastes by landfill, dumping and incineration have variously led to soil, groundwater, marine and atmospheric pollution.

Environmental pollutants are implicated, also, in effects on human health. These effects are most indisputable and stark in the case of industrial accidents, such as the Bhopal disaster in 1984, when a leak of methyl gas led to the death of 2000 people, and injured 200 000 more. But longer-term, chronic impacts have also occurred. During the 1950s and early 1960s, for example, atmospheric pollution in London and other European cities resulted in the death of many thousands of people and contributed to respiratory disease in hundreds of thousands of others. In the mid-1970s, sulphur oxide pollution is estimated to have caused 24 000 deaths annually in the USA (e.g. Mendelsohn and Orcutt, 1979). In other cases the effects remain still unproven and contentious: for example, the relationship between radioactive emissions from nuclear energy installations and human leukaemia or the health effects of nitrate pollution in drinking water.

In all these instances, understanding of the geography of environmental pollution is clearly a vital need. Information is required on levels of pollution in order to help define appropriate quality standards and limits. Knowledge of the current distribution of pollutants is required to identify human populations which may be at risk and to target action at the areas of greatest concern. Pollution sources need to be defined in order to take effective preventive action by controlling pollution at point of release. Rates of change need to be assessed in order to evaluate the efficiency of current control measures, and to predict likely future problems. Pathways of pollution dispersal and transfer need to be understood in order to model the potential effects of future pollution incidents—and thereby to make appropriate response plans. In addition, where the health effects of the pollutants are still uncertain, information on the geography of pollution is required to help define possible links with health outcomes, and thus to provide a baseline for detailed epidemiological research.

Environmental monitoring

In the light of this need, considerable investment has been made in Europe in systems of environmental monitoring. Many national and regional networks have been set up, for example, to monitor both air and water quality. The effectiveness and quality of these systems are nevertheless variable. Environmental monitoring is costly, and the benefits are not easy to define or assess. As a consequence, monitoring systems are often limited in both their comprehensiveness and scope. The density of monitoring sites and the frequency of measurement may be low. Many sources of error and inconsistency also affect the data which are produced: sampling and measurement methods may vary, measurement instruments may not be adequately calibrated or maintained, procedures for analysing and reporting the results may differ. Many of the data which are obtained are subject to restrictions of confidentiality, for commercial, military or political reasons.

The information provided by existing monitoring networks is therefore far from ideal, and is not adequate (nor is it intended to be adequate) for all possible applications. This paper outlines the data sources which are available, discusses the quality of the data, and considers the implications for attempts to assess potential impacts on human health. Attention is focused on the two main pathways by which humans are exposed to environmental pollution, and those for which most data exist: air and water pollution.

Air pollution

Air pollution is a product of emissions from a wide variety of anthropogenic and natural sources. For most pollutants the major sources comprise fuel combustion (e.g. by industry, transport or domestic uses), industrial processing and manufacture (e.g. chemical activities) or product use and disposal (fertilizer application, waste dumping, etc.). Once in the atmosphere the pollutants are then dispersed by a combination of diffusion and mass transfer, being diluted and often undergoing reactive change on the way, before being removed by wet or dry deposition or gaseous exchange. Monitoring of air pollution may thus take place at a variety of points in the pollution stream: as measurements of emission (at source), as measurements of concentration (in the ambient atmosphere), or as deposition rates or loads. Increasing attention is now being given to the assessment of pollution deposition and—by comparing these with the sensitivity of the receiving environment—the calculation of critical loads. This approach is being developed, especially, in relation to acid deposition (e.g. Bull, 1991; UNEP, 1991), but could logically be extended to human exposure and health. Currently, however, the majority of available data relate to measurements of emission or concentration.

Atmospheric emissions

Direct measurements of pollutant emissions into the atmosphere are extremely rare. Although monitoring is undertaken at many industrial installations—most especially major combustion sites—little of this information is readily available because of the constraints of commercial confidentiality. Even where it is accessible, moreover, it provides only an incomplete picture of total emissions since it is restricted to major point sources: comparable emission data either for smaller point sources (e.g. domestic sites) or for non-point sources such as transport and agriculture are not available.

Emission models In the absence of routine and spatially comprehensive monitoring, most data on emissions are derived indirectly, using modelling techniques. In the past, all countries in Europe have developed such models for application at the national level (e.g. Centraal Bureau voor de Statistiek, 1987). Though these have varied in detail and scope, they all followed a broadly similar form. Emissions are estimated as the product of fuel combustion rate and unit emission rate, taking account of both combustion process and fuel type.

In an attempt to regularize these national emission models and develop a consistent pan-European scheme, the European Commission set up the CORINAIR project, under the auspices of the CORINE Programme (e.g. Briggs, 1991; Commission of the European Communities, 1992). This established a standard classification of emission sources and a common framework for assessment. It was initially applied to estimate regional emissions of SO_2, NO_x and volatile organic compounds (VOCs) for the reference year 1985, but is now being extended to other pollutants and other years, at a finer spatial scale.

Two major sources of error and inconsistency nevertheless exist in emission modelling which the CORINAIR system has only partially resolved. The first relates to the emission factors used. These are assessed for different combustion processes and fuel types on the basis of controlled analyses under test conditions. As such, they are open to some degree of error, depending upon the representativeness of the test conditions. This error undoubtedly varies both from one country and one substance to another; in The Netherlands it is estimated to be less than 10% in the case of SO_2, up to 25% for NO_x, but between 25% and 100% for CO and hydrocarbons (Centraal Bureau voor de Staistiek, 1987). In recognition of these errors, adjustments may be made to the emission factors as new test data become available. In the UK, for example, repeated revision of the factors for both SO_2 and NO_x from mobile sources occurred between 1983 and 1990. As a result, the estimated emission total for mobile sources in the UK was revised upwards several times: the NO_x value for 1983 rose from 1.62 million tonnes (Department of the Environment, 1984) to 2.23 million tonnes (Department of the Environment, 1990)—an adjustment of over 25%. Variations in emission factors also occur between countries. Standard emission factors for carbon dioxide from diesel oil, for example, range from 70 t CO_2/TJ in Luxembourg to 75 t/TJ in Ireland; values for hard coal range from 90 t/TJ in the UK to 95 t/TJ in Denmark and Germany (Statistical Office of the European Communities, 1991). Insofar as these reflect true differences in fuel composition and combustion process they are clearly valid and do not undermine the model results. In part, however, they appear to be due to different model assumptions and test conditions, and as such imply small inconsistencies in estimated emissions from different countries. For these reasons, comparisons across national boundaries need to be undertaken with care.

More significantly, uncertainties tend to exist about the quality of the energy data used to run these models. Often, direct measurements of energy consumption in different activity sectors are not available, and energy statistics must therefore be derived indirectly from surrogates (e.g. employment or production statistics). Reliable estimates of the error involved are not available, but some indication is given by comparing national energy consumption statistics from different official publications. These imply a margin-of-error of at least 10–20%, an error which is likely to be transmitted into national emission estimates. Even larger errors may occur for subnational areas, since energy statistics are often incomplete at the regional scale. In the CORINAIR study, for example, regional estimates had to be derived from national statistics in some cases, using data on population and employment as a basis for disaggregation. How reliable such estimates are is open to some doubt.

Dispersion models Estimates of emissions, whether derived from at-site monitoring or from modelling procedures, provide information only on pollutant releases into the environment at source; they do not indicate the distribution of pollutants in the open environment and consequently cannot be used directly to assess human exposure. For this purpose it is necessary to add a further stage of analysis, modelling the dispersion of the pollutant from its source.

In the case of a single point source, relatively simple models may be used: the simplest is perhaps to assume that concentrations fall uniformly in all directions away from the source, such that an essentially circular concentration field exists. It is this assumption which in principle underlies those epidemiological studies which seek inflated mortality or morbidity levels within a circular zone around a putative point source. Nevertheless, whilst possibly a valid model of simple diffusion processes—for example, those operating in areas of relatively uniform terrain under conditions of stable and calm atmospheric conditions—this approach clearly does not provide an adequate model of most dispersion systems, and is likely to give only poor estimates of the actual geography of air pollution.

More realistic models thus take account of a wider range of local atmospheric and site factors, including the emission rate, emission temperature, atmospheric temperature, turbulence and surface topography (e.g. Finzi *et al.*, 1984; Andresen and Kyaw Tha Paw, 1985). These models may then be applied to the estimation of long-term average pollution distributions around a site, or to predictions of likely short-term pathways of pollutants released during a single event (e.g. an industrial accident). In either case, given the availability of adequate site and meteorological data, model performance may be good. Reliability is nevertheless limited in areas of highly dissected terrain—such as urban environments—where local wind and shadow effects may occur, generating complex dispersion patterns. Such models are also of limited use in the presence of multiple emission sources or where non-point sources are involved, though attempts have been made to estimate diffusion from transport networks (e.g. Beiruti and Al-Omishy, 1985).

Broad-scale models have also been developed to assess dispersion at inter-regional scale, most notably the transfer models developed by EMEP as part of the long-range air pollution programme (e.g. Hanssen *et al.*, 1990). Typically, these involve compartment models, assessing transfers between arbitrarily defined grid cells on the basis of general wind patterns and atmospheric circulation. As such their resolution is generally low, and the estimations they provide no better than rough orders-of-magnitude.

Air quality

Monitoring networks   Monitoring of air quality is carried out routinely by all countries in Europe. Many countries operate several networks, designed to monitor different aspects of air pollution for different purposes. For example, as part of the EMEP programme on long-range pollution, many countries run a rural network, aimed at assessing background levels of pollution. This focuses especially on pollution relating to acid deposition. All countries also run one or more urban networks; pollutants covered by these typically include smoke or particulates, SO_2, NO_x, CO_2, CO, ozone and lead. In addition, other *ad-hoc* surveys may be run to provide data on specific policy issues.

   The design and extent of these surveys, and the quality of the data they provide, vary considerably. Some degree of consistency is ensured by the requirement to submit data on smoke (or particulates) and SO_2 to the European Commission, in accordance with Directive 80/779 (Commission of the European Communities, 1986). Significant inconsistencies nevertheless occur in site location, sampling, measurement method and data treatment, not only from one substance to another but also from country to country (and in some cases from town to town). Measurements of particulates, for example, may be based on fundamentally different definitions: in Belgium they relate to particulates less than 7 μm in size; in Italy the maximum size varies from one town to another—it is 20 μm in Rome and 60 μm in Milan (OECD, 1991). In the UK the number of routine monitoring sites ranges from two for hydrocarbons to 287 for smoke and SO_2 (Table 1). In France each town runs its own network, often using different equipment and sampling designs (Agence pour la Qualité de l'Air, 1991). Moreover, because sites are normally located in areas of known high pollution, they cannot provide an indication of average urban conditions. Muschett (1981) for instance, estimated that averaging concentrations at sampling sites overestimated actual mean particulate pollution in US cities by up to 12% as a result of locational bias in the network. For these reasons comparisons either between countries, or between towns, are liable to be misleading.

Spatial interpolation   For all their inadequacies the urban pollution networks

Table 1 Air pollution monitoring stations in the UK

Pollutant	Number of stations
Ozone	17
Carbon monoxide	5
Nitrogen oxides	11
Hydrocarbons	2
Smoke/sulphur dioxide	287
Lead	19

Data from Department of the Environment, 1990

remain the best available source of air pollution data in most circumstances. Indeed, their very bias towards urban areas is in many cases an advantage, since it is in urban areas which most people are likely to receive their main air pollution dose. If the data are to be used for epidemiological studies, or to generate assessments of health risk, however, some form of spatial interpolation is necessary to generate area coverages from the point data sets. Given the often clustered distribution of the monitoring sites, and the complex urban terrains across which interpolation must be performed, this is far from easy.

Various methods have been employed for this purpose. The most common has been to conduct a simple form of contouring, using either manual or automatic techniques. Typically, this is based on the assumption of an underlying linear trend. The US Environmental Protection Agency (1977), for example, recommends a range of mapping, plotting and smoothing techniques, all for use with linear interpolation. Similarly, Muschett (1981) noted that 'Linear interpolation commonly is accepted in an urban area inasmuch as most locations are affected by multiple, interacting point sources of pollution, including industrial processes and combustion from residential, automobile and industrial sources.' Whether linear models are actually valid in relation to ground-level pollution, however, seems far from certain, and there is reason to believe that strong local variations in pollution level occur as a result of street-canyon and shadow effects.

Various alternative methods for spatial interpolation certainly exist, though as yet few have been used with air quality data. One of the most promising is the use of plate-spline techniques. These provide the facility to construct locally fitted polynomial surfaces which can be linked to give a continuous surface. Hutchinson and Bischoff (1983), for example, used them to generate rainfall maps across Australia. As this example showed, the methods appear to be especially robust and effective in situations where the data are strongly clustered; by incorporating information on the length of the weather record they were also able to weight the data according to their local variances, thereby combining data of variable reliability without reducing the overall quality of the modelled surface. Both these facilities are valuable for air quality mapping in urban areas, where sites are often clustered and pollution records of variable completeness and length.

Kriging, similarly, provides a flexible technique for spatial interpolation—though, again, one which has not yet been widely applied for air pollution modelling. It comprises a suite of procedures, each adapted to different empirical conditions and data types. At its base is the assumption that spatial variation can be disaggregated into three different components: a regional trend (or drift), a local but spatially correlated variation (such that neighbouring sites tend to be more similar to each other than do more distant sites), and a truly stochastic variation (or noise). Kriging operates by removing the regional trend (if it exists), then analysing the relationship between inter-site distance (lag) and inter-site differences in the measured variable, to identify the spatially correlated component of variation, via the construction of a variogram. The remaining variation (the nugget variance) represents the unresolvable randomness in the data.

Kriging was originally developed by Matheron (1971) for geological prospecting applications, but has since been used is a wide variety of spatial interpolation problems, especially in the fields of agriculture and soil survey (e.g. Burrough and Webster, 1980; Oliver, 1991; Webster and Oliver, 1989). As noted above, relatively few examples are available of its use for air pollution modelling, although it was applied by Webster et al. (1991) to map rainfall chemistry across the UK. Nevertheless, kriging seems to have several advantages over more traditional techniques—not least the fact that it is an 'exact interpolator' and fits the modelled surface exactly to the measured data without smoothing, thereby retaining the most reliable data available.

In recent years a number of comparisons have been made between spline techniques and kriging, along with other interpolation methods such as trend surface analysis and choropleth mapping (e.g. Kuilenberg et al., 1982; Laslett et al., 1987; Abbass et al., 1990). No clear conclusions emerge, except that relative performance seems to depend upon specific conditions of data type and quality, sample design and computing power. For broad-scale spatial interpolation of air quality, where the surfaces to be fitted are relatively smooth, and the noise component small, both kriging and spline interpolation may be expected to be satisfactory. In urban areas, however, the stochastic element may be much greater, more disjunct patterns of variation may occur and statistical methods of interpolation may be much less effective. In these circumstances there is undoubtedly a need to develop a clearer understanding of the nature of spatial variation, and its relationship to factors such as urban morphology, land use and microclimate.

Water pollution

Pollution pathways

Water pollution occurs in a variety of ways and from a range of different sources: from industry, in sewage and stormwater drainage, as a result of runoff and leaching of agricultural chemicals, and by deposition from the atmosphere. In the case of surface freshwaters, industrial and urban wastes have been major causes of concern in the past. Phosphates and nitrates in sewage waters, for example, have helped to cause widespread eutrophication, while organic pollutants have led to a significant loss of biodiversity in many streams and lakes. Heavy metal contamination in seepage and wastewaters from industry has also been a problem in many traditional industrial areas, though this is now declining as industrial structure and technology have changed.

In recent years, however, attention has tended to shift towards agricultural sources. Fertilizers and livestock wastes, in particular, appear to be contributing to a marked increase in nitrate concentrations in surface freshwaters. Of the 26 stream monitoring sites in the European Community reporting to the OECD for the period from 1975 to 1985, 21 show a rise in nitrate levels (OECD, 1991). Similarly, pollution of groundwaters has increased substantially in many areas, primarily as a result of leaching of fertilizer and pesticide residues under intensive agricultural systems.

Short-term pollution events, arising from the deliberate or accidental release of chemicals into the aquatic environment have also increased in recent years. In England and Wales, for example, the number of reported incidents more than doubled between 1981 and 1988. Of the almost 27 000 cases in 1988, about 38% were related to industrial activities, 17% were attributed to agriculture and 19% to sewage treatment and handling (Department of the Environment, 1990).

Similar accidental discharges occur at sea, especially from oil exploration, extraction and handling. These, too, have increased in recent years, reflecting the expansion of oil extraction activities in European waters. Total spillages reported in UK waters rose from 366 in 1985 to 764 in 1989; spills from oil operations in the North Sea alone rose from 91 in 1985 to 307 in 1989 (Department of the Environment, 1990). In relation to human health effects, however, greater concern probably attaches to the longer-term effects of runoff from land-based sources. The problems are most acute in relatively enclosed seas, such as the Mediterranean and Baltic, where turnover of water is slow and inputs from major rivers high. Agricultural and urban wastes, for example, seem to be increasing the extent and frequency of algal blooms (e.g. the 'red tides') in these areas, and are believed to be contributing to rising rates of fish death and damage to marine and coastal ecosystems.

Human exposure to these various forms of water pollution may occur in a number of ways. A common form of exposure is likely to be during bathing in contaminated seawaters or freshwaters (e.g. Cabelli, 1989; Fewtrell, 1991), though such incidents are likely to be poorly reported, not easily detected and often of only minor health significance. More important is exposure via drinking water supply (e.g. Kay and McDonald, 1991). In this context, rising levels of nitrates in both ground- and surface-water sources has given cause for considerable concern. By the early 1980s, for example, over 8% of the population in Denmark were being supplied with water the NO_3 concentration of which exceeded the EC guideline limit of 50 mg/l (Commission of the European Communities, 1987). Although the health implications of nitrate nitrogen at such concentrations (e.g. methaemoglobinaemia and stomach cancer) remain contentious, a number of policy initiatives have since been taken in the European Community to reduce nitrate contamination, leading to the adoption of the Nitrates Directive in 1991.

Environmental water pollution may similarly result in human exposure to contaminants which enter the food chain (Jones, 1991). The most direct pathway in this case is probably via fish and other aquatic organisms which are caught for human consumption. Filter feeders and bottom-dwelling organisms, especially, tend to accumulate large quantities of pollutants from the water or sediments, which can then be passed into the human food chain. Further accumulation may also occur in birds, or via domesticated animals fed on fish compounds.

Data availability and quality

Monitoring of drinking water quality is typically carried out by the supply companies or by ministries of public works—normally at point of withdrawal, treatment and/or storage. This monitoring is normally able to identify major pollution effects before the water is released to public consumption; in recent years, several reservoirs have been temporarily closed, for example, as a result of contamination by toxic algae. Pollution within the supply network is more difficult to detect. Possibly the main problem relates to the release of contaminants from the distribution system itself—for example, lead in domestic plumbing. In addition, however, accidents during water supply may cause serious pollution of drinking water downstream of the routine monitoring point. In these cases contamination may go undetected, and human exposure may occur before the problem is recognized (e.g. the Camelford incident in the UK in 1991).

Monitoring of surface water quality is undertaken by a range of different agencies in different countries in Europe. In the UK, for example, the main responsibility for monitoring of stream and bathing water quality lies with the National Rivers Authority in England and Wales, and with the Water Purification Boards in Scotland. In France, surface water quality in the main rivers is monitored by the six basin agencies; smaller streams are monitored by the Ministry of Agriculture.

Despite the existence of the EC Directive on the Exchange of Information on Fresh Surface Water Quality, and the Bathing Water Directive—both of which lay down procedures for monitoring and reporting water quality— the scope and character of the data collected by these different national and regional agencies vary substantially. In the case of the bathing water network, for example, major differences exist in the selection of sample sites, the methods for sample extraction, the timing and frequency of sampling, methods for data storage, transport and pretreatment, the parameters measured and the measurement techniques. The measurement accuracy of some parameters (e.g. nitrates, bacteria) is known to be low in some cases, whilst the quality standards applied in each member state vary so that reported values of compliance levels cannot be directly compared. Individual sites also tend to be added to, or dropped from, the network from one year to another so that time trends, equally, cannot easily be assessed.

Similar problems tend to afflict data on stream water quality, albeit to a lesser degree. Some differences occur in the parameters measured, measurement methods and procedures for data treatment and reporting. The major weaknesses, however, generally relate to the location and frequency of sampling. In particular, the spatial representativeness of the sampling sites is often uncertain, and many smaller streams are not monitored on any regular basis. One consequence of this is that reliable statistics on overall water quality are difficult to compile (and generally impossible to compare). Another is that pollution in minor headwater streams may go undetected. The frequency of monitoring is similarly often low (only once per month or less in many cases), and, except in the few automatically monitored sites, early-warning systems, capable of detecting chemical or other releases, do not exist. Short-term pollution events are thus readily missed. Together with the low density of monitoring sites, this also means that pollutants spilled or released into the stream network may have spread widely through the system before the effects are noticed and, after detection, it is often difficult to identify reliably the source of specific water pollution incidents. Of the nearly 27 000 pollution incidents reported in England and Wales in 1968, therefore, only 327 led to prosecutions—188 against farms, 133 against industrial establishments and a mere six for sewage incidents (Department of the Environment, 1990).

The geography of exposure

The limited range, quality and resolution of the environmental data currently available clearly restricts their use in studies of health impacts. Whether the concern is to map areas of health risk, to assess the relationship between pollution levels and disease, or to model potential impacts of pollution events, the available data are subject to serious limitations. Rarely, if ever, are the data at a sufficient level of spatial or temporal detail, or sufficiently wide-ranging in terms of the substances measured or their geographical coverage, to meet the needs of the epidemiologist or health analyst.

Much of this problem relates to the mechanisms by which humans are exposed to pollutants, and the scales at which this exposure occurs. Human exposure takes place in a wide variety of environments—domestic, occupational, outdoor. Exposure occurs as individuals move through or rest within these environments, encountering, absorbing, and ingesting the pollutants which exist. Exposure thus depends upon the residence time and nature of activity in each contributory environment. These patterns of activity—and the resultant interactions with individual pollutants—are notoriously difficult to define. They are themselves highly dynamic and diverse. They vary according to the economic and social characteristics of the people involved—their class, occupation, gender, race and age. They are influenced by information and perception, and by personal experience and whim. They are a partial response also to the nature of the surrounding environment, and to the cultural mores and legal controls which exist. Nor is the level of exposure a perfect index of the resultant health effect. In many cases this relationship is overlaid and confused by other, confounding factors (e.g. of lifestyle or quality of health service support). It depends, similarly, upon the toxicity of the pollutants concerned, the exact site of accumulation in the human body, and the synergistic effects which might occur as a result of multiple exposure to different substances. Measures of environmental exposure for a definable human group thus give only a blurred picture of the total degree of health risk.

A major part of this uncertainty is a product of the spatial and temporal scales involved. Exposure to pollutants, and their consequent impacts on health, vary greatly in their spatial and temporal character. In some cases they may be the result of prolonged exposure over a wide area; in other cases to repeated exposure at a specific site (or set of sites); in yet other cases to brief high-dose exposure at a particular locality. The lag between exposure to pollution and development or recognition of symptoms may similarly vary.

It follows that, to be useful for epidemiological applications especially, information on the distribution of environmental pollution must satisfy somewhat contradictory requirements of both resolution and extent. In terms of its *spatial* character, for example, it must be available for a broad geographic area to include all important sources of exposure, but must also be sufficiently detailed to allow local variations in levels of exposure (e.g. pollution hotspots) to be identified. In terms of its *temporal* character, it must cover a long enough period to permit estimation of historic exposure, but must also provide sufficient temporal detail to identify short-period, high-exposure events. These requirements clearly vary from one pollutant to another, depending on the nature of the health effects. Rarely, however, do routine data on environmental pollution come close to meeting these requirements in their raw form. For this reason one of two approaches must be adopted in attempts to describe the geography of environmental pollution for health-related studies. Either specific, purpose-designed studies must be undertaken, aimed at collecting the environmental data needed; or modelling techniques must be used to extend the available data to give the spatial and temporal scale required.

The former approach clearly has many advantages, in that it provides direct control over both what aspects of the environment are measured and the way in which measurement is done. Sample size, sample layout, frequency and measurement provision can all be adjusted, therefore, to meet the specific needs. Nevertheless, purpose-designed sampling can be inherently time-consuming, thereby delaying the progress of the work. It can also be extremely costly, especially where intensive surveys are required. In many cases, however, low-cost sampling devices can be applied if demands for accuracy can be relaxed. Moss-bags collectors (e.g. Goodman and Smith, 1975; Archibold and Crisp, 1983), corrosion plates (Yocum, 1962) and solution tablets (Jaynes and Cooke, 1987), for example, have been widely used in the past for the monitoring of air pollution, while lichen have widely been applied as natural monitors of sulphur dioxide concentrations (e.g. Nyangobobo, 1987). More recently, diffusion tubes have also been used to measure atmospheric NO_2 (Campbell, 1988), while similar devices are currently being developed for both ozone and SO_2. Although the accuracy of such devices is inevitably limited—quoted reproducibilities for diffusion tubes are *ca.* $\pm 10\%$ for NO_2 and $< 30\%$ for SO_2—and they do not give time-specific measures of concentrations, they do have the advantage of allowing much denser networks of sample sites to be established, and provide useful time-integrated measures of average conditions over several weeks (and, in the case of lichen, over several years).

Nevertheless, the main limitation of purpose-designed surveys of this type is that—with the possible exception of lichen—they only provide estimates of present (or recent) pollution levels, and do not give any readily interpretable indication of previous conditions. To obtain historic information, other methods thus need to be used. The first need is to identify materials which preserve dateable evidence from the past. Reservoir sediments, lake sediments, peat bodies, ice cores and even museum specimens are all useful in this context, and a number of attempts have been made to reconstruct pollution histories from such sources (e.g. Elliott *et al.*, 1988, Pavoni *et al.*, 1987, Reczynska-Dutka, 1986, Rose, 1990, Schintu *et al.*, 1989). Such materials are generally only available for a few locations, however, and these are rarely representative of the wider area. Their use in estimates of past exposure is therefore limited, unless the information derived from them can be extrapolated regionally to give an indication of the historic pollution surface.

These general limitations with purpose-designed surveys mean that it is often difficult to avoid reliance on existing data sources: most especially, the results from routine monitoring networks. In these cases the spatial limitations of the environmental data need to be recognized and resolved. If attempts are to be made to assess levels of human exposure, the environmental data must be matched to the details of human distribution and behaviour. If the health effects of pollution are to be investigated, environmental data must be refined to the scale and resolution of the health information. For these purposes spatial modelling techniques are essential. Major strides have been made in recent years to develop statistical interpolation methods, which can undoubtedly improve the mapping of pollution patterns. The complexity of many environments is nevertheless such that we need to improve equally our knowledge of the physical processes of pollution dispersal if we are to devise an accurate and reliable picture of the geography of environmental pollution.

References

Abbass T El, Jallouli C, Albouy Y and Diament M (1990) A comparison of surface fitting algorithms for geophysical data. *Terra Nova*, *2*, 467–475

Agence pour la Qualité de l'Air (1991) La qualité de l'air en 1990. *Bulletin d'Information de l'Agence pour la Qualité de l'Air*, *13* (June), 1–6

Andresen J and Kyaw Tha Paw U (1985) Modelling of sulfur dioxide emissions and acidic precipitation at mesoscale distances. *Journal of the Air Pollution Control Association*, *35*, 1159–1163

Archibold OW and Crisp PT (1983) The distribution of airborne metals in the Illawara region of New South Wales, Australia. *Applied Geography*, *3*, 331–344

Beiruti AAR and Al-Omishy HK (1985) Traffic atmospheric diffusion model. *Atmospheric Environment*, *19*, 1519–1524

Briggs DJ (1991) Establishing an environmental information system for the European Community: the experience of the CORINE Programme. *Information Services and Use*, *10*, 63–75

Bull K (1991) *Critical Loads Maps for the United Kingdom*. Critical Loads Advisory Group to the Department of the Environment.

Burrough PA and Webster R (1980) Optimal interpolation and isarithmic mapping of soil properties. I. The semiovariogram and punctual kriging. *Journal of Soil Science*, *31*, 315–332

Cabelli VJ (1989) Swimming-associated illness and recreational water quality criteria. *Water Science and Technology*, *21* (2), 13–21

Campbell GW (1988) Measurements of nitrogen dioxide concentrations at rural sites in the United Kingdom using diffusion tubes. *Environmental Pollution*, *55*, 251–270

Centraal Bureau voor de Statistiek (1987) *Luchverontreiniging emissies door verbranding van fossiele brandstoffen in vuurhaarden 1980–1985*. CBS-Publikaties, 's-Gravenhage

Commission of the European Community (1986) *EC Directive 80/779 (EEC). A study of network design for monitoring suspended particulates and sulphur dioxide in the Member States. Report EUR 10647*. Office for Official Publications of the European Communities, Luxembourg

Commission of the European Communities (1987) *State of the environment in the European Communities, 1986*. Office for Official Publications of the European Communities, Luxembourg

Commission of the European Communities (1992) *CORINAIR: Final report of a CORINE project to map atmospheric emissions in the European Community*. Commission of the European Communities, Directorate General for the Environment, Civil Protection and Nuclear Safety, Brussels

Department of the Environment (1984) *Digest of Environment Protection and Water Quality Statistics*. HMSO, London

Department of the Environment (1990) *Digest of Environment Protection and Water Quality Statistics*. HMSO, London

Elliott JE, Norstrom RJ and Keith JA (1988) Organochlorines and eggshell thinning in northern gannets (*Sula bassanus*) from eastern Canada. *Environment and Ecology*, *16*, 247–256

Fewtrell L (1991) Freshwater recreation: a cause for concern? *Applied Geography*, *11*, 215–226

Finzi G, Bonelli P and Bacci C (1984) A stochastic model of surface windspeed for air quality control purposes. *Journal of Climate and Applied Meteorology*, *16*, 247–256

Goodman GT and Smith S (1975) Relative burdens of airborne metals in South Wales. In *Report of a collaborative study on certain elements in air, soil, animals and humans in the Swansea–Neath–Port Talbot area together with a report on a moss bag study of atmospheric pollution across South Wales*. HMSO and Welsh Office, Cardiff, pp. 337–361

Hanssen JE, Pederson U, Schaug J, Dovland H, Pacyna JM, Semb A and Skjelmoen JE (1990) *Summary report from the Chemical Co-ordinating Centre for the Fourth Phase of EMEP*. EMEP/CCC—Report 2/90. Norwegian Meteorological Institute, Lillestrøm

Hutchinson MF and Bischoff RJ (1983) A new method for estimating the spatial distribution of mean seasonal and annual rainfall applied to the Hunter Valley, New South Wales. *Australian Meteorological Magazine*, *31*, 177–184

Jaynes SM and Cooke RU (1987) Stone weathering in southeast England. *Atmospheric Environment*, *21*, 1601–1622

Jones F (1991) Public health aspects of the water cycle: a review. *Applied Geography*, *11*, 179–186

Kay D and McDonald AT (1991) Water quality issues. *Applied Geography*, *11*, 171–186

Kuilenberg J van, de Gruijter JJ, Marsman B and Bouma J (1982) Accuracy of spatial interpolation between point data on moisture supply capacity, compared with estimates from mapping units. *Geoderma*, *27*, 311–325

Laslett GM, McBratney AB, Pahl PJ and Hutchinson MF (1987) Comparison of several prediction methods for soil pH. *Journal of Soil Science*, *38*, 325–350

Matheron G (1971) The theory of regionalised variables and its applications. *Les Cahiers du Centre de Morphologie Mathematique de Fontainbleu*. Ecole Nationale Supérieure des Mines de Paris, Paris

Mendelsohn R and Orcutt G (1979) An empirical analysis of air pollution dose-response curves. *Journal of Environmental Economics and Management*, 6, 85–106

Muschett FD (1981) Spatial distributions of urban atmospheric particulate concentrations. *Annals of the Association of American Geographers*, 71 (4), 552–565

Nyangobobo JT (1987) Lichen as monitors of aerial heavy metal pollution in and around Kampala. *Bulletin of Environmental Contamination and Toxicology*, 38, 91–95

OECD (1991) *OECD Environmental Data Compendium 1991*. OECD, Paris

Oliver MA (1991) Disjunctive kriging: an aid to making decisions on environmental issues. *Area*, 23, 19–24

Pavoni B, Donazzola R, Marcomini A, Degobbia D and Orio AA (1987) Historical development of the Venice Lagoon contamination as recorded in radiodated sediment cores. *Marine Pollution Bulletin*, 18, 18–24

Reczynska-Dutka M (1986) Ecology of some waters in the forest-agricultural basin of the River Brynica near the Upper Silesia industrial region. 4: Atmospheric heavy metal pollution in the bottom sediments. *Acta Hydrobiologica*, 27, 359–373

Rose NL (1990) A method for the extraction of carbonaceous particles from lake sediments. *Journal of Palaeolimnology*, 3, 45–53

Schintu M, Sechi N, Sarritzu G and Contu A (1989) Reservoir sediments as potential sources of heavy metals in drinking water (Sardinia, Italy). *Water Science and Technology*, 21, 1891–1894

Statistical Office of the European Communities (1991) Proposal for a harmonized set of working emission factors for carbon dioxide. Working Group Statistics on the Environment, 9, 10 and 11 July 1991. Eurostat, Luxembourg

UNEP (1991) *United Nations Environment Programme. Environmental data report*. Blackwell, Oxford

United States Environmental Protection Agency (1977) *Guidelines in Procedures for Constructing Air Pollution Isopleth Profiles and Population Exposure Analysis*. US Environmental Protection Agency, Office of Air Quality Planning and Standards, EPA-450/2-77-024a

Webster R and Oliver M (1989) Disjunctive kriging in agriculture. In Armstrong M (ed.) *Geostatistics*, Vol. 1. Reidel, Dordrecht, pp. 421–432

Webster R, Campbell GW and Irwin JG (1991) Spatial analysis and mapping the annual mean concentrations of acidity and major ions in precipitation over the United Kingdom in 1986. *Environmental Monitoring and Assessment*, 16, 1–17

Yocum JE (1962) Effects of air pollution on materials. In Stern AC (ed.) *Air Pollution*, vol. 1. Academic Press, London, pp. 199–219

Congenital anomalies and the environment

Helen Dolk, *London School of Hygiene and Tropical Medicine, UK*

Introduction—the scope of the discussion

Congenital anomalies are an important cause of perinatal mortality and physical and mental handicap in European countries. The dimensions of congenital anomalies as a public health problem are undergoing considerable change. Improvements in surgery and treatment may reduce the level of disability for the individual and increase the number of disabled individuals surviving through childhood and into adulthood. Prenatal diagnosis is leading to the selective termination of affected pregnancies for conditions where effective treatment is not available. Demographic changes can themselves lead to changes in prevalence, as evidenced by the effect of trends towards delayed childbirth on the prevalence of Down's syndrome.

Perhaps at least as great a change is produced by a changing perception, definition and diagnosis of congenital anomalies. They are a group of conditions that have in common only that they are 'present at birth'. It is well known that certain congenital anomalies (such as many cardiac anomalies) may be diagnosed only after the neonatal period, and that some anomalies may never manifest themselves. Prenatal and neonatal screening are bringing forward the age at diagnosis of many anomalies, so that their congenital nature is more likely to be recognized in health statistics. Moreover, the boundaries between what is and what is not classed as congenital seem to be changing. Cerebral palsy, long thought to be a condition linked to events at birth, has now been recognized to be due in the majority of cases to prenatal events (Editorial, 1990). It is only a short conceptual distance to move from conditions which are totally determined by prenatal events to conditions which are partially determined by prenatal events, as suggested by recent research which implicates intrauterine life and maternal factors in the risk of childhood cancers (Gilman *et al.*, 1989) and adult disease such as cardiovascular disease (Barker, 1990).

Whatever we include under the umbrella term of 'congenital anomalies', a few main pathways through which environmental exposures can exert their effect can be considered. The mutagenic pathway involves preconceptional (and possibly postconceptional) maternal and paternal exposures. Genetic syndromes which are well recognized at birth, including Down's syndrome and some autosomal dominant syndromes, are an obvious endpoint to consider, although we are also concerned with the general mutational load in the population. The teratogenic pathway involves somatic effects on the developing fetus. As well as maternal exposures during the first trimester of pregnancy, it is also possible that exposure of the mother during any part of her life may change the maternal environment and thus indirectly the development of the fetus. This effect has been suggested, for example, by the observation that short maternal height is a risk factor for neural tube defects (Anderson *et al.*, 1958).

The environment and public health policy

In order to have an impact on the development of effective public health and environmental policies in Europe, we need to identify the levels of environmental concern, quantify the effects of the environment at each of these levels on congenital anomalies in their widest sense, identify intervention strategies, and provide constant monitoring of both exposures and the effects of interventions.

For the purposes of this discussion, four broad environmental 'levels' can be identified. First there is the personal environment, including nutrition, occupation, stress, drugs, alcohol and smoking. Second, there is the local or community environment, including air pollution, industrial wastes, radon, and water pollution. Third, there is the European environment, including environmental exposures with supranational effects (Chernobyl, acid rain, the siting of industry on a European level). Finally there is the world or global level (the greenhouse effect, environmental degradation, the threat of nuclear war, the siting of different forms of economic activity). Exposures on one level are of course determined in part by the levels above, and appropriate interventions would take this into account. Appropriate strategies for reducing environmental risks may be based on identification of high-risk individuals, on population-wide changes in individual exposure-related behaviour, on modifying the sources of environmental exposure, or on changing the economic relationships between communities.

Research and surveillance

The EUROCAT project

EUROCAT (European Registration of Congenital Anomalies and Twins) was set up in 1979 as a Concerted Action of the EEC for the epidemiological surveillance of congenital anomalies. It was initially an experiment in European surveillance, to assess the feasibility of pooling data across national boundaries, both in terms of standardization of definitions, diagnosis and terminology, and in terms of confidentiality arrangements.

The project is based on a network of regional registries, coordinated by a central registry in Brussels (Dolk *et al.*, 1991). In 1991, 25 registries in 14 countries of Europe (including EC countries as well as Yugoslavia, Malta and Switzerland) were participating in the network, covering altogether 350 000 births per year. The registries are population-based in design (although local approximations to this end are sometimes necessary). Most importantly, multiple sources of information are used for case-ascertainment and for the validation and elaboration of diagnoses. Because of this intensive data collection effort it is also possible for many of the registries to collect data on terminations of pregnancy following prenatal diagnosis of congenital anomalies, and to collect information on anomalies diagnosed after the neonatal period.

Regional registries were emphasized over national registries in order to collect better-quality data for small to medium-sized populations which could then be pooled across Europe, sharing the cost of the enterprise. The existence of a standard protocol for data collection facilitated the setting-up of registries in countries where previously there had been no information system covering congenital anomalies.

For research into environmental exposures on the individual or personal level, collaborative studies can be conducted, for example an ongoing case–control study of occupational exposures in six centres (Cordier et al., 1989). In the field of identification of teratogenic drug exposures and medical procedures, the network provides a response mechanism to reports of associations based on small numbers (EUROCAT, 1991a, b). In terms of evaluation of interventions, the surveillance network can be used, for example, to monitor the effectiveness of the regulation of teratogenic drugs; and is ready to monitor the results of eventual interventions following the confirmation of the importance of periconceptional vitamin and folic acid intake in the prevention of neural tube defects (MRC Vitamin Study Research Group, 1991).

On a local community level, perhaps the main contribution of EUROCAT remains the provision of well-validated baseline information against which to assess apparent localized risk increases.

On a European level a coherent European surveillance network provides a mechanism for giving a unified response to environmental concerns such as Chernobyl. With a 10% sample of the population of western European countries the EUROCAT system was able to provide a systematic evaluation of the impact of the accident on the prevalence of Down's syndrome (De Wals et al., 1988) and central nervous system anomalies (EUROCAT Working Group, 1988), and so place in context the inevitable reports of isolated clusters occurring in Europe.

SAHSU

The Small Area Health Statistics Unit (SAHSU) in London, which evaluates the health effects near point sources of environmental pollution (see p. 247), provides a contrast in terms of what can be achieved at a national rather than European level.

SAHSU's main concerns are risks at the local community level, in particular residence near industrial sites. This project is designed as a screening system which can rapidly detect localized risks, according to a standardized methodology, using existing routinely collected data. However, the more events we survey, the more unusual events we will discover, simply by the laws of probability. The problem is to distinguish between random local clusters and clusters which may be related to local environmental exposures. The general approach therefore must be to prioritize analyses in such a way that each investigation starts off with as strong as possible a prior hypothesis and/or should lead to a real possibility of independent confirmation. A prior hypothesis may be strong because of the accumulation of evidence from animal studies or occupational or other epidemiological studies about an exposure. A possibility of confirmation is provided when a number of different localities can be identified with similar exposure, so that the study can be replicated from within the SAHSU database.

The next development in the SAHSU system is to integrate the birth and congenital anomaly data for the UK. There are a number of advantages of looking at congenital anomalies rather than adult diseases in such a system. Exact annual denominators by postcode can be provided by the births, so that problems of extrapolation in time from census data are avoided. Furthermore, at least some of the pathways of environmental effect involve a relatively short interval between exposure and diagnosis of the anomaly, so that the population effects will be less diluted or subject to bias from migration.

Nevertheless, the usefulness of this approach to the study of congenital anomalies will be determined by the extent to which the system will generate false-positives and false-negatives. These will relate particularly to the quality of the data, which come from a national reporting system of congenital anomalies diagnosed within the first week of life in England and Wales (OPCS, 1991), and from computerized neonatal discharge records in Scotland (Cole, 1983). Comparisons of the results of the OPCS system in England and Wales with multisource regional registries have suggested that the OPCS data are of relatively poor quality for a range of anomalies. Nevertheless, the great strength of the system is its exhaustive geographic coverage, which is clearly essential, and it may be that multisource regional registries can provide external standards for use in the evaluation of results. For specific conditions, national registries which depend on essentially one virtually complete source of information have been started. A recent initiative in England and Wales is the establishment of a national Down's syndrome registry based on information supplied by cytogenetic laboratories (Mutton *et al.*, 1991), and a surveillance system for very rare conditions based on information supplied by paediatricians (BPSU, 1989).

Final comment

Initiatives such as EUROCAT and SAHSU are useful starting points for research and surveillance, and demonstrate the complementary nature of different information systems. It is important, however, that information systems should have the flexibility to respond to the changing dimensions of congenital anomalies as a public health problem, and that this should be reflected in our methods of research and surveillance. It is doubtful that we really have the capability in Europe at present to answer some of the major questions concerning congenital anomalies and the environment. This is, of course, dependent not only on the availability of appropriate health information, but also on the availability of appropriate environmental exposure measurements and methods of estimation.

References

Anderson WJR, Baird D and Thomson AM (1958) Epidemiology of stillbirths and infant deaths due to congenital malformation. *Lancet*, *1*, 1304–1306

Barker DJP (1990) The fetal and infant origins of adult disease. *British Medical Journal*, *301*, 1111

British Paediatric Surveillance Unit (1989) *Annual Report*

Cole SK (1983) Evaluation of a neonatal discharge record as a monitor of congenital malformations. *Community Medicine*, *5*, 21–30

Cordier S, Goujard J and De Wals P (1989) *EUROCAT Guide 4*. Collaborative study of environment and pregnancy. Guidelines for participants. Department of Epidemiology, Catholic University of Louvain, Brussels

De Wals P, Bertrand F, De La Mata I and Lechat MF (1988) Chromosomal anomalies and Chernobyl. *International Journal of Epidemiology*, *17*, 230–231

Dolk H, Goyens S and Lechat MF (1991) *EUROCAT Registry Descriptions 1979–90*. Commission of the European Communities Report EUR 13615 EN, Luxembourg

Editorial (1990) Cerebral palsy rarely caused by birth trauma. *British Medical Journal*, *301*, 781

EUROCAT (1991a) Holoprosencephaly and exposure to topical retinoids. *EUROCAT Newsletter*, *5*, 1

EUROCAT (1991b) Methylene blue and atresia and stenosis of the ileum and jejunum. *EUROCAT Newsletter*, *5*, 2

EUROCAT Working Group (1988) Preliminary evaluation of the impact of the Chernobyl radiological contamination on the frequency of central nervous system malformations in 18 regions of Europe. *Paediatric and Perinatal Epidemiology*, *2*, 253–264

Gilman EA, Kinnier Wilson M and Kneale GW, Waterhouse JAH (1989) Childhood cancers and their association with pregnancy drugs and illnesses. *Paediatric and Perinatal Epidemiology*, *3*, 66–94

MRC Vitamin Study Research Group (1991) Prevention of neural tube defects: results of the Medical Research Council Vitamin Study. *Lancet*, *338*, 131–137

Mutton DE, Alberman E, Ide R and Bobrow M (1991) Results of the first year
    (1989) of a national register of Down's syndrome in England and Wales. *British
    Medical Journal*, *303*, 1295–1297
OPCS (1991) *Congenital Malformation Statistics 1989*. Series MB3, No. 5. HMSO,
    London

Occupational mortality studies in Switzerland: potential and limitations

Felix Gurtner and Christoph E. Minder, *University of Berne, Switzerland*

Introduction

In 1989 a report, written on request of the Minister of Internal Affairs (who
is responsible for health, environment, education and social security),
listed and evaluated routine health statistics in view of their suitability for
monitoring health effects of environmental pollution, especially air pollution
(Morin and Ackermann-Liebrich, 1990). The authors concluded that, out
of the available routine health statistics on a national level, only mortality
statistics met the requirements for monitoring health effects of air pollution
and environmental pollution in general. The main reason for this opinion
was that other data sources did not cover the whole country and did not
include sufficient base-level information, and it was given in spite of the
obvious disadvantages of mortality statistics, like long latency, absence of
individual exposure information apart from proxy data, and (compared to
symptoms or diseases) reduced sensitivity to environmental factors.

Occupation is among the items of information recorded on every death
certificate. Some occupations can be considered as proxies for extreme
forms of the physical environment of the deceased person, and all occupations
are indicators of the social environment.

Three examples, typical for the situation of an advanced, European
country in the transition phase from an industrial to a post-industrial society
are presented.

Material and methods

The information on death certificates of all Swiss men, deceased from 1979
to 1982, and data of the 1980 census were used to compute standardized
mortality ratios (SMR) by occupation, economic sector, employment grade,
and grouped together by social class emulating the British Registrar General's

social class definitions (Office of Population Censuses and Surveys, 1970). Swiss data do not allow reliable discrimination between partly skilled and unskilled workers, so SMRs were calculated for social classes IV and V combined. The numerator–denominator bias arising from different sources of information on occupation was assessed, and correction factors for every occupation and social class were determined by linking a stratified random sample of death certificates of the year 1981 with the census records (Beer *et al.*, 1986).

The data of the first example were drawn from death certificates of the years 1950, 1955, 1960 and 1970 in 20 municipalities with foundry industry. These data permitted a proportional mortality analysis of lung cancer by occupation (Schnorf and Minder, 1991). Tuberculosis incidence data of the second example are based on the register of all new cases of tuberculosis, which is kept at the Swiss Federal Office of Public Health. Tuberculosis is one of the notifiable communicable diseases with compulsory individual named notification by laboratories and physicians, and all notifications concerning the same patient have been linked since 1988. This case register includes medical and demographical information (e.g. nationality) (Federal Office of Public Health, 1990).

Worksite accidents mentioned in the third example are covered by a mandatory insurance scheme, and minimal information on each accident, as well as more detailed information on a subsample, is kept for statistical analyses with the aim of drawing preventive conclusions (Burkhalter, 1988).

Results

Lung cancer mortality of foundry workers

In 1950, 20% of Swiss foundry workers who died in 20 municipalities with a foundry industry died of lung cancer, compared to 4% only of the Swiss male population in the same municipalities (Schnorf and Minder, 1991). The resulting proportional mortality ratio (PMR) of 5 fell to 1.42 in 1970 and 1.27 in 1979–1982 (Figure 1). This time the lung cancer PMR was calculated from all death certificates and the SMR was also calculated, as occupation data were available for the population at risk. The SMR corrected for misclassification of the occupation was 1.59.

For 1979–1982 the lung cancer mortality of foundry workers and that of other metal workers was calculated by age group. Foundry workers have the highest mortality from lung cancer in late working age and immediately after retirement, while other metal workers, assumed to have similar lifestyles, have a moderately elevated risk for all age groups.

It was concluded that:

1. The excess of lung cancer in foundry workers is real (consistent over

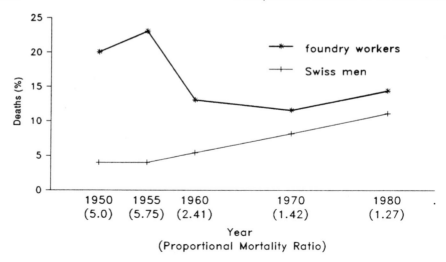

Figure 1 Lung cancer deaths as a percentage of all cancer deaths, Swiss foundry workers and all Swiss men, 1950–1980 (from Schnorf and Minder, 1991)

    years, misclassification taken into account, consistent with reported results of other studies).
2. The age pattern is typical for a disease which is not entirely lifestyle-associated, but also related to occupational exposure.
3. While the problem has not disappeared, the lung cancer risk of foundry workers has dramatically decreased from 1950 to 1970.

Item 3 was explained partly by substantial structural changes in the foundry industry: large-scale mass casting was gradually replaced by smaller-scale specialty foundry work, and the absolute number of employees in foundry industry has fallen from about 36 000 in 1966 (earliest available numbers) to about 26 000 in 1981. Both developments reflect the worldwide concentration of the metal and steel industry in lower-salary countries as a response to over-capacity; what remains is specialty foundry work in the context of the whole production process (e.g. railway engine production). Improvement of working conditions in general also occurred, even though the special lung cancer risk of foundry workers has not been a subject of preventive considerations.

Mortality and incidence of tuberculosis

Tuberculosis is a classical indicator for socioeconomic conditions underlying disease. The distribution among different groups of the population, as well

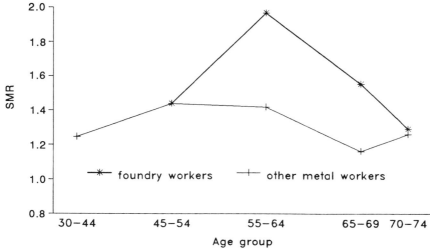

Figure 2 Age-specific SMRs of lung cancer for foundry workers and other metal workers, Swiss men aged 15–74, 1979–1982 (from Schnorf and Minder, 1991)

as comparisons of incidence and mortality, give some interesting findings as a basis for reasoning about the living conditions of particular groups.

In a country where optimal chemotherapy is available for all new cases of TB, tuberculosis mortality is very low (1.7/100 000), and is affecting mainly older people. Specific subpopulations, however, had a substantially higher mortality than others in 1979–1982: a steep social class gradient was observed (Figure 3). There were small differences between the different

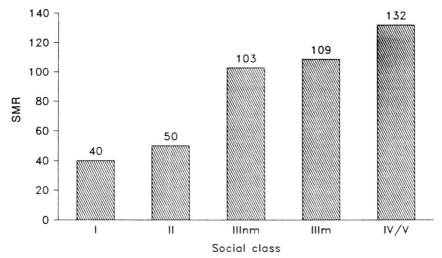

Figure 3 SMR of tuberculosis by social class, Swiss men aged 15–74, 1979–1982

economic sectors, with the agricultural sector being at the top; within each economic sector, big differences between management and workers were observed (Figure 4). Foreign nationals had only a slightly elevated mortality of tuberculosis (Figure 5).

In 1989 a total of 504 new cases among Swiss nationals and 427 cases among foreign nationals were reported to the Federal Office of Public Health. Two different endemics can be distinguished: the first among old Swiss and foreign nationals, and the second one almost exclusively among young foreign nationals (Figure 6) (Federal Office of Public Health, 1990). The rate ratio between foreign and Swiss nationals over all age groups is 4.1, but is much higher in children and young adults, and lower in people aged 45 and over.

The estimated prevalence of *Mycobacterium tuberculosis* infection in the Swiss population is 1.0% in the age group of 15–24 years, 3.4% from 25 to 34 years and 11.1% from 35 to 44 years, but 60% and more in the age group over 65 years (Rieder *et al.*, 1990). This pattern reflects the ageing and disappearance of the age cohorts who have experienced high infection risks of *M. tuberculosis*, and explains the actual character of tuberculosis of Swiss nationals as a disease of old age.

The population of young foreigners with high incidence rates merits further reflections: 67% of them come from five Mediterranean countries; two of those are countries of origin of many political refugees: the former

Figure 4 SMR of tuberculosis by economic sector, Swiss men aged 15–74, 1979–1982

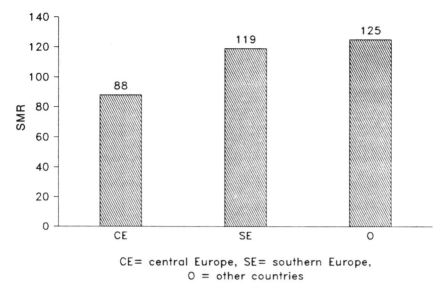

CE= central Europe, SE= southern Europe,
O = other countries

Figure 5 SMR of tuberculosis, foreign nationals aged 15–79, 1979–1982

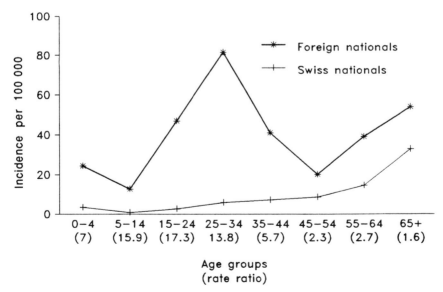

Figure 6 Age-specific tuberculosis incidence 1989, Swiss and foreign nationals, based on figures published in Federal Office of Public Health (1990)

Yugoslavia and Turkey; the three remaining (Italy, Portugal and Spain), and also Yugoslavia are recruitment countries for seasonal migrant workers who work for a maximum of nine months per year, mainly in the construction sector, in tourism and in agriculture. The rates mentioned above were calculated by using as a denominator the average number of foreign nationals (without refugees) and Swiss, and they are bound to be much higher for people from specific countries, especially from Yugoslavia and Turkey.

If tuberculosis mortality is taken as an indicator of socioeconomic status, why does mortality not affect these young foreigners who come from high-prevalence countries and probably also from high-risk socioeconomic groups? Obviously only the fittest people emigrate. If they do not recover completely from their tuberculosis they will not return to work in the consecutive seasons, and eventually die in their country of origin. The foreign nationals, on the other hand, who died of tuberculosis in Switzerland in 1980, seem to have come from a similar socioeconomic background to the Swiss population.

The social class paradox

As probably in all societies, a gradient exists in Swiss men between social classes with regard to overall mortality. In contrast to the situation in England and Wales, however, skilled manual workers instead of unskilled workers experience the highest SMR, which is almost twice as high as the one of professionals (class I) (Minder *et al.*, 1986; Egger *et al.*, 1990).

In the Canton of Zürich, the business centre of Switzerland, where the service sector is more important than the industrial sector, it is the social class of the non-manual skilled workers where the highest SMR was observed (Figure 7).

This paradox must be viewed by taking into account the foreign national population. They represent 25% of the male workforce, but they are unequally distributed to the different social classes: while they constitute approximately 10% of classes I, II and IIInm, they make up 24% of class IIIm, and 40% of class IV/V (Table 1) (Egger *et al.*, 1990). By the end of 1980 a total of 374 864 foreign men aged 16 and over lived in Switzerland; between about 40 000 (winter) and 100 000 (summer) men were working as seasonal workers. About 60 000 men were commuting from the neighbouring countries (Federal Bureau of Statistics, 1981). Few of the seasonal and none of the commuting workers are counted in the censuses which take place usually in December, i.e. after the summer and before the winter season, and cover the population living in Switzerland on this date only.

Information on the population, on which mortality statistics are based, is thus incomplete. Therefore, it is not possible to calculate reliable rates

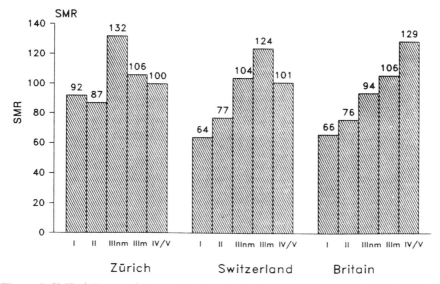

Figure 7 SMR (all causes) by social class for Swiss men aged 15–74, 1979–1982, and from British men aged 20–64, 1979, 1980, 1982, 1983 (Office of Population Censuses and Surveys, 1986)

Table 1 Percentage of Swiss and foreign nationals in social classes I to IV/V, 1980

Social class	No.	Swiss (%)	Foreign nationals (%)
I (professional)	43 994	90.3	9.7
II (middle class)	532 667	88.3	11.7
IIInm (skilled non-manual)	344 737	90.2	9.8
IIIm (skilled manual)	464 868	76.0	24.0
IV/V (partly/unskilled)	747 282	59.5	40.5

Excluded: 110 122 in agriculture and 152 685 without social class assignment
From: Federal Bureau of Statistics and Central Registry of Foreign Nationals (1981), with permission

for foreign nationals, due to the numerator–denominator bias, although information on cause of death, nationality and occupation is available for all deaths occurring in Switzerland. In addition, a second bias must be taken into account: many foreign nationals are staying in Switzerland only for as long as they are fit and able to work, but will leave the country as soon as they fall ill, when they reach the age of retirement or have saved enough money for building up a new existence in their country of origin. The mortality of the foreign nationals is thus at least in parts exported.

All foreign nationals were excluded from the occupational mortality analysis for these two reasons. The fact that the 60% of Swiss men among the un- and semi-skilled workers may have a privileged position or occupy more favourable jobs compared to the 40% foreign workers classified as the same, may be one explanation for that paradox. In the 'business' canton of Zürich this development may already also have affected the skilled manual workers.

This interpretation is supported by the difference in accident rates in the construction sector; they were, in 1982: 158‰ for Swiss and 230‰ for foreign nationals (Burkhalter, 1988).

Discussion

Three examples of occupational mortality analyses with regard to environmental factors associated with health inequalities were given along with possible conclusions. They demonstrate:

1. Mortality analyses can detect associations of occupational and socioeconomic factors of the past with specific pathology now.
2. The socioeconomic changes and technological progress of recent decades probably make the occupational environment (and maybe also the physical environment in general) less dangerous for health. Better worksite standards, automatization and containment of dirty or dangerous production, but probably also export of such production to countries with less stringent labour force protection and environmental laws, result in reduced risks associated directly with industrial production in central Europe. As the absolute number of workers in industrial production decreases in favour of jobs in administration and supervision of production robots, the attributable risk fraction is further reduced. Increasing job rotation accompanying the technological development spreads and dilutes the remaining risks to a larger population. As the inequalities remain, and can be seen not only in countries which experienced economic difficulties, but also in rich countries such as Sweden and Switzerland, the reason must be sought mainly in the socioeconomic rather than the physical environment.
3. Rapid changes in technology itself, change and increase in the number of materials processed and used for production, and an increasing number of jobs a given person occupies during his/her professional life make causal conclusions out of mortality statistics increasingly more difficult; individual exposure assessment for analytical studies is also becoming more and more difficult.
4. Migrant workers are not taken sufficiently into account in many routine statistics. The disease burden of rich countries associated with

socioeconomic inequalities, however, may be carried to a large extent by this group. On the other hand, they escape unemployment in their own country, and unemployment is still a worse health risk than the great majority of jobs.

European integration, with free exchange of goods and a free labour market, will bring a boost to migration, and people originating from eastern Europe and developing countries may offer themselves as a cheap labour force for dangerous or underprivileged jobs. Deprived areas in and outside Europe, on the other hand, will accept dangerous or polluting production or waste processing plants. It is therefore urgent that we create surveillance systems which are able to deal with the transfer of noxious agents, disease, risks and populations across Europe.

References

Beer V, Greusing Th and Minder Ch E (1986) Berufsbezogene sozio-ökonomische Gruppen für die Schweiz: sozialwissenschaftliche Grundlagen und Untersuchungen zur Validität. *Sozial- und Präventivmedizin*, *31*, 274–280

Burkhalter R (1988) *Arbeitssicherheit, Arbeitsgestaltung und technologische Entwicklung im Baugewerbe* (National Research Programme 15). Schweizerischer Nationalfonds, Bern

Egger M, Minder Ch E and Davey Smith G (1990) Health inequalities and migrant workers in Switzerland (Letter). *Lancet*, *336*, 816

Federal Bureau of Statistics (1981) *Statistisches Jahrbuch der Schweiz 1981*. Federal Bureau of Statistics. Birkhäuser Verlag, Basel, pp. 82–92

Federal Office of Public Health (1990) Tuberkulose—Schweiz, 1989 bis 1989. *Bulletin SFOPH*, *43*, 700–703

Minder Ch E, Beer V and Rehmann R (1986) Sterblichkeitsunterschiede nach sozio-ökonomischen Gruppen in der Schweiz 1980: 15- bis 74jährige Männer. *Sozial- und Präventivmedizin*, *31*, 216–219

Morin G and Ackermann-Liebrich U (1990) Epidemiologische Datenquellen in der Schweiz unter besonderer Berücksichtigung der mit vertretbarem Aufwand erschliessbaren Daten über mögliche Auswirkungen der Luftverschmutzung auf die Gesundheit der Bevölkerung in der Schweiz. *Abteilung für Sozial- und Präventivmedizin der Universität Basel*

Office of Population Censuses and Surveys (1970) *Classification of Occupations*. HMSO, London

Office of Population Censuses and Surveys (1986) *Occupational Mortality, decennial supplement 1979–1980, 1982–1983*. HMSO, London

Rieder HL, Zimmermann H, Zwahlen M and Billo NE (1990) Epidemiologie der Tuberkulose in der Schweiz. *Schweizerische Rundschau Medizin (Praxis)*, *79*, 675–679

Schnorf J and Minder Ch E (1991) Lung cancer mortality of Swiss foundry workers. Dissertation, University of Bern

Life expectancy and mortality by causes of death in Estonia, Latvia and Lithuania: socioeconomic and environmental factors and health policy issues

Juris Krúminš, *University of Latvia, Riga, Latvia*

Introduction

There are many factors associated with the stagnation of mortality analysis in the Baltic States in the postwar period, among them: preoccupation with the decline of the birth rate, reduction of access to statistical data on population, restrictions in publication of results of analysis. The official Soviet view also considered health and mortality conditions as satisfactory. Thus the government of the USSR regarded mortality and life expectancy as acceptable according to the 6th UN monitoring report of 1987 (UN, 1987, p. 164).

The purpose of this paper is to examine trends and differentiation of life expectancy and mortality by causes of death, and review recent studies on socioeconomic mortality differentials in the three Baltic States—Estonia, Latvia and Lithuania. This paper summarizes the first results from the more general study of mortality transition and regional differentiation in the Baltics. This analysis is mainly based on information obtained on 1990 and partly on 1991. Taking into consideration that information is fuller, and mortality researches more advanced in Latvia, the analysis of Latvian mortality patterns is more detailed.

Mortality transition in the Baltic States—general remarks

The first reliable data on mortality in the ethnic area of Balts are traced back to the end of the eighteenth century (Birziska, 1922; Jasas and Truska, 1972; Zvidrins, 1978; Palli, 1977). Life expectancy for both sexes in the Karuse parish in Estonia for real cohorts born 1712–1724 was 34.4 years, and for hypothetical cohorts of 1783–1794 it was 28.6 years. Mortality decrease began in Latvia and Estonia about half a century earlier than in Lithuania and in European Russia, where it started at the beginning of the 1890s and intensified at the turn of the century (Krumins *et al.*, 1992). Life tables for all Baltic provinces calculated on the basis of the 1881 census indicate that life expectancy in 1880–1883 for males was 39.1 years and for females 42.7 years (Besser and Ballod, 1897, p. 107).

Estonia, Latvia and Lithuania have much in common in their historical development. A relatively high standard of public health care, sanitary culture, and economic development in the Baltics determined a higher life expectancy of its population in comparison with other regions of the European Russia. Life expectancy in the Baltic provinces, in which 72–93% of the populations were native peoples, was the highest among 11 nationalities of former European Russia in 1896–1897 (Ptoukha, 1928). On the eve of the twentieth century, life expectancy in the Baltics was over 10 years higher than the average in 50 provinces of European Russia, and even exceeded the level of several developed nations.

During the period of independence (1918–1940) life expectancy in the Baltic States grew remarkably. Its level was essentially higher than in Russia, Ukraine and the European part of the USSR in the 1920s (Table 1). In the 1930s, life expectancy in Estonia and Latvia was higher than in many countries of eastern and southern Europe, it was approximately equal to that of Austria and Finland, and lagged a few years behind several western European countries. Life expectancy in the eastern regions of Estonia and Latvia at this time was lower than in the other parts because of less developed social infrastructure.

After 1940, when the Baltic States were incorporated into the USSR, they still retained a leading position among other Soviet republics in many respects judged by a number of socioeconomic characteristics (Krumins and Zvidrins, 1992). It seems that the first 15–20 years of the Soviet regime did

Table 1 Changes in life expectancy at birth (both sexes), three Baltic republics, Belorussia, Russia, Ukraine and the former USSR, 1926/1927–1989

	1926–1927	1958–1959	1978–1979	1986–1987	1988	1989
Baltic republics						
(total)	51.9	68.3	69.6	71.6	71.3	70.8
Estonia	51.7[a]	68.4	69.6	71.0	71.0	70.6
Latvia	53.7[b]	69.1	69.1	70.9	71.0	70.4
Lithuania	50.5[c]	68.4	70.6	72.5	72.4	71.8
Belorussia	52.7	69.8	71.4	72.0	71.7	71.8
Russia	42.9	67.9	67.7	70.1	69.9	69.6
Ukraine	47.1	69.3	69.8	71.1	70.9	70.9
USSR (total)	44.4[d]	68.6	67.9	69.8	69.5	69.5

[a] 1922; [b] 1924–25; [c] 1925–26; [d] European part
Note: If the life expectancies for both sexes are absent, they are computed as an average of men's and women's life expectancy at birth as follows: $E(0) = 0.512\, Em + 0.488\, Ef$

Calculated from: Ptoukha (1960), pp. 412, 414; *Tablitsi smertnosti i ozhidajemoj prodolzhitelnosti zhizni naseleniya* (Moscow, 1989); *Naseleniye SSSR, 1988* (Moscow, 1990), p. 390; *Demograficheskij ezhegodnik SSSR, 1990* (Moscow, 1990), p. 390; national life tables for the 1920s and 1950s.

not have a negative effect on the level of normal civilian mortality in the Baltic countries, if we ignore mortality caused directly by the war and the mass repressions in the 1940s and the beginning of the 1950s (Valkonen *et al.*, 1991, p. 63). At the end of the 1950s, life expectancy in the Baltic republics (68.3 years) was higher than in eastern Europe (66.5 years) and southern Europe (66.2 years), but for females it was higher (71.8 years) than the average in all Europe (70.4 years). However, in the course of the following decades this position was lost, and the tendency of lagging behind developed countries became more evident for males.

Changes in mortality by causes of death

Cause-specific mortality analysis for the three Baltic republics in the time period before the Second World War has not been reported. It is an urgent task for the near future. Since no published cause of death statistical data are available for 1950–1979 for Estonia and Lithuania more attention is paid to mortality analysis by causes of death in Latvia (Krumins, 1990; Zvidrins and Krumins, 1990).

The decrease in life expectancy in Latvia in 1964–1979 occurred mainly due to an increase in mortality from diseases of the circulatory system, and accidents, injuries and poisoning. Until the end of the 1970s mortality from accidental deaths was the main reason for the large gap in male and female life expectancy in Latvia. In the mid-1980s restrictions were placed on use of alcohol, which resulted in reduced consumption of alcoholic beverages. This led to a decrease in traumatism, an essential decrease in male excess mortality from accidental deaths and a radical change in the evolution of mortality. The same phenomenon was observed in Estonia, Lithuania and other republics of the former Soviet Union.

Age-standardized death rates from diseases of the respiratory system showed a considerable decrease in the Baltic republics in the 1980s. The level achieved is lower than it was in the countries of eastern and northern Europe and the USSR. However, circulatory disease mortality shows a different picture. In Latvia, mortality from diseases of the circulatory system was still increasing until the mid-1980s, and only then did it start to decrease slightly. This latter category is perhaps the most disturbing, and has attracted the attention of researchers, since the trends here represent a radical departure from those presently observed in most of the western world. A similar situation can also be observed on other eastern European countries and the former USSR (Krumins and Zvidrins, 1992). Changing dietary habits, greater stress and a higher smoking rate are among the factors hindering progress in mortality from diseases of the circulatory system in Eastern Europe (Rychtarikova *et al.*, 1988). There is reason to consider that the high proportion of deaths from circulatory diseases in the Baltic States may have been the result of miscertification. Data from 1989 indicate that in Jonava region (Lithuania) the age-standardized cardiovascular mortality rate in verified death cases constituted 72% of the standardized death rate in non-verified cases of disease (Stalioraityte *et al.*, 1990). A noticeable growth in death rates from neoplasms for males is present in the Baltic States.

Territorial differentiation of mortality in the three Baltic States shows that regions of excess mortality are: in Estonia—counties located on the Baltic coast; in Latvia—northeastern and western counties; in Lithuania—southeastern and Western counties. Excess mortality is found in the region around Joniskio county both in Latvia and Lithuania. Large differentiations on mortality are usually found between large cities, where the situation is relatively good, and surrounding rural areas, for example, around Tallinn, Riga and Vilnius. The residual excess of rural mortality may be due mainly to differences in standards of hygiene and to poorer medical services.

Socioeconomic and environmental factors that have affected people's health and health policy issues

The socioeconomic and environmental aspects of mortality differentiation still remain insufficiently investigated in the Baltic States. Yet, on the basis of population data in Latvia, calculations have been done, and a number of indices are obtained to characterize this aspect of mortality differentiation. The results of the analysis show substantial socioeconomic differentials in mortality.

In 1969–1970 the standardized death rates according to social groups adopted in Soviet statistics in Latvia were as follows: non-manual employees, 9.1‰; manual workers, 11.5‰; collective farmers, 12.6‰. According to the 1978–1979 Latvian data, mortality in the working ages among workers engaged mainly in physical labour was about twice as high for males, and for females 1.5 times as high as in intellectual professions (Zvidrins and Krumins, 1990). These differences are clearly greater in rural than in urban areas. This can be explained by an inadequately developed system of labour protection for the manual workers and by the worker's self-preservation behaviour. The above-mentioned differences are greater in Latvia than in many European countries (Valkonen, 1987).

A very important problem in the Baltic States in strengthening the status of health is the ever-increasing level of air and water pollution. The impact of industrial pollution on the environment is particularly obvious in many areas of Estonia (Kohtla-Jarve, Narva, Tallinn), of Latvia (Riga, Ventspils) and in the northwest, the central part and the major cities of Lithuania. There is no strong correlation between environmental damage and overall mortality in the Baltic States. Higher levels of infant mortality, morbidity and impaired physical development in the environmentally damaged regions are shown by some studies in Latvia.

Compulsory collectivization changed the way of life and reduced the concern of the rural population for the land and for the preservation of nature. Depositories used in agriculture are mainly below standard. Leakage from these storage devices is one of the main reasons for the pollution surface water basins (*World War II*, 1990, p. 50).

The coastal Baltic Sea is heavily polluted at many locations. The recreational use of the coastal sea waters in many resorts (Haapsalu, Parnu, Saulkrasti, Vecaki, Jurmala and others) is currently considerably limited. In some areas pollution of the subsoil water has begun. Among the main causes of environmental damage in the Baltic States are: centralized socioeconomic planning which ignores local interests, backward technology, the destruction of traditional rural agricultural settlements and subordination of human values to the priorities of the mercantile interests of producers.

The situation of people's health can be improved by a radical revision of the whole system of measures aimed at providing normal functions in activities in all spheres of life. A radical change in the system of health care and social security is necessary. Basic plans have already been made in the Baltic countries, particularly after their declaration of independence in 1990. The Ministry of Health Care and the Ministry of Social Security were combined to form the Ministry of Social Welfare in Latvia in November 1991. The main strategic goal of this reorganization envisages the introduction of a united system of health care and social security, based on an insurance system.

Unfortunately, a new decrease of life expectancy in 1992 is expected, caused by the further worsening of the socioeconomic situation. It is expected that in 1992 in Latvia, as in Estonia and Lithuania, the supply of many essential medicines and medical instruments will end. As a result it will not be possible to treat many degenerative and acute diseases or to do necessary operations (*Laiks*, 1992). In the long-term perspective the Baltic nations are looking with optimism, and hope to restore their place among other European nations which they had before Soviet occupation.

Acknowledgements

I thank Uldis Ushackis and Elmira Senkane (the Latvian Committee of Statistics), Kalev Katus and Mall Leinsalu from Estonia, and Gindra Kasnauskiene from Lithuania, for providing me with data on mortality for the three Baltic States. I thank Professor Barbara A. Anderson for helpful comments during my work on the final version of the paper; I also gratefully acknowledge the editorial assistance of Douglas D. Johnson in preparation of this paper.

References

Besser L and Ballod K (1897) *Smertnost, vozrastnoy sostav i dolgovecnost pravoslavnogo narodonaselenya oboego pola v Rossii za 1851–1890* (Mortality, age structure and longevity of both sexes of the orthodox population of Russia in 1851–1890). Sankt Peterbourg (in Russian)

Birziska V (1992) Iz Lietuvos gyventoju statistikos XVIII amziaus gale. *Mosu senove*, 4/5, 675–684 (in Lithuanian)

Jasas R and Truska L (1972) *Lietuvos Didziosios kunigaikitystes gyventoju suraiymas 1790* m. Vilnius (in Lithuanian)

Krumins J (1990) Stanovlienie sovremennogo tipa smertnosti naselenya Latvii (Formation of contemporary mortality pattern of population in Latvia) *Proceedings of the Latvian Academy of Sciences*, 8, 75–84 (in Russian, English summary)

Krumins J, Zvidrins P, Katus K and Stankuniene V (1992) Mortality trends in Estonia, Latvia and Lithuania: the 19th and 20th centuries. *Proceedings of the Latvian Academy of Sciences* (forthcoming)

Krumins J and Zvidrins P (1992) Recent mortality trends in the three Baltic republics. Population, London (forthcoming)

Laiks (Latvian newspaper in the USA) (1992) Latvija draud veselibas krize (Health crisis threatens Latvia), vol. XLIV, no. 4, p. 7

Palli H (1977) Vosproizvodstvo naselenya Estonii v XVII–XIX vv. (Reproduction of population of Estonia in 17th–19th centuries). Brachnost, rozhdaemost, smertnost v Rossii i v SSSR (Marriage, fertility, mortality in Russia and in the USSR). Statistika, Moscow (in Russian)

Ptoukha M (1928) *Smertnost 11 narodnostey E. Rossii v konce XIX veka* (Mortality of population of 11 nationalities of European Russia at the end of the 19th century). Harkov-Kiev (in Russian)

Ptoukha M (1960) *Ocherki po statistike naselenya* (Treatise on population statistics). Goskomstat CSU SSSR, Moscow (in Russian)

Rychtarikova J, Vallin J and Mesle F (1988) Comparative study of mortality trends in France and the Czech Republic since 1950. Population. *English Selection*, 44 (1), 291–321.

Stalioraityte E, Bernatonyte E, Neimantas R and Pangonyte D (1990) Cardiovascular diseases as cause of death in rural population. Paper presented at the International Conference on Health, Morbidity and Mortality by Cause of Death in Europe, Vilnius, 3–7 December

United Nations (1987) *Global Population Policy Database*. UN, New York

Valkonen T (1987) Social inequality in the face of death. Paper presented at the European Population Conference

Valkonen T, Krumins J and Zvidrins P (1991) *Mortality Trends in Finland and Latvia since the 1920s*. Yearbook of population research in Finland, Population Research Institute, Helsinki, vol. 29, pp. 61–72

World War II and Soviet Occupation in Estonia (1990) A damage report. Periodika Publishers, Tallinn

Zvidrins P (1978) O demograficheskom perehode v Latvii (On demographic transition in Latvia). *Proceedings of the Academy of Sciences of Latvian SSR*, 4, 40 (in Russian)

Zvidrins P and Krumins J (1990) Morbidity and mortality in Estonia, Latvia and Lithuania in the '80s. Paper presented at the East–West Workshop, September

Epidemiology in the assessment of environmental hazards

PART (i) ACUTE INCIDENTS AND CHRONIC EXPOSURE*

Susana Sans and Paul Elliott, *London School of Hygiene and Tropical Medicine, UK*

The forthcoming unified European market will bring changes in production, manufacturing, distribution and consumption of goods and changes in the use of energy resources. These changes are likely to carry unforeseen health effects related to potential toxic exposures through air, soil, water and food. In this chapter we briefly introduce the epidemiological approach and discuss its application to the study of the health effects related, on the one hand, to acute high-level exposures to environmental contaminants and, on the other, to chronic low-level exposures. A number of examples are discussed.

The epidemiological approach

Epidemiology is the study of the distribution of health and disease and their determinants in human populations (MacMahon and Pugh, 1970), and is a key scientific discipline that informs public health decision-making and policy. Environmental epidemiology focuses on the study of the effects on human health of social, physical, biological and chemical factors in the external environment.

Chronic exposure to potentially toxic substances is a fact of modern life. Only a small proportion of the more than 60 000 synthetic chemicals currently in use have been extensively tested for toxicity. Of the 800 or so chemicals that have been assessed for carcinogenicity, about two-thirds have been classified as carcinogens in rodents, and around 30 in humans (Gold *et al.*, 1984; IARC, 1987). Extrapolation of results from animal experiments to humans requires caution not only because of biological diversity, but also because the relative doses used in toxicological experiments are usually orders of magnitude higher than human exposure. Whenever possible,

---

* An earlier version of this paper was presented at a meeting organised by the International Programme on Chemical Safety, held at the London School of Hygiene and Tropical Medicine on February 20–21, 1992.

animal experiments and chemical toxicological data need to be viewed alongside human data, but these are often lacking where available data on human exposure are more likely to have been obtained through observational studies of occupational cohorts than of populations exposed to environmental pollution.

The classical epidemiological approach starts by describing the frequency of disease, measured in terms of morbidity or mortality in different groups, places and time. Variations in the distribution of disease in time and space may reflect differences in exposure to environmental factors, to lifestyles and behaviour or, to a lesser extent, to genetic factors. Based on these observations, hypotheses may be formulated concerning the aetiology of diseases which can then be tested in *ad-hoc* analytical studies, e.g. case–control or cohort (follow-up) studies, in which individual exposures to putative risk factors are measured and related to disease frequency.

In interpreting geographical variations in disease, it cannot be assumed that they are due to differences in the distribution of an environmental risk factor. Firstly, the differences observed could be due to chance. Secondly, environmental or occupational risks need to be disentangled from the effects of lifestyle-related factors such as smoking or diet. This is especially so when the long-term effects of low-level chronic exposures are being assessed. For example, the higher rates of lung cancer found in urban compared to rural environments need to be evaluated with regard to the different smoking patterns in the two settings (Doll and Peto, 1981). Thirdly, occupational or environmental risk may vary depending on lifestyle factors, e.g. the risk of lung cancer is many-fold higher in individuals exposed to both asbestos and cigarette smoking than in those exposed to one of these two risk factors (Selikoff *et al.*, 1968).

Epidemiology, like any other human science, seldom permits direct inferences about causation. Rather the totality of evidence from a range of disciplines (human, animal, experimental, chemical, toxicological) needs to be assessed as a whole, and a judgement made as to causality. Epidemiology seeks to identify and control for extraneous factors that may distort or modify a causal relationship, often in circumstances where an experimental approach is limited by, or impossible because of, practical or ethical considerations. Bradford Hill (1965) set out several criteria that should be considered when addressing the question of causality in epidemiological studies: chance; temporal sequence; strength, specificity and consistency of the association; period of exposure; dose–response relationship; effects of removing the suggested cause; biological plausibility of the association, and coherence of the findings.

Epidemiological response to acute and chronic exposures to environmental pollutants

Acute high-level exposure

Following a chemical or nuclear accident, acute short-term exposure to high levels of environmental contaminants may occur. The epidemiologist charged with studying the possible health effects has to work under emergency conditions, with all the problems consequent upon the disruption of political and administrative control. The main concern of the authorities following such an event is to identify those individuals who are acutely ill, and provide immediate medical attention and humanitarian relief. Generally, very little thought and resources are given to the needs of scientific research.

As Andersson *et al.* (1988) point out in relation to Bhopal, the emergency measures taken to regain control in the immediate wake of a disaster produce additional and sometimes insuperable difficulties for the epidemiologist. Inaccurate and unsubstantiated assertions about the cause and extent of the disaster may be made, and these can distort estimates of the two fundamental epidemiological parameters—namely, exposure and effect. Thus, at the outset, the value of any scientific endeavour may be compromised, even before attempts are made to account for the effect of modifying (confounding) factors or missing data.

Often, little is known in advance about the pathology and clinical picture of diseases produced by acute and high-level exposure to environmental contaminants. Previous knowledge of the expected symptomatology and disease outcome may be lacking, or may have to be inferred from the effects of chemically similar agents. Often the investigation of environmental catastrophic events involving human exposure is unable to delimit and quantify exposures accurately (as occurred at Seveso or Bhopal) or may give inconclusive or incomplete results concerning causality (e.g. toxic oil syndrome). These examples are discussed briefly below.

Seveso   A cloud of toxic chemicals from a plant synthesizing trichlorophenol (TCP) was released over nearby residential areas during the night of 10 July 1976 in Seveso, northern Italy. The toxic cloud included TCP as well as dioxin (TCDD). A few days later, effects upon vegetation, birds, domestic animals and children were noted, including burns, caustic lesions and swellings on uncovered parts of the body. The affected areas were classified into three exposure zones (A, B, and R) according to decreasing but overlapping measured soil levels of TCDD, as well as distance from the plant. The purpose was to seal off the areas heavily contaminated and hence avoid further exposure of the population consequent upon the long half-life of dioxin. Different intervention strategies were employed among people living in the three zones.

The exposure zones defined for the immediate intervention were later used as exposure categories for epidemiological research, but it was soon realized that the correlation between clinical symptoms and other ecological damage did not correspond well with the soil measurements (Merlo *et al.*, 1986). Any misclassification of areas would have diluted the estimated health effects of the accident.

TCDD has recently been measured in frozen serum samples collected soon after the accident in an attempt to validate the exposure categories measured by geographical zones and TCDD soil measurements. However, only very few samples were analysed and these were purportedly collected from severely ill persons, or according to other unclear criteria.

Clinically ill persons or pregnant women were followed up for long-term effects during the first years after the incident. It was not until several years after the accident that a cohort design was adopted, with all the inherent problems of having to reconstruct the population resident in the area at the time of the accident. More recently, a second attempt was made, whereby any person registered as resident at any time since the accident in the municipalities affected, was defined as at risk, and was considered available for follow-up. Length of residence is being used as a surrogate for duration of exposure, which is particularly important in this case given the long half-life of dioxin. The study has been hampered by the difficulty of locating and tracing subjects *a posteriori* (Bertazzi *et al.*, 1992).

Toxic oil syndrome On 1 May 1981, five members of a family of eight, who were resident in Torrejon de Ardoz, a town on the outskirts of Madrid, Spain, were taken seriously ill with respiratory symptoms; one of them died on admission to hospital. In the following weeks an epidemic of cases of a previously unknown syndrome characterized by a non-cardiogenic pulmonary oedema, fever, exanthema, eosinophilia and high IgE spread in the environs of Madrid and the provinces to the northwest of the capital. The epidemic of cases reached a peak by mid-June and then vanished by the end of the month. More than 25 000 people were affected. Some of them developed a chronic phase with neurological and scleroderma-like symptoms, and more than 600 people died. The epidemic was associated with the consumption of adulterated oil containing anilines and fatty acid anilides (WHO, 1984). Traces of trichlorethylene and chloride were also detected in some oil samples (Kilbourne *et al.*, 1988).

The suspicion that illegally sold oil might have been related to the outbreak was officially announced on television 40 days after the first diagnosed case. A massive operation was organized to exchange suspected oil carafes for pure olive oil, regardless of whether family members were affected by the syndrome. The records of these exchanges were kept, but were inaccurate; hence the opportunity for precise exposure measurement was lost. Furthermore, chemical analysis was carried out only on occasional samples of oils, which were generally selected because of severity of illness and other anecdotal criteria (and which probably resulted in selection bias). There were later efforts to characterize the origin of the oil samples collected, which eventually led to fruitful investigations (Anonymous, 1982), but the accuracy of the census of the exposed population is uncertain.

As the clinical and pathological features of the syndrome were previously unknown, a definition of who was an epidemic-related case had to be established. This definition included not only the clinical characteristics but also the exposure category of cases, thus preventing proper effect assessment. Thus, the opportunity to investigate properly the cause of this toxic outbreak, both from the epidemiological and the toxicological point of view, was lost.

Bhopal   During the first week of December 1984 a toxic cloud releasing methylisocyanate (MIC) escaped from the Union Carbide plant producing carbamate pesticides in Bhopal, India. The effects included eye irritation and blindness. It is estimated that more than 200 000 people were exposed to the gas cloud.

In contrast to the long half-life of dioxin, the half-life of MIC is only two minutes; therefore it was not possible to define exposure based on environmental measurements. Proximity to a cluster of high mortality measured two weeks after the disaster was used as a proxy indicator of exposure to MIC (Andersson *et al.*, 1988). Problems of follow-up of the exposed population have been immense, both because of the difficulties of exposure estimation and also because of large-scale inward and outward migration to and from the study area. Scientific study was also hampered by the many political and legal ramifications of the accident.

Comment

These three acute toxic events have a number of characteristics in common. They were the result of high doses of contaminant affecting large numbers of the general population. The resulting clinical pictures were poorly recognized or were unknown previously, with biological mechanisms that were not well understood. The episodes created great social concern and anxiety and had large economic and political impact. Underlying all three events were economic, political, social and cultural conditions that favoured weak enforcement of safety regulations, and a poorly coordinated response to the disaster.

As enquiries concerning symptoms and health effects were carried out some time after the events had taken place, and within the framework of discussion about compensation, it was difficult if not impossible to obtain reliable exposure and effect data for scientific epidemiological studies. In all three episodes, manipulation of exposure categories for the purposes of compensation interfered with the characterization of the exposed population. Thus, in Bhopal, families ran away from their houses during the acute episode. Some of the worst-affected people never came back, and their dwellings were occupied by other families in the weeks after, especially once rumours had started about possible compensation. In Spain, many carafes of cheap oil not related to the adulteration episode were exchanged for olive oil, and people claimed compensation afterwards. Taken together, these factors would tend to have produced underestimates of the health effects.

Another factor in common was the obvious need to follow up all the exposed persons, and not only those who became ill immediately after the acute event. In order to study long-term effects it is necessary to set up appropriate population and disease registers. However, when the toxic effects of an environmental agent are poorly understood, it is difficult to establish what health effects to follow up over time. In Bhopal, the eye was chosen as a sentinel organ, and in Seveso and Spain, mortality, cancer incidence, congenital malformations and abortions are being studied. Outpatient clinics were established in Bhopal and in Spain to provide specialized care to victims. Such a system is a useful framework for this type of research; however, without a proper epidemiological perspective there is the danger of carrying out more intensive follow-up of the exposed than the non-exposed population, and hence introducing large biases into the analysis. In addition, in these examples there were questions of liability and other legal implications, as well as international ramifications: for example in Bhopal there was foreign shareholding of the plant, and in the case of the toxic oil, some of the adulterated rapeseed oil had been refined in and imported from France.

Chronic low-level exposure

The problems of assessment of long-term effects of low-level exposure are also considerable and include, among others, the technological difficulties, costs and poor geographical coverage of environmental measurements, the lack of specificity of most health outcomes, confounding socioeconomic and socio-behavioural factors, and the time of follow-up necessary to observe any effects. Attempts to overcome some of these difficulties include the development of biological markers of exposure and effect (e.g. DNA adducts) (Hulka *et al.*, 1990), but these have not been fully evaluated, and their relationship to disease end-points consequent upon environmental exposure is uncertain. Another approach is to establish a monitoring and surveillance system able to detect possible adverse health effects at an early stage. For example, it could be used to study the geographical distribution of diseases in relation to point sources of environmental pollution, or to investigate clusters of diseases in small geographical areas, and place them in a wider context. In the UK, the Small Area Health Statistics Unit (SAHSU) has been funded by government to carry out rapid initial investigations of health effects around point sources of environmental pollution—see accompanying paper by Elliott, for further discussion). Potentially, a further advantage of such a system is that it allows for the study of long-term effects following accidental high-level exposure (should this occur) without the problems associated with *ad-hoc* systems established after an accident. Its establishment requires (Elliott *et al.*, 1992):

1. The existence of high-quality routine health data, i.e. mortality and cancer registrations, with the ability to locate individual events to the place of residence at diagnosis, death, or birth.
2. Access to small area population demographic information (e.g. from census) for the calculation of disease rates.
3. Availability of adequate computer hardware and software and skilled computer manpower.
4. Appropriate high-level epidemiological and statistical expertise.

Conclusions

The ability to evaluate health effects associated with exposure to environmental hazards is currently limited. The evaluation of health effects related to catastrophic environmental events is usually severely constrained by the demands of the emergency situation. In any case these studies do not address the problem of chemical and toxic agents in the environment generally, for which better measurements or estimates of human exposure are required. Existing disease registries and vital statistics systems with geographically referenced data are now being used to assess the public health impact of point sources of environmental pollution.

References

Andersson N, Kerr Muir M, Mehra V and Salmon AG (1988) Exposure and response to methylisocyanate: results of a community based survey in Bhopal. *British Journal of Industrial Medicine*, 45, 469–475

Anonymous (1982) Contribucion del programa del CSIC al estudio de la etiologia y patogenia Sindrome Toxico. In *Symposium Nacional Sindrome Toxico*. Ministerio de Sanidad y Consumo, Madrid, pp. 514–533

Bertazzi PA, Pesatori AC and Zocchetti C (1992) The Seveso accident. In Elliott P, Cuzick J, English D and Stern R (eds), *Geographical and Environmental Epidemiology: methods for small-area studies*. Oxford University Press, Oxford, pp. 342–358

Doll R and Peto R (1981) *The Causes of Cancer*. Oxford University Press, Oxford

Elliott P, Kleinschmidt I and Westlake AI (1992) Use of routine data in studies of point sources of environmental pollution. In Elliott P, Cuzick J, English D and Stern R (eds), *Geographical and Environmental Epidemiology: methods for small area studies*. Oxford University Press, Oxford, pp. 106–114

Gold LS *et al.* (1984) A carcinogenic potency database of the standardized results of animal bioassays. *Environmental Health Perspectives*, 58, 9–319

Hill B (1965) The environment and disease: Association or causation? *Proceedings of the Royal Society of Medicine*, 58, 295

Hulka B, Wilcosky TC and Griffith JD (eds) (1990) *Biological Markers in Epidemiology*. Oxford University Press, Oxford

IARC (International Agency for Research on Cancer) (1987) *IARC Monographs on the Evaluation of Carcinogenic Risk to Humans*. Overall evaluations of carcinogenicity: an updating of IARC Monographs, vols 1 to 42, Suppl. 7. IARC, Lyon, France

Kilbourne, EM *et al.* (1988) Chemical correlates of pathogenicity of oils related to the toxic oil syndrome epidemic in Spain. *American Journal of Epidemiology*, 127, 1210–1227

MacMahon B and Pugh TF (1970) *Epidemiology: Principles and Methods*. Little Brown, Boston

Merlo F, Puntoni R and Santi L (1986) The Seveso episode: the validity of epidemiological enquiries in relation to the definition of population at risk. *Chemosphere*, 15, 1777–1786

Selikoff IJ *et al.* (1968) Asbestos exposure, smoking and neoplasia. *Journal of the American Medical Association*, 204, 106–112

WHO (1984) Toxic oil syndrome mass food poisoning in Spain. Report on a WHO meeting. Madrid, 21–25 March 1983. WHO, Copenhagen

PART (ii) THE SMALL AREA HEALTH STATISTICS UNIT

Paul Elliott, *London School of Hygiene and Tropical Medicine, UK*

Introduction

Environmental pollution and its possible effects on health have become a major public health issue throughout Europe. Concern has focused on the potential for a major accident such as occurred at Seveso and Chernobyl, and on the effects of chronic low-level pollution. An obvious and readily identifiable source of pollution (e.g. a plume from an industrial plant) may come under public scrutiny, and apparent clusters of disease which may be identified locally may then be attributed to that source. Other potential sources of pollution, e.g. nuclear installations, may stimulate similar levels of public anxiety. Risks from the *external* environment, which are perceived as being outside individual control, are generally considered to be more threatening than risks related to individual lifestyle and behaviour. This is despite the fact that only a small proportion of cancers are estimated to be due to pollution, the majority being attributed to individual diet and tobacco use.

Considerable *scientific* uncertainty also exists concerning the risks to human health of chemicals and radiation in the environment. Of the many thousands of chemicals, by-products and combustion products released into the environment, relatively few have been assessed for toxicity: some have been classified as likely or possible human carcinogens (IARC, 1987). Risk assessment is often based on chemical or animal data alone, as human data on exposure are largely lacking. The human data that do exist may be derived from an occupational setting in which levels of exposure may be orders of magnitude higher than those experienced by the general population. Nonetheless, low levels of environmental pollution experienced by large numbers in the general population could result in large numbers of attributable cases, especially for common cancers such as lung cancer; however, the level of risk may be too low to be detectable.

Risk assessment concerning the health effects of environmental pollution needs to be informed by human data from epidemiological studies. A classical epidemiological approach is to investigate the geographical variability in disease rates in areas with contrasting levels of exposure. Unfortunately data on levels of pollutants in the environment are usually available for only a few monitoring sites around the country (see contribution by Briggs).

A useful first step might be to examine the health effects near point sources of pollution, where levels of pollution would be expected to be higher than for the general population. For example, disease rates close to the source could be compared with some external standard, e.g. regional or national rates, or with rates in an unexposed control area. Such studies were until recently expensive and time-consuming, since the routine reporting of health statistics was available only for large administrative areas (e.g. district or region): disease rates in small localities near a point source could not readily be obtained. However, recent developments in computing and database management can potentially make available geographically referenced data on health events at much higher levels of resolution than hitherto; this enables the initial analysis of the health statistics around point sources to be largely automated. In the remainder of this chapter, the work of the Small Area Health Statistics Unit (SAHSU) in the UK is described, and examples of the type of study undertaken are given.

The Small Area Health Statistics Unit

In 1983 a television programme alleged that the incidence of childhood leukaemia was raised near the nuclear reprocessing plant at Sellafield (then Windscale). The government set up an independent enquiry under the Chairmanship of Sir Douglas Black (Black, 1984). Recommendation 5 of the report called for an organization:

> to coordinate centrally the monitoring of small area statistics around major installations producing discharges that might present a carcinogenic or mutagenic hazard to the public. In this way, early warning of any untoward health effect could be obtained.

Subsequently, the Small Area Health Statistics Unit (SAHSU) was established as an independent facility at the London School of Hygiene and Tropical Medicine, funded by government departments of health and environment, and the Health and Safety Executive. Its terms of reference are as follows:

1. To examine quickly reports of unusual clusters of disease, particularly in the neighbourhood of industrial installations, and advise authoritatively as soon as possible.
2. In collaboration with other scientific groups, to build up reliable background information on the distribution of disease amongst small areas so that specific clusters can be placed in proper context.
3. To study the available statistics in order to detect any unusual incidence of disease as early as possible and, where appropriate, to investigate.
4. To develop the methodology for analysing and interpreting statistics relating to small areas.

SAHSU works closely with the Environmental Monitoring Project at the Office of Population Censuses and Surveys (OPCS), to include joint staff appointments, the transfer of data for England and Wales to SAHSU, and the exchange of computer programs and expertise. There are also close working relationships with data providers in Scotland and Northern Ireland, the Welsh Office, and with the various cancer registries which feed data into the national cancer registration scheme.

Most of our attention has focused on methods for the study of point sources. We have been particularly concerned with the study of disease around multiple sites, either to replicate an enquiry conducted *post-hoc* around one site (by studying other sites in Britain producing similar discharges) or to test hypotheses related to particular industrial processes. The various components of the SAHSU system are described below.

Geography

In the 1970s the Post Office introduced a comprehensive system of postcodes, covering the whole of the UK, to improve the efficiency of delivering mail. Postcodes are allocated through a hierarchy. In the UK there are 120 postal areas, and approximately 2700 districts, 9000 sectors and 1.6 million unit postcodes representing 22 million postal addresses. Unit postcodes uniquely define areas containing on average only 14 households each. Many vital statistics and health events in the UK are now routinely postcoded.

Although the postcode relates to too small an area for analyses in its own right, it serves as a building block for the entire system. It can be used to locate events in administrative areas such as local government district, or in arbitrary areas such as a circle around a point source of pollution. Standard directories give a map grid reference (accurate to 100 m) for each postcode. There are also approximate geographical links to enumeration districts (EDs), the smallest census unit available, and hence to the relevant population data. (In Scotland there are direct links between postcodes and EDs; in England and Wales following the 1991 census, the census office will be able to assign postcodes directly to EDs, although some postcodes will span more than one ED.)

Health events

Postcoded data sets held by SAHSU include:

1. Deaths, live births and still births for England and Wales from 1981, for Scotland from 1974 and for Northern Ireland from 1986. The information on births provides accurate year-by-year denominator data for perinatal and childhood events. OPCS (but not SAHSU) has link files which enable information on infant mortality to be collated for particular individuals.
2. Cancer registrations for England and Wales from 1974. These were originally collected by the 12 regional cancer registries, and enhanced by a large retrospective postcoding exercise undertaken by the Environmental Monitoring Project at OPCS. SAHSU also holds Scottish data from 1975, and data on childhood leukaemia and non-Hodgkin lymphomas in Great Britain from 1966, supplied by the Childhood Cancer Research Group in Oxford.
3. Congenital malformations for England and Wales from 1983.

In addition, the Environmental Monitoring Project at OPCS holds some data items which for legal and confidentiality reasons cannot be passed to SAHSU, e.g., data on abortions.

For each individual event, SAHSU holds postcode of residence, diagnosis (ICD code, and histology code for cancer registrations), age in years and months, and an identifier allowing OPCS to link to individual records. A similar system is in place for Scottish data.

Populations

The population data come mainly from the decennial census. Population statistics were published for wards in 1971 and at the level of ED in 1981. There are approximately 10 000 wards and 130 000 EDs in Britain, each ED containing on average about 150 households and 400 individuals. A system of 'census tracts' based on 1981 geography links areas between the two censuses. Similar data from the 1991 census will be published for EDs together with some small area aggregated postcode data. Standard directories are available to relate EDs to wards and higher-level administrative units such as health authorities, local government districts or parliamentary constituencies. Tables giving socioeconomic information for EDs have also been abstracted from the census small area statistics (e.g. car ownership, proportion unemployed). These data allow some control in the statistical analyses for social and demographic confounding variables.

Computer hardware and software

The SAHSU system runs under Unix on a RISC (Reduced Instruction Set Computer) Digital (DEC) 5500 super-microcomputer, with about 24 mips of processing power and installed data storage of around 10 500 Mbytes. We use the Oracle relational database management system and implement algorithms in C with 'embedded' SQL for access to the database. Further analysis is done in the statistical packages Gauss, 'S' and SAS.

Statistical methods

Currently only a simple dispersion model around a point source is used, although extension to other models (to take account, for example, of prevailing wind patterns) is feasible. Thus a range of circle sizes around a source is chosen *a priori*, and the numbers of events observed, and the numbers expected, are calculated for the bands between adjacent circles. Expected numbers are calculated from national rates, regionally adjusted, standardized for age and sex, and with and without adjustment for Carstairs' index, a measure of the socioeconomic profile of small areas (Jolley *et al.*, 1992). Two statistical tests are carried out. The first is based on the Poisson distribution, to give observed/expected (O/E) ratios and 95% confidence intervals for two adjacent bands close to, and more distant from, the source.

The second uses Stone's (1988) method for data over a range of circles, to test whether there is evidence of decreasing risk with distance from the source. Data from a number of installations can readily be pooled and tested in the same way.

Examples

1. *Mortality from mesothelioma and asbestosis near Plymouth dockyards.* Mortality from pleural mesothelioma and asbestosis for 1981–1987 was examined near the naval dockyards at Plymouth, southwest England, where it was known that occupational exposure to asbestos had occurred historically. For men, O/E ratios of over 11 for mesothelioma (four deaths) and 40 for asbestosis (two deaths) were found within 1 km of the docks (Figure 1), and overall the excess was highly significant ($p < 0.00001$). For women there were few deaths from mesothelioma, and none from asbestosis. Review of death certificates confirmed that most of these cases had worked at the docks, suggesting in this case that occupational rather than environmental exposure was the likely cause (Elliott *et al.*, 1992a).

2. *Incidence of cancer of the larynx and lung near incinerators of waste solvents and oils in Britain.* A report of cancer incidence near a defunct incinerator of waste solvents and oils at Charnock Richard, Coppull, Lancashire, northwest England, suggested that there was an apparent cluster of five cases of cancer of the larynx nearby. This *post-hoc* finding was examined, and the enquiry extended to all 10 eligible incinerator sites in Great Britain that could be identified as burning a similar type of waste. The excess of cancer of the larynx near Charnock Richard was found in our analysis to be within chance limits. In the pooled analysis over all 10 sites no statistically significant excess of either cancer of the larynx or lung was found. It was concluded that the apparent cluster of cancer of the larynx previously observed at Charnock Richard was unlikely to be due to its former incinerator (Elliott *et al.*, 1992b).

Conclusion

There is considerable public and scientific concern about the health effects of environmental pollution. The availability of high-quality national data sets with high-resolution geographical information has enabled the initial screening and analysis of health data around point sources of industrial pollution to be largely automated. SAHSU is the first example of a national system dedicated to the study of small area health statistics. If a disease excess is found near a particular site, replication around sites with similar discharges (if such can be found) can be carried out from within the

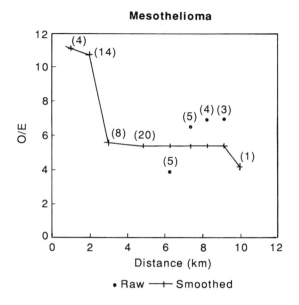

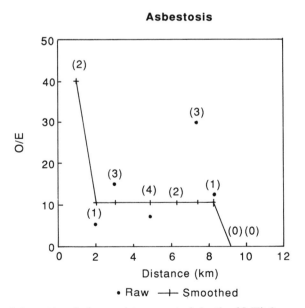

Figure 1 Plot of the ratio of observed to expected deaths (O/E) for men in different bands by distance from Plymouth docks. The points give the observed O/E ratios. The smoothed line joins the estimated values of O/E subject to the constraint that the risk is a decreasing function of distance. Numbers in parentheses are the observed number of deaths at each distance

database. Alternatively, disease around multiple sites can be examined *a priori*, and the study replicated if necessary around other sites, to investigate the risks associated with a particular industrial process or set of installations (e.g. municipal incinerators). Confirmatory field studies may then be required, to include environmental measurements, and assessment of possible confounding factors such as smoking, alcohol consumption, housing quality and occupational histories. Examples of studies under way include investigation of the health effects related to vinyl chloride plants, coke works and municipal incinerators.

References

Black, Sir Douglas (Chairman) (1984) Report of the Independent Advisory Group. *Investigation of the Possible Increased Incidence of Cancer in West Cumbria.* HMSO, London

Doll R and Peto R (1981) *The Causes of Cancer: Quantitative Estimates of Avoidable Risks of Cancer in the United States Today.* Oxford University Press, Oxford.

Elliott P, Westlake AJ, Hills M, Kleinschmidt I, Rodrigues R, McGale P, Marshall K and Rose G (1992a) The Small Area Health Statistics Unit: a national facility for investigating health around point sources of environmental pollution in the United Kingdom. *Journal of Epidemiology and Community Health*, *46*, 345–349

Elliott P, Hills M, Beresford J, Kleinschmidt I, Jolley D, Pattenden S, Rodrigues L, Westlake A and Rose G (1992b) Incidence of cancer of the larynx and lung near incinerators of waste solvents and oils in Great Britain. *Lancet, 339*, 854–858

International Agency for Research on Cancer (IARC) (1987) IARC Monographs on the Evaluation of Carcinogenic Risk to Humans. Overall evaluations of carcinogenicity: an updating of IARC monographs, vols 1–42, Suppl. 7, IARC, Lyon, France

Jolley D, Jarman B and Elliott P (1992) Socio-economic confounding. In Elliott P, Cuzick J, English D and Stern R (eds), *Geographical and Environmental Epidemiology: methods for small area studies*. Oxford University Press, Oxford, pp 115–124

Stone RA (1988) Investigations of excess environmental risks around putative sources: statistical problems and a proposed test. *Statist. Med. 7*, 649–650

Workshop discussion report

Sir Richard Doll, *Imperial Cancer Research Fund, Oxford, UK*

The impact of the total environment on health cannot be considered solely in physical, chemical and biological terms, but must also take account of the effect of social, cultural and psychological factors. Social factors are among the most important, and policies for improving the environment should give priority to the alleviation of poverty, illiteracy and feelings of personal helplessness in the face of fate.

Even so, the establishment of the European Environment Agency provides an opportunity for a re-examination of policies for monitoring chemical exposures. These need to be regularly reviewed by expert groups of scientists, including those with an understanding of the aetiology of human disease.

Quality control of monitoring procedures is essential to ensure comparability of data in different areas and at different times. Precision in a few sites is less important than widespread coverage by methods that give comparable results.

Monitoring procedures need to be sufficiently flexible to respond to changing situations and be able to trigger intensive investigations when accepted levels of pollution are exceeded.

The European Environment Agency should seek to establish administrative arrangements with bodies responsible for monitoring in other European countries outside the European Community to ensure that comparable data of uniform reliability are collected throughout Europe.

Monitoring of exposures to environmental hazards without comparable monitoring of health effects is of little value. Data indicative of health status needs to be made available, for research purposes, for the smallest units for which population statistics are reliable.

Not all health indicators can be effectively monitored routinely on a national scale, and there is also a need for the surveillance of complex health outcomes, such as the prevalence of congenital abnormalities that is currently monitored by EUROCAT.

International collaboration between research groups studying the relationship between health and the environment should be encouraged through the World Health Organization centres for Environmental Health at Bilthoven and Rome in order to facilitate the identification of common problems, to improve the comparability of data, and to generate hypotheses. Research workers throughout Europe should be encouraged to make use of the specialized data that may be available in individual countries.

Good quality monitoring of environmental hazards, and their effects on health, require people with skills in environmental epidemiology and environmental health policy. An initiative for the training of this core of skilled workers is needed at the European level.

The recognition of environmental hazards often requires access to medical data relating to individuals. Access to such data is hindered in some parts of Europe by legal and administrative regulations for the preservation of the confidentiality of personal medical information. Such regulations should not be allowed to prevent access for bona-fide medical research workers for the purposes of research in the public interest, under conditions that require the research workers to treat the personal information as strictly confidential.

The removal of frontiers within Europe has many implications for the control of environmental hazards. For example, the transport of toxic wastes that has occurred across frontiers within Europe should not be allowed to be replaced by its transport outside Europe.

The impact of environment on health now has to be considered on a global and not only a local scale. Increases in populations in the developing countries and in per-capita national product in the developed countries are altering the global environment in ways that will eventually seriously affect standards of health and the quality of life by the destruction of the atmospheric ozone layer, the build-up of greenhouse gases, the acidification of rainfall, and the destruction of national resources. European and other countries with a high standard of living must accept responsibility for initiating the reversal of the process by action within their own countries, and by providing incentives for less-favoured countries to improve their standard of living in ways that have the least deleterious impact on the global environment.

Nutrition, diet and food standards

Food supply patterns in Europe

Michel Rotily and *Suraiya Ismail, *Centre Alpin de Recherche Epidemiologique et de Prevention Sanitaire, Grenoble, France, and *London School of Hygiene and Tropical Medicine, UK*

In 1982 Malassis and Padilla prepared a worldwide typology of food supply patterns. On the basis of food supply figures compiled by the Food and Agriculture Organization (FAO) for 1975–1977 they characterized six European patterns (Anglosaxon, Continental European, Scandinavian, eastern European, Mediterranean European, and Mediterranean 'Japanese'). Blandford (1984), using cluster analysis on OECD data for 1977–1979, derived country groupings on the basis of similarities in dietary structure indicated by daily per capita supply of calories obtained from eight major food groups. Although some differences were noted, he concluded that there was a general tendency for dietary structure to become increasingly similar across the majority of the OECD countries. However, European countries such as Greece, Yugoslavia and eastern countries were not taken into account, while some non-European countries (USA, Australia and Japan) were included in the analysis. As a result, Japan's very different pattern of high cereal supply and low supplies of fats, oils, meats and eggs, tended to mask dissimilarities between European regions. More recently, James (1989) proposed three European food patterns (eastern, northern and southern), using FAO's food balance sheets (FBS) for 1979–1982, and related these to morbidity and mortality figures.

This study attempts to define food supply patterns across 26 countries of Europe on the basis of the latest FAO FBS (1984–1986), using multivariate analysis. The findings are compared to those described in the earlier studies mentioned above.

Methods

FAO's supply data on 13 food groups for all European countries (Table 1) were extracted and averaged for the three most recent years for which data were available.

Europe Without Frontiers. Edited by C.E.M. Normand and P. Vaughan
© 1993 John Wiley & Sons Ltd

Table 1 Food groups, countries and abbreviations

Food groups

CER — Cereals	RTB — Roots and tubers
PUL — Pulses	MEA — Meat and offal
VEG — Vegetables	VOF — Vegetable oils and fats
FRU — Fruits	AOF — Animal oils and fats
EGG — Eggs	SUG — Sugar, honey, syrups
NUT — Nuts	MLK — Milk and milk products
CAL — Total calories	FSH — Fish and seafood

Countries

ALB — Albania	NL — Netherlands
AUS — Austria	NOR — Norway
BEL — Belgium	POL — Poland
BUL — Bulgaria	POR — Portugal
CZE — Czechoslovakia	EGR — East Germany
DK — Denmark	WGR — West Germany
FIN — Finland	ROM — Romania
FRA — France	SP — Spain
GRE — Greece	SWE — Sweden
HUN — Hungary	SWI — Switzerland
IRL — Ireland	UK — United Kingdom
ITA — Italy	USSR — Soviet Union
MAL — Malta	Yug — Yugoslavia

The statistical analysis consisted in performing a principal-component analysis (PCA) of a matrix comprising the calorie contributions of the food groups for each European country. As the total variance could be well summarized by the first four principal components (PC) which accounted for 80% of total variance, and in order to derive groups of countries on the basis of overall similarity in food supply patterns, a Ward's minimum variance cluster analysis (CA) was performed with coordinates of each country on the first four PC's (Kendall, 1980; Lebart *et al.*, 1982). The analysis was repeated for the same countries but using the calorie contributions of fats derived from food groups defined above.

Results

Calories supplied by each food group are shown in Table 2; it can be seen that on average cereals contribute more calories (31.4%) to total calories supply than any other food group. Meats provide the next greatest contribution (14.2%), followed by sugar (10.3%) and vegetable oils (9.8%). Calories supplied by fish and seafood (1.2%), pulses (0.9%), nuts (0.9%) and animal fats (7.6%) show the most important inter-country variations. Table 3 is the matrix of the correlation coefficients between food groups.

Table 2 Calories from food groups (kcal per capita daily) by country

	CER	RTB	PUL	VEG	FRU	MEA	EGG	VOF	AOF	SUG	NUT	MLK	FSH	CAL
ALB	1757	64	56	20	80	151	15	132	46	191	20	191	7	2730
AUS	685	112	6	47	149	494	56	370	368	396	49	351	16	3160
BEL	746	191	25	74	102	746	53	380	463	396	27	309	34	3612
BUL	1473	57	42	63	130	349	54	370	161	375	30	269	18	3404
CZE	1047	146	8	61	78	476	67	252	315	407	15	299	16	3197
DK	727	135	9	59	81	778	58	231	327	423	27	319	65	3286
FIN	710	188	10	25	91	494	41	162	243	377	14	459	66	2916
FRA	757	141	16	79	94	457	60	288	288	388	31	377	37	3036
GRE	1126	126	53	143	186	466	43	595	33	338	31	339	33	3571
HUN	1069	91	39	59	94	486	71	180	444	404	77	269	11	3287
IRL	897	242	29	55	73	639	42	231	300	535	13	378	30	3486
ITA	1130	72	39	99	142	387	44	520	142	300	15	330	33	3292
MAL	946	39	47	74	94	351	56	333	111	393	36	274	32	2801
NL	651	162	20	51	117	388	54	372	367	389	37	388	19	3073
NOR	789	148	12	34	110	365	46	349	194	411	31	479	98	3125
POL	1144	199	21	69	44	317	46	164	262	454	30	414	41	3183
POR	1244	176	50	87	66	335	22	401	50	265	0	137	75	2941
EGR	954	270	10	57	101	554	69	254	444	421	22	280	28	3472
WGR	740	144	11	57	147	536	64	299	343	430	15	320	22	3187
ROM	1451	131	42	111	107	295	60	223	181	281	42	246	23	3177
SP	846	198	52	102	132	511	61	527	51	284	45	268	55	3145
SWE	680	131	9	37	97	317	50	271	250	456	35	490	62	2923
SWI	673	91	11	63	157	651	47	285	222	427	47	457	29	3222
UK	641	191	24	60	76	495	47	379	227	480	38	331	27	3038
USSR	1263	196	24	59	70	337	56	222	176	467	22	269	67	3238
YUG	1628	96	48	54	76	278	34	284	270	352	13	254	10	3403
Mean	991	144	27	65	104	448	51	310	242	386	29	327	37	3190
STD	321	57	17	27	33	147	13	115	125	75	16	87	23	224
CV	0.32	0.40	0.62	0.41	0.32	0.32	0.26	0.37	0.52	0.19	0.54	0.26	0.63	0.07

Table 3 Correlation matrix — total calories from food groups

	CER	RTB	PUL	VEG	FRU	MEA	EGG	VOF	AOF	SUG	NUT	MLK	FSH
CER	1.00	-0.34	0.70	0.14	-0.22	-0.68	-0.41	-0.17	-0.44	-0.56	-0.33	-0.65	-0.30
RTB	-0.34	1.00	-0.35	-0.03	-0.33	0.36	0.15	-0.09	0.32	0.41	-0.28	0.14	0.33
PUL	0.70	-0.35	1.00	0.48	0.03	-0.46	-0.43	0.33	-0.65	-0.65	0.09	-0.67	-0.22
VEG	0.14	-0.03	0.48	1.00	0.04	0.08	0.15	0.65	-0.36	-0.29	0.45	-0.29	-0.06
FRU	-0.22	-0.33	0.03	0.40	1.00	0.21	0.20	0.64	-0.13	-0.19	0.83	0.19	-0.18
MEA	-0.66	0.36	-0.46	0.08	0.21	1.00	0.42	0.11	0.53	0.46	0.19	0.25	0.06
EGG	-0.41	0.15	-0.43	0.15	0.20	0.42	1.00	-0.02	0.56	0.42	0.03	0.14	-0.14
VOP	-0.17	-0.09	0.33	0.65	0.64	0.11	-0.02	1.00	-0.37	-0.24	0.76	-0.07	0.09
AOF	-0.44	0.32	-0.65	-0.36	-0.13	0.53	0.56	-0.37	1.00	0.56	-0.34	0.26	-0.27
SUG	-0.56	0.41	-0.65	-0.28	-0.19	0.46	0.42	-0.24	0.56	1.00	-0.10	0.56	0.11
NUT	-0.33	-0.28	0.09	0.45	0.83	0.19	0.03	0.76	-0.34	-0.10	1.00	0.15	0.01
MLK	-0.65	0.14	-0.67	-0.29	0.19	0.25	0.14	-0.07	0.26	0.56	0.15	1.00	0.31
FSH	-0.30	0.33	-0.22	-0.06	-0.18	0.06	-0.14	0.09	-0.27	0.11	0.01	0.31	1.00

Table 4 shows the fat calories supplied by food group and by country; on average meats and vegetable oils are the two highest contributors to the total fat supply, respectively 28.2% and 27%, followed by animal fats (20.8%) and milk and milk products (15.1%).

Results of the PCA over all the food groups show that the two first principal components account for about 60% of total variance, the first one accounting on its own for 34%. The third and fourth PCs explain a further 12.4% and 10% respectively of the total variance.

Tables 5 and 6 classify European countries according to the PCA on the first three axes (PC1, PC2, PC3). PC1 contrasts supplies of cereals and pulses in southern Europe with those of sugar, meat, animal fats and milk in northern Europe. Hungary and the USSR show features of both the

Table 4 Fat calories (kcal per capital daily) from food groups

	CER	MEA	EGG	VOF	AOF	NUT	MLK	FSH
ALB	59	106	10	135	47	18	108	2
AUS	25	342	35	376	369	40	188	8
BEL	26	596	33	385	467	22	156	13
BUL	46	236	34	377	161	24	159	7
CZE	36	335	42	256	318	12	145	6
DK	28	655	37	234	331	22	164	22
FIN	29	404	26	165	247	11	238	24
FRA	31	286	38	293	292	24	218	12
GRE	40	347	27	606	34	59	205	9
HUN	38	344	45	183	444	10	164	5
IRL	29	491	26	235	305	13	208	12
ITA	34	253	28	529	143	29	187	11
MAL	38	262	35	338	111	29	150	13
NL	23	261	34	377	371	26	197	6
NOR	31	283	29	354	197	25	262	29
POL	37	218	29	167	265	0	238	12
POR	40	259	14	408	50	15	70	19
EGR	35	386	44	257	449	11	123	11
WGR	28	381	40	304	346	34	168	9
ROM	50	195	38	226	181	15	120	9
SP	29	403	38	537	51	37	139	15
SWE	26	217	32	274	254	29	244	25
SWI	25	517	30	290	225	37	265	15
UK	24	381	30	386	230	30	179	8
USSR	45	233	35	225	179	16	140	25
YUG	57	182	22	289	270	10	145	4
Mean	35	330	32	315	244	23	176	13
STD	10	129	8	118	126	13	49	7
CV	0.28	0.39	0.26	0.37	0.52	0.54	0.28	0.57

Table 5 Classification of countries by PC1, PC2

Southern	Northern
Cereals, Pulses	Sugar, milk, meat animal fats
POR, ROM, BUL, MAL, GRE, ITA, SP, ALB, YUG	EGR, DK, IRL, SWE, BEL, NOR, UK, NL, SWI, AUS, WGR, POL, FIN, CZE, FRA

Nuts, fruit, vegetables, Vegetable oils	Cereals	Cereals	Nuts, fruit, Vegetables, Vegetable Oils
GRE, ITA, SP	ALB, YUG	POL, FIN, CZE	SWI, AUS, WGR

Table 6 Classification of countries by PC1, PC3

Southern	Northern
Cereals, pulses	Sugar, milk, meat, animal fats
POR, ROM, BUL, MAL, GRE, ITA, SP, ALB, YUG	EGR, DK, IRL, SWE, BEL, NOR, UK, NL, SWI, AUS, WGR, POL, FIN, CZE, FRA

Fish	Animal fats, eggs	Animal fats, eggs	Fish
POR	ROM, BUL, YUG	HUN, CZE, EGR, WGR, AUS	NOR, FIN, SWE, USSR

northern and southern supply patterns. PC2 and PC3 create further divisions within the northern and southern groups of countries, but not all countries are well differentiated by these axes.

The results of the cluster analysis on the first four PCs are shown in Table 7. The disaggregation of the overall European food supply pattern into northern and southern patterns occurs at a very low level. Albania and Portugal also branch off early because of their singular patterns: Albania characterized by a pattern of high cereal supply and low supplies of vegetable, vegetable oils and all animal products, Portugal by low supplies of fruit and

Table 7 Cluster medians of total calories (mean for Cluster 6) in kcal per capita daily

Cluster		CER	RTB	PUL	VEG	FRU	MEA	EGG	VOF	AOF	SUG	NUT	MLK	FSH
1	POL USSR IRL DK UK	897	196	24	59	73	495	47	231	262	467	22	331	41
2	BEL EGR CZE HUN	1000	169	17	60	97	520	68	253	444	405	15	289	22
3	SWE FIN NOR	710	148	9	34	97	364	46	270	243	411	30	479	66
4	FRA NL AUS WGR SWI	685	140	11	57	147	494	55	299	343	396	42	378	22
5	ITA BUL MAL ROM YUG	1451	72	42	74	107	349	54	333	161	352	30	269	23
6	ALB POR	1757 1244	64 175	56 50	20 87	80 65	151 335	15 22	132 400	46 50	191 265	20 22	191 137	7 75
	SP GRE	985	161	52	122	160	488	52	560	42	311	61	303	44

High -------- Level of linkage -------- Low

milk and an ample supply of fish. Six clusters of two or more countries each are retained to a moderately high level, after which individual countries or pairs of countries branch off quite rapidly. Interestingly, four pairs of countries remain close to a very high level, as regards their overall food supply patterns: Denmark and the United Kingdom, France and the Netherlands, Malta and Bulgaria, and Austria and West Germany.

Table 7 provides the median values of the calories supplied by each food group by cluster (means are provided for Cluster 6). Clusters 1 and 2 show dissimilarities in that Cluster 1 has greater supplies of sugar, milk and fish, while Cluster 2 has more ample supplies of fruit, meat, eggs and animal oils; Clusters 3 and 4 differ mainly in that Cluster 3 has more fish and milk; and Cluster 5 is distinguished from Cluster 6 in that Cluster 6 has rich supplies of roots and tubers and vegetable oils, and lower supplies of animal oils.

The second part of the analysis considers the calories from fat contributed by the various food groups (Table 4). Roots and tubers, pulses, fruits and vegetables were omitted due to their small contributions to the total fat supply. Results from the PCA show that the first three PCs account for 76% of the total variance (PC1 = 33%, PC2 = 26%, PC3 = 17%). Table 8 illustrates the results of the cluster analysis on the first four PCs. As with the cluster analysis of total calories, cluster analysis of fat calories produces also six clusters. There is, however, no early dissaggregation into northern and southern Europe. The first branch to emerge is a cluster comprising the Nordic countries (Finland, Norway and Sweden), Switzerland, Poland, the USSR and Ireland. This cluster (Cluster 1) is characterized by rich fat supplies from fish and milk. The remaining clusters branch off fairly soon after Cluster 1. Clusters 2 and 3 are characterized by their high levels of fat contributions from meat and especially animal fat. Clusters 4 and 5 differ from each other in their supplies of fat from animal fats and vegetable oils.

As for the analysis on total energy supplies, some pairs of countries remain close at a high level, in terms of their patterns of fat supplies: Sweden and Norway, Czechoslovakia and Hungary, West Germany and the United Kingdom, Austria and The Netherlands, Bulgaria and Malta, and Romania and Yugoslavia. It is interesting to note that Sweden's supply pattern is very close to Finland in the total calorie analysis, whereas it is near Norway in the fat analysis, with Finland closer to Ireland. Similarly Switzerland, which clusters with Austria and West Germany in the energy analysis, clusters rather with Norway and Sweden in the fat analysis.

Discussion

Reservations about the reliability and use of FBS as proxies for food consumption data have been noted (Dowler and Seo, 1985; Pacey and

Table 8 Cluster medians of fat calories (mean for Cluster 6) in kcal per capita daily

Cluster		CER	MEA	EGG	VOF	AOF	NUT	MLK	FSH
1	SWI⌐ NOR⌐⌐ SWE⌐ POL⌐ USSR FIN IRL⌐	29	283	29	235	247	16	238	24
2	EGR⌐ CZE⌐ HUN⌐	36	344	44	256	444	11	145	6
3	BEL DK	27	626	35	310	399	22	160	18
4	WGR⌐ UK⌐ FRA AUS⌐ NL⌐ ITA BUL⌐ MAL⌐	29	274	35	376	261	29	183	8
5	GRE⌐ SP⌐	34	375	33	571	42	48	171	12
6	ALB⌐ ROM⌐ YUG⌐	57	182	22	226	181	15	120	4
	POR	40	260	14	407	50	15	70	19
High					Level of linkage				Low

Payne, 1985). Seo (1981) has shown that in Japan over a 30-year period, discrepancies between household consumption surveys (HCS) and FBS calorie-equivalent data increased as the GNP increased, FBS providing higher figures than HCS at all times. Pacey and Payne (1985) have also shown that an increasingly complex food system can introduce more opportunities for loss or waste within the system as a whole. The household food wastage not taken into account in FBS data might be an additional reason for such discrepancies.

Unfortunately, however, data from nationally representative food consumption surveys are sparse in some countries and totally absent in others. Certainly the available data would not permit an analysis of time trends, or an analysis of dietary patterns across Europe for any one time period. Differences in survey methodology limit the validity of both inter-country comparisons and of statements regarding changes in dietary patterns within one country.

By using multivariate analyses such as PCA and CA, we have obtained a classification of the European food supply patterns and an indication of the degree of closeness between these patterns. We have examined the patterns as a whole by analysing the energy and fat contributions of the various food groups, the two analyses providing different information regarding similarities between the patterns.

Geographical distance is not always sufficient to explain differences between patterns. For instance, Albania, Yugoslavia and Bulgaria, which are geographically and culturally close to Greece, have different patterns as regards their supplies of nuts, fruit, vegetables and vegetable oils, which are lower, while cereal supply is greater. These three countries have lower GDPs than Greece, and centrally planned economies. Portugal, geographically close to Spain, is, however, far from it as regards cereal supply, and is closer to Albania and Yugoslavia in terms of fat supply as well as GDP. Cereal supplies and GDPs in Europe show a strong negative correlation ($r = -0.8$; $p < 0.001$). This fits in well with Blandford's finding that further expansion in the share of animal products in total food consumption was possible with income growth in the majority of OECD countries, although the rate of such expansion was falling (Blandford, 1984).

Somewhat surprisingly, Kelly (1986) found that Ireland is closer to Finland than to the United Kingdom; we find similar results when we consider the cluster analysis of fat supplies, but in terms of total calorie supply Ireland seems to be closer to the group composed of the United Kingdom and Denmark. Kelly has also noted the comparative closeness of Germany, France, Switzerland and Austria, reflecting the relative importance of meat in their national diets and also the fact that cereals are less important. On the basis of the overall national supply pattern we disagree with the inclusion of France in the southern European group (James, 1989). For both the total food and the fat cluster analyses, France is clearly closer to the more northern countries of Europe, in particular to the Netherlands. Furthermore its supply of fruit, one of the features of a Mediterranean diet, is lower than that found elsewhere in the Mediterranean. Blandford has pointed out that since the mid-1950s most European countries, and especially France and Denmark, have moved towards a pattern shared by Australia, Canada, New Zealand and the United States of America.

Malassis and Padilla (1982) and James (1989) attribute a common food pattern to all countries of eastern Europe, with Malassis and Padilla adding Switzerland and Austria to this group of countries. We find that there is not a single supply pattern, but rather several patterns in eastern Europe. First there is an 'animal product' pattern represented by the more northern of these countries (Czechoslovakia, Hungary, East Germany, Poland,

USSR), and secondly a 'vegetable pattern' in the southern countries (Albania, Bulgaria, Romania, Yugoslavia). In the northern group, Czechoslovakia, Hungary and East Germany are close to each other and close also to Belgium and Denmark, largely because of their substantial supplies of animal fats, eggs and meat, while Poland and the USSR are closer to the Scandinavian countries because of higher fish and seafood supplies. Within the southern group, Yugoslavia and Romania have greater supplies of eggs and animal fats; Bulgaria has a food supply pattern close to that of Italy. Finally, we find that Switzerland and Austria cannot be considered as close to the eastern European countries, but rather as close to countries such as West Germany, Netherlands and France.

Both Malassis and Padilla (1982) and Blandford (1984) have combined some food groups, such as cereals with roots and tubers, fruits with vegetables, meat with eggs. Table 3 shows that the respective correlations are not strong enough to justify such combinations, especially the correlation between cereals and roots and tubers ($r = -0.34$ in our table, -0.31 at the time of the study by Malassis and Padilla, 1975–1977). Malassis and Padilla also place together Spain and Portugal; while their supplies of roots and tubers are very similar, their supplies of cereals and fruit are very different, respectively 846 and 132 kcal per capita daily in Spain and 1244 and 65 kcal per capita daily in Portugal. Because of greater supplies of vegetable oils, meats, sugar and milk, Spain is closer to Greece than to Portugal. Secondly, the origin of oils and fats—vegetable or animal—was not taken into account; this factor is important because the distinction between the northern and southern countries is made upon the basis of dissimilarities in supplies of animal and vegetable oils and fats. We have also examined if one reason for the discrepancies between our study and that of Malassis and Padilla could be the different time periods analysed; we repeated our analyses using data from 1975–1977, and found that the 1975–1977 typologies are indeed somewhat different to those for 1984–1986: France has come closer to West Germany, Switzerland and Netherlands; Hungary to Czechoslovakia, East Germany and Belgium; the patterns of Poland and the USSR, which were close to those of Portugal and the Scandinavian countries (the latter to a lesser extent), approached those of Ireland, Denmark and the United Kingdom. Nevertheless, even taking account of these trends, the lack of homogeneity of the patterns of the eastern European countries remains striking.

A definition of the Mediterranean diet was described recently as being high in cereals (>60% of total energy), low in total fats (<30% of total energy), with moderate amounts of added fats, predominantly olive oil, and relatively high in fruits and vegetables (Ferro-Luzzi and Sette, 1989). Our study has not examined diets of all Mediterranean countries, but it does highlight the heterogeneity that characterizes the southern European countries, with supplies of cereals and pulses ranging from 27% to 64% and 1.25–2.3% of total energy respectively. Within this heterogeneity, our cluster analysis has proposed two groupings (Table 1): one comprising Spain, Greece and Portugal, and the other the remaining countries. It is noteworthy that in terms of fat supplies Italy and Malta are closer to the country grouping made up of France, Austria and West Germany. For Italy it could be due to either the importance of northern Italy or a trend towards a pattern richer in meat and animal fats as suggested by Blandford (1984) for France and Denmark, i.e. a move towards a more 'anglophonic' pattern.

A closer examination of clusters raises some important epidemiological issues. For instance Switzerland, which seems to have a fat supply pattern similar to the patterns of Sweden and Norway, has half the mortality from coronary heart disease (CHD) among men aged 30–69 years. Can this difference be partly explained by supplies in fruit and vegetables which have been excluded in carrying out the fat CA, and which are twice as high in Switzerland as in Sweden and Norway? The closeness of the total French pattern (as well as fat supply pattern) to that of the Netherlands, Austria and West Germany, whose CHD mortality rates are nearly twice that of France, also needs explanation. This latter difference in CHD mortality rates cannot be attributed to overall supplies in fruits, vegetables, and roots and tubers. As within most countries food supply patterns show regional variations (i.e. Belgium: French- and Dutch-speaking population groups; France: olive oil on the Mediterranean coast and butter in the northwest region; northern and southern Italy). It may be that sub-national regional variation in patterns could be greater than intercountry variations, and this could contribute to explaining some epidemiological discrepancies.

Bibliography

Blandford D (1984). Changes in food consumption patterns in the OECD area. *Euro R Agr Eco*, *11*, pp 43–65

Dowler EA and Young OS (1985). Assessment of energy intake. Estimates of food supply vs measurement of food consumption. *Food Policy*, *10*, 278–288

Dupin H and Rouaud (1983). L'alimentation des français. *La Recherche*, *146* (14), 964–971

FAO (1984). *Food Balance Sheets 1979–1981 Average*. Food and Agriculture Organization of the United Nations, Rome, pp v–xviii

Ferro-Luzzi A and Sette S (1989). The Mediterranean diet: an attempt to define its present and past composition. *European Journal of Clinical Nutrition*, *43*, suppl 2, pp 13–29, 1989

James WPT (1989). *Implications for Agriculture and Food Production in Europe of New Concepts of Healthy Nutrition*. European Food Policy Paper. World Health Organization, Copenhagen

Kelly A (1986). *Nutrition Surveillance in Europe: a Critical Appraisal*. Report of an EC Workshop, Athens, Greece, 22–23 May 1986

Kendall M (1980). *Multivariate Analysis*. Charles Griffin, London and High Wycombe

Lebart A, Morineau L and Fenelon JP (1982). *Traitement des donnée statistiques*. Méthodes et programmes, Dunod, Paris

Malassis L and Padilla M (1982). *Typologie mondiale des modèles agro-nutritionnels*. Institut National de la Recherche Agronomique. Serie Etudes et Recherches. Numero 72. Montpellier

Pacey A and Payne P (1985). *Agriculture Development and Nutrition*. Hutchinson, London, pp 79–81

Seo YO (1981). The pattern of nutrition indicators at different stages of national development. PhD Thesis, Faculty of Medicine, University of London

Souci, Fachmann and Kraut (1969). *Die Zusammensetzung der Lebensmittel*. Nahrwert-Tabellen

USDA (1983). *Composition of Foods Raw, Processed and Prepared*. BK Watt and AL Merril. United States Department of Agriculture, Agriculture Handbook N°8

Nutrition, diet and food standards: informing consumers and producers

John S. Marsh,, *University of Reading, UK*

This paper concentrates on three major issues:

1. The importance of our perception of 'good' nutrition.
2. The role of food standards in relation to consumption.
3. The implications of food standards for food producers.

There are many other relevant issues; for example the problems of defining 'good' nutrition, of measuring what people actually eat and of describing and enforcing food standards, which are relevant to this theme but are not attempted here. The approach is that of a social scientist, an economist, rather than of a natural or medical scientist. There will be much more to be said about this theme when this paper is complete.

Perceptions of 'good' nutrition

There is no doubt that what we eat is important. Consumption of food which contains poisons or spreads disease can have catastrophic consequences. Thus the protection of society from food-borne risks becomes a government responsibility in line with protecting the citizen from crime or war. More difficult is the impact of diets consisting of foods which are individually safe but which, together, constitute a diet which is conducive to chronic diseases.

Such diseases are of great significance for the health and prosperity of the community but legislative intervention may not be straightforward. Several problems are involved.

First, general statements about diet tend to be wrong. What constitutes an optimum diet for one individual may be wholly inappropriate for another. Nutritional requirements vary with the level of physical activity, with genetic inheritance and with the environment. People vary greatly in their opportunities and inclination to take exercise; within both homes and workplaces many have become accustomed to temperatures which avoid excessive heat or cold. Where food intake exceeds a reduced energy requirement then obesity is likely to threaten health. We need thus to recognize that indiscriminate statements about what constitutes a sensible diet are likely to be misleading and, in some cases, may be seriously wrong.

A second problem stems from the infirmity of our understanding of the relationship between diet and health. There are various aspects of the nutritional debate for which this is important. Targets set for diets are likely to be formulated in terms of their nutrient content. Consumers do not buy nutrients, they buy foods or even meals. Thus they have to translate relatively precise statements about calories and fat into decisions about particular items they eat. It is impractical to assess the nutrient content of each mouthful so the consequence tends to be that some food items are classified as bad whilst others assume a mantle of virtue. During the war consumers were reminded of the great value of milk. Today butter, cream and full-fat milk are seen as major contributors to heart disease. Early slimming guidance said much about cutting down carbohydrates, the message was to eat less bread and potatoes. Now the potato and the brown loaf have been rehabilitated and advice suggests that more of these items, together with more fruit and vegetables, would be beneficial. To be operational advice has to be conveyed in such terms, but because our scientific understanding changes, the message to the consumer may become confused and misinterpreted. The consumer may end up with a bad diet consisting wholly of 'good' foods.

Professionals understand well the need to revise and improve dietary advice in the light of advances in science. The problem is sometimes to understand what is an 'advance' and always to determine how to 'get the message across'. There is a danger that, since science advances unevenly in various relevant disciplines, a new discovery may hit the headlines and assume an importance in the scientific debate, and in research funding, unrelated to its significance in the broad field of nutrition and diet. For the layman fresh discoveries or the scrapping of old advice may make it hard to distinguish between a dietary crank and an important new insight.

Even when science has evolved a balanced message which incorporates new understanding about dietary issues it has to be conveyed to those whose actions will affect consumer behaviour. Many of these may be resistant to changes which appear to threaten their authority or to jeopardize their investments. Public education, advertisements and statements by ministers probably do affect the more informed and sensitive members of society but they may be ignored by the bulk of the population. The apparent failure of vulnerable groups to respond to government-sponsored advertisements about AIDS, a much more immediate threat than diet, illustrates the weakness of such an approach. Greater impact may result once a new dietary message is translated into 'good' products where a health message can enhance the likelihood that they will be profit-earners. The switch to reduced-fat milk represents one such success. The proliferation of 'healthy' processed foods and high-fibre breakfast cereals is a similar industrial response.

Unfortunately the message is never simple. A product which may score highly in one nutritional dimension may cause anxiety on another. For example, products which are high in fibre and low in fat may nevertheless contain a high proportion of salt. Thus the most effective agent for changing consumption patterns may not be readily controllable by those who wish to ensure that a more healthy diet results. The nutritionist and the regulator may have to accept some uncomfortable compromises.

A third area of difficulty arises because our understanding of the relationship between how we produce food and its effect on human health is poor. In the absence of such understanding, groups who argue for some particular method of production on health grounds, such as for 'organically' produced food, can neither prove their case nor have it disproved on accepted objective grounds. In such a situation the possibilities of the greedy making a profit from the credulous are substantial.

Although our understanding of these matters is imperfect our ability to diagnose some of the relevant elements has steadily improved as methods of analysis have enabled smaller and smaller quantities of substances to be detected. This is important in relation to the use of farm chemicals, especially those which by definition have some toxic effect, pesticides and herbicides. It is also relevant to the use of additives in foodstuffs designed to improve flavour or colour or to extend shelf-life. Both farm chemicals and food additives add greatly to the productivity of industry and so lower both the cost and the price of food. Concern is justified where residues may damage human health, but the present methods of measurement are capable of identifying such substances in quantities which have no detectable effect on health, even though in larger quantities the same materials might be dangerous. There is thus a risk that legislative prohibitions may be based on scientific evidence which gives rise to groundless concerns and has the effect of making food more expensive than it needs to be. Higher prices damage most the welfare of those people in society who spend the highest proportion of their income on food: the poor and especially those with large families. Such regulation may also limit imports of food and so reduce the incomes of producers in other countries.

A fourth problem area lies more fully within the social science arena; it is the extent to which we can properly impose restrictions on the majority in order to safeguard a minority. The issue is readily illustrated in the case of drug addiction. Most countries ban, sometimes with severe penalties, trade in and the use of such drugs as heroin, cocaine and cannabis. In the West, at least, they do not ban alcohol, although the evidence of damage to some individuals from its abuse is compelling. Clearly a judgement has been made that the costs of enforcement and the limited effectiveness of an alcohol ban outweigh the benefits—despite the fact that the lives of many individuals who suffer from alcohol addiction are most seriously damaged.

Legislative requirements applied to food are much less dramatic but the principle is similar. To prohibit some ingredient to which some section of the population may be allergic, imposes a cost on the rest of the community. Even to require that products are labelled in a way which enables potential sufferers to identify materials to which they are allergic imposes a cost which has to be borne by the consumers of the product as a whole. Since, even for some common food substances there are a small number of people who have an allergic reaction, governments have to decide how far they are justified in imposing such requirements on food manufacturers and traders. Complete listing in a form which is understood by all consumers is probably impossible, but even a comprehensive description of the contents of a food product may demand considerable label space and induce a rigidity in the ingredients used in manufacture in a way which adds significantly to costs. It is even more difficult to apply to meals eaten outside the home. What is right in this context must reflect the judgement of society as a whole, but unless there is a good understanding of the issues involved, pressure groups may treat such legislative intervention as of 'no cost' and as such demand ever more detailed requirements of food producers. We need, but so far do not possess, a satisfactory system of cost–benefit analysis of each proposed measure.

The role of food standards in relation to consumption

Food standards can protect and inform the consumer and can provide a level playing-field for industry. Each of these elements needs further examination.

One of the earliest reasons for imposing standards relating to food was to prevent adulteration and to ensure that consumers were not deceived by misleading packaging, incorrect weights or false labelling. From the mixing of sand with sugar to the addition of water to milk, unscrupulous food retailers found ways of cheating the consumer. Such deceit imposed a cost on those who bought the food but it might also occasion them severe damage. The substitution of cheaper mineral oils for vegetable oil has caused illness and even death. There are therefore very strong grounds for seeking to enforce minimum standards.

Difficulties arise, however, where standards ossify, preventing the emergence of competitive products which are neither deceitful nor lethal. Rules about the way in which beer is made in Germany provide one example. Requirements to add vitamins to bread in the UK afforded another. Legislation which was designed to protect consumers who derived a high proportion of their total food intake from a limited range of products may become irrelevant as richer populations enjoy more varied diets. However, there is always likely to be an interest in its retention by firms who wish to avoid competition from newer products or processes.

Protective legislation may have a growing and much more complex role in an environment in which a greater proportion of food is purchased in a highly processed form. The individual consumer, even with the aid of labels, is ill-equipped to assess the safety of food products he is offered. The story of 'E' numbers makes the point. A device intended to signal both that the additives used had been tested and found 'safe', and to alert the vulnerable minority to substances to which they might be allergic, became used as a symbol of the inclusion of 'dangerous chemicals' in human food. As a result manufacturers have tended to advertise food as 'additive-free' even though the absence of these materials might add significantly to the risk that stored products could become microbiologically unsafe.

Consumers, or those who claim to speak on their behalf, may also demand protection from non-existent risks. From the point of view of governments, permission to sell products which have been subject to tightly controlled doses of irradiation represents a significant political risk. Consumers have to rely on 'experts'. A major problem for the food industry is the credibility of the 'experts'. Those who have most to lose from any failure of food safety are the food producers and distributors. The slightest suspicion that a food is not safe may involve its immediate removal from shelves and long-run damage to a brand name. Such firms know most about what has been done in preparing and marketing the product. However, consumers, aware of their financial interest, may fear that the food industry itself will be reluctant to publicize any potential problem, unless it is of an inescapable, immediate and catastrophic nature.

Governments may be more independent of financial interests but they have a political interest both in the fortunes of the food industry and in avoiding any appearance of neglect of food 'safety'. Should a problem arise they may be suspected of being more concerned to ensure that they are not blamed than to inform the public of a potential hazard. In the UK recent concern about the possible effect of bovine spongiform encephalopathy (BSE) on human health illustrates the problem. The government have followed a policy of full and prompt disclosure of the evidence as it has become available. Even so some of the media have tended to suggest that 'there is something to hide'. Independent experts, university research units, for example, may have a more credible image but they may lack both the scientific resources and the ready access to data which industry and governments enjoy. On the basis of imperfect information opinions of such experts, although given great weight by the media, may be seriously flawed. No decisions are free from risk, so political pressure will tend to favour the imposition of consumer 'protection' and may do so when there is no objective scientific justification.

An important attribute of food standards is that they permit food legislation to be enforced. Precise definition relating to all aspects of food—for example, its weight, volume, purity, ingredients, shelf-life and chemical composition—are a precondition of imposing penalties on those who infringe them. In the United Kingdom the 1990 Food Safety Act, with its attendant concept of 'due diligence', represents a major step forward in consumer protection. Since all involved in the production and distribution of food have to be able to demonstrate that they have observed appropriate practices, consumers are more likely to be confident that the food they buy meets contemporary requirements for safety, whether chemical or microbiological.

Food standards provide a shorthand for much complex information which is relevant to consumers. In addition to confidence about the safety of food, consumers who wish to adopt nutritionally sound eating habits look to standards, and particularly labelling requirements, to give them in a simple form the information they need about the contents of the products they propose to buy. Such shorthand information plays an important part in many other consumer purchases. For example, the car buyer may want to know about the petrol consumption, power output and weight of his motor car if he is to combine something he can afford with a vehicle capable of towing a caravan. In fact the data he receives are all surrogates for the questions he is actually attempting to answer, and depend for their usefulness on other information and concepts which the customer must supply—how much he can afford, what is the weight of his caravan, in what sort of country he intends to tow—before he can use it to reach a sensible decision. The food consumer, similarly, may be told about the energy, fat and vitamin content of a product but he needs to bring to this concepts about how this will affect his health, knowledge about what other foods he intends to eat and an awareness of the impact of his lifestyle on his food requirement.

The problem for those who wish to make available nutritional information is not just what data to provide but in what form the data should be offered.

Consumers vary greatly in their interest and education in dietary matters. Most will bring much less understanding to their decisions than the medical world or the food industry. Redundant information can be confusing and so counterproductive. There is a need to identify what information the consumer needs about food, to see how far this can be offered in the shorthand form of food standards and to update this in the context not only of better nutritional science, but also the developing level of understanding and interest of the food consumer.

The food industry operates in a competitive environment. If it cannot offer consumers the products they want at a price and of the quality they seek, its business will be lost to other suppliers. However, not all aspects of quality can be directly observed. The method of production, any long-term risks to health which might result from consumption and the chemical constitution of the product are relevant to what many consumers would regard as 'quality', but not self-evident. Food standards can provide that reassurance and should help to make products which conform more competitive. Within a country such legislation generally applies to all businesses. There may be exceptions in the case of some very small businesses, such as farm-gate shops or farmhouse cheese and bacon, but these normally represent only a tiny fraction of the market. Between countries, however, there may be substantial differences in legislation and in the degree to which it is enforced. Such differences may become non-tariff barriers offering businesses within a country protection from external competition. In the European Community, following the principles established in a European Court judgement relating to Cassis de Dijon, such barriers no longer afford protection to businesses which face a more demanding domestic food standard environment than those of other member countries. Cassis de Dijon established the principle of mutual recognition; that a product which could legally be sold in any one member country could not be prevented from being offered for sale in any other.

This approach to food standard legislation has been criticized on the grounds that it will lead to a gradual reduction of standards to the least demanding level in order to allow food businesses to compete within the wider European market. Such a complaint contains an important implication. It can be valid only if in fact consumers do not prefer the food produced to higher standards. This may well be the case. Where, as is the case, for example with Cassis de Dijon, the difference is only in the proportion of alcohol in the product, it might be a matter of no concern. In contrast, if it relates to the safety of food, governments might argue that any decline in standards is unacceptable.

The route away from such entanglements, which is also consistent with creating a level playing-field for all the firms in the EC food sector, would be to substitute common standards for those currently operating in each member state. This process, known as harmonization, has been under way for a long time within the Community. It has given rise to a great deal of complaint that the EC bureaucracy is interfering in an unreasonable way in the daily life of citizens. This is the origin of alarms about the Euro-sausage, the abolition of the pint and the restrictions placed on the use of geographical labels to describe products which have long been produced in areas far away from the place which has given its name to the product.

For those whose concern is nutrition, it is important to recognize that this type of legislation is essentially trade-related. It has nothing to do with the need to promote a healthier diet. Thus, for example, the recently proposed Yellow Fats Regulation, which includes 18 permitted different designations for products which are spread on bread, originates in DG-III, the Commission Directorate responsible for trade. The designation grid, which is proposed, divides spreads according to the proportion of fat, and whether they are based on butter, a blend or on margarine. There is, for example, no indication as to whether the fat is saturated or polyunsaturated, information which would concern most nutritionists. The primary object is to facilitate competition across EC frontiers. A secondary intention is to improve the ability of butter to compete with the growing number of low-fat blends and margarine in the Community market—an intention which flies in the face of current nutritional advice.

Even with good, well-designed food standards, which take account of nutrition, there is no guarantee that this will lead consumers to choose a healthy diet. For the consumer such information is only one of the items which has to be considered. Of greater immediate importance is likely to be income and the tastes of the family. Income levels vary considerably within all EC countries but most people are able to afford sufficient food to avoid hunger. There is, however, less certainty that they can afford an interesting diet which is also 'healthy'. That a nutritionally sound diet can be bought at low cost has been shown by my colleague Dr Spencer Henson (1990). However, the diet which can be afforded is not gastronomically exciting. Even for those for whom shortage of money is not an obstacle, the determination to seek out a nutritionally sound diet may be more related to social pressures to approximate to the norm that 'slim is beautiful' than to an understanding of the impact of particular patterns of consumption on health, especially in relation to longer-term health concerns such as heart disease and cancers. For many people, especially successful executives, what they eat may be determined by the practice of the 'business lunch' and the overnight stay in hotels in strange cities. Such eating is difficult to control if it is likely to obstruct good communication with someone with whom business is to be done. Whilst there may be opportunities to balance consumption over time by reduced intakes of undesirable nutrients at home, even here, excessive fussiness and the rejection of food prepared within the family may itself be a cause of stress.

Such reservations do not mean that food standards related to sound nutritional practice are unimportant; they do imply that the task facing those who seek to improve eating habits is much larger and longer-term than simply providing information. In time, as understanding spreads more widely within the community, new lifestyles and changed expectations will remove some of these problems. Whilst legislation to raise food standards has an important role, it cannot alone achieve the sorts of change in personal habit which are needed if present understanding of the relationship between diet and health is to be translated into longer and healthier lives for the population as a whole.

The implications of food standards for producers

Producers have an inescapably ambivalent attitude to food standards. Most are well aware that if a particular food item is convicted of causing illness, then it will not only be the firms that produced that particular product who suffer, but all who seek to sell products of the same type. In recent years yoghurt sales for all sellers were damaged by an outbreak of botulism attributed to one particular supplier who had used an infected ingredient. National egg sales fell sharply following remarks by a government minister concerning the presence of salmonella in some fresh eggs. Beef producers have faced lower sales and depressed prices because of the infection with BSE of a relatively small proportion of the national herd of cattle. Food standards may form an important means of preventing such events. As such they are likely to be welcomed by the food industry, especially if they are enforced and apply to all suppliers, domestic and imported.

Food standards impose costs on producers. Some of these costs are implicit in ensuring that the productive process itself is satisfactory. Some of them result from the need to be able to show that the standards have been observed. Without such evidence, enforcement is impossible, but because enforcement must be able to detect even a small number of marginal infringements, the bureaucratic requirement may itself be onerous and costly. Still more, in an industry which relies on innovation as a major instrument of competition some types of food standards may impose a rigidity on production methods which has no justification in relation to consumer safety or the provision of information to consumers.

The food industry faces a challenge to offer the consumer new food products which combine the insights of the nutritionist with the demand for foods which are attractive to consumers. In such a situation, inflexible food standards can represent an obstacle to the improvement of diet. However, if consumers are to be protected from bogus claims, the level of information required increases. Confusion may result from the use of such terms as 'natural', 'contains no additives' or 'low cholesterol'. The choice may have to be made either to constrain the language used on labels, for example, by the tighter definition of such terms or their replacement by a more precise technical language, or by the imposition of standards to which every product has to conform.

Two examples of industrial responses to the demand for a healthier diet illustrate how confusion may arise and how important standards have become.

Farmers and animal breeders may breed strains of animals which have a lower fat content in their carcases. Such animals may offer potential nutritional advantages but these will be realized only if the animal is appropriately fed and exercised during its life. There are good nutritional reasons to encourage such a breeding policy in the agricultural industry, but to label such products as 'low-fat' beef, sheep meat or pork may be misleading. Again, much may depend on the distribution of fat in the carcase. For gastronomic purposes it may be important that it is widely distributed in meat which is described as marbled. For nutritional purposes it may be more helpful if it is concentrated in lumps which may be cut off before the product is eaten. A food standard specification which classifies meat in terms of its overall fat content may thus fail to provide the essential information—can the consumer avoid the fat?

There is a growing body of evidence that it is more important to distinguish between the various types of fat than to simply aim at a reduction in the overall fat content of the diet. This has been recognized by food manufacturers who may label products 'high in polyunsaturated fats' or 'low in saturated fat'. The development of such products and their advertisement as part of an attractive, healthy lifestyle may play a major part in improving the diet of the nation. The biochemistry of such fats is complex and likely to be very imperfectly understood by most consumers. Some consumers may fear that they are being 'blinded with science'. Standards which are independently devised and monitored may be needed if full advantage is to be taken of progress within the food industry. Such standards are unlikely to imply fewer claims for a food product than reputable manufacturers would wish to make. However, they may be essential to prevent unscrupulous producers deceiving the public and so undermining confidence in claims which are fully justified.

In an affluent market, such as the UK, food retailers and manufacturers prosper by identifying subsections of the whole to which they can target products specifically designed for their needs. Such niche marketing grows in importance as richer consumers are prepared to pay more for goods which are more convenient, which match more precisely their own preferences or which enable them to enjoy meals which have hitherto been beyond their normal expectation. There are already a number of diet-related niche markets. Substantial shelf space is occupied with baby foods. Foods which are low in sugar may be offered not just to diabetics but to all who wish to become 'slimmer'. The marketing message with such products stresses their relevance for the particular purpose in mind. There is considerable scope for the development of more such diet-related niches which correspond to the varying lifestyles, ages and inclinations of other groups within the population. Already the frozen-food cabinets of most supermarkets contain a diversity of products, some of which are named in ways designed to attract such custom, 'Healthy Options', 'Lean Cuisine' and 'Hungry Man', for example. Opportunities may arise to build these designer products into packages which represent a substantial proportion of the total diet of an individual: for the supplier there is the attraction of building an element of customer loyalty; for the consumer an assurance that within the product range the foods match his own nutritional needs. Should markets develop in this way the importance of the nutritional content of food standards is likely to be increased. It would provide an opportunity to make a substantial improvement in the quality of diet provided the specifications are not so restrictive as to prevent commercial firms innovating, nor so vague as to deny the logic of a 'good food package'.

Nutrition, diet and food standards

Most citizens of the world's developed countries have the opportunity to choose among a very wide range of food products.* The food industry is adept at responding to nuances of consumer demand in order to secure market share. If people choose a 'healthy diet' the food needed to provide this will be supplied. If they do not, the availability of such items will not secure a healthy diet.

This places the emphasis on consumer perception. However, given the complexity of information involved, both about what is a healthy diet and what are the physiological needs of individuals, decisions about what is eaten are likely to continue to rely on general statements which convey the nutritional message in an abbreviated and greatly simplified form. A good outcome requires that the consumer has a good understanding of these statements and is able to relate them to his purchases. For that to be the case food standards are needed. They need to be appropriate to the requirements of the consumer and the commercial realities of the food industry. They must also command consumer and producer confidence.

---

* One UK food supermarket chain advertises that it has 30 000 items on its shelves.

This paper started with a reminder that there are many issues which are relevant to nutrition and diet, which it makes no attempt to discuss. It ends with an assertion that, in translating improved scientific understanding of the relationship of food consumption to health, food standards have an important part to play. Both consumers and producers need such standards, and for both there must be a procedure which allows change to occur without destroying the credibility of the standards themselves. This is a sophisticated requirement even for an affluent society. It is likely to require both a better-educated public and responsible restraint in reports by the media on the food industry.

Reference

Henson SJ (1990) *The Use of Linear Programming for the Economic Analysis of Human Diets.* Department of Agricultural Economics and Management, University of Reading

Related reading

Burns J and Swinbank A (eds) (1986) *Food Policies and the Food Industries,* Food Economics Study No. 3, Department of Agricultural Economics and Management, University of Reading

Cottrell R (1987) *Food and Health: Now and the Future.* Proceedings of the Eighth British Nutrition Foundation Annual Conference. Parthenon, Lancs

Department of Health (1991) *Dietary Reference Values for Food Energy and Nutrients for the United Kingdom.* Report on Health and Social Subects 41. HMSO, London

European Community Food Legislation (1991) Background Report, ISEC/B2/91. Commission of the European Communities (CEC), 6 February

Food Advisory Committee (1990) Report on a Review of Food Labelling and Advertising. Ministry of Agriculture, Fisheries and Food, FdAC/REP/10. HMSO, London

Guild of Food Writers and Coronary Prevention Group (1991) 'Eat Well . . . Live Well'. Contribution to the Healthy Eating Campaign, July.

Miller FA (ed.) (1990) Food safety in the human food chain. CAS Paper 20, Centre for Agricultural Strategy, University of Reading

Workshop Discussion Report

Michael J. Gibney, *Trinity College Medical School, Dublin, Ireland*

The workshop accepted at the outset the pivotal role which nutrition and food safety both play in health. A number of policies and policy instruments deal with food safety, but existing public policies do not generally take account of nutrition.

There are some policy areas *outside* the health sector which significantly influence food and nutrition. These sometimes act directly on health, as in food safety legislation, and at other times indirectly, in agricultural and trade policies which affect the food supply, such as the Common Agricultural Policy and the General Agreement on Tariffs and Trade. ('Food labelling', often regarded as a health-related policy, is in fact a measure to facilitate international trade in foods.)

The workshop agreed that nutrition considerations should be integrated into *all* relevant policies across Europe; while for food standards the aim should be to maintain the present global approach. All aspects of nutrition, policy, education and promotion should be based as far as possible on research, and as little as possible on untested assumptions about food–health links. Central to achievement of this aim is the collection of data on food and nutrient intake and the assessment of nutritional status. As far as possible these data should become more comparable and more available in the European countries.

Nutrition and relevant practical skills should be integrated into education at all levels. The workshop was particularly anxious that, in the pursuit of health policy objectives, those involved in health promotion should develop a better understanding of the relationship between diet and health than is presently the case. This should help avoid the oversimplification of issues in public debate, and also allow for more sophisticated approaches to policy development.

In terms of research, it was agreed that nutrition research has too low a priority and that greater funding should be available. The notion that 'we know it all and that we have a consistent message' is naive, in view of current research on fats and antioxidant nutrients. The following areas of research were identified:

1. Societal and individual determinants of food choice.
2. Better understanding of mechanisms underlying the effects of diet on health.
3. Impact assessment of current and proposed policies.

4. Economic analysis of policy options in relation to nutrition and health.
5. Objective measurements of nutritional status.

The workshop would like to see more Europe-wide collaborative studies in nutrition, which are more extensive than many realize, but which should be strengthened and extended.

Policy on licit substances

Europe without frontiers? Balancing pharmaceutical interests

David G. Taylor, *King's Fund Institute, London, UK*

Legislation exists to control the supply and use of many potentially dangerous but licit substances, ranging from bulk agrochemicals and industrial chemicals and explosives to solvents, household chemicals, fuels and even fireworks sold at the retail level. Alcohol, cigarettes and pharmaceutical products share a distinctive common characteristic in that their primary function is to deliver pharmacologically active substances into the bodies of those who use them. They differ in as much as the consumers' objective in drinking alcohol and smoking is normally taken to be to gain pleasure, while in the case of medicines and allied goods it is usually believed to be to maintain or regain health or reduce disease.

The purpose of legislation may also vary between the social and medical drug fields. In the case of alcohol use, for instance, limitations on access arguably owe their primary origin to a desire for social control, the prevention of disruptive behaviour and the maintenance of labour force discipline. Price and allied interventions stem from the need to ensure fair trading (which was present even in medieval society) and subsequently to raise taxation. Promotion of tobacco use was, in the early twentieth century, seen as an active contributor to social order, and subsequently as a fiscal asset. Both alcohol and tobacco helped through their status as licit cultural 'super-drugs' to define the identity of industrial societies such as twentieth-century Britain and that of adults within them; it has only been very recently that State policy towards them has begun fully to reflect awareness of their role as a way of death as well as of life.

Legislation on drugs used in health care has always been more openly based on a recognition of their dangers (Griffin, 1989). This is in part because it has been in the interests of groups such as doctors, pharmacists, governments and pharmaceutical companies (not to mention the regulators themselves) openly to recognize this aspect of medicinal substances. For

Europe Without Frontiers. Edited by C.E.M. Normand and P. Vaughan
© 1993 John Wiley & Sons Ltd

instance, awareness of risk helps legitimate prescriber and dispenser authority (and income) and market interventions which may inhibit competition and/or favour national interests. Even price controls can be two-edged swords, keeping health care costs down on the one hand, but on occasions subsidizing companies or encouraging research on the other (Taylor and Maynard, 1990).

Against this background this paper presents information relating to the use of pharmaceuticals in the EC, and the nature of national and recent community wide initiatives (see Table 1) designed to promote public interests in this field. It then identifies some key health- and pharmaceutical-related policy issues which should be debated in Europe during the early 1990s.

Pharmaceutical consumption in Europe—some key determinants

Table 2 and Figures 1–3 give outline data relating to spending on medicines (in manufacturers' price terms) and pharmaceutical trading and direct employment in EC member states, for the year 1989 (ABPI, 1990; Taylor, 1992). The statistics presented are subject to a variety of possible distortions, but even so provide a reasonably reliable outline framework. Significant observations include:

1. Health care tends to behave as a luxury good, with richer EC states spending more of their greater wealth on it than do poorer ones. Pharmaceutical spending shows a somewhat less positive income elasticity. Richer countries usually incur greater absolute drug costs on them than do poorer ones, but as a proportion of all health spending medicine outlays are highest in the least wealthy states. This effect is most obvious in comparisons involving industrialized as against non-industrialized/developing nations, but is apparent in the EC data.
2. Medicine prices and volume sales appear to be inversely related within the EC. How and from which end the relationship is driven is open to some debate. Germany has, however, historically combined high prices with above-average domestic sales volumes.
3. EC countries with strong balances of trade in pharmaceuticals have higher medicine prices than those with weaker trade balances. Holland is an exception.
4. Over-the-counter (OTC) medicine sales have historically been highest in northern Europe, where health care systems are traditionally less dependent on high-volume usage of medicines. In the UK, Germany and Denmark OTCs, valued in manufacturers' returns, accounted for about 20% of the overall pharmaceutical market in 1989; equivalent figures for Portugal, France and Italy were 5–10%. In the US the OTC market accounts for about 30% of manufacturers' sales by value. The extent to

Table 1 Major EC pharmaceutical initiatives

1965	First directive on human medicinal products established a general framework for subsequent national and EC legislation.
1975	Second directive led to the establishment of the EC's Committee for Proprietary Medicinal Products in 1976. First EC licensing procedures thus established.
1975–1985	Limited developments—for example, in 1983 a council recommendation introduced preclinical and clinical guidelines, and medicine information and data requirements were amended.
1985	The Delors white paper put forward 13 proposals relating to pharmaceuticals.
1987	The biotech. and high-tech. directive established a new means of authorizing and protecting products that might not have patents. It established the first pan-EC arrangements for licensing certain types of medicine.
1989	The 'transparency' directive, which came into force in January 1990, sought to ensure that national decisions on medicine pricing and reimbursement are fair and made on a visible basis. It laid down a framework for cooperation and information exchange, and required the commission to present before January 1992 further proposals to eliminate distortions in the EC market.
1991	Directives on the rational use of drugs, affecting wholesaling, harmonization of legal status, and labelling and package information are nearing adoption. Also, a directive on pharmaceutical advertising has been prepared; it affects matters such as financial inducements and the distribution of free samples to professionals, as well as advertising to the public, but will not now prevent companies from sponsoring medical meetings.
Under consideration	Future systems for drug authorization, which at first will probably involve three approaches: a European Medicines Agency will be established in an as yet undecided location to handle centralized applications. The commission's proposals on supplementary protection certificates for medicines patents are under consideration—see text—along with suggested controls on homoeopathic medicines and international drug-testing harmonization; and a consultation document on clinical trials, aimed at controlling fraudulent practices and raising ethical standards, is in circulation. There are no proposals yet on the control of postmarketing surveillance initiatives and allied marketing interventions other than those in the 'future systems' package.

Table 2 Costs and consumption of pharmaceuticals in EC countries, 1989

Country	Percentage of gross domestic product spent on health services*	Percentage of health resources spent on pharmaceuticals	Percentage gross domestic product spent on pharmaceuticals	Relative price of medicines, 1990 (EC = 100)*	Implied volume of pharmaceutical consumption (UK = 1)
Denmark	6.3	6.8	0.47	129	0.8
Germany	8.2	10.6	0.87	128	1.6
France	8.7	10.8	0.94	72	2.7
Belgium	7.2	9.9	0.71	89	1.6
Netherlands	8.3	5.5	0.46	133	0.7
Italy	7.6	12.5	0.95	80	2.1
United Kingdom	5.8	11.5	0.67	117	1
Spain	6.3	13.8	0.87	73	1.4
Republic of Ireland	7.3	10.8	0.79	132	0.6
Greece	5.1	20.9	1.06	74	0.9
Portugal	6.3	23.6	1.48	68	1.1

Column 2 relates all pharmaceutical consumption (including over-the-counter drugs) valued at manufacturers' prices to all health care spending, public and private. In columns 1 and 3 gross domestic product is measured at market prices. The index of prices used is based on retail costings. Countries are ranked in order of gross domestic product per head, compared at 1989 exchange rates unadjusted for internal purchasing power variations. Population aged ≥65 (high drug users) ranges from 11% in the Republic of Ireland to nearly 16% in Germany, United Kingdom, and Denmark. *Data from Taylor, 1992

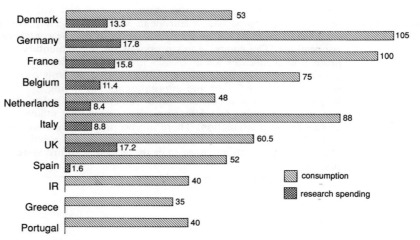

Figure 1 EC pharmaceutical consumption (manufacturers' prices) and research spending, 1989, £ per capita

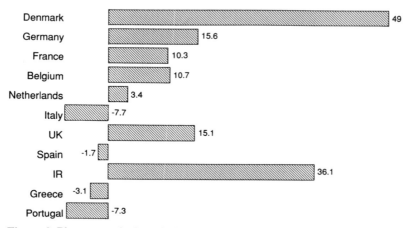

Figure 2 Pharmaceutical trade balance, £ per capita, EC countries (1988)

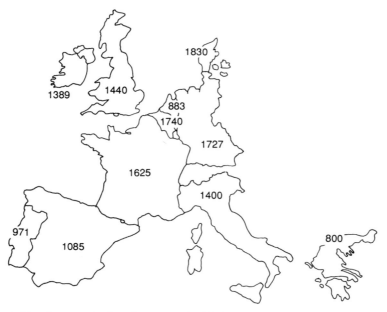

Figure 3 Employment in the pharmaceutical industry—workforce/million population (1989)

which this last reflects access restraints affecting poorer health service users is uncertain, as are its consequences.

5. Advertising spend relative to domestic sales appears to be unusually low in the UK (due essentially to Department of Health interventions) and relatively high in low unit cost–high volume consumption countries such as France. (The proportion of GDP spent on pharmaceutical promotion in the UK in 1989 was 0.07%, compared with 0.2% in France.) The German market's apparently atypical behaviour and the arguably limited performance of its research-based companies might perhaps be related to high promotional spending in a domestic arena dominated by local suppliers. Failure of German pharmaceutical supply-side representatives to negotiate constructively in this area may have been linked to governmental decisions to move away from free pricing in the late 1980s, although the impact of German reference pricing has so far been limited.

6. Relative to home market size, spending on pharmaceutical research and development (R&D) is highest in the UK and Denmark. This in part reflects their successful foreign trading, and in part their domestic policies and (arguably) their health service structures.

7. Holland's approach to pharmaceuticals, most recently illustrated in its reference pricing system, has helped to keep its medicines to health spending ratio the lowest in Europe. (Another factor may have been the professional status of pharmacists in The Netherlands.) The extent to which the Dutch are seeking drug cost minimization as distinct from therapeutic efficiency maximization can be questioned, however; some industry-linked observers suggest that the government there is pursuing a 'free-ride' relative to global pharmaceutical research costs. Certainly there seem to be political tensions in Holland associated with a historic combination of a liberal domestic pricing policy and a near-zero balance of trade in pharmaceuticals.

8. French policies on pharmaceuticals are widely regarded as unsatisfactory (Thomas, 1989; Redwood, 1992). They combine a very high-volume use of drugs with low prices for internationally successful products, despite overall high spending. Special structural factors include the attitude and status of the French medical profession, and also perhaps the strong influence of locally owned companies and interests in national policy-making. The proportion of French GDP going on pharmaceuticals (in MSP) is twice that of Denmark.

9. Italy and Spain are also examples of larger EC States with relatively low unit medicine costs and high or 'highish' volume consumption rates. Significant factors once again include the nature of the doctor–patient relationship, and levels of consumer education and expectation. In looking at prescribing practices it is important to recognize how underlying differences in medical and popular culture work alongside factors such

as promotional effort and health service structure. (This is also true, of course, in respect of societies such as Japan. There a relatively authoritarian medical approach, coupled with doctor dispensing and medical incomes related directly to prescribing costs, has for many years promoted high-volume usage of, and expenditure on, drugs. This pattern seems to be gradually being modified in line with a long-term global pharmaceutical strategy, as might be expected in a planned state-capitalist system.)

Harmonization

Patent protection is arguably the area in which Europe is most visibly moving towards a harmonized system, with EC supplementary protection certificates for pharmaceutical products likely to be introduced in the coming year or so (Sauer, 1990). It now seems almost certain that these will permit an effective extension of five years, up to an overall 'on the market' patent life of 15 years.

However, intellectual property law changes have been taking place worldwide, backed not only by strong industrial lobbying but also associated US government pressure. Seen in this light the EC's patent reforms do not appear a particularly dramatic step, or one which is representative of moves to harmonize the overall pharmaceutical/health sector. Rather, European pharmaceutical policies in general remain highly fragmented.

Some progress has, for instance, been made towards a common medicines authorization system; but in practice responsible officials/agencies in each member state still appear reluctant to trust each other's judgements or to permit any future single EC-wide medicines regulatory agency to have too great a final control over local licensing decisions.

To a degree such caution may be justified—it would clearly be wrong to break down member state drug safety controls for the purpose of enhancing trade at the expense of consumers' well-being (*Lancet*, 1991). It would also be wrong to transfer too much power to a single European administrative centre, were this to prove inaccessible to ordinary people and their representatives but open to high-level lobbying from multinational companies and similar quarters. Yet in practice neither danger seems likely to materialize. Instead, a greater hazard may prove to be that local vested interests, including bureaucracies and professional establishments not known for their commitment to open democratic process, will be able to perpetuate their influence in a way which could continue to distort trade.

Similar conclusions apply, perhaps with even more force, in the context of medicine price controls (Burstall, 1990). EC member states are experimenting with a wide variety of possible mechanisms for enforcing public health sector medicines cost restraints—see Table 3. Despite Commission-level attempts to explore the possibilities for harmonization these differ widely in nature, and member states are said to be unwilling or unable to participate constructively in efforts to determine how a more unified approach to medicines price and cost control might be achieved. In time the movement of pharmaceutical goods across internal EC borders will help force reductions in price disparity, but policies on issues like patient charging/drug reimbursement are likely to remain variable. Differences in policy structured into arrangements such as reference price schemes could perpetuate European pharmaceutical market distortions indefinitely.

In analysing questions relating to both EC medicine licensing and cost control it is pertinent to note that key 'stakeholders' in the area include:

1. The medical profession: existing power base significantly dependent on retention of prescribing control; benefits from EC fragmentation?
2. Pharmacists: do not have control over access of consumers to the good/service at the centre of their profession. Strategies: could extend OTC/P medicines lists; take a central role in prescription drug cost control by substitution, etc., increase expertise to become able to identify each patient's tailored drug needs?
3. Nurses: could enhance status by taking on prescribing/supply functions. For example, for chronically ill patients?
4. Governments: want to control public health spending, but also to strengthen local pharmaceutical sector and support 'worthwhile' research. Export revenues and inward capital investment welcome; may offer subsidies for them. Health gain a priority? Dependent on consumers (see below) for votes.
5. The Eurocracy: wants strong overall European pharmaceutical sector, level internal playing-field, elimination of anti-competitive or otherwise wasteful local structures, and increase in central power? Could bargain with international industry to counter local member state interests, but simultaneously encourage cross-boundary flows of goods to harmonize prices. Health gain a priority?
6. Industry: seeks financial profit more openly than other stake holders. EC fragmentation allows protection, EC production rationalization cost savings for 'winning' players. Smaller and larger companies' interests conflict, as may those of Euro and non-Euro concerns. Industry desires high free prices, fears regulatory interventions that 'excessive' drug costs may engender. Longer planning horizons and greater issue endurance than any other group of players?
7. Regulators: survival considerations may make them dependent on retention of local structures alongside extended job opportunities in Euro institutions.

Table 3 Approaches to public health medicines cost limitation

Product by product price control   This is the most common EC model, used in France, Belgium, Italy, Spain, Greece, and Portugal. In many cases it has been used to support local industry. (Reference pricing, now being introduced in Germany and in a particularly rigorous form in The Netherlands, sets a basic price for entire drug classes. More expensive products in a given group have to be paid for directly by patients.)

Company-by-company profit and cost control   This is unique to the United Kingdom, where the Department of Health's pharmaceutical price regulation scheme has helped to achieve low promotion spending coupled with high research outlays.

Positive and negative lists   Examples of one or the other now exist in all EC nations. Their effect is either to restrict prescribing for patients of the public health care system to products approved on positive lists, or to block their access to medicines on negative ones. Controls over entry of products to such national lists—or local formularies—may limit the influence of the medical profession. (The introduction of needs clauses in medicine licensing procedures, as in Norway, can be seen as a form of strict negative listing.)

Patient copayment systems   Countries such as Belgium, Denmark, Greece, Italy, and Portugal vary the amount of prescription payment due inversely with the perceived value of the medicine. High levels of exemptions, as in the United Kingdom, decrease the impact of such systems. So too do back-up private insurance systems to cover public service costs, as is most obvious in France.

Generic or therapeutic substitution, or both   Generic prescribing has been strongly encouraged in Denmark, The Netherlands, the United Kingdom, and to a lesser extent Germany. Mandatory generic or therapeutic substitution (in which doctors' prescriptions are filled with products other than those actually specified) does not yet exist in the EC.

Prescriber budgets   Pioneered in the United Kingdom's fundholding and indicative prescribing schemes, prescriber budgets can increase prescribers' awareness of medicine prices without imposing rigid limitations on their judgement. Provided that the sums allocated are adequate, and provision is made for unpredictable cost increase, this approach should combine the pursuit of cost restraint with respect for professional and consumer therapeutic choice.

Privatization   Encouraging the use of over-the-counter medicines and the private purchase of prescription drugs shifts costs away from the public purse. The United Kingdom and Germany already have sizeable over-the-counter markets, although no European country has—in relative terms—as great a volume of non-prescription sales as the United States. Denmark has a large over-the-counter market, coupled with private purchase of about a quarter of all prescribed medicines.

8. Academics: interests sometimes lie in maintaining complexity (and existence) of problems to analyse. As with all other groups above, health gain may or may not be a significant priority. Sufficient incentive to help deliver pragmatic 'fixes'?

9. Consumers: health gain a priority, but divided between sectional interests. Representatives may seek temporary high-profile coverage rather than long-term effective progress. Dependent on all other actors for services as patients, taxpayers, electors, workers, etc. Industry and allied medicines research reflects (sometimes unrealistic) hopes of sick and dying, cost-controlling governments the preferences of the healthy living?

Conclusions—towards market solidarity

The social significance of pharmaceuticals as both therapeutic tools and as economic goods is considerable. For example, including distribution payments they account for over 15% of all EC health spending. Drug sales to the rest of the world contribute over £4 billion net to the EC's trade balance; and medicine manufacturers employ directly about 500 000 people in the Community.

Such figures, taken together with the population's natural concern to gain effective treatments for disease, emphasize the need for policies in this area to be as informed and balanced as is possible. But there remain significant questions as to how the Community's pharmaceutical best interests can in practical terms be identified, much less effectively pursued.

In addition to the multiplicity of often-conflicting sectional groups involved, the problem of determining 'right' R&D expenditures illustrates the inherent weakness of naive rational planning approaches. Whatever the past welfare returns of medicines research investments, the rewards they will in future generate remain uncertain. Thus to a substantial degree relevant policies must be based on conviction rather than scientific (or quasi-scientific) calculation.

Similarly, individual medicine and other licit drug consumption behaviour can only to a limited degree be considered 'rational' or based on firm knowledge. This is not just because of factors such as potentially remediable information asymmetries and deficiencies. The consequences of many personal choices in areas such as health care are inevitably uncertain; also, factors other than knowledge and rational analysis may well influence consumers' preferences. In the case of tobacco and alcohol, for instance, the potential for addiction and short-term pleasure to overwhelm concerns about longer-term cost is generally recognized.

Such considerations raise fundamental questions regarding the role of disciplines such as health economics in licit and illicit substance policy formation, as well as the ethical basis of 'consumer protection' and other risk-related legislation. But as far as EC pharmaceutical policies in the 1990s are concerned, their more prosaic immediate relevance is that there seems good reason to believe that there will be no swift movement to a single view of what is 'correct'. The EC's regulatory and allied structures will tend to remain fragmented, and influenced to a substantial degree by opportunistic political and allied propagandist interventions made by the various special interests active in the sphere.

However, underlying this the increasingly free movement of pharmaceutical goods in the Community will in time help bring a degree of *de-facto* pricing uniformity. This could ultimately have 'knock-on' effects on medicine supply and health care delivery arrangements generally. With this medium- to long-term market unification in mind, options and possibilities which may currently be worth analysis include:

1. The degree to which medicines promotion content and expenditure controls could in themselves, if coherently established throughout the EC, help structure the internal pharmaceutical market in a desired manner and ensure reasonable overall expenditure limitation. To what extent might they negate the perceived need for other forms of price control?
2. If free pricing balanced by increased patient co-payments and/or direct payments (private prescriptions, shift to OTC, etc.) were to become established as a generally accepted way of restraining demand for, and public spending on, medicines in the EC, what would be the effect of this? Would poor consumers/ communities suffer, even if such an approach worked well for most people in northern Europe? Could the EC establish a regional public medicines costs support scheme to help nations such as Greece and Portugal, and internally could nations support poorer consumers without turning publicly funded pharmaceutical programmes into stigmatized 'poor-law' systems? Are positive/negative lists for public care acceptable if private consumers have a full choice of effective medicines?
3. What effect will schemes like the UK's fundholding and indicative pharmaceutical amount schemes have on doctor–patient relationships? Can a new form of committed doctor–patient partnership be developed throughout the EC during the 1990s, through which matters of individual choice and preference and community-wide welfare maximization can more satisfactorily be integrated than is at present the case?

In many respects the emergence of a new (or true) professionalism is an exciting prospect. If the financial and other interests of medicine prescribers, and the patients and the populations they serve, can somehow be brought to a closer unity it is possible to imagine the gradual emergence of something not far short of a 'perfect' pharmaceutical market in a future harmonized Europe. In the realm of the more probably achievable, however, the most likely prospect is slow decay of national-level price and other regulations and a general EC-wide drift towards more direct patient payments for medicines on the one hand, backed by a range of residual pharmaceutical access support provisions for less advantaged consumers on the other. The best-case outcome of this might be termed (common) market solidarity.

References

Association of the British Pharmaceutical Industry (ABPI) (1990) *Pharma Facts and Figures*. ABPI, London
Burstall ML (1990) *1992 and the Regulation of the Pharmaceutical Industry*. Institute of Economic Affairs, Health and Welfare Unit, London
Griffin JP (ed.) (1989) *Medicines Regulation Research and Risk*. The Queen's University of Belfast, Belfast
Editorial (1991) European drug regulation—anti-protectionism or consumer protection? *Lancet*, **337**, 1571–1572
Redwood H (1992) *The Dynamics of Drug Pricing and Reimbursement in the European Community*. Oldwicks Press, Felixstowe
Sauer F (1990) *The European Community's Pharmaceutical Policy*. Commission of the European Community's Directorate General for Internal Market and Industrial Affairs, Brussels
Taylor D and Maynard A (1990) *Medicines, the NHS and Europe*. The King's Fund Institute and the Centre for Health Economics, London and York
Taylor D (1992) Prescribing in Europe—forces for change. *British Medical Journal*, **304**, 239–242
Thomas LG (1989) *Spare the Rod and Spoil the Industry*. Columbia University, New York

Policy on licit substances: the case of tobacco

Nick Bosanquet and Andrew Trigg, *Royal Holloway and Bedford New College, University of London, UK*

The aim of this paper is to assess the policy outlook for reduction in tobacco use in Europe between now and 2000. The policy target set by the WHO is that a minimum of 80% of the population should be non-smokers and that tobacco consumption should be reduced by 50% by 1995 (WHO, 1987).

How realistic is this target in relation to the current levels of addiction and in relation to the current policy agenda?

Evidence from the US and the UK would suggest that once smoking rates start to decline the most noticeable impact would be among younger people. Among older people day-to-day health problems may well make smoking a much less pleasant habit, and some older people may not have taken up the habit in the first place. Smoking rates for the under-40s are a much more telling indication of whether there is going to be a non-smoking future. Older people will give up anyway. The variation in decision to quit is likely to be found among younger people.

The 25–39 age group should show a high demand for health where decisions can affect life expectancy and infant well-being. Fifty-three per cent of men in this age group and 40% of women smoked in 1987–1989 and high levels of smoking are not just found in the South (CEC, 1989). Forty-seven per cent of women in this age group in The Netherlands smoke, and 43% in West Germany. Smoking would seem to have increased recently among women in most EC countries.

Reductions in smoking in the US and the UK did not take place evenly. There were certain lead groups which gave up early and the change diffused more widely in society. Above all the medical profession in Britain and the US played leading roles. There are few signs that the medical professions are prepared to take this role even three decades later.

There may even be some complacency about the possible effects. Yet WHO projections suggest that deaths from smoking-related disease would increase from 0.8 million in 1988 to 2 million in 2025 (Peto, 1988). There has already been a 25% rise in mortality from lung cancer in France and Germany in the 1980s (UK Parliament, 1991). Detailed evidence is available from the US on the costs of smoking and the gains from abstention. As a result of the anti-smoking campaign the Surgeon General estimated 789 000 deaths were postponed during 1964–1985; 112 000 in 1985 alone. The average increase in life expectancy was 21 years (Surgeon General, 1989).

There will be high inescapable costs from past decisions. Without a strong policy response over the next three years such costs are in fact likely to grow markedly as rising real incomes lead to more smoking. We turn now to the current and likely policy response.

There is now a great deal of experience of anti-smoking policies in the US, the UK and Scandinavia, and the evidence points to some very clear conclusions about effective as against ineffective policy (Bosanquet and Trigg, 1991).

1. A rise in the relative price of cigarettes is a powerful and effective means of reducing consumption. Our recent research showed that a 14% increase in cigarette prices such as might result from tax harmonization can reduce

expenditure from between 6% and 14%, depending on the choice of elasticity.

2. Authoritative statements about the health consequences of smoking, either from Government or from the medical profession, attract a great deal of free publicity and can alter smoking behaviour. The Surgeon General's Reports in the US, and those of the Royal College of Physicians in the UK, are examples of such initiatives.

3. New research on the effects of passive smoking has strengthened the case for restrictions on smoking in public places and at workplaces.

These three findings can be used as a test for the effectiveness of policy both for the EC as a whole and for individual members. EC policies seemed to be shaping up promisingly with a clear priority to pricing issues. The Commission's original proposals were on pricing as part of fiscal harmonization designed to produce similar rates of taxation across the internal market. The process received some new impetus in the late 1980s as policy-makers became more aware of the health issue. Proposals in 1989 set target rates designed to increase taxation on cigarettes in southern Europe. However, such rates would have had perverse effects on reducing prices in the north. The Council's new proposals simply set a minimum tax of 57% and a ratio of specific duty to total tax of at least 25%. These conditions are not likely to compel any strong increase in prices.

The main thrust of EC policy has shifted from the issue of pricing towards the issue of advertising. Much publicity has surrounded the initiative by the Social Affairs Commissioner. As part of the EC's policy of extending the internal market the Commission has proposed a complete ban on advertising apart from advertising in retail shops.

The Europe Against Cancer campaign has led to a number of useful moves and has provided a framework for policy moves on tar yield, labelling and advertising. Measures on labelling are designed to strengthen warnings and to extend them to products other than cigarettes. The EC has also set standards for reducing smoking in public places.

There has certainly been an increase in concern, but the overall impact of EC policy is likely to be inadequate in relation to the resistance likely to be encountered. Our simulations of the impact of various policies would suggest that the total impact of current EC policies is likely to reduce the rate of increase in smoking arising from growth in real income rather to bring about absolute reductions in smoking.

Much depends on the policy choices made by national governments. In terms of the policy criteria to qualify as effective, national governments would have at least to bring about a substantial increase in the real price of cigarettes and sponsor the production of authoritative reports on smoking.

There is some hope of a clearer and stronger strategy in France where successive governments have shown greater concern about the rising costs of smoking (Hirsch *et al.*, 1988). France has introduced new measures to restrict advertising and to limit smoking in public places, with accompanying fines. However, there appears to be no current plan for the most vital step of raising the real price of cigarettes. The issue has received less attention in Germany where discussion has tended to focus on the lighter types of policy measure involving peer group influence through sports stars and pop idols. There are signs that Germany is now adopting WHO targets, but this is not linked to any change in policy which would achieve these targets before 1995 or even 2000. The UK and Ireland stand out as having developed more effective approaches with links between fiscal decisions and health issues so that the real price of cigarettes has increased. In other countries, whatever the current levels which differ, there has been no increase in the real price of cigarettes, and concern about inflationary consequences may make such increases even less likely in the future.

The second test of effective policy was whether it maximized the impact of government and professional opinion. Here the UK and Ireland stand out with the strong lead given by professional associations. The RCGP and the BMA have shown exemplary and strong leadership. The Government record in the UK started poorly. A recent review by the former Chairman of the Independent Scientific Committee on Smoking and health concluded of the early period that 'With the harsh judgment of hindsight government, in their policies on smoking, were poor custodians of the public interest in the 1950s and 1960s' (Froggatt, 1989). The record in the 1990s has improved. In other EC member countries there has not been a strong or effective lead from professional associations.

The policy challenge is set to grow in the 1990s. Any increases in real income are likely to lead to some further increases in smoking. There are continuing conflicts of interest between agricultural policy and health issues within the EC, with community spending on subsidies to tobacco growers, £800 million, still vastly greater than spending on the Europe Against Cancer campaign (£50 million). The outlook for eastern Europe and Russia is even worse, as there may be few competing forms of consumption over the next few years and a 30-year lag in information about smoking.

Research has now clarified the incentives which influence the smoking habit. In our earlier UK report for the Health Education Authority we set out a six-point programme which builds on this knowledge and which could move Europe towards the WHO target at least by 2000.

1. There should be a Euro-equivalent of the Surgeon General's office—an organization which would produce authoritative reports on smoking in Europe. This could be an important new role for the WHO.
2. Strong use should be made of price incentives over the next three years.

In Britain and in northern Europe an increase in the real price of cigarettes of about 20% over three years is required if there is to be substantial progress by the year 2000.

3. There should be an extensive media campaign on smoking and its effects.
4. There should be a programme to mobilize medical support to reduce smoking among doctors. The BMA and other professional associations throughout Europe could associate themselves in a joint initiative. This would help to start the diffusion process.
5. The insurance industry should be encouraged to give realistic discounts to non-smokers.
6. There should be a new drive to reach young people and schools to promote the message that there can be a smoke-free generation in Europe.
7. This would represent strategy of concentration on a few powerful initiatives.

References

Bosanquet N and Trigg A (1991) A smoke free Europe in the year 2000: wishful thinking or realistic strategy? RHBNC/St Mary's Discussion Paper 4. Carden Publications, London

CEC (Commission of the European Communities) (1989) *Smoking and the Wish to Stop*. EC, Brussels

Froggatt P (1989) Determinants of policy on smoking and health. *International Journal of Epidemiology, 18*(1), 1–9

Hirsch A, Hill C, Frossart M, Tassin J-P and Pechabrier, M (1988) *Lutter Contre le Tabagisme*. La Documentation Francais, Paris

Peto R (1988) Total tobacco mortality. In *1985 Estimates and 2025 Projections*. WHO, Copenhagen

Surgeon General (1989) *Reducing the Health Consequences of Smoking: 25 years of progress*. US Department of Health and Human Services, Washington

UK Parliament: Department of Health (1991). *The Health of the Nation, A consultative document for health in England* (Cm 1523). HMSO, London

World Health Organization (1987) *A 5-year Action Plan: Smoke-free Europe*. WHO, Copenhagen

A policy for licit substances

M.N. Graham Dukes, *University of Groningen, The Netherlands*

Introduction

It is very natural that as part of the growing together of Europe the entire approach to health policy, as it has developed in each of the nation states, should be reviewed. Some parts of that policy have been notably more successful than others; a few require very careful rethinking, rather than taking the practice developed in individual countries as a basis for a European model. Policy with respect to pharmaceuticals is one field where there is every reason for thorough re-evaluation. One needs to be entirely sure that whatever policy approaches have been developed in such an area in the past have truly served the interest of public health; and where medicines are concerned that assurance is very difficult to provide.

No-one with an interest in public health needs to be reminded of the fact that policy on medicines has evolved largely as a response to things which have gone wrong. The horrifying history of thalidomide—the drug which when taken in pregnancy caused gross deformations of the unborn child (Sjöström and Nilsson, 1972)—was the accident which precipitated much drug legislation as we currently know it. But there had been problems with medicines, and regulatory reactions to them, for centuries before that (Mann, 1984); laws on apothecaries had been passed in the Middle Ages because they had been found selling spurious goods; advertising legislation early in this century arose because of commercialized quackery in the field of venereal diseases and tuberculosis; modern drug laws in the United States were passed in 1938 largely because a sulphanilamide preparation sold in an untested solvent had killed a great many people. More problematical is that even modern drug regulation has not put a stop to the problems, though it has clearly helped to prevent their growing worse; drugs such as benoxaprofen, diethylstilboestrol and triazolam have wreaked havoc in an age of regulation, it is important to know why, before we go any further.

What is drug policy?

In deciding what drug policy is or should be, it is important to return to the basic challenge. Legislation and regulation on licit drugs must be a part of overall health legislation; they are not an end in themselves. What that means is that the drug is not truly the subject of the policies we need to develop. The subject is the patient or the health individual, and he or she must be in the middle of the picture all the time. The difference is not merely a rhetorical one. If you put drugs in the centre of the stage, your policy centres on their characteristics—their quality, efficacy and safety, and the information which is given with respect to them—all very much the components of drug policy to date. If, however, you take the individual as a starting point, you find yourself also confronted with the problems which may arise if drugs are poorly distributed or stored, recklessly advertised, wrongly prescribed, sold at an immoral price, incorrectly dispensed, or improperly taken. These problems and others like them should equally be components of health policy as it relates to drugs.

In that respect I have to make some fundamental reservations about medicines policy as it found its way into the European Communities from 1965 onwards. Because Community thinking at the time, and for long afterwards, was economically orientated, attuned to the free movement of goods and services, the basic harmonization of practice which grew up was inevitably directed to a uniform practice in drug registration. In many minds, that *was* drug policy.

The WHO notion of drug policy

In 1969 a historic meeting was convened in Oslo, largely on Scandinavian initiative, but involving the World Health Organization's Regional Office for Europe. It was devoted to something quite basic: methods of studying drug utilization. National pharmaceutical policies, as they had grown up and been exercised up till that time, had been put into effect largely in the dark. Whereas the pharmaceutical industry had developed its own systems for determining which drugs were being prescribed for which indications, by whom, in what doses, and why, government policy-makers and regulators often did not know these things. The information was in many cases denied them; it was regarded as a commercial secret. The problems which thus arose in determining where official measures were needed, and what their effects were, are obvious; in the absence of clear information as to what was going on in the field, policies were likely to be theoretical, problems were likely to be recognized only very late, and the effects of any measures taken remained uncertain. The people meeting in Oslo in 1969 recognized that problem; they created what was to become the Drug Utilization Research Group, in order to open up these things and document the medicines situation in such a way that one knew where the trends and problems lay.

That, in a sense, was the start of a hesitant move within WHO to defining what drug policy was. Drug utilization studies were an essential input, which had hitherto been neglected. What about the output? The answer which emerged from a great deal of consultation is summarized in Figure 1. Four forms of output were defined. Drug policies needed to concern themselves with *education*, including both the training of prescribers and other health professionals and the teaching of the public; next, policy needed to tackle the problem of providing true and objective *information* on medicines; thirdly, there was a need to tackle some forms of *research*, including the study of adverse drug reactions and interactions and the maintenance of ethical standards in clinical investigation. Finally there was a need for appropriate *regulation*, which was clearly proving its value but which was not necessarily in the centre of the picture.

That was the scene as it developed by about 1980. It was necessarily an incomplete picture, since it concentrated largely on the issues which had become of clear and identifiable concern in relatively well-to-do western European countries. It left out of consideration some important matters which did not merit international attention because they had either been solved by the private sector (manufacturing quality, for example, was no longer a great problem in most western countries) or because member states seemed to have them reasonably well in hand—for example the inspection of pharmacies. The five-pronged picture painted by WHO also soon became dated; by the mid-1980s a great many countries were so concerned about the financing of their national health services that drug pricing and cost containment with respect to prescribing were becoming matters of economic interest and often conflict; no-one in the United Kingdom needs to be reminded of the major battle being waged between the pharmaceutical industry and the Government by 1984 with respect to the Limited List of

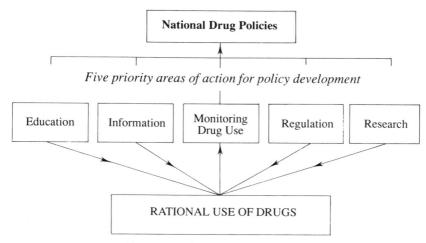

Figure 1 Definition of drug policy

prescribable drugs (Haaijer-Ruskamp and Dukes, 1991). Similarly, by the late 1980s a rising tide of litigation brought against doctors and the pharmaceutical industry (Dukes and Swartz, 1988) for alleged drug-induced injury strongly suggested that something was wrong in the drug scene. It was clear that WHO's picture of 1980 had been an excellent starting point to understanding pharmaceutical policies, but that it did not go nearly far enough, even for western Europe.

An integral approach to drug policies

From the basic picture provided by Figure 1 it is a rude shock to be presented with the immensely more complicated scene summarized in Figure 2. Even this is not by any means complete, but it gives a much closer indication as to where we should be going with pharmaceutical policies, and some of the problems we shall encounter on the way.

A general point, which springs to the fore when one merely glances at a scheme like this, is that national drug policies are conceived as having as their fundamental aim the rational use of medicines. That means that the right drugs must be available, and that they must be properly made, distributed, prescribed, dispensed and used. In most countries things are in

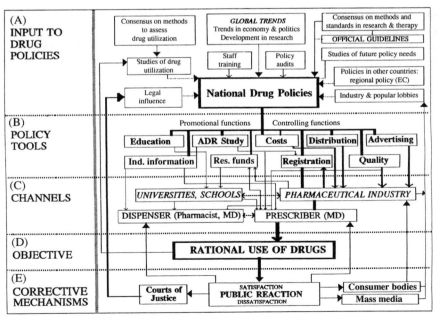

Figure 2 The scheme of drug policy development

fact deficient at various points in that scheme of things; we know, thanks to the immense volume of work on drug utilization now performed, that even in the best of industrial societies medicines are largely over-used and inappropriately used. We also know—and the experience with the Limited List in Britain is only one example—that any attempt to modify the situation in any way is likely to run into conflicts with habit, prejudice and vested interest.

Let us, all the same, take a look at several of the various processes which are sketched in this scheme of things.

Input to drug policies

We have already seen that up-to-date knowledge of *drug utilization* patterns is an essential piece of input to policy; that in turn will require ongoing study of the best way of obtaining and using data on utilization. Similarly, one will need to build policy around consistent *guidelines*, in which the standards set are made known, as much for the sake of the pharmaceutical industry as the professions; the input to those guidelines will have to come from scientific consensus, if policy is to be in touch with current knowledge. Beyond that one will need constant *auditing* of policy if one is to be sure that one is on the right lines. It is surprising to see how little effort has been devoted to examining the practical effects on society, even of something as prominent as the process of drug approval; the one critic will assert that regulation is destroying research (Marcus, 1980); the other will point to the fact that regulation is still not sufficiently strict to ensure safety (Medawar, 1980). Again the WHO has done rather better, with a series of studies to measure regulatory achievement; summarized some years ago in a small book (Dukes, 1985), these essentially showed that regulation, though not perfect, had done a lot of good, and not nearly as much harm as its critics asserted. While such auditing looks back, *policy studies* will need to look forwards; The Netherlands authorities may be unique in having commissioned, very recently, a well-financed study of the long-term future of medicines in health care, as a basis for future policy development. Finally, among the inputs to drug policy one will need to have proper training of policy-makers and regulators; it may be uncharitable to say that many of these people have come into the field because of their failure to settle elsewhere, but it is not untrue; very few people go into this sort of important work because they feel a call to do so, and most will need some very careful training if they are to do it properly and come to do it with enthusiasm.

Outputs of drug policy

The four outputs of policy listed a decade ago are still to be found here—*education, information, research and regulation*. Each of those four has undergone a great deal of development in the past decade. A new approach to educating prescribers, for example, has been put into effect in a massive international programme coordinated by our own university at Groningen, with the collaboration of the WHO in Geneva. Regulation has advanced in many countries to become better organized through semi-independent but government-controlled institutes with adequate finance. But one also sees here listed some of the other essential outputs of policy—*cost containment, distribution, advertising* and the control of *quality* among the players on the stage, whether they be manufacturing, prescribing or dispensing. All these policy outputs naturally have their repercussions for the four main parties on the scene—the industry, the universities, the prescribers and the dispensers. It will sometimes be less than easy to persuade them that policy measures which change their world or encroach unavoidably upon their traditional freedoms do nevertheless serve the general good.

Corrective mechanisms

The last section of Figure 2 points to the principal corrective mechanisms which come into play if the aim of pharmaceutical policies, i.e. the rational use of drugs, is not considered to have been attained. Views on that will necessarily differ; rightly or wrongly, the patient may believe that policies must change or that he or she has been injured, defrauded or overcharged. The result may be litigation, pressure through the consumer organizations or the mass media, or simply direct protest by the patient to the prescriber or dispenser. All these processes play an important role in correcting imbalances; they also render the scene of medicines policies an unusually lively one.

The scene today

It is almost impossible to summarize briefly the present-day scene with respect to the growth of policies on licit substances. It is immensely complex and changing all the time. Clearly, some things are constantly calling for correction. The influence of the manufacturer on prescribers, through massive promotion and other forms of inducement, is widely considered to be improper. The role of the pharmacist is shifting subtly; he is becoming an adviser rather than a compounder of medicines, though his future role is immensely complicated by his financial interests. Research funding clearly too often comes from the wrong sources; perfectly good research may be funded by large profits derived from the sale of medicines which should no longer be on the market. Above all, however, there is the problem that government policies in no country truly encompass the entirety of this scheme, and that the policies of one agency all too readily conflict with those of another; if one body is concerned about the sheer financial waste resulting from over-prescribing, it is disconcerting to see another government agency at the same time trying to save money by economizing on the very things which might improve prescribing, such as drug information services and teaching in clinical pharmacology. One encouraging trend is emerging at Brussels; the Community is still drug-centred in these matters, but it is becoming increasingly concerned with research, pricing and promotion, and it is planning to assume a more positive role in health as a whole. That is all to the good. Licit drugs occupy a large place in medical care, and thus in its costs, its achievements and its failures. For that reason they must be the subject of policies which reflect a proper understanding of what they are about.

References

Dukes MNG (1985) *The Effects of Drug Regulation*. MTP, Lancaster

Dukes MNG and Swartz B (1988) *Responsibility for Drug-Induced Injury: A reference book for lawyers, the Health Professions and Manufacturers*. Elsevier, Amsterdam

EC (1965) Council Directive 65/65/EEC of 26 January 1965 on the approximation of provisions laid down by law, regulation or administrative action relating to proprietary medicinal products *Official Journal*, No. 22, 9 February

Haaijer-Ruskamp FM and Dukes MNG (1991) *Drugs and Money: the problem of cost containment*, 6th edn. For the University of Groningen and the World Health Organization: Styx Publications, Groningen

Mann RD (1984) *Modern Drug Use: An Enquiry on Historical Principles*. MTP, Lancaster

Marcus AW (ed.) (1980) *Risk and Regulation in Medicine: the fettered physician*. Association of Medical Advisers in the Pharmaceutical Industry, London

Medawar C (1992) *Power and Dependence: Social Audit on the Safety of Medicines*. Social Audit, London

Sjöström H and Nilsson R (1972) *Thalidomide and the Power of the Drug Companies*. Penguin, Harmondsworth, Middx

Workshop discussion report

Klaus Mäkelä, *Finnish Foundation for Alcohol Studies, Helsinki, Finland*

Licit substances are a heterogeneous category. Alcohol and tobacco are used as recreational drugs and are part of our daily social life. At the same time they are dependency-producing drugs, and connected to considerable health hazards. Among pharmaceuticals, psychotropic substances pose problems which are similar in part to those attached to alcohol and tobacco. In general, however, issues related to the pharmaceutical markets form a category of their own. The two groups of licit substances will therefore be discussed separately.

Tobacco and alcohol

There are studies indicating that very moderate amounts of alcohol may help to prevent heart disease, but the evidence is still doubtful. The risk for more adverse consequences of smoking and drinking is a direct function of intake with no clear threshold values.

There is much evidence to show that policies affecting the general population have simultaneous impact on heavy consumers. It is thus problematic to draw a sharp line between policies affecting the general population and measures specifically directed at heavy consumers.

Smoking is a clearly recognized major health problem, but one which lacks policy momentum in today's Europe. Not only will it be difficult to reach the goal set by WHO of reducing the proportion of smokers in the population to 20% by the year 2000, but massive increases in smoking may be imminent in eastern Europe.

The experience of several countries has helped to identify the following key components in effective policies on tobacco:

1. Increasing the real price of cigarettes.
2. Authoritative statements about the health consequences of smoking from the government and representative bodies of the medical profession.
3. Warning labels.
4. Bans on advertising.
5. Mobilizing the concerns of non-smokers about passive smoking.

Drinking is part of European culture, and is often regarded as a sociable activity. Alcoholic beverages may also form a prominent part of the daily diet. Nevertheless, in most countries alcohol-related conditions contribute significantly to the overall mortality rate and to the use of health services.

The widely varying cultural traditions and patterns of drinking make it important to find a proper balance, sensitive to national circumstances, between health education and restrictive alcohol policies. Price policies are, however, an important component of any public health policies with respect to alcohol.

Because of the economic significance of alcohol and tobacco, public health concerns have so far had little weight in the policies adopted by the European Community. Processes towards diminishing differences in price would tend to increase price levels in southern European countries, but they would also have the effect of lowering prices in northern Europe. Should the Scandinavian countries be forced to abolish their restrictive alcohol policies, substantial increases in consumption and alcohol-related problems will most probably follow.

With respect to alcohol and tobacco policies, the medical profession has a key role, not only in advising individual patients, but also in public health advocacy. The most permanent reductions in smoking have been achieved in countries where the medical profession has taken an active stand.

Pharmaceutical markets

In a normal market situation the buyer assesses the quality of what the seller offers, and makes a choice accordingly. In the market for pharmaceuticals the seller, chooser, user, buyer and assessor are all different parties. Regulating the market is therefore extremely complicated.

The market functions well in some respects. In affluent countries it ensures a wide range of drugs and it finances new product research and development. In other respects the market functions badly. Cost containment is difficult, and expenditure on advertising and promotion much exceeds that on research.

Different countries in Europe have different drug-use traditions. In general, more is used in the south than the north.

Countries tend to react only when disasters occur, or when the money runs out.

Ideal policies would comprise a fair mix of regulation, self-regulation, persuasion, information and education, with appropriate intersectoral mechanisms.

Important tasks in the immediate future include the following:

1. Ensuring access to essential drugs in all countries of Europe.
2. Rising professional standards in prescribing.
3. Cost containment by, for example, limiting public reimbursement to flexibly defined essential drugs.

Research priorities

More information is needed both on the actual use and the incidence of adverse consequences of various substances, and on the determinants of public policies with respect to these substances. The following types of study therefore deserve high priority:

1. Regular comparable surveys of levels and patterns of use of licit and illicit substances in all European countries. It is important that the use of all types of substances is monitored within a common frame of reference.
2. Studies aiming at a common framework for determining the public health effects of the use of different substances.
3. Studies of the economic interests and policies related to various substances.

Policy on illicit substances

Drug problems and policies: comparative perspectives

Peter Reuter, *RAND Corporation, Washington DC, USA*

The nations of western Europe and North America have adopted quite varied means to control the use of prohibited psychoactive drugs. Some have adopted what might be called 'tolerant' policies, reserving criminal sanctions not for users but almost exclusively for those who sell drugs. These nations give most policy emphasis to minimizing the harms the drug-dependent do to themselves and the rest of society, as well as using education to prevent initiation. Other countries have adopted more punitive policies, using criminal law aggressively against users as well as dealers, with less emphasis on harm reduction and treatment of current users.

This variation should provide an opportunity for nations to learn from each other. Yet systematic comparative descriptions of the drug control experiences of developed nations are hard to find. No published study compares the severity and nature of the drug problems of different countries, nor is there much available on how various nations have attempted to control such problems.* Consequently little has been learned from the national experiences.

This paper summarizes data, description and analysis on the experiences with illegal psychoactive drugs of ten nations.† The first section focuses on the nature and extent of the problems of these nations, while the second section describes and analyses how the 10 countries have tried to control the use of, and harms associated with, these substances.

---

* A forthcoming WHO–Europe study that will present a good deal of comparative data on European nations.
† The 10 nations are Canada, France, Germany, Great Britain, Holland, Italy, Norway, Spain, Switzerland and the United States.

Europe Without Frontiers. Edited by C.E.M. Normand and P. Vaughan
© 1993 John Wiley & Sons Ltd

Comparing problems

The data on the past two decades of drug problems are relatively easy to summarize. Most of the nations included here have experienced at least one heroin epidemic, starting between about 1965 and 1985; Norway is probably the only nation in our study that has not had a period of substantially elevated initiation into frequent heroin use. The heroin epidemics have all come to an end, in the sense that the rate of initiation into heavy heroin use appears now to be much lower than it was at its peak. However, the problems of heroin addiction, as indicated by the number of heroin-related deaths and arrests, seem to be still rising in most countries; The Netherlands is an exception in that respect. Initiation rates may be down but it seems that most of those who became heroin addicts are still addicted.

No western European nation has yet experienced an epidemic of heavy cocaine use, despite the large and rapidly growing amounts seized. Marijuana use is endemic at a fairly high level among adolescents and young adults; however few marijuana users continue heavy use for long periods of their life. Some nations have modest problems with synthetic drugs, mostly amphetamines.

The pattern of health and behavioural problems related to drugs is more complex. In a 'Mediterranean crescent' consisting of Spain, southern France and Italy, intravenous drug users (IVDU) constitute a major source of the HIV infection; between a third and a half of known IVDU are seropositive. In the rest of Europe, except for the German-speaking part of Switzerland, there is generally a low association between IVDU and HIV.

Heroin addiction is strongly associated with crime in all nations, i.e. the criminally active have much higher rates of addiction than the rest of the population and much of their crime seems to be related to the financing of drug consumption itself. These statements are true even of harm reductionist Netherlands. However, there is generally only a modest level of violence associated with drug use and with the sale of drugs.

The United States has been, in every sense, more severely affected by drugs than the other countries studied. The heroin epidemic started earlier and was more severe, in the sense that the peak prevalence of heroin addiction there was higher than in any of the western European countries or Canada. Heavy cocaine use has been a major health and crime problem at least since 1985. Both the cocaine and heroin epidemics have come to an end, in the sense that the rates of initiation are much lower now than they were at their peak. Nonetheless the rates of prevalence of heroin and cocaine dependence are extremely high by international standards. Marijuana use, though declining from extraordinary levels in the late 1970s, remains much higher than in any other nation. What is also striking is the fact that a high percentage (more than a quarter in recent cohorts of 18-year-olds) of those who experiment with marijuana become frequent users for at least a few months. A variety of synthetic drugs (such as PCP [phencyclidine] and methamphetamine) are in wide use in a few cities; for example Washington, DC has had a particularly high prevalence of PCP use, and San Diego a high rate for methamphetamines.

The extent and severity of user and distributor crime are much higher in the United States than in the other nations. In particular, the level of violence surrounding drug distribution in American cities is unmatched anywhere else. Of more than 20000 homicides reported annually, 5000 might be related to drug marketing. IVDU is a primary source of the very high prevalence of HIV in the United States. Seventeen per cent of reported AIDS cases give IVDU as the primary risk factor, a percentage that has been growing in recent years. Again it is worth noting that the percentage varies a great deal across cities, being much higher around New York City than in any other part of the nation.

Canada is strikingly different from both the United States and western Europe. Indicators of heroin addiction are at very low levels and always have been. There is little to suggest much use of synthetics. Some cocaine indicators, notably those related to enforcement, have risen sharply, but there is little evidence of much heavy use of that drug. Of illegal psychotropic drugs, only marijuana is widely used. Canada is still little affected by the HIV infection.

Different national perspectives

Nations differ not only in the nature and severity of their drug problems but in their conceptions of what those problems are. That in turn, we conjecture, may account for some of the differences in the ways that they attempt to control drug use.

For some nations the use of psychoactive drugs is viewed primarily as a health problem, and hence should be dealt with primarily through public health measures. Moral issues are seen as secondary and crime is seen as a function of factors other than drug use itself, such as poverty, alienation and the high price of the drugs. That is fairly explicitly the view of the Dutch and, somewhat less explicitly, of the Canadian and Spanish governments.

For other nations crime is viewed as much more central. For example, polls in France point to illicit drugs as a major source of fear, and drugs are associated with a sense of a deteriorating social environment. In the United States the drug problem has become almost synonymous with crime in popular perceptions. Government policy tends to be responsive to this concern.

In Scandinavia, apart from Denmark, the drug problem has still another configuration. Drug use is seen as in itself bad behaviour that should be deterred; even marijuana use, particularly among the young, is dealt with seriously, regardless of whether marijuana users tend to commit more crime or suffer more health problems.

Differences in the salience of different elements of the drug problem may be captured by the extent to which illict drugs are separated from licit substances, particularly alcohol. For example, the Canadian government's drug campaign is administered by an office that also deals with alcohol, while the recently established US Office of National Drug Control Policy explicitly avoids any consideration of alcohol (except as it involves use by youth below the legal drinking age) or tobacco problems. The relative prominence of health and justice ministries in different countries may also be indicative of the national perception of the drug problem. Thus the principal Dutch office for drug policy is in the Health Ministry, while in France the Ministry of Justice has tended to have the primary role.

Comparing policies

The United States has taken, throughout the 1980s, an increasingly intolerant stand towards drugs, spurred on by the rapid increase in cocaine-related problems. More emphasis is given now to detecting drug use both in the workplace and the criminal justice system; for example, drug testing of job applicants has become routine for large corporations. Police departments throughout the nation have developed innovative programmes for punishing arrested drug users, for example by seizing the cars of those buying drugs in street markets. Colleges have been under pressure to increase their efforts to detect and punish drug use on campus. Though most drug users face little risk of jail, there is a substantial effort to increase their risk of other kinds of penalties. Very harsh penalties for drug traffickers have become the norm, with Congress invoking the death penalty as an allowed statutory penalty for an increasing range of drug trafficking-related offences.

Although The Netherlands has received most attention as the leader of tolerant policies in Europe, Italy (until mid-1990) and Spain have formal laws that were more explicitly tolerant. In both nations it appears that there were no criminal sanctions against persons possessing psychoactive drugs for personal use. Italy, after an intense parliamentary debate in the summer of 1990, reintroduced the criminal sanctions that it removed in 1974. In Spain controversy currently rages over the effort of municipal governments to introduce administrative penalties for use of drugs in a public setting. Both countries emphasize the wide variety of nationally funded treatment and social services available to their addict populations.

At the other extreme lie most of the northern European nations. Scandinavia, with the exception of Denmark, where pockets of open drug trading have been allowed to exist for the past decade, has adopted a strict prohibitionist policy, making extensive use of the criminal sanction against drug users. The same is generally true of Germany, though some Lander (notably Hamburg) are moving towards more harm-reductionist stances.

Britain, often held up as an example of a tolerant nation, actually falls in between the two groups. The primary difference is the right of properly licensed medical practitioners to dispense heroin or cocaine to their addicted patients, a right that is infrequently used. In other respects it looks little different from the rest of northern Europe, with an aggressive arrest and sentencing policy. Punitiveness is also emphasized in the rhetoric of drug policy in Britain.

The arrival of the HIV infection has affected policy attitudes in a number of European nations; as yet it has had minimal impact on the United States. Both Britain and The Netherlands have been explicit in their willingness to sacrifice drug control goals to reduce the prevalence of AIDS. Needle-exchange programmes have been implemented in both countries with little controversy. This contrasts sharply with the highly divisive debate that has characterized the issue in the United States, a debate that has prevented all but the most fledgling of exchange schemes from being implemented there.

In Italy and Spain needles have always been cheaply available from retail pharmacies, but that has not prevented the spread of HIV in the addicted population. It has, however, led to an interest in more aggressive efforts to reduce needle-sharing among addicts in treatment programmes. France, generally a hardline country with respect to drug control, permitted the sale of needles starting in 1987 as a means for controlling the spread of AIDS. In other respects it appears not to have changed drug policy to reflect AIDS concerns.

One measure of policy differences would be the relative emphasis of government drug control expenditures on enforcement as opposed to treatment and prevention. Unfortunately it is almost impossible to put together estimates of total government expenditures on drug programmes for any country. Even in the US, where the appropriate emphasis is a matter of considerable debate, there are data only for the federal government, though most drug control expenditures are financed by state and local governments. At the federal level enforcement-related programmes receive between 70% and 75% of total expenditures; despite considerable political concern about this emphasis on enforcement, recent years have not seen much increase in the share going to treatment and prevention programmes. State and local governments probably spend an even smaller share on treatment and prevention. We estimate that direct government drug control expenditures in 1988 totalled approximately $28.5 billion, of which three-quarters went to enforcement.

In Europe there are a few indicators that provide an impression of differences in policy emphasis. For example, in Norway the Oslo police department has a drug squad of about 100 officers, possibly the largest of any European city, and the total number of drug offence arrests was 3000; only 500 persons were in treatment slots. In Italy, on the other hand, there were 47 000 persons in treatment in 1988, compared to 23 000 arrests. Though the Italian arrests were all for trafficking offences (since possession of drugs for personal use at that time was not a criminal offence), this suggests that the Italian government gives substantially less emphasis to enforcement than does the Norwegian government.

Conclusion

This has been an essentially descriptive and generally cautious paper, being an early product of a larger project with higher analytic and policy ambitions. In this section we offer a few analytic and policy speculations.

First, the differences in drug policy are real and have their roots in very distinct views of the dangers presented by drug use. The US view, which shows some signs of modification at home just as its export potential is being realized in Europe, is that the prevalence of drug use itself must be reduced because the extent of problematic drug use is driven by that prevalence; the more marijuana experimenters today, the more crack addicts tomorrow. The view of the more tolerant European nations is that the extent of problematic drug use is only slightly related to the prevalence of drug use itself and that little effort, either rhetorical or real, should go to controlling the broader behaviour, which poses little risk to either the individual or society.

Second, it is hard to find evidence that targeted policy affects prevalence of drug use or addiction. The usual comparison is between tolerant Holland, with its low rate of drug use and associated problems, and the intolerant US, with extraordinarily high rates of use, addiction and every conceivable related problem. However, one might just as readily compare tolerant Italy, with a heroin death rate that is still growing rapidly, with harsh Norway, with modest levels of use and addiction.

If there is any simple relationship between drug policy and problems, we suggest that it has the opposite causal direction; severe problems lead generally to more punitive policies. Dutch tolerance has not been strained by any evidence of worsening problems; the Italian reaction to the increase in heroin-related deaths in the 1980s was to reach for the criminal prohibition, and the Spanish are apparently in the throes of the same experience. A corollary is that nations will leave their drug policy, whether tolerant or punitive, unchanged if there is no evidence that the problems are worsening. What prevents Europe from sliding into a punitive stasis is the (sensible) belief that AIDS control requires a policy milieu that focuses on ensuring that injecting drug users keep in contact with health and social services.

Bibliography

Albrecht H-J and Van Kalmthout A (eds) (1989) *Drug Policies in Western Europe*, Max Planck Institute, Freiburg

Co-operation Group to Combat Drug Abuse and Illicit Trafficking in Drugs (Pompidou Group) (1987) *Multi-city Study of Drug Misuse: Final Report.* Council of Europe, Strasbourg

Leuw E (1991) Drugs and drug policy in the Netherlands. In Tonry M (ed.) *Crime and Justice: A Review of Research*, Vol. 14, University of Chicago Press, Chicago

Office of National Drug Control Policy (1992) *National Drug Control Strategy* Washington, DC

Reuband K-H (1990) Drug use and drug policy: a cross-national comparison. Paper presented at the Conference of the USSR Academy of Science, Institute of Sociology, on Problems of Deviant Behavior, April

Health policies, drug control and the European Communities

Nicholas Dorn, *Institute for the Study of Drug Dependence, London, UK*

Introduction

Can a specifically European approach to policies on illegal drugs be identified? And, if so, to what extent can the Institutions of the European Communities, such as the Commission, Council and European Court of Justice, said to be shaping those policies?

The process of European Union is evolving, from its primarily economic focus as outlined in the founding treaties, through a series of social implications of those economic concerns, to a wider set of political objectives as agreed in Maastricht in December 1991. The five objectives of European Union were summarized at Maastricht in the following terms:

1. To promote economic and social progress . . . through the creation of an area without internal frontiers . . . the establishment of *economic and social union* including a single currency.
2. To assert its identity on the international scene, in particular through the

implementation of a *common foreign and security policy* which shall include the eventual framing of a common defence policy.
3. To strengthen the protection of the rights and interests of the nationals of its member states through the introduction of a *citizenship of the Union*.
4. To develop close cooperation on *justice and home affairs*.
5. To maintain in full the 'acquis communautaire' (evolving legacy of EC-developed principles and laws) . . . [Article B, *Political Union*, Presidency Conclusions, op. cit.; 1, emphasis added].

Commentaries on the significance of the EC for the development of European drug policy tend to focus only on some implications of just part of the first of these objectives, that is *on the abolition of internal frontiers* by the beginning of 1993. This focus has led some, including the European Parliament in its well-known reports, to shift from a balanced view to one focusing upon the dangers of the abolition on internal frontiers. The first report of MEPs on drugs issues was by Stewart-Clark (1986). This useful report revealed the varied interests of Members of the European Parliament in drugs issues. By 1991, increasing xenophobia in Europe had provided a framework for another report by MEPs (Bowe, 1991), which showed much more hysteria about the consequences of lowering internal frontiers.

EC competence on economic union: minimal coordination of health policies

'Health promotion'

Health and health aspects of illegal drugs is mentioned in the text of the recent Maastricht agreement on European Union between EC member states as they concern public health. There is encouragement towards cooperation and coordination, 'excluding any harmonization of the laws and regulations of the member states' (European Community, 1991a). The text says:

> The Community shall contribute towards ensuring a high level of human health protection by encouraging cooperation between the Member States and if necessary, lending support to their actions. Community action shall be directed towards the prevention of disease, in particular the major health scourges, including drug dependence, by promoting research into their causes and their transmission, as well as health information and education. *Health protection requirements shall form a constituent part of the Community's other policies* (European Community, 1991b).

The last phrase (the emphasis was not in the original) reflects the fact there is very little EC health policy as such, and virtually no direct health care policy. This is because neither the enhancement of health, nor the provision of health services, were objectives of the Treaty of Rome, or of the Single European Act or of the Maastricht Treaty.

The four freedoms and health policy

Such EC health policy as there is arises primarily from the 'four freedoms of movement' involved in creation of an economic area without internal frontiers which are: (a) free movement of goods; (b) freedom to provide and receive services; (c) free movement of labour; (d) free movement of capital. Each of these freedoms of movement has some implications for health policy generally, and for health-related policy on illegal drugs in particular.

Movement of goods

In relation to the free movement of goods, attention has focused on the effects of lowering internal border controls on the standardization of standards of quality, of weights and measures, and the harmonization of tax levels. This has all kinds of implications for trade in licit drugs such as alcohol and cigarettes, and for medical technology and pharmacological products, including medicines containing controlled substances. Two Commission proposals for Directives submitted to the Council in January 1990 were on the distribution and issuing of medicines including those containing substances classified as narcotics or psychotropic substances within the terms of the International Conventions (EC Council document 10234/1/90, CELAD 126, on the European Plan to Combat Drugs). As far as illegal drugs are concerned there is no question of free movement of goods, but the Commission's competence in matters of trade has led it to draw up draft legislation regulating the movement of precursor chemicals—licit chemicals which may be misused to produce or refine illegal drugs (CEC, DG Customs Union and Indirect Taxation, Draft proposal for a Council Regulation on laying down measures to discourage the manufacture of certain substances needed in the illicit manufacture of narcotic drugs and psychotropic substances, Commission Doc XX1/22/90-EN Rev 2).

Services

Providers of services available in one EC country should be equally free to provide them to consumers in other EC countries, and consumers should be free to receive services in the country of their choice (Nielsen and Szyszczak, 1991). Thus, for example, no EC government can prevent its citizens travelling to another member state to consume a health service, such as an abortion or drug treatment.

However, the EC has agreed that member states retain powers which potentially restrict the right of EC nationals to move between EC countries. Article 3 of Council Directive 64/221, on Special Measures Concerning Movement and Residence, allows that a national of one EC member state, who travels to another EC country either to pursue employment or to receive services, may be refused entry to that country or expelled from it *if considered a threat to public policy or public security*. Drug addiction is amongst the conditions that 'might threaten public policy or public security' (Annex section B of the Directive). However, it is incumbent on the member state concerned to show that any exclusion is a response to the 'personal conduct of the individual concerned'. Hence, for example, a drug-using EC national who enters another EC country in order to use health services might possibly be expelled if his or her ongoing conduct is considered a present threat to public policy. Drug possession or drug consumption, as distinct from addiction, are not generally sufficient grounds for public health exclusion (for instance, *Regina v. Bouchereau*, case 30/77 before the Court of Justice of the EC, 2 *Common Market Law Reports*; 800–825).

Also, according to Article 4 of the same Directive, persons may be refused entry to a member state, or even expelled, if they are in a state of *disease or disability which might endanger public health*. In the case of those already resident, a government's power to expel is limited to a shortlist which includes 'infectious diseases' as well as drug addiction (Annex sections A and B to the Directive). Hence, an HIV-positive EC national seeking entry to another EC country in order to consume public or private health care services might be denied entry for public health reasons, or expelled once resident in the country.

Labour

Freedom of movement of labour means that any EC national can establish themselves and work in any EC country. There are, however, some restrictions.

As far as the freedom of drug-using EC workers is concerned, there are restrictions of at least two sorts:

1. The above Council Directive provides that people may be refused entry to a state, or deported, when they travel to another country to pursue employment if their personal conduct constitutes a serious threat to public policy. On the basis one member state, Belgium, expelled a number of women working as prostitutes. The European Court of Justice held that this particular action was unjustified, since the Belgian government

expelled them as a group. Instead member states must examine the personal conduct of each individual (*Adoui v Belgium State and City of Liege*, joined cases 115 and 116/81, reported 1982 in *European Community Reports* 1665, also in Nielsen and Szyszczak, 1991, pp. 61–62).

2. More broadly, a preliminary ruling of the European Court of Justice has narrowed the scope of the right to travel within the EC in search of work by *excluding* former drug users employed in Dutch sheltered work premises (European Court of Justice, 1989, Case 388/87, *Bettray vs. Staats-secretaris vorr Justice*, 31 May, cited in Van Hamme, 1991). Participation in such schemes was held to be rehabilitative or educational rather than strictly employment, so employment-related rights of free movement accorded by Article 48 of the Treaty of Rome were held not to apply.

In the case of certain professions, for example medicine and nursing, the EC has established equivalence of qualifications. In addition, the General Systems Directive has established as valid for EC-wide professional practice all qualifications recognized in any member state and acquired through study of three years duration or more (Council Directive of 21 December 1988 on a General System for the Recognition of Higher-Education Diplomas Awarded on Completion of Professional Studies and Training of at least Three Years Duration. Official Journal, 24 January 1989. For discussion see Orzack, 1991). Generally, therefore, European countries can be expected to experience an increasing interchange between EC health and welfare professionals.

However, the British government has decided to stick with a *social work* training period of two years. Hence, British social workers taking these qualifications will not be professionally mobile in the EC. However, comparability of *medical and nursing* qualifications will permit practice throughout the EC. As far as workers in the field of drug problems are concerned, a dichotomy may be opening up, with those on the medical and paramedical side having the ability to practise in Europe, go on exchanges, etc.—whilst those on the social work side may not be able to in future. This may lead to a gradual remedicalization of the drug field in Britain, after a period in which social workers have played a leading part.

Movement of capital

The implications for health care of the free movement of capital are broadly similar to the implications for the free movement of services. There can be no restriction on capital from one EC country investing in health services, including drug treatment, rehabilitation, counselling or advice services, in other EC countries. What these broad possibilities might mean for services relating to drug problems is anybody's guess at present. It seems that any change will be in the direction of greater variety in service provision and in service cost, reflecting the variety of forms of capital investment.

Thus, in summary, the health protection implications of European Union appear mixed, with tendencies to guarantee customer access to a variety of services being potentially offset by powers of restriction.

EC citizenship

The objective of EC citizenship, recently agreed at Maastrict, seems likely to consolidate, rather than extend, existing travel rights of the citizens of member states. But it will *not* place any obligation on member states to provide services, and Community legislation is, if anything, *reducing* the rights of EC citizens if they are drug users (see above). External border controls and internal police checks will focus upon non-EC citizens. EC citizenship is an important topic, but its implication for health policy may be limited—except in the negative, exclusionary sense—and it may focus on health protection measures for non-EC nationalities.

Justice and foreign policy issues

Anti-trafficking coordination falls primarily in the areas of Common Foreign and Security Policy (CFSP), and Justice and Home Affairs (JHA)—both of which are argued by some to fall outside any present or future competence of the EC and its Commission. The UK government, in particular, has been keen to stress that cooperation in these two latter areas takes place in intergovernmental meetings and not within the policy-making arena of the EC.

However, other observers—termed 'maximalists' because of their enthusiasm for European integration in all spheres of policy—foresee a degree of integration on JHA and CFSP into the EC framework of institutions. How things will work out in future must remain a matter of some conjecture at this time. But there are evidently some ways in which aspects of intergovernmental cooperation relating to JHA and CFSP are being pulled into the ambit of the EC.

Justice and home affairs: money laundering

The Commission, for example, has initiated Community legislation on money-laundering, hence insisting on its competence to rule on a matter that is central to JHA concerns. This legislation would *require* EC member states to make money-laundering a criminal offence, to lift bank secrecy in all suspected cases of laundering, and to request them to inform the judicial authorities. In this manner the EC uses its competence in an aspect of Economic Union to legislate in matters of JHA (Proposal for a Council Directive on Prevention of the Financial System for the Purpose of Money Laundering, COM[90] 106 final SYN 254). Similarly, the EC has legislated in respect of trade in precursor chemicals.

More generally, however, drug enforcement remains the province of member states and by means of cooperation between them through various bilateral and multi-lateral agreements for political cooperation and police cooperation (SCHENGEN, TREVI, etc.). The EC has observer status on many such working groups but has little real influence (work in progress is to be published in a volume edited by Ernesto Savona and Jorgen Jepsen; for a view of the importance of drugs enforcement in the UK and centralising tendencies, see Dorn et al., 1992).

Common foreign and security policy: terms of trade and crop substitution

The competence of the Communities in relation to economic and trade aspects of external relations gives them leverage in some matters of CFSP. The EC already offers improved terms of trade to Andean countries as an inducement to cooperate in crop substitution programmes. These programmes, which have an enforcement side, may in future bring the EC more into the arena of international drug enforcement.

The above are some points of creative tension that may yet subordinate much of European anti-trafficking policy to the EC. There is a lack of any EC institutional focus that is capable of bringing together the drug-related policies as these relate to the five objectives of European Union.

The commission, past and future

The impasse of DG-Ve

It has been possible to write this paper on EC drug policy without so far referring to DG-Ve—the health and safety section in the Employment, Education and Social Affairs Directorate of the Commission—which has a brief for drugs and alcohol issues. This arises because DG-V has had little impact on either alcohol or drug policies, which is not necessarily a criticism of DG-V. It is simply that drug issues are too wide-ranging to be captured by one such Directorate, especially one that receives poor political support. One area in which DG-Ve might, in future, have influence is in relation to its formal area of competence—health and safety at work. Occupational drug testing has become an issue in some employment contexts. European experts distinguish between two quite separate arguments for testing: (a) discipline and (b) work safety. A test service justified on health and

safety grounds would have to withhold any test results on past drug use—
where the latter is strictly irrelevant from a health and safety point of
view—whilst reporting on any current intoxication, or post-intoxication
impairment, which is affecting safety.

However, the EC has now spawned a Community Institution which will
most probably act as a focus for EC drug policy formation.

The Observatoire

The European Drugs Monitoring Centre, or drugs *Observatoire* as it is
sometimes called in recognition of the French roots of this initiative, will
have the task of bringing together on an EC-wide basis all relevant
information on illegal drugs, problems and policies. It is expected to operate
on three levels:

1. Political covering restricted and enforcement (i.e. strategic intelligence)
   information on drug problems and policies.
2. Professional information from epidemiological surveys, other research
   and the scientific literature.
3. Public information on illegal drugs.

The details are still subject to feasibility studies but certain key aspects are
emerging, such as a possible site (Portugal); the institutional basis of the
Observatoire (an entity under EC law); and its preliminary focus on
epidemiological surveys of drug use. The EC *Observatoire*'s initial priority
on epidemiological research on drug users represents something of a political
coup by The Netherlands, since it brings into centre stage all health-related
issues related to drug users, drug consumption, drug treatment needs, and
HIV prevention schemes, such as needle exchanges.

Such an information centre might appear politically unproblematic, but
that would overlook the fact that information is power. The future of EC
drug policy is of concern to several member states. Some fear that a tightly
coordinated European drug policy might lead to adoption of US-style drug
policies, which is a concern of the Dutch. Others fear that the *Observatoire*
might lead to too great a degree of harmonization in relation to drug
treatment, perhaps leading to EC standards in health care generally, a
British reservation. Some fear that the *Observatoire* will give the Commission,
European Parliament and European Court of Justice a 'foot in the door' in
national policy matters, a fear of several Interior Ministries.

An entity under Community Law

Such scenarios may appear far-fetched, but they are not entirely without basis. This can be shown, by analogy, by referring to the area of environmental policy. Although the ECs 'environmental protection requirements shall be a component of the Community's other policies', just as 'health protection requirements' are, community legislation on environmental protection has blossomed, and a European Environmental Agency (EEA) has been set up (Council Regulation 1210/90, of 7 May 1990, on the Establishment of the European Environmental Agency and the European Environmental Information and Observation Network, reference *OJ—Official Journal of the European Communities* – No. L 120/1, especially the Preamble and article 20). It has been suggested that 'The establishment of the EEA deserves special prominence, not for what it has already achieved, but for what it potentially might become' (Hagland, 1991).

In the longer term the EEA may become involved in the enforcement of minimum environmental standards. Thus, given time, the drug *Observatoire* – for which the EEA is the institutional model—may become involved in EC policy formulation and a focus for coordinated EC action on drugs. Drug control, as always, appears to be a part of much wider policy developments.

Conclusion

The drive towards European Union involves both the creation of an economic Single Market and a wider set of political initiatives. Both aspects have implications for drug policies.

Firstly, on the economic side, the Treaty of Rome, initiated by the Single European Act and solemnized by Maastricht, does not include a health policy as such. Instead, the pursuit of the 'four freedoms' implies harmonization of the opportunities for competition of goods, services, labour and capital. This complex process of economic harmonization implies a variety of developments in health and health care. There is no part of the EC that is concerned with pulling together, synthesizing or directing these varied developments. Health *per se* is not the aim of the Union. As one observer puts it

> In sum, health is an EC-policy issue of minor priority, and selected aspects are scattered in various Directorates General (DG), the main administrative bodies of the Commission . . . . Health and health system impacts of the European integration are not being monitored under the responsibility of a specific EC authority, and information about impacts is not reported to those responsible (Leidl, 1990).

Such fragmentation is reflected in the Maastricht Treaty. Vague and unspecific references to public health prevention and 'health protection' illustrate the limits of Community competence in relation to health. It is interesting that 'drug dependence' is the only 'major health scourge' mentioned by name. It seems that this particular scourge was added to the Treaty text at the last moment during the Maastrict meeting. One wonders if Maastricht would have had anything specifically on health had there not been this particular peg to hang it on.

Secondly, once we move beyond the Single Market agenda and examine the broader aspects of the drive to political union, references to policy on illegal drugs become less anodyne—and also much more politically contentious. European drug policy will be greatly influenced by political union. For example, by cooperation in justice and home affairs and the setting up of a European Police Office, whose first task will be to collate drug enforcement information; by the Common Foreign and Security Police, and its relationship to external relations (of trade) and to international action against drug production and trafficking; and by the role of the drugs *Observatoire* in bringing information, monitoring, evaluation and policy-making together in these and the health areas.

In summary, we might suggest that the health policies of EC member states on drug users and on health protection are only weakly coordinated through the Single Market process. The real action is taking place in the wider areas of political cooperation. The present paper is an early attempt to analyse the ways in which European Union is shaping health, law enforcement and other policy frameworks for drug control.

NOTE: For further discussion please contact the author at ISDD, 1 Hatton Place, London EC1N 8ND, UK, or telephone + (44 0)71 242 1878.

References

Bowe D (1991) *Report Drawn up on Behalf of the Committee into the Spread of Organised Crime Linked to Drugs Trafficking into the Member States of the European Community*. European Working Document

Commission of the European Communities (no date) *Feasibility Study for a European Drugs Monitoring Centre*. Report to CELAD

Commission of the European Communities (1991) *European Drugs Monitoring Centre: feasibility study phase II*. Brussels

Dorn N, Murji N and South N (1992) *Traffickers: Drug Markets and Law Enforcement*. Routledge, London

European Community (1991a) *Treaty on Political Union* (English draft). Articles 129 (4) 68

European Community (1991b) *Treaty on Political Union* (English draft). Articles 129 (1) 67

Hagland P (1991) *Environmental policy*; In Hurwitz L and Lequesne C (eds) *The*

State of the European Community. Lynne Rienner, Longman, Colorado, pp. 259–272

Hendriks A (1990) The right to freedom of movement and (un)lawfulness of AIDS/HIV specific travel restrictions from a European perspective. *Nordic Journal of International Law, 59,* 186–203

Leidl R (1990) 1992 and the challenge for health systems. Paper for EC/WHO EURO, Workshop on the Future of Health Services Research

Nielsen L and Szyszczak C (1991) *The Social Dimension to the European Community.* Handelshojskolens Forlag, Copenhagen, pp 54–66

Orzack L (1991) The general system directive and the liberal professions. In Hurwitz L and Lesquesne C (eds) *The State of the European Community.* Lynne Rienner, Longman, Colorado, pp 137–152

Stewart-Clark J (1986) *Report Drawn up on Behalf of the Committee into the Drugs Problem in the Member States of the Community.* European Communities Working Documents A 2-114/86/Corr

Van Hamme A (1991) The European Court of Justice. In Hurwitz L and Lesquesne C (eds) *The State of the European Community.* Lynne Rienner, Longman, Colorado, pp 45–64

Van Overbeek J (1990) AIDS/HIV infection and the free movement of workers in the European Economic Community. *Common Market Law Review, 27,* 791

Prevention of illicit drug use in Poland

Czeslaw Czabala, *Institute of Psychiatry and Neurology, Warszawa, Poland*

Nobody knows the exact range of drugs use in Poland. Approximate statistical estimates pertain to drug abusers only. According to police statistics the number of drug-using offenders amounts to about 15 000. Some 4000–5000 persons are treated at various health care and MONAR facilities, which allows assessment of the probable number of drug users to range at around 20 000 to 25 000 (World statistics indicate that every fourth drug user undergoes treatment). Estimates made by the Ministry of Health and Social Welfare suggest that at least 200 000 to 250 000 people are users of intoxicating substances.

The only precise data are those provided by police statistics and by the Institute of Psychiatry and Neurology. The latter pertain to hospitalized patients only: in 1990 there were 3161 drug-dependent persons treated on an inpatient basis. Compared to 1989, their number has increased by 14.6% (and in that number there have been 22.4% more first admissions). The indicator per 100 000 inhabitants amounts to 7.99. The distribution of drug-dependent inpatients over years indicates that the peak frequency was in 1984, gradually decreasing to 1989 (with the lowest index of 6.98), while in 1990 a considerable increase was noted, amounting to the 1985 rates.

Among those hospitalized in 1990, the most numerous was the group of opiate-dependent persons (80.2%), then of sniffers (7.6%) and of those dependent on over-the-counter medicines and pills (6.0%). This means that in comparison to 1989 rates the number of opiate-dependent persons has increased by 18.1%, and that of sniffers has increased by 28.3%. Only 16.8% of drug-dependent inpatients were able to remain in treatment or rehabilitation centres for over a month. In 43.3% of cases the mean duration of hospitalization was under seven days.

According to data reported by the National Institute of Hygiene 2074 Polish citizens were infected with HIV in January 1992. In that group 1522 were injecting drug users. Out of the total of 87 persons with AIDS, 42 died. There is a tendency for constant growth in the number of HIV-infected persons: in October 1991 there were 27 such cases, of whom 22 were injecting drug users, in November the figures were 49 and 32, respectively; in December 1991, 37 and 24, and in January 1992, 74 and 44. As regards new cases of AIDS, the distribution was as follows: October 1991, none; November, 7 (six males, one female, in that number three were drug users, and two homosexuals); in December, none; in January 1992 there were two (both homosexual).

The majority of drug-dependent persons have a blue-collar family background (about 60–70%), while the minority come from farmers' families. Predominant among those in treatment are male patients (75%) and young persons (80% are under 30 years of age, and about a half are under 24, according to the official statistics of the Ministry of Health and Social Welfare).

At the start of the 1980s the most popular drug was the so-called 'compote', i.e. Polish heroin, home-brewed from poppy and poppy straw. It was produced by drug-dependent persons themselves and destined for their own consumption. The number of 'compote' users has decreased in recent years. The youngest drug users are most often sniffers (of glue, paint, solvents, etc.), while young adults prefer amphetamines and marijuana. There are sporadic cases of cocaine dependence and of using hallucinogenic mushrooms. According to the Society for Preventing Drug Dependence, import of considerable amounts of cocaine to Poland is expected. A synthetic version of cocaine (kreg) has recently appeared. Another threat consists in the constantly growing output of amphetamine produced in Poland. The drug is produced and trafficked by gangs striving for financial profits. Detection and conviction of these gangs is almost impossible.

The legal act governing prevention and treatment of drug dependence in Poland is the Law issued on 31 January 1985. The Law is based on three main assumptions (Chruściel and Korozs, 1988):

1. Organs of the State are duty-bound to undertake comprehensive actions

aimed at preventing drug dependence and to support the activity of social organizations and religious unions in this area.

2. Undertaking of appropriate educational and preventive activities; control of agents which may lead to drug dependence; treatment and rehabilitation of drug-dependent persons.
3. Establishment of a Fund for Preventing Drug Dependence. The Fund provides means for, among other things, indispensable assistance to drug-dependent persons and their families.

As regards preventive activity, special emphasis is laid by the Law on:

1. The care for appropriate development of children and youth (their attitudes, life goals, providing them with care and support).
2. Spreading information on the hazards of drug dependence, via schools and mass media.
3. Reduction of habit-forming substances supply (regulations concerning poppy and hemp growing, permits for production of intoxicants and psychotropic drugs).

As for treatment and rehabilitation, responsibilities are assumed by the State following the 1961 and 1971 conventions, these are carried out by health services, social and religious organizations and by citizens. Treatment of drug dependence may be only voluntary, with the following exceptions: compulsory treatment is permissible in the case of drug dependent persons under 18 years of age, and on judicial decision in the case of convicted offenders.

According to the penal law provisions, distribution of intoxicant drugs is an offence liable to punishment by imprisonment of up to eight years, while intoxicant drug use is not punishable.

Practical realizations of the law provisions was reduced mostly to an increased availability of treatment to drug-dependent persons. This pertains, above all, to inpatient treatment, most often limited to a short detoxification. As indicated by the previously cited statistics, only a small percentage of drug-dependent persons were subject to this form of treatment. Similarly, a small percentage of drug users choose voluntary self-referral to a MONAR rehabilitation centre and remain in treatment later on. These are the only facilities offering a specified rehabilitation programme to drug-dependent persons. As regards preventive activities, practically nothing has been done. There are no preventive programmes at schools, as far as informing, behaviour shaping and assistance to persons at risk for drug dependence are concerned. The only prophylactic actions aimed at pointing out hazards of drug dependence have been conducted by MONAR, but even these were only occasional. Some preventive steps—although definitely insufficient—

have been undertaken by social organizations, e.g. by the Association of Families of Drug Dependent Persons, 'Recovery from D'; or by the Society for Preventing Drug Dependence. On the other hand, some research projects have been launched, including epidemiological surveys and investigation of socio-psychological factors in drug dependence.

The socio-political situation in Poland has changed dramatically over the past two years. The changes have also had their impact on drug-dependence problems. The major change in this respect consists in the emergence of an intoxicant drugs market. Production of amphetamine in Poland, appearance of groups gaining profits from trade in illicit drugs, and—in consequence— availability of cocaine on the market. Detection and controlling of production and trade in drugs are difficult. In earlier years drugs were produced by drug users themselves, for their own and their colleagues' consumption. At present both drug production and traffic are better organized and therefore it is much more difficult to identify the offenders. Police forces are less efficient than at the time of the militia, which had practically everything under control. The police have neither the time nor means to deal effectively with continually growing crime rates (i.e. thefts, burglaries, use of arms, embezzlements, etc.). Besides, the police seem to underestimate the dangers connected with trade in drugs. They also lack the skills required to detect gangs, often having international connections. Even courts are not adequately prepared for penal proceedings in the case of suspected production and trade in illicit drugs.

Another change consists in the growing number of young people using inhalants. This is probably due to the economic situation of the country. There is much unemployment among young, uneducated people, as well as lack of perspectives for a career after vocational training in trades for which there is little demand. It should be noted that about 60% of young people either have no specific vocation (trade), or are trained for trades for which there is no demand at all.

Due to all these factors a need for changes in the preventive policy concerning drug dependence is more and more often recognized. In Parliament amendments to the Law on Preventing Drug Dependence are currently being developed. New penal law provisions are proposed, e.g. possession of narcotic drugs is to be included among punishable offences; in the case of drug-dependent offenders imprisonment may be replaced by compulsory treatment; poppy growing is to be totally prohibited.

A very important bridging plan for the prevention and control of AIDS has been developed in cooperation with the WHO Global Programme on AIDS. The plan includes a number of specific provisions concerning epidemiological assessment, laboratory services, health promotion in the general public and in specific populations (among them the group of injecting drug users).

Further steps involve development and publication of materials (intended for the general public) on the problems of drug use and drug dependence. However, due to financial shortages, translation, development and publication of such materials is not feasible on a large scale.

The contribution of schoolteachers in preventive activities requires changes. Teachers lack not only sufficient knowledge of the problems of drug dependence, but also skills necessary to shape desired attitudes in their students. Besides, they share with the majority of the society in Poland hostility against drug users and drug-dependent persons. In consequence of all these factors the hazards of drug dependence are not taken into consideration in the education process. Sometimes hostile attitudes towards drug users are even directly instilled in pupils taught to treat the latter like dirt or outcasts. Such beliefs are remnants of the former political regime in Poland. Since they are popular, it is extremely difficult to get many people involved in the prevention of drug use.

However, various programmes have recently been started with the aims of changing public opinion, as well as teaching skills required for the prevention, treatment and rehabilitation of drug dependence.

For example, a teacher training programme has been launched. Its goals are to improve teachers' educational skills so that they could develop in their students behaviours and attitudes reducing the need for drugs and alcohol use. The training is conducted by teachers themselves, after a special preparation for this role provided by, among others, the Institute of Psychiatry and Neurology, as well as by the Teachers' and the Youth Fund 'Ferry'. The Fund cooperates with teachers from Lithuania, and as regards the contents of its activities, receives assistance from some centres in Europe. It is our belief that activities referring to the Health Promoting Schools Project should also be introduced.

Special educational programmes have been started in local communities. The goal of these programmes is to involve local authorities, the local police, social and religious organizations in the preventive activities. The programmes also strive to develop ways of cooperation between these various institutions, on the grounds of which should be formed lobbies on behalf of drug-dependent persons as well as local support groups for them.

Another element of coping with the problem of drug dependence consists in a recently launched research project on methadone use (in cooperation with WHO), and the planned Polish–American research project on the use of clonidine and buprenorphine for treatment of opioid-dependent patients.

A very important constituent of more efficient coping with the problem of narcotic drugs use is the issue of receiving full information, as well as the coordination of activities of various agencies. The seriousness of risks connected with drug dependence as a health and social problem is still underestimated, therefore relatively few efforts have been made in this area by the government. Activities of particular centres are fragmentary and uncoordinated; experiences of other European countries are not sufficiently heeded. Participation in all-European activities is necessary, as well as development of a specific plan of action. We hope that the more and more frequent visits of WHO representatives to our country, and a more marked participation of Polish scientists in joint research projects and shared programmes (such as the bridging plan for AIDS prevention) would help to develop a sensible policy of preventing drug dependence. Our cooperation should include, above all:

1. Methods of epidemiological data collection and of monitoring prophylactic actions and therapeutic interventions.
2. Shared methodology of research into socio-psychological problems associated with drug use.
3. Training of personnel who later would conduct training in prevention and rehabilitation in Poland, designed for various groups of trainees.
4. Training of the police in drug use prevention.
5. Availability of relevant publications addressed to professionals as well as to young drug users and their families.
6. Popularization of methods of preventing drug use, via mass media (radio, TV, press).
7. Constant cooperation of Polish representatives with appropriate European organizations.

References

Chrusciel TL, Karozs L (1988) *Zapobieganie narkomanii w swietle polskiego prawa* (Polish law regulations of drug abuse prevention). Warsaw
Sikorska-Godwood C (1991) Uzaleznienia lekowe w Polsce—epidemiologia (Drug Abuse in Poland—epidemiological data). Unpublished report of the Institute of Psychiatry and Neurology. Warsaw

AIDS and drugs in Europe: a research agenda

Virginia Berridge and Demetra Nicolaou, *London School of Hygiene and Tropical Medicine, UK*

Increasing use of illict drugs has been a matter of cross-European concern from the early 1980s. The advent of AIDS among intravenous drug users has made that concern more urgent. This is the mode of transmission of HIV which appears to be accelerating both in the United States and in many European countries. The spread of the virus through non-sterile needles and syringes facilitates the ease of blood-to-blood transmission.

Table 1 gives the breakdown for specific European countries up to the autumn of 1991. From these figures four issues are clear: firstly that numbers of reported and estimated cases are lower relative to population in Europe than in Africa; but secondly that European countries fall within what has been termed pattern 1a of the epidemic. This is a development of pattern 1 in which the majority of early cases were among homosexual men. The rate of infection now appears to be levelling in that group; and the major increase in infection has come from among intravenous drug users. The issue of spread among drug users brings with it the possibility of continuing spread of the virus into the heterosexual population with increasing numbers of women and babies infected. A third issue, apparent from these figures, is the particular concentration of AIDS in a belt of southern Europe covering Spain, southern France and Italy. In these, and in some eastern European countries (Poland, for example), the major take-off for the syndrome has occurred among drug users. This is also true of individual cities elsewhere in Europe, with Edinburgh the most obvious example. In some southern

Table 1 Cumulative AIDS cases in selected European countries and their major transmission groups (reported by 30 September 1991)

Country	Total cases	Injecting drug user (intravenous) (%)	Homo/bisexual drug user (intravenous) (%)	Hetero-sexual (%)	Homo/bisexual (%)
France	16 552	20.8	1.8	11.5	51.6
Italy	10 584	65.8	2.6	15.0	2.6
Spain	10 101	64.3	2.8	4.6	16.1
Germany	6 968	12.5	0.7	4.4	69.9
United Kingdom	5 065	4.4	1.6	7.6	77.5
Switzerland	2 086	36.2	1.9	13.1	43.0
Netherlands	1 857	8.1	1.1	6.5	78.2
Belgium	977	4.4	0.7	42.0	38.5
Denmark	870	5.1	1.0	10.2	76.3
Portugal	746	13.4	0.0	25.6	44.9
Austria	639	28.2	0.6	10.6	40.8
Sweden	617	5.2	0.6	9.2	70.0
Greece	528	4.0	0.8	20.5	51.3
Poland	78	34.6	0.0	9.0	56.4

From AIDS Surveillance in Europe Quarterly Report No. 31, 30 September 1991, by the European Centre for the Epidemiological Monitoring of AIDS, with permission.

European countries intravenous drug use is the predominant means of transmission. In Spain in 1991, 67.1% of all AIDS cases were among drug users, and three-quarters of all the female AIDS cases. A fourth and final issue emerging from this pattern of transmission is that a high prevalence of infection among drug users appears to lead quickly into second-generation heterosexual transmission; that is, to infection among those with no direct overlap with high-risk groups. In Europe, as in the US, a pattern is beginning to emerge of increasing prevalence in disadvantaged groups and areas. In Italy, for example, the spread of the disease to the south means that AIDS has underlined the existing north/south disparities of wealth and economic status in that country. The background is thus one of increasing spread among European intravenous drug users; of second-generation heterosexual transmission; and of the connection with poverty and disadvantage (Blaxter, 1991).

Against that background this paper aims briefly to survey current trends in research into AIDS and drug use in Europe, both by country and by examining the cross-national studies which have been mounted in recent years. Its aim is not for all-inclusiveness or a comprehensive literature review. It aims simply to identify what seem to be the dominant current tendencies in research and their relationship to past trends. The paper will conclude with an outline of future directions which research in this area could take.

AIDS/drugs research in individual European countries

First, research on the AIDS/drug connection in individual European countries. Research on drug misuse was not well developed in many of these countries prior to AIDS (Berridge, 1990). Individual countries had particular research 'traditions' (for example, the stronger 'policy studies' tradition in the northern European and Scandinavian countries). Overall, research was often identified with epidemiology. HIV/drugs research has built on those traditions and certain general trends can be outlined. There has been an emphasis on 'basic epidemiological data', in particular in researching data on seroprevalence among drug injectors in particular localities and over time. For example, studies of drug use in Bari, Italy, in 1982, revealed a 5% prevalence of HIV, rising by 1985 to 76%. In Edinburgh HIV was first detected among drug users in 1983; by 1985 prevalence was 51%. Similarly, in other major cities such as Barcelona and Milan the percentage of drug injectors known to have become HIV infected ranges from 50% to 60% (Strang and Stimson, 1990). In Italy the number of cases of AIDS among drug users overtook the number among homosexuals at the end of 1985; in 1989 80% of cumulative cases were attributed to drug use, if heterosexual contact with drug users, and the children of drug users, were included (Blaxter, 1991). Another related strand of research has looked at behavioural risk factors for HIV infection among intravenous drug users. These include frequency of injection, sharing injecting equipment, sexual behaviour, and questions of socioeconomic status, years of injection, imprisonment, and perhaps gender (Friedman and Des Jarlais, 1991).

A major area of research has been on the evaluation of preventive strategies in the HIV/AIDS/drugs arena. HIV/AIDS has led to the introduction of new policy objectives of 'harm minimization' for drug use in a number of European countries. AIDS has been perceived as a greater threat to the public health than drug misuse. Consequently policies designed to prevent the spread of HIV through needle sharing rather than the spread of drug misuse itself have become acceptable. Harm minimization strategies are varied, and range from teaching users safer practices to sterilization of injecting equipment, easier availability of needles and syringes, or their exchange, and the use of methadone maintenance to reduce engagement in risky injecting behaviour. Many European countries have adopted variants of these practices—from Denmark, The Netherlands, Austria, through to France and Poland so far as syringe availability goes (the nature of availability can vary according to local circumstances) (Buning et al., 1988; Farrell and Strang, 1992). The UK needle exchange experiment attracted world-wide attention; and research there, as elsewhere, has focused on the evaluation of the effectiveness of needle exchange as a harm-minimization strategy. Other trends in research have focused on the impact of other interventions—the provision of bleach for cleaning, for example, and the role of outreach work. There is also a strand of what can be called 'clinical epidemiology' in research, quantitative descriptions of HIV-infected drug users in treatment (Hart, 1989). There are a few European studies of HIV-infected drug users in prison (Harding, 1990).

Collaborative European studies on AIDS/drugs

These general trends in country research must be set against a number of cross-European studies which have developed in recent years. Coordination has been provided both by the European Community and by WHO-Euro. Existing collaborative projects, in particular the multi-city study sponsored by the Pompidou Group, have also continued (Pompidou Group, 1987). Research collaboration was fostered initially by a series of meetings, in particular one in Stockholm at the end of 1986 organized by WHO-Euro, which among other urgent business sketched out a research agenda for country and collaborative work (WHO, 1986). This focused on epidemiological studies. Other early collaboration stimulated by WHO focused on basic information exchange. WHO-Euro produced in 1989 an overview of selected AIDS policies and programmes in the 32 European member states (WHO,

1989). This did not focus specifically on AIDS and drug use, but included some information on relevant policies. Other documents have surveyed the AIDS/drugs situation in a selection of countries; and the provision of care for HIV-infected drug users (WHO, 1991a,b; Brenner *et al.*, 1991). Information provision of this type has been one strand of European research.

A number of collaborative studies are also under way. The MRC and WHO are jointly funding a serial Period Prevalence Study which began in London in January 1990. This three-year project aims to measure HIV prevalence, associated risk behaviour and knowledge of AIDS among injecting drug users in a number of large cities around the world; these include Rome, Madrid and London (Crosier, personal communication, 1991; Papaevangelou *et al.*, 1991). An EC-funded study which began in 1989 is looking at the assessment of HIV/AIDS preventive strategies in EC/COST countries. One of six working groups is collecting information about prevention strategies, broadly conceived, in European countries. Their preliminary report has information on media campaigns; testing and counselling; methadone programmes; prison programmes; behavioural studies; and sexual behaviour (EC, 1991). Other collaborative studies are also in operation, for example 'Managing AIDS: The role of private non-profit institutions and non-governmental organisations in public health and welfare policy', based in Vienna, which aims to survey the role of voluntary organizations in AIDS work in European countries. Drug use is not a primary focus here, but does enter incidentally into the survey. The advent of AIDS has also led to a survey of the organization and operation of methadone programmes in six countries, including France, The Netherlands and the UK (WHO, 1989). Some work has begun on the local and city responses to drug use and AIDS (Bennett, 1991).

After AIDS: all change in the drugs research agenda?

How can we assess the general trends in AIDS/drugs research in European countries? In a recent editorial, John Strang, Gerry Stimson and Don Des Jarlais (1992) have argued that AIDS has brought a radical change in the drugs research agenda. Their evidence is not confined to Europe. But they cite, as illustration of this point, research on the mechanics of injecting behaviour; the association between drug use and sexual behaviour, the feasibility of change within on-going drug taking; and the factors which determine the choice of route of drug use. They argue that AIDS has brought a true inter-disciplinary mix in the AIDS/drug research arena. Much of this, excepting the latter point (for the language of multi-disciplinary endeavour has characterized drugs research for 20 years or more) is indeed the case.

But this paper will argue for considerable areas of continuity in research both pre- and post-AIDS. In particular if one examines the form and nature of research, very little seems to have changed. A number of general conclusions can be drawn. Epidemiological and quantitative research has always predominated in the drugs area, but AIDS has intensified this tendency to a marked degree. Surveys and statistical analyses of the AIDS/drug connection predominate, often on a localized basis. Friedman and Des Jarlais (1991), in their analysis of AIDS prevention programmes, comment on the way in which these have focused on the individual drug injector, to the neglect of larger social processes or structures. The same tendency is visible in the AIDS/drugs research arena. Although AIDS has led to a marked expansion of drugs research in Europe, by far the greater proportion still comes from the United States, again continuing a tendency which was well established prior to AIDS (Berridge, 1989, 1990).

Epidemiological measures in various forms, evaluations and attempts to develop common measures (as in the WHO/MRC study) are all features of current research (Loimer, 1992). But there have been few attempts to locate these initiatives in policy context, to look more broadly at strategies of response over time and to see what lessons can be drawn. There are very few studies of the overall policy context in European countries. Those which do exist, focus *either* primarily on drug policy in individual countries *or* on AIDS policies, with drugs as a subsidiary theme. One example of the first tendency is the Rand Corporation comparative study of drug policies in western European countries. The latter tendency is represented by the cross-national study of AIDS policies in the US, Sweden and the UK by Fox, Day and Klein (1989), or the comparative study of AIDS policies (including European countries) edited and written by Misztal and Moss (1990) and by Misztal (1991). Very few studies have looked at the AIDS/drugs policy connection in depth (Berridge, 1993; Uchtenhagen, 1991), AIDS is now at the end of its first decade as a European as well as a world-wide phenomenon. Yet mostly the primary research establishing significant relationships between knowledge, interests and policy formation has still to be carried out.

A future research agenda

Any proposed research agenda must take into account that the general trends in current work will continue. This is the case both at a European and country and local levels. The European Observatory planned as an EC agency to coordinate data on a cross-European basis will continue the epidemiological strand of research. Most funding bodies, in particular those with a local remit (such as the health authorities which are increasingly funding AIDS research in the UK), will want specific locally based studies for planning purposes. However, some other lines of research needing development at a European level can also be suggested.

Basic information exchange

The information exchange function of research is already present, but there are a number of ways in which this can be strengthened

1. Literature reviews and country surveys.
2. Information on cross-European research collaboration.

Literature reviews   Research has proliferated—but as yet few analytical literature reviews exist, and none with a European focus. The annual surveys of AIDS/drugs presentations at the international AIDS conference are a useful guide to current research findings. At the end of 10 years it is perhaps time to produce consolidated analyses of key findings on a cross-European basis. There are national journals and research efforts (in particular in eastern Europe) which are barely known. Existing reviews tend to be dominated by the larger volume of US research. It is important that cross-fertilization occurs between different European countries, and especially between East and West.

Cross-European research collaboration   AIDS has complicated the existing cross-European picture so far as research collaboration goes. There are AIDS networks, drugs networks, and a multitude of cross-European bodies are involved, primarily the EC and WHO-Euro. It would be important to have a central reference point which could bring together information on AIDS/drugs networks from both these areas. The European network of drugs research centres being coordinated by WHO-Euro may help in this process.

Descriptive analysis of AIDS/drugs practice

Descriptions of the shape of services and of treatment responses are notable by their absence and we currently lack, for most European countries, any sense of the overall size and shape of services; or of what is *really* happening in treatment post-AIDS. The basic descriptive function of research needs to be strengthened. It is important in the evaluation of policy to be able to assess what is actually happening, the translation of policy into practice. Both the health and penal aspect of drug policy suffer from a lack of examination in this respect.

Policy analysis on a national and cross-European level

Policy studies at various levels are necessary in order to raise the level of debate and to contribute to the improvement of practical responses. 'Policy' is used here not in the sense of descriptions of particular programmes or institutional responses. It is used to encompass the dynamics of political, cultural, organizational, professional and other factors which shape responses at local, national and international levels. Overviews of the AIDS/drugs area in European countries are one possibility. We also need to expand our understanding of particular aspects of policy on a cross-European basis, for example the AIDS/drugs connection in prisons and policy responses to it; the role of the voluntary sector in this area; or the relationships between drugs and other service areas which have developed because of AIDS (genito-urinary medicine, for example, in the UK). Policy issues around testing of drug users and the national differences in response are another important area, in particular because of the ethical issues which are raised. The current individual and quantitative dimension of research needs to be linked to a sense of policy context.

Area studies

The local dimension of the AIDS/drugs connection has been important within Europe. Area studies could compare the development of policies in different areas which have experienced different AIDS/drugs scenarios, for example Edinburgh and Glasgow or Liverpool in the UK, to analyse what has determined particular forms of response and effectiveness. Existing studies of this type tend to take a Euro/US framework (Grund *et al.*, 1992).

The research/policy connection

AIDS has brought research into a closer relationship with the drug policy agenda than had been the case for some time before (Berridge, 1992a,b). The advantages, and the dangers of a policy-driven research agenda have been much discussed. It is perhaps time for an analysis of the connection in the AIDS/drugs area both at a practical and at a theoretical level; AIDS/drugs provides a case study of the interrelationship. Again cross-national or local studies would be useful here.

Conclusion

Drugs research in the early 1990s at national and European level shows distinct continuities with pre-AIDS tendencies. The advent of AIDS has led to an expansion of research across Europe, but the previous focus, at country level, on the quantifiable and the individual, has remained constant. The 'search for numbers' at local and national levels has been intensified by AIDS. Cross-nationally the move to develop comparable indicators continues (also a pre-AIDS tendency) (Loimer, 1992; Farrell and Strang,

1992). US research still predominates, but the evidence which would enable us to compare strategies of response and derive lessons from successes or failures is currently lacking. As Misztal and Moss (1990) comment: 'Rational health policies on AIDS are constructed within the spaces offered by local history, social organisation, and culture.' It is at this level, as well as at the individual one, where our research agenda should be set.

References

Bennett T (1991) *Drug Misuse in Local Communities: perspectives across Europe.* Police Foundation, London

Berridge V (1989) *Drug Research in Europe.* ISDD, London

Berridge V (1990) *Drugs Research and Policy in Britain: a review of the 1980s.* Gower, Aldershot

Berridge V (1992a) AIDS, drugs and history. *British Journal of Addiction, 87,* 363–370

Berridge V (1993) AIDS and British drug policy: continuity or change? In Berridge V and Strong P (eds) *AIDS and Contemporary History.* Cambridge University Press, Cambridge, (in press)

Blaxter M (1991) *AIDS: World Wide Policies and Problems.* Office of Health Economics, London

Brenner H, Hernando-Briongos P and Goos C (1991) AIDS among drug users in Europe. *Drug and Alcohol Dependence, 29,* 171–181

Buning EC, Van Brussel GHA and Van Santen G (1988) Amsterdam's drug policy and its implications for controlling needle sharing. In Battjes RJ and Pickens RW (eds) *Needle Sharing Among IDUs: National and International Perspectives.* NIDA, Washington

EC (1991) EC Concerted Action: Assessment of the AIDS/HIV Preventive Strategies (unpublished document).

Farrell M and Strang J (1992) Alcohol and drugs. *British Medical Journal, 304,* 489–491

Fox D, Day P and Klein R (1989) The power of professionalism: policies for AIDS in Britain, Sweden, and the United States. *Daedalus, 118,* 93–112

Friedman SR and Des Jarlais DC (1991) HIV among drug injectors: the epidemic and the response. *AIDS Care, 3*(3), 239–250

Grund J-P, Stern S, Kaplan CD, Adriaans NFP and Drucker E (1992) Drug use contexts and HIV consequences: the effect of drug policy on patterns of everyday drug use in Rotterdam and the Bronx. *British Journal of Addiction, 87,* 381–392

Harding T (1990) HIV infection and AIDS in the prison environment: a test case for the respect of human rights. In Strang J and Stimson G (eds) *AIDS and Drug Misuse.* Routledge, London, pp. 197–207

Hart G (1989) Injecting drug use, HIV and AIDS. *AIDS Care, 1*(3), 237–245

Loimer N (1992) Drug addiction and AIDS: highlights of the first European Congress. *AIDS Care, 4*(1), 111–114

Misztal BA (1991) HIV/AIDS in Poland: a society in need of the State. *European Journal of Social Policy, 1*(2), 79–91

Misztal BA and Moss D (1990) *Action on AIDS. National Policies in Comparative Perspective.* Greenwood, New York

Papaevangelou, G *et al.* (1991) HIV prevalence and risk factors for infection among IVDUs in the European Community. Abstract M.D. 4074 presented at International AIDS Conference

Pompidou Group (1987) *Multi-city Study of Drug Misuse in Amsterdam, Dublin, Hamburg, London, Paris, Rome and Stockholm.* Council of Europe, Strasbourg

Strang J and Stimson G (eds) (1990) *AIDS and Drug Misuse.* Routledge, London

Strang J, Stimson G and Des Jarlais D (1992) What is AIDS doing to the drug research agenda? *British Journal of Addiction, 87,* 343–346

Uchtenhagen A (1991) Drug abuse policies against the background of the AIDS epidemic. EUR/ICP/GPA 04917

WHO (1986) *AIDS Among Drug Abusers.* Report on a consultation. Stockholm, 7–9 October. ICP/ADA/535 9713F

WHO (1989) *Options for the Use of Methadone in the Treatment of Drug Dependence.* WHO/MNH/DAT 89.2

WHO (1989) *AIDS Policies and Programmes in the European Region.* ICP/GPA 040

WHO (1991a) *AIDS among Drug Abusers in Europe: a review of recent developments.* EUR/ICP/GPA 049(B)

WHO (1991b) *Providing Care for HIV-infected Drug Users.* EUR/ICP/GPA 089

Workshop discussion report

Cees Goos, *World Health Organization, Copenhagen, Denmark*

Illicit drugs are one of the most regulated areas of public health, and one with the highest policy profile. Both nationally and internationally a battery of legislation covers drug use; but, unusually for a public health issue, this regulation falls within both criminal justice and health systems.

While drug abuse seems to be levelling off in some parts of the European regions there is an increase in other parts, especially in southern and eastern Europe. Of particular significance is the role which drug abuse plays in the increased incidence of communicable diseases, AIDS, hepatitis B and tuberculosis.

From a public health perspective it is important that policies and programmes are being implemented which aim explicitly at the reduction of harm resulting from drug abuse. This has become even more urgent to contain the HIV epidemic.

Features of the current European situation

European national drug abuse policies show considerable variation from approaches which are tolerant to those which place emphasis on reduction of supply.

These variations have been described to some degree but serious attempts at assessing the relative impact of policies have been rare, if not entirely absent. There is a real challenge for comparative research for which the opportunities are now much better than ever before.

There is a small information base for policy formation and the link between research and policy needs to be strengthened.

The local community perspective is an essential dimension for a true understanding of this particular problem. Research efforts with this particular focus are needed.

The public health dimension of drug abuse policies has not always received the support which it needs. High prevalence rates of HIV infection and other communicable diseases have made it even more important to take drug abuse on board as a public health issue.

Current developments in Europe

A number of developments are taking place in Europe which may have great influence on drug policy.

There are loosening controls in general in central and eastern European countries, in the wake of which more liberal policies are likely to be put in place which could lead to a worsening of the drug abuse situation. In a country such as Poland the situation is already quite dramatic, as there the AIDS epidemic is more or less equal to the drug abuse epidemic.

There is continuing pressure towards more individual rights and less State interference, which is already having its impact on 'consumer rights' for drug users.

There are increasing doubts over the effectiveness of policies which rely predominantly on controlling the availability of psychoactive substances in contrast to policies which emphasize the importance of demand reduction strategies.

The typical public health response to the control of communicable disease (hepatitis B, AIDS, tuberculosis) has stressed policies aiming at reducing harm related to drug abuse rather than aiming at reducing drug abuse itself.

Parallel to these developments there is increasing international cooperation at a sub-regional level. The Balkan countries are currently developing cooperation activities; so are the countries around the Baltic Sea and the new republics of the CIS. Very intensive cooperation is taking place between the European Community countries, where a major information resource centre is being established as a Commission agency. The European Community has declared drug abuse to be a major public health issue.

Issues for policy development

The eastern European situation is clearly urgent. Given the fact that resources are very scarce in this part of the region a massive input from outside is needed to implement preventive action. Drug abuse is also a priority for the EC countries, and has been declared such by the Commission. This gives an opportunity to strengthen the public health contribution.

It is also important to integrate drug abuse not only into public health but into studies of tobacco and alcohol. The European survey of health behaviours among school children is a good example of this integrated approach.

Research topics

Several items of a research agenda are already implicit in our preceding comments.

1. The analysis of the effectiveness of policies requires cross-national policy comparisons.
2. Improving the information base for policy requires better mechanisms of information exchange.
3. The advent of HIV among drug users has thrown policy into a state of flux; it is important that evaluation and cost-effectiveness studies of different areas of policy, for example prison or the police response, are made (particularly in relation to HIV infection). AIDS has highlighted the link between research and policy, and these interconnections should be developed.
4. The establishment of European research networks makes possible more research coordination than has taken place in the past. There should also be some consideration in that context of levels of research coordination at a European, a regional or a local level.

Europe is a natural laboratory for the testing of drug policies. It is important that research focuses on this area in coming years.

People's role in health policy

Consumers and health care services: the right to information and access

Elizabeth Hayes, *International Organization of Consumers Unions, The Hague, The Netherlands*

Introduction

The World Health Organization has defined health as

> a state of complete physical, mental, social well-being, not merely the absence of disease or infirmity . . . . Health is, therefore, seen as a resource for everyday life, not the objective of living. Health is a positive concept emphasising social and personal resources, as well as physical capacities (World Health Organization, 1986).

Health is the consumer's most precious commodity because it profoundly affects quality of life. That explains why consumers demand so much from their health care services. Not only do they expect care providers to diagnose correctly and treat their minor ailments, but also, if necessary, to save them from death or the prospect of lifelong sickness. No other service is as valuable to consumers—or demands so much of their trust. Health care must satisfy a consumer's right to basic services, acceptable safety, adequate information, health education and choice of care. It should also be affordable and accessible to all (Cook, 1989).

Consumer organizations such as International Organization of Consumers' Unions (IOCU) view health care from the perspective of the patient who is, after all, a consumer of health care goods and services. Such a viewpoint applies to all of the processes and systems that are used to treat health problems and improve people's health. This means not only professional medical care but also treatment with medicines, mental and social treatment and access to care. Today's European consumers seek high standards at a time when issues such as the growing number of elderly, the spiralling costs of health care, inadequate insurance, the irrational use of drugs and environmental effects on health are causing mounting concern (Snijder 1989).

Europe Without Frontiers. Edited by C.E.M. Normand and P. Vaughan
© 1993 John Wiley & Sons Ltd

The importance of the consumer voice

The consumer voice is a relatively new one in the health sector, and it is one that needs to grow much stronger. Producers and suppliers of goods and services in the health care industry are well organized and knowledgeable but have their own viewpoints and interests—and the power to pursue them. Organizing consumers to speak up for their own needs and priorities is a way of correcting a long-standing imbalance. With so much political and economic change taking place in Europe today, all players in the health care system need to recognize that consumers must have an active role in formulating health policy, as they are the ultimate users of it.

Consumer interests have long been expressed as a set of basic rights. They inform and guide the work of the international consumer movement. Thirty years ago, former US President John F. Kennedy proclaimed four basic consumer rights: the right to safety, the right to be informed, the right to choose and the right to be heard. In recent years, IOCU has added four more. All eight can be directly applied to the promotion of good health care and conditions that improve health (Wells and Tiranti, undated).

The right to safety: consumers should be protected from products, processes or services that could be hazardous to their health or life. Health procedures, medication and devices must be safe for consumers to use.

The right to be informed: this means consumers have the right to be given factual information in order to make informed choices and decisions. Consumers deserve to understand their own health condition and how best to improve and maintain it. They must be given complete, understandable information at their own level so that they can take the best possible care of themselves.

The right to choose: consumers should have access to a variety of products and services at competitive prices and, in the case of monopolies, to have assurance of satisfactory quality and service at a fair price. Today, consumers are faced with more and more choice on health care. This can, at times, be overwhelming and confusing, particularly for those who are just gaining access to the plenitude of western health services and medicines. Consumers need to have adequate choice about medicines and health services so they can make the best possible decision in light of their own preferences and needs.

The right to be heard: this means participation in decision-making regarding things that affect their interests. Consumers need to play an active part in developing European health policy. As users of health care goods and services it is crucial for consumers to have a say in how health decisions are discussed and decided. For example, national and international drug approval committees, advertising regulations, labelling and care standards should all have consumer input in their work.

The right to the satisfaction of basic needs: in this context, this means access to basic health care services. This care should also be affordable for consumers.

The right to redress: consumers have the right to fair settlement of just claims. When health care is negligent or substandard, consumers should be able to obtain redress. Some critical issues are drug-induced injuries, uninformed consent complications and other areas where the consumer is placed in a passive role, dependent upon health experts.

The right to consumer education: consumers must be able to acquire the knowledge and skills they need throughout life. To do this they need the support of institutions and adequate resources. Today, European consumers are much more assertive about their own health care than 20 years ago, but they are still at a profound information and expertise disadvantage. It is important for consumers to learn more about health care choices and their rights. Only by being fully aware of their rights as well as responsibilities as a consumer of health services can a true health care partnership be forged.

The right to a healthy environment: this means consumers should have a physical environment that will enhance their quality of life. The interplay between environmental issues and health has never been as obvious as it is today. Dirty air, chemical dumping, fouled water and temperature changes endanger the health of millions of Europeans. Because it is impossible to change industrial operating practices quickly, consumers' health stands at great risk of bearing the brunt of environmental damage.

Health's special problems

It is difficult to organize consumers so that they become more active in their own health care. Few people want to discuss medication and health care options when they are healthy; and once they are sick, consumers may find it difficult to argue effectively for their own interests. Instead, because they *need* a drug or service, consumers become highly dependent upon their health care providers.

On a national level, consumer organizations are playing an increasingly active part in the spheres of health care and health promotion. The UK's Consumers' Association, for example, has recently published articles on topics ranging from X-rays and information for outpatients on how to switch doctors. In fact, health issues are such a high priority, the organization has a whole magazine, *Which? Way to Health* devoted to the subject. Many national consumer organizations have also been actively involved in the development of charters on patients' rights to ensure that consumers are aware of their rights and responsibilities as patients. This issue has become a high priority in Europe and has also been taken up by the World Health

Organization's (WHO) Regional Office for Europe. Well aware of disparate national levels of protection for patients, this WHO office is now developing a European Declaration on the Rights of Patients. Many IOCU regional members have already contributed comments to its first draft version.

Consumer organizations are also becoming more active in the health field at the international and European level. IOCU's regional office for Europe and North America recently started a health working group to enable national consumer organizations to exchange information on their health work and concerns. The group is also starting to develop regional research and policy projects on current health topics that can be used on both a national and international level. The work of the group intends to focus on all health issues, but to date has focused mainly on consumer issues involving pharmaceuticals. Because of that emphasis, the rest of this paper will use pharmaceuticals as an example to illustrate how the consumer interest relates to health issues.

Consumers and pharmaceuticals

At a national level the use and abuse of pharmaceuticals has been the subject of a growing number of investigations. The Consumers' Association (1991a) has published an in-depth study on the subject of generic drugs, and carried out an extensive survey on the quality of advice given by UK pharmacists (Consumers' Association, 1991b). The Dutch consumer group, Consumentenbond, has also been active in the health field. In 1991 it published a booklet advising elderly consumers on the underlying risks surrounding the use of medicines. It also counselled consumers against using unnecessary pharmaceuticals and highlighted the continuing problem of some drugs' high prices (Consumentenbond, 1991a,b,c).

Internationally, pharmaceuticals have been a focus of consumer interest for many years. The possible problems stemming from the use, distribution, production, export and licensing of pharmaceuticals have prompted the United Nations to adopt special provisions on them in its *Guidelines for Consumer Protection* adopted by the UN General Assembly in 1986 (United Nations, 1987). Ensuring the rational use of drugs has been IOCU's longest-running health campaign. IOCU continues to work with WHO and Health Action International, a global network of consumer, health and development groups, to promote the proper use of drugs. IOCU believes that pharmaceuticals are a special area of concern for today's consumers. The following consumer concerns and proposals regarding pharmaceuticals show some of the risks and power imbalances which European consumers currently face in the health care marketplace. The issues also highlight some of the areas that must be addressed by European governments, health professionals, consumers and industry in the upcoming years.

By their very nature, pharmaceuticals differ from other products available to consumers. Under usual circumstances the consumer chooses, uses and pays for a product. This does not happen with prescription drugs. Instead, these three actions are usually divided among different players. The doctor chooses a medication, the consumer uses it and the State, through insurance, usually pays for it (Murray, 1992).

There is no doubt that pharmaceuticals have given major benefits to patients; but it is often difficult to find a direct correlation between consumption of drugs and consumer well-being. That is to say, just because a patient takes a medication does not guarantee that his health will improve; or that taking more of a drug means his health will improve more quickly. Furthermore, the consequences when things go wrong are more drastic than with practically every other product available to consumers. Consumers need to understand that *all* medication is potentially dangerous. Finally, people taking drugs usually have little access to information on them. Most of that information is held by health professionals and the pharmaceutical industry (Murray, 1992).

Drugs and consumer protection

Countries often suffer from an inconsistent tracking of adverse drug reactions. With so many health changes planned to take effect at the end of 1992, now is the time for a more consistent drug adverse reaction tracking method to be introduced in Europe. Under such a system, drugs sold within a number of countries (such as the EC region) could be monitored for possible problems, and adverse effects could be more quickly spotted. This could be done in addition to information gathered from national agencies that see fewer incidents due to their smaller population size.

It is crucial for consumers to have a voice among drug manufacturers in order to make sure that the consumer interest is protected during all phases of production—including research, clinical trials, the drafting of product information, advertising, marketing and post-marketing. However, this type of activity requires strong, well-funded consumer organizations to support efforts made to counterbalance industry's power.

Drug promotion

This issue is already raising many questions, and it only promises to become more widely debated after 1992. Promotion affects both health care providers and consumers. Therefore, advertisements need strong regulation and complete information to fully inform and protect consumers; and consumers and health care professionals both need access to factual drug information.

The boundaries between promotion and factual information must remain clear. Drug information and drug advertising are two different things.

Better drug information

Consumers need to be informed about their treatment up to the level that they wish. Just as consumers have a right to receive full information about their own care and options, they also have the right to refuse information. When information is requested and received, it is often inadequate. For example, although many countries detail in legislation what doctors and pharmacists should tell consumers about a given drug, such lengthy conversations rarely happen in practice. Consumers are at a clear disadvantage here.

The need for greater openness

Very little information on drug licensing and approval filters down to the people taking medicines. There is a lack of consumer information at the licensing stage, and industry controls clinical trial data. Consumers need to be represented on the committees making decisions about drug approval. The quality of information that reaches consumers is often inadequate. Some countries have placed prohibitions on the flow of information in areas such as licensing and the reason for a drug's withdrawal from the market, for commercial reasons.

The drug pricing system also lacks transparency. Currently, different schemes are employed in each European country, which leads to a wide variance in price. Pharmaceutical firms can negotiate their basic profitability and can manipulate the overall basket of prices so that a price does not always reflect the actual value of a drug, and some branded drugs remain much more expensive than their generic equivalents.

The future of European health

The consumer movement is working to help consumers judge the health changes taking place around them. Consumers need good information and adequate choice in a spectrum of health areas. Yet these are often the essential elements missing when consumers make their health decisions.

As Europe faces new health care challenges the information available to consumers must reflect that fact. Information must give patients sufficient knowledge to become intelligent and assertive consumers of health care services. Consumers need more information on how they can stay healthy, recognize their own illnesses and take a more active part in their own treatment. Good consumer information should also instruct patients on the most effective way to communicate with their health care providers, including the kinds of questions they must be sure to have answered (Cook, 1989).

Responsibility for people's health lies not only with governments and health care professionals, but with consumers themselves. Education efforts must continue to be made so that consumers possess sufficient information and confidence to act in their own best interest, and receive the best possible health care.

References

Consumentenbond (1991a) Medicijnen: word er niet ziek van. Consumentenbond and Stichting, COMAC

Consumentenbond (1991b) Tien vragen over pijn: Pijnstiller niet altijd nodig. *Consumentengids*, November, pp 714–718

Consumentenbond (1991c) Sommige geneesmiddelen zijn nog steeds te duur. *Consumentengids*, December, p. 810

Consumers' Association (1991a) Are you getting the right medicine? *Which?*, November, pp. 646–649

Consumers' Association (1991b) Pharmacists: how reliable are they? *Which? Way to Health*, December, pp. 191–194

Cook K (1989) Responsible health care—everyone's right. World Consumer Rights Day Kit. International Organization of Consumers' Unions

Murray J (1992) Lecture before colloquium: medicines in Europe after 1992. Pharmaceutical Group of the E.C. (24 January)

Snijder S (1989) *Consumer Aspects of Health Care and Proposals for IOCU ROENA—Summary*. International Organization of Consumers Unions, p. 2

United Nations (1987) *Guidelines for Consumer Protection*. HMSO, London, p. 6

Wells T and Tiranti D (undated) *IOCU: Giving a Voice to the World's Consumers*, p. 8

World Health Organization (1986) Ottawa Charter for Health Promotion. Canadian Public Health Association, Ottawa

Attitudes and consumer food choice

Richard Shepherd, *AFRC Institute of Food Research, Reading, UK*

In order to be able to intervene in modifying behaviours to improve health we need a better understanding of the processes involved in decision-making by consumers. Measuring the attitudes and beliefs held by consumers offers one means for understanding how decisions are made, but it is necessary to have a coherent theoretical framework within which to measure and relate beliefs, values and attitudes to behaviour. The theory of reasoned action developed by Ajzen and Fishbein (1980) offers such a framework, and has proved useful in leading to a better understanding of the reasons for a number of food choices. There are several modifications and extensions to this basic model, including perceived control, habit, and self-identity, which offer the prospect both of a better understanding of the reasons for choices and more effective ways of targeting health interventions.

This type of approach implies careful balancing of costs and benefits of actions and, although it describes a number of types of choices well, there are alternative decision strategies which rely much less on this analytical approach. In some cases these simpler 'rules of thumb' may be used by consumers in making decisions. Different types of strategies are likely to be used for different types of choices, and it is important to know what types of considerations are important in order to intervene effectively.

Introduction

Many public health policies are designed to try to influence the behaviour of people. Providing people with appropriate information concerning risks to health might be expected to lead to a change in their behaviour, but this turns out to be far from simple. In order to implement recommendations on modifying behaviour we need to understand why people behave as they do, and how they make decisions about what behaviours to perform. In this paper the examples will all be related to diet, but many of the insights gained in this area will also have implications for other behaviours associated with good or poor health.

Food choice is obviously a major concern to those involved in producing and manufacturing foods, since in order to make profits they must sell food products to consumers. However, it is increasingly being recognized that there are also important nutritional questions related to food choice. Food choice determines nutritional status and, in so far as there are influences of diet on health and disease (WHO, 1991), it is of vital importance to understand the processes by which choices are made. In particular, only with an adequate understanding of the reasons for the choices of foods by consumers can we effectively attempt to change choices and hence influence dietary patterns.

Factors influencing food choice: beliefs and attitudes

Food choice, like any complex human behaviour, is influenced by many interrelating factors. Although authors have put forward models trying to explain food choice (e.g. Khan, 1981), in general these are not quantitative, nor do they explain the likely mechanisms of action. As catalogues of the likely influences they can be useful in pointing to the variables to measure, but they do not offer a framework within which to design studies or a basis upon which to build theories of human food choice (see review by Shepherd, 1989).

Many of the influences on food choice are likely to be mediated by the beliefs and attitudes held by consumers (Shepherd, 1989). Thus sensory attributes of taste, texture, etc. are mediated by preferences for these attributes, and beliefs about the nutritional and health effects of a food may be more important than the actual health consequences in determining a person's choice. Although attitudes are generally assumed to be causally related to behaviour, the evidence for this relationship has not always been apparent.

In the nutritional literature, for example, a number of attempts have been made to relate attitudes to consumption of foods, with many studies adopting a framework known as 'knowledge–attitudes–practice' (behaviour). Here there is a clear expectation that knowledge affects attitudes, which in turn influence behaviour. If this were true then changes in behaviour could be brought about by increasing knowledge, and many interventions are based upon this assumption. Although this seems a simple and appealing formula the evidence for such a link is rather poor. A meta-analysis takes the results of a number of studies and integrates them in an effort to estimate what the correlation between the variables would have been if one large study had been conducted with all of the people in the individual studies. Axelson *et al.* (1985) conducted such an analysis of studies attempting to relate knowledge to attitudes and dietary intake, and found evidence for statistically significant but small associations between these variables; the correlation between attitudes and behaviour was 0.18, and that between knowledge and behaviour was even lower at only 0.10.

The theory of reasoned action

The same lack of a clear attitude–behaviour link in social psychology led to the development of a number of structured attitude models. One example is 'the theory of reasoned action' developed by Ajzen and Fishbein (1980). This offers a 'rational' account of attitude formation where the potential advantages and disadvantages of performing a behaviour are weighed up by the individual before a decision is made. This is one example of a set of theories known as expected-utility theories.

The theory of reasoned action seeks to explain behaviour which is volitional (i.e. is under the control of the individual). With volitional behaviours, intention to perform a behaviour is seen as the best single predictor of behaviour. Intention, in turn, is predicted by two components: the person's own attitude (e.g. whether the person sees the behaviour as good, beneficial, pleasant, etc.) and perceived social pressure to behave in this way (termed the 'subjective norm'). These relationships are shown schematically in Figure 1. The attitude is in turn predicted by the sum of products of a set of beliefs about outcomes of the behaviour, and the evaluation of these outcomes as good or bad. The subjective norm is predicted by the sum of products of normative beliefs, which are perceived pressure from specific people or groups (e.g. doctors, family) and the person's motivation to comply with the wishes of these people.

This model has been applied to a range of food choice issues (e.g. Shepherd and Farleigh, 1986; Shepherd, 1988, 1989) and strong relationships between food choice and attitudes have been shown (Shepherd, 1989). In these studies the consumer's own attitude has been found to be far more important than perceived social pressure. In general, beliefs concerning the taste and flavour of foods have been the most important in determining the selection of foods (e.g. Shepherd and Farleigh, 1986; Towler and Shepherd, 1992a). One exception is the finding in a study of low-fat milk consumption, where nutritional beliefs were the most important influence on consumption, although sensory and suitability aspects were still important (Shepherd, 1988).

Sheppard *et al.* (1988) carried out a meta-analysis of 87 studies using this model, including around 12000 subjects. They found an estimated correlation of 0.53 between intention and behaviour, and a multiple correlation of 0.66 between attitude plus subjective norm against intention. Thus this model

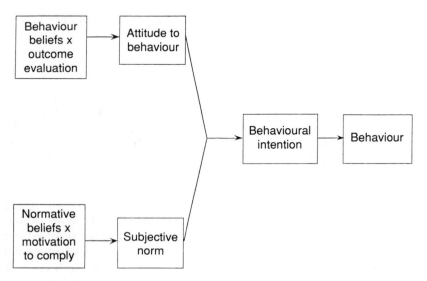

Figure 1 Schematic representation of the Fishbein and Ajzen theory of reasoned action

has validity in the study of a range of behaviours and specifically of food choice.

Extensions to the theory of reasoned action

Although the theory of reasoned action has proved successful in many applications in the food choice area, the model can be modified and extended in a number of ways. Ajzen (1989) has argued for the inclusion of perceived control, which extends the model to include non-volitional behaviours, goals and outcomes. There is evidence for the importance of perceived control for various health-related behaviours (Ajzen and Timko, 1986), consumption of organic vegetables (Sparks and Shepherd, 1992b), and consumption of biscuits, although not wholemeal bread (Sparks et al., 1992). Hence, for certain choices of foods, perceived control may be a variable worthy of attention.

Habit is another factor considered likely to play an important role in predicting behaviours, especially if they are frequently performed. It may not play a major role in the initiation of a particular behaviour, where attitudes are more likely to be important, but when a behaviour is established it may be that habit is a key factor in its maintenance (Ronis et al., 1989). Thus habit may serve as a barrier to change. In the food context, habit has been shown to be significantly related to the consumption of sweet, salty and fatty foods (Tuorila and Pangborn, 1988) and the consumption of chips (Towler and Shepherd, 1992b).

Thus although the basic theory of reasoned action has proved reasonably successful in the food choice area, there are a number of possible modifications which may improve its predictive ability.

Exceptions to expected-utility theories

One major criticism of all expected-utility theories, such as the theory of reasoned action, is that people could not, and would not, perform the computations necessary in order to make most decisions. There is evidence that in some instances indeed people do make decisions which go against the predictions of such theories. This has led to development of alternative theories of decision-making, which apply particularly when there is some uncertainty involved in the decision. Much of this work has taken the ideas developed by Kahneman and Tversky (1984) on heuristics (or 'rules of thumb'), framing and prospect theory as its starting point. Some examples of this type of research will be described briefly, but more detailed consideration can be found elsewhere (Kahneman and Tversky, 1984; Sparks and Shepherd, 1992a).

One example of a heuristic is the availability heuristic, where information that comes readily to mind has a disproportionate influence on decision-making. This is illustrated in a study which examined the perceived causes of a car's failure to start (Fischhoff *et al.*, 1978), where subjects were presented with a fault tree of possible causes and then asked to guess what proportion of failures to start would fall under the category 'all other problems'. When the fault tree was 'pruned' by 50%, the proportion of failures allocated to this 'all other problems' category did not significantly increase. Apparently what was out of sight was effectively out of mind.

There is also evidence of what has come to be known as an optimistic bias in risk perception, where people underestimate the personal risk to themselves of a number of hazards (e.g. Weinstein, 1989). When asked to respond to questions such as 'Compared to other men/women my age, my chances of getting [e.g. food poisoning] in the future are . . .', there was a consistent trend to mark personal risk as below average. The reasons for this phenomenon are, as yet, far from clear, although the implications for preventive action programmes are considerable.

The wording of information is also important in influencing people's decisions. The following is an example of such a 'framing' effect (taken from Kahneman and Tversky, 1984). Subjects are presented with one of two scenarios. They are asked to imagine that there will be an outbreak of an unusual disease, which is expected to kill 600 people. Two alternative programmes to combat the disease have been proposed. If one group of subjects is offered the alternatives of a programme where 200 people will be saved, or one where there is a one-third probability that 600 people will be saved and a two-thirds probability that no people will be saved, 72% chose the first option, hence going for the certainty of saving 200 lives. In a separate group of subjects the choice is posed as a programme where 400 people will die against a programme with a one-third probability that nobody will die and a two-thirds probability that 600 people will die; in this case only 22% chose the option of 400 dying with certainty. Here, the same problem elicits different decisions, depending on whether it is couched in terms of lives or deaths. The reason for this is that people weight gains and losses differently.

Observations of such instances where the weighing-up of costs and benefits does not apply, and the implications of phenomena such as framing effects for dietary interventions, need to be explored further.

Conclusions

The attempt to model food choice via an understanding of people's beliefs and attitudes requires a structured framework. The theory of reasoned action generally shows good prediction of behaviour, and can be used to determine the relative importance of different factors in influencing food choice. There are, however, a number of possible modifications and extensions which need to be further developed and tested. In particular perceived control and habit potentially have important implications for attempts to modify behaviour.

When choices do not have to be made quickly, or are particularly important, or are irreversible, decision-making strategies may well be relatively analytical, as in the theory of reasoned action. However, strategies may be qualitatively different when decisions are mundane, run-of-the-mill, in need of being made quickly and relatively inconsequential. It has to be recognized that such choices are often made using quick heuristics or 'rules-of-thumb' rather than a careful balancing of the costs and benefits.

Only with an understanding of how consumers do make decisions of different types concerning foods can we hope to intervene effectively to change dietary patterns. The research described in this paper offers some pointers to how consumers make certain types of decisions, but more research is required, specifically investigating the validity of these theories and models and how they can be applied to dietary interventions.

References

Ajzen I (1989) *Attitudes, Personality, and Behaviour*. Brooks-Cole, Andover, Hants
Ajzen I and Fishbein M (1980) *Understanding Attitudes and Predicting Social Behavior*. Prentice-Hall, Englewood Cliffs, NJ
Ajzen I and Timko C (1986) Correspondence between health attitudes and behavior. *Basic and Applied Social Psychology*, 7, 259–276
Axelson ML, Federline TL and Brinberg D (1985) A meta-analysis of food and nutrition-related research. *Journal of Nutrition Education*, 17, 51–54
Fischhoff B, Slovic P and Lichtenstein S (1978) Fault tree: sensitivity of estimated failure probabilities to problem representation. *Journal of Experimental Psychology: Human Perception and Performance*, 4, 330–334
Khan MA (1981) Evaluation of food selection patterns and preferences. *CRC Critical Reviews in Food Science and Nutrition*, 15, 129–153
Kahneman D and Tversky A (1984) Choices, values, and frames. *American Psychologist*, 39, 341–350
Ronis DL, Yates JF and Kirscht JP (1989) Attitudes, decisions, and habits as determinants of repeated behavior. In Pratkanis A, Breckler S and Greenwald A (eds) *Attitude Structure and Function*. Erlbaum, Hillsdale, NJ, pp. 213–239
Shepherd R (1988) Belief structure in relation to low-fat milk consumption. *Journal of Human Nutrition and Dietetics*, 1, 421–428
Shepherd R (1989) Factors influencing food preferences and choice. In Shepherd R (ed.) *Handbook of the Psychophysiology of Human Eating*. John Wiley, Chichester, pp. 3–24
Shepherd R and Farleigh CA (1986) Attitudes and personality related to salt intake. *Appetite*, 7, 343–354
Sheppard BH, Hartwick J and Warshaw PR (1988) The theory of reasoned action: a meta-analysis of past research with recommendations for modifications and future research. *Journal of Consumer Research*, 15, 325–343

Sparks P and Shepherd R (1992a) Public perceptions of food-related hazards: Individual and social dimensions. (Submitted)

Sparks P and Shepherd R (1992b) Self-identity and the theory of planned behavior: assessing the role of identification with green consumerism. *Soc Psych Q* (in press)

Sparks P, Hedderley D and Shepherd R (1992) An investigation into the relationship between perceived control, attitude variability and the consumption of two common foods. *European Journal of Social Psychology*, 22, 55–71

Towler G and Shepherd R (1992a) Application of Fishbein and Ajzen's expectancy-value model to understanding fat intake. *Appetite*, 18, pp 15–27

Towler G and Shepherd R (1992b) Modification of Fishbein and Ajzen's theory of reasoned action to predict chip consumption. *Food Quality and Preference*, 3, pp 37–45

Tuorila H and Pangborn RM (1988) Behavioural models in the prediction of consumption of selected sweet, salty and fatty foods. In Thomson DMH (ed.) *Food Acceptability: International Symposium Proceedings*. Elsevier, London, pp. 267–279

Weinstein ND (1989) Optimistic biases about personal risks. *Science*, 246, (493S); 1232–1233

WHO (1991) *Diet, Nutrition, and the Prevention of Chronic Diseases*, WHO, Geneva

Workshop discussion report

Louise J. Gunning-Schepers, *University of Amsterdam, The Netherlands*

The working group decided on a change in its title from consumers' *view* to consumers' *role*, to emphasize an active rather than a passive approach. In discussion it became clear that particular terminology, e.g. 'consumer', could easily imply particular assumptions which both biased and limited the range of enquiry required to address issues of health and health promotion at all levels from the individual to the European population. It also became clear that consumer involvement was not limited to health or health promotion, but also applied to health services and lay care. Hence the use of the word health policy. In the light of this discussion the group's focus and title became 'People's role in health policy'.

Process

The *logic* of the group's discussion followed four steps:

1. *Identifying valued aspirations for the people's role and influence.* We aspire towards societies which: (a) affirm the importance of health as a resource to life; (b) recognize both collective and individual responsibility

for achieving health for all; (c) establish the conditions necessary for promoting a population's health; (d) enable citizens to shape these conditions in the fields of environment, lifestyle and health services; (e) establish rights to use services which are beneficial. This ordering of aspirations seeks to give prominence to health promotion over service provision and to collective as well as individual rights and responsibilities. It needs to be reflected also in terminology* which recognizes that everyone has a part to play, and appreciates the overlapping but different connotation of the words patients, user, consumer and citizen in different cultures. The actual measures proposed will differ for each level.

2. *Reviewing current performance against these aspirations.* We identified the extent to which the current situation falls short of the aspirations and identified the barriers to effective influence by ordinary people in: (a) the relative lack of power in relation to 'economic' forces and provider interests; (b) major inequalities between population groups; (c) distortion of health policy by the sometimes over-enthusiastic preoccupation with medical treatment; (d) the difficulty in weighing the interests of different groups, especially those that are not well organized.

3. *Assessing opportunities and risks in the changing Europe for improving consumer participation.* We pooled our understanding of Europe and scanned the policy agenda for opportunities and risks to consumer participation strategies at a European level.

4. *Identifying issues for further learning and research.*

Results

Step (3) provided the main focus for our discussion and recommendations. Looking across *health promotion, health services* and the *lay provision* of care and self-care, we identified basic requirements for people's participation as being:

1. Information – understandable and pertinent.
2. Choices – in health services; in shaping a healthy environment.
3. Organization – to mobilize consumer power.
4. Rights and responsibilities – the interest of the individual and that of society.

Out of that discussion the following points emerged: *opportunities* of a

---

* When we use the term consumer in this text it is meant to stand for people.

Europe without frontiers seemed to concentrate on making information for consumers more plentiful, the sharing of experiences between countries easier and choices more apparent through comparisons. *Risks*, on the other hand, seem to be too much information (sometimes misleading), the lack of a proper democratic structure within Europe to weigh the different interests, and the risk of the majority ignoring cultural diversity. Also shopping around for services on the one hand provides extra choices for consumers, but may also place unacceptable burdens on those countries that have their health services well organized and attractive to consumers. This also applies to long-term care and possible support for home care.

Recommendations

1. Since we agree that health is central to life, there is a general responsibility for health, and people should help shape a healthy environment and help shape health services, we recommend an active policy to achieve consumer participation in health policy at a European level.
2. The following elements are prerequisites for such a consumer participation: (a) government support, (b) sufficient education, (c) consideration for the diversity and values within Europe.
3. To achieve effective consumer participation sufficient information, choices, organization and rights should be available for health promotion, use of health services and involvement in lay care.
4. To strengthen consumer participation we propose the following research agenda: (a) comparative studies of strategies for consumer group effectiveness at different levels; (b) research on the role of professionals in making consumer participation work; (c) development of vocabularies for engaging people in the health dialogue and consumer-oriented standards for evaluation, (d) research on consumer choices in relation to information provision, including the role of the mass media; (e) experimental studies of effectiveness of patient/consumer-oriented methods (e.g. of information presentation, patient record-keeping, patient advocacy).

Overview

An overview: looking to the future

Sir E. Donald Acheson

London School of Hygiene and Tropical Medicine, UK

First I would like to congratulate all involved both in the presentation of the papers in the plenary sessions and in the exemplary workshop reports. I also congratulate those who participated in the lively and constructive discussion. Happily for me, to make a final statement does not necessarily imply that I have composed a balanced summary. Instead I shall employ an unashamedly personal approach by selecting a few issues that have struck me as of a particular significance. My remarks will not claim to be comprehensive.

The scale of the problems and opportunities

The Forum opened with addresses giving a clear indication of the scale both of the problems and the opportunities in the field of health which face Europe at present. We were reminded that Europe contains no fewer than 850 million people, and that within the past two years the number of countries in Europe which wish to be represented within the World Health Organization has increased from 31 to 50. In view of recent events it is not surprising that the problems of central and eastern Europe have dominated our discussions. These problems include a decline in national product varying from 10% to 50%; inflation of up to 400%; massive unemployment with, in some places, collapse of the social infrastructure and health services, an antiquated industrial system and the resurgence of nationalism. It has been said, with some justice, that to meet the needs a new Marshall plan is really required.

In relation to the problems of central and eastern Europe I wish to make three points. First, I regard it as questionable whether the scale of the need for aid both in terms of cash and skills has yet been recognized by the more fortunate countries in this region. Second I think some of the issues are so urgent that, rather than pinning hopes on new *ad hoc* institutions which would take time to create, we must make the best possible use of institutions which are currently in existence and available to help such as the EC, WHO, the World Bank, OECD and the European Development Bank. The third

Europe Without Frontiers. Edited by C.E.M. Normand and P. Vaughan
© 1993 John Wiley & Sons Ltd

point is that the widening gap in health between western Europe and certain central and eastern European countries presents unprecedented opportunities for research. This widening gap also raises the issue of gross and increasing degree of inequality within Europe. This creates a perspective which seems to make the progress towards competence for health promotion within the draft Maastricht Treaty pale almost into insignificance. Nevertheless the EC is and will remain a key player in solving the problems of Europe as a whole, not only in financial terms but by the provision of skills. I was particularly interested to hear that under the terms of Maastricht new public policies originating within EC countries may be subject not only to environmental impact assessment but to an assessment of their impact upon health. As far as health surveillance is concerned, the first priority under Maastricht may be a pilot project of surveillance of acute outbreaks of communicable disease. I hope such a project would be extended to the rest of Europe as soon as practicable.

Organization of health services

Although it is well known that even effective and efficient health services are not the most important determinants of health, the political reality is that the provision of health services is usually perceived as more urgent than is health promotion. Thus, for example, the public are difficult to interest in campaigns against smoking and unhealthy diet as long as the hospital services which deal with injury and acute illness are in disarray. We were reminded that health care policy is a key area for the participation of the citizen who needs to be involved and to be given choices.

There was little emphasis in the discussions on the importance of a credible primary care system as gatekeeper for hospital services. A system of primary care can provide a wide range of preventive and therapeutic services close to home, which have much higher costs if carried out in hospital. I believe those countries which have previously had a centralist system where doctors received salaries from the state may be too ready to accept a fee-for-service system as the only alternative. Experience in North America, for example, has shown that 'fee-for-service' systems tend to lead to inflation of unnecessary treatments and costs. Furthermore, hospitals working within such systems tend to lack a sense of mission or duty to a defined population. It may be worth looking at intermediate options involving salaries with performance-related pay and incentives.

The 1990s will undoubtedly be an era when indicators of the outcome of health care are developed and refined. The alternative is waste of valuable resources on unhelpful procedures and ultimately the bankruptcy of health services. As an example of what the future may hold, a set of tested outcome indicators for the treatment of diabetes both at home and in hospital has recently become available. Outcome indicators relating to a wide range of surgical procedures and to the treatment of coronary heart disease and high blood pressure are also likely to become available shortly.

Lack of information of all kinds

Within the working groups a common theme emerged of frustration about lack of comparative information of all kinds. This included lack of information about mortality and morbidity, effective and safe medicines, nutrition and food distribution, the use of illicit substances, evaluation of technologies, the differing roles of nurses and doctors and other health care professionals and about the consumption of health services. The starting point of the solution of a problem is often the demonstration of differences between groups and areas. Later it may be possible to define a hypothesis which leads to a reduction in these differences. Thus the demonstration in previous work of gross differences in hysterectomy and caesarean section rates between areas without parallel differences in morbidity had led to the hypothesis that the higher rates were undesirable. In another field, differences between countries in the duties of nurses had led to the hypothesis that in some places more of the clinical work could be done as effectively and more cheaply by nurses than by doctors. It was agreed that, rather than set up new data banks, it was important to extend and improve harmonization in those banks that already existed. Examples of existing data banks include those held by WHO's European office on mortality, communicable disease notifications and on effective and safe medicines. WHO's European Centre of Environment and Health with its centres in Bilthoven, Rome and Nancy is assembling data banks on, e.g., air and water pollution and food contamination, and also offers advice. It was emphasized that in respect of design and management of health services there was an urgent need to set up clearing houses to reduce the confusion caused by the large numbers of overlapping bilateral projects.

The health gap

A number of indicators show that health in the populations in central and eastern Europe is worse than that in the West, and that over the last 10–15 years the gap has widened in some areas. This discovery has created an important new area for research. It is urgent to achieve a successful analysis of the causes of this situation in order that appropriate policies to improve health may be introduced. In view of the serious degree of air and water pollution in parts of central and eastern Europe it is tempting to blame everything on the recent deterioration of the environment. Unhealthy lifestyles including smoking, diet, and lack of physical exercise and deterioration in the social infrastructure and health services are probably at least as important.

The environment

As far as the environment is concerned, although the effect of air pollution as a causative factor in chronic lung disease cannot be denied, more emphasis is needed on the key role of housing and on urban design with, for example, better facilities for recreation, on health. The issue of sustainability and our responsibility to future generations in the spirit of Brundtland was also emphasized. Future development must take into account the problem of diminution of the atmospheric ozone layer, the build-up of greenhouse gases and the destruction of natural resources. In the 'sulphur triangle' of Silesia and parts of Czechoslovakia, the use of brown coal has created very high levels of air pollution due to sulphur dioxide. An important project involving the EC, the European Development Bank and WHO is addressing this problem, with the object of reducing economic dependence on this material in this part of Europe.

Health promotion

It was accepted that the case that prevention is better than cure had been made, and the principles of the Ottawa Charter and their application are as important to the improvement of health in central and eastern Europe as in the West. The importance of obtaining the commitment of the citizen and the community in the improvement of health was emphasized. Policies on tobacco, to take one important example, must be strong everywhere, and in these days of satellite-based mass media, controls on advertising must be international if they are to be effective. There is no conflict between health promotion and medical treatment. The objective of both is to improve health.

The 'Health-For-All' policy and public health targets

WHO's European regions document on 'Health-For-All' provides a comprehensive health policy describing 48 targets which cover the determinants of health, the organization and management of health services, quality, evaluation of technology, and most recently ethics and patients' rights. The emphasis of the policy is on a multi-sectoral approach to health involving all parts of government, an emphasis on primary care and on community participation. The rhetoric of the 'Health-For-All' policy has been criticized, but its content has never been successfully challenged on intellectual grounds. Indicators have been set and progress evaluated twice in the past decade, and the text has recently been revised. I submit that 'Health-For-All' is an appropriate policy framework for improving health in Europe; but there is a key trade-off between the policy ideas and skills of the World Health Organization and the regulatory powers of the EC. Each should be a constructive partner of the other. Provided we engage all the key players including the EC, the World Bank, the European Bank and the bilateral agencies, and seize the opportunities for research, and improve our information base and coordinate our activities, there are grounds for optimism.

I hope this seminar will raise the profile of the huge and testing health problems which face Europe today, and facilitate progress towards their solution.

Index

Index compiled by Geoffrey Jones